Edition **DETAIL** Green Books

Green building certification systems

Assessing sustainability
International system comparison
Economic impact of certifications

Thilo Ebert
Natalie Eßig
Gerd Hauser

Imprint

Authors:
Thilo Ebert, Dipl.-Ing. (FH)
Natalie Eßig, Dr.-Ing. Architect
Gerd Hauser, Prof. Dr.-Ing.

Co-authors:
Oliver Baumann, Dipl.-Ing.
Sebastian Eberl, Dipl.-Ing. (FH) M. Sc.
Tajo Friedemann, B. Sc.
Thorsten Huff, Dr.-Ing.
Jochen Schäfer, Dipl.-Ing.
Heike Schlappa
Arend von Stackelberg

Project management:
Jakob Schoof, Dipl.-Ing.

Editorial work:
Kim Ahrend, Dipl.-Ing.
Jakob Schoof, Dipl.-Ing.

Editorial assistants:
Julia Bauer
Katinka Johanning, M. A.
Sandra Leitte, Dipl.-Ing. (FH)
Jana Rackwitz, Dipl.-Ing.

Translations:
Sharon Heidenreich, Dipl.-Ing. (FH)
Roderick O'Donovan, B. Arch.

Proofreading:
Feargal Doyle, B. Arch.

Illustrations:
Ralph Donhauser, Dipl.-Ing.
Cedric Ehlers

Layout:
Cornelia Hellstern, Dipl.-Ing. (FH)

DTP & layout:
Roswitha Siegler, Simone Soesters

Reproduction:
ludwig:media, Zell am See

Print:
Aumüller Druck, Regensburg
1st edition 2011

Institut für internationale
Architektur-Dokumentation GmbH & Co. KG
Hackerbrücke 6, D-80335 München
Tel.: +49/89/38 16 20-0
Fax: +49/89/39 86 70
www.detail.de

© 2011 Institut für internationale
Architektur-Dokumentation GmbH & Co. KG, Munich
A specialist book from Redaktion DETAIL

ISBN: 978-3-920034-54-6

Contents

"Sustainability is the concept of a lasting forward-looking development of all economic, ecological and social aspects of human existence. These three pillars of sustainability are interdependent and require a balanced coordination." This is the most common definition of sustainability which was formulated by the Enquete Commission of the German Bundestag on the "Protection of Humanity and Environment". Sustainability therefore embraces all aspects of human life.

The building industry in particular has a considerable impact on the sustainable actions of our society since immense amounts of energy are consumed and large volume flows are required. Furthermore, construction materials and buildings are extremely durable and therefore have an influence on our environment and society for long periods of time.

Since society is sensitive to environmental issues, much can be achieved by making use of public opinion. Attitudes and behaviours change and even radical, far-reaching measures can be implemented. In describing "environmental sins", reference is made to concentration levels of pollutants or other contaminants, of which there are specified levels that may not be exceeded. Energy Performance Certificates (EPCs) defining the quality of buildings in terms of their energy efficiency have become obligatory almost throughout the whole of the EU.

However, up until now there has been a lack of widely acceptable, tried and tested comparison tools for a holistic assessment of a building's sustainability.

For a long time, the considerable complexity made it almost impossible to perform a truly comprehensive assessment and to provide a transparent rating of a sustainable building. Yet, these are prerequisites to motivate people and ensure that our everyday actions improve sustainability. In a similar way to the consumption of energy, where Energy Performance Certificates form a basis for comparison, a building's sustainability also requires a simple and clear but, at the same time, reasonably precise assessment method.

The beginnings of these eco-assessment and certification systems date back to the early 1990s. Their development throughout the world has gained increasing momentum in recent years. Some general trends highlighting the conflicting priorities currently surrounding building certification stand out:

- The aim of certificates is to make the sustainability of buildings transparent for society and economically feasible for investors and clients. The development and application of the systems is therefore not only being promoted by governments, there are also economic drivers. In several cases, the forces are coordinated, in others the two interest groups have taken a different approach and are following different paths. The foundations for the German Quality Label for Sustainable Building (Deutsches Gütesiegel Nachhaltiges Bauen) were for example developed in a cooperation between the Federal Ministry of Transport, Building and Urban Development (BMVBS) and the German Sustainable Building Council (Deutsche Gesellschaft für Nachhaltiges Bauen e.V., DGNB). Today, however, it is used by both parties independently with different names (DGNB Certificate and BNB) and the onward development is being carried out separately.
- Certification systems define and describe the requirements of the criteria and the objectives of sustainable building in a clear and comprehensible way. These guidelines then function as valuable design and quality assurance tools supporting clients and planning teams in their aim to erect sustainable buildings.
- The assessment methods are becoming more and more complex; the definition of criteria and the process involved in achieving objectives ever more precise. Nevertheless, it is necessary to make sure that the application of a certification system does not complicate the design process. Sustainability will only gain further acceptance if building certification remains feasible, if there is added value and the requirements continue to be transparent and comprehensible for all participants.
- Building certification sets new standards in areas of construction that have, up until today, only been a minor issue or indeed of no importance. It stands to reason that some planning participants are slightly sceptical about whether rating systems will lead to a rationalisation of all planning matters forcing design aspects to take a backseat. However, numerous completed, certified buildings negate this theory.
- On the one hand, the individual systems and their operating companies or associations are cooperating, on the other hand, they are competing for a share of the global market. In years to come, this could lead to a gradual convergence of system structures and the basic approaches as well as the benchmarks for the fulfilment of individual criteria. Still, it can hardly be expected that a global, uniform certification system will emerge in the foreseeable future.
- Measured against the global construction volume, certified buildings are still in the minority. However, the role model

effect of these buildings exceeds the volume by far giving the building sector new impetus and creating a market for new products.

- Certification systems must be adapted to meet the needs of regional climate, social and economic conditions. Yet, at the same time, they must be designed to compare the sustainability of buildings worldwide. The ability to cope with this apparent contradiction is one of the main challenges which future development faces.
- The aim of certification systems is to provide transparency and clarity in the field of sustainable development. However, new systems are constantly being introduced. It follows that there is an urgent need for an up-to-date guide to the world of established sustainability labels.

This book is designed to meet this need. It conveys practical knowledge on the various assessment and certification systems and helps to highlight the differences and the fields of application. The focus is on presentation of the systems with the widest distribution worldwide and in Europe and on those that are most advanced in terms of approach and structure.

The introductory chapters explain the global conditions and aims of sustainable building, which form the basis of all important assessment methods, as well as the historical development and the institutional background of building certification. This is followed by a detailed description of the systems, BREEAM, LEED, DGNB, CASBEE, MINERGIE, HQE and the EU GreenBuilding Programme. Each description includes the objectives and the structure of the assessment method, past and current developments, the criteria and the respective definitions, the certification process as well as the certification costs.

The two following chapters delve deeper into the more important aspects of building certification, illustrated by examples based on the BREEAM, LEED and DGNB systems. Aspects covered in comparisons of the three systems include planning processes, documentation requirements and the main criteria in the assessments. In addition, the chapter "System comparison" describes the status quo of international standards in the field of sustainable building.

The economic aspects, as explained in the chapter "Economic aspects and market potentials", are fundamental factors for the success of a certification system and the suitability for future use. The aim is to balance the extra costs incurred through certification with the cost savings achieved through improved building operation, possible additional income due to better rentability and value stability of the property. Tajo Friedmann sums up the current situation in his statement: "Investors and tenants have discovered the significance of sustainability certificates to advance their own interests. Consequently, assessment methods have become established as standard in some market segments. However, the expense and time required as well as the necessity to involve an external consultant (auditor, specialist engineer) are counteracting a quick establishment of already marketable certificates in a number of different market constellations."

So long as building certification is not a statutory requirement, as with residential buildings in the United Kingdom, sustainability labels seem to appeal mostly to upmarket office buildings and commercial properties. This is documented clearly by the reference buildings described in the second to last chapter of this book. The main focus here is on a holistic presentation of the buildings and the planning sequences. Alongside the process of building certification, the chosen examples explain the design philosophy, the technical concepts and the knowledge gained from each project.

The final chapter of the book takes a look into the possible future of building certification and sustainable development. Existing trends include moves to broaden the perspective to incorporate entire building complexes, estates or urban districts since in some instances the potential for improvements in sustainability can only be achieved at this higher level. A second phenomenon is the increasing number of courses dealing with the subject of sustainable building offered by universities and other educational institutions. Naturally, these also include offers arising out of the introduction or use of certification systems.

Standardisation of the various systems at an international level is not yet within sight due to the prevailing regional differences. If this standardisation were achieved, the result would not only be considerable synergies and cost saving, but also a maximum degree of transparency and comparability of sustainability in buildings. On the other hand, the current situation has its advantages: the principle "competition is good for business" also applies to building certification. The variety of approaches available today is beneficial for the content-related further development of all systems and gives those already tried and tested fresh impetus.

Sustainable building

To secure the quality of life for future generations we must ensure the sustainable and efficient use of our planet's resources. This requirement applies to architecture as well as to land use and urban planning [1]. Today and in future, the goal must be to achieve architecture of the best possible quality, while at the same ensuring maximum protection of resources. Sustainable architecture is often described in terms of "ecological planning" and "energy-efficient building". However, ecology and energy efficiency are only some aspects of sustainable development. The field of sustainable building encompasses a considerably more complex range of themes. While the aspects of ecology, economy and society form the classic dimensions of sustainable planning and building, sustainable architecture at both national and international levels is increasingly characterised by categories such as quality of technology and processes as well as functional and location-specific aspects [2].

In recent years, a variety of tools has been developed to measure and compare the quality of sustainable building. These labels, certificates and assessment systems, the most important of which are introduced in this book, should, however, always be seen in terms of their dependence on the social, political, cultural and climatic situation of the nation or the region for which they were developed To understand the content and objectives of such tools and the theme of sustainable building as a whole, it is therefore necessary to take a closer look at the international situations that have arisen as a result of global change and which, in the last few years, have helped to shape sustainable development at a global level.

Global change

Recent decades have shown that our lifestyle and our demands on the architecture of our homes, workplaces and leisure facilities have changed radically since the start of the industrial revolution and that the rapid development of new technologies in the energy production and information sectors has brought with it considerable social changes. Since the end of the 18th century in Europe and the USA, and since the late 19th century also in Japan and other parts of Asia, industrialisation introduced the transition from an agricultural to an industrial society. Newly industrialising countries such as China and India have been experiencing a similar development in recent decades, but in a far more radical manner and at a much faster pace. Enormous economic growth and increasing poverty, population growth and the ageing of society as well as urbanisation all reflect this development. Climate change, the loss of biological diversity, increasing soil degradation and land use, air pollution as well as the shortage and pollution of drinking water are signs of critical changes in our natural environment that are continuing worldwide.

The prosperity of the industrialised nations is still based on the use of finite fossil energy sources. In addition the use of resources and the consumption of energy are very unevenly distributed in different regions. Since the first oil crisis in the 1970s the dependence of humankind on economic growth and fossil fuels has become drastically clear [3] (Fig. 1.1). This realisation has for some time now been leading to new developments in the area of building construction that also have far-reaching effects on the future planning, construction and operation of buildings. Environmental technologies and sustainable processes nowadays form an important part of sustainable building [4].

However, sustainable planning and building does not take place just at regional and national levels, but is determined by international boundary conditions. These are subject to constant change and differ from generation to generation and according to history, culture, climate and the political situation (Fig. 1.2). Consequently, sustainability in building must be defined differently for different epochs and it must be constantly adapted to suit new developments. This is possible only by observing global processes of change, which on the one hand influence each other to a considerable extent and also exert an effect on national and international building activity (Fig. 1.3):

· social change: demographic changes, population growth, ageing, urbanisation, migration, spatial separation in cities and social restructuring processes in cities and regions (gentrification)
· ecological change: global environmental changes, warming, deforestation, loss of biodiversity, acidification of the seas
· political change: agreements on protecting the climate and the environment, legislation on saving energy and resources as well as with regard to sustainability and renewable energies
· economic change: changes in the building industry labour market (new professions), new environmental technologies in the building sector, funding schemes for ecological and energy-efficient buildings, as well as consideration of the entire life cycle of properties (construction and running costs)

Social change

Social change results from global population growth, demographic change, urbanisation and migration. All of these aspects have significant effects on architecture and the building industry.

Demographic change and population increase

Demographic change and population growth are very closely related. Since the beginning of the 19th century, improved living conditions and medical progress have together led to a decrease in child mortality and increased life expectancy. This, in turn, has led to growth in world population that is still continuing and will remain a factor in future, as is clearly shown by a report of the United Nations Population Division (2006 revision). Whereas in 2007, 6.7 billion people (that is 547 million more than in 2000) lived on earth, by 2050 the United Nations expect the world population to increase to around 9.2 billion (Fig. 1.4, p. 10). This represents a global population growth figure of around 30 million people each year [5].

After the exponential population growth in the 20th century – from 1.5 billion to four times this figure in barely one hundred years – demographic development in the 21st century will be marked by a gradual decline in growth rates and a distinct ageing process. According to prognoses of the UN population fund, UNFPA, the often prophesied "population explosion" will not, in fact, happen. What is known as the demographic transition plays an important role in stabilising population growth. This phase is characterised by a reduction in birth rates, lower mortality rates, increasing life expectancy and weaker population growth. While the wealthy industrial nations of Western Europe went through this phase over one hundred years ago, other countries are only at the start. In Africa demographic transition is taking place more slowly than in Asia or Latin America, but in general we can assume that the trend will stabilise and by 2050 will have been established world-wide (Fig. 1.7).

In the industrial nations, the phenomenon of ageing in particular is defining societal change. At present, the majority of those in work in these countries are only about 12 years away from retirement. In 2007 around 20 % of the world population was older than 60, by 2050 this figure will

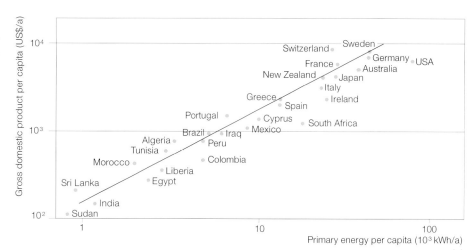

1.1

Global change

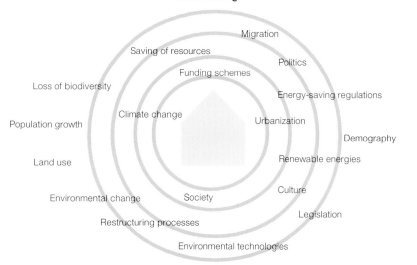

1.2

Aspects	Individual phenomena
Social change	• Demographic changes • Population growth • Ageing • Urbanisation • Spatial segregation in cities • Social restructuring processes of urban districts and regions (gentrification) • Migration
Ecological change	• Global environmental change • Warming • Deforestation • Loss of biodiversity • Acidification of the seas
Political change	• Kyoto protocol • Legislation on energy-saving and sustainability, saving resources and renewable energies • Certificate trading
Economic change	• Changes in the labour market in the building industry • New environmental technologies in the building sector • Subsidy programme for ecological and energy-efficient buildings and urban planning • Consideration of the entire life cycle of properties (construction and running costs)

1.3

1.1 Correlation between gross domestic product and primary energy requirements for selected countries in 1970

1.2 Sustainable architecture in relation to global change

1.3 Aspects of global change

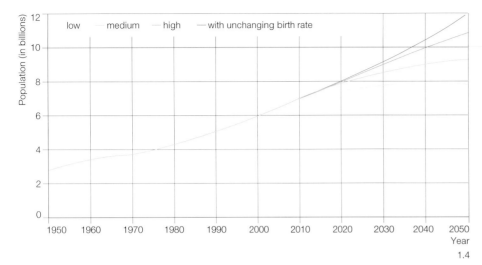

1.4

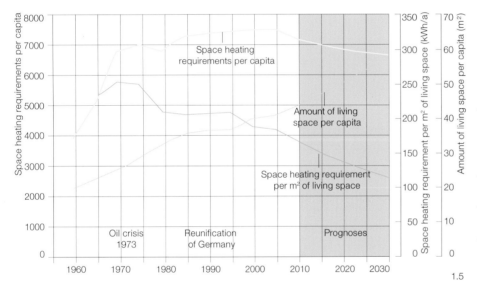

1.5

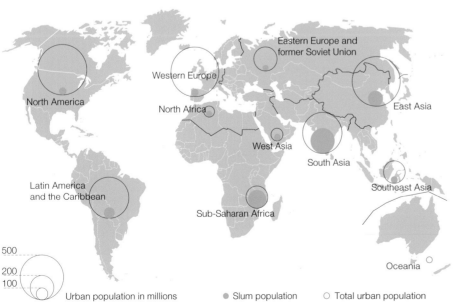

500
200
100
Urban population in millions ● Slum population ○ Total urban population

Oceania ○

1.6

have risen to 33% (Fig. 1.11, p. 12) [6]. The ageing of society imposes new demands on our buildings for work, leisure and living. The elimination of physical barriers in both work and private life will become an increasingly important factor in the area of sustainable building. Declining population figures and demands for greater comfort in our homes and lives are leading to a rise in the average per capita area of living space. Since the 1960s, the amount of living space per capita in Germany has risen from around 20 m^2 to a new high (2007) of about 42 m^2 (Fig. 1.9). And, as a comparison with other countries shows, in this area Germany by no means tops the ranking [7]:

- United States: 68.1 m^2
- Denmark 50.6 m^2
- Sweden: 44 m^2
- Switzerland: 44 m^2
- Great Britain: 44 m^2
- Germany: 41.9 m^2

The per capita living space figure has risen, even though the amount of new housing construction in Germany continues to decline. An important reason for this increased figure is that newly constructed single-family houses and double-family houses as well as owner-occupied apartments now make up more than three-quarters of all new housing construction, and in this sector the floor area of the average dwelling is larger than in rented housing construction. This tendency illustrates a contradiction in our society and in the current sustainability debate: everyone talks about sustainability but is reluctant to cut back on personal luxury. Although the annual space heating requirement (per square metre of living space) is sinking due to legal regulations and new technologies, the Germans continue to use more space and more energy (Fig. 1.5) [8].

Urbanisation
The world has been urbanising increasingly since the start of the 20th century. In 1900, there were only eleven cities in the entire world with more than one million residents. By 1950, there were already 80 cities with a population of one million or more; in 2000, there were 400 such cities, and in 2015 there will probably be around 550 cities of this size throughout the world (Fig. 1.10). Whereas in 1900, city dwellers amounted only to 14% of the world's total

population, now, at the start of the 21st century, around 50% of the world's population lives in cities. According to estimates from the UN/DESA (United Nations – Department of Economic and Social Affairs), by 2050 the proportion of urban population will rise further to a figure of almost 69% [9].

The process of urbanisation differs from one continent to another. In Europe there are only a few metropolis-like major cities such as London, Moscow and Paris. The population has tended to settle in conurbations where cities sprawl into the surrounding region. In contrast, on the American continent numerous "megacities" have developed with populations of more than 15 million, e.g. São Paulo, Buenos Aires, Mexico City, New York and Los Angeles. In Australia and New Zealand, 75% of the population already lives in cities. In Asia, in particular, the pace of urbanisation has increased rapidly in recent decades. It has been estimated that around ten mega-cities throughout the world will reach the 20 million mark by 2020 (e.g. Bombay, Karachi, Shanghai, Dhaka, Jakarta, and Tokyo). In Africa the development of cities differs greatly from region to region, but here, too, there are huge urban centres such as Kinshasa, Cairo or Lagos. Many of these centres consist mostly of slums whose growth is accompanied by social tensions and ecological problems (Fig. 1.6).

Development in the industrialised nations, above all in Europe, is different and in each case is strongly dependent on the regional and economic circumstances (Fig. 1.8). Whereas a number of conurbations such as Munich, Paris or London continue to show population growth, population figures in other cities and regions in Europe are decreasing drastically and, in some cases, entire urban districts are disappearing. In Eisenhüttenstadt, for example, the population decreased by 32% between 1989 and 2004. This development was accompanied by the demolition of 4500 apartments up until 2010. Especially the eastern regions of Germany are severely affected by the process of shrinking towns, whereas in the north-west and south of the country, population figures, in particular in large urban centres such as Hamburg, the Rhine-Main metropolitan area, Stuttgart or Munich, are clearly increasing [11].

In addition, spatial segregation and social restructuring processes (gentrification)

also shape urban planning today. Since the introduction of the social housing policy after 1918, the even distribution of various social and professional groups has been a fixed goal of urban development, but even today there is still no completely even distribution of social groups in urban space. The mix of different social classes is one of the most important strategies and goals of the European Council's sustainability policy [12]. Sustainable urban development functions only when economic growth, social cohesion and justice as well as the elimination of social segregation work together as equal partners [13].

Urbanisation also leads to increasing mobility. Mobility is an important precondition for the proper functioning of our working society. Traffic, which in Germany represents the second largest energy consumption sector after building, today moves not only between the buildings in a city but increasingly extends across regional and national boundaries.

The process of continuous urbanisation places a strain on non-renewable energy sources as enormous amounts of electricity and gas are used for the industry as well as for the heating and air conditioning of buildings. This, together with the enormous increase in individual motorized traffic in cities and conurbations, leads to increased air pollution and noise and thus endangers health and the environment.

A comparison of the per capita energy use of different cities shows a clear relationship between urban density and energy efficiency. For example, densely populated cities such as Singapore or Hong Kong have an energy consumption level that is up to eight times less than that of less densely populated cities, such as Houston or Phoenix. However, once a figure of 75 persons per hectare is exceeded, this effect grows weaker (e.g. Berlin, Munich). With more than 150 persons per hectare, only a minimal saving is possible [14] (e.g. Paris). In addition, modern day slums and shanty towns with more than 1000 persons per hectare, some of which must do without drinking water and energy, show that urban density is not always advantageous and can, indeed, lead to major ecological and social problems that are difficult to solve. To counteract this trend, sustainable building must extend far beyond the area of architecture and must begin with regional and urban planning. Sustainable

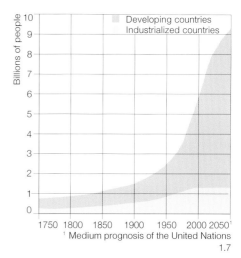

1.7

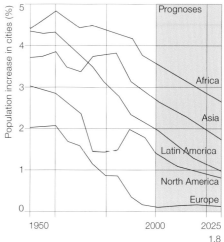

1.8

Year	Area/person
2007	41.9 m^2
2006	41.6 m^2
2005	41.2 m^2
2004	40.8 m^2
2003	40.5 m^2

1.9

Year	Cities with more than 1 million inhabitants
1900	11
1950	80
1990	276
2000	400
2015	550

1.10

1.4 Prognoses of population growth
1.5 Correlation between living area, per capital heating energy requirements and square metres of living space
1.6 Urban and slum population in various regions
1.7 Development of population growth up to 2050 in the industrialized and developing countries
1.8 Population increase in the cities: the cities will grow more slowly
1.9 Development of per capita living area in Germany
1.10 Number of cities with a population of over one million in the world between 1900 and 2015

urban development is therefore more necessary than ever before.

Migration
The phenomenon of population movements is thousands of years old. The reasons behind such movements were and remain very diverse: natural catastrophes, the search for better living conditions, the pure delight in adventure, or mass expulsions. Alongside emigration and war refugees, there is today a new wave of migration: climate refugees. Already more than 20 million people are fleeing from natural catastrophes, the rise in sea levels caused by climate change and shortage of drinking water. Prognoses from the "German Advisory Council on Global Change" (WBGU), which advises the German federal government, forecast that by 2050 the number of climate refugees could rise to between 80 and 400 million [15]. The thousands of refugees from Africa who are stranded every year on the Italian coast and the inhabitants of South Pacific island states who apply for asylum represent only the spearhead of a development which, in a few years, could lead to world-wide climate conflicts and wars. Increasing migration brings about an ethnic mix of the population and with it numerous new challenges for those countries who take in the migrants or whose

population figures are decreasing. This also has an impact on architecture which in this case must take on an important role. It must contribute to the integration and identification processes and counteract the social tensions that result from the current waves of migration.

Ecological change
Experts have been warning for decades about increasing environmental pollution and the associated, irreversible damage to our planet. Among the effects are global warming, natural catastrophes. (flooding, storms) extensive clearing of forests, increasing land use, the loss of biodiversity and shortage of drinking water. This damage results primarily from [16]:
· rapid population growth
· wasteful use of raw materials and fossil energy sources
· increasing decline in the quality of air, water and ground
· the exorbitant increase in the volume of waste

The building sector, too, has enormous effects on the environment, as the following figures clearly present: the European building sector uses around 50 % of the world's natural resources as well as 40 % of the energy and 16 % of the water. In addition, building construction causes

around 60 % of all waste produced, and around 40 % of worldwide greenhouse gas emissions result from the production and use of buildings [17].

Climate change
Meteorological measurements over the last few decades show that our planet is growing warmer. In the past 100 years, the average global temperature rose by about 0.8 °C. The last fifteen years were among the warmest since measurements began to be taken. According to scientific scenarios, by the year 2100, the figure for global warming in our part of the world (in comparison to 2000) will lie between 1.5 and 5.8 °C. This represents an enormous change for such a short period of time: during the last Ice Age, 15 000 years ago, the temperatures were only about 5 °C colder than today.
In its fourth report published in 2007, the UN climate council IPCC (Intergovernmental Panel on Climate Change) pointed out that the greenhouse effect has increased significantly since the 19th century and established a connection between global climate change and the increased emissions of greenhouse gases caused by humankind (Fig. 1.12). Since then this fact has been generally accepted and recognised by politicians. Above all, the increase in the concentra-

Proportion of people over 60 (prognosis for 2050)
  0–10%   10–20%   20–25%   25–30%   over 30%

1.11

tion of CO_2, which since 1750 has risen by 36 % to a current figure of 383 ppm (parts per million), is responsible for the greenhouse effect. The year 1750 serves as a reference year as it marks the approximate start of industrialisation. At present, the CO_2 concentration is rising annually by 2.5 ppm [18].

Other gases also contribute to exacerbating climate change. In this context, mention should be made of methane (CH_4), nitrogen oxide (N_2O), fully halogenated chlorofluorocarbons (H-CFCs), partially halogenated chlorofluorocarbons (CFCs) and sulphur hexafluoride (SF_6). On account of the ozone damage they cause, the chlorofluorocarbons used in refrigeration and cooling plants are to be completely prohibited in the EU from 2015.

But what effects do changing climate conditions have on our environment and the earth's sensitive ecological systems? Today the debate about climate has attained new dimensions, to which politics, business, but also every individual human being, must react. Even today numerous consequences of climate change are evident: the melting of glaciers and polar ice caps, flooding, mudslides and storms. These natural catastrophes, which in recent years have occurred with greater frequency, and the damage that they cause have a measurable influence on the economy and the gross domestic product, in particular those of very poor countries. To prevent the further advance of climate change or, at the very least, to weaken it, our consumption patterns and economic behaviour, but also our building practices, will have to change radically within the next few years [19].

Land use
In the last 40 years the amount of land required for settlement and transport in Germany has almost doubled (8.0 % for housing, 4.9 % for transport; Fig. 1.13, p. 14). Despite stagnating population figures, in the last decade, a further 120 hectares of land were on average used every day for housing and transport. This represents about 52 hectares per 100 000 inhabitants, per year. In comparison with other European countries, such as England, where the relevant figure is 14.3 hectares per 100 000 inhabitants, this gives an idea of the enormous extent of sealed surfaces in Germany. Although

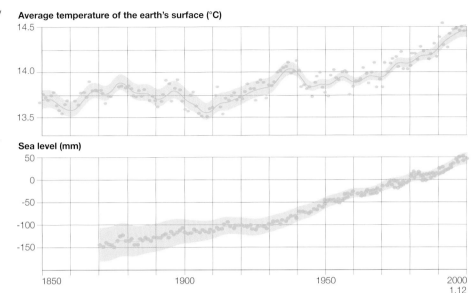

1.12

Area type	Total	% of the land area
Settlement areas		
• Areas covered by buildings	27 634 km²	7.7 %
• Areas for communal use	1106 km²	0.3 %
Traffic areas		
• Traffic and transport (supra-regional traffic and local main traffic arteries)	7638 km²	2.1 %
• Areas of filled ground and excavations	2199 km²	0.6 %
• Areas for supplies and disposals	605 km²	0.2 %
• Other areas	6807 km²	2.0 %
Green areas and areas used for agricultural purposes		
• Green areas	7686 km²	2.2 %
• Agriculture	191 119 km²	53.5 %
• Forestry	105 432 km²	29.5 %
• Water	6749 km²	1.9 %

1.13

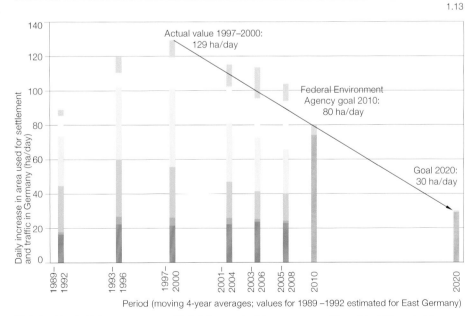

1.14

1.11 Number of people over sixty as a proportion of total population (prognosis for 2050)
1.12 Effects of climate change

1.13 Distribution of land use in Germany (as of 2004)
1.14 Daily increase in area used for settlement and traffic in Germany

13

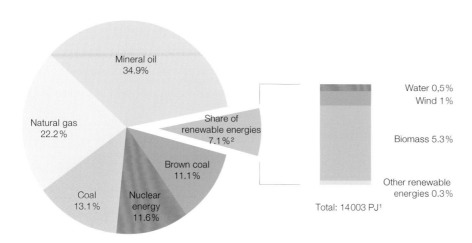

Mineral oil
34.9%

Natural gas
22.2%

Share of
renewable energies
7.1%[2]

Water 0,5%
Wind 1%

Biomass 5.3%

Coal
13.1%

Nuclear
energy
11.6%

Brown coal
11.1%

Other renewable
energies 0.3%

Total: 14003 PJ[1]

[1] Consumption 2008. Status: February 2009
[2] Calculated according to physical energy content method: 9.7%

1.15

the sustainability strategy of the federal government calls for a drastic reduction in the amount of land required for the purposes of settlement and transport to 30 ha/day by 2020, this goal is still far from being reached (Fig. 1.14, p. 14) [20]. Within the various federal states, the proportion of sealed surface area varies considerably. It is highest in the city-states Berlin (69.6%), Hamburg (59.0%) and Bremen (56.6%), and lowest in Mecklenburg-Vorpommern, where the figure is only 7.3% [21].

Use of resources
The sources of raw materials and energy existing on earth are described as resources. A difference is made between reserves and resources: the term "reserves" is used to describe known deposits that can be extracted using technology available today, for example deposits of mineral fuels. Resources, on the other hand, are those deposits that can probably be exploited with the technology that will become available in the future without consideration of cost efficiency. These include energy commodities whose existence can be assumed on the basis of geological indicators but have not yet been proven, or which, given the cost of extracting them or the lack of the requisite technological means, cannot yet be exploited in an economically viable way [22].

Today the industrialised nations and the emerging countries are highly dependent on the availability of energy commodities. Since the end of the Second World War humankind has used more fossil raw materials than in its entire previous history. So far more than half the resources have been used in the industrialised countries, in the future this balance will swing in favour of the emerging and developing countries. At present, non-renewable energy sources account for approximately 80% of the total consumption of primary energy worldwide (Fig. 1.17) [23]. In Germany this figure is as high as 93% (Fig. 1.15) [24].

According to a prognosis made by the German Federal Ministry for Economics (BMWi), in 2030 four-fifths of the world's energy requirements will still be met by fossil fuels. The most important primary energy source will continue to be mineral oil, gas will take second place. Although the absolute consumption of non-fossil energy sources will continue

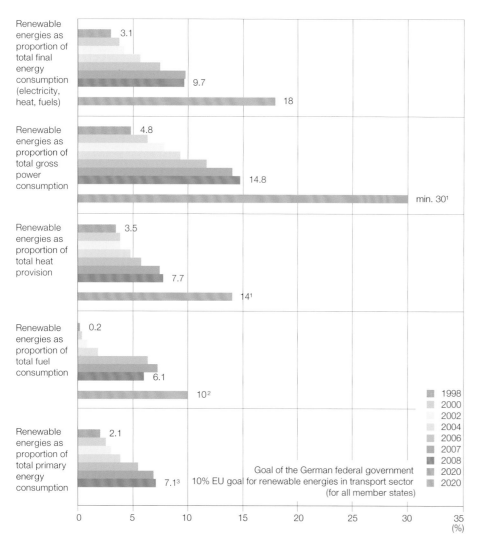

Renewable energies as proportion of total final energy consumption (electricity, heat, fuels)

3.1

9.7

18

Renewable energies as proportion of total gross power consumption

4.8

14.8

min. 30[1]

Renewable energies as proportion of total heat provision

3.5

7.7

14[1]

Renewable energies as proportion of total fuel consumption

0.2

6.1

10[2]

Renewable energies as proportion of total primary energy consumption

2.1

7.1[3]

Goal of the German federal government
10% EU goal for renewable energies in transport sector
(for all member states)

1998
2000
2002
2004
2006
2007
2008
2020
2020

0   5   10   15   20   25   30   35
(%)

[1] Sources: Renewable Energy Sources Act (EEG 2009) and Renewable Energies in the Heat Sector Act (EEWärmeG) from 2008
[2] Source: EU directive to promote the use of energy from renewable sources
[3] Proportion of primary energy consumption calculated according to (the official) physical energy content method; according to the partial substitution method: 9.7%

1.16

to grow, their proportion of the total world energy consumption will decrease, as energy consumption will rise faster than the use of renewable energies [25]. These statistics conflict with the statistical range of conventionally exploitable, non-renewable energy reserves. According to prognoses, existing mineral oil reserves will be exhausted in 50 years time, the deposits of natural gas in 70 years, and coal deposits in 190 years [26]. A reduction in the consumption of energy and the use of energy-efficient technologies in the building sector are therefore more urgently necessary than ever before. Since the mid-1970s, on account of the dramatic rise in the prices of fossil energies, new technologies, alongside historic forms of the use of biomass, wind and water energy, have increasingly become established in the area of renewable energies. The safety problems with regard to nuclear energy and the Chernobyl disaster in 1986 have encouraged this development. As a consequence of political frameworks such as the Renewable Energy Sources Act (EEG) and the Renewable Energies Heat Act (EEWärmeG), which are intended to increase the proportion of renewable energies used for the generation of electricity to at least 30%, and in the areas of heating and cooling to at least 14% by the year 2020, a clear growth in the use of renewable energies such as solar radiation, hydroelectric power, wind energy, geothermal energy and biomass can already be observed today. In Germany, a continuous increase, particularly in the areas of gross electricity consumption and final energy, is clearly visible (Fig. 1.16) [27]. At present the proportion of renewable energies in Germany amounts to approximately 10% of the total heat, electricity and fuel consumption (final energy) (status 2009) [28, 29].

Various studies and scenarios, such as the AEO 2010 prognosis (Annual Energy Outlook 2010) [30] or the Advanced Energy Revolution Scenario [31] assume an increase in the use of renewable energies of around 80% by the year 2035 or latest 2050. A study by the German Renewable Energy Research Association (FVEE) [32] even comes to the conclusion that a 100% provision with renewable energies is possible in Germany by 2050.

Timber industry
Forests have always been and today still

remain one of our planet's most important resources. At present around 1.6 billion people depend on forests for their livelihood. Around 70% of all known animal and plant species in the world live in forests. The start of industrialisation, the dramatic rise in population and the increasing use of land initiated the process of deforestation, i.e. the worldwide transformation of woodland areas into other kinds of land use. Often the consequence was a reduction in the variety of species in the animal and plant world, or even the extinction of individual species. The deforestation of our planet combined with the burning of fossil fuels is one of the most significant causes of global warming.

Today woods and forests cover an area of around four billion hectares, which represents around 30% of the earth's total land area. However, to use the wood and land, humankind every year destroys 15 million hectares of forest, i.e. every minute an area the size of 44 football pitches. Between 1990 and 2005, the world lost approximately 3% of all its forests. In particular primary or old-growth forests, including tropical rain forests, are vanishing. Forest loss is increasing in an uncontrolled fashion above all in countries outside Europe. The greatest amount of forest loss (even taking into account afforestation and reforestation) is being recorded in Latin America, above all in Brazil, where every year 4.3 million hectares of forest are cleared and, in comparison to the 1990s, deforestation has accelerated by 500,000 hectares per year. A further focal point of deforestation is Southeast Asia, in particular Indonesia and Papua New Guinea. In Africa, too, the annual loss of forests amounts to about 4 million hectares.

The only areas of the world which have been able to record a continuous growth in the area covered by forests over the past number of years are China and Europe. At present China, in response to numerous natural catastrophes and the threat posed by desertification, is undertaking the largest afforestation campaign in the world. More than 20 million hectares of new forests were planted between 2000 and 2005. By the year 2020, the People's Republic intends to increase the area of forest by a further 40 million hectares. [33].

But afforestation and plantations are only substitute measures and often lead to a

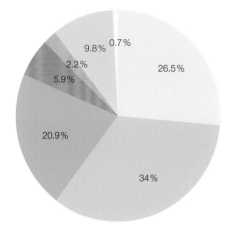

- Coal/turf
- Mineral oil
- Natural gas
- Nuclear energy
- Water power
- Biomass and waste
- Other

1.17

Country	Annual change (1000 ha/year)
Brazil	-3103
Indonesia	-1871
Sudan	-589
Myanmar	-466
Zambia	-445
Tanzania	-412
Nigeria	-410
DR Congo	-319
Zimbabwe	-313
Venezuela	-288
Total	**-8216**

a

Country	Annual change (1000 ha/year)
China	4058
Spain	296
Vietnam	241
USA	159
Italy	106
Chile	57
Cuba	56
Bulgaria	50
France	41
Portugal	40
Total	**5104**

b   1.18

1.15 Structure of primary energy consumption in Germany in 2008
1.16 Proportions and development of renewable energies in the supply of energy in Germany
1.17 World primary energy consumption in 2007 according to energy sources
1.18 Countries with the highest deforestation and afforestation rates worldwide 2000–2005
a deforestation
b afforestation

decline in global biodiversity. This is shown by the example of the United States which, although it can demonstrate a positive balance in terms of reforestation, occupies seventh place in the world as regards the loss of primary forest. Here primary forests are being replaced by plantations that are unable to recreate former habitats or to restore the former richness of plant and animal life.

This makes sustainable forestry all the more important. A first start is represented by certificates such as the FSC-Label (Forest Stewardship Council). The intention behind this certificate is to prevent uncontrolled felling of trees, violations of human rights and environmental pollution. To date, 10 million hectares in 25 countries have been certified by the FSC. This certificate is increasingly being used in the area of building, too [34].

Drinking water
One of the most important resources – and one that is growing increasingly scarce – is clean drinking water. On the one hand, many countries have enough water and there is no need to fear a shortage in future, while on the other hand, more than one billion people have no access to clean drinking water today. For example Asia, where 60 % of the world's population lives, has only 30 % of the world's drinking water resources. In other countries, above all in Africa, a large proportion of the population today suffers from chronic water shortage (Fig. 1.19). Current prognoses forecast that the availability of drinking water, above all in Africa, Asia and southern Europe, will decline dramatically by 2025.

According to UN figures, which assume a constant increase in consumption, in 20 years time, 1.8 billion people will live in regions with an absolute shortage of water. Whereas poor sectors of the population save water, the wastage of this essential resource is increasing with better living standards. At present Europeans consume between 100 and 200 litres daily. The water consumption of an American is on average 300–400 litres daily. The top position is held by the Australians, who use around 1000 litres of water per capita every day. To ensure the continuing availability of clean drinking water, we must use this resource in an efficient and sensible way. Measures such as the use of grey water and rain water, ensuring the proper functioning of plants and pipelines, as well as combating water pollution are first steps towards efficient use [35].

In addition to shortage of drinking water, the quality of water is a major problem. Today worldwide around 90 % of waste water and 70 % of industrial waste enters surface water untreated. According to figures provided by the UN, every year around four million people die from illnesses caused by dirty drinking water. Above all in developing and emerging countries, in addition to using technology to identify sources of water, it must increasingly be used to treat local water supplies [36].

The climate model of the 2008 IPCC study shows that in the 21st century the intensity of both rainfall and dry periods will change globally. Both the amount of precipitation and the number and lengths of dry periods will increase substantially. While the intensity of rain will increase in all climate zones, in particular the continents Africa and America but also southern Europe and Asia will have to anticipate longer dry periods. [37].

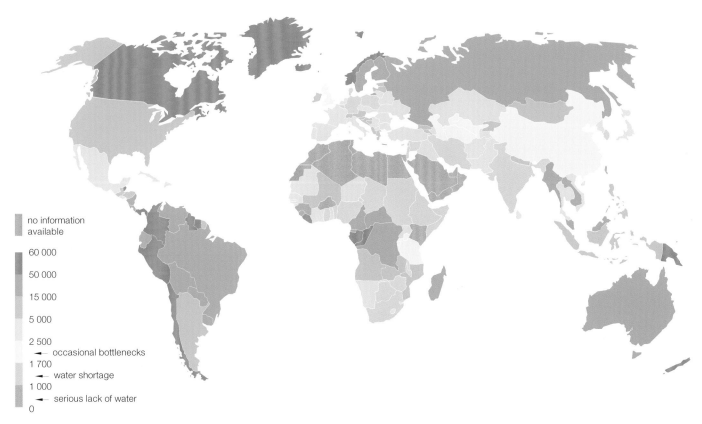

no information
available

60 000

50 000

15 000

5 000

2 500
◄── occasional bottlenecks
1 700
◄── water shortage
1 000
◄── serious lack of water
0

1.19 Availability of freshwater (in m² per person/year, situation in 2000)
1.20 International climate conferences

1.19

Volume of waste

The amount of waste that we produce increases with our growing use of resources. The building industry in particular is today a major producer of waste. Three-quarters of the current volume of waste is created in the industrialized nations. Whereas in Germany numerous waste management laws have been passed since the beginning of the 1970s, at international level there are still hardly any legal regulations relating to domestic and industrial waste. The first international agreement was the Basel Convention of the 1980s, which came into being under the patronage of the United Nations and which has been signed by 165 countries. However up to the present day most countries do not provide any statistics regarding the use of waste. In addition illegal waste transports of, above all, environmentally hazardous waste to Asia and Africa are creating a situation in which developing countries are increasingly functioning as the scrap yard of the world [38].

Political change

There is a direct relationship between humankind's actions, the destruction of the natural environment and current climate change. Awareness of this fact and the consciousness of the population at large have clearly improved in recent decades. This process was aided above all by politics and by the media. The terms climate change, energy efficiency and sustainability are today on everyone's lips. The current goals and measures of international climate protection policy are based largely on the results of the climate convention of 1992 (United Nations Framework Convention on Climate Change, UNFCCC) (Fig. 1.20). The Intergovernmental Panel on Climate Change (IPCC), established in 1988 by the United Nations Environmental Programme (UNEP) and the World Meteorological Organization (WMO), is regarded as the most important expert body on the subject of climate change. It does not itself conduct any scientific activity but compiles data on climate change, evaluates the risks of global warming and develops adaptation strategies, taking into account ecological, economic and social aspects. To date this body has produced four expert reports that form the current basis for the political and scientific discussion of global warming. The IPCC

Year	Conference/Event
1988	Founding of the Intergovernmental Panel on Climate Change (IPCC)
1990	Negotiations at the General Assembly of the UNO on a framework convention about climate protection
1992	UN Conference on the Environment and Development ("Earth Summit") in Rio de Janeiro: signing of the Framework Convention on Climate Change
1994	Framework Convention on Climate Change comes into force
1995	Berlin (COP 1): "Berlin Mandate"
1996	Geneva (COP 2): Ministerial Declaration
1997	Kyoto (COP 3): Kyoto Protocol
1998	Buenos Aires (COP 4): Plan of Action
2001	Marrakech (COP 7): negotiations
2002	World Summit on Sustainable Development in Johannesburg: October
2002	New Delhi (COP 8): relationship between sustainable development and climate protection
2003	Milan (COP 9): fund to encourage the development, spread and use of environmentally-friendly technologies
2004	Buenos Aires (COP 10): tenth anniversary of Framework Convention on Climate Change
2005	Montreal (COP 11): complete implementation of the Kyoto Protocol and introduction of a negotiation process for the period after 2012
2007	Bali (COP 13): Conference of the Parties on the development of a strategy for a climate agreement to follow the Kyoto Protocol
2009	Copenhagen (COP 15): Climate Summit in Copenhagen to establish a global climate agreement for the period from 2012
2010	Cancún (COP 16): Conference of the Parties

1.20

plans to issue its next report in 2014 [39]. At the 1992 UN conference in Rio de Janeiro 150 states agreed for the first time to limit emissions of greenhouse gases. Whereas at the "Earth Summit" of 1992 the main focus was on social and cultural aspects, the Kyoto Summit in 1997 emphasized the setting of practical goals. In the Kyoto Protocol, an additional protocol to the Framework Convention on Climate Change adopted in 1997, the industrialised nations present, committed themselves to setting legally binding targets for reductions in the emission of greenhouse gases. The aim of the climate protection agreement, which came into force in 2005, and will expire in 2013, is for industrialised countries to achieve an average 5.2 % reduction in their annual greenhouse gas emissions from the level in 1990, within what is known as the 'first commitment period' (2008–2012) [40]. At the climate summit in 2007 on the Indonesian island of Bali, the participating nations agreed upon a strategy for a successor agreement to the Kyoto Protocol. This proposed concluding the negotiations by the 2009 climate conference in Copenhagen. However, in Copenhagen the parties could not agree on a binding climate agreement and merely passed a non-binding declaration of political intent known as the "Copenhagen Accord". Even at the 16th climate conference in Cancún the following year, no successor

agreement to the Kyoto Protocol has been passed [41].

Although the Kyoto Protocol forms an important milestone in international climate protection policy, its objectives are far from adequate. Worldwide greenhouse gas emissions today are around 25 % above the level in the baseline year 1990. To limit the increase of the world-wide average temperature to what is regarded as the critical boundary of 2 % the industrialised nations would have to reduce their CO_2 emissions by the year 2050, to one quarter of today's figure. If the objectives which were agreed in the Kyoto Protocol were to be implemented in their entirety, this would reduce the global warming figure calculated for 2100 by only 0.06 °C, and to achieve just this all the nations involved would have to reach the agreed targets. However, the failure of the negotiations at the Copenhagen Climate Summit has shown how great the resistance to lowering CO_2 emissions actually is [42].

To provide an international role model the EU has committed itself to reducing its greenhouse gas emissions by the year 2020, to 20 % below the level for 1990, or, to 30 % if other industrialized nations commit themselves to comparable reductions in emissions as well as the economically more advanced developing countries also making their contributions. The most important aspect in the redution of greenhouse gas emissions should be a 20% increase in energy efficiency, and a tripling of renewable energy's share of European final energy consumption to a figure of 20% by 2020.

As 40% of the total consumption of energy in the EU is accounted for by the building sector, the reduction of energy consumption, and the use of energy from renewable sources in buildings, play a vital role in reaching the targets of the Kyoto Protocol. To achieve this, and in the course of harmonising standards, the EU member states committed themselves to translating the requirements of directive 2002/91/EG (Energy Performance of Buildings Directive, EPBD) of the European Parliament, regarding the overall energy efficiency of buildings, into national law. In May 2010 the European Parliament passed the revised building directive 2010/31/EU (EBPD 2010), which states that from 2021 onwards all new buildings throughout the EU must be nearly zero energy buildings.

In Germany it is planned to implement the new EU directive on the overall energy efficiency of buildings by revising the energy conservation regulations in 2012 (EnEV 2012) (Fig. 1.21). The first version of these energy conservation regulations (EnEV 2002) came into force on February 1, 2002 and combined the previous thermal insulation regulations (WSchV), and the heating plant regulations (HeizAnlV) . New versions of the EnEV came into force in 2004, 2007, and most recently in autumn 2009. The goal of EnEV 2009 is to reduce energy, heating and warm water requirements in new buildings by approx. 30% as against EnEV 2007 [43].

Economic change

The goal of our economy today is continuous growth. In our society growth is understood as increasing the gross national product (GNP) or the gross domestic product (GDP). However extreme economic growth generally takes place at the expense of the environment, as is clearly indicated by the cases of the newly industrialized countries such as China or India. As early as 1972 the study "Limits of Growth" by the Club of Rome questioned the sense and the feasibility of unrestricted growth. In this study the authors pointed out that, if

environmental pollution and the exploitation of natural raw materials were to continue unchanged, the absolute growth limits of our ecological system would be reached in the course of the next hundred years [44].

Whereas in the past, the incompatibility of sustainable, ecologically responsible activity with permanent economic growth was regularly pointed out, since the mid-1980s most ecologists see no contradiction between sustainability and economic success. Sustainable development incorporates complex efficiency in terms of resources, energy and materials as well as the efficient use of those factors that influence production (e.g. staff). Businesses, too, no longer see sustainability as an obstacle to growth, but as an opportunity for the future. In particular the Rio Conference in1992 introduced a change in thinking in this respect. As part of the Agenda 21, in addition to recommendations for ecological and social action, economic goals for trade and industry, such as support of environmentally friendly production or entrepreneurship with a sense of responsibility, were defined [45, 46].

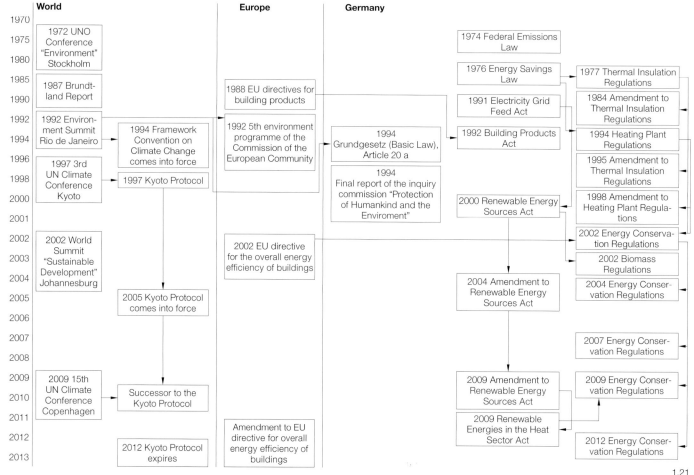

1.21

The Stern Report, which appeared in 2006, undertook the first economic assessment of climate change [47]. In this report the former head economist of the World Bank and later head of the British Government Economic Service, describes and calculates the consequences of global warming from an economic perspective. According to Stern the costs of climate change, i.e. the impact of rising sea levels, reductions in agricultural yields, natural catastrophes and major migration movements, would in the medium term mean a loss of between 5 and 20% of the global gross domestic product. Above all developing and newly industrialized countries would, he wrote, be negatively affected to a disproportionate extent by the economic effects of climate change [48]. According to Stern early action, increased use of renewable energies, the implementation of low CO_2 technologies and a clear increase in energy efficiency could mitigate the consequences of climate change.

Environmental technologies as a growth market
Today the main protagonists in the economy are fully aware that implementing and integrating resource-saving production processes allows them to optimise industrial processes, while at the same time improving their own image and developing characteristics that clearly distinguish them from their competitors. Thus environmental protection and economic growth are no longer necessarily in conflict with each other, but in fact are closely connected. Environmental technologies are among the most important future markets of the 21st century.
This development is shown in the Lead Market Initiative for Europe (LMI), launched by the EU Commission in 2007, the objective of which, is to strengthen the European market and to more than double the size of the economy by 2020 [49].In the process six lead markets were defined:
· e-health
· protective textiles
· sustainable construction
· recycling
· bio-based products
· renewable energies

The aim is that the energy-efficient and sustainable building market in particular should contribute to the advancement of

European and national economic markets. Aspects of environmental protection (e.g. efficient electrical appliances and heating plants), health questions (e.g. air quality in buildings) and user comfort (e.g. mobility of elderly people) are the principle focus of attention [50]. In addition the goals of the lead market 'Sustainable Construction' relate to the following areas [51]:
· transformation of national standardisation to reflect a more performance-based building approach
· further development of the EU directive on the overall energy efficiency of buildings

Europe-wide efficiency goals include:
· further development of national and European building legislation
· consideration of life cycle costs as well as the environmental characteristics of building products and buildings in the procurement policies of state bodies
· development of instruments and incentives to encourage sustainable building
· integration of aspects of sustainability in European standards
· further development of building product regulations
· development of assessment standards and aids to evaluate the sustainability of buildings

The tasks and goals for the lead market 'Sustainable Construction' were compiled in the 'Action Plan for Sustainable Construction' [52].
The environmental technology atlas for Germany, 'GreenTech made in Germany 2.0' (2009), also makes clear that the theme of sustainable building will capture an important share of the market in the future [53]. Prognoses suggest that at national level the turnover of environmental industries will almost double by 2020. In 2007 their share of the German GDP amounted to 8%, by 2020 this proportion should increase to 14%. The following environmental technology lead markets have developed on the global world market (Fig. 1.22):
· lead market energy efficiency
· lead market environmentally friendly energies
· lead market raw material efficiency
· lead market recycling management
· lead market sustainable water resources management
· lead market sustainable mobility

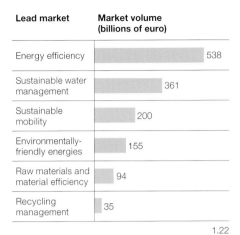

Lead market	Market volume (billions of euro)
Energy efficiency	538
Sustainable water management	361
Sustainable mobility	200
Environmentally-friendly energies	155
Raw materials and material efficiency	94
Recycling management	35

1.22

The double-figure growth rates with which these branches achieved a global market volume of around 1,400 billion euro in 2007 confirm the increasing importance of the role played by these six lead markets.

Economic change in the building sector
Today it is becoming clear that economic change also has a considerable impact on the building industry. Hence building owners as well as users are increasingly conscious that aspects of sustainability should be considered in the erection of new buildings, the renovation of existing, and in the operation of buildings. On the other hand, numerous new approaches to the erection and marketing of buildings reflect the call for an ever-increasing level of flexibility, with shorter payback periods and the separation of the roles of investor and user.
This increased consideration of aspects of sustainability in construction projects is supported on the one hand by numerous state subsidy programmes, such as, in Germany, the KfW programmes and the urban planning subsidy programme 'Stadtumbau West', as well as by new loan facilities from the banks. Since the reform of procurement law in Germany in the context of Green Public Procurement (GPP), social, environmentally-related and innovate aspects must be taken into consideration in public procurement processes. A study of the EU Commission [54] from 2010 showed that, through the implementation of GPP throughout Europe, not only can, on average, 25% of CO_2 emissions be avoided, but GPP also enables cost reductions in comparison

1.21 Development of requirements in the areas of energy and sustainability
1.22 Volume of world markets for environmental technologies 2007

to standard procurement policies. At present the greatest effects are achieved in the area of specifications and tenders for buildings (minus 10%).

With the technical means available to us today, it is possible to reduce consumption of energy and drinking water, as well as the production of waste by about one half, and to mitigate the environmental impact of noise and pollutants in the air and water [55]. Although these technologies involve higher acquisition costs, overall they result in short and long-term savings. This also applies to the building sector. In planning decisions, however, the main focus is often on construction costs. However, lower building costs and the lower building quality associated with them lead to a situation in which operation and maintenance costs can often outstrip investment costs within only a few years. With the use of sustainable technologies in the building sector and more environmentally friendly products we can reduce not only CO_2 emissions (Fig. 1.23), but also a building's running cost over its entire life cycle. Today the consideration of a property's entire life cycle already plays an increasingly important role in planning. In addition to running costs the emphasis here is on aspects such as adaptability for use by third parties, high suitability for conversion (possibility to refit the building for different kinds of uses, or modularity of the building), flexible design of the spatial structure, such as the adaptability of the electrical, media, heating and water supply, and disposal systems.

Surveys conducted amongst project developers, investors, designers and users show that sustainability will become an important criterion for decision-making as regards the design and marketing of buildings (Fig. 1.24). Although a sustainable property does not always necessarily mean a higher selling price or rental income, nevertheless buildings that are erected or renovated taking into account ecological, economic, and societal aspects and which can certify this with a sustainability certificate, such as LEED, BREEAM or DGNB, are easier to market (Figs. 1.25 and 1.26, p. 22). However surveys have also indicated that in the future the market will be willing to pay higher prices for sustainable buildings with proven lower CO_2 emissions [56, 57]. The increased use of environmental technologies and sustainable planning and

construction processes in the building sector also encourage the development of new job markets. Planning and consultancy services will have an important share of these. Alongside the energy consultant a new profession will become established, that of the sustainability consultant (Fig. 1.27, p. 22). These new professional fields demand additional specialist knowledge from engineers and designers, who will have to be integrated at an early stage in the new educational and training measures.

Sustainable development

The current term sustainability was shaped largely by the World Commission on Environment and Development, known as the Brundtland Commission. The Brundtland Report 'Our Common Future', which dates from 1987, describes as sustainable the kind of development that "meets the needs of the present without compromising the ability of future generations to meet their own needs" [58]. But in fact the idea of sustainable development is not a phenomenon of our society but can be traced back to forestry in the 18th century.

The first approaches to our present day thinking about sustainability were developed as early as the 1970s. At that time the economic model of the industrialized nations in particular was questioned. The book 'The Limits to Growth' (1972) by the Club of Rome drew attention to increasing environmental pollution and damage as well as to the resulting necessity to combine protection of nature with economic development. In the same year the first United Nations conference on the theme of humankind and the environment, (the Conference on the Human Environment) was held in Stockholm. The term 'sustainable development' (SD) on the other hand was first used within the context of the World Conservation Strategy in 1980 [60]. At the 1992 UNCED (United Nations Conference on the Environment and Development), known as the 1992 Rio Conference, the Rio Declaration and the Agenda 21 (an internationally valid development and environmental policy programme of action for sustainable development in the 21st century) were formulated. At international level numerous cities and towns have prepared a local Agenda 21 since 1992. The results of the theoretical and practical implementation in the individual

countries were presented at the World Summit on Sustainable Development 2002 in Johannesburg, which was the Rio+10 World Summit [61].

Europe's sustainability strategy
Based on the movement launched in Rio de Janeiro in 1992, the EU heads of state and government set up the EU Sustainable Development Strategy in 2001. This strategy is continually examined and modified by the European Commission. In June 2006 the following seven thematic areas were defined in the context of the modified "Renewed Strategy" [62]:
- climate change and clean energy
- sustainable development of transport
- sustainable consumption and sustainable production
- protection and management of natural resources
- public health
- global challenges with regard to poverty and sustainable development
- society, demography and migration

National sustainable development strategy in Germany
The European Commission is endeavouring to link the overall European approach with the national strategies of the member countries. The member states are called upon to establish conformity between national and European strategies, without losing sight of special regional features and characteristics. Germany's national sustainable development strategy was published in 2002 under the title 'Perspektiven für Deutschland' (Perspectives for Germany) and has been continuously developed since that time. The federal government has regularly published progress reports in this context. The national sustainable development strategy is based on the awareness that sustainable development cannot be decreed from above but that the state can only support its direction and implementation. In this sense the government has defined the following areas of action [63]:
- energy/climate
- environmentally-friendly mobility
- healthy production and nutrition
- shaping demographic change
- innovation and global responsibility

Approaches and strategies of sustainable development
The linking of sustainable development to growth and profit has today become

acceptable to many people, as it allows a fairer distribution of profits and a more considerate use of natural resources. In the area of industry sustainable development has gradually become reality in recent years. Businesses are becoming more and more aware that the implementation and integration of ecological factors enable industrial production processes to be upgraded, as well as allowing them to improve their image and standing, and to distinguish themselves from their competitors [64].

The different protagonists are approaching the model of sustainable development using different strategies, instruments, contents and definitions [65]:

- Three-column model [66]:
  equal priority for the ecological, economic and social dimension
- Magic triangle [67]:
  equal consideration given to ecological, economic and social aspects
- Tetrahedron of sustainability
  an institutional dimension is added to the classic three-column model (co-determination, participation)
- Five levels of sustainability:
  the incorporation of a cultural and spiritual basis alongside ecological, economic and social aspects
- Pentagon of sustainability:
  social stability and justice, sustainable economic methods, ecological capacity, securing and developing cultural qualities, as well as human health

Due to its simplicity and easy comprehensibility the three-column model appears to be successfully establishing itself. The origins of this approach cannot be precisely determined [68]. However, the final report of the inquiry commission "Schutz des Menschen und der Umwelt" of the German Bundestag from 1998 is also based on the essential features of this approach. The goal of the report was to operationalise the sustainability model for the areas of building and housing with regard to ecological, economic and societal aspects [69].

Within the context of the sustainability debate a distinction must be made between weak and strong sustainability. Weak sustainability describes the approach that balances ecological, economic and social resources against each other. According to this view nature is replaceable and can be technically recreated, i.e. the ecological damage and neg-

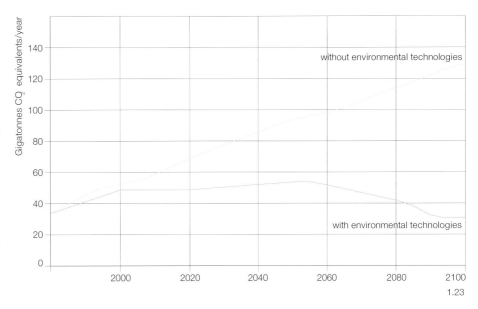

1.23

Is "green building" or the sustainability of real estate an important theme for your business?

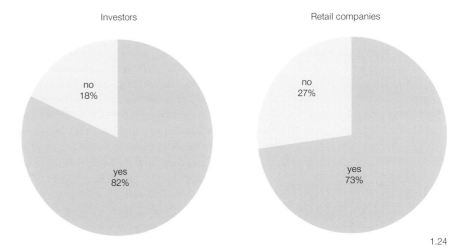

1.24

To what extent is the decision to buy a particular property influenced by aspects of sustainability?

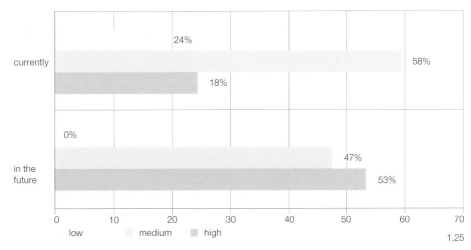

1.25

1.23 Prognoses for the development of global CO_2 emissions up to 2010 with the use of sustainable technologies and without the use of environmental technologies

1.24 "Green building" and the sustainability of real estate are important themes for the building sector (survey conducted among approx. 200 managers in the German real estate industry 2008)

1.25 Influence of aspects of sustainability on decisions about acquiring real estate (survey conducted among approx. 200 managers in the German real estate industry 2008)

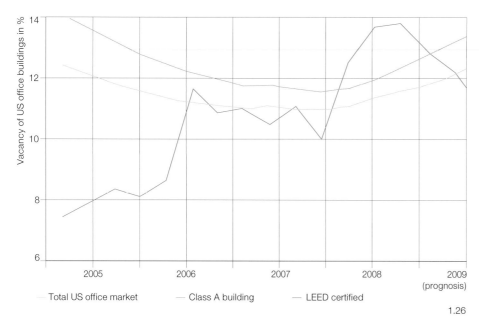

Total US office market — Class A building — LEED certified

1.26

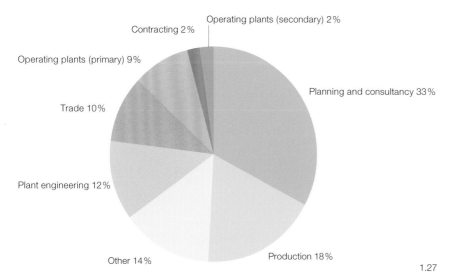

1.27

Year	Document
1993	The Declaration of Interdependence for a Sustainable Future UIA/AIA World Congress of Architects, Chicago
2007	The ACE Policy on Environment and Sustainable Architecture Architects' Council of Europe – Conseil des Architectes d'Europe (ACE-CAE)
2007	The Leipzig Charter on Sustainable European Cities EU ministers meeting on urban development and territorial cohesion
2008	The Council Conclusions on Architecture: Culture's Contribution to Sustainable Development European Forum for Architectural Policies (EFAP-FEPA)

1.28

1.26 Development of vacancy in LEED certified buildings in comparison to total US office market (status 2008)
1.27 Focus of activity of firms in the area of environmental technologies
1.28 Important declarations and agreements by international associations on sustainability in architecture and urban planning

ative effects of human economic activity can be compensated for at any time [70]. In contrast strong sustainability is a more theoretical approach, which asserts that the ecological crisis is caused by the squandering of natural resources, i.e. according to this interpretation finite resources should no longer be used in the future.

Closely related to these theories are the efficiency, sufficiency and consistency strategies:

• Efficiency: the efficiency approach calls for an extreme increase in resource productivity combined with a simultaneous reduction of resource consumption by means of innovative technologies, savings and increased efficiency, as our present infrastructures, goods and services are too energy and material-intensive.

• Sufficiency: the sufficiency strategy in contrast says that the consumption of energy and materials is determined by lifestyle and consumption habits. Consequently an extreme restriction of energy consumption as well as a reduction in the use of remaining resources is called for, i.e. consumers should behave responsibly and consciously do without energy-intensive products and services.

• Consistency: the objectives of the consistency strategy are to harmonise the flows of material and energy with the cycles of nature, and the development of products and processes such as, for example, the use of renewable energy supplies.

The goal of all strategies is to reduce the ecological footprint, i.e. to use fewer resources and to produce less waste. However, sustainable development cannot be achieved merely by implementing a number of individual strategies, but must be based on a combination of all three approaches and their reciprocal effects. Only a clear reduction in the consumption of energy and materials, as the result of efficiency and sufficiency measures, forms the basis for meeting remaining resource and energy demand through the use of renewable materials and renewable energy sources (consistency) [71].

Sustainable architecture

The call for the requirements of sustainability to be observed is today applicable to every kind of building activity. Consequently in the age of climate change, CO_2 emissions and the rapid increase in surface sealing, the sustainability debate plays an increasingly important role in architecture and town planning [72]. The first so-called low-tech architecture developed as a result of the first oil crisis in the 1970s. Numerous environmental initiatives sprang up, above all in the area of housing and in educational and cultural facilities. Materials such as timber and earth as well as planted roofs and facades began to (re) establish themselves in architecture. The 1968 movement, too, introduced new approaches in the area of social housing.

At about the same time what is known as high-tech architecture developed. In the area of office building in particular, spectacular buildings of metal and glass were built, using enormous amounts of energy and resources. In the past decade, however, a different direction has been adopted. Since the beginning of the 1990s, the implementation of ecological principles, the optimization of room climate and comfort with the help of energy-efficient concepts, as well as the use of renewable energies has gradually been developing into standard practice. Above all in Europe today a "golden mean" between low-tech and high-tech architecture is becoming apparent [73]. The combination of traditional materials with innovative industrial products and sustainable energy concepts has acquired considerably more relevance in the building sector.

Above all in Central and Northern Europe, numerous environmental laws and initiatives have been introduced in the construction industry since the 1980s. These range from energy saving, to waste separation, to water management. In Germany the important milestones in these efforts were the development of thermal insulation and energy saving regulations, as well as concepts for low energy, passive, and energy plus houses.

Although sustainable construction has a positive effect on the development of buildings' asset values, everyday practice still lags far behind the possibilities available. Consequently in 2001 the building ministry (BMVBS) introduced the guideline "Nachhaltiges Bauen" (Sustainable Building), which was re-issued in 2010. Based on the three-column model mentioned above, this guideline presents recommendations for action with regard to

ecological, economic and socio-cultural aspects, and reviews the entire life cycle of a building, from the planning and production of building products to construction and operation, and to its demolition. During the 1993 World Congress of the Union Internationale des Architectes (UIA), as a consequence of the Rio de Janeiro UN conference of 1992, the 'Declaration of Interdependence for a Sustainable Future' was published. According to this declaration sustainable architecture can not only minimize the impact of humankind on its environment but at the same time can also improve quality of life and promote economic prosperity [74]. Building on the basis established by this declaration, The Architects' Council of Europe (ACE), formulated the following goals for architecture (Fig. 1.28) [75]:

- to change current practices in design and construction
- to integrate the themes of sustainability into the planning process
- to promote sustainable design: combining aspects of sustainability with architectural competitions and tenders as well as to award prizes for sustainable art and architecture
- to support environmental and educational sustainability programmes in the building industry such as the integration of sustainability as a focal theme in courses given at universities and further education institutions
- to implement regulations and laws such as the development of environmental and energy guidelines for sustainable architecture
- collaboration at an interdisciplinary level, including the encouragement of research into sustainability through cooperation with industry, the business world, and the research institutes
- to encourage the idea of sustainability at both national and international level through collaboration with international organisations

Through publications such as 'A Green Vitruvius: A Sustainable Architectural Design' [76] in 1999 and 'Architecture and Quality of Life' [77] in 2004, the ACE has made it clear that the sustainability of public and private buildings, and security of public spaces have an effect on the well-being and the social structures of our society. Therefore, in the development of our built environment, it is necessary to

take all aspects of sustainability; socio-economic, ecological and cultural, into account.

Building assessment and certification

We know today that sustainable architecture consists of more than ecological, resource-saving and energy-efficient building. Aspects such as aesthetics, design methods and integral planning, location and socio-cultural criteria must be taken into account, as well as the economic, functional and technical characteristics of a building. This makes it impossible to implement sustainable building according to rigid principles. Some building projects require specific concepts with different approaches to solutions, which are tailored to suit the respective building [78].

Since the end of the 1980s, to implement ecological and energy-related aspects in the building sector, Germany and Austria have introduced energy saving regulations and promoted the construction of low energy buildings and passive houses, i.e. a scientifically oriented ecological approach. In other countries, such as France, Great Britain or the USA, environmental goals in the building industry were, in contrast, defined with the aid of catalogues of criteria i.e. in quantative terms, which after a practical testing phase were further updated and adapted to match current technological levels [79].

Planning instruments
To design buildings in a sustainable way and to describe and assess them as regards ecological, economic and societal aspects tools, and aids are required which depict the entire life cycle of a property and which make the relevant information available during the planning process [80]. In recent years a considerable number of such instruments have been developed, which are used to assess the sustainability of buildings and building products, and which have been adapted to suit the climatic, cultural and legal boundary conditions of individual nations. These instruments can differ quite considerably, depending on the target group at which they are aimed (planners, building clients, project developers, the building industry), the areas to be assessed (ecology, economy, societal aspects), and the phases of the life cycle to be reviewed (planning, erection, use, demolition, disposal).

Despite differing initial conditions it is still possible to identify and categorise different types of systems according to [81].

- the kind of property to be examined and assessed: housing, office buildings, sports buildings.
- the goals of the assessment: ecological, economic and social aspects etc.
- the framework of the examination and assessment: temporal, spatial, historical etc.
- the method used: legal requirements, agreed boundary and target values, national emphasis, access to databanks etc.
- target groups: architects, building clients, politicians etc.
- the form in which the results of the assessment are to be presented: tables, vectors, grades etc.

Within the framework of the sustainability assessment, instruments with concrete goals and guideline indicators are required. These should enable the planning team to recognize the effects and interactions of influential ecological, economic and social factors, and to take these into consideration in the planning or construction phase. The instruments available for the assessment of sustainable buildings can be categorized in the following groups [82]:

- product declarations: building products and building supplies e.g. EPD (Environmental Product Declaration), Blauer Engel, NaturePlus etc.
- element or building part catalogues: the assessment of building parts and elements (environmental parameters, building physics data etc.) e.g. standard details of software programmes for energy certificates or the building elements catalogue SIA D 0123 of the Swiss Association of Engineers and Architects
- specification aids: ecologically oriented specifications, e.g. WECOBIS/WINGIS (Germany), ECO-DEVIS (Switzerland)
- energy certificates: description and assessment of the energy efficiency of buildings, e.g. Energieausweis (Germany) [83], Energy Performance Certificate (Great Britain)
- checklists and guidelines: definitions of goals, principles and models for energy efficient, ecological planning and construction, e.g. guidelines for sustainable building from the Federal Ministry of Transport, Building and Urban Development

- holistic planning and assessment tools: interactive tools for decision making, for instance by calculating the eco-balance or lifecycle costs, e.g. LEGEP, GaBi (ganzheitliche Bilanzierung/life cycle assessment), or Bauloop
- building labels, evaluations or certificates: building assessment with regard to ecological, economic and societal aspects (e.g. LEED, BREEAM, DGNB)

The development of building labels and certificates (Fig. 1.29) represented an important step forward in assessing sustainability. These labels allow the comprehensive assessment of a building as an entire system. They combine existing planning instruments and aspects of sustainable building (energy-efficiency, ecological balance, life cycle costs etc.), and are built up on the basis of existing national standards and legislation. They enable planners and those who commission buildings to make a project assessment at an early stage, from which guidelines can be then derived for achieving sustainable planning goals and improving the building's sustainability during the design stage. Upon completion of the building such building certificates provide users and operators with clearly understandable documentation of the sustainable quality of their building. In addition to the objective assessment of the building's quality, the certification itself, i.e. the fact that accredited auditors and certification bodies examine the building documentation, represents a further assurance of quality [84].

Systems and methods of assessing sustainable building quality

Today sustainability assessment occupies a central place in planning and building. In the last two decades the number of assessment and certification systems, as well as the total number of certified buildings has increased enormously worldwide. In addition to standards, guidelines and planning goals in providing sustainable buildings for companies, institutions or ministries, there now exist worldwide more than 600 methods to assess the quality of a building in terms of its sustainability [85, 86]. These methods have numerous advantages [87]:

- reduction and control of the environmental damage caused by buildings [88]

- aid in determining sustainable planning goals [89]
- ensuring that building quality can be described on a comparable basis [90]
- improving the transparency of the planning process by describing the sustainability quality and providing information for operators and users [91]
- ensuring the implementation of sustainable building quality through monitoring and by aiding integrative planning processes [92]
- quality assurance of the building by examination of the planning, execution and operation concepts, as well as the materials used [93]
- high level of competitiveness throughout the entire life cycle [94]
- lower life cycle costs and insurance premiums [95]

Most of the seals of quality so far have been developed to meet the needs of individual nations and therefore take into account these countries' climatic, cultural and legal situations. The assessment models used as a basis differ greatly and illustrate sustainability in the building sector in very different ways. To date, systems have only assessed partial aspects of sustainability, such as energy efficiency, ecology or quality of location, or assessments have been restricted to only part of a building's life cycle, e.g. to the planning of its individual phases, to the assessment of completed buildings or, in a holistic sense, to all life cycle phases. The most important internationally recognized systems are listed below according to country:

- Australia: NABERS, Green Star
- Belgium: BREEAM Belgium
- Brazil: LEED Brasil, AQUA, BREEAM Brasil
- China: GBAS, Three Star, HK-BEAM (Hong Kong)
- Germany: DGNB, BNB, TÜV Süd SCoRE
- Finland: PromisE
- France: HQE, Escale; BREEAM France
- Great Britain: BREEAM
- Hong Kong: HK-BEAM
- India: LEED India, TGBRS India
- Italy: Protocollo Itaca
- Japan: CASBEE
- Canada: LEED Canada, Green Globes (Green Leaf)
- Mexico: LEED Mexico, SICES
- Netherlands: BREEAM Netherlands
- New Zealand: Green Star NZ

- Austria: Total Quality
- Poland: BREEAM Poland
- Portugal: Lider A, SBTool Portugal
- Russia: BREEAM Russia
- Switzerland: MINERGIE
- Singapore: BCA Singapur Green Mark
- Spain: VERDE, BREEAM Spain
- South Africa: SBAT, Green Star SA
- Taiwan: ABRI
- Czech Republic: SBTool CZ
- United States: LEED, Green Globes
- United Arab Emirates: LEED Emirates, BREEAM Gulfs
- Europa: Green Building, LEnSE, Open House, Super Building

Market penetration of the systems
Of all the seals of quality and assessment methods for sustainability, two methods in particular, BREEAM (BRE Environmental Assessment Method) and the American method LEED (Leadership in Energy and Environmental Design), have been able to establish themselves at international level (Fig. 1.32, p. 26). However, more recent systems, such as the DGNB certificate, are also increasingly making their way onto the global market. On account of its successful marketing strategy the american LEED label is at present the best known certification system worldwide. With about 4,000 certified and 25,000 registered buildings (as of 2009) [96] it does not, however, come close to matching the registration and certification figures of the British method BREEAM. The high figure of around 115,000 certified and over 800,000 registered buildings (as of 2009) [97] for BREEAM is due, in part, to the fact that the British government has introduced regulations and standards for sustainable building in Great Britain, which are based on the BREEAM requirements. Mention should be made here of the 'Sustainable Procurement Action Plan', which was passed in 2006, and which requires that all new state buildings and all renovations of such buildings should meet the BREEAM Excellent Standard. Also the legal regulation 'The Code for Sustainable Homes', introduced in May 2008, requires that certain predetermined sustainability goals be met for all new housing, and that these buildings should be assessed upon completion. At present the main focus of BREEAM certification is clearly on housing construction, as the number of assessments up to the year 2008 clearly shows: in the area of housing construction 109,450 dwelling

Product declarations: building products and supplies
+ Element catalogues: building elements (functional unit) in built-in state
+ Tender document aids: ecologically oriented specifications
+ Check lists and guidelines: formulation of goals, principles and models for energy-efficient, ecological planning and building
+ Energy certificate: description and assessment of the energy efficiency of buildings
+ Holistic planning and assessment tools: instruments to assess ecological balance and life cycle costs (decision-making)

= **Building labels, evaluations or certificates: building assessment e.g. DGNB Certificate**

1.29

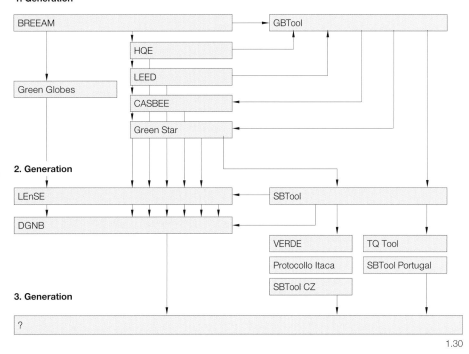

1.30

Assessment tool	Country	Based on
BREEAM (Building Research Establishment Environmental Assessment Method)	Great Britain	– (first assessment system)
HQE (Haute Qualité Environnementale)	France	BREEAM
LEED (Leadership in Energy and Environmental Design)	USA	BREEAM
Green Globe	Canada	BREEAM
CASBEE (Comprehensive Assessment System for Building Environmental Efficiency)	Japan	BREEAM, LEED
Green Star (Green Building Council of Australia)	Australia	LEED, BREEAM
GBAS (Green Building Assessment System)	China	LEED, BREEAM, CASBEE
DGNB (DGNB Zertifikat)	Germany	BREEAM, LEED, CASBEE, HQE, Green Star
Protocollo Itaca	Italy	SBTool
TQ (Total Quality)	Austria	SBTool
SBTool Portugal	Portugal	SBTool
SBTool CZ	Czech Republic	SBTool
VERDE	Spain	SBTool

1.31

1.29 Planning instruments, data sources and individual proofs for sustainable building and their interaction in creating building labels and certificates
1.30 Relationship of the international assessment methods to each other
1.31 How the international assessment methods are derived from each other

units have been certified to date, in the area of non-housing construction only 1,358 buildings [98].

Historical development of building certification

The assessment methods currently recognized in the international building sector are, for the most part, built up on each other and incorporate experience and knowledge gained from their predecessors. The pioneer among the certification systems was the British method BREEAM from the Building Research Establishment (BRE), whose assessment catalogue was published back in 1990. The French equivalent, HQE (Haute Qualité Environnementale), followed in 1996, but, up to the present, substantial parts of this method are only available in French. In 1998 the North American label LEED from the U.S. Green Building Council (USGBC) began with the first assessments in the area of new office and administration buildings. Based on the experience of BREEAM and LEED, in 2001 the Japanese method CASBEE (Comprehensive Assessment System for Building Environmental Efficiency) was developed, followed closely in 2002 by the Green Star assessment method in Australia. The labels mentioned here are the first generation of assessment methods, i.e. instruments that were developed as the first certification systems in the 1990s and

which primarily evaluate the "green", i.e. ecological and energy-related, criteria of a building's quality (the 'green building' approach, refer to the comparison of systems, p. 94). The assessment methods of the second generation, such as the Deutsche Gütesiegel Nachhaltiges Bauen (DGNB) from 2008 are based on experience gained from the instruments of the first generation but are in part still at the testing stage. These assessment tools not only take into account a building's ecology and energy efficiency, but also evaluate its holistic quality, i.e. ecological and economic aspects, socio-cultural criteria, technology, location and process quality, throughout the entire life cycle (planning, construction, start of operation, use and demolition) (Figs. 1.30 and 1.31) [99].

International competition between systems

Although numerous initiatives to develop a uniform international method for assessing the sustainability of buildings have already been launched, no uniform seal of quality has yet been established. At national level, too, different assessment methods exist alongside each other (e.g. Australia: Green Star, NABERS or Germany: DGNB, BNB, TÜV SÜD SCoRE). It seems as if, in the future buildings will be evaluated according to national or international market orientation using not only one but several seals of quality.

Certification systems such as LEED or BREEAM, which are already in use internationally, have in recent years made more and more efforts to establish themselves globally. For example, with LEED, buildings have already been registered for certification in 76 countries. LEED here takes two paths. At international level, LEED certifies according to the criteria of the American main catalogue, i.e. according to standards and values suited to the conditions in North America. On the other hand, subsidiary systems have been developed on the basis of the American method, e.g. LEED Brazil, LEED Canada, LEED Emirates, LEED India or LEED Mexico, which have been modified to suit local climatic and political conditions, and adapted by the Green Building Councils of the respective countries. In contrast BREEAM has issued special European and international framework catalogues such as BREEAM Europe or BREEAM BREEAM International. These appear to be increasingly gaining a foothold in the market, as demonstrated by a figure of more than 10,000 certified buildings worldwide [100]. On the basis of these framework catalogues, international systems such as BREEAM have already established themselves in numerous countries, for example BREEAM Belgium, BREEAM Brazil, BREEAM France or BREEAM Netherlands. The more recent DGNB Certificate is pursuing a similar

1.32 Timeline showing development of assessment and certification systems
1.33 Development from Green Building Tool to Sustainable Building Tool

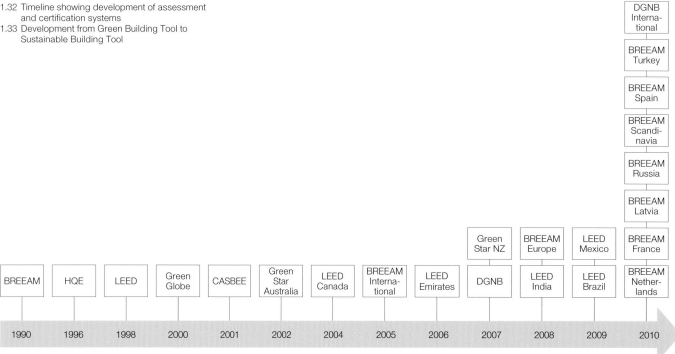

1.32

	Green Building	Sustainable Building
Use of non-renewable energies	▮	▮
Water consumption	▮	▮
Land use	▮	▮
Consumption of materials	▮	▮
Greenhouse gas emissions	▮	▮
Other atmospheric emissions	▮	▮
Influences on the ecology of the location	▮	▮
Solid waste / liquid waste products	▮	▮
Quality of indoor air, light, acoustics	▮	▮
Longevity, adaptability, flexibility	▮	▮
Operation and maintenance	▮	▮
Social and economic aspects		▮
Urban planning / aspects of relevance for planning		▮

1.33

goal, and with the aim of becoming international has undertaken cooperation with partners in Austria, Bulgaria and China. Furthermore DGNB intends to use the German system in countries such as Italy, Switzerland, Turkey and Poland.

International organisational framework of building certification

Many companies that operate the assessment systems listed here belong to the international umbrella organization, the World Green Building Council (WorldGBC). In addition to the WorldGBC there are several other organisations that also promote sustainable building at international level. With the founding of the Green Building Challenge (GBC), today known as Sustainable Building Challenge (SBC), a worldwide network was established based on joint research objectives, conferences and publications related to the theme of sustainable architecture. The GBC was set up by the initiative iiSBE (International Initiative for a Sustainable Built Environment) [102] in 1996 [103]. One of the most important conferences worldwide on the theme of sustainable building, which the SBC helps to organise, is the World Sustainable Building Conference (SB02 Oslo, SB05 Tokyo, SB08 Melbourne) [104].

The Sustainable Building Alliance (SB Alliance), an international network of universities, research institutes, environment organisations and the business world, was founded with the objective of developing sustainable building and the planning and assessment tools needed for it.

In addition to the networks mentioned above, more recently, international environment programmes such as UNEP (United Nations Environment Programme), international architects associations such as the UIA (Union Internationale des Architectes), and engineers' associations such as IB (International Council for Building) have recognized the importance of the theme of sustainable building [105].

In Europe the European Union is the driving force behind the development of a uniform seal of quality. In 2004 the EU introduced the label GreenBuilding [106] for buildings outside the field of housing. This was followed in 2008 by the method LEnSE [107], which is subsidised by the EU in the framework of a subsidy programme, and assesses building quality with regard to ecological, economic and social aspects. To arrive at a common standard for sustainability assessments throughout Europe, the EU has now set up research projects such as OPEN HOUSE [108] and SUPER BUILDING, for the period from 2010 to 2013.

World Green Building Council (WorldGBC)
To support the development of national methods of assessment and the work of the national Green Building Councils (GBCs)a global umbrella organization for sustainable building, the World Green Building Council (WorldGBC), was set up in 1998 [109]. This non-profit organization currently represents 20 Green Building Councils worldwide (as of July 2009), to pursue the goal of encouraging the real estate sector in the direction of sustainability [110]. The WorldGBC supports the development of sustainability standards, technologies, products and certification systems at international level. It does not promote a special assessment system but endeavours to integrate important aspects of relevance for sustainability in the development of national assessment systems and, through collaboration with the national Green Building Councils, to establish an adequate reference to the climatic, political and cultural circumstances of the respective country.

A number of steps are involved in attaining the official status of a Green Building Council. These lead from the initial Expression of Interest to Emerging Member Status and on to Established Member Status. Numerous assessment methods such as LEED, BREEAM, CASBEE, Green Star or DGNB, are already united under the umbrella organisation of the WorldGBC, while other countries have already submitted an application for membership or expressed their interest.

International Initiative for a Sustainable Built Environment (iiSBE)
The goal of the network International Initiative for a Sustainable Built Environment (iiSBE) is the development of a common, comparable assessment tool as a means of promoting and comparing the sustainability of buildings at international level. What is known as the Sustainable Building Tool (SBTool), was developed from 1996 onwards in the context of the 'Green Building Challenge (GBC)' by a group consisting of more than 15 national teams, and is still being tested today in numerous case studies. Although this initiative was founded by Natural Resources Canada, in 2002 responsibility was transferred to iiSBE. The method of the SBTool adopts a different approach to that used by systems such as LEED or BREEAM. The assessment matrix of the SBTool is intended to represent the basis for national assessment methods so as to make buildings comparable at international level [111]. However, the original aim to establish a globally comparable assessment method failed in the practical implementation. Despite an initial common starting point, after being adapted to national circumstances i.e. to the respective climate , the legal directives, national standards and the respective building culture, the criteria were no longer comparable with each other.

In response to suggestions from national teams the structure and goal of this assessment framework tool have undergone many changes in recent years. The original approach of the Green Building Tool (GBTool), with its focus on energy-efficiency, ecology and location-specific factors, was expanded by including social, economic and urban aspects to become the SBTool (Fig. 1.33) (see Comparison of systems, p. 88). As an international framework tool it offers a common catalogue of criteria for new assessment methods, such as, for example, the Austrian certificate Total Quality (TQ), the Spanish assessment instrument VERDE, the Italian Protocollo Itaca, the Czech SBTool CZ or the SBTool Portugal [112].

Sustainable Building Alliance (SB Alliance)
The Sustainable Building Alliance (SB Alliance) is an international, non-profit network of universities, research centres, Green Building Councils, and the international building industry (see Comparison of systems, p. 88). This initiative is funded by the UNESCO Chair for Sustainable Buildings, the UNEP-SBCI (United Nations Environment Programme-Sustainable Buildings and Climate Initiative), the WFTAO (World Federation of Technical Assessment Organizations), as well as by the iiSBE (International Initiative for a Sustainable Built Environment) and the ECTP (European Construction Technology Platform) [113]. The SBA, like the organisations described above, pursues the goal of promoting sustainable building and the use of assessment methods at international level. At the same time, the aim is to develop a uniform matrix for the comparison of existing assessment methods, and to support international standardisation in the field of sustainable building. In a comparison of existing European assessment methods carried out by the institutions BRE (BREEAM, Great Britain), CSTB (HQE, France), DGNB (DGNB Zertifikat, Germany), FCAV (AQUA, Brazil), VTT (Finland), and NIST (USA), in 2009 the first core indicators were developed for the assessment of the ecological quality of buildings for their entire life cycle (production, construction, operation and end of life) [114].

UNEP-SBCI (United Nations Environmental Programme – Sustainable Buildings and Climate Initiative)
Within the framework of the United Nations' environment activities, the UNEP (United Nations Environment Programme) has created its own platform for sustainable buildings: the Sustainable Buildings and Climate Initiative (SBCI) [115]. This initiative, which bridges the boundaries between different branches, is intended to support aspects of sustainability and new environmental technologies in the building sector worldwide. Its focus are

themes of energy- efficiency and greenhouse gas emissions, taking into account the entire life cycle of buildings, as well as the implementation of pilot studies at local, national and international levels. The main protagonists of the UNEP-SBCI are the building industry, government organisations, local authorities, research initiatives, experts and associations. In particular the development of the 'Sustainable Building Index (SB Index)' [116] and the 'Common Carbon Metric' [117], are important tools for promoting and developing sustainability in building construction at international level.
The UNEP SB Index is not, in the strict sense, an instrument to assess a building's level of sustainability, but rather a framework that produces directives and recommendations in annual sustainability reports for the building industry, on the basis of the following core indicators: energy-efficiency and greenhouse gas emissions, water, materials, biodiversity, as well as social and economic aspects. With the support of numerous institutions such as the World Resources Institute (WRI), the SB Alliance, the World Green Building Council (WGBC) or the iiSBE, the UNEP-SBCI developed the calculation tool known as the Common Carbon Metric. With this tool energy use and CO_2 emissions during the operational phase of a building's life (heating, cooling, ventilation, lighting etc.) are measured accoring to a consistent method worldwide. The Metric is calculated on the basis of kilograms of CO_2 equivalents per square metre per year (kg CO_2 equivalents/m^2/a) and can be correlated to specific building types and climate regions. The first pilot versions of the Common Carbon Metric were presented at the UN Climate Conference (COP 15) 2009 in Copenhagen and were implemented at the beginning of 2010.

References:

[1] Gauzin-Müller, Dominique: Nachhaltigkeit in Architektur und Städtebau. Basel 2001, p. 5f.
[2] Hegger, Manfred u. a.: Energie Atlas. München/ Basel 2007, p. 39
[3] Wissenschaftlicher Beirat der Bundesregierung für globale Umweltveränderungen (WBGU). http://www.wbgu.de/wbgu_globalerwandel.html
[4] As note 2, p. 19
[5] United Nations Population Division. http://www.un.org/popin/data.html
[6] Colin, Armand: Atlas der Globalisierung. Berlin 2007, p. 39
[7] ifs Institut für Städtebau, Wohnungswirtschaft und Bausparwesen: Pro-Kopf-Wohnfläche weiter gestiegen. http://www.ifs-staedtebauinstitut.de/ hi/hi2006/hi02.pdf
[8] Venjakob, Johannes; Hanke, Thomas: Neue Phase im Wettstreit zwischen Energieeffizienz und Wohnraumbedarf. In: E & M, 15 May 2006. http://www.wupperinst.org/uploads/tx_ wibeitrag/bild-des-monats_05-06.pdf
[9] United Nations – Department of Economic and Social Affairs (UN/DESA): World Urbanization Prospects: The 2009 Revision. http://esa.un.org/unpd/wup/index.htm
[10] Bundesministerium für Verkehr, Bau und Stadtentwicklung (BMVBS): Renaturierung als Strategie nachhaltiger Stadtentwicklung. Bonn 2009, Heft 62, p. 41. http://d-nb.in- fo/997406372/34
[11] Bundesinstitut für Bau-, Stadt- und Raumforschung (BBSR): Raumordnungsprognose 2025. http://www.bmvbs.de/Raumentwicklung, 1501.1053603/Raumordnungsprognose-2025. htm
[12] Häußermann, Hartmut: Segregierte Stadt. http://www.bpb.de/themen/ OXHCW8,0,Segregierte_Stadt.html
[13] Franke, Thomas u. a.: Integrierte Stadtentwicklung als Erfolgsbedingung einer Stadt. http://www.bak.de/userfiles/bak/download/ studie_integrierte_stadtentwicklung.pdf
[14] As note 2, p. 49
[15] As note 3, http://www.wbgu.de/gc_portal/ global_change_portal_de.html
[16] As note 1, p. 15
[17] European Union: European Directive on the Energy Performance of Buildings. Guideline 2002/91/EG. Brussels 2002. http://eur-lex.europa.eu/LexUriServ/LexUriServ. do?uri=OJ:L:2003:001:0065: 0071:DE:PDF
[18] Intergovernmental Panel on Climate Change (IPCC): Fourth Assessment Report. Genf 2004, http://www.ipcc.ch/publications_and_data/ar4/ syr/en/contents.html
[19] As note 2, p. 46
[20] Umweltbundesamt (UBA): Flächenverbrauch, ein Umweltproblem mit wirtschaftlichen Folgen. Berlin 2004
[21] Statistisches Bundesamt: Zunahme der Sied- lungs- und Verkehrsfläche: 114 ha/Tag. http://www.destatis.de/jetspeed/portal/cms/ Sites/destatis/Internet/DE/Presse/pm/2006/11/ PD06__492__85,templateId=renderPrint.psml
[22] Bundesministerium für Wirtschaft (BMWi): Energie in Deutschland. Berlin 2009. http://www.energie-verstehen.de/Dateien/ Energieportal/PDF/energie-in-deutschland, property=pdf,bereich=energieportal,sprache= de,rwb=true.pdf
[23] International Energy Agency (IEA): Key World Energy Statistics. Paris 2009. http://www.iea.org/textbase/nppdf/free/2009/ key_stats_2009.pdf
[24] Deutsche Energieagentur (dene): Thema Energie. http://www.thema-energie.de/ typo3temp/pics/7c2f97c03a.jpg
[25] Bundesministerium für Wirtschaft (BMWi): Die Entwicklung der Energiemärkte bis zum Jahr 2030 (EWI-Prognos-Studie). Berlin 2005. http://www.bmwi.de/BMWi/Redaktion/PDF/ Publikationen/Dokumentationen/ewi-prognos_ E2_80_93studie-entwicklung-der- energiemaerkte-545,property=pdf,bereich=- bmwi,sprache=de,rwb=true.pdf

[26] As note 2, p. 41
[27] Bundesministerium für Umwelt, Naturschutz und Reaktorsicherheit (BMU): Erneuerbare Energien 2008 in Deutschland. Berlin 2009
[28] Ergebnis der Arbeitsgruppe Erneuerbare Energien Statistik (AGEE-Stat). http://erneuerbare-energien.de/inhalt/5468/
[29] BMU: Erneuerbare Energien behaupten sich in der Wirtschaftskrise. http://www.erneuerbare-energien.de/inhalt/45805/5466
[30] U.S. Energy Information Administration: Annual Energy Outlook 2010. Washington 2010. http://www.eia.doe.gov/oiaf/aeo/pdf/0383%282010%29.pdf
[31] European Renewable Energy Council and Greenpeace: Energy Revolution, A Sustainable Global Energy Outlook. http://www.greenpeace.org/raw/content/international/press/reports/energyrevolutionreport.pdf
[32] Altgeld, Horst u. a.: Vision des FVEE für ein 100 % erneuerbares Energiesystem. Berlin 2010
[33] Food and Agriculture Organization (FAO): Global Forest Resources Assessment 2005. Rome 2005, p. 21. ftp://ftp.fao.org/docrep/fao/008/a0400e/a0400e00.pdf
[34] Forest Stewardship Council: Arbeitsgruppe Deutschland e. V. http://www.fsc-deutschland.de/fsc/was-macht-fsc/#8
[35] As note 6, p. 19
[36] Bundesministerium für Bildung und Forschung (BMBF): Wasser – Ressource für das Leben. http://www.bmbf.de/de/3934.php
[37] Intergovernmental Panel on Climate Change (IPCC): Climate Change and Water. Genf 2008. http://www.ipcc.ch/pdf/technical-papers/climate-change-water-en.pdf
[38] As note 6, p. 31
[39] As note 18, http://www.ipcc.ch/organization/organization.htm
[40] BMU: Protokoll von Kyoto zum Rahmenübereinkommen der Vereinten Nationen über Klimaänderungen. Kyoto 1997. http://www.bmu.de/files/pdfs/allgemein/application/pdf/protodt.pdf
[41] BMU: UN-Klimakonferenz in Kopenhagen 2009. http://www.bmu.de/15_klimakonferenz/doc/44133.php
[42] As note 6, p. 16
[43] Maas, Anton; Hauser, Gerd: Energieeinsparverordnung 2009. Kassel 2009
[44] Meadows, Dennis L. u. a.: Die Grenzen des Wachstums. Stuttgart 1972
[45] Kresse, Dodo; Schauer, Kurt; Wallner, Hans Peter: Erfolg mit der Business Agenda 21. Munich 2004
[46] Lovins, Amory u. a.: Faktor vier. Doppelter Wohlstand – halbierter Naturverbrauch. Munich 1995
[47] Stern, Nicholas: The Economics of Climate Change: The Stern Review. Cambridge 2006
[48] As note 2, p. 40; As note 47
[49] http://ec.europa.eu/enterprise/policies/innovation/policy/lead-market-initiative
[50] BBSR: Europäische Leitmarktinitiative Nachhaltiges Bauen. http://www.bbsr.bund.de/nn_623536/BBSR/DE/Bauwesen/NachhaltigesBauen/Leitmarktinitiative/start.html
[51] Lützkendorf, Thomas: Grundlagen zur Beurteilung der Nachhaltigkeit von Immobilien. Karlsruhe 2009. http://www.intergeo.de/archiv/2009/Luetzkendorf.pdf
[52] As note 49
[53] BMU: GreenTech made in Germany 2.0, Umwelttechnologieatlas für Deutschland. München 2009. http://www.bmu.de/files/pdfs/allgemein/application/pdf/greentech2009.pdf
[54] PricewaterhouseCoopers (PwC) in collaboration with Significant and Ecofys: Collection of statistical information on Green Public Procurement in the EU. http://www.pwc.de/fileserver/RepositoryItem/CollstatinfGPP-resultFIN.pdf?itemId=9207780
[55] As note 52
[56] Studie zur Zahlungsbereitschaft für nachhaltige Gebäude in Deutschland: Ergebnisse einer Befragung von ca. 200 Führungskräften aus der deutschen Immobilienwirtschaft im Rahmen der 15. Handelsblatt Jahrestagung Immobilienwirtschaft. Berlin 2008

[57] Pressemitteilung: Deutsche Immobilienbranche sieht weiterhin grün. Berlin 2008. http://www.immobilien-forum.com/pdf/pb_2008.pdf
[58] World Commission on Environment and Development (WCED): Our Common Future. New York/ Oxford 1987
[59] As note 44
[60] Ott, Konrad; Döring, Ralf: Grundlinien einer Theorie starker Nachhaltigkeit. In: Umwelt-Handeln. Munich 2006, pp. 89–127
[61] Heinrich Böll Foundation: Erdgipfel Rio 1992. Johannesburg 2002. http://www.worldsummit2002.de/web/joburg/167.html
[62] BMU: Nachhaltigkeitsstrategie Europa. Berlin 2009, http://www.bmu.de/europa_und_umwelt/eu-nachhaltigkeitsstrategie/doc/print/6733.php
[63] Die Bundesregierung: Fortschrittsbericht 2008 zur nationalen Nachhaltigkeitsstrategie. Berlin 2008. http://www.bundesregierung.de/nn_774/Content/DE/Publikation/Bestellservice/2008-11-17-fortschrittsbericht-2008.html
[64] As note 1, p. 14f.
[65] Lang, Annette: Ist Nachhaltigkeit messbar? Stuttgart 2003
[66] Deutscher Bundestag: Schlussbericht der Enquete-Kommission. Berlin 1999. http://www.bundestag.de/gremien/welt/glob_end/
[67] Huber, Joseph: Nachhaltige Entwicklung. Berlin 1995
[68] As note 65, p. 61
[69] As note 66
[70] OECD: Glossary of statistical terms. http://stats.oecd.org/glossary/detail.asp?ID=6611
[71] As note 2, p. 50f.
[72] Eßig, Natalie: Nachhaltigkeit von Olympischen Bauten. Stuttgart 2010, p. 47
[73] As note 1, p. 19
[74] Union Internationale des Architectes (UIA): Declaration of Interdependence for a Sustainable Future. Chicago 1993. http://www.uia-architectes.org/texte/england/2aaf1.html
[75] ACE: Architecture and Sustainability. Brussels 2009. http://www.danskeark.org/om_par/2009_ACE_Architecture_Sustainability.pdf
[76] Lewis, J. Owen: A Green Vitruvius – Principles and Practice of Sustainable Architectural Design. London 1999
[77] ACE: Architecture & Quality of Life. Brussels 2004
[78] Bundesamt für Bauwesen und Raumordnung (BBR): Leitfaden nachhaltiges Bauen. Bonn 2001. http://www.bmvbs.de/architektur-baukultur
[79] As note 1, p. 19f.
[80] Lützkendorf, Thomas: Umsetzung von Prinzipien einer nachhaltigen Entwicklung im Baubereich. In: Darmstädter Nachhaltigkeitssymposium. Darmstadt 2003, pp. 32–40
[81] Lützkendorf, Thomas: Nachhaltiges Planen, Bauen und Bewirtschaften von Bauwerken. Karlsruhe 2002
[82] As note 2, p. 191
[83] Hauser, Gerd; Maas, Anton; Lüking, Rolf-Michael: Der Energiepass für Gebäude. Herausgegeben von Gesellschaft für Rationelle Energieverwendung e. V., Kassel 2004
[84] As note 72, p. 228
[85] Hájek, Petr: Complex Methods for Life Cycle Analysis (LCA) and Life Cycle Cost (LCC) Assessments. Prague 2005. http://www.cideas.cz/free/okno/technicke_listy/1uvten/EN_1221.pdf
[86] Reed, Richard; Bilos, Anita; Wilkinson, Sara; Schulte, Karl-Werner: International Comparison of Sustainable Rating Tools. http://www.costar.com/josre/journalPdfs/01-Sustainable-Rating-Tools.pdf
[87] As note 72, p. 226
[88] U.S. Green Building Council: LEED – New Construction & Major Renovation, Version 2.2. Reference Guide. Washington 2006
[89] As note 72, p. 226
[90] ibid.
[91] Hauser, Gerd: Mehrwert und Marktchancen von Zertifikaten im Vergleich zu Energieausweisen. Frankfurt 2008, pp. 76–84. http://www.enreso2020.de/fileadmin/enreso/downloads/statements/Statement_Hauser.pdf

[92] Cole, Raymond J.: Building environmental assessment methods. In: Building Research and Information. issue 27, 1999, pp. 230–246
[93] As note 72, p. 226
[94] Lechner, Robert; Fröhlich, Thomas: Immo-Rate, Leitfaden für das Immobilienrating nachhaltiger Wohnbauten. Melk/Donau 2006. http://www.ecology.at/files/berichte/E08.458.pdf
[95] Braune, Anna; Sedlbauer Klaus: Kurzstudie. Potenziale des Nachhaltigen Bauens in Deutschland. Leinfelden-Echterdingen 2007
[96] U.S. Green Building Council: About USGBC. http://www.usgbc.org/DisplayPage.aspx?CMSPageID=1720
[97] BREEAM Communities: sustainable assessment framework. http://www.breeam.org/filelibrary/BREEAM_Communities_-_Fact_Sheet_v2.pdf
[98] http://www.breeam.org
[99] As note 72, p. 230f.
[100] BREEAM: What is BREEAM international. http://www.breeam.org/page.jsp?id=203
[101] As note 70, p. 50
[102] iiSBE: SB/GB Challenge. http://www.iisbe.org/sb_challenge
[103] Green Building Challenge. http://greenbuilding.ca/gbc98cnf
[104] As note 102
[105] As note 72
[106] EU Commission: Greenbuilding – Improved Energy Efficiency for Non-residential Buildings. http://www.eu-greenbuilding.org
[107] http://www.lensebuildings.com
[108] http://www.openhouse-fp7.eu
[109] http://www.worldgbc.org
[110] As note 95
[111] iiSBE: About iiSBE. http://www.iisbe.org/sb_challenge
[112] As note 72, p. 228
[113] SB Alliance: The SB Alliance. A research based assessment oriented organization. Paris 2008. http://www.sballiance.org/?page_id=9
[114] http://www.sballiance.org/
[115] http://www.unep.org/sbci/index.asp
[116] http://www.unep.org/sbci/pdfs/SYM2010-UNEP-SBCI_SB_Index_Briefing.pdf
[117] http://www.unep.org/sbci/pdfs/UNEPSBCI CarbonMetric.pdf

BREEAM (Building Research Establishment Environmental Assessment Method)

The first certification system to assess the sustainability of buildings was the Building Research Establishment's Environmental Assessment Method (BREEAM) which was published in the United Kingdom (UK). The system was developed and administered by the British Building Research Establishment (BRE). BREEAM can be regarded as the model for all certificates of the first generation since the contents and assessment methods for most of these are based on this system. The US American system LEED was also originally derived from BREEAM. The similar structure of the individual criteria and the possibility of being awarded further credits for innovations are aspects that have been adopted in LEED.

System origin

BREEAM was developed at the end of the 1980s and introduced to the market in 1990. Originally designed as a national system for office and residential buildings, the certification system is now used worldwide for a range of different building types. Over the years, BREEAM has been revised, extended to incorporate additional building types and internationalised. The version currently valid for the UK was issued in 2008 [1]. According to BRE, any building throughout the world can be assessed with BREEAM [2].

breeam

2.1

BREEAM also offers the possibility to certify buildings not included in the categories of predetermined uses or building types.

Organisation

Founded in 1921, the Building Research Establishment [3] was originally a state-run business, at that time called Building Research Station. It was formed to investigate various building materials and housing schemes as well as to develop rules and regulations in this field. There were further organisations, such as the Forest Products Research Laboratory (FPRL) and the Fire Research Station, which were also carrying out research work on timber products and fire prevention. In 1972, the Building Research Station merged with the institutes for timber research and fire prevention to form the Building Research Establishment (BRE). BRE was privatised in 1997. At first BRE was owned by the Foundation for the Built Environment (FBE), which was later renamed BRE Trust. Members of the foundation come from widely varying sectors of the building industry. This deliberately broad representation strengthens the aim of the organisation to be completely impartial. After being privatised, BRE focussed more on the assessment and certification of building products and buildings. These activities were brought together under the name BRE Certification. Following the first certification of an international project in 2006, BRE Certification was renamed BRE Global. The BRE Group [4] has since been created to incorporate the operations of BRE, BRE Global and BRE Trust.
Alongside certification schemes, BRE Global today undertakes testing and approval of fire prevention and safety measures as well as performs quality

assurance checks according to, for example, ISO 9001 and ISO 14001. Furthermore, BRE conducts research and offers training on a range of topics [5] and provides the training and exams necessary to become a BREEAM Assessor.

Market penetration

Even though the system is being applied in different countries worldwide, the main focus is still quite clearly on the UK. The certification schemes, particularly for residential buildings, have led to a wide acceptance of BREEAM and in consequence to a large number of registrations and certifications. The extensive implementation in the UK is supported by government regulations, which, for example, require that all residential buildings completed after 1 May 2008 should be certified according to a specific standard of the "BREEAM Code for Sustainable Homes". If the certification has not been obtained, the vendor of a property is obliged to provide the owner or buyer with a document, which explicitly states that the building has been constructed according to applicable standards, but that it does not meet the higher BREEAM system standards, for example, in terms of energy and water efficiency.
In comparison to other systems, BREEAM has the highest number of registered (i.e. buildings that have applied for certification) and certified buildings. By 2009 [6], 818,943 residential buildings and 22,972 other buildings were registered worldwide, and more than 115,000 buildings had already been certified in the UK [7], the larger proportion of these being residential buildings.
Outside the UK, 14 buildings have currently been certified according to the BREEAM International system [8]. Apart from one property in the USA, the certi-

fied buildings are mainly in Europe, with examples in Germany, Spain, Turkey, Luxembourg, Italy, Belgium and France. One example in Germany is the Centrum Galerie in Dresden, the first shopping centre in Europe outside the UK to receive the "BREEAM Excellent" award (Fig. 2.10, p. 37).

The development of special schemes, such as BREEAM Gulf, shows that the system is currently being adapted to markets outside Europe. In order to encourage even greater international acceptance, links were established with different countries, such as Brazil, Russia, the Netherlands, Norway, Sweden and Turkey. Cooperation agreements were reached with the national organisations abroad, generally these are the so-called Green Building Councils. The overall aim is the adaptation of the BREEAM system to meet the local requirements, such as legal specifications and climate conditions.

Certification process

As with other systems, the BREEAM certification process covers the various work stages of design and construction. The assessment methods based on these phases currently differ for national and international BREEAM projects. The following assessments are available in the UK [9]:

- Design and Procurement: Assessment within the planning phase, e.g. for new build or extensive refurbishment projects.
- Post Construction: Review of the assessment performed at design stage on completion of the construction phase ensuring that all BREEAM criteria specified have been implemented.
- Fit-out: Specifically for let property in office or retail buildings, the fit-out of rented floor space can also be assessed.
- Management and Operation: The certification of certain types of existing building is regarded as optional if the assessment is carried out whilst the building is in use. In this case, in addition to the physical properties of the building, the policy guidelines and operating procedures are considered.

In the case of BREEAM Europe, there is no separate assessment of building operation or the fit-out of rented property. The assessment process only incorporates

Certification system	Building use	Field of application
In the United Kingdom		
BREEAM Offices	Office buildings	BREEAM Offices can assess new builds or major refurbishments of offices at the design stage, post construction or in use.
BREEAM Retail	Retail buildings	BREEAM Retail can assess new builds or major refurbishments of retail buildings post construction, as tenant fit-out, existing (occupied) or in use.
BREEAM Education	Education buildings	BREEAM Education can assess new schools, major refurbishment projects and extensions at the design stage and post construction.
BREEAM Industrial	Industrial buildings	BREEAM Industrial can assess storage & distribution buildings, factories and workshops at the design stage and post construction.
BREEAM Healthcare	Healthcare buildings	BREEAM Healthcare can be used to assess all healthcare buildings containing medical facilities at different stages of their lifecycle.
BREEAM Prisons	Prisons	BREEAM Prisons can assess security prisons at the design stage and post construction.
BREEAM Courts	Courts	BREEAM Courts can assess new builds and refurbishments of court buildings.
BREEAM Other Buildings	Other building types	BREEAM Other Buildings can assess buildings that fall outside the standard BREEAM categories at the design stage and post construction. These include, for example, leisure complexes, laboratories and hotels.
The Code for Sustainable Homes	Residential buildings	Since April 2007, the Code for Sustainable Homes is to be applied for the certification of new homes.
BREEAM Ecohomes	Residential buildings	Since April 2007, the original evaluation system for residential buildings is only to be used for homes undergoing major refurbishment.
BREEAM Ecohomes XB	Residential buildings	BREEAM Ecohomes XB is a tool to administer existing buildings.
BREEAM Multi-Residential	Halls of residence	BREEAM Multi-Residential can assess student halls of residence, sheltered housing for the elderly and other accommodation with similar functions at the design stage and post construction.
BREEAM Communities	Urban planning / development proposals	BREEAM Communities is intended to evaluate and improve development proposals concerning their sustainability.
BREEAM Domestic Refurbishment	Residential buildings (in progress)	This new evaluation system assesses the refurbishment of existing buildings.
Outside the UK: BREEAM International		
BREEAM Europe Commercial	Different building types	This evaluation system has been developed for European countries outside Great Britain.
BREEAM Gulf	Different building types	BREEAM Gulf is the response to the volume of construction work in the Gulf region.
BREEM International Bespoke	Any building type	This evaluation system allows any building throughout the world to be certified according to individually specified and tailored standards.
BREEAM In-Use	Different existing buildings	BREEAM In-Use is an easy-to-use system to assess portfolios and improve the sustainability of existing buildings.

2.2

BREEAM rating	Overall fulfilment
Unclassified	< 30 %
Pass	≥ 30 %
Good	≥ 45 %
Very good	≥ 55 %
Excellent	≥ 70 %
Outstanding	≥ 85 %

2.3

2.1 BREEAM logo
2.2 Overview of the European and international BREEAM assessment schemes

2.3 BREEAM certification ratings each with their corresponding degree of overall fulfilment

Criteria		Minimum number of credits for the BREEAM ratings				
		Pass	Good	Very good	Excellent	Outstand-ing
Man 1	Commissioning	–	–	–	1	2
Man 3	Impact on the building site	–	–	–	1	2
Man 4	Building user guide	–	1	1	1	1
Hea 4	High frequency lighting	1	1	1	1	1
Ene 1	Energy efficiency	–	–	–	6	10
Ene 2	Metering of energy consumption	–	–	1	1	1
Ene 5	Renewable energies	–	–	–	1	1
Wat 1	Water consumption	–	–	1	1	2
Wat 2	Metering of water consumption	–	–	–	1	1
Wst 3	Storage of recyclable waste	–	–	–	1	1
LE 4	Impact on the site's ecology	–	–	–	2	2

2.4

BREEAM sections	Weighting (%)	
	New builds, extensions, refurbishments	Fit-out
Management – Man	12	13
Health & Wellbeing – Hea	15	17
Energy – Ene	19	21
Transport – Tra	8	9
Water – Wat	6	7
Materials – Mat	12.5	14
Waste – Wst	7.5	8
Land Use & Ecology – LE	10	–
Pollution – Pol	10	11
Innovation – Inn Extra credits for exceptional performance	10	10

2.5

Submission stages	Partial perform-ance	Partial amount	Total
Design and Procurement	Registration Certification	£650 (approx. €750) £850 (approx. €975)	£1,500 (approx. €1,725)
Post Construction Review	Registration Certification	£650 (approx. €750) £380 (approx. €435)	£1,030 (approx. €1,185)
Post Construction Assessment	Registration Certification	£650 (approx. €750) £850 (approx. €975)	£1,500 (approx. €1,725)

2.6

2.4 Minimum requirements for the BREEAM certification stages using the BREEAM Europe Commercial scheme 2009 as an example
2.5 Weighting of the sections in the BREEAM Europe scheme
2.6 Structure of fees for the BREEAM International scheme as of September 2009

two stages (Design and Procurement and Post Construction). As in the UK, assessments can be carried out for new builds, conversions/refurbishments, fit-outs as well as shell and core. Here there is differentiation between the design stage (DS) and the phase following completion (Post Construction Stage, PCS) [10].

The assessment during the planning phase can only relate to the aspired quality of the building and naturally cannot refer to the actual features of the finally completed building. In order to ensure that the assessment is based on the most likely outcome, information should be submitted when the design is well advanced, for example during the building application phase. A pre-certificate, in this case a so-called interim certificate, is awarded at this stage.

The assessment after the completion reviews the building as constructed. There are two different procedures: one possibility is a review of the assessment performed during the design phase. The aim of this method is to confirm the results of the original assessment. The other possibility is to carry out a full assessment following completion. The latter method is selected if an interim certificate was not applied for during the design phase.

The actual assessment and certification process is carried out as follows: at first, the project is registered for a specific BREEAM certification scheme. Then the information necessary to fulfil the individual criteria of the certificate is gathered and compiled. The assessor determines the certification rating based on these documents. Subsequently, the documents are handed over to BREEAM to be counter-checked. Assuming there are no discrepancies, this process usually takes at the very most three weeks. Having completed the review, the assessor is notified and the relevant certificate, interim or final, is delivered to the owner of the building.

The procedure concerning the certification scheme BREEAM Bespoke is a special case (see Certification schemes, p. 33) since an assessment scheme is drawn up in conjunction with BRE for the specific building.

Fees

In the UK, the fees vary according to the scheme and the type of building or number of dwellings. The fees do not

relate to the size of the building, e.g. they are not calculated according to the gross floor area. The fees for BREEAM are broken down into a fee for the registration and one for the certification. The total fees for the submitted assessments are approximately as follows [11]:
- Design and Procurement: £850–1,140 (approx. €975–€1,300)
- Post Construction Review: £380–500 (approx. €435–€575)
- Post Construction Assessment: £1,230–1,640 (approx. €1,400–€1,900)
- Management and Operation: £850 (approx. €975)

The fees for BREEAM International and BREEAM Europe are also split between registration and certification (Fig. 2.6). If some documents are not provided in English, there may be additional costs for translation. These are usually around £1,500 (approx. €1,725).

Certification levels
The certification ratings for BREEAM (Europe) are dependent on the overall performance (Fig. 2.3, p. 31). The ratings may also, in part, be depicted by star awards. Alongside the overall performance percentage, it is also necessary to meet minimum standards on individual criteria. For example, for a building to achieve the BREEAM Excellent rating, it must have been awarded at least six credit points in the assessment criterion energy efficiency [12].
To achieve the certification rating Outstanding, the building must score a percentage of at least 85% and meet the minimum standards for this rating as presented in Fig. 2.4. In addition, a case study or project description of the scheme, which BRE has the right to publish, must be provided. The aim is to present these outstanding projects as guiding lights or role models for use by other planners as reference material.

Certification schemes
BREEAM offers special certification schemes for a selection of different uses (Fig. 2.2, p. 31). In the UK, there are standard versions for common uses in non-residential buildings:
- BREEAM Offices
- BREEAM Retail
- BREEAM Industrial (factories and warehouses)

- BREEAM Educational (schools)
- BREEAM Healthcare (medical facilities)

In residential buildings, there is a differentiation between the following schemes, which are sometimes country specific:
- BREEAM EcoHomes (refurbishments in England, now builds in Wales and Scotland)
- BREEAM EcoHomesXB (a tool for housing associations etc.)
- The Code for Sustainable Homes (new single-family homes and apartments in England)
- BREEAM Multi-Residential (student halls of residence, sheltered housing, youth hostels etc.)

There are further versions for other special building types such as courts or prisons as well as systems specifically developed for individual companies.
A special feature, in contrast to other certification methods, is the possibility to adapt the assessment criteria to a particular type of building: in the event that none of the available schemes meet the requirements of a particular project, such as a hotel or laboratory building, the certification scheme Bespoke is applied. In agreement with BRE and based on the existing standard versions, an individual certification scheme can be drawn up.
The scheme BREEAM International has been developed for buildings outside the UK and currently includes the following versions:
- BREEAM Gulf (all building types within the Gulf region)
- BREEAM Europe (selected European countries; office and retail buildings)
- BREEAM Communities (urban developments)

BREEAM International has also been extended to include the Bespoke version which accommodates modified certification schemes for specialised properties. The project Centrum Galerie in Dresden (Fig. 2.10, p. 37) was for example certified according to BREEAM International Bespoke.
The scheme BREEAM In-Use, which can also be used internationally, stands out because of the special approach. It has been developed for a comparatively quick assessment of a whole portfolio or an estate. In contrast to the other certification schemes, this internet-based

assessment process is intended for a fairly sketchy assessment of several buildings. The assessment, in this case, is performed by the owner or his/her representative and on completion is reviewed and confirmed by a BREEAM assessor.
The participation of an assessor is mandatory for all BREEAM schemes. This expert, who has been trained and approved by BREEAM, in a similar way to the DGNB Auditor or the LEED Accredited Professional, is responsible for performing an objective assessment and ensuring a consistent degree of quality within the certification process. The BREEAM report for the certification can only be submitted to BRE by an assessor.

Documentation requirements
The requirements in terms of documentation for BREEAM are comparable to those for other certification systems. When performing an assessment according to BREEAM, the documentation is particularly dependent on the project phase. Since certain evidence cannot be provided during the design stage, the documentation presented tends to take the form of a declaration of intent drawn up by the client. Documents already on hand, such as plans and calculations, are to be handed in at design stage.
On completion of the project, the actual documentary evidence of the hitherto aspired structural features must be submitted. Based on the individual criteria, these include, for example:
- Confirmations from the planning team (explanations, photographic evidence)
- Documents such as the Operation and Maintenance Manual, specification sheets of used products, etc.
- Confirmations or measuring records from surveyors (e.g. building acoustics specialist)
- Inclusion of official documentary evidence such as the Energy Performance Certificate (in the UK), which is comparable with the German EnEV certificate

If an interim certificate was submitted, the planning approach and the calculations must be confirmed in writing by the client or the appropriate planner in the final certificate. The confirmation through an assessor is a special feature of BREEAM. On completion, the assessor inspects the building and collects photographic evidence. If the building's qualities correspond to those aspired, the assessor confirms to BRE that the building conforms with the requirements of the certificate.

System structure

Within BREEAM Europe, as is also the case for other BREEAM schemes, the criteria are set out initially in general terms. The requirements for specific areas of application are contained in the detailed descriptions. These are:

- Whole new buildings
- Major refurbishments to existing buildings
- New build extensions to existing buildings
- Shell and core
- Fit-out of existing and new buildings
- Similar buildings within one estate
- Combinations of new build and refurbishment
- New build or refurbishments which are part of a larger mixed use building

The assessment is performed with a two-stage credit point system, which includes awarding credits in nine different categories for criteria met (Fig. 2.7).

Each one of these categories is assigned a different number of criteria. However, depending on the field of application, not all of these are brought into the assessment. The following explanation is based, as an example, on the criteria relevant for office buildings using the scheme BREEAM Europe. The criteria for other schemes can vary in scope and content and this is apparent from the non-consecutive numbering of the criteria. Within the overall system, the greatest weight is attached to energy efficiency. Full presentations and explanations are provided in the respective assessor manuals. Different issues are checked and rated in the individual categories:

- Management: the impact and effect of manufacturing processes
- Health and wellbeing: the different impacts the building has on the user
- Energy: different aspects concerning energy saving features
- Transport: the influence the building and its location have on private transport

- Water: reduction of water consumption and various other aspects concerning an efficient use of water
- Materials: the negative impact of materials
- Waste: the issues concerning waste during the construction process as well as during later use
- Landuse and ecology: the building footprint and the impact this has on the environment regarding ecological features
- Pollution: the various negative emissions such as noise, light or pollutants
- Additional section for exceptional achievements: Additional credits can be awarded when, due to special innovation, the requirements of individual criteria are exceeded (Fig. 2.7).

Exemplary contents of BREEAM Europe

The contents of the BREEAM Europe scheme are also a fundamental component of all other BREEAM schemes. However the requirements of the BREEAM Europe system for office and retail buildings exceed the requirements of BREEAM Office in the UK.

Energy efficiency

The credits available for the criterion energy efficiency can be obtained using various methods. If the country concerned has a standard calculation tool for energy efficiency, the number of credits can be determined according to the improvement in energy efficiency. The improvement is calculated by comparing the energy efficiency of the actual building (so-called Building Energy Performance Index, BEPI) with that of a reference building (Current Standards Building Energy Performance Index, CSBEPI). Figure 2.8 (p. 36) shows the available credits for a building differentiating between a new build and refurbishment [13].

If there is no such national calculation guideline, the expected energy efficiency can also be determined by using a dynamic simulation method, which must, however, be BREEAM-approved. In this case, the available credits are calculated by comparing the simulated value with the energy efficiency of a standard building where this has been calculated according to country-specific standards. If there are no available standards, it is possible to resort to the US American standard ASHRAE 90.1-2007, Appendix G. The third possibility is to determine

the number of credits using a checklist of measures influencing the energy efficiency. In this case, however, the maximum of credits is limited to 10 rather than 15.

Life cycle costs

The life cycle costs (LCC) are determined by applying a simplified procedure. There are no benchmark comparisons involved and the assessment is based on whether an LCC calculation was undertaken and how the findings were implemented. The BREEAM assessment method does not, therefore, attach the same importance to the LCC calculation as, for example, the DGNB system. There is no clearly defined calculation method in the case of BREEAM. However, the LCC calculation must observe the following ground rules:

- The LCC calculation must be based on the final design.
- It must consider the construction phase and the utilisation phase including building operation, maintenance and recycling.
- The first scenario covers a 25 or 30-year period; a second scenario to be examined covers a 60-year period.
- At least two of the following building elements must be considered: structure, envelope, building services or fit-out.
- When selecting a structural option, in addition to the lowest life cycle costs, at least one of the following factors must be considered: low energy consumption, reduction of maintenance expenses and effort, better durability of building components, reuse of structural elements.
- The calculation method must be updated during the subsequent planning phases.

An additional credit point is awarded if the results of the life cycle cost calculation are implemented on site.

Life cycle assessment

As an alternative analysis method to the Green Guide, a life cycle assessment (LCA) can be used to evaluate the criteria of Mat 1 and Mat 2 (see Standards, guidelines, data sources, p. 37). It is permitted to apply existing national LCA methods. However, the methods currently used in Germany are not yet listed and must be approved by BRE Global prior to their application.

BREEAM section	Weighting	Index	Criterion	Max. credits	Percentage
Management	12.0%	Man 1	Commissioning	2	2.18%
		Man 2	Constructors' Environmental and Social Code of Conduct	2	2.18%
		Man 3	Construction site impacts	4	4.36%
		Man 4	Building user guide	1	1.09%
		Man 12	Life Cycle Cost Analysis	2	2.18%
Health & Wellbeing	15.0%	Hea 1	Daylighting	1	1.07%
		Hea 2	View out	1	1.07%
		Hea 3	Glare control	1	1.07%
		Hea 4	High frequency lighting	1	1.07%
		Hea 5	Internal and external lighting levels	1	1.07%
		Hea 6	Lighting zones and control	1	1.07%
		Hea 7	Potential for natural ventilation	1	1.07%
		Hea 8	Indoor air quality	1	1.07%
		Hea 9	Volatile Organic Compounds (VOC)	1	1.07%
		Hea 10	Thermal comfort	2	2.14%
		Hea 11	Thermal zoning	1	1.07%
		Hea 12	Microbial contamination	1	1.07%
		Hea 13	Acoustic performance	1	1.07%
Energy	19.0%	Ene 1	Energy efficiency	15	11.87%
		Ene 2	Sub-metering of substantial energy use	1	0.79%
		Ene 3	Sub-metering of high energy areas and tenancy	1	0.79%
		Ene 4	External lighting	1	0.79%
		Ene 5	Low-zero carbon technologies	3	2.38%
		Ene 8	Lifts	2	1.58%
		Ene 9	Escalators and travelling walkways	1	0.79%
Transport	8.0%	Tra 1	Provision of public transport	2	1.78%
		Tra 2	Proximity to amenities	1	0.89%
		Tra 3	Alternative modes of transport	2	1.78%
		Tra 4	Pedestrian and cyclist safety	1	0.89%
		Tra 5	Travel plan	1	0.89%
		Tra 6	Maximum car parking capacity	2	1.78%
Water	6.0%	Wat 1	Water consumption	3	2.00%
		Wat 2	Water meter	1	0.67%
		Wat 3	Major leak detection	1	0.67%
		Wat 4	Sanitary supply shut-off	1	0.67%
		Wat 6	Irrigation systems	1	0.67%
		Wat 8	Sustainable on-site water treatment	2	1.33%
Materials	12.5%	Mat 1	Material specifications (major building elements)	4	3.85%
		Mat 2	Hard landscaping and boundary protection	1	0.96%
		Mat 3	Re-use of building facade	1	0.96%
		Mat 4	Re-use of building structure	1	0.96%
		Mat 5	Responsible sourcing of materials	3	2.88%
		Mat 6	Insulation	2	1.92%
		Mat 7	Designing for robustness	1	0.96%
Waste	7,5%	Wst 1	Construction site waste management	3	3.21%
		Wst 2	Recycled aggregates	1	1.07%
		Wst 3	Recyclable waste storage	1	1.07%
		Wst 5	Composting	1	1.07%
		Wst 6	Floor finishes	1	1.07%
Land Use & Ecology	10.0%	LE 1	Re-use of land	1	1.00%
		LE 2	Contaminated land	1	1.00%
		LE 3	Ecological value of site & protection of ecological features	1	1.00%
		LE 4	Mitigating ecological impact	5	5.00%
		LE 6	Long term impact on biodiversity	2	2.00%
Pollution	10.0%	Pol 1	Refrigerant GWP - building services	1	0.83%
		Pol 2	Preventing refrigerant leaks	2	1.67%
		Pol 4	NO_x emissions from heating source	3	2.50%
		Pol 5	Flood risk	3	2.50%
		Pol 6	Minimising watercourse pollution	1	0.83%
		Pol 7	Reduction of night-time light pollution	1	0.83%
		Pol 8	Noise attenuation	1	0.83%
Innovation	10.0%	Inn 1	Innovations (1 credit per innovation, max. 10 credits)	10	10.00%

2.7

**Primary energy demand of the building
undercut in per cent in comparison to local requirements**

BREEAM credits	New builds	Refurbishments
1	1 %	-50 %
2	3 %	-32 %
3	5 %	-20 %
4	7 %	-9 %
5	11 %	0 %
6	15 %	8 %
7	19 %	15 %
8	25 %	21 %
9	31 %	28 %
10	37 %	36 %
11	45 %	45 %
12	55 %	55 %
13	70 %	70 %
14	85 %	85 %
15	100 %	100 %
Additional credit 1	Carbon-neutral building (on balance)	
Additional credit 2	Zero-emission building	

2.8

BREEAM section	Credits achieved per section	Possible credits per section	Achievement in per cent	Weighting of section	Section result
Management (Man)	7	10	70 %	0.12	8.40 %
Health and wellbeing (Hea)	11	14	79 %	0.15	11.79 %
Energy (Ene)	10	21	48 %	0.19	9.05 %
Transport (Tra)	5	10	50 %	0.08	4.00 %
Water (Wat)	4	6	67 %	0.06	4.00 %
Materials (Mat)	6	12	50 %	0.125	6.25 %
Waste (Wst)	3	7	43 %	0.075	3.21 %
Landuse and ecology (LE)	4	10	40 %	0.1	4.00 %
Pollution (Pol)	5	12	42 %	0.1	4.17 %
Innovations (Inn)	1	10	10 %	0.1	1.00 %
Overall result					**55.87 %**
BREEAM rating					**Very good**

Minimum requirements for BREEAM "Very good"	Fulfilled?
Man 4 Building user guide	yes
Hea 4 High frequency lighting	yes
Ene 2 Sub-metering of substantial energy use	yes
Wat 1 Water consumption	yes

2.9

2.8   Number of credits assigned in the case of the criterion energy efficiency, which is dependent on the percentage by which the local minimum requirements are undercut.

2.9   Exemplary results of BREEAM's scoring and rating process

2.10   South view of Centrum Galerie, Dresden

The following basic conditions must be observed as minimum requirements when performing an LCA:
- At least three environmental indicators must be defined.
- The assessment must consider the entire life cycle including the operation phase and end-of-life.
- The LCA must be performed according to international standards (ISO 14040, ISO 14044 and others).

Site factors
In a similar way to LEED, various site factors are included in the overall assessment of the building. These are, for example, the proximity to public transport facilities or public amenities, such as shopping facilities.

Assessment process
The assessment, in the case of BREEAM, is performed in two stages. The example presented in Figure 2.9 illustrates the process: at first, each criterion has a maximum number of credits that can be awarded. Then the achieved credits for the individual criteria within the sections are summed. The totals are then expressed as percentages of the maximum number of credits achievable in the respective section. These percentages indicate the degree of fulfilment in each section. The example shows 70 % fulfilment in the management section. Pre-defined weighting factors are applied to the section percentages to give weighted performance rates for each individual section. The selected example shows a result of 8.40 % for the management section due to a weighting factor of 0.12. The sum of all weighted percentages is the overall degree of fulfilment, here 55.87 %. The final result, the overall assessment, (in the example "very good") derives from this figure but also depends upon the achievement of minimum levels of fulfilment in individual criteria. Only if the minimum scores are met by the criteria - in the example this is the case - the calculated overall assessment level can actually be recognised.

Standards, guidelines, data sources
The applicable guidelines depend on which BREEAM scheme has been selected and differ considerably. For the schemes in the UK, local standards and guidelines must be observed. Basically

these are the British Standards (BS). In addition, documents are applied such as BSRIA Commissioning Guides [14], Considerate Constructors Scheme (CCS), Good Practice Guide, Carbon Trust, BCO-Guide or the Energy Performance Certificate (EPC).

The requirements are supplemented by tools, for example devices to measure water consumption or the tables to evaluate the ecological value of a plot.

In contrast, BREEAM Europe specifically excludes national standards and guidelines and refers only to international ISO or EN standards. These have generally been introduced as DIN standards in Germany so that the design results in Germany can also be applied as evidence. DIN EN ISO 7730 is referred to, for example, to determine the standard of thermal comfort; DIN EN 13779 to establish the indoor air quality.

BREEAM has compiled lists for comparison of standard requirements and these indicate the degree of conformity between the different national standards and guidelines. If a national standard is missing, it can, in certain circumstances, be proven that the contents of the criteria correspond to those on the list. One example is the subject of commissioning, which must first of all be performed according to national standards and guidelines, but then also has to meet the minimum requirements stated in BREEAM. If there are no standard guidelines for commissioning, the planning team must prove the conformity with British or other European standards.

To a greater extent than for the BREEAM schemes in the UK, various checklists are supplied for international schemes. The lists spare the need for standard references in the case of numerous criteria.

A further feature specific to BREEAM is the inclusion of tools, which were developed by BRE partly outside the certification system and support sustainable construction work. In this context, it is necessary to mention Green Book Live, Smart Waste and BRE Green Guide.

Green Book Live

Green Book Live is an online databank which provides users with the information necessary to identify environmentally friendly products and the relevant services. It contains, for example, lists of organisations certified according to ISO

14001 or information about building materials. The aim is to give end users and users the opportunity to select environmentally friendly products and services [15].

Smart Waste

The Green Book also includes a reference to the tool Smart Waste, which amongst other things includes the Smart Waste plan. This tool developed by BRE facilitates the development and application of Site Waste Management Plans (SWMP), now compulsory in the UK [16].

BRE Green Guide

BRE Green Guide is a tool which helps to assess building materials and products according to their environmental impact. The results of these evaluations are directly relevant to two criteria in the BREEAM assessment [17].

Outlook

BRE is seeking to continue the internationalisation of its certification system. On the one hand, this is expressed in the development of schemes for special markets in Europe and the Gulf States, on the

other hand, it has become apparent through the cooperation agreements concluded with numerous national organisations.

In 2008, BRE Global founded the SB Alliance with the French organisation CSTB (Centre Scientifique et Technique du Bâtiment), a year later the International Sustainability Alliance (ISA) [18]. Furthermore, in 2009, BREEAM signed a Memorandum of Understanding with CSTB with the aim of developing a common European assessment system.

2.10

Centrum Galerie in Dresden, 2009
Architects: T+T Design in cooperation with Peter Kulka, Dresden, and De Architekten Cie., Amsterdam
Client: Multi Development Germany GmbH, Duisburg

Assessor: Drees & Sommer Advanced Building Technologies GmbH, Stuttgart
The shopping centre received the BREEAM Excellent award (76.5%) according to the certification scheme BREEAM International Bespoke.

LEED (Leadership in Energy & Environmental Design)

LEED (Leadership in Energy & Environmental Design) is a certification programme which is intended to define high-quality, ecological building methods for healthier, more environmentally-friendly and profitable buildings (Fig. 2.11).
The aim of the LEED Green Building Rating System is to provide building owners and operators with a structured framework to identify and implement practical and measurable solutions for the design, construction, operation and maintenance of sustainable buildings. Although originally developed specifically for the American market, LEED is now used worldwide.

System origin

LEED was developed by the USGBC (U.S. Green Building Council), a non-profit organisation located in Washington D.C. and started with a pilot project in 1993. The first version of LEED was then published at the end of the 90s. The LEED Green Building Rating System Version 2.0 for new builds (LEED-NC 2.0) was brought to the market in March 2000. Additional systems were developed over the years, which, apart from new buildings and major renovations, also cover the certification of existing buildings. It has also become possible to meet the requirements of special building types, such as schools, shopping centres or hospitals.
The motivation for the development of LEED was the demand for a system which could be used to assess and compare buildings according to their sustainability. USGBC functions as an independent authority, which sets and monitors standards. A further aim was to encourage the development of the building trade in the USA towards a more sustainable approach and therefore improve the availability of appropriate materials and efficient facilities and installations. In addition, there was a need to raise public awareness in these matters. Primarily, LEED covers all ecological and sociocultural aspects of sustainability. It focuses mainly on energy and water efficiency, the reduction of CO_2 emissions, a healthy and comfortable indoor climate and the conservation of resources. It also assesses the building operations as well as the quality of the site (Fig. 2.12).

Organisation

Originally USGBC was solely responsible for all aspects of LEED. This included the onward development of existing rating systems and the development of new ones, the organisation and implementation of training programmes and examinations on LEED and sustainable building, the review of submitted project documents and the awarding of certificates. Since January 2008, GBCI (Green Building Certification Institute) has been affiliated into the larger organisation as an independent subsidiary and the responsibilities have been shared between USGBC and GBCI. GBCI has taken on the active business area, which includes the certification, and is responsible for the entire certification process right up to completing and awarding the certificates. From the beginning, the integration of the building industry into the development process of LEED has been a key factor. Technical Advisory Groups (TAGs) bringing together experts from within the industry were introduced precisely for this purpose. These groups work on a voluntary basis on the further development of the certification system and answer technical questions (Credit Interpretation Requests, CIRs) put by project teams during the course of the certification process (Fig. 2.13).
Apart from the certification process and the review of submitted project documents, GBCI is responsible for the development of exam questions, the accreditation of LEED Green Associates, LEED Accredited Professionals (AP) and LEED Accredited Professional Fellows. LEED Green Associate is the first stage of the accreditation process. Basic knowledge about LEED and sustainable building is imparted which is then tested in exams. The requirements for the admission to the exam to become a LEED Green Associate are the participation in a LEED project or work experience in a field dealing with sustainability.
The LEED AP then has to specialise in a specific LEED rating system and once again demonstrate the in depth knowledge in a further exam. This specialised training is reflected in an addition to the title, for example LEED AP (O&M), indicating detailed knowledge about the system LEED-EB: O&M (LEED for Existing Buildings: Operation & Maintenance). For their registration, LEED APs must provide proof of their active participation in a LEED project. Both accreditations are valid for two years and can be renewed by supplying evidence of further training programmes, work on registered LEED projects, publications concerning LEED or the sustainability of buildings. The highest accreditation level is LEED Fellow. It is only awarded to LEED APs that have held their credential for at least eight years and have professional experience of at least 10 years in the green building field (Fig. 2.14).
Up until the middle of 2009, the only title available was LEED Accredited Professional (LEED AP). All LEED APs may retain their title and are under no obligation to provide evidence of updates to their accreditation. However, up until the autumn of 2011, there is the possibility to specialise in a specific rating system by taking a further exam or providing evidence of further training measures.
LEED accreditation is not mandatory for the preparation and submission of LEED documents to GBCI. However, it does make sense to involve a LEED AP in the project team. Their experience in the field of sustainable building and knowledge of the particular rating system support the project participants in translating the requirements purposefully into the design. The cooperation with a LEED AP is awarded one point in the assessment process.
External certification institutes review the submitted project documentation on behalf of GBCI. To ensure high quality, GBCI reserves the right to examine all reviews performed by external certification institutes. If the quality is not up to standard, GBCI may request the responsible institute to repeat the inspections.
USGBC is a member of the World Green Building Council, which is an affiliation of individual national Green Building Coun-

2.11

cils. Several countries worldwide have adopted the LEED certification system and adapted it in part to cater for country-specific conditions and requirements. Amongst these are India (LEED India), Canada (LEED Canada), Brazil (LEED Brazil) and Italy (LEED Italy).

Market penetration

In April 2010, 27,696 commercial and office buildings were registered for a LEED certification; 5,462 of these buildings have been certified. The majority of the registered buildings – almost 90 % – are located in the USA. Following a moderate start, a significant increase in the number of registrations has been noted since 2007 (Fig. 2.17, p. 41).

The system LEED for Homes introduced in 2007 has also experienced a high level of acceptance in the market. 24,939 residential buildings were registered in April 2010, 5,988 of these certified. The increase in recent years is, on the one hand, due to many US American authorities demanding at least a LEED Silver Certificate as a minimum for new builds and, on the other hand, reflects the fact that the market has recognised the benefits of sustainability certifications. Due to the increasing number of certified and sustainable buildings in the USA, there is pressure on the owners of existing buildings to also obtain certification.

The number of members is also rising: approximately 18,000 companies and organisations were registered as USGBC members in April 2010. Worldwide, more than 160,470 persons have been successful in passing the exam to qualify as a LEED AP. The LEED APs function as catalysts for the transfer of knowledge into the industry and private sector. Furthermore, they are frequently active members in one of the numerous local USGBCs (Fig. 2.18, p. 41).

Certification process

In the following, the certification processes are described for the LEED rating systems New Construction, Core and Shell (new builds without tenant fit-out) and Existing Buildings. Differences to the other LEED rating systems are highlighted and explained.

New Construction and Major Renovations (LEED-NC)

The certification process for new construction work (LEED-NC) is divided into

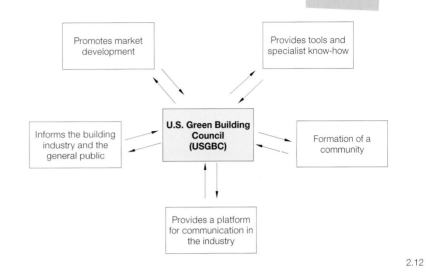

2.12

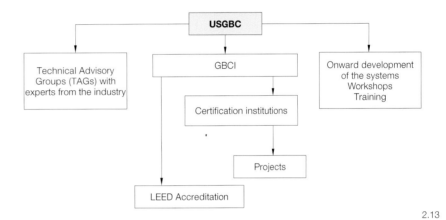

2.13

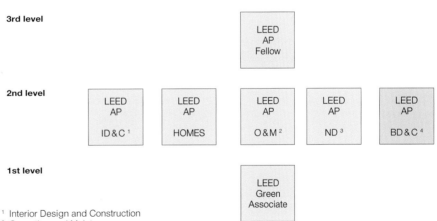

³rd level · 2nd level · 1st level

¹ Interior Design and Construction
² Operation and Maintenance
³ Neighbourhood Development
⁴ Building Design and Construction

2.14

LEED certification rating	Points
Certified	40–49
Silver	50–59
Gold	60–79
Platinum	> 80

2.15

2.11 LEED logo
2.12 Focus areas of the U.S. Green Building Council (USGBC)
2.13 Organisational structure of the USGBC
2.14 Stages of the LEED accreditation
2.15 Certification levels dependent on the number of points achieved in LEED 2009 (uniform throughout all systems)

two phases: the design phase and the construction phase (Fig. 2.16 and 2.19a). The prerequisites and credits, which can be evaluated on the basis of the design documents and location of the building, are documented and reviewed in the design phase. This documentation is then submitted to the Green Building Certification Institute (GBCI) for review before construction work commences. The result of the review is that the listed credits are either rejected or approved by the GBCI on condition that precisely these credits are actually realised on site. There is no clearly defined time for the design review. It can also be performed at the same time as the construction review on completion of the building. However, in this case, there is no possibility to adapt the design to the results of the design review.

The further credits which are related to the applied building materials, products and sequence of building operations are checked towards the end of the construction phase. On completion of the building, the documentation concerning the construction phase is submitted. If applica-

ble, a confirmation is issued stating that the construction was performed according to the documentation submitted for the design review. If this is not the case, the submittal documentation must be updated to reflect the alterations for the construction review.

Whereas there is no specific timing for the submission of the documentation at the end of the design or construction phase, the procedures concerning the review are clearly detailed. Once the documents have been submitted to GBCI, they are inspected in a first review process. If the proof or supporting documents for some credits are incomplete or unsatisfactory, the project team is granted a 25-day period to amend and revise the documentation. The amended documentation is resubmitted and evaluated in a second review. On completion of the review, the project team must accept the result within 25 days or otherwise lodge an appeal (Fig. 2.20, p. 42).

Due to the many different certification levels and the various weightings of the individual assessment categories and credits, the LEED certification can be

implemented for a wide range of applications and in many different situations within the project. On many projects, an assessment is carried out as a first step. This initial assessment gives the client and the project team an insight into the LEED certification system and enables them to judge the chances of a certificate being granted. The individual measures for a successful LEED certification are determined on the basis of this assessment.

Core & Shell (LEED-CS)
The same phases apply for the LEED rating system Core and Shell (LEED-CS) as for New Construction. In addition, it is possible, as an option, to obtain pre-certification from GBCI at an early stage of the project, for example before the design phase. In this case, a declaration of intent for all credits is submitted to GBCI with the planned objectives of the building features. The requirements concerning the requested documentation correspond with the early design phase of the project. The pre-certificate may be useful for marketing the project (Fig. 2.19b).

Introduction	Rating system	Type of use	Example
2000	**LEED-NC**	New Construction & Major Renovations	New builds and major refurbishments of office buildings and buildings with mixed use (e.g. offices, dwellings, restaurants, etc.)
2004	**LEED-EB: O&M**	Existing Buildings: Operation & Maintenance	All different kinds of existing buildings
2004	**LEED-CI**	Commercial Interiors	Tenant fit-out (e.g. offices, chemist's, banks, etc.)
2006	**LEED-CS**	Core & Shell	New builds including office buildings and buildings with mixed use (offices, dwellings, restaurants, etc.); only the shell and the basic fit-out is considered in the certification.
2007	**LEED-H**	Homes	Single and multi-family dwellings
2007	**LEED for Schools**	Schools	Primary and secondary schools
2010	**LEED-ND**	Neighbourhood Development	Urban developments
2010	**LEED Volume Certification**	Volume Certification	All building types that fall into the categories LEED-NC, LEED-EB: O&M, LEED-CI and LEED-Retail, e.g. branches of banks and supermarkets
2010	**LEED-Retail (NC and CI)**	Retail: New Construction & Commercial Interiors	Shopping centres, supermarkets, chemist's, etc.; either new build or tenant fit-out
2011	**LEED for Healthcare**	Healthcare	Hospitals, sheltered housing for elderly people, care homes for physically and mentally disabled, etc.

2.16

2.16 Current LEED rating systems (as of April 2011)
2.17 LEED building registrations (January 2010; cumulative numbers)
2.18 USGBC's company members (as of September 2009)

2.19 Certification process for
a New Construction & Major Renovations (LEED-NC)
b Core & Shell (LEED-CS)
c Existing buildings (LEED-EB: O&M)

Existing Buildings (LEED-EB: O&M)
The certification process for the rating system Existing Buildings (LEED-EB: O&M) is divided into an implementation period and a performance period (Fig. 2.19c).

The steps necessary to achieve the various credits are taken during the course of the implementation phase, whereas their fulfilment is documented in the performance period.

Taking the water consumption of sanitary fittings as an example, the fittings or volume flow regulators are installed during the implementation phase in order to achieve the specified reduction in domestic water consumption. The volume flow is then verified in the performance period either by performing several spot checks or by reference to manufacturers' specification sheets. The findings are then compared with the baseline preset by LEED. A further example is the implementation of environmentally-friendly cleaning agents: in the implementation phase, the products previously used are checked according to their compliance with the requirements of the corresponding LEED credit and, if necessary, replaced by more environmentally-friendly products. The costs for the cleaning agents are monitored and the purchases are recorded for a defined period during the performance phase. The requirements for the credit concerning cleaning agents are fulfilled, if at least 30 % of the expenses for cleaning products is spent on environmentally-friendly ones.

The period of the performance phase is at least three months for the majority of credits. An exception is the credit for energy efficiency, which has to be assessed over a period of at least twelve months. On completion of the performance phase, the documentation must be submitted to GBCI within 60 calendar days.

To maintain LEED-EB: O&M certification, re-certification is required once in every five years. Re-certification does not involve a new certification process, but, depending on the type of credit, confirmation of compliance with the original requirements at the time of re-certification or proof of previous compliance. In the case of the domestic water consumption of sanitary fittings, it is only necessary to confirm that the equipment has not been changed. However, in the case of cleaning agents, evidence must be provided that more environmentally-friendly agents have been used for the entire period

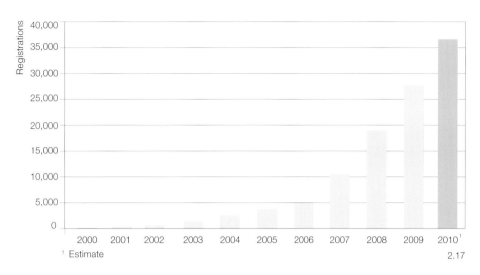

2.17
¹ Estimate

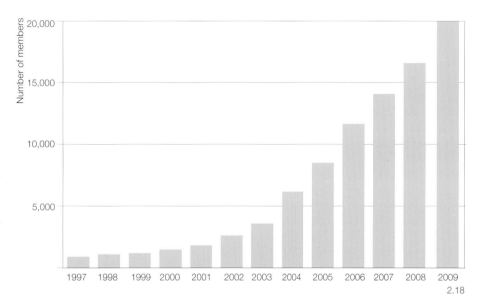

2.18

LEED-NC (New Construction and Major Renovations)

a

LEED-CS (Shell & Core)

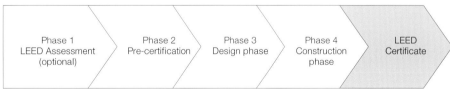

b

LEED-EB: O&M (Existing Buildings)

c

2.19

41

since receiving certification. Alterations to the building services prior to re-certification are incorporated in the assessment of the building's energy efficiency. All certification processes are based on the requirements of the currently valid version of the rating system. Credits which were not part of the original certification scheme can be incorporated and considered in the re-certification.

System structure

The LEED certification is based on a point system. Points are awarded for the fulfilment of individual credits. With the exception of the rating systems LEED-ND and LEED Homes, all of the systems divide the predetermined credits into seven categories:

- Sustainable Sites, SS
- Water Efficiency, WE
- Energy & Atmosphere, EA
- Materials & Resources, MR
- Indoor Environmental Quality, IEQ
- Regional Priority, RP
- Innovation & Design, ID

The weighting of the categories differs slightly between the rating systems (Fig. 2.21).

Apart from the minimum number of points required for the level of LEED certification aimed at, there are so-called prerequisites which must be met. In the case of the rating system LEED-NC, the following prerequisites are mandatory:

- Sustainable Sites (SS-P1): reduce dust generation, waterway sedimentation and soil erosion caused by construction activities
- Water Efficiency (WE-P1): reduce water consumption by 20% in comparison to the LEED baseline value [19]
- Energy and Atmosphere (EA-P1): fundamental commissioning of building energy systems
- Energy and Atmosphere (EA-P2): compliance with minimum requirements for energy efficiency based on the standard ASHRAE 90.1-2007
- Energy and Atmosphere (EA-P3): zero use of CFC-based refrigerants
- Materials and Resources (MR-P1): provide a dedicated area for storage and collection of recyclables during the operation phase, at least including the recycling of paper, corrugated cardboard, glass, plastics and metals
- Indoor Environmental Quality (IEQ-P1):

meet minimum requirements of indoor air quality based on the standard ASHRAE 62.1-2007 [20]
- Indoor Environmental Quality (IEQ-P2): prohibit smoking in the entire building except in designated areas

Dependent on existing environment protection requirements and local building standards in the individual countries, even the minimum requirements, for example concerning the required energy efficiency, are a real challenge. Construction projects in Germany usually meet the minimum requirements due to the prevailing high standards. However, the requirements concerning the protection of non-smokers must be considered at an early stage and the commissioning, still made little use of in Germany, must also be incorporated into the design and construction phase at an early planning stage.

In the following, the contents of the individual categories are described in detail and, using the LEED-NC rating system as an example, all credits are listed with the number of achievable points. In the case of LEED, it is not possible to meet only a proportion of a credit's requirements; the

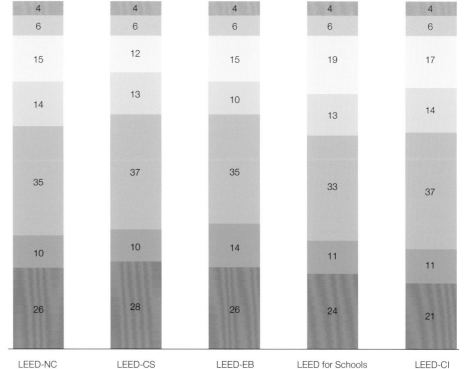

2.20 Timescale of a LEED review
2.21 Weighting of the categories according to the different LEED rating systems
2.22 List of categories and credits including the number of points attainable using LEED-NC (New Construction & Major Renovations) by way of example

requirements of the credit are either met or not. The only exception is made for the credits WE-3 – Water Use Reduction, EA-1 – Optimise Energy Performance and EA-2 – On-site Renewable Energy. The number of points awarded for these credits depends on the degree of fulfilment. In the case of LEED, there is no multiplying system similar to those for other rating systems and points are awarded directly (Fig. 2.22).

Sustainable Sites
The category "Sustainable Sites" focuses on the location of the building. Protecting land resources by selecting an already developed site or even contaminated building land and protecting or rehabilitating parkland is rated positively. The location of the property and its environment has direct influence on traffic reduction; good access to public transportation and proximity to residential areas offering public services is rated highly.

Water efficiency
The aim of the aspect "Water Efficiency" is to reduce the consumption of water during the operation of the building. This can be achieved by installing water-saving sanitary fittings, using rain or greywater and planning the exterior landscape in such a way that it requires little or no irrigation (Fig. 2.25, p. 45).

Energy and Atmosphere
The main aspects of the category "Energy and Atmosphere" are the credits Optimise Energy Performance and On-site Renewable Energy, which together can contribute as many as 26 points towards the maximum of 110 points. The energy efficiency is generally determined by performing a dynamic simulation of the building based on hourly weather data throughout the course of a whole reference year in accordance with the ASHRAE Standard 90.1-2007, Appendix G [21]. In contrast to the German Energy Performance Directive (Energiereinsparverordnung, EnEV), not the primary energy demand is evaluated but the savings in energy costs in relation to a reference value. All energy flows within the building are considered. Apart from the energy demand for building services and lighting, LEED also takes account of the energy demand to cover office equipment, kitchen appliances, exterior lighting, etc. (Fig. 2.23, 2.24 and 2.26).

Index	Category/Credit	Points
SS	**Sustainable Sites**	**26**
SS-P1	Construction Activity Pollution Prevention	R
SS-1	Site Selection	1
SS-2	Development Density and Community Connectivity	5
SS-3	Brownfield Redevelopment	1
SS-4.1	Alternative Transportation - Public Transportation Access	6
SS-4.2	Alternative Transportation - Bicycle Storage and Changing Rooms	1
SS-4.3	Alternative Transportation - Low-Emitting and Fuel-Efficient Vehicles	3
SS-4.4	Alternative Transportation - Parking Capacity	2
SS-5.1	Site Development - Protect or Restore Habitat	1
SS-5.2	Site Development - Maximize Open Space	1
SS-6.1	Stormwater Design - Quantity Control	1
SS-6.2	Stormwater Design - Quality Control	1
SS-7.1	Heat Island Effect - Non-roof	1
SS-7.2	Heat Island Effect - Roof	1
SS-8	Light Pollution Reduction	1
WE	**Water Efficiency**	**10**
WE-P1	Water Use Reduction by 20%	R
WE-1.1	Water Efficient Landscaping: reduction of domestic water consumption by 50%	2
WE-1.2	Water Efficient Landscaping: no use of domestic water	2
WE-2	Innovative Wastewater Technology	2
WE-3	Water Use Reduction by 30%/35%/40%	4
EA	**Energy & Atmosphere**	**35**
EA-P1	Fundamental Commissioning of Building Energy Systems	R
EA-P2	Minimum Energy Performance	R
EA-P3	Fundamental Refrigerant Management	R
EA-1	Optimise Energy Performance	19
EA-2	On-site Renewable Energy	7
EA-3	Enhanced Commissioning	2
EA-4	Enhanced Refrigerant Management	2
EA-5	Measurement and Verification	3
EA-6	Green Power	2
MR	**Materials & Resources**	**14**
MR-P1	Storage and Collection of Recyclables	R
MR-1.1	Building Reuse - Maintain 55% of Existing Walls, Floors and Roof	1
MR-1.1	Building Reuse - Maintain 75% of Existing Walls, Floors and Roof	1
MR-1.1	Building Reuse - Maintain 95% of Existing Walls, Floors and Roof	1
MR-1.2	Building Reuse, Maintain 50% of fit-out	1
MR-2.1	Construction Waste Management, 50% of all waste is recycled	1
MR-2.2	Construction Waste Management, 75% of all waste is recycled	1
MR-3.1	Materials Reuse, 5%	1
MR-3.2	Materials Reuse, 10%	1
MR-4.1	Recycled Content, 10%	1
MR-4.2	Recycled Content, 20%	1
MR-5.1	Regional Materials, 10%	1
MR-5.2	Regional Materials, 20%	1
MR-6	Rapidly Renewable Materials	1
MR-7	Certified wood	1
IEQ	**Indoor Environmental Quality**	**15**
IEQ-P1	Minimum Indoor Air Quality Performance	R
IEQ-P2	Environmental Tobacco Smoke (ETS) Control	R
IEQ-1	Outdoor Air Delivery Monitoring	1
IEQ-2	Increased Ventilation	1
IEQ-3.1	Construction Indoor Air Quality Management Plan—During Construction	1
IEQ-3.2	Construction Indoor Air Quality Management Plan—Before Occupancy	1
IEQ-4.1	Low-Emitting Materials - Adhesives and Sealants	1
IEQ-4.2	Low-Emitting Materials - Paints and Coatings	1
IEQ-4.3	Low-Emitting Materials - Flooring Systems	1
IEQ-4.4	Low-Emitting Materials - Composite Wood and Agrifiber Products	1
IEQ-5	Indoor Chemical and Pollutant Source Control	1
IEQ-6.1	Controllability of Systems - Lighting	1
IEQ-6.2	Controllability of Systems - Thermal Comfort	1
IEQ-7.1	Thermal Comfort - Design	1
IEQ-7.2	Thermal Comfort - Verification	1
IEQ-8.1	Daylight and Views - Daylight, 75% of the Surface	1
IEQ-8.2	Daylight and Views - Views, 90% of the Surface	1
ID	**Innovation & Design**	**6**
ID-1.1–1.5	Innovation in Design	5
ID-2	LEED Accredited Professional	1
RP	**Regional Credits**	**4**
RP-1.1–1–4	Regional Priority	4

R = requirement

2.22

2.23

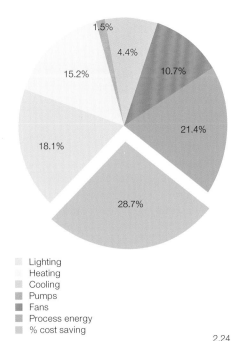

◻ Lighting
◻ Heating
◻ Cooling
◻ Pumps
◼ Fans
◻ Process energy
◻ % cost saving

2.24

2.23 Exemplary 3D model as a basis for the dynamic
building simulation. This is applied to assess the
energy efficiency according to ASHRAE 90.1,
Appendix G
2.24 Exemplary presentation of the energy cost
shares of different services in a new building as
well as the energy costs saved in comparison to
a reference building according to ASHRAE 90.1-
2004, Appendix G
2.25 Maximum limits for flush and flow volumes as
determined in the Energy Policy Act 1992
2.26 Analysis of energy efficiency according to LEED:
exemplary comparison of the final energy consumption in a planned project with the reference
values according to ASHRAE 90.1-2004, Appendix G. The process energy (for office equipment,
lifts, kitchen, etc.) has been set at the same level
as the reference value.
2.27 Certification fees for members of the USGBC

Materials and Resources
The category "Materials and Resources"
incorporates recycling during the construction phase and the development of a
recycling concept for the duration of the
building's useful phase. Due to the statutory requirements and the cost saving that
can be achieved through recycling, a
recycling rate of 75 % for construction
waste can be achieved for projects in
Germany. All quantities of waste must be
recorded and registered. A central site
waste management system simplifies this
process considerably. The second focus
of this category is on the reuse of existing
building components and the selection of
materials with a large proportion of recyclable or regional material.

Indoor Environmental Quality
This category addresses the sociocultural
factors of sustainability with the aim of providing a healthy indoor climate in a comfortable environment. Good air quality can
be achieved through low-emitting adhesives, paints, varnishes, floor coverings,
etc. and a sufficient volume of fresh air
supply. The requirements for the thermal
climate are determined by the standard
ASHRAE 55, which is based on EN
ISO 730 [22]. Matters considered are the
room temperature, local air velocity, radiant temperature asymmetry, air humidity
as well as the clothing and activity level of
the building's occupants. In order to perform an evaluation, the PPD index (Predicted Percentage of Dissatisfied) is
applied. In this case, the ten per cent mark
is not to be exceeded. Visual comfort as
well as the possibility for the users to control thermal comfort and lighting in their
own environment are further important
issues.

Innovation in Design
By implementing new technologies that
have not yet been applied or by exceeding
the targets set for individual credits, innovation points can be awarded. An additional point is awarded if, for example, the
proportion of recycled materials amounts
to more than 30 % instead of the required
20 %. However, the number of innovation
points achieved through overfulfilment is
limited to three out of five possible points.
A sixth point is awarded if a LEED AP par-
ticipates in the certification process.

Regional Priority
In order to give recognition to regional dif-

ferences, regional credits have been
determined for all communities in the
USA based on post codes. The criteria for
these cover factors which have a positive
impact on the local environment. For
example, due to the drought in Phoenix,
Arizona, a 30 % water reduction, based
on the requirements of credit WE3, is
rewarded with an additional point in the
appropriate category.
Since November 2010, international
projects can achieve regional priority
credits. The following six credits have
been selected regardless of the location
of the project: WEc1, WEc2, WEc3, EAc1,
EAc3 and EAc5. A maximum of four
regional points may be awarded for each
construction project.

Fees
Registration and certification fees accrue
in the context of a LEED certification,
which are directly payable to USGBC.
The fees can be broken down into design
review and construction review and are
calculated according to the gross floor
area of the building. Companies which
are members of USGBC generally receive
a discount. The discount is also granted if
the company of the LEED AP, accompanying the certification process, is a member. The total fees for LEED-NC start at
US$3,400 and end at a maximum sum of
US$25,900 for members (based on a
separate review performed after each the
design and construction phase). A lump
sum of US$3,250 for members and
US$4,250 for non-members is charged
for the review of documents in the context
of a LEED-CS pre-certification (as of April
2010; Fig. 2.27).

Certification levels
The assessment is based on a point system with only whole points awarded for
the fulfilment of the issues considered in
the credits. There are no points for meeting the mandatory minimum requirements. Since 2009, the maximum number
of points attainable is 110 (including the
innovation and regional priority points)
and, in relation to this, the certification
levels silver, gold and platinum are
awarded (Fig. 2.15, p. 39).

Rating systems
LEED currently offers ten rating systems.
The individual systems are described in
detail in the following paragraphs and the
differences to the basic rating system,

LEED-NC, are explained (see System structure, p. 42ff.).

Existing Buildings: Operations & Maintenance (LEED-EB: O&M)
LEED-EB: O&M offers the possibility to certify existing buildings. In contrast to LEED-NC, this rating system is designed for the building's operation and maintenance. Apart from considering the energy and water efficiency, it assesses the environmental compatibility of cleaning methods and agents and the purchasing of sustainable materials including their recycling.
In line with all rating systems, most of the points in LEED-EB: O&M are awarded for energy efficiency. An energy-efficient building can receive up to 18 points (out of a total of 110 points). A further six points are awarded for purchasing or producing renewable energies. An energy audit, which reveals measures to reduce energy consumption, constitutes a part of the certification. Commuters using alternative transportation to cars to reduce CO_2 emissions and traffic is ranked very highly. This credit is based on an occupants' survey and is worth up to 15 points. Measures to reduce the use of cars range from jobtickets and home office to supporting carpools by offering a reserved car park or reduced parking fees.
The section Materials and Resources rewards the purchasing of sustainable, i.e. regional or recycled, office supplies and furniture as well as energy-efficient equipment for office applications and low-mercury lamps.

Core & Shell (LEED-CS)
LEED-CS differs from LEED-NC in that this certification system is limited to aspects that can be influenced by the client. LEED-CS offers the opportunity to certify buildings where the client is not responsible for the fit-out or the proportion of let space falls below 50% and therefore below the required minimum value for a certification according to LEED-NC.

Commercial Interiors (LEED-CI)
The LEED-CI rating system, which is used to certify tenant fit-outs, is an addition to LEED-CS. The matter considered is limited to the tenant's rented space. This rating system can be used for space in new builds as well as space in existing buildings.

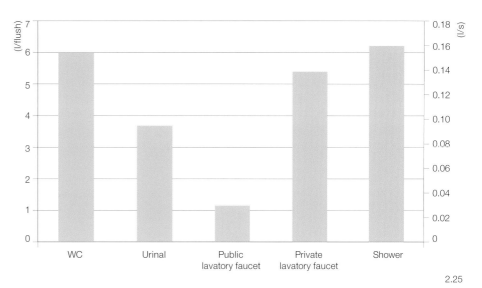

2.25

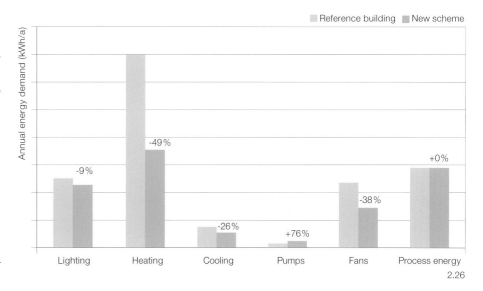

2.26

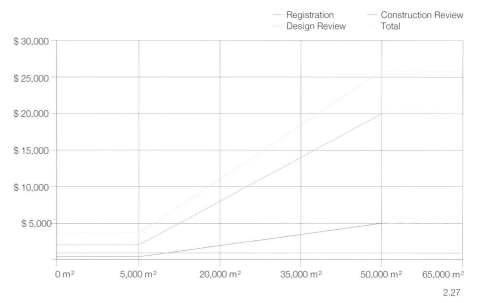

2.27

Differences are made in the assessment of the energy efficiency. In contrast to the simulation of the total building, as is the case for a LEED-NC certification, different aspects, such as lighting, lighting control, heating, ventilation and air-conditioning devices as well as the technical building equipment, are assessed separately in LEED-CI. A special feature in LEED-CI is the reward of an extra point, if the requirements concerning the pollutant emission of furniture are observed or if the tenancy agreements are concluded for periods of at least ten years.

Retail (LEED-Retail NC or CI)
LEED-Retail has been developed as an independent rating system to meet the specific needs of retail space. The credits for LEED Retail NC or LEED Retail CI are based on the systems for new builds or tenant fit-outs. However, some of the requirements have been adapted to cater for the distinctive features of retail space. This rating system, for example, also considers all of the electric kitchen appliances operated in the building and the installation of sustainable materials, such as the furniture.

Healthcare (LEED for Healthcare)
The special requirements of buildings for healthcare facilities are catered for in a separate rating system, LEED for Healthcare. The system is generally based on the requirements of LEED-NC and the Green Guide for Healthcare [23], which was first published in 2003. The Green Guide for Healthcare also awards points, like LEED, however, without defining certification levels.

Schools (LEED for Schools)
LEED for Schools has been adapted to meet the special needs of schools. The rating system LEED-NC has been used as a basis, however, with higher requirements in certain areas. LEED for Schools, for example, has additional requirements concerning room acoustics, room air quality and avoidance of mould formation. The system can currently only be used for new builds. LEED-EB: O&M is applied for the refurbishment of existing schools.

Homes (LEED-H)
LEED for Homes is a rating system for single-family and multi-family dwellings. This rating system differs from other LEED systems in the user-specific require-ments, as well as the process used to obtain certification. In this case, involvement of an approved LEED for Homes Provider in the certification process is paramount. On completion of the building, an independent agent, the so-called Green Rater, inspects whether all the measures have been implemented as described. The Green Rater accompanies the entire building process and performs at least one site inspection during the construction phase and one on completion. This system can currently only be used in the USA.

Neighbourhood Development (LEED-ND)
LEED-ND has been developed especially for the certification of larger and connected developments. With a few minor exceptions, these categories and credits are not comparable with the building-related rating systems. It has been specifically developed for projects in urban areas. Amongst others, the requirements include the planning of footpaths within the district, the proximity to schools and other public amenities.

Portfolio Certification (LEED-Volume)
The LEED Portfolio Program is a rating system for companies, which are developing the same type of building in different locations, for example banks, supermarkets or retail chains. Depending on the building type, a portfolio certification can be applied to the rating systems LEED-NC, LEED-EB: O&M or LEED for Retail. LEED for Retail will presumably play a major role within the CSR strategy (Corporate Social Responsibility) of enterprises as this scheme allows for an inexpensive certification of a large number of buildings.
In a first step, the company must be consistent in deciding which criteria are to be identical throughout the portfolio buildings. These are recorded in detail in a standard building description and determine the requirements of materials (e.g. colour, timber, regional materials), floor plans, basic fit-out, characteristic values of the facade, the efficiency of technical equipment and more. In addition to the standard building description, a reference manual must be compiled for quality control purposes and for the training of staff members and project participants. These must then be implemented and observed within the context of the selected LEED rating system.

The standard building description and the manual compiled by the company are then reviewed for compliance on completion of the construction work. If assessed positively, the same documents can be reused for each of the follow-up projects. The result is a certification with a determined certification target, which can be used for all of the following, similar-type buildings. It is no longer necessary to perform a whole new assessment process for each individual project. However, a few random checks are performed on buildings selected from the portfolio in order to check the implementation of the standard building description and manual. At least three out of a portfolio certification program with 50 projects are subject to random checks. If the requirements of the LEED rating system change, the respective manual must be revised to meet the new requirements at least once every two years.
The costs for a portfolio certification are as follows (as of August 2010):
· US$ 35,000 for the certification of the reference manual
· US$ 25,000 for the first 25 buildings
· US$ 10,000 for each of the next 50 buildings

According to USGBC, a LEED Portfolio Program is not economically viable for portfolios with less than approximately 25 buildings.

Documentation requirements
As with all rating systems, the documentation is uploaded onto LEED's internet platform from where it can be retrieved by the GBCI and checked. The documentation must be compiled in English. It is not necessary to translate all of the plans and documents so long as the submitted documentation explains the contents thoroughly and conclusively. A PDF submittal form has to be completed for every minimum requirement and for each individual credit. The form contents must confirm compliance with the requirements and/or provide detailed information. Depending on the documentation requirements of the individual credits, the following additional documents must be submitted:
· Confirmations from the design team regarding the compliance with various requirements
· Certificates from product manufacturers, for example concerning the proportion of recycled or regional material in a product

- Floor plans and schematic drawings
- Report concerning the building energy simulation
- Photographic evidence confirming the implementation of requirements during the construction phase
- Measurements of the indoor air quality or a certificate with evidence of a flush-out
- Summary of all activities performed in the context of commissioning

Standards, guidelines and data sources
The LEED rating system was originally developed for the American market and therefore refers to a number of US-American standards and guidelines. The three most important standards are ASHRAE Standard 90.1 – Energy Efficiency, ASHRAE 62.1 – Ventilation for Acceptable Indoor Air Quality [24] and ASHRAE 55 – Thermal Comfort [25].

Outlook
Apart from developing new rating systems for special types and uses of buildings, USGBC is working steadily on the improvement and further development of already available rating systems. The objectives are thereby adjusted continuously taking into account ongoing technical innovation (Fig. 2.28). The requirements for the next version of the rating systems (LEED 2012) are currently being developed and compiled. The next LEED version will refer to the standard ASHRAE 90.1-2010 with energy efficiency requirements that have increased by approximately 30 % in comparison to ASHRAE 90.1-2007. Up until now, the energy efficiency has been determined according to the annual energy costs. In future, however, the energy efficiency will refer to the primary energy demand similar to the German Energy Performance Directive (Energieeinsparverordnung, EnEV). USGBC is planning to give greater weight to the life cycle in future versions and to integrate a life-cycle assessment. This is currently being tested on the market in a pilot process with the pilot credit "Life Cycle Assessment of Building Assemblies and Materials".

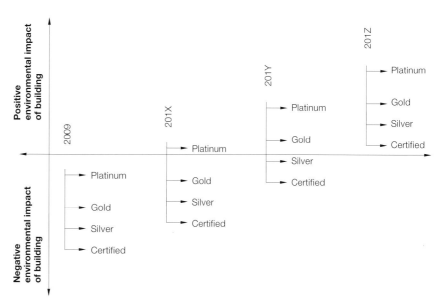

2.28

2.29

Opernturm in Frankfurt am Main, 2010
Architects: Prof. Christoph Mäckler Architekten, Frankfurt am Main
Client: Tishman Speyer, Frankfurt am Main
LEED Consultant: Ebert-Consultung Group GmbH & Co. KG, Munich

The aspired certification level is a gold rating according to LEED-NC 2.2. The high-quality facade and the efficient technical systems, such as the hybrid heating/cooling ceiling, undercut the energy demand stipulated by the German EnEV by 23 %.

2.28 Further development of the requirements in future LEED versions
2.29 Aerial view, Opernturm, Frankfurt am Main

DGNB (DGNB Certificate)

The DGNB certificate (up until June 2010 called "Deutsches Gütesiegel Nachhaltiges Bauen") follows a holistic approach in which not only ecological, economic and sociocultural aspects of sustainability form a part of the assessment, but also technical, process-oriented and site-specific factors are considered. It is for this reason that the German Sustainable Building Certificate is regarded as a rating system of the second generation (see System comparison, p. 86ff.) (Fig. 2.30 and 2.31).

System origin

Whereas numerous methods and approaches to assess and certify the performance of ecological and energy-efficient features in buildings were developed around the world during the 80s (see Principles, p. 23ff.), the German certification system, first introduced in 2007, was a relatively late entrant to the national and international property market. The first steps towards more energy-efficient, resource-saving and sustainable building with quantitative design and assessment procedures, such as LEED or BREEAM (see LEED, p. 38ff., and BREEAM, p. 30ff.), had been taken more than 15 years earlier in the USA and the UK. These methods and the experience gained as a result were used as a basis for the development of American and British standards and guidelines for sustainable construction work, for example the "Code for Sustainable Homes" for new residential buildings in the UK.

The approach in Germany was quite different. The oil crisis and the German student movement of 1968 gave stimulus in the 1970s to environmentally-friendly construction. The introduction of the Thermal Insulation Regulation (WSchVO) in 1977 functioned as a standard to improve energy efficiency in the building sector.

The Thermal Insulation Regulation was updated in 1982 and 1995 and finally replaced by the German Energy Saving Ordinance (Energieeinsparverordnung, EnEV) in 2002.

Further developments are currently taking place in this field and a move from low-energy and passive houses to zero-energy buildings [26] is evident. In order to increase the energy efficiency of properties, energy assessments of buildings became mandatory under the German Energy Saving Ordinance 2009 (EnEV). The calculations for the assessment are based on the standard DIN V 18599 [27]. Albeit the above mentioned assessment tools only cover a part of sustainability, namely the energy efficiency aspect. Recent developments in the international property market have however shown that holistic evaluation systems to assess all aspects of sustainability in the building sector are sought after and applied. In recent years, design and assessment tools, such as LEED or BREEAM, which are based on the respective American and British standards, are trying not only to gain a foothold in international markets, but also in the German property market. The DGNB certificate, available since 2007 and specifically designed to meet the needs of German standards, is counteracting this trend (Fig. 2.34, p. 50).

The German Sustainable Building Council (DGNB) was founded in Stuttgart in 2007 with the intention of developing a German system to assess the sustainable performance of buildings and to firmly establish sustainability aspects in the German and international building sector. At the same time, the Federal Ministry of Transport, Building and Urban Development (BMVBS) also began working on a rating system for sustainable buildings. At a fairly early stage, DGNB and BMVBS decided to collaborate and share the task of developing an appropriate system. The foundations of the German system therefore lie in the work of groups of experts and numerous preceding research papers and publications. The teams are made up of experts from a number of different fields and various interest groups, amongst these are architects, engineers, specialists from the construction industry, building physicists, building ecologists, energy consultants, as well as building product manufacturers, investors and scientists.

The first list of criteria developed jointly by DGNB and BMVBS in 2008 for the former

Deutsches Gütesiegel Nachhaltiges Bauen [28] was based on:
- the practical experience of the teams
- current international and European standardisation work for sustainability [29] (see Standardisation activities, p. 86f.)
- the quality verification and certification of building products
- the environmental declarations based on the international standard ISO 14025
- the results of the round-table discussion for sustainable building (Runder Tisch Nachhaltiges Bauen)
- the BMVBS's Guideline for Sustainable Building (Leitfaden Nachhaltiges Bauen)

The round-table discussion "Runder Tisch Nachhaltiges Bauen" was set up by the Federal Ministry of Transport, Building and Urban Development in 2001 in order to further develop different thematic priorities in sustainable building. The members came from associations, the construction industry, public building authorities and scientific institutes. Insights gained hereby have contributed towards the development of federal sustainability strategies for the building industry, the BMVBS's Guideline for Sustainable Building (Leitfaden Nachhaltiges Bauen) and the DGNB certificate [30].

The Guideline for Sustainable Building was published by the BMVBS in 2001. It is currently being updated based on the experience gained from the pilot phase of the DGNB certificate. The Guideline for Sustainable Building addresses the basic principles of sustainable building and relates to the total life cycle of a property [31].

Based on the above-mentioned results, an assessment tool was made available at the end of 2008 to be used for the certification of newly built office buildings in a first pilot phase. A total of sixteen new builds were certified according to this set of criteria and twelve pre-certificates were issued [32]. In the context of a second joint test-run, the current occupancy profile "New construction of office and administration buildings, version 2009" was developed (Fig. 2.35, p. 50).

Organisation

Despite the joint development of the system and implementation of the pilot phases, DGNB and the federal institution decided to go their separate ways after the second pilot scheme. It was decided, and this still applies today, that both insti-

2.30

tutions would be permitted to continue the onward development of the German certification system based on the jointly developed list of criteria. DGNB has continued using the system calling it "DGNB Certificate", while the Federal Ministry's certificate is called "Bewertungssystem Nachhaltiges Bauen" (BNB – rating system for sustainable building). DGNB is primarily responsible for the private building sector and internationalisation of the system. BMVBS, on the other hand, focuses on buildings of significance in the public sector. Parallel to this, BMVBS provides guidelines for a public recognition procedure for the certification system [33] under which an additional title is awarded stating that it is a "Federal Government-approved Certificate of Sustainable Building" (von der Bundesregierung anerkanntes Gütesiegel Nachhaltiges Bauen) [34] .

German Sustainable Building Council (DGNB – Deutsche Gesellschaft für Nachhaltiges Bauen)
The association's main task is the awarding of certificates in respect of sustainable buildings. The aim of DGNB's certification system is to foster the concept of sustainability in terms of design, construction and operation of buildings in Germany and abroad. Apart from awarding the DGNB certificate, further developing and updating the certification system and the occupancy profiles, the DGNB is also responsible for training auditors, running the certification office and managing quality assurance. For this purpose, the association is divided into different bodies [35]: DGNB's main organisational elements are the board of directors and the administrative office. The board of directors presides over all committees, whereas the administration coordinates the processes involved with the certification system. A specialist committee supports the administrative office of the DGNB in questions concerning contents and the onward development and application of the system. The committee helps the DGNB teams to determine the contents of criteria for new occupancy profiles. The teams are interdisciplinary groups made up of architects, consultants, representatives from the real estate industry and business and auditors.

Federal Ministry of Transport, Building and Urban Development (BMVBS – Bundesministerium für Verkehr, Bau und Stadtentwicklung)

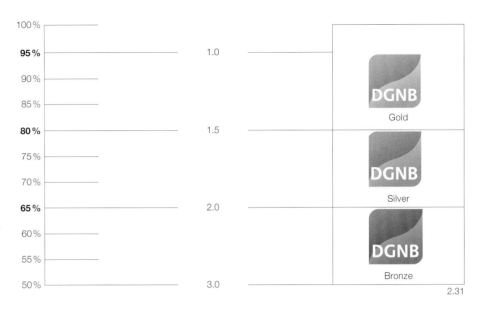

DGNB occupancy profiles	Status
New office and administrative buildings	available occupancy profile
Modernisation of office and administrative buildings	available occupancy profile
New retail buildings	available occupancy profile
New industrial buildings	available occupancy profile
New residential buildings	available occupancy profile
New educational buildings	available occupancy profile
New hotel buildings	available occupancy profile
New mixed city districts	available occupancy profile
New mixed-use buildings	available occupancy profile
Branches/tenant fit-out	in progress
New hospitals	in progress
New laboratories	in progress
Architecture-related structures/Design objects	in progress
New assembly buildings	in progress
New production sites	in progress
New infrastructure buildings	in progress
New leisure facilities	in progress
New multi-storey car park	in progress
New terminal buildings	in progress

2.32

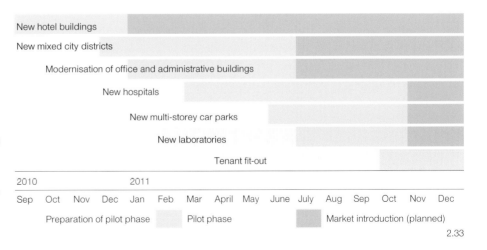

2.33

2.30 DGNB Certificate's logo
2.31 DGNB rating levels dependent on the degree of fulfilment

2.32 Currently available and future occupancy profiles of the DGNB Certificate (as of 2011)
2.33 Schedule for the development of new occupancy profiles

DGNB Certificate

2001	Round-table discussion for sustainable building (Runder Tisch Nachhaltiges Bauen), The Federal Ministry of Transport, Building and Urban Development (BMVBS) introduces Guideline for Sustainable Building (Leitfaden Nachhaltiges Bauen)
2007	
June	Celebration of DGNB's foundation, the German Council for Sustainable Building (Deutsche Gesellschaft für Nachhaltiges Bauen) Development of DGNB Certificate by DGNB and BMVBS
2008	
February	Member of the World Green Building Council
June	DGNB Congress "Consense"
September	Start of pilot certifications
2009	
January	First awarding of certificates within the framework of the Messe BAU 2009
March	Development of new certification versions by DGNB
July	Start of the DGNB auditor training programme/centres

2.34

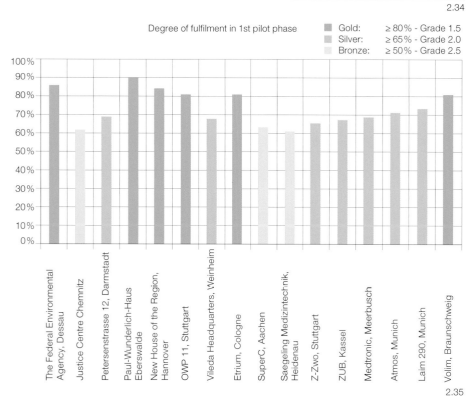

Degree of fulfilment in 1st pilot phase

Gold: ≥ 80% - Grade 1.5
Silver: ≥ 65% - Grade 2.0
Bronze: ≥ 50% - Grade 2.5

2.35

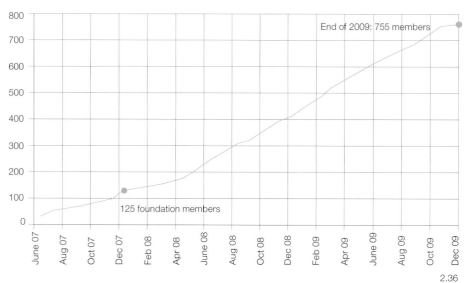

2.36

2.34 Development of DGNB Certificate
2.35 Overview of the first pilot certifications with the DGNB Certificate (main certificate)
2.36 Development of DGNB memberships since June 2007 (as of end of 2009)

Since 2009, all tasks concerning the federal government's sustainable building work have been performed by the newly established Federal Institute for Research on Building, Urban Affairs and Spatial Development (BBSR) in the Federal Office for Building and Regional Planning (BBR). The institute's responsibilities include advising the BMVBS on policies and offering support on topics relating to sustainable building, the organisation of the round-table discussion for sustainable building as well as looking after and updating the information portal "Sustainable Building" (Nachhaltiges Bauen) [36]. Furthermore, the institute is responsible for coordinating the contents of the new assessment system (Bewertungssystem Nachhaltiges Bauen, BNB) and the assessment of all public buildings. The certification system, which has been renamed as "Sustainable Building Assessment System for Public Buildings" (Bewertungssystem Nachhaltiges Bauen (BNB) für Bundesgebäude), is, in addition to the Guideline for Sustainable Building (Leitfaden Nachhaltiges Bauen), a holistic quantitative assessment procedure for office buildings. The intention of the information portal "Sustainable Building" is to provide information on further developments and updates with regard to the sustainability criteria, the system rules and additional information [37].

Market penetration

The German Sustainable Building Council (DGNB) was founded in 2007 by a group of initiators who wanted to promote a concept of sustainability for the design and construction of buildings in Germany. The current members of the DGNB represent the entire value chain of the construction industry: architects, engineers, project managers, contractors, investors and scientists [38]. The number of DGNB members is rising continuously (Fig. 2.36). More than 850 new members have since joined the original 125 founding members (total membership as of June 2011: 1000) [39].

The widening appeal of the certificate can be seen from the continuous increase in the number of project registrations and certifications. Since the beginning of the pilot phases, 220 buildings have been registered in Germany for certification with the occupancy profile "New office and administration buildings" and the pilot phase of "New retail, industrial and educational buildings" (as of August 2010). Within this number, 88 buildings in their design phase received a pre-certificate and 32 completed buildings the main certificate [40]. The market penetration of the DGNB certificate is not only making progress in Germany, but also abroad. This is not just due to the demand for certificates but also requests from partner organisations abroad for adaptations of the DGNB system to meet country-specific needs. This development is reflected in the signing of first contracts between the DGNB and partner organisations in Austria, Bulgaria and China and memoranda of understanding with organisations in a number of further countries [41]. Close cooperation with the Austrian partner organisation, Austrian Society for Sustainable Real Estate (Österreichischen Gesellschaft für Nachhaltige Immobilienwirtschaft, ÖGNI), at the end of 2009, led to the adaptation of the DGNB certification system to meet the needs of the Austrian market.

The newly created international DGNB core system is the basis for the internationalisation of the DGNB system. This catalogue of criteria is based, almost without exception, on the European Union's statutory requirements, standards and technical guidelines. German standards have only been applied in areas for which there are no EU-wide guidelines, for example in the case of fire prevention and protection.

The DGNB partner organisations, in cooperation with the DGNB main office, adapt the certification system to meet the needs of their respective countries. If there is no set standard on which to base a change to a specific DGNB criterion, there is the possibility to revert to the requirements listed in the DGNB's international core system. The same procedure applies to important calculations, such as the life cycle assessment of a product: if there is no country-specific data for a certain building product, the corresponding international data records included in the core system may be used. At the same time, the international core system provides the basis for cross-border comparisons between buildings. The requirements for a DGNB bronze certificate are normally set according to the prevailing building practices in the respective country. The DGNB gold certificate, in contrast, is based on a uniform international scale which is climate and market neutral. According to the DGNB, a "gold" building in Southern Europe fea-

tures the same qualities as a "gold" building in East Asia.

At institutional level, DGNB is also assuming responsibility for the international development of sustainable building by being a full member of the World Green Building Council (WorldGBC). As the worldwide umbrella organisation of the Green or Sustainable Building Councils, the WGBC pools and coordinates all international activities of the individual associations and functions as a mouthpiece in politics and business. In this regard, the WGBC's strategy is one of decentralisation. European interests are to be represented by the two full members, DGNB and UKGBC (United Kingdom Green Building Council), through the WGBC European Network Offices set up in Stuttgart and London respectively [42].

Occupancy profiles

Once the joint pilot phases of BMVBS and DGNB had been completed and evaluated, the final draft "New construction office and administration, version 2009" was introduced onto the market in the middle of 2009. Since then, DGNB has extended the certification system to include other building types – new builds as well as existing buildings – incorporating new occupancy profiles. These are currently being tested in pilot phases, for example, for retail, industrial and educational buildings (Fig. 2.32, p. 49). At present (June 2011), the DGNB system is available for eleven occupancy profiles:
· New office and administration buildings
· Modernization of office and administration buildings
· Existing office and administration buildings
· New retail buildings
· New industrial buildings (production + logistics))
· New educational buildings)
· New residential buildings
· New hotels
· New mixed-use city districts
· Masterplan certification for new retail buildings, new industrial buildings, new educational buildings, new residential buildings and new hotel buildings
· New mixed-use buildings

Further occupancy profiles for sports facilities, laboratories and hospitals, airports, assembly buildings and infrastructural buildings as well as for the fit-out of branch offices or stores, are still underway (Fig. 2.33, p. 49).

Certification process

The certification of buildings according to the DGNB system is voluntary. There is a difference between the pre-certificate and the actual certificate. The intention of the pre-certificate is to determine objectives and criteria for buildings that are still in their design phase. The actual certificate is awarded on completion of the building once an audit has been performed to determine whether construction was executed as planned and the sustainability objectives have been achieved. If the client or investor is planning to have a building assessed and certified, a DGNB auditor must be commissioned (Fig. 2.38, p. 52). This is usually an architect, consultant or engineer, who has either completed an additional training programme at the DGNB or at a DGNB-approved educational institute for the appropriate DGNB occupancy profile. In addition to the work performed in connection with the audit itself during the design and construction phase, the auditor is responsible for the documentation and evaluation of the registered building (pre-certificate and certificate), for all organisational matters concerning the certification process, including the registration of the building and the submission of the documents to the appropriate DGNB certification body [44]. Subsequently, the documents and the process itself are subject to a so-called conformity inspection by experts from the DGNB. If all criteria have been fulfilled, the client, depending on the project phase, either receives a pre-certificate or a certificate and a plaque for the building (Fig. 2.37, p. 52). The pre-certificate can be used for marketing purposes and public relations work. However, the client is then obliged to follow through with the entire certification programme on completion of the building. If all criteria have been fulfilled in the completed building, the pre-certificate is replaced by a permanent full certificate.

Documentation requirements

The type and extent of the project documentation for a certification programme is determined by the DGNB. The documentation includes design documents, a detailed building description and precise information concerning the building services. Furthermore, the proof documents must be compiled in accordance with the rules of the DGNB certification system's profiles (see DGNB certification process,

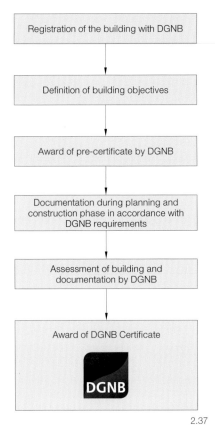

2.37

Business relationship

2.38

2.37 Certification process
2.38 Role of the DGNB auditor during the certification process
2.39 DGNB certificate's criteria and weighting factors for the occupancy profile "New office and administrative buildings" (2009)

p. 82ff.). The documents are supplied by the client as well as the planners and consultants involved in the project, compiled by the auditor and forwarded to the certification body. According to the DGNB, almost 80% of the documents to be submitted for certification are the same as those required during a conventional design and construction process. However, the fact remains that for most buildings, these have not been prepared and compiled in a form suitable for the application. Apart from the actual certification, the clear documentation of building facts and data according to the rules of the DGNB criteria catalogue is a further attribute of the certification system. During both the building's planning process and the operational phase, the documents can be used as a source of particular and clear information concerning specific characteristic features of the property. With the aid of DGNB software, the documentation can be submitted directly to the certification body.

Fees

When considering the costs of certification, it is necessary to distinguish be-tween the certification fees charged by the DGNB certification body, the auditor's fees and the construction costs. In the DGNB system, the auditor's fees, the certification fees and possible excess building costs are extremely dependent on the project. The certification fees cover the handling of the entire certification process through the DGNB. The fees therefore include the various reviews undertaken in relation to the conformity inspection, essentially the review of the documents submitted by the auditor, and the awarding of the certificate. No costs are incurred for the registration. There is a further differentiation of fees according to the building's occupancy profile and the type of certificate (pre-certificate or certificate). For all projects, the level of certification fee is dependent on the size of the building and ranges from €3,000 to €28,000 for the main certificate (see Certification fees, p. 103) [46]. The costs for the auditor's services (only the audit) are dependent on the type of project as well as the extent and timing of the certification. On average one should reckon with three to four man months purely for the auditing (without sustainability consulting) and with one to two months for a pre-certificate. Over and above this, it is necessary to consider the

additional design requirements, such as the life cycle assessment or the life cycle cost analysis, which must be prepared according to the system's requirements, as well as the costs for any extra work undertaken by consultants in this regard. It is also difficult to make a general statement regarding the construction costs. According to investors and the government, up to 8% can be added to the construction costs for designing, building and certifying a sustainable building.

System structure

The German sustainability certificate is not an additional, new tool, but a method which pools the existing national design and assessment tools for sustainable building, such as life cycle assessment, thermal simulations or eco assessments performed according to DIN V 18599, in 63 sustainability criteria and builds upon existing standards and rules (Fig. 2.39). 48 of the 63 criteria can already be applied. The remaining 15 criteria, for example concerning the building services, have been put on the back burner, since there is still need for further research. However, benchmarks are currently being developed for these criteria and they will gradually be integrated in the new versions.

In terms of sustainability, the certification system builds on the experience of existing international assessment methods. The life cycle of the building is an integral part of the assessment, which means that, alongside the phases of production, design and construction, the operation, management and removal (end of life) of the building are also considered [47]. A life cycle of 50 years has been selected as the average service life for all buildings. The aim of the certificate is to protect common property, such as the environment, resources, health, economy as well as cultural and social aspects. This concept is derived from the three pillars of sustainability: the ecological, economic as well as the sociocultural and functional quality. There are therefore clear links between the German assessment system and national sustainability strategies. The technical quality and the process quality are also included in the assessment as so called intersection qualities. The quality of the location, in contrast, is not part of the overall assessment of the building. It is evaluated as a sixth aspect, separately from the five categories concerning the quality of

Main criteria group	Criteria group	No.[1]	Criterion	Criterion points Achieved	Criterion points max. possible	Weighting [2]	Adjustment factor [3]	Weighted points Achieved	Weighted points max. possible	Fulfilment	Group points Achieved	Group points max. possible	Fulfilment	Group weighting	Total fulfilment
Ecological Quality	Life cycle assessment	1	Global warming potential (GWP)	10.0	10	3	1	30	30	100 %	173.5	195	89 %	22.5 %	
		2	Ozone depletion potential (ODP)	10.0	10	1	1	10	10	100 %					
		3	Photochemical ozone creation potential (POCP)	10.0	10	1	1	10	10	100 %					
		4	Acidification potential (AP)	10.0	10	1	1	10	10	100 %					
		5	Eutrophication potential (EP)	7.1	10	1	1	7.1	10	71 %					
	Impact on global and local environment	6	Risks to the local environment	8.2	10	3	1	24.6	30	82 %					
		8	Sustainable use of resources/timber	10.0	10	1	1	10	10	100 %					
		9	Microclimate	10.0	10	1	0	0	10	100 %					
	Utilisation of resources and arising waste	10	Non-renewable primary energy demand	10.0	10	3	1	30	30	100 %					
		11	Total primary energy demand and proportion of renewable primary energy	8.4	10	2	1	17	20	84 %					
		14	Domestic water consumption and volume of waste water	5.0	10	2	1	10	20	50 %					
		15	Area demand	10.0	10	2	1	20	20	100 %					
Economic Quality	Life cycle costs	16	Building-related life cycle costs	9.0	10	3	1	27	30	90 %	47	50	94 %	22.5 %	
	Value stability	17	Suitability for third-party use	10.0	10	2	1	20	20	100 %					
Sociocultural and Functional Quality	Health, comfort and user satisfaction	18	Thermal comfort in winter	10.0	10	2	1	20	20	100 %	251.1	280	90 %	22.5 %	86.4 % Gold
		19	Thermal comfort in summer	10.0	10	3	1	30	30	100 %					
		20	Indoor hygiene	10.0	10	3	1	30	30	100 %					
		21	Acoustic comfort	10.0	10	1	1	10	10	100 %					
		22	Visual comfort	8.5	10	3	1	26	30	85 %					
		23	Occupants' extent of control	6.7	10	2	1	13	20	67 %					
		24	Building-related outdoor quality	9.0	10	1	1	9	10	90 %					
		25	Safety and risk prevention	8.0	10	1	1	8	10	80 %					
	Functionality	26	Accessibility for disabled persons	8.0	10	2	1	16	20	80 %					
		27	Efficient use of space	5.0	10	1	1	5	10	50 %					
		28	Suitability for conversions	7.1	10	2	1	14	20	71 %					
		29	Accessibility	10.0	10	2	1	20	20	100 %					
		30	Convenience for cyclists	10.0	10	1	1	10	10	100 %					
	Quality of the design	31	Staging of an architectural competition to ensure creative and urban quality	10.0	10	3	1	30	30	100 %					
		32	Artwork	10.0	10	1	1	10	10	100 %					
Technical Quality	Quality of technical configuration	33	Fire protection	8.0	10	2	1	16	20	80 %	74	100	74 %	22.5 %	
		34	Sound insulation	5.0	10	2	1	10	20	50 %					
		35	Quality of building envelope's thermal and moisture insulation	7.7	10	2	1	15	20	77 %					
		40	Structure's suitability for upkeep and repair	7.1	10	2	1	14	20	71 %					
		42	Suitability for deconstruction, recycling and reuse	9.2	10	2	1	18	20	92 %					
Process Quality	Quality of planning	43	Quality of project preparation	8.3	10	3	1	25	30	83 %	188.6	230	82 %	10.0 %	
		44	Comprehensive planning	10.0	10	3	1	30	30	100 %					
		45	Optimisation and completeness in the planning approach	8.6	10	3	1	26	30	86 %					
		46	Evidence of sustainability aspects in the tendering process	10.0	10	2	1	20	20	100 %					
		47	Provision of conditions for perfect use and operation	5.0	10	2	1	10	20	50 %					
		48	Construction site/construction phase	7.7	10	2	1	15	20	77 %					
		49	Quality of executing firms, pre-qualification	5.0	10	2	1	10	20	50 %					
	Quality of construction activities	50	Quality assurance of workmanship	10.0	10	3	1	30	30	100 %					
		51	Systematic commissioning	7.5	10	3	1	23	30	75 %					

Site quality: separate assessment, not included in overall rating

Main criteria group	Criteria group	No.	Criterion	Achieved	max. possible	Weighting	Adjust. factor	Achieved	max. possible	Fulfilment	Group Achieved	Group max. possible	Fulfilment		
Site Quality		56	Risks in the micro environment	7.0	10	2	1	14	20	70 %	93.3	130	72 %		
		57	Conditions of microclimate	7.1	10	2	1	14.2	20	71 %					
		58	Image and condition of site and neighbourhood	1.0	10	2	1	2	20	10 %					
		59	Traffic connections	8.3	10	3	1	24.9	30	83 %					
		60	Vicinity to user-specific facilities	9.7	10	2	1	19.4	20	97 %					
		61	Utilities and site development	9.4	10	2	1	18.8	20	94 %					

Grade 1.0 95 %
Grade 1.5 80 %
Grade 2.0 65 %
Grade 3.0 50 %
Grade 4.0 35 %
Grade 5.0 20 %

[1] The numbers missing are categories still in progress.   [2] uniform for all occupancy profiles   [3] user-specific, is determined for all occupancy profiles separately

must be filled   is calculated automatically   fixed values

2.39

the building, since the impact the building has on the location is fairly limited.

The five categories of the building assessment are evaluated separately and then, once multiplied with their appropriate weighting factor, added up to a total sum. The same weighting of 22.5 % is applied for the ecological, economic, the sociocultural and functional and the technical quality in the overall assessment. The quality of the process accounts for 10 %. This breakdown offers the opportunity to not only present the evaluation of the main criteria groups as a single overall grade, but also separately [48] (Fig. 2.40).

Ecological quality
The results of the building's life cycle assessment function as a basis for the evaluation of the ecological quality:
• Gobal warming potential
• Ozone depletion potential
• Photochemical ozone creation potential
• Acidification potential
• Eutrophication potential
• Non-renewable primary energy demands
• Total primary energy demands and proportion of renewable primary energy

The criteria are determined by using suitable methods and tools. A period of 50 years is applied. The calculations are based on:
• The data basis of the Ökobau.dat (databank of the Federal Ministry of Transport, Building and Urban Development) for material-specific properties [49]
• The useful life of components and building services systems according to the recommendations in BMVBS's Guideline for Sustainable Building (Leitfaden Nachhaltiges Bauen)
• The quantity survey according to the cost groups 300 and 400 (DIN 276)
• The final energy demand for electricity and heat calculated according to DIN V 18599

In the context of the ecological quality, criteria such as the freshwater consumption and sewage volume or land use are also assessed. The aim of calculating the environmental impact products have on the immediate environment according to information provided by the Environmental Product Declaration (EPD) is to avoid the use of halogen, heavy metals, organic solvents, biocides and products marked as environmentally hazardous in buildings. The criterion "Sustainable use of

resources / timber" requires certificates such as FSC (Forest Stewardship Council) or PEFC (Programme for the Endorsement of Forest Certification) for timber products used in order to provide evidence of a controlled and sustainable management of the source forest.

Economic quality
The economic quality incorporates aspects such as life cycle costs and suitability of the building for third-party use. The primary aim is to reduce the operating costs. The life cycle costs are made up of the construction costs and the operation costs. The construction costs are estimated according to DIN 276 (selected cost groups 300 and 400). The operation costs are determined by a building-specific present value (Euro/m$^2_{BGF}$) calculated according to DIN 18960 over a period of 50 years. This method includes aspects such as utilities, cleaning and upkeep of the building as well as the operation, inspection and servicing of building installations. In addition, these cost groups take into account maintenance and repair of the built structure and the building services in terms of costs for replacement or renewal of components that have a shorter useful life than the period under consideration. The useful lives of building components are listed in BMVBS's Guideline for Sustainable Building. The deconstruction and removal costs are not yet considered in the current versions of the certificate.

Sociocultural and functional quality
The sociocultural and functional quality focuses mainly on aspects such as health, comfort and user satisfaction. This category is also used to assess the functionality and design quality of the building. Characteristic values for the comfort of the occupants are determined by taking measurements of physical criteria, such as thermal, acoustic and visual comfort or room hygiene. User satisfaction is based upon the extent to which the building occupants, at their work place, are able to control ventilation, sun and glare protection, temperature, natural daylight and artificial light. Further aspects in this category are the quality of the building in relation to the exterior space and the factors, safety and risk of accidents, with an emphasis on risk prevention. According to the DGNB system, the functionality of a building is defined by criteria such as accessibility for disabled persons, effi-

cient use of space, suitability for conversions, accessibility for the general public and the convenience for cyclists. The staging of an architectural competition and the stipulation for artwork on the building serve to ensure creative design.

Technical quality
The criteria for the technical quality include minimising the energy demand, maintaining thermal comfort, preventing structural damage and optimising the building envelope. This category also considers actions to safeguard the quality of fire prevention measures and improve sound insulation. Thorough cleaning, upkeep, inspection and maintenance and repair help to extend the service life of materials to the maximum. The criterion "Suitability for deconstruction, recycling and reuse" is intended to prevent ecologically damaging waste and encourage the use of building products suitable for recycling. The assessment of the building services systems within this category, technical quality, is in progress and not yet available.

Process quality
The quality of the design, the construction process and building operation are the primary concern of the category process quality. Aspects inspected and evaluated are the approach towards a building-related planning process, the consideration of sustainability features in the concept and tender documents as well as the comparison of alternative approaches (energy, water, waste concept, etc.). The aim is to optimise the building and its components. With regard to construction work, minimising the impact on the surrounding environment has priority (waste, noise and dust prevention on the building site) as well as verifying and documenting the agreed planning objectives. Controlled operation is to be ensured through systematic commissioning, i.e. the setting and adjusting of building services by a specialist firm and the compilation of a user's manual with instructions on maintenance, inspection, operation and upkeep.

Site quality
The site quality is evaluated separately. The important factors within this assessment category are the relationship between the micro and macro location of the building as well as the risks resulting therefrom. The image and the condition of the area are also considered. The crite-

rion relating to traffic connections is to ensure and improve the accessibility of the building using public transport. The category also considers the proximity and range of user-specific facilities, such as restaurants, local amenities, parks, educational institutions, etc., all of which are significant for the user's quality of life. The availability of utilities and the possibilities concerning site development are to be considered for the scheme concerned as well as for possible extensions in order to reveal alternative energy and water concepts and secure sufficient supply facilities for further building sections.

Certification levels

The DGNB certificate, in particular, offers the possibility to perform a comprehensive assessment of a building with a holistic approach. It will soon be extended to incorporate the sustainable development of quarters, towns and regional areas. Due to consideration of the entire life cycle of a building and the application of quantifiable criteria and indicators, the DGNB system is a uniform and easily comprehensible certification system. A significant improvement in comparison to previous methods is that not only the main criteria groups are weighted against one another but also that the individual criteria are provided with different factors of importance. According to the significance of national or building-specific aspects, individual criteria have been assigned different weighting factors such as 1, 2 or 3. The total number of points is determined on completion of the assessment. This then leads to the degree of fulfilment, which constitutes the relationship between the achieved points and the total number of achievable points. The score is shown as a grade, which in turn corresponds to either a bronze, silver or gold award. If a building achieves at least 50% of the achievable number of total points, the bronze certificate is awarded. The silver award requires a degree of fulfilment of at least 65%, the gold award at least 80% [50]. The final grade therefore considers ecological and economic as well as sociocultural and functional aspects and, at the same time, assesses the technical and design qualities of a building.

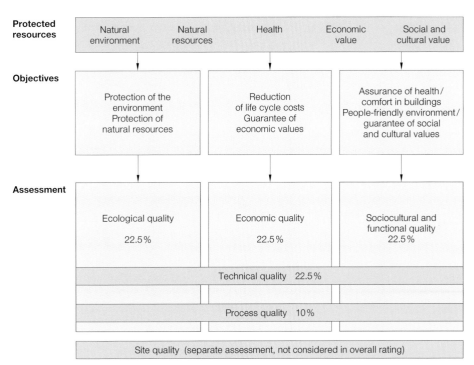

2.40

2.41

2.40 Structure of the DGNB certificate with weighting factors
2.41 Aerial view (photomontage), district administration and county council, Eberswalde

District administration and county council, Eberswalde, 2007
Architects: GAP Generalplaner, Berlin
Client: Kreisverwaltung Barnim, Eberswalde
Auditor: sol.id.ar planungswerkstatt Dr. Günther Löhnert, Berlin

The building complex was one of the first to be awarded the gold DGNB certificate. The overall rating was 1.2 and the rating for the quality of the location 1.6. The ground is used as the exclusive source for heating and cooling the building.

CASBEE (Comprehensive Assessment System for Building Environmental Efficiency)

CASBEE (Comprehensive Assessment System for Building Environmental Efficiency) was developed in Japan to evaluate the sustainability of buildings (Fig. 2.42). The system is focused on a comprehensive assessment bringing together the environmental performance (Q, Building Environmental Quality & Performance) and the environmental impact (L, Building Environmental Loadings) of the building.

In Japan, CASBEE is used by architects, planners, building operators or owners as a planning tool on a self-assessment basis. Numerous Japanese town and local authorities have adopted the CASBEE assessment method in a modified form and it has become an integral part of the planning application. At the same time, CASBEE is a certification system. Independent certification bodies check the qualities of a building based on one of the assessment tools and award an appropriate certificate.

System origin

There are some very close ties in Japan between government and industry. Based on these traditions, the Japan GreenBuild Council (JaGBC) and the Japan Sustainable Building Consortium (JSBC) were created in 2001 as a result of a joint initiative by industry, government and various other research institutions. As part of a joint research and development project, they created the CASBEE assessment system. The development work focused on the following aims:

- The assessment method should be structured to give recognition to outstanding, sustainable buildings, thereby enhancing incentives for other planning teams and decision makers to follow suit and design sustainable buildings.
- The assessment system should be simple and easy to use. It should furthermore be applicable for a wide range of different buildings and uses.
- It should take into consideration the special issues and requirements of Asia and in particular Japan.

2.42

The Japan Sustainable Building Consortium (JSBC) is responsible for the onward development and administration of CASBEE. The Japanese Institute for Building Environment and Energy Conservation (IBEC)[51] is in charge of carrying out the certification processes and dealing with the training and accreditation of CASBEE auditors. IBEC is supported in this task by eleven external organisations.

Market penetration

CASBEE is used on a wide range of buildings in Japan as a means of voluntary self-assessment. Here it functions as a design tool to help classify and optimise the building concerned. CASBEE is based on local Japanese standards and regulations, is easy to use and can be applied from the very early design stages in a very constructive way.

Due to the demand for an independent certification system, a formal certification process was launched in 2005 and applied to a range of different building types. Town and local authorities in Japan have contributed significantly towards propagating the system since they adopted it to implement the state environmental policies. Up until February 2010, 88 buildings had been certified; up until March 2009, 3,859 assessments had been submitted to the authorities as part of the building application.

Certification process

In common with other rating systems, the CASBEE assessment for new constructions is divided into three stages. The system can be applied to evaluate the sustainability of a building during the course of any design or construction phase. The first assessment is performed at pre-design stage. The planners and clients involved establish the objectives of the building's components in relation to the criteria assessed under CASBEE. The assessment is updated at the end of the design stage and on completion of the building. Subsequently, a final assessment is performed and the documentation is compiled (Fig. 2.45).

If the aim is to obtain certification, the planning team prepares the necessary documents and has them compiled by an approved CASBEE auditor. The client submits these documents at the end of the design phase and on completion of the building to the appropriate certification body. The applicable certificate is awarded on the basis of these documents. The validity of a certificate is limited: a period of three years from the date of issue applies for new builds; five years for existing building stock.

In the case of CASBEE, the assessment criteria are mostly quantitative. However, some criteria require a qualitative appraisal for which detailed knowledge concerning application of the system is necessary. It was for this reason that IBEC developed a training and accreditation programme for CASBEE auditors. The auditors are obliged to participate in a training programme, must complete the final exam successfully and officially register with IBEC. The costs for training and accreditation amount to approximately €400 (JPY 50,000, exchange rate 125 JPY/€). There are currently 3,800 approved CASBEE auditors in Japan (as of March 2010).

Fees

In Japan, CASBEE is used mainly as a voluntary benchmarking standard by the planning team, but many town and local authorities have also made it a statutory requirement for building applications. In these cases, no costs accrue. If certification is requested by an independent certification body, registration and certification fees are charged. The level of fees is dependent on the size of the project and the number of different uses fulfilled by the building. They range from €5,400 – €14,360 (JPY 630,000 – JPY 1,795,000). A fee of €6,300 (JPY 787,500) is, for example, charged for a school with a gross floor area of 10,000 m^2; €9,828 (JPY 1,228,500, exchange rate 125 JPY/€) for a building complex with a shopping centre and a hotel with a gross floor area of 50,000 m^2.

Certification levels

The ranking of a building is based on the indicator Building Environmental Efficiency (BEE), which is the quotient of Q (Building Environmental Quality and Performance) and L (Building Environmental Loadings). The range of the Building Environmental Efficiency is subdivided to give five quality levels or rankings. The highest level S, which is the equivalent to "outstanding", applies to buildings satisfying the highest standards set for sustainable buildings. The rating B+, equivalent to the result "good", is the benchmark value of the system and corresponds to average standards for new builds in

Japan. The lowest rating C, equivalent to the result "poor", applies to buildings which only just comply with statutory requirements (Fig. 2.43).

System variants

CASBEE may be used for a variety of building types and uses and offers assessment tools for new constructions, existing buildings, temporary buildings and whole urban districts (Fig. 2.44). The CASBEE assessment tool for office buildings has been available since 2002. CASBEE for new construction was developed in 2003, CASBEE for existing buildings in 2004 and CASBEE for renovations in 2005 (Fig. 2.46, p. 58). The assessment tool for new construction can be applied to a range of different uses, in which case the weightings of the individual categories and criteria vary according to the building's use. In factories, the assessment is limited to the areas intended for use by persons. The production process itself is not considered.

CASBEE also offers an assessment tool appropriate for buildings or building complexes with mixed uses (Fig. 2.47, p. 58). In this case, the criteria are assessed separately for the individual uses. The assessment result for the complex is determined in a second step by weighting the results according to the proportion of the total area occupied by the respective uses and adding them together:

· Assessment of mixed-use development = assessment of individual use × proportion of total area covered

This formula can be applied to schemes where several buildings share a common site as well as a single building complex with different uses.

Documentation requirements

In the case of a certification, the documents, which must be written in Japanese, are submitted to the IBEC or one of the eleven external organisations by an approved CASBEE auditor. In order to support the documentation process, IBEC offers appropriate software free of charge. The same software is also available in English and can be accessed via the IBEC website. The software application displays the CASBEE results clearly and thoroughly in the form of graphical diagrams. All of the assessment results, including those of separate criteria categories, are therefore visible and clearly detailed.

Rating	Assessment	BEE indicator	Label
S	Excellent	BEE ≥ 3.0 or Q ≥ 50	* * * * *
A	Very Good	BEE = 1.5…3.0	* * * *
B+	Good	BEE = 1.0…1.5	* * *
B-	Fairly Poor	BEE = 0.5…1.0	* *
C	Poor	BEE < 0.5	*

2.43

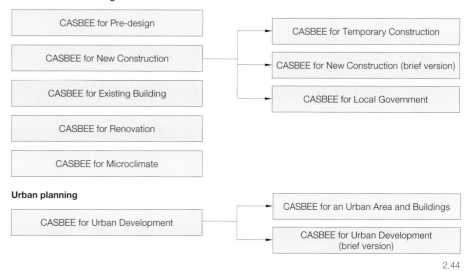

2.44

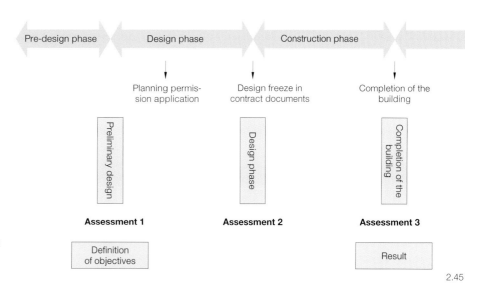

2.45

2.42 CASBEE logo
2.43 Overview of CASBEE certification levels
2.44 Assessment tools are divided into residential buildings, non-residential buildings, urban planning
2.45 Assessment phases for the system CASBEE for New Construction

Building type	Application	Example
Non-residential buildings	Office and administration	Office buildings, government buildings, libraries, museums, post offices, etc.
	Schools	Primary schools, secondary schools, universities, vocational schools and other educational facilities
	Retail	Shopping centres, supermarkets, etc.
	Restaurants	Restaurants, canteens, cafés, etc.
	Halls	Lecture theatres, halls, buildings for events, such as bowling centres, leisure centres, theatres, cinemas, amusement arcades, etc.
	Factories	Factories (excluding production space), garages, warehouses, viewing stands, wholesale markets, etc.
Residential buildings	Hospitals	Hospitals, assisted living for the elderly, care homes for the physically and mentally disabled, etc.
	Hotels	Hotels, hostels, etc.
	Dwellings	Apartments, etc.

2.46

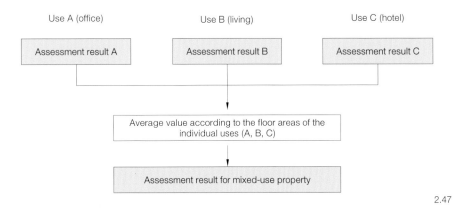

2.47

System structure

CASBEE focuses on the following fields: energy efficiency, resource efficiency, local environment and indoor environment. The individual criteria are then assigned either to the assessment category "Building Environmental Quality and Performance" or "Building Environmental Loadings". The separation is performed in relation to a hypothetical system boundary, which is defined, on the one hand, by the site boundary and, on the other hand, by the impact of the sustainability aspects under consideration. The Building Environmental Quality and Performance (Q) evaluates the "improvement in living amenity for the building users, within the hypothetical enclosed space (the private property)." In contrast, the Building Environmental Loadings (L) assesses the "negative aspects of environmental impact which go beyond the hypothetical enclosed space to the outside (the public property)" (Fig. 2.48).

The evaluation is based on six main assessment categories, which are assigned either to Q or LR: Indoor Environment (Q1), Quality of Service (Q2), Outdoor Environment on Site (Q3), Energy (LR1), Resources and Materials (LR2) and Off-site Environment (LR3) (Fig. 2.50 and 2.51).

CASBEE is based on a complex rating method and uses weighting coefficients in order to balance the individual criteria. These are used at each evaluation level. The result is that all six main categories are weighted according to their significance for the respective building type and use (Fig. 2.49). The weighting factors have not only been based on scientific findings, but express the relevance that professionals (architects, planners, building owners, operators, representatives from local building authorities) attribute to the individual criteria. The aim of IBEC is to ensure that the assessment of sustainability achieves the broadest possible social consensus by the groups involved.

The categories Q1, Q2 and Q3 refer to the environmental performance of the building, the categories LR1, LR2 and LR3 to the environmental impact of the building. The Building Environment Efficiency (BEE) is calculated by dividing the numerator Q (Building Environment Quality and Performance) by the denominator L (Building Environmental Loadings). The higher the environmental performance

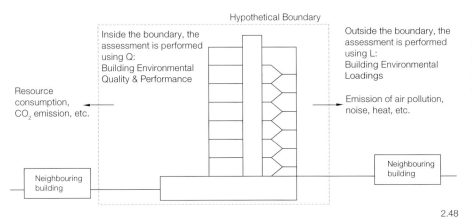

2.48

Code	Category	Factory	Others
Q1	Indoor Environment	0.30	0.40
Q2	Quality of Service	0.30	0.30
Q3	Outdoor Environment on Site	0.40	0.30
LR1	Energy	0.40	0.40
LR2	Resources & Materials	0.30	0.30
LR3	Off-site Environment	0.30	0.30

2.49

and the lower the negative environmental impact of the building, the higher the performance of the building is in terms of the sustainability objectives of the system. In the case of CASBEE, this is expressed as the Building Environmental Efficiency (BEE). A high BEE factor distinguishes a property displaying particularly positive qualities in regard of sustainability (Fig. 2.52):
• BEE = Q (quality)/L (load)

The values for Q and L are determined by the number of total points achieved in the respective categories, Building Environment Quality and Performance (SQ) and Reduction of Building Environmental Loadings (SLR). The determined assessment figure, ranging between 1 and 5, is then transposed for both categories to numbers between 0 and 100 by applying the following formula:
• $Q = 25 \cdot (SQ - 1)$
• $L = 25 \cdot (5 - SLR)$

The Building Environmental Efficiency (BEE) is at the heart of a CASBEE assessment. It allows for a transparent presentation of the achieved sustainability level. The result is displayed graphically in an x/y diagram. Q is shown on the y axis, L on the x axis. The gradient of the straight line in the x/y diagram passing through the origin (0, 0) and the score (Q, L) indicates the achieved Building Environmental Efficiency. The steeper the gradient in the diagram, the more sustainable the building is. Figure 2.52 presents an example of a building with a quality Q of 77 ($SQ = 4.08$: $Q = 25 \cdot (4.08 - 1)$) and a load L of 38 ($SLR = 3.48$: $L = 25 \cdot (5 - 3.48)$). The result is a BEE rating of 2.0 and therefore a class A, which complies with "very good".
Each one of the six main criteria categories is divided into several subcategories each with its own set of individual criteria. Depending on the achieved performance, each criteria is given a score between one and five points. The lowest level with the smallest number of points represents the minimum statutory and normative requirements in Japan. A score of three points is used as the benchmark as it corresponds approximately to an average new building in Japan. Similar to the way in which the main criteria categories are weighted, the groups of criteria on the second tier as well as the individual criteria are weighted according to their significance in relation to the type of building and its use. Figure 2.53 (p. 60) presents the criteria as well as the corresponding weighting coefficients for an office building using the assessment tool CASBEE for New Construction. The objectives of the six main criteria categories are as follows:

Indoor Environment Q1
The quality of the indoor environment has a considerable impact on the health, comfort and productivity of the building's occupants. Therefore, the main criteria category Q1 assesses the aspects influencing the quality of the indoor environment, such as noise and acoustics, thermal comfort, lighting and illumination as well as air quality.

Quality of Service Q2
The focus, in this case, is on the functional aspects of the interior and the building services facilities, which influence the occupants' wellbeing (e.g. the space provided at the workplace, availability of kitchenettes, safety hazards and risks, such as earthquake resistance, durability of the applied components as well as the flexibility and suitability of the building for future conversions).

Outdoor Environment on Site Q3
This category evaluates the improvement in the outdoor environment within the site boundary and in its immediate surroundings due to measures performed that are immediately related to the scheme. These include the preservation and creation of biotope, the urban and landscape design as well as outdoor facilities for the occupants, such as protection against rain, wind or sun, and communal facilities. However, the aesthetics and the architecture of these outdoor facilities are not considered.

Energy LR1
This main criteria category assesses the energy demand during the useful period of the building. The aim is to minimise the consumption of non-renewable energies. The reduction of the global warming potential is considered in the main criteria category Off-site Environment (LR 3).

Resources and Materials LR2
In this case, the assessment concerns the materials consumed during the production of the building, the demand for

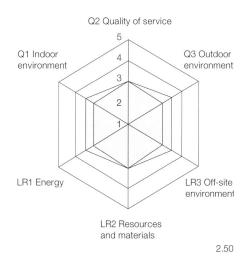

2.50

Code	Assessment category
Q 1	Indoor Environment
Q 2	Quality of Service
Q 3	Outdoor Environment on Site

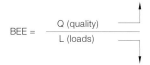

Code	Assessment category
LR 1	Energy
LR 2	Resources and materials
LR 3	Off-site environment

2.51

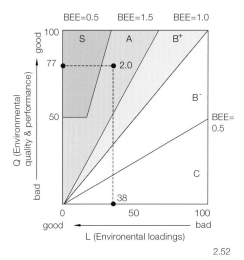

2.52

2.46 The building types and uses that can be assessed by the tool CASBEE for New Construction
2.47 CASBEE assessment method for mixed use
2.48 Definition of environmental performance and the impact the building has on the environment according to the hypothetical system boundary
2.49 Weighting coefficients of the main criteria categories
2.50 The radar chart of CASBEE's main criteria categories displays the strengths and weaknesses of a building
2.51 Determination of the Building Environmental Efficiency (BEE)
2.52 Determination of the rating level: the assessment of a building with an A rating and therefore the result "very good" has been used as an example

No.	Main criteria category	Weighting coefficient	No.	Criteria category	Weighting coefficient	No.	Criterion	Weighting coefficient
LR1	Energy	40%	1	Building Thermal Load	30.0%			
			2	Natural Energy Utilisation	20.0%			
			3	Efficiency of Building Service System	30.0%	3.1	HVAC system	45%
						3.2	Ventilation system	15%
						3.3	Lighting system	30%
						3.4	Hot water supply system	5%
						3.5	Elevators	5%
			4	Efficient Operation	20.0%	4.1	Monitoring	50%
						4.2	Operation & management system	50%
LR2	Resources & Materials	30%	1	Water Resources	15.0%	1.1	Water saving	40%
						1.2	Rainwater & greywater	60%
			2	Reducing Usage of Non-renewable Resources	63.0%	2.1	Reducing usage of materials	7%
						2.2	Continuing use of existing building skeleton etc.	24%
						2.3	Use of recycled materials as structural frame materials	20%
						2.4	Use of recycled materials as non-structural materials	20%
						2.5	Timber from sustainable forestry	5%
						2.6	Reusability of components and materials	24%
			3	Avoiding the Use of Materials with Pollutant Content	22.0%	3.1	Use of materials without harmful substances	32%
						3.2	Avoidance of CFCs and halons	68%
LR3	Off-site Environment	30%	1	Consideration of Global Warming	33.3%			
			2	Consideration of Local Environment	33.3%	2.1	Air pollution	25%
						2.2	Heat island effect	50%
						2.3	Load on local infrastructure	25%
			3	Consideration of Surrounding Environment	33.3%	3.1	Noise, vibration & odour	40%
						3.2	Wind damage & sunlight obstruction	40%
						3.3	Light pollution	20%
Q1	Indoor Environment	40%	1	Noise & Acoustics	15.0%	1.1	Noise	40%
						1.2	Sound insulation	40%
						1.3	Sound absorption	20%
			2	Thermal Comfort	35.0%	2.1	Room temperature control	50%
						2.2	Humidity control	20%
						2.3	Type of air conditioning system	30%
			3	Lighting & Illumination	25.0%	3.1	Daylighting	30%
						3.2	Anti-glare measures	30%
						3.3	Illuminance level	15%
						3.4	Lighting controllability	25%
			4	Air Quality	25.0%	4.1	Source control	50%
						4.2	Ventilation	30%
						4.3	Operation plan	20%
Q2	Quality of Service	30%	1	Service Ability	40.0%	1.1	Functionality & usability	40%
						1.2	Amenity	30%
						1.3	Maintenance management	30%
			2	Durability & Reliability	31.0%	2.1	Earthquake resistance	48%
						2.2	Service life of components	33%
						2.3	Reliability	19%
			3	Flexibility & Adaptability	29.0%	3.1	Spatial margin	31%
						3.2	Floor load margin	31%
						3.3	Adaptability of facilities	38%
Q3	Outdoor Environment on Site	30%	1	Preservation & Creation of Biotope	30.0%			
			2	Townscape & Landscape	40.0%			
			3	Local Characteristics & Outdoor Amenity	30.0%	3.1	Attention to local character & improvement of comfort	50%
						3.2	Improvement of the thermal environment on site	50%

2.53

domestic water during the building's operation phase and the avoidance of environmentally-harmful building materials and products.

Off-site Environment LR3
This main criteria category evaluates the measures to reduce the negative impact of the building on the global and local environment as well as the area immediately beyond the boundary of the property. Measures to avoid the contamination of the ground and groundwater are not included in CASBEE's assessment since these aspects are already covered by statutory regulations in Japan. The assessment of the building's CO_2 emissions (criterion: Consideration of Global Warming) is based on a life cycle assessment. The calculation method applied by CASBEE considers the production phase, the operation phase as well as the deconstruction of the building. The annual CO_2 emissions per square metre of gross floor area serve as a basis for the evaluation. The achieved assessment result depends on the relation between the CO_2 emissions of the building and a benchmark value (Fig. 2.54).

Standards, guidelines and data sources
CASBEE relates mainly to Japanese standards and guidelines. The assessment of thermal comfort is based on the comfort zone as defined by the US standard ASHRAE 55 [52] and POEM-O [53] (a Japanese method used to assess buildings during operation). The specifications for the assessment of the air exchange rates are in line with the Japanese standard SHASE-S102-2203 [54]; the eco-assessment is performed according to the provisions of the Japanese energy saving order.

Outlook
The objectives and the requirements of the individual criteria are subject to continuous further development. Furthermore, they are adapted to meet the changing statutory requirements and technical possibilities. According to official statements, the Japanese Green-Building Council and IBEC are not making any attempts at present to internationalise the CASBEE assessment system despite the system being used by Japanese planners for projects abroad.

Level 1	CO_2 emissions are 125 % or more than the reference value.
Level 2	
Level 3	CO_2 emissions correspond with the reference value.
Level 4	
Level 5	CO_2 emissions are 75 % or less than the reference value.

2.54

2.55

2.53 CASBEE for New Construction: structural configuration of the category Q (Building Environmental Quality and Performance) and the category L (Building Environmental Loadings) presented by using an office building as an example
2.54 Assessment system for the criterion LR 3-1 "Consideration of Global Warming" based on a life cycle assessment of the building's CO_2 emissions
2.55 Aerial view, Breezè Tower, Osaka (J)

Breezè Tower in Osaka (J) 2008
Design architect: Ingenhoven Architects, Düsseldorf
Master planner: Mitsubishi Jisho Sekkei, Inc., Japan
Client: Sankei Building Cooperation, Osaka, Japan
Auditor: Mitsubishi Jisho Sekkei, Inc., Japan
The certification result of the building is S, "outstanding" (BEE = 3.17). A double glass facade with exterior sun protection is used to naturally ventilate the interior. Planted exterior walls reduce the urban heat island effect.

MINERGIE

System origin

The development of the Swiss label for energy-efficient buildings took place in the 1990s parallel to similar activities in other countries, such as the establishment of LEED in the USA and BREEAM in the UK. As with LEED and BREEAM, MINERGIE is a registered brand, which alongside the environmental factor, energy, considers the user requirements of comfort, value conservation and economic and operational efficiency (Fig. 2.56).

System origin

One of the most important sustainability targets in Switzerland is the reduction of the energy consumption of buildings. National energy programmes (SwissEnergy) [55] or initiatives, such as the 2000-Watt Society [56], which are demanding a considerable contribution from the building sector to reduce the consumption of fossil fuels, support these targets. These attempts and efforts in the Swiss building sector have been supported by MINERGIE since 1998 [58]. MINERGIE is a label for new and refurbished buildings. The aim is to achieve a high-level of comfort for the occupants living and working in the building while, at the same time, having efficient use of energy using renewable energy sources. The requirements of MINERGIE are based on existing Swiss standards and guidelines [59]. Following private initiatives and pilot projects, the Swiss Cantons Zurich and Bern took over the label in 1998 and, as a result, it gained official status. Since then, all rights have been transferred to the MINERGIE association, also founded in 1998, which is now responsible for the certification process and marketing of the brand. Due to the large network of members, professional partners and sponsors as well as support from the government and the economic sector, the brand has become established as a sought-after standard for energy-efficient building.

Organisation

MINERGIE is structured as an association (non-profit) and is sponsored jointly by the government, the cantons and the industry.

The association currently has 360 members. The MINERGIE network consists of the following organisational institutions:
- MINERGIE head office
- Building Agency (Agentur Bau)
- MINERGIE agencies in Romandie and Italian Switzerland
- MINERGIE certification bodies and the cantonal energy offices
- MINERGIE professional partners

The MINERGIE head office and the Building Agency [60] are responsible for the operational management. The head office is in charge of marketing, communication and trademark protection. Further responsibilities include the organisation of events, all work relating to memberships, sponsorships and finances. The MINERGIE Building Agency, on the other hand, provides technical input, in particular, concerning the development of MINERGIE standards and guidelines. Other priorities are the vocational training and further training of professional partners at universities and in planning offices as well as quality assurance. The MINERGIE Building Agency, founded in 1999, has since established branch offices in Romandie and Tessin, which are responsible for incorporating characteristics specific to the different regions of Switzerland. The cantonal MINERGIE certification bodies, simply called energy offices, are centres for all matters concerning the certification of buildings with the MINERGIE label. They are responsible for all technical questions concerning the certification, such as the certification process itself, grants, subsidies, etc. The investors, clients and planners are supported in the design and implementation of MINERGIE certifications by so-called MINERGIE Professional Partners (Fachpartner). They must have practical experience drawn from participation in at least two MINERGIE projects or must provide evidence of having taken part in a MINERGIE (Fachpartner) training programme. The status "MINERGIE Fachpartner" has to be renewed every three years by either taking part in a training programme or by providing MINERGIE references [61].

System structure

MINERGIE is a voluntary building standard. Approximately 13% of all new builds and 2% of all refurbishments are currently being certified according to MINERGIE in Switzerland. The majority of these are residential buildings. The basic MINERGIE standard is in parts comparable with the German low-energy standard.

The four standards available today, MINERGIE, MINERGIE-P, MINERGIE-ECO and MINERGIE-P-ECO, differentiate, on the one hand, between new builds and refurbishments and, on the other hand, between building categories. Apart from the mentioned standards for buildings, MINERGIE also offers certifications for building services installations and structural components, such as windows, doors or wall and roof elements. The application of these MINERGIE modules is intended to simplify the MINERGIE certification of a whole building. However, the use of the modules is by no means compulsory. All of the twelve building categories covered by the Swiss standard SIA 380/1 "Thermal Energy in Buildings" (2009) qualify for the basic MINERGIE certification. Apart from indoor swimming pools, all of the mentioned building types can be assessed according to the MINERGIE-P standard. The ECO standard is currently available for new office buildings, schools, single and multi-family homes (Fig. 2.57). The basic MINERGIE standard defines six basic requirements for the building based on the standards SIA 380/1 (2009) and SIA 380/4 "Electrical Energy in Buildings" (Fig. 2.58a) [62]:
- Ensure a sustainable construction; the primary requirements concern the building envelope
- Air exchange by using a comfort ventilation system
- MINERGIE limiting values (weighted energy factors for the final total energy consumption for heating, domestic hot water production and air exchange)
- Information regarding the thermal comfort in summer
- Additional requirements, depending on the building category, for lighting as well as the generation of heat and cold
- Limitation of additional construction costs to a maximum of 10% of the costs for comparable conventional properties

The MINERGIE-P standard was introduced in 2001. It is used to certify buildings that strive for an even lower energy consumption, i.e. heat demand and weighted energy factors, than required by the basic MINERGIE standard. The extra costs, in this case, may not exceed 15% of the costs for a comparable conventional building. The Swiss MINERGIE-P label is comparable to the German Passive House Standard. In

Mehr Lebensqualität, tiefer Energieverbrauch
Meilleure qualité de vie, faible consommation d'énergie

2.56

addition to the basic MINERGIE require-
ments, the following aspects must be ful-
filled (Fig. 2.60, p. 64):
· Specific heat demand
· Use of renewable energies
· Airtight building envelope
· Use of energy-efficient electrical house-
hold appliances

Since 2006, the assessment system MIN-
ERGIE-ECO has been used in Switzerland
for offices, schools, single and multi-family
homes. It follows the criteria for the SIA recommendation 112/1 "Sustainable Building".
An addition for refurbishments is currently
being developed. The building label supplements the basic MINERGIE standard
with qualities concerning health and building ecology [63]. It was developed in a cooperation of the associations eco-bau, a
platform for public clients, cantons, communities, and MINERGIE.
The assessment criteria for MINERGIE-
ECO comprise the MINERGIE assessment
for the evaluation of the operational energy
consumption and a questionnaire to enable environmental and health-oriented aspects of the construction method to be
evaluated. The questionnaire incorporates
the main criteria, building ecology (environmental load, resources and deconstruction)
and health (air quality, lighting and noise)
(Fig. 2.59 and 2.61, p. 64) [64, 65].
In the context of MINERGIE-ECO, the website, www.eco-bau.ch, provides a list of
eco-tools to help select the right materials:
ECO-BKP 2009 pamphlets (Merkblätter
Ökologisch Bauen) [66], the ecological
specification, eco-devis [67] and SIA D
0200 "SNARC: System for an environmental sustainability assessment of architecture projects" [68].
With regard to selection of building materials, an additional module defines the requirements and criteria concerning the
most suitable components for deconstruction and the use of recycled building materials and products.
The health aspects are assessed according to a questionnaire (e.g. concerning indoor air quality measurements) and the following standards: noise (SIA 181 "Noise
protection in buildings"), lighting (SIA 380/4
"Electrical Energy in Buildings") as well as
indoor air quality (SIA 382/1 "Performance
requirements for ventilation and room-con-
ditioning systems", SWKI 2003-5). Furthermore, MINERGIE-ECO buildings must comply with conditions excluding the use of
specific materials, such as the avoidance

Building categories	MINERGIE	MINERGIE-P	MINERGIE-ECO	MINERGIE-P-ECO
Homes I (multi-family dwellings)	■	■	■	■
Homes II (single-family dwellings)	■	■	■	■
Office buildings	■	■	■	■
Schools	■	■	■	■
Retail	■	■		
Restaurants	■	■		
Assembly places	■	■		
Hospitals	■	■		
Industry	■	■		
Storage facilities	■	■		
Sports facilities	■	■		
Indoor swimming pools	■			

2.57

	Category	Energy weighting factor	Primary requirement (heat demand)	Air-handling system	Additional requirements
I	Homes, multi	38 kWh/m² for H, DHW, el. ventilation [1]	$Q_h \leq 90\% \ Q_{h,ll}$ [2]	conditional	no requirements recommendation for household appliances: energy label class A
II	Homes, single	38 kWh/m² for H, DHW, el. ventilation [1]	$Q_h \leq 90\% \ Q_{h,ll}$ [2]	conditional	no requirements recommendation for household appliances: energy label class A
III	Office	40 kWh/m² for H, DHW, el. ventilation [1]	$Q_h \leq 90\% \ Q_{h,ll}$ [2]	conditional	lighting acc. to SIA 380/4
IV	Schools	40 kWh/m² for H, DHW, el. ventilation [1]	$Q_h \leq 90\% \ Q_{h,ll}$ [2]	conditional	lighting acc. to SIA 380/4

[1] Heating, domestic hot water, electric ventilation
[2] $Q_{h,ll}$ = limiting values acc. to SIA 380/1
a

	Category	Energy weighting factor	Primary requirement (heat demand)	specific thermal output (air heating)	Air-handling system	Airtightness (n50 value)	Energy-efficient electrical appliances	Additional requirements
I	Homes, multi	30 kWh/m²	$Q_h \leq 60\% \ Q_{h,ll}$ [1] or $Q_h \leq 15$ kWh/m²	10 W/m²	yes	0.6 h	yes	–
II	Homes, single	30 kWh/m²	$Q_h \leq 60\% \ Q_{h,ll}$ [1] or $Q_h \leq 15$ kWh/m²	10 W/m²	yes	0.6 h	yes	–
III	Office	25 kWh/m²	$Q_h \leq 60\% \ Q_{h,ll}$ [1] or $Q_h \leq 15$ kWh/m²	10 W/m²	yes	0.6 h	yes	lighting acc. to SIA 380/4 ventilation/climate acc. to SIA 380/4
IV	Schools	25 kWh/m²	$Q_h \leq 60\% \ Q_{h,ll}$ [1] or $Q_h \leq 15$ kWh/m²	10 W/m²	yes	0.6 h	yes	lighting acc. to SIA 380/4 ventilation/climate acc. to SIA 380/4

[1] $Q_{h,ll}$ = limiting value acc. to SIA 380/1
b

2.58

2.56 MINERGIE logo
2.57 Building categories MINERGIE, MINERGIE-P,
    MINERGIE-ECO and MINERGIE-P-ECO
2.58 Requirements for new builds
    a MINERGIE
    b MINERGIE-P

MINERGIE-ECO			
MINERGIE		**ECO**	
higher quality of living	Comfort • high level of thermal comfort due to insulated and airtight building envelope • high level of comfort due to summer heat protection • systematic air exchange, preferably with comfort ventilation system, in new builds and residential refurbishments	Health • optimised daylight conditions • low noise immission • low pollutant load in room air caused by emissions from building materials • low immission due to ionizing radiation (radon)	Light
			Noise
			Air quality
lower environmental load	Energy efficiency For a defined use, the • total energy consumption must be at least 26 % and the • consumption of fossil fuels at least 50 % below the average standard	Building ecology • good availability of raw materials and a large proportion of recycled materials • building materials with a low environmental load in the production and processing • simple deconstruction with building materials that can be reused or removed in an environmentally-friendly way	Raw materials
			Production
			Deconstruction

2.59

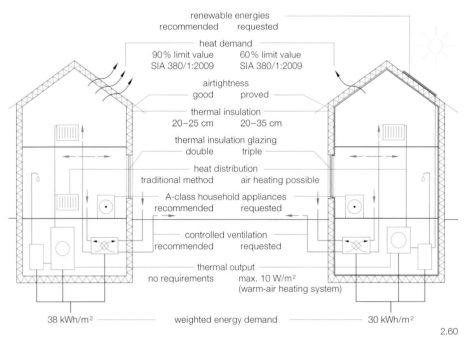

MINERGIE			MINERGIE-P

renewable energies
recommended / requested
heat demand
90 % limit value / 60 % limit value
SIA 380/1:2009 / SIA 380/1:2009
airtightness
good / proved
thermal insulation
20–25 cm / 20–35 cm
thermal insulation glazing
double / triple
heat distribution
traditional method / air heating possible
A-class household appliances
recommended / requested
controlled ventilation
recommended / requested
thermal output
no requirements / max. 10 W/m² (warm-air heating system)
38 kWh/m² — weighted energy demand — 30 kWh/m²

2.60

Criteria		Design tools as a basis for the questionnaire	Overall result of the MINERGIE-ECO certificate
Health	Light	SIA 380/4 Electrical energy in buildings (daylight)	Health
	Noise	SIA 181 Noise protection in buildings	
	Air quality	Indoor air quality, SIA 382/1, SWKI 2003-5	
	Extras	e.g. indoor air quality monitoring	
Building ecology	Raw materials	BKP pamphlets, eco-devis, recycled building materials module, SIA D 0200 SNARC	Building ecology
	Production		
	Deconstruction	Suitability for deconstruction module	
	Extras	Competition acc. to SNARC, labels for building products	

2.61

of biocides and wood preservatives in the building interior, as well as achieve minimum levels in relation to set criteria (Fig. 2.62, p. 65).

In 2008, as a further development of MINERGIE-ECO, a systemised approach was introduced. The aim was to simplify and improve the presentation of a building's label and make it applicable to refurbishments as well as new builds. The life cycle assessment allows for a quantitative evaluation of as many criteria as possible. The system combines the monitoring and evaluation of the energy consumption, the environmental load caused by building materials and health aspects in a single software tool. In addition, the assessment system incorporates the Energy Performance of Buildings Directive (EPBD). The basic principles of the earlier evaluation system, operational energy, building ecology and health, have been adopted, however, the method has been revised thoroughly (Fig. 2.63) [69].

Certification process

The certification process and proof procedure for all buildings that are awarded a MINERGIE label are performed according to a predetermined pattern. Apart from the traditional assessment process based on the Swiss standard SIA 380/1, it is possible, in the case of the basic MINERGIE standard, for residential buildings with a treated floor area (TFA) of up to 500 m² to resort to a standard solution. This is a simplified procedure under which one of five standard solutions may be selected. There is an additional EDP-based questionnaire for the evaluation of MINERGIE-ECO projects. For all MINERGIE standards, the path to certification is divided into four steps [70]:

1st step: Application
• MINERGIE and MINERGIE-P: The application, which is based on the planning permission application, is submitted to the cantonal certification body (calculations performed according to the standard SIA 380/1 "Thermal energy in buildings" and MINERGIE or MINERGIE calculations)
• MINERGIE-ECO: The certification of the property according to MINERGIE-ECO must be applied for at the cantonal certification body by using the "ECO planning dossier"

2nd step: Assurance – provisional certification
• MINERGIE, MINERGIE-P and MINERGIE-ECO: Examination of the documents by the certification body with

certification agreed in principle, i.e. issuance of provisional certificate

3rd step: Confirmation – realisation
- MINERGIE: Notification of completion of the building work (with the certificate of completion) and of realisation in compliance with design
- MINERGIE-P: additional implementation and recording of the blower door test
- MINERGIE-ECO: additional submission of the updated ECO dossier on the construction operations prior to the completion of the building

4th step: Definitive certification
- MINERGIE, MINERGIE-P and MINERGIE-ECO: Awarding of the label or examination of the ECO dossier and performance of random tests, either during construction or following completion, to check the quality and performance of the building, approval of label

Market penetration

In the same way as the certification methods LEED, BREEAM and DGNB, MINERGIE standards enjoy wide acceptance in Switzerland due to the way in which they provide high living comfort, a cost-benefit ratio and the complete freedom of design. Up until the end of 2009, 14,686 buildings had been certified according to MINERGIE, 538 according to MINERGIE-P, 60 according to MINERGIE-ECO and 52 according to MINERGIE-P-ECO [71]. MINERGIE standards are also starting to become established outside Switzerland. In December 2006, MINERGIE opened a branch office in France.

Fees

The fees for the issue of a MINERGIE certificate are payable to the certification body. The level of fees depends on the MINERGIE standard, the building category as well as the number of applications (e.g. single or multiple in the case of standard or system houses). The fees depend on the square metres of treated floor area (TFA) in the building and vary between € 600 (SFr 900) and € 10,250 (SFr 15,500) (as of 2010) [72].
Some cantons and Swiss banks subsidise the construction of MINERGIE buildings and offer grants and low-interest loans, such as green mortgages, MINERGIE home loans or environment-related loans. The subsidies are generally dependent on the economic efficiency of the building. For example, support may cover certification fees, the costs for the blower door test or installations to generate renewable energy [73].

Health:
User-related exclusion criteria
- biocides and wood preservatives in the building interior
- certain solvent-containing products
- large areas of timber products emitting formaldehyde
- the use-related criteria are to be fulfilled in the useful area of the building (office, classroom, living room, etc.)

Building ecology:
Definite exclusion criteria
- heavy-metal-containing building materials (lead or large areas of blank copper, titanium zinc or galvanized steel sheet on the building's exterior without a metal filter for accumulating rainwater)
- no use of recycled concrete (if available within a distance of 25 km)
- timber materials from outside Europe without a sustainability certificate
- soundproof glazing with SF_6-gas filling
- spray foam insulation

2.62

Overall result of assessment system

Building materials / methods	Operational energy	Comfort/health
ECO exclusion criteria	MINERGIE assessment topic: operational energy	ECO exclusion criteria
Questionnaire topics: choice of materials, building concept		Questionnaire topics: noise, pollutants, daylight
Life cycle assessment of building materials	Life cycle assessment of operational energy (primary energy factors)	Room module topics: total VOC, formaldehyde

2.63

2.64

2.59 Structure of the MINERGIE-ECO standard
2.60 Differences between the requirements for the MINERGIE and MINERGIE-P standard
2.61 MINERGIE-ECO design tools and criteria
2.62 MINERGIE-ECO exclusion criteria
2.63 Assessment system for the further development of MINERGIE-ECO
2.64 North-west elevation, multi-family dwelling, Liebefeld (CH)

Multi-family dwelling in Liebefeld (CH) 2007
Architects: Halle 58 Architekten, Peter Schürch, Bern
Client: Halle 58 Architekten, Peter Schürch, Bern
Auditor: Gartenmann Engineering, Bern
The building meets the MINERGIE-P-ECO standard. The pellet heating was complemented by an approx. 20 m^2-large solar thermal array consisting of roof-mounted flat-plate collectors. In combination with the storage tank in the cellar, it covers approx. 75 % of the energy demand to heat domestic hot water.

HQE (Haute Qualité Environnementale)

In recent years, in the French property market, numerous tools have been developed to evaluate the quality of sustainable buildings. The most frequently applied certification scheme in France is the HQE standard. The abbreviation HQE stands for "Haute Qualité Environnementale" which corresponds to the translation "high environmental quality". Due to the fact that a large proportion of the system is only available in French, the contents of the HQE label are not very well known outside France. It was not until a few years ago that various documents were made available in English.

System origin

The origins of the HQE sustainability label reach back approximately 15 years (Fig. 2.66). The trademark "HQE" was registered at INPI (French Patent Office) in December 1995, the HQE Association was founded in the following year and recognised as a not-for-profit organisation in 2004 [74]. Membership of the HQE Association is limited to public institutions and building associations; companies and individuals are excluded. The aim is to represent the full range of participants in the building industry (clients, contractors, manufacturers, planners, etc.) in order to improve and develop the ecological quality of buildings [75].

The French construction products association AIMCC (Association des Industriels de Matériaux, Produits, Composants et Equipements pour la Construction) [76, 77] is the owner of the protected trademarks "HQE" and "Démarche HQE", whereby HQE stands for the sustainability standard itself and Démarche HQE for the associated certification process. According to a license agreement concluded with the association AIMCC in 1999, the HQE Association has free and exclusive right of use to the HQE label [78].

The HQE Association deals only with the high level conceptual aspects concerning the quality standard. The institution AFNOR Certification has been commissioned to administer the actual certifications [79]. Amongst other things, AFNOR is responsible for marketing the label "NF" (Norme Française, the French national standard), which certifies that products and services conform with French standards [80]. As a result of an agreement concluded in 2004 between the HQE Association and AFNOR Certification, the HQE standards and criteria have become an integral part of French standards and the abbreviation NF has been integrated in the logo of the French label (Fig. 2.65) [81].

The institution AFNOR Certification has put the companies Certivéa, Céquami and Cerqual in charge of compiling the HQE manuals and profiles as well as certifying buildings and issuing the respective labels (Fig. 2.71, p. 69). These companies are subsidiaries of the not-for-profit association Qualitel and the state-owned French Building Research Center (CSTB, Centre Scientifique et Technique du Bâtiment) [82, 83, 84].

System structure

All HQE certification schemes are based on two components, which form the main pillars of the process and the target-oriented approach of the French system (Fig. 2.67):
- SMO (Système de Management de l'Opération): Operations Management System
- QEB (Qualité Environnementale du Bâtiment): Environmental Building Quality

The Operations Management System (SMO) incorporates all organisational and process-oriented construction procedures, which allows the client to compile a requirement profile for the Environmental Building Quality (QEB). QEB is based on 14 assessment targets, which in turn are broken down into 42 sub-targets and 159 indicators (Fig. 2.72, p. 69). The 14 HQE targets are arranged according to the following four categories:
- Eco construction (integration of the building into its local surroundings, consideration of building methods and materials in the design phase, etc.)
- Eco management (energy and water consumption, waste management and maintenance of the building)
- Comfort (humidity, acoustics, light and occupant well-being)
- Health (sanitary installations, air and water quality)

The approach is similar for all building types. The contents of the categories, however, are adjusted to meet the needs of the relevant building and life-cycle phase and, if required, supplemented by additional evaluation aspects. The contents and procedures for the certification are described in manuals and various guidelines for the respective types of building to be evaluated:
- General NF standards
- HQE certification regulations in the NF standards
- Manual for the Operations Management System
- Manual for the Environmental Building Quality: description of the 14 assessment targets and indicators
- Handbook for the manual, Environmental Building Quality
- Further guidelines

Certification levels

There are numerous environmental assessment methods evaluating the quality of buildings according to fulfilment grades or with awards such as gold, silver and bronze. The French HQE label follows a different approach: instead of assessing the building according to fulfilment levels, the HQE standard certifies compliance with predetermined targets. In contrast to other assessment methods, which provide weighting factors for the individual criteria or categories, the HQE method treats each objective equally and merely divides them into three levels. For each of the 14 assessment targets, on which the Environmental Building Quality (QEB) is based, it is possible to achieve either a very good, good or basic rating [85]:
- Basic rating: conforms to current regulations and technology standards
- Good rating: superior building construction
- Very good rating: the currently best possible building construction and technology

Compliance with the building-specific minimum requirements relating to the Environmental Building Quality (QEB) and the guidelines of the Operations Management System (SMO) is part of the assessment process. The minimum standards set for the objectives vary depending on the building type, however, it is mandatory to achieve at least the basic rating level in all categories. Furthermore, all

BÂTIMENTS TERTIAIRES

2.65

building types and certification variants must conform to a so-called minimum environmental profile. This requires that a rating of very good must be achieved in at least three of the 14 assessment targets, at least four targets must have a good rating and the remaining seven can be at basic level (Fig. 2.68) [86].

Despite the lack of an award and an overall rating, it is possible to compare HQE-certified buildings: when performing the assessment of the 14 Environmental Building Quality targets, one of the three rating levels is assigned to each criterion of the HQE building certificate. Various institutions have developed special presentation methods for non-residential buildings (with the exception of industrial buildings; French: bâtiments tertiaires) to facilitate a better comparison of the overall HQE certification results. The certification body Certivéa [87, 88], for example, provides overviews of all certified buildings in this building sector and assigns a special assessment result to the environmental profile of each building. The graphical results are based on a colour code with dark blue for a very good rating, light blue for a good rating and grey for a basic rating.

DTZ, a company operating on the property market, has developed its own assessment tool for the comparison of non-residential buildings [89]. In this case, each of the 14 assessment targets is assigned a grade ranging from one to three (Fig. 2.69):
- Grade 1 for results with a basic rating level
- Grade 2 for results with a good rating level
- Grade 3 for results with a very good rating level

A separate standard has also been developed for the assessment of logistics centres. In addition to the HQE assessment method, these can also be rated in accordance with the AFILOG system. AFILOG was founded in 2001 to represent the interests of the logistics industry in the building sector [90]. The method is based on HQE's system to evaluate the Environmental Building Quality (QEB). In addition to the 14 QEB assessment targets, two further thematic aspects are of relevance:
- Aspect A: labour conditions
- Aspect B: the building's adaptation to the processes relevant to logistics (opti-

Year	Event
1995	Registration of HQE trademark (owner of the trademark: AIMCC)
1996	Foundation of the HQE Association
1999	License agreement between AIMCC and the HQE Association
2002	Introduction of the HQE certification system through the HQE Association
2003	Protection of trademark "Démarche HQE"
2004	Agreement between AFNOR Certification and HQE Association to jointly use the trademarks "NF Ouvrage" and "Démarche HQE"
2004	Recogntion of the HQE Association as a not-for-profit organisation
2005	Launch of the HQE certification scheme for non-residential buildings (new build and refurbishments)
2007	Launch of the HQE certification scheme for single-family homes (new builds)
2007	Launch of the HQE certification scheme for multi-family dwellings, dwelling units and residential estates (new builds and refurbishments)
2008	Foundation of the SB Alliance through BRE and CSTB
2009	Agreement signed by BRE and CSTB to align the labels BREEAM and HQE
2009	Launch of HQE certification scheme for in-use phase of existing non-residential buildings
2010	Launch of HQE certification scheme for single-family homes (refurbishment)
2010	Launch of HQE certification scheme for urban districts

2.66

2.67

2.68

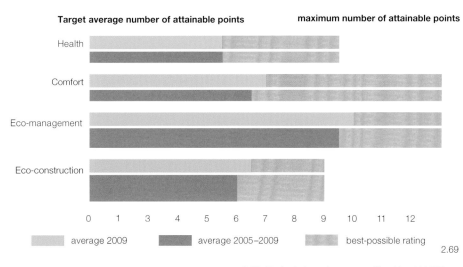

2.69

2.65 HQE logo
2.66 Development of HQE label
2.67 Pillars of the HQE certification system for new builds and refurbishments of non-residential buildings (NF Bâtiment Tertiaire – Démarche HQE)

2.68 Ecological requirement profile of the 14 HQE targets presented by using a non-residential building as an example
2.69 The DTZ assessment scale indicates the maximum number of attainable points and the average number of points achieved by all non-residential buildings in the respective years

Sector	Certification office	Status	Certification system/label	Type of building	Validity period
Non-residential buildings (excl. industrial buildings)	Certivéa	available system	NF Bâtiments Tertiaires – Démarche HQE "Bureau/Enseignement"	new office buildings and educational institutions	unlimited
		available system	NF Bâtiments Tertiaires – Démarche HQE "Etablissements de santé"	new buildings for health care	unlimited
		available system	NF Bâtiments Tertiaires – Démarche HQE "Commerce"	new buildings for trade and retail	unlimited
		available system	NF Bâtiments Tertiaires – Démarche HQE "Hôtellerie"	new hotels	unlimited
		available system	NF Bâtiments Tertiaires – Démarche HQE "Plateforme logistique"	new logistics buildings	unlimited
		pilot phase (test version)	NF Bâtiments Tertiaires – Démarche HQE "Salle multisports"	new sports facilities	unlimited
		in progress	NF Bâtiments Tertiaires – Démarche HQE "Bâtiments en Rénovation – Bâtiments Tertiaires"	refurbishments of non-residential buildings	unlimited
		available system	NF Bâtiments Tertiaires en Exploitation – Démarche HQE	non-residential buildings in use	5 years, renewable
Single-family homes	Céquami	available system	NF Maison Individuelle – Démarche HQE	new single-family homes	building: unlimited contractor: 3 years, renewable
		available system	NF Maison Rénovée – Démarche HQE	refurbishment of single-family homes	building: unlimited contractor: 3 years, renewable
Multi-family dwellings	Cerqual	available system	NF Logement – Démarche HQE	new multi-family dwellings,/apartments	building: unlimited contractor: 3 years, renewable
Residential estates	–	available system	HQE Aménagement	residential estates	

2.70

misation of the surfaces, functional arrangement, concept of the loading zone, etc.)

The AFILOG rating is performed in a similar way to HQE and can, in addition, be awarded a maximum of three stars.

System variants

The HQE certification system can be applied to the public, as well as the private, building sector and can be divided into three system variants (Fig. 2.70):
- Certifications for non-residential buildings (since 2005)
- Certifications for single-family houses (since 2007)
- Certifications for multi-family houses and residential estates (since 2007)

The company Certivéa is responsible for the certification and the drafting of HQE rules for non-residential buildings. The standard can be applied to new builds, refurbishments and existing properties during the operation phase. The HQE assessment process is currently being used for:
- Offices and educational institutions
- Buildings for health care
- Trade and retail
- Hotels
- Logistics buildings
- Sports facilities

2.70 List of current and future HQE system variants
2.71 HQE's organisational structure
2.72 Overview of HQE categories and targets

Newly erected non-residential buildings are assessed according to the HQE standard procedure "NF Bâtiment Tertiaire – Démarche HQE". Since 2009, existing building stock can be evaluated during its occupancy period with the certificate "NF Bâtiments Tertiaires en Exploitation – Démarche HQE" [91]. Alongside the two standard pillars "Operations Management System – in use" (Système de Management de l'Exploitation, SMEx) and "Environmental Building Quality – in use" (Qualité Environnementale des Bâtiments en Exploitation, QEBE), which have been especially adapted to the building during operation, a third aspect is added in this variant to assess the environmental quality of occupant behaviour (Qualité Environnementale des Bâtiments en Exploitation, QEBE). In this case, the Operations Management System for the in use phase (SMEx) is based on a variant of the international environmental management standard ISO 14001, which has been adapted to meet the demands of the HQE system. The Environmental Building Quality for the in use phase (QEBE) is based on the already mentioned 14 assessment targets of the HQE system. Alongside the environmental aspects (QEIB), for example acoustic comfort, thermal comfort, etc., it also assesses operational criteria such as the recording of consumption data, building maintenance as well as everyday building management and use (QEE) (Fig. 2.73, p. 70).
New builds and refurbishments of single-

family homes are certified by the certification body, Céquami. Since 2007, new builds have been receiving the label "NF Maison Individuelle – Démarche HQE", refurbished building stock the label "NF Maison Rénovée – Démarche HQE". The organisation Cerqual is responsible for the HQE certification of multi-family dwellings and residential estates. They have been awarding the label "NF Logement – Démarche HQE" since 2007. The assessment of residential buildings may only be performed by registered construction companies, which have received the approval "NF Maison Individuelle – Démarche HQE" or "NF Logement – Démarche HQE" from the respective certification bodies, Céquami and Cerqual. The approved construction company, in cooperation with the client, develops an Operations Management System (SMO) adapted to meet the needs of the specific building project and, in line with the certification procedure for non-residential buildings, determines the levels of the 14 assessment targets concerning the Environmental Building Quality (QEB).
As an addition to the existing labels for new and existing buildings in the French building sector, the HQE Association introduced a further label at the beginning of 2010. The aim of the new label "HQE Aménagement" is to encourage the ecological and sustainable design of urban developments [92]. The label caters in particular for issues concerning residential estates and urban planning. It is also

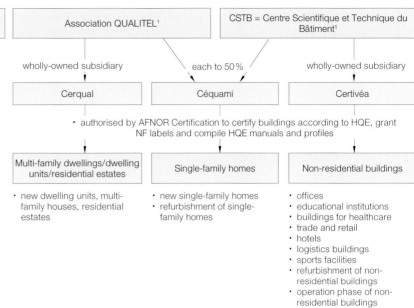

HQE Association	AFNOR Certification[1]	Association QUALITEL[1]	CSTB = Centre Scientifique et Technique du Bâtiment[1]
• commissions AFNOR Certification with certification operations	• has commissioned Cerqual, Céquami and Certivéa with the implementation of certifications, granting of labels and the compilation of manuals and profiles		

	wholly-owned subsidiary	each to 50%	wholly-owned subsidiary
	Cerqual	Céquami	Certivéa

• authorised by AFNOR Certification to certify buildings according to HQE, grant NF labels and compile HQE manuals and profiles

Multi-family dwellings/dwelling units/residential estates	Single-family homes	Non-residential buildings
• new dwelling units, multi-family houses, residential estates	• new single-family homes • refurbishment of single-family homes	• offices • educational institutions • buildings for healthcare • trade and retail • hotels • logistics buildings • sports facilities • refurbishment of non-residential buildings • operation phase of non-residential buildings

[1] Members of the HQE Association's expert group

2.71

Aspects	Criteria (targets)	Objectives (sub-targets)
Eco-construction (Eco-construction)	1 Harmony of building and environment	1.1 Sustainable embedding of site in urban development 1.2 Quality of outside space for building occupants 1.3 Impact of the building on the neighbourhood
	2 Integrated choice of construction process and products	2.1 Constructive measures to increase durability and flexibility of the building 2.2 Constructive measures to ease upkeep and maintenance of building 2.3 Reduction of environmental impact through target-oriented selection of building materials and products 2.4 Reduction of impact on health through selection of building materials and products
	3 Low-nuisance construction site	3.1 Optimisation of management concerning construction site waste 3.2 Reduction of nuisance caused by construction site 3.3 Reduction of environmental impact and consumption of natural resources on site
Eco-management (Eco-gestion)	4 Energy management	4.1 Reduction of energy consumption through the energy concept and architectural design 4.2 Reduction of primary energy demand 4.3 Reduction of pollutant emission into atmosphere
	5 Water management	5.1 Reduction of water consumption 5.2 Optimisation of rainwater management 5.3 Waste water management
	6 Process waste management	6.1 Optimisation of waste recycling during the building's operation phase 6.2 Quality of the waste management system during the building's operation phase
	7 Maintenance	7.1 Maintenance of heating and cooling systems 7.2 Maintenance of ventilation systems 7.3 Maintenance of lighting systems 7.4 Maintenance of water supply
Comfort (Confort)	8 Hygrothermal comfort	8.1 Architectural measures for the optimisation of hygrothermal comfort in summer and winter 8.2 Provision of hygrothermal comfort in winter 8.3 Provision of hygrothermal comfort in summer in areas without cooling (separately for office and educational buildings) 8.4 Provision of hygrothermal comfort in summer in areas with cooling
	9 Acoustic comfort	9.1 Optimisation of acoustic installations to minimise acoustic disturbance 9.2 Improvement of acoustic quality dependent on the area's utilisation • rooms for education • single, group, open-plan offices • unfinished office space • other rooms in office buildings (conference and seminar rooms, relaxation room, corridors, canteen)
	10 Visual comfort	10.1 Optimisation of natural lighting 10.2 Well-being through artificial lighting
	11 Olfactory comfort	11.1 Provision of efficient ventilation 11.2 Minimisation of olfactory discomfort and improvement of indoor air quality
Health (Santé)	12 Cleanliness of the internal environment	12.1 Minimisation of electromagnetic radiation 12.2 Provision of specific hygienic conditions
	13 Air quality	13.1 Provision of efficient ventilation 13.2 Inside air pollution control 13.3 Outside air pollution control
	14 Water quality	14.1 Quality and durability of the water supply network 14.2 Concept and protection of water supply network 14.3 Monitoring of water supply network temperature 14.4 Inspection of water treatment 14.5 Monitoring of water extraction and reuse

2.72

based on the two standard pillars of the HQE system: Operations Management System and Environmental Building Quality. The "HQE Aménagement" label includes 17 evaluation categories concerning the environmental quality, which are divided into the three following groups [93]:
- Harmony between estate and environment
- Protection of natural resources and promotion of environmental and health-based qualities in the regional and urban development
- Encouragement of social neighbourhood structures and economic growth

Certification process
The certification process of HQE standards differs fundamentally from all other assessment systems. There are also significant differences between the applied assessment variants. In the HQE certification process, a difference is made between the assessment of new builds and refurbishments of non-residential buildings, the certification of residential buildings and the evaluation of existing buildings in use (non-residential buildings).

Non-residential buildings, that are certified with the HQE system, must pass through a three-step assessment programme in order to receive the label "NF Bâtiment Tertiaire – Démarche HQE" from the Certivéa certification body. It is the client and planning team's task to implement the Operations Management System and construct the building according to the HQE environmental targets. An auditor from the Certivéa certification body is then responsible for inspecting the documents and the execution of the works. The auditor compiles an audit report for each of the three project stages (shown below), and the building receives a certificate corresponding to the respective certification phase [94]:

- Application (programme)
- Design (conception)
- Execution (réalisation)

In the case of residential buildings, it is not the building which is actually certified with the HQE label, but the property developer or the building contractor. When implementing the HQE targets in a new build or a refurbishment of a single-family home, the building contractor is responsible for carrying out the HQE certification. The company must have received the license "NF Maison Individuelle – Démarche HQE" from the Céquami certification body. To apply the HQE label to multi-family homes, the organisation Cerqual awards the license "NF Logement – Démarche HQE" to the property developer. To obtain this license, the authorised building contractors and property developers must provide proof of their experience in developing ecological residential buildings. In order to ensure consistent quality standards, the organisations Céquami and Cerqual perform regular inspections of the compliance with HQE guidelines in the planned residential buildings as well as at the approved building contractors. The licenses of the property developers and building contractors must be renewed every three years.

The holder of the HQE certificate for the in use phase of an existing property can either be the building owner, operator or occupant of the building. This person is responsible for ensuring compliance with the requirements of the label. The certification is performed by Certivéa auditors. After assessing the audit report, the applicant is awarded the certificate "NF Bâtiments Tertiaires en Exploitation – Démarche HQE". In contrast to the HQE label for new builds and refurbishments, this award is only valid for five years and

must be renewed thereafter. During the five-year period, the certification body performs annual follow-up audits to check whether the HQE guidelines are being observed.

Fees
Reflecting the different certification procedures of the HQE variants, the certification costs can differ considerably. In the case of non-residential buildings, the fixed costs are made up of a fee for the inspection of the admission requirements (€623 plus VAT) and a fee for the registration of the project (€1,245 plus VAT). The additional certification fees charged by the certification offices are dependent on the building type and the usable floor area. The overall auditing tariffs for new office buildings currently range between €9,618 and €42,245 (Fig. 2.75). The costs for the certification of public service buildings in use follow the fee structure for the assessment of new builds and depend on the building type and the net floor area. There are additional fees each year in respect of the annual follow-up audits.

The certification fees for single-family homes and other residential buildings vary according to the building contractor or the property developer and are dependent on their respective annual volume of work. The license fees are made up of charges for the first application, the license renewal and the continuous monitoring of license holders. In addition, there are flat rates for each concluded HQE construction contract (single-family home or completed apartment built according to HQE standards). For a property developer with an annual construction output of, for example, approximately 200 apartments, the certification body Cerqual states an admission fee of approximately €4,600 plus tax. This fee includes the audits. In addition, costs of €162.50 plus tax are charged per certified HQE dwelling unit [95].

Market penetration
The first HQE certifications for new office buildings were performed in 2005. More than 400 certificates have since been awarded to non-residential buildings (Fig. 2.74) [96]. Approximately 50% of all non-residential buildings in Greater Paris (Île-de-France) completed in 2009 have been assessed according to HQE. Outside France, only four office buildings have received the French label: two of these projects are located in Luxembourg

2.73

and one each in Belgium and Algeria [98]. Since the introduction of the HQE label for buildings in use in 2010, eight buildings have been certified [99]. At present, 86 building contractors in France are licensed according to Céquami and therefore entitled to erect new single-family homes according to HQE standards [100]. Since 2007, approximately 1,000 single-family homes have been awarded the HQE label [101].

The label "NF Maison Rénovée – Démarche HQE" for refurbishments of residential buildings was not introduced on the market until 2010. So far only two building contractors have obtained the license for this HQE label [102, 103].

In 2007, the system variant "NF Logement – Démarche HQE" was introduced to assess multi-family dwellings and residential estates. 15 property developers are currently licensed to construct multi-family homes and residential estates according to this HQE standard [104]. According to the Cerqual certification body, 39 residential building projects have been constructed according to the HQE standard and 2,212 dwelling units have been certified with the HQE label [105].

Outlook

In order to ensure the future construction and operation of ecological and sustainable non-residential buildings in France and to avoid certifications being performed with other labels, the British certification office BRE and the French institution CSTB signed a cooperation agreement in June 2009. The aim is to align the two assessment methods, BREEAM and HQE, and to adapt the British certification system to meet French demands. The harmonisation of the two certificates started in 2010 and is to take place in three phases:

• Phase 1 (six months): adaptation of BREEAM to correspond with the French initial situation through CSTB (Certivéa)
• Phase 2 (36 months): determination of Certivéa as the French certification body for BREEAM France and investigation regarding the possible use of the French BREEAM certificate in place of the French equivalent "NF Bâtiments Tertiaires – Démarche HQE"
• Phase 3: final consolidation of BREEAM France and HQE to develop a uniform French third-generation assessment method based on the international standards and guidelines for certification systems

		Current certification phases		
	Total	Application (Programme)	Design (Conception)	Execution (Réalisation)
Offices and educational institutions	376	157	147	72
Buildings for health care	1	0	1	0
Trade and retail	5	3	2	0
Hotels	5	1	4	0
Logistics buildings	10	2	3	5
Sports facilities	0	0	0	0
Total	**397**	**163**	**157**	**77**

2.74

Certification costs for the audit (of an office building, as of 2010)

Net floor area in m²	Total amount of audit plus taxes	
< 1,500 m²	€ 9,618	
1,500 m² < area < 45,000 m²	fixed costs	€ 8,494
	variable costs	€ 0.75 / m² net floor area
> 45,000 m²	€ 42,245	

Explanation:
• For a building with a net floor area of 1,000 m², the certification costs are paid as a lump sum of € 9,618.
• For a building with a net floor area of 40,000 m², the certification costs are € 8,494 + 40 000 m² × € 0.75 / m² = € 38,494.
• For a building with a net floor area of more than 45,000 m², the certification costs are paid as a lump sum of € 42,245.

2.75

2.76

2.73 Pillars of the HQE certification system for the in-use phase of non-residential buildings
2.74 Number of HQE-certified buildings (as of April 2010)
2.75 Costs for certification presented by using an office building as an example
2.76 Street view, office building "270", Paris/Aubervilliers (F)

Office building "270" in Paris/Aubervilliers (F) 2005
Architect: Brenac & Gonzales, Paris
Client: ICADE Direction de l'International, Paris
Auditor: Certivéa certification office
The building "270", which was designed in close cooperation with CSTB, was one of the first to receive a HQE label. It has a net floor area of 9200 m².

EU GreenBuilding Programme

The European Commission has developed the EU GreenBuilding Programme to encourage owners and users of public and private non-residential buildings to increase energy efficiency in their properties and use renewable energies. In contrast to other rating systems, this programme tends to concentrate on the promotion and assessment of energy efficiency during building operation and demands a significant reduction of energy consumption and CO_2 emissions. Additional environmental and sociocultural sustainability issues are not considered. In contrast to other sustainability certificates, such as BREEAM, LEED or DGNB, the certificate is not awarded to the building. On the contrary, the company or the client investing in the energy efficiency or increasing the use of renewable energies is awarded the status "GreenBuilding Partner".

System origin

A key component of the European Union's policy on energy and climate protection is increased efficiency in energy consumption and promotion of the use of renewable energies. The European Commission Directorate General Energy and Transport is supporting this goal through a series of measures within the programme "Intelligent Energy – Europe". The GreenBuilding Programme is one of these measures. It was introduced early in 2005 by the European Commission [106] as a voluntary programme.

Organisation

The European Commission has set up national agencies for the GreenBuilding Programme in 13 of the 27 EU Member States. Up until May 2010, the responsible agencies in Germany were the German Energy Agency (Deutsche Energie-Agentur GmbH, dena) [107] and the Berlin Energy Agency (Berliner Energieagentur, BEA) [108]. In Germany, the use of the GreenBuilding Programme is promoted by the Federal Ministry of Transport, Building and Urban Development.

Market penetration

Currently there are 180 GreenBuilding Partners in Europe with a total of 300 buildings. Among these, 65 partners are in Germany (as of March 2010) some of which have received the GreenBuilding Partner status for more than one building.

Certification process

All organisations that reduce the energy consumption in their buildings, invest in energy efficiency and increase the use of renewable energies can achieve the GreenBuilding Partner status if the following programme objectives are met:

- New builds must undercut the statutory requirements concerning the consumption of primary energies by at least 25 %
- Refurbishments must undercut the former consumption of primary energies by at least 25 %

The process necessary for the assessment incorporates four stages, which differ in scope and content according to the type of building (Fig. 2.80). The procedure applied for refurbishment and modernisation of existing building stock differs from that for new builds. However, the process generally includes an analysis of the existing or planned building in terms of energy and the drafting of an energy management plan for the future operation of the building.

If the planned measures comply with the programme's requirements, the GreenBuilding Partner status is awarded on submission and approval of the documents. The GreenBuilding Partner status is granted prior to executing the planned measures on condition that the financing of the project has been approved. Subsequently, the applicant instigates the building work in accordance with the approved action plan, applies the energy management plan to the building operations and reports on the implementation following completion. The national agencies and/or the EU Commission check whether the agreed action plan complies with the information included in the submitted final report. If this is not the case or if the applicant does not submit a final report, the EU Commission is entitled to revoke the GreenBuilding Partner status. It is generally recommended to involve an external specialist firm as a GreenBuilding consultant to provide support and execute the necessary assessment stages accurately. However, it is by no means compulsory to commission an external specialist.

Fees

The EU Commission and the national agencies responsible for awarding the GreenBuilding Partner status do not charge any fees for the registration or certification. Apart from the actual costs to compile and implement the action plan, no further costs are incurred.

Certification levels

The EU GreenBuilding Programme does not make use of differentiated certification levels. It merely highlights the commendable energy efficiency of the building. Nor does it make a statement concerning the extent of the potential for savings in excess of the programme's minimum requirements.

The GreenBuilding Partner status is granted if a new building's primary energy demand for heating, cooling, ventilation, domestic hot water and lighting undercuts the statutory minimum requirements (in Germany these are defined in the Energy Performance Directive) by at least 25 % at the time of the building application. In the case of refurbishments to existing building stock, the primary energy demand must be 25 % less than the values before work commenced. By comparison, Fig. 2.79 shows the actual improvements that were achieved in 85 buildings surveyed between 2008 and 2010. The vertical lines indicate the overall range of savings; the horizontal bar indicates the area of savings weighted average amongst all buildings surveyed in each category.

System variants

The GreenBuilding Programme is flexible and can be used for most building types and uses in the EU irrespective of the site's climate zone. The EU programme does not offer system variants to cater for different types of building. However, a distinction is made between existing

2.77

Handbook and module description

Guidelines for Energy Audit

Guidelines for Energy Management

Module Financing

Building Envelope

Sustainable Summer Comfort

Heating

Combined Heat and Power

Solar Hot Water and Heating

Air Conditioning

Lighting

Office Equipment

2.78

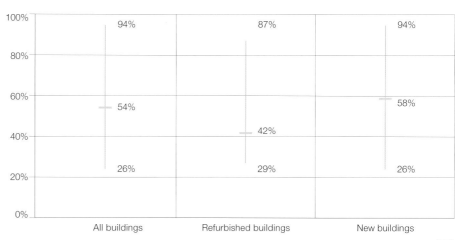

2.79

Refurbishment of existing building stock

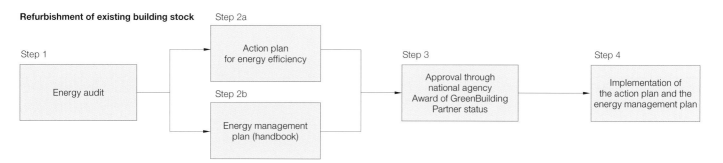

New build

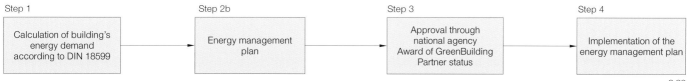

2.80

2.81

2.77 EU GreenBuilding logo

2.78 Guidelines, handbooks and technical modules provided for the EU GreenBuilding programme

2.79 Improvements in energy efficiency achieved in 85 EU GreenBuildings surveyed between 2008 and 2010

2.80 Certification processes

2.81 Visualisiation, AHB Park, Ingolstadt, Germany

AHB Park in Ingolstadt (D) 2010

Architect: Architekturbüro Franz Bauer, Ingolstadt

Client: AHB Immobilien GmbH & Co. KG, Ingolstadt

EU GreenBuilding consultant: Ebert-Consulting Group GmbH & Co. KG, Munich

The new build of this office and retail centre (GFA approx. 9 000 m²) undercut the statutory requirements of energy consumption by approx. 34 % and an energy management plan was compiled to optimise the building operations in terms of energy.

The building is heated and cooled with a regenerative heat source using ground piles. The EU GreenBuilding Partner status was awarded to AHB Immobilien GmbH & Co. KG in 2010.

building stock, new builds and buildings that were refurbished during the five-year period prior to the application. The process steps and requirements depend on the building category. Different assessment criteria are applied for existing building stock and new builds. The programme can be adapted to the differing local and national requirements and framework conditions.

Documentation requirements

To obtain the GreenBuilding Partner status, detailed documentation of the project must be submitted to one of the national agencies or directly to the EU Commission. The appropriate forms must be submitted in English. Enclosures and plans may be compiled in the national language if the documents are submitted to a national agency. The application documents and the project documentation must include the following:
- Application form
- Voluntary declaration of commitment signed by the client concerning the planned energy saving measures
- General building information
- Information concerning the physical parameters of the building envelope
- Information concerning the implemented building services
- Comprehensive description of the planned energy saving measures including a list of the corresponding investment costs
- Energy management plan

Additional documents for refurbishments:
- Energy demand analysis
- Action plan for energy saving measures

Additional documents for new builds:
- Calculation of the building's energy demand according to the country-specific energy performance directive (in Germany according to DIN V 18599)
- Description and explanation of the selected technical facilities which contribute towards meeting the aspired targets.

The application documents can be obtained from the national agencies or directly from the EU Commission. The application documents are submitted together with the required documentation to the national agencies, where a preliminary examination is undertaken. The documents are then forwarded to the European Commission.

System structure

The individual processing steps required for an existing building are described in the following paragraphs (Fig. 2.80, p. 73). In the case of new builds, the energy demand determined according to legally binding calculation methods (in Germany the DIN V 18599) together with a description and an explanation of the implemented technologies replaces the processing steps 1 and 2a, which are necessary in the case of existing buildings.

Step 1: Survey of energy flows
A survey of energy flows, also referred to as energy audit, includes the inspection of all energy consuming systems in order to determine ways of using energy more efficiently. This is the first obligatory step towards participating in a EU GreenBuilding Programme. The aim is to identify the items showing the greatest potential for improved energy efficiency, to set priorities concerning the profitability of planned measures and to address the mutual dependencies of specific measures. The European Commission has published guidelines for the energy audit which is required in the context of the GreenBuilding Programme [109].

Step 2a: Action plan for energy efficiency
Based on the survey, an action plan must be compiled describing the measures to improve energy efficiency. The measures may concern all or only a few of the building's systems that are relevant for the consumption of final energy. The systems selected for the action plan should generally be responsible for a significant proportion of the building's overall energy consumption (electricity, heating) since the aim is to reduce the total demand of primary energy. The action plan describes the precisely specified measures, for example the replacement of systems, a more efficient approach concerning maintenance and inspections or an optimisation of operating methods.

Step 2b: Energy management plan
This plan determines the guidelines for energy management. The EU Commission's handbook includes recommendations concerning the structure and contents of the energy management plan required for the programme [110]. The handbook suggests measures that contribute towards understanding energy efficiency as a management task lasting

throughout the entire life cycle of a building. It includes the building design, the selection of components, the execution of building work and installation of systems, the commissioning of the building, the operation, energy contracting, training and motivation of staff and monitoring of the energy flows after commissioning.

Step 3: Awarding the GreenBuilding Partner status
The application documents and the documentation are submitted to a national agency or directly to the EU Commission. The agencies verify the submitted documents and forward them to the EU Commission for a final review unless the application was submitted directly. The GreenBuilding Partner status is granted on approval of the submitted documents.

Step 4: Implementation of the action and energy management plan
The GreenBuilding Partner compiles a final report describing and proving the execution of the individual measures and the implementation of the energy management plan during the operation of the building.

During the course of the EU GreenBuilding Programme, the European Commission assists interested persons by providing handbooks, technical modules and guidelines (Fig. 2.78, p. 73). The technical modules also contain useful information for the compilation of the action plan required for the second processing step.

GreenBuilding Endorsers

Companies supporting GreenBuilding Partners in implementing the objectives of the GreenBuilding Programme, can become Green Building Endorsers. To become an endorser, the following five-stage process must be completed [111]:
- Compilation of a GreenBuilding Promotion Plan
- At least one organisation must have been supported in obtaining the GreenBuilding Partner status.
- The European Commission approves the GreenBuilding Promotion Plan
- GreenBuilding Promotion Plan is implemented and a report is drawn up for the European Commission
- The GreenBuilding Endorser status is renewed by the Commission after three years on condition that at least one further organisation was supported in becoming a GreenBuilding Partner

References:

[1] BREEAM: About BREEAM Buildings. http://www.breeam.org/page.jsp?id=13

[2] BRE: BREEAM Europe Commercial 2009 Assessor Manual, p. 12

[3] BRE: Our history. http://www.bre.co.uk/page.jsp?id=1712

[4] ibid.

[5] BRE: BRE global. http://www.bre.co.uk/page.jsp?id=383

[6] BRE: Ten things you might not know about the BRE Group. http://www.bre.co.uk/page.jsp?id=1707

[7] BRE: BREEAM Europe Commercial 2009 Assessor Manual, p. 9

[8] Enquiry to BRE

[9] BREEAM: Getting a building BREEAM assessed. http://www.breeam.org/page.jsp?id=31

[10] see ref. 2, p. 19

[11] BRE Global: Fee Sheet FS036

[12] see ref. 2, p. 38

[13] see ref. 2, p. 102

[14] The Building Services Research and Information Association. http://www.bsria.co.uk

[15] BRE: Green Book Live. http://www.greenbooklive.com

[16] BRE: SMARTWaste. http://www.smartwaste.co.uk

[17] BRE: Green Guide. http://www.thegreenguide.org.uk

[18] BREEAM: Global real estate leaders join the International Sustainability Alliance. http://www.breeam.org/newsdetails.jsp?id=608

[19] The Energy Policy Act (109th Congress H.R.776. ENR, abbreviated as EPACT92)

[20] ANSI/ASHRAE Standard 62.1: Ventilation for Acceptable Indoor Air Quality SHAPE

[21] ANSI/ASHRAE/IESNA Standard 90.1: Energy Standard for Buildings Except Low-Rise Residential Buildings.

[22] EN ISO 7730: Ergonomics of the thermal environment – Analytical determination and interpretation of thermal comfort using calculations of the PMV and PPD indices and local thermal comfort criteria.

[23] Green Guide for Healthcare. http://www.gghc.org

[24] see ref. 20

[25] ANSI/ASHRAE/IESNA Standard 55: Thermal Environmental Conditions for Human Occupancy

[26] German Energy Agency: EPBD Directive. EU Directive with stricter demands on the building and the energy certificate. http://www.zukunft-haus.info/de/planer-handwerker/fachwissen-bauen-und-sanieren/gesetze-und-verordnungen/epbd-richtlinie.html

[27] Passive House Institute: Criteria for passive houses with residential use. Certification as "Quality-approved Passive House", http://www.passiv.de

[28] Eßig, Natalie: Die Bemessung der Nachhaltigkeit. In: Deutsche Bauzeitung 05/2009, p. 62–65

[29] e.g. the international ISO TC 59 SC 17: Sustainability in Building Construction and the European CEN/ TC 350: Sustainability of construction works; both currently still in progress

[30] Federal Ministry of Transport, Building and Urban Development (BMVBS): round-table discussion "Runder Tisch Nachhaltiges Bauen". http://www.nachhaltigesbauen.de/nachhaltiges-bauen/runder-tisch-nachhaltiges-bauen.html

[31] Federal Office for Building and Regional Planning (BBR): Guideline for Sustainable Building (Leitfaden Nachhaltiges Bauen). Bonn 2001.

[32] German Sustainable Building Council (DGNB): Certified properties. http://www.dgnb.de/_de/zertifizierung/zertifikat/projekte/index.php?Sortierung=Objektbewertung

[33] German Sustainable Building Council (DGNB): DGNB und BMVBS stellen Form der weiteren Zusammenarbeit vor. http://www.dgnb.de/de/news/presseinfos/detail.php?we_objectID=2894

[34] Hegner, Hans-Dieter: Bewertungssystem als Planungshilfe. In: DBZ, 12/2009

[35] www.dgnb.de

[36] Information portal for sustainable building (Informationsportal Nachhaltiges Bauen). http://www.nachhaltigesbauen.de

[37] ibid.

[38] German Sustainable Building Council (DGNB): DGNB at a glance. http://www.dgnb.de/de/news/presseinfos/detail.php?we_objectID=2388

[39] German Sustainable Building Council (DGNB): Memberships. http://www.dgnb.de/de/mitgliedschaft/mitgliederverzeichnis/index.php

[40] see ref. 32

[41] German Sustainable Building Council (DGNB): Internationalisierung schreitet rasch voran. http://www.dgnb.de/de/news/presseinfos/detail.php?we_objectID=3708

[42] German Sustainable Building Council (DGNB): DGNB network. http://www.dgnb.de/_de/verein/international/netzwerk.php

[43] German Sustainable Building Council (DGNB): Bespoke certificates. http://www.dgnb.de/_de/suche.php?we_objectID=4712&pid=1928

[44] German Sustainable Building Council (DGNB): DGNB certificate – step by step. http://www.dgnb.de/_de/zertifizierung/weg/index.php

[45] German Sustainable Building Council (DGNB): DGNB software. http://www.dgnb.de/_de/zertifizierung/software/index.php

[46] German Sustainable Building Council (DGNB): Certification fees. http://www.dgnb.de/_de/zertifizierung/index.php

[47] König, Holger et al.: Lebenszyklusanalyse in der Gebäudeplanung. Munich 2009, p.102

[48] Gertis, Karl: Was bedeutet Platin? In: Bauphysik, 04/2008, p. 244–255

[49] http://www.nachhaltigesbauen.de/baustoff-und-gebaeudededaten/oekobaudat.html

[50] see ref. 28

[51] Institute for Building Environment and Energy Conservation. http://www.ibec.or.jp

[52] ANSI/ASHRAE Standard 55: Thermal Environmental Conditions for Human Occupancy

[53] POEM-O: Post-Occupancy Evaluation Method for Office

[54] SHASE-S102-2203: Society of Heating, Air-conditioning and Sanitary Engineering of Japan

[55] Swiss Federal Office of Energy (SFOE): Energie-Schweiz für eine intelligente und effiziente Energiezukunft. http://www.bfe.admin.ch/energie/index.html

[56] http://www.2000watt-gesellschaft.org

[57] novatlantis: 2000-Watt Society. http://www.novatlantis.ch/index.php?id=26

[58] MINERGIE: 10 Jahre MINERGIE - Die Zukunft des Bauens 2008. http://www.minergie.ch/tl_files/download/MINERGIE_Info_04.2008.pdf

[59] http://www.minergie.ch/was-ist-minergie-105/articles/das-wichtigste-1025.html

[60] MINERGIE: 10 Jahre MINERGIE – eine Erfolgsgeschichte. http://www.minergie.ch/tl_files/download/Festschrift_10_Jahre_MINERGIE_2008.pdf, p. 27 and 47

[61] ibid., p. 47

[62] ibid., p. 42–44

[63] Schweizer Bau Dokumentation: Das Gebäudelabel MINERGIE und MINERGIE-P. Blauen 2006. http://www.minergie.ch/tl_files/download/Schweizer_Baudoc_Minergie_P.pdf

[64] Swiss Association of Engineers and Architects (SIA): SNARC: System for an environmental sustainability assessment of architecture projects. Zurich 2004. http://www.eco-bau.ch/resources/uploads/SNARCD.pdf

[65] MINERGIE: MINERGIE-ECO, MINERGIE-P-ECO. http://www.minergie.ch/minergie-eco.html

[66] eco-bau: Sustainability in public buildings. http://www.eco-bau.ch/index.cfm?js=1

[67] eco-bau: ECO-BKP guidelines. http://www.eco-bau.ch/index.cfm?Nav=15&ID=15

[68] eco-bau: eco-devis. http://www.eco-bau.ch/index.cfm?Nav=15&ID=16

[69] Swiss Federal Office of Energy (SFOE): MINERGIE-ECO assessment system. Final report. Bern 2008, p. 16

[70] see ref. 60, p. 42–44

[71] http://www.minergie.ch/statistik.html

[72] http://www.minergie.ch/tl_files/download/Gebuehren_ME_ME_P_ME_ECO.pdf

[73] http://www.minergie.ch/finanzhilfen.html

[74] http://www.assohqe.org/association_presentation.php

[75] http://www.assohqe.org/association_liste_adherents.php

[76] http://www.aimcc.org

[77] http://www.assohqe.org/autres_documents_historique_de_la_marque.php

[78] ibid.

[79] http://www.assohqe.org/documents_certifications_hqe.php

[80] http://fr.wikipedia.org/wiki/Norme_fran%C3%A7aise

[81] http://www.assohqe.org/autres_documents_historique_de_la_marque.php

[82] http://www.marque-nf.com/pages.asp?Lang=English&ref=reseau_organismes_mandates

[83] http://www.qualitel.org/qui-sommes-nous/nos-activites

[84] http://www.wissenschaft-frankreich.de/informationen/forschung_in_frankreich/offentlichen_forschungseinrichtungen/cstb/index.htm

[85] http://www.certivea.com/uk/documentations/simplificado.pdf

[86] http://www.certivea.com/uk/documentations.php

[87] http://www.certivea.fr/op_certifiees/HQE.pdf

[88] http://www.certivea.fr/op_certifiees/EXPLOITATION.pdf

[89] http://www.paris-region.com/adminsite/objetspartages/liste_fichiergw.jsp?OBJET=DOCUMENT&CODE=42994995&LANGUE=0&RH=PUBLICATIONS

[90] http://www.afilog.org/about

[91] http://www.certivea.fr/documentations/HQE_EXPLOITATION_A4.pdf

[92] http://www.assohqe.org/docs/DP%20HQE%20Amenagement.pdf

[93] http://www.assohqe.org/docs/depliant-2.pdf

[94] http://www.certivea.fr/documentations/etapes_cles_de_la_certification_NF_BT_HQEV012009.pdf

[95] http://www.cerqual.fr/cerqual/nf/prix-des-prestations/

[96] http://www.certivea.fr/certif_HQE.php

[97] http://www.certivea.fr/documentations/BROC_HQEIAL.pdf, S. 6

[98] http://www.certivea.fr/presse/v1CP_1eres_operations_etrangeres_NF_Batiments_Tertiaires_demarcheHQE_050309_EG.pdf

[99] http://www.certivea.fr/op_certifiees/EXPLOITATION.pdf

[100] http://www.cequami.fr/Qualite-globale-environnementale.html

[101] http://www.cequami.fr/Qualite-globale-environnementale.html

[102] http://www.mamaisonrenoveecertifiee.com/Trouver-un-professionnel.html

[103] http://www.cequami.fr/Qualite-globale-environnementale.html

[104] http://www.cerqual.fr/cerqual/nf/promoteurs-titulaires/

[105] http://www.cerqual.fr/newsletter_maj/lettres/visu.php?id=19&perso=1

[106] European Commission DG Joint Research Centre. http://www.ec.europa.eu

[107] German Energy Agency (Deutsche Energie-Agentur GmbH, dena). http://www.dena.de

[108] Berlin Energy Agency (Berliner Energieagentur GmbH, BEA). http://www.berliner-e-agentur.de

[109] European Commission: GreenBuilding Programme – Energy audit guidelines, version 1. Ispra 2005

[110] European Commission: GreenBuilding Programme – Energy management manual, version 1. Ispra 2004

[111] GreenBuilding Programme's endorser manual. http://www.dena.de/fileadmin/user_upload/Download/Dokumente/Projekte/BAU/GreenBuilding_Unterstuetzer-Leitfaden.pdf

Planning process

Assessment and certification systems are designed to help describe and determine the quality of design objectives. On the one hand, the assessment systems function as tools to evaluate a building's performance in terms of environmental, energy and holistic aspects and, on the other hand, they support planners in making decisions on the design. These range from aids to define the shape and appearance of the building to tools which help select technical building equipment and materials.

Application of these tools has resulted in new process sequences, planning methods and documentation requirements which affect the total life cycle of a building. The challenge now is to integrate these into today's planning process. In recent years, these changes have led to the involvement of new professional groups in the planning and construction process, for example auditors and environment and sustainability consultants.

Integrated planning

Rising levels of complexity as well as increasing specialisation in all areas of planning and construction make it necessary for experts from various technical disciplines to be brought together at the start of a project [1]. The involvement of consultants, construction companies, potential users and the public at an early planning stage is one of the fundamental features of integrated planning (derived from the Latin word "integer" meaning complete, entire). This concept has gained greater acceptance over the last few years. Today the integrated planning approach is a key feature of sustainable building, and its application is considered highly in the assessment for building certification.

An integrated planning approach ensures the following (Fig. 3.3) [2]:
- Implementation of quantitative and qualitative planning objectives
- Integration and realisation of contributions made by different technical consultants
- Incorporation of building related characteristics throughout the total life cycle
- Consideration of the interests of potential users and neighbours

Life cycle-oriented design process

The involvement of competent partners and specialists is necessary from the very beginning of a project in order to deal with aspects such as comfort, energy efficiency, environmentally-friendly technologies and the smooth commissioning and operation of the building. Additional and increasing requirements in relation to building services, safety and security, material efficiency and barrier-free access influence the design. At the same time, it is necessary to provide and adhere to reliable cost plans for the construction and operation of the building. Alongside the design of a property, it is therefore necessary today to plan and control the construction process and to consider the entire life cycle of the project from day one. The overall cost efficiency of a project can only be influenced effectively in the initial design phases, i.e. through decisions affecting costs for the construction, operation and upkeep of the building (Fig. 3.7, p. 80) [3].

The consideration of the life cycle is gaining considerable importance in the assessment and certification of sustainable buildings. However, it is an aspect not yet included in all rating systems. In this context, the DGNB certificate differs significantly: the development of the criteria for the occupancy profile Office and Adminis-

tration (new build) has long been based on an average service life of 50 years. The service life of a property can naturally never be determined in advance and the assessment is therefore based on average values, which vary according to the building type and selected construction materials (Fig. 3.1 and 3.2).

In a life cycle analysis, reference projects are used to determine and calculate the expected effects of ageing and depreciation over the entire service life of the building. As part of this, for example, strategies for renovation and conversion are considered from the very beginning in an attempt to eliminate or cushion the effects of any future problems which may arise. The life cycle of a building is structured according to the following phases:
- Production phase (products and building)
- Utilisation phase (operation and upkeep)
- End-of-life phase (deconstruction)

These main phases are broken down further to include detailed process stages (Fig. 3.4, p. 78) [4].

Certification and life cycle

The early phases of the design process, in particular, have a considerable impact on the appearance, the costs, the total life cycle and the ability of a building to meet future needs [5]. The first service phases of a building, the brief, the preliminary design and the final design, are the most important for the implementation of sustainability objectives in buildings [6]. The greatest potential to optimise the building in terms of sustainability is in these early design phases This applies particularly to the influence that can be exerted on costs, construction, materials and the concept for energy efficiency and building operation. For this reason, procedures have been developed at national and international levels which enable the assessment of sustainability of early design concepts and competition entries. The criteria catalogues provided by established rating systems are suitable for this purpose since they are intended to determine design objectives and, during the project development phase, make a statement regarding the sustainability performance of the planned property (Fig. 3.7, p. 80). The pre-certificate "Interim BREEAM Certificate" provided by the British assessment method BREEAM can, for example, be used to assess the design objectives of a building in the design phase. The implementation of the concept is then rated with the "Final BREEAM Certificate" on completion of the building (see Certification process, p. 31f.). The American method LEED offers the possibility to determine design objectives by means of a scorecard. However, LEED currently only provides pre-certification for the system variant "Core & Shell". The actual certification, as in the case of BREEAM, is performed on commissioning of the building (see Certification process, p. 40). The DGNB certificate allows for design objectives to be defined and assessed during the design phase in the context of a voluntary pre-certification programme. These are then inspected during the main certification process once the building has been commissioned (see Certification process, p. 51). Even though the inspection of the awarded certificates renders importance to a smooth and sustainable operation during the utilisation phase of a building, re-certifications, i.e. the inspection of main certificates during the utilisation phase, are not yet requirements of the individual rating systems. However, it is possible to perform an independent assessment of the operation using system variants from established certification systems. In this context, some rating systems, require re-certification after a period of only 5 years, for example LEED with the variant "LEED for Existing Buildings: Operation & Maintenance" (LEED-EB: O & M) [7].

During the course of the design process, the certifications are therefore arranged according to the following structure (Fig. 3.5, p. 78):

• Pre-assessment:
  A first quick check during the project

Building component/component layer	Life expectancy from – to (years)	Average life expectancy (years)
1 Foundations, concrete	80–150	100
2 Exterior walls/posts		
Concrete, reinforced, exposed	60–80	70
Natural stone, exposed	60–250	80
Brick, clinker, exposed	80–150	90
Concrete, concrete block, brick, sandlime brick, not exposed	100–150	120
Light-weight concrete, not exposed	80–120	100
Grouting, exposed masonry	30–40	35
Steel	60–100	80
Softwood, exposed	40–50	45
Softwood, not exposed; hardwood, exposed	60–80	70
Hardwood, not exposed	80–120	100
3 Interior walls, interior posts		
Concrete, natural stone, brick, clinker, sandlime brick	100–150	120
Light-weight concrete, not exposed	80–120	100
Steel	80–100	90
Softwood	50–80	70
Hardwood	80–150	100
4 Floors, stairs, balconies		
Concrete, exposed	60–80	70
Concrete, not exposed, outside or inside	100–150	100
Vaults and arches made of brick, clinker	80–150	100
Steel inside	80–100	90
Steel outside	50–90	60
Load-bearing structure for timber stairs inside, softwood	50–80	60
Load-bearing structure for timber stairs inside, hardwood	80–150	90
Load-bearing structure for timber stairs outside, softwood	30–50	45
Load-bearing structure for timber stairs outside, hardwood	50–80	70

3.1

Building type	Economic life (years)
Single-family homes Two and three-family homes Terraced houses (dependent on their structural quality; shorter life spans apply to light construction methods)	60–100
Prefabricated houses, solid	60–80
Prefabricated houses, frame or panel systems	60–70
Detached or terraced house in residential development	50–60
Timber houses Simple houses (solid structure)	50–60
Rental housing privately financed council housing	60–80 50–70
Mixed-use buildings with up to 80 % leased for retail	50–70
Office and administration buildings, schools and kindergartens	50–80
Retail and industrial buildings (with flexible and future-oriented designs)	40–60
Petrol stations	10–20
Shopping centres/stores	30–50
Hotels/sanatoriums/hospitals	40–60

3.2

Agents of the integral planning approach	
Client/operator	
Occupants and other persons affected	
Architect/planner	
Energy consultant	
Sustainability consultant	
Auditor/certifier	
Consultants	• Building services engineer • Light designer • Structural engineer • Acoustics planner • Fire safety consultant
Construction companies and contractors	
Facility manager	
Politicians	
Town and regional planners	
Landscape architects and ecologists	
Financiers and banks	

3.3

3.1 Examples of life expectancies for different structural elements (according to Enclosure 6 of the Guideline for Sustainable Building (Leitfaden Nachhaltiges Bauen)
3.2 Overview of different building types and their average economic life
3.3 Agents of the integral planning approach

development phase helps to make a decision on whether a certification programme is to be performed, which result might be attainable and which certification scheme or system variant is applicable.

- Pre-certification:
Pre-certification during the design phase is performed to determine and assess design objectives and to define aspired characteristics of the building.
- Certification:
On completion or on commissioning of the building, the scheme is documented according to the criteria of the proposed label and the incorporated benchmarks incorporated. The documentation and monitoring of the demanded targets during the tendering and contracting phase, the construction processes and commissioning of the building contribute towards the sustainability performance of the building.
- Re-certification:
A review of the main certificate during the utilisation phase of the building contributes towards maintenance of the building's level of sustainability during operation.

Certification and building documentation

Various data acquisition and logging systems are available today. The ways in which they are integrated into the planning and operation process differ. Building certification, in particular, usually requires detailed building documentation to be compiled in the form of an "operation manual" or a "property CV" [8].
In addition to the evaluation of data, building certificates bring together existing data gathering and logging systems and design tools. Interim results of individual criteria offer objective, directly related and verifiable information that can be used as a specific source of information by consultants, construction companies, occupants, tenants and buyers [9].

Principles of building documentation
A systematic, conclusive and constantly updated documentation of a building for its entire life cycle is an important foundation for the communication amongst project participants (architect, client, consultants) and third parties (surveyors, tenants, auditors). Documentation encour-

ages the sustainability performance of buildings since it allows for a transparent and clear presentation of all facts important to the design and operation process. It furthermore provides a cost and time-efficient basis for cost calculations and for later refurbishments, conversions and deconstruction work. Building documentation reveals information regarding functionality, environmental protection and the sustainability of the building and helps to maintain the value of the property. The graphs contained in the building documentation clearly illustrate the building's management concept as well as the sources and routes of energy supplies. They also provide a basis for the on-going collection and evaluation of building-related energy flow data and aspects of sustainability [10].
In recent years, it has become possible to more effectively link together the traditional building descriptions, consisting of drawings (layouts, sections, elevations), calculations (cost calculations, energy calculations, etc.) and lists (e.g. specifications), thereby facilitating communication between planning partners. The development of a general interface, Building Infor-

Production			Use (supply and disposal, upkeep)			End-of-life (deconstruction)
Project development	Design	Construction	Commissioning	Operation	Modernisation	Deconstruction
• site • use • existing building stock • financing • useful period • demand	• preliminary design • design: minimise energy demand sustainability (ecology, economy and social aspects) • selection of materials: manufacture pollutants durability deconstructability • production information: minimised use of materials • specifications • contract award	• construction • supervision • waste recycling • quality assurance	• acceptance • documentation • building certificate	• use • energy demand (supply and disposal) • monitoring • facility management • servicing • maintenance/ upkeep • repair	• retrofit • adaptation/fit-out • conversion • refurbishment	• removal • recycling • disposal

Life cycle phases of a building

3.4

Pre-assessment/quick check	Pre-certification	Certification	Re-certification
Life cycle phase: project development Aim: decision aid to determine possible results and to select type and level of certificate	Life cycle phase: preliminary design and final design Aim: definition of sustainable design objectives	Life cycle phase: after completion, commissioning Aim: audit of the implemented sustainability features, monitoring	Life cycle phase: in use Aim: inspection and monitoring of pre-determined sustainability features

3.5

mation Modelling (BIM), has been a major step forward. It links the graphical CAD acquisition programmes with calculation tools and data banks to record, for example, the energy consumption or environmental impact of building materials [11]. However, these methods have not yet become fully established since the required CAD programmes, the comprehensive tender database with more than 30,000 work items, component catalogues as well as design and assessment tools are still only available in part with very little coordination. Architects and engineers are still using a variety of programmes and databases even when working on large-scale projects.

To meet future needs in relation to planning and building certification, there is an urgent requirement for linked digital planning tools. The following aspects of sustainable building can only be ensured long-term if these links are established (Fig. 3.6) [12]:

- Detailed consideration of the building throughout all life phases, production, operation and disposal
- An integrated planning approach achieved by linking the design tools, software and database (construction and operation costs, energy demand and costs, environmental impact)
- Guaranteed consistency of data and a smooth project run achieved by a common interface
- Safekeeping of data and avoidance of problems in connection with long-term archiving, e.g. due to lost or missing data caused by incomplete building documentation, frequent changes of ownership and a lack of updates
- Improvements concerning the thoroughness and clarity of the documentation for third parties
- Recording of energy, material and cost flows with automatic updating for alterations and information concerning the type of construction, building processes as well as aspects relevant to building physics, health and waste removal

Data collection for assessments

Alongside the assessment and audit of the building's sustainability performance, data collection is an important element in building certification. It involves the determination of facts and figures about the building in relation to the specific performance criteria demanded by the certification body. All data has to be verified

Building documentation		
General information		• site, client, owner, architect, completion date / modernisation date • documentary evidence: list of consultants and construction companies
Legal aspects		• land use plan, planning permission, information regarding buildings with preservation orders • documentary evidence: extract from development plan
Property		• premises, prior use, information concerning contamination, site development (water supply, water disposal, gas, district heat, etc.), distances • documentary evidence of public transport: site plan
Exterior space		• information concerning access, accessibility for disabled persons, rainwater infiltration system, public utility lines, lighting, parking, green space, playgrounds • documentary evidence: description of exterior space, site-specific wastewater concept
Building	General description	• gross cubic volume (GCV), enclosed space, number of storeys, information regarding useful floor space (living, office, others), areas (gross floor area GFA; net floor area NFA; useful area UA, etc.), surface-area-to-volume ratio (SA:V), GCV/GFA ratio, information regarding basement construction • documentary evidence: floor plans, sections
	Building construction	• natural subsoil, groundwater, foundation, exterior basement walls, exterior walls, load-bearing interior walls, partition walls, floor slabs, stairs, roof, windows, doors, sun protection devices • documentary evidence: extract from ground survey, building space utilisation book, building description
	Structural stability / load-bearing capacity	• permissible imposed load (offices, habitable space, corridors, etc.), fire protection • documentary evidence: building statics, fire protection concept
	Utilisation of daylight, artificial light	• proportion of window area, illuminance depending on space utilisation, luminosity factors dependent on work space and surrounding area • documentary evidence: lighting concept
	Thermal protection/energy demand	• annual heat requirement, primary energy demand, measures for summer heat protection, use of renewable energies, energy concept • evidence: energy supply concept, EnEV statement, proof of energy requirements, evidence of summer heat protection, cooling load calculation, explanations concerning the energy concept, etc.
	Noise protection	• protection against noise from adjacent rooms (airborne sound insulation, impact sound insulation), protection against exterior noise and noise from building services (water installations, etc.) • documentary evidence: noise protection proof
	Ventilation	• information regarding natural ventilation (cross ventilation, shaft ventilation), mechanical ventilation (air supply and removal with or without heat recovery), ventilation requirement • documentary evidence: explanatory notes on the ventilation concept and characteristic values of energy yield and applied ancillary energy
	Water	• water consumption • documentary evidence: water saving concept
	Waste management	• waste disposal system • documentary evidence: waste disposal concept
	Fit-out	• information concerning lifts, underground parking, accessibility for disabled persons, floor finishes, surface finishes, fit-out • documentary evidence: description of the sanitary and kitchen facilities, explanations concerning the interior fit-out
	Building services	• electrical installations, communication technology, heating, hot water production, sanitary installations, ventilation system, waste water facilities, use of renewable energies • documentary evidence: description of building services
Inspection/upkeep/ maintenance		• information on facilities and components and on the schedule for inspections/ upkeep and maintenance work • documentary evidence: explanatory notes concerning the schedule for inspections and maintenance measures, documentation of repair work
Operating costs		• costs for cleaning, water supply/waste water, heating/cooling, electrical energy, operation, maintenance, inspection, repair work, etc. • documentary evidence: compilation of operating costs

3.6

3.4 Life cycle phases of a building
3.5 Phases of a certification process
3.6 Contents of a building's documentation

(according to Enclosure 7 of the Guideline for Sustainable Building (Leitfaden Nachhaltiges Bauen))

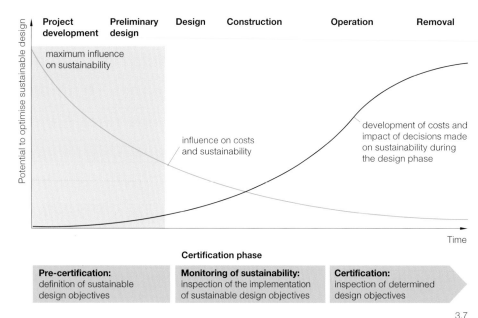

Project development	Preliminary design	Design	Construction	Operation	Removal

Certification phase

Pre-certification: definition of sustainable design objectives	Monitoring of sustainability: inspection of the implementation of sustainable design objectives	Certification: inspection of determined design objectives

3.7

Basic principles and tools for the assessment and documentation of buildings

Data	Information on building products and materials, e.g. Environmental Product Declarations (EPDs)	
	Information for tender items, e.g. bills of quantities	
	Information on components	Data for the construction phase (pieces and quantities), e.g. component-related structuring according to cost groups (according to DIN 276)
		Data for the operation phase, e.g. building-related services concerning supply and disposal (according to DIN 18960)
		Component-related services, e.g. cleaning, maintenance and inspection work, refurbishments, etc.
Database	Database for the useful life expectancy of structural components, e.g. Guideline for Sustainable Building (Leitfaden Nachhaltiges Bauen)	
	Database for information on life cycle assessment, e.g. Ökobau.dat	
Information and component catalogues	Hazardous substance information system, e.g. WINGIS	
	Building product information system, e.g. WECOBIS	
	Component catalogue, e.g. component catalogues from design software to assess the building performance in terms of energy efficiency	
Design tools and calculation programmes	Design tools to support the planning process, e.g. CAD software, tendering, letting and billing software, tools to calculate energy consumption	
Planning and assessment tools	Tools for the integrated planning approach to life cycle costs (LCC) and performance of a life cycle assessment (LCA)	

3.8

3.7 Life cycle and certification process: Development and possible influence on overall costs and the potential for a sustainable design
3.8 Basic principles and tools for the assessment and documentation of buildings

3.9 Assessment methods regarded as summarised building documentation
3.10 Extract from the documentation requirements according to BREEAM, system variant: BREEAM Europe Commercial

by providing appropriate evidence or certificates. These are defined as criteria or indicators and are phrased and drafted in a way that enables impartial institutions, i.e. the certification body, to verify the information. The facts and figures concerning the building indicate the result of the sustainability audit and are adopted in the actual rating. Thus the process of assessing and rating the building is a summary, consolidation and interpretation of building-specific information. The results can lead to the awarding of a certificate, which in itself is a concentrated documentation of the building (Fig. 3.9) [13].

In the case of today's certification systems, software tools and data platforms are provided to aid data collection and then forward the gathered information to the appropriate certification body. However, up to now, there is a lack of interface between these tools and already well-established design tools, such as CAD software, tools to perform life cycle assessments or calculate life cycle costs, building simulation programmes and database providing information on energy-efficient, physical and ecological components and values (Fig. 3.8). This shortcoming increases the time and effort required for the data collection and evaluation necessary in the context of a building assessment since the data has to be retrieved, compiled and entered repeatedly.

Dependent on the selected certification system and the respective system variant, the following information is usually requested by most well-established assessment methods:
- Fundamental planning documents:
  - building description
  - up-to-date plans (detail drawings, construction drawings, building statics, etc.)
  - information on the client, consultants and occupants
  - area and volume calculations
- Environmental aspects:
  - material and quantity specifications
  - drinking water and waste water concept
  - waste disposal concept
  - analysis concerning deconstruction and recycling
  - calculations of land use and land efficiency
- Economic efficiency:
  - statement and summary of construction and operation costs

– evidence of the suitability for conversion
- Social factors:
  - information on the accessibility for disabled persons
  - safety certificates and concept
  - design concept (innovation)
  - documents concerning aspects such as health and comfort
  - evidence concerning thermal comfort and occupants' scope of influence
  - light simulations and calculations
  - documents concerning the monitoring of indoor air quality
  - evidence of noise protection measures
- Energy and building services:
  - energy concept and simulation concerning the reduction of CO_2 emissions
  - statement concerning the use of renewable energies
  - building physics
  - fire protection proof
  - description of building services
- Process:
  - information concerning the design process
  - staging of architectural competitions and analysis of alternatives
  - incorporation of sustainable aspects in the design
  - closely linked planning team
  - evidence of the inclusion of sustainable aspects in the tender documents
  - description of construction site operations
  - documentation of commissioning and building operation
- Site:
  - documentation of traffic connections
  - description of site-specific factors and neighbourhood
  - evidence concerning the reuse, rehabilitation and remediation of developed sites (brownfields redevelopment) and measures of decontamination
  - information on the improvement of biodiversity and site ecology

BREEAM certification process

In a similar way to the LEED and DGNB systems, the BREEAM certification process is divided into two stages and must be performed by an approved BREEAM Assessor. The assessor is also responsible for submitting the documentation to the certification body:

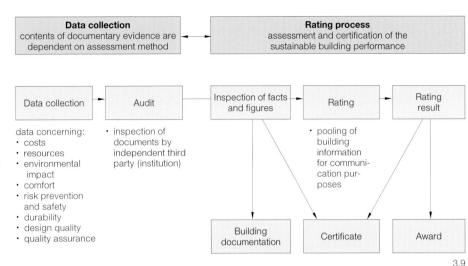

3.9

Documentation requirements for BREEAM certification

Standard

- comprehensive description of the building services
- evidence of planned glare protection
- description of the ventilation concept
- daylight and artificial light concept
- monitoring concept
- lift concept
- documentation of the implementation of hygienic requirements (domestic water, ventilation)
- documentary evidence of energy efficiency (in Germany the calculation can be performed according to valid version of the Energy Performance Directive)
- water supply and wastewater concept
- waste concept
- documentary evidence of the applied refrigerants
- noise protection proof

Additional mandatory requirements

- documentary evidence of high-frequency halogen lamps
- documentary evidence of thermal comfort

Additional documentary evidence to improve rating

- documentation of the commissioning process
- evidence of standards observed by contractors (e.g. safety and neatness of construction site, considerations of neighbours)
- documentation of the impact of the construction site (e.g. CO_2 emission, water consumption, etc.)
- compilation of a user manual
- life cycle cost calculation
- daylight calculation/simulation
- documentary evidence of view out
- documentary evidence of low-pollutant construction materials
- acoustic measurements
- thermal simulation
- energy simulation
- site-related evidence (distance to public transportation facilities and public amenities)
- car-sharing concept
- irrigation concept for exterior planting
- material certificates according to BREEAM Green Guide
- life cycle assessment according to ISO 14040ff.
- documentary evidence of reused structural components
- documentary evidence of sustainable construction products
- documentary evidence of waste volume
- compilation of a site waste management plan (standard in GB)
- documentary evidence of the proportion of recycled materials
- documentary evidence of the site's ecological value

3.10

- BREEAM Interim Certificate: preliminary assessment performed at design stage based on first results for the scheme
- BREEAM Certificate: final assessment performed on completion of the building at post construction stage

The general approach with a pre-assessment phase performed prior to the actual certification process and the implementation of workshops with the design team as part of the BREEAM consultancy services is comparable to the processes applicable to a DGNB certification (see p. 84). The BREEAM Interim Certificate, awarded on the basis of an assessment performed at design stage, rates criteria on the basis of the preliminary design. In order to perform a full assessment, the design must be sufficiently far advanced for the BREEAM Assessor to verify and document clearly the building characteristics in accordance with the system documentation requirements. This design stage assessment is generally completed prior to commencement of construction work. The post construction assessment, which is the basis for building certification, is performed on completion of the construction work and can be carried out as either:

- a post construction review of the preliminary design stage assessment
- a post construction assessment

The aim of the post construction review is to confirm and update the preliminary BREEAM rating awarded during the design phase. The design stage assessment is optional and is only carried out if there is a request for an interim certificate. If this is not the case, a full post construction assessment is performed on completion of the building and submitted to the certification body.

Documentation
The certification is based on extracts from the design and construction documentation (e.g. description of the building services), statements made by the design team and/or the client, additional surveys or calculations (e.g. analysis of life cycle costs), documentation from the BREEAM Assessor's site inspection (e.g. letter of acknowledgement and photographic evidence of the number of parking spaces and the type of car parking) as well as a written statement from the BREEAM Assessor confirming conformity of the submitted documents with the building.

The site inspections performed by the assessor are fundamental in furnishing proof for a number of different criteria. Via the assessor, BREEAM provides manuals and technical checklists to simplify the assessment process and the target-oriented evaluation (Fig. 3.10).

LEED certification process

In principle, the certification process for the system variant LEED-NC (New Construction & Major Renovations) is comparable to that of BREEAM and DGNB. It is divided into two phases: the design phase and the construction phase. At the end of the design phase, the criteria, which can be fully documented on the basis of available design results, can be compiled (e.g. criteria concerning energy efficiency, water efficiency, etc.) and submitted to the GBCI (Green Building Certification Institute). The GBCI confirms the criteria so long as they are consistent with the requirements and on condition that they are then implemented during the construction phase.

The remaining criteria, which basically refer to the work performed on site and the applied building products and materials, are submitted to the certification body and checked on completion of the construction work.

The submission at the end of the design phase, the design review, is not obligatory. The client or the project team are also entitled to submit the full documentation to the GBCI only once, namely for a construction review on completion of the building. The certificate is awarded once the audit of the criteria has been performed.

The awarding of a pre-certificate is exclusive to the LEED rating system, Core & Shell (LEED-CS). The intention of the pre-certificate is to support the client and investor in successfully marketing the property.

A project team administrator (generally this is the respective LEED consultant) is responsible for the communication between the project team and the certification body or the appropriate inspector. In contrast to the DGNB certificate, where only approved auditors are entitled to carry out the audit, LEED does not require that this function is performed by a LEED AP (Accredited Professional). However, the cooperation of the project team with an experienced LEED AP is beneficial and recommended.

Documentation
The documentation required for building certification is uploaded onto the U.S. Green Building Council's internet platform, LEED Online, and released for verification by the project team administrator [14]. It is not necessary to submit the documentation in hard copy. All documents must be prepared in English. The scope of the requested documents (descriptions, plans and calculations) must enable the inspector to form an opinion on the implementation of the LEED requirements in the project. Concise explanations or calculations as well as statements by the design team confirming conformity with LEED requirements usually suffice as evidence.

The certification is based on US American standards and guidelines. When LEED assessments are performed outside the USA, for example in Germany, additional proof must be submitted since the calculation methods prescribed by LEED can, in part, differ significantly from those abroad. For a LEED certification, the energy efficiency of a building, for example, must be verified using the calculation method determined in ASHRAE 90.1-Appendix G. This method differs considerably from calculations specified under the Energy Performance Directive in Germany.

Depending on the aspired certification level, the rating can be improved by furnishing additional proof, for example air pollution measurements taken prior to building occupation (Fig. 3.11).

DGNB certification process

The certification process to obtain a DGNB certificate is divided into two steps and must be performed by a DGNB-trained and approved auditor (Fig. 3.13, p. 84):

- Pre-certifcate: definition and assessment of design objectives during the design phase
- Main certificate: evaluation of the implemented measures on completion of the building

A so-called pre-assessment is usually performed prior to the actual building certification process. The intention of this first quick check is to assess the performance of the building and determine the possible certification result during the preliminary design stage.

Documentation requirements for LEED certification

Standard

- up-to-date plans
- building description
- description of building services
- information on client and occupants
- description of implemented energy concept
- ground survey
- waste concept
- water supply and wastewater concept

Additional mandatory requirements

- compilation of an "Erosion and Sedimentation Control Plan" (ESC) for all construction work and presentation of all measures in a detailed construction site plan
- photographic evidence of the implementation of the above-mentioned measures
- calculation of the project's water consumption based on the Energy Policy Act of 1992
- documentary evidence of the flush and flow volumes of sanitary installations by means of appropriate certificates
- confirmation that no CFC-based refrigerants or gas are used in the fire extinguishing plant
- confirmation of the fulfilment of the energy efficiency requirements according to ASHRAE 90.1-2007
- fundamental commissioning:
  – description of the technical plant and report on the commissioning results
  – compilation of the commissioning plan and confirmation that the requirements were incorporated in the planning documents
- recycling and waste disposal concept for the operation phase of the building
- calculation providing evidence of the fulfilment of indoor air requirements according to ASHRAE 62.1-2007
- description of the refrigeration plant, including diagram
- confirmation of no-smoking ban throughout the building or, if smokers' room is provided, confirmation of the fulfilment of all ventilation and indoor air quality requirements, including ventilation diagram, building sections, records of pressure difference to the surrounding rooms

Additional documentary evidence to improve rating

- documentation of privileged car parking for low-pollutant and fuel-efficient vehicles and for car pools in the site plan and with photos on completion of the project
- documentation of shower and changing facilities as well as bicycle parking areas in the floor plans and the site plan
- calculation of the water consumption for the irrigation of exterior planting
- description of the used plants and the irrigation system
- performance of building simulation according to ASHRAE 90.1-2007, App. G and summary of results in a report
- enhanced commissioning:
  confirmation and documentary evidence proving that
  – the person responsible for commissioning checked all planning documents and tenders
  – the staff responsible for the building operation and future occupants were trained accordingly
  – the person responsible for commissioning checks the building operation within the first ten months after completion
- submission of measurement and monitoring concept according to IPMVP Volume III [1]
- evidence confirming that the measurement and monitoring concept was implemented for at least one year
- certificate proving that the power supply is from renewable resources
- confirmation of a minimum contract period for the power supply of at least two years
- presentation of the recyclability of existing building stock in floor plans including the appropriate calculations
- manufacturer's certificates confirming the implementation of regional and recycled materials
- presentation of FSC certificates (Forest Stewardship Council) for all timber products applied
- product certificates and product-related manufacturer confirmations providing evidence of the use of low-pollutant materials
- documentary evidence of the illuminance in the exterior by performing dynamic simulations
- manufacturer's certificate or measurement of the reflective level (Solar Reflectance Index) of the roof's surface material
- performance of pollutant measurements prior to building use

[1] International Performance Measurement & Verification Protocol Volume III, April 2003

3.11

3.11 Extract from LEED's documentary requirements for system variant LEED-NC

Documentation requirements for DGNB certificate

Standard

- up-to-date planning documents
- building description
- description of building services
- information regarding client, consultants and occupants
- calculation of areas according to DIN 277
- EnEV calculation based on DIN V 18599
- energy concept
- drinking water and wastewater concept
- daylighting and artificial light concept
- waste scheme
- noise protection proof
- safety and risk prevention concept and evacuation plan
- accessbility concept for disabled persons according to DIN 18024
- SiGePlan (safety, risk and health coordination on building sites)
- ground survey
- evaluation of design alternatives
- systematic commissioning including adjustments and plant optimisation

Additional mandatory requirements

- life cycle assessment:
  - based on the building-specific useful life expectancies as determined in the individual occupancy profiles
  - construction phase: quantity surveying of components and heat generation plant (cost groups 300 and 400 according to DIN 276), links to database Ökobau.dat
  - building utilisation phase (relevant cost groups according to DIN V 18599): supply and disposal (DIN V 18599), maintenance and upkeep according to the Guideline of Sustainable Building (Leitfaden Nachhaltiges Bauen) and VDI 2076
  - end-of-life: material-specific scenarios based on the database Ökobau.dat
- life cycle cost calculation:
  - based on the building-specific useful life expectancies as determined in the individual occupancy profiles
  - for construction costs (relevant cost groups 300 and 400 according to DIN 276): construction and building services
  - for utilisation costs (relevant cost groups according to DIN V 18599): operation costs (supply and disposal, upkeep, operation, inspections and maintenance) and repair costs

Additional documentary evidence to improve rating

- list of construction materials: documentation and evidence of Environmental Product Declarations (EPDs)
- timber: FSC/PSFC and CoC certificates
- thermal building simulation
- indoor air flow simulation
- daylight and artificial light simulation
- indoor air monitoring for TVOC and formaldehyde content
- utilisation of roof surface
- staging of architectural competition
- artwork
- blower-door test
- concept for deconstruction, recycling and disposal
- upkeep and maintenance concept
- control and monitoring concept
- integration of sustainability aspects in the tendering documents
- inclusion of sustainability aspects when selecting companies
- building documentation (according to Enclosure 7 of the Guideline for Sustainable Building (Leitfaden Nachhaltiges Bauen) or similar)
- instructions for the maintenance, inspection, operation and upkeep of the building
- compilation of a facility management and user manual
- project diary
- concept for a low-waste and noise, and environmentally-friendly construction site
- implementation of a pre-qualification process
- functional test of commissioning performed by independent third party (Commissioning Management)

3.12

Pre-certificate	Certificate	
		Pre-certificate determination of design objectives
assessment workshop with project participants (auditor, planners, consultants, client, etc.): determination of design objectives	assessment workshop with project participants (auditor, planners, consultants, client, etc.)	
	site inspection and data collection	
evidence of design objectives through data collection		
data evaluation and determination of possible result: approximate life cycle assessment, life cycle cost calculation, definition of physical aspects, etc.	data evaluation and determination of possible result: life cycle assessment, life cycle cost calculation, definition of physical aspects, etc.	
	intermediate meeting with project participants (auditor, planners, consultants, client, etc.) determination of missing documents, uncertainties, etc.	
submission of requested documentation		
audit performed by third party	submission of requested documentation	**Certificate** documentation of results
	audit performed by third party	

3.13

With the aid of the DGNB pre-certificate, it is possible to determine and assess building-specific design objectives as early as during the design phase. The pre-certificate can furthermore be used by the client or investor as a marketing tool. In order to ensure a high level of sustainability, the pre-certification should be performed at an early design stage, however, at the latest prior to HOAI's 5th service phase, i.e. before compiling the production drawings (Fig. 3.14). Pre-certification is optional, however, it does commit the applicant to carrying out the main certification process.

In line with the pre-certification procedure, the auditor has the task of registering the building for the main certificate and is in charge of submitting the application to the DGNB office. The auditor is furthermore responsible for the communication between the certification body and the design team. The certification workshop performed at the beginning of a DGNB certification process is an important aspect with regard to the assessment and integrated planning approach. The auditor or sustainability consultant uses the workshop to introduce the design team, made up of planners, consultants, the client, etc., to the contents and processes of the label. It is furthermore used to rate first design objectives and assessment criteria. Other important aspects of the certification process are the final site inspection, the advice offered throughout the tendering and construction period, random checks of construction work on site and the coordination of the required building documentation with the design team and the construction companies.

Alongside the data collection to furnish proof of criteria, the auditor's main tasks include the evaluation of the obtained data and the determination of the assessment result. On completion of the assessment, the documentation is forwarded to the DGNB certification body by the auditor. Once the audit has been completed by the DGNB, the client is awarded the appropriate building certificate (Fig. 3.14).

Documentation

The building documentation for the DGNB certificate is compiled using a software package developed by DGNB. It is then forwarded to the certification body in printed and digital format.

The certification is based on German standards and guidelines and does not therefore include any DGNB-developed calculation methods. The intention of the certificate is to pool the results of well-established design tools and legally-prescribed data records in order to provide clear and transparent documentation of the building. The calculation performed according to DIN V 18599, for example, is the basis for assessing the building's performance in terms of energy efficiency. The applicant is furthermore obliged to perform a life cycle assessment and calculate the life cycle costs according to DGNB requirements. If a high rating level is aspired, increased efficiency and evidence is requested, for example the compilation of a material list with information concerning the environmental impact of products (EPDs), indoor air monitoring or a simulation of the thermal, visual or acoustic comfort (Fig. 3.12) [15].

References

[1] König, Holger; Kreißig, Johannes; Kohler, Niklaus; Lützkendorf, Thomas: Lebenszyklus-analyse in der Gebäudeplanung, p. 78
[2] Hegger, Manfred et al: Energie Atlas. Munich/Basel 2007, p. 187
[3] ibid. p. 186
[4] see ref. 1, p. 19
[5] Eßig, Natalie: Nachhaltigkeit von Olympischen Bauten. Stuttgart 2010
[6] Federal Office for Building and Regional Planning (BBR): Guidline for Sustainable Building (Leitfaden nachhaltiges Bauen). Bonn 2001, p. 2. http://www.bmvbs.de/architektur-baukultur
[7] see ref. 5
[8] Geissler, Susanne: Leitfaden zum Umgang mit Energieeffizienz und weiteren Nachhaltigkeitsparametern in der Immobilienwertermittlung. 2010, p. 14. http://www.fh-wien.ac.at/fileadmin/daten/studienangebot/immo/News/LeitfadenfuerWertermittlerzumUmgangmitEnergieeffizienzundweiterenNachhaltigkeitsparametern.pdf
[9] Geissler, Susanne: Gebäudebewertungen mit Nachhaltigkeitsanspruch. Vienna 2009, p. 5, and Geissler, Susanne; Bruck, Manfred: Eco-Building. Vienna 2001, p. 43
[10] see ref. 2, p. 183
[11] see ref. 1, p. 19f.
[12] see ref. 1, p. 78, 94
[13] see ref. 9
[14] http://www.leedonline.com
[15] acc. to profiles of the German Sustainable Building Council (DGNB)

3.12 Extract from DGNB's documentation requirements
3.13 Process for DGNB's pre-certification and certification programme
3.14 Process of the DGNB certification in accordance with DVP and HOAI phases

Project phases according to DVP[1]	HOAI service phases	DGNB certification process
1. Project preparation	Project development and 1st service phase (establishing the basis of the project)	Pre-assessment (quick check): first assessment of building's performance in terms of sustainability
2. Design	2nd to 4th service phase (preliminary design, final design, building permission application)	Pre-certificate
3. Preparatory measures for construction	5th service phase (execution drawings)	Monitoring of design objectives during the phase of preparing execution drawings
	6th and 7th service phase (preparation of contract award and assisting award process)	Monitoring of design objectives during the procurement phase
4. Construction	8th service phase (project supervision)	Monitoring of design objectives during the construction phase
5. Project completion	9th service phase (project control and documentation)	Certificate

[1] German association of project managers in the real estate and construction industry (DVP, Deutscher Verband der Projektmanager in der Immobilien- und Bauwirtschaft e.V.)

3.14

Structural comparison

At present, there is no broad international consensus regarding the composition and structure of assessment tools. Each sustainability label is based on its own individual structure. Hence, there is not a recognised "best system" since direct comp arison of the currently available assessment methods is often not possible and the individual systems have been specifically developed to meet an individual country's needs in terms of cultural, climatic and political conditions. Numerous studies have been undertaken at international and European levels to improve the content of the various assessment systems and facilitate comparison. The certification organisations, research institutes and the construction industry play important roles in this, as do international, European and national standards.

Standardisation activities

The aim of the international (ISO), European (CEN) and national (DIN) standardisation activities in relation to the assessment of a building's sustainability is the development of uniform and comparable parameters for already available and new certification systems. The intention is to structure the basic principles, requirements, guidelines and terminology not only for the sustainability of buildings (assessment methods) but also for the environmental and heath-related information concerning construction products (Environmental Product Declaration, EPD) [1].

There are currently two standardisation organisations working at international and European level: the technical committee ISO TC59/SC17: Sustainability in building construction for international standardisation and the technical committee CEN/TC 350: Sustainability of construction works for European standards [2]. The work performed on standards by ISO/TC59/SC17 forms the basis for the work of CEN/TC 350 and the respective national standards. Most recently introduced assessment methods, such as the DGNB Certificate, took into account the early versions of the international and European standards in the development of their systems. Systems, such as BREEAM and LEED, that have been on the market for longer, are progressively incorporating the standards into their new versions [3].

The main contents of an international and European standard are a description of the basic principles as well as the respective calculation and evaluation methods. The aim is to establish quantifiable indicators, a modular life cycle analysis (design, production, construction, operation and management as well as end-of-life) and a performance-oriented approach. The standards, however, do not make any statements regarding evaluation criteria and benchmarks since these are to be determined by national standards or assessment systems. ISO TC 59/SC17 and CEN/TC 350 have been developed according to a similar structure (Fig. 4.1), which includes three levels [4]:

· general principles
· building aspects
· product aspects

It is based on the three pillars of sustainability:

· environment
· society
· economy

The international standard, ISO 15392 "Sustainability in building construction – General principles" [5] defines the basic principles of sustainable building. The standard differs between the sustainability assessment of buildings and the environment and health-relevant properties of construction products (Environmental Product Declarations, EPDs). In both cases, the standard so far only provides guidelines for the environmental assessment. The international standard does not yet make any statements concerning social or economic indicators [6].

The European standardisation of CEN/TC 350, which is based on international guidelines, has adopted a similar approach. The three pillars of the assessment also refer to the environmental, social and economic performance of buildings and construction products. Alongside these three main pillars, CEN/TC 350 also considers technical and functional sustainability aspects [7]. CEN divides the individual dimensions of

4.1   Structure of standards
      a ISO/TC 59/SC 17: Sustainability in building
        construction
      b CEN/TC 350: Sustainability of construction
        works

sustainability into several parts. In order to assess the environmental performance of buildings and provide clear guidelines concerning calculation methods and procedures, the first preliminary standard, prEN 15978 was published in early 2010: Assessment of environmental performance. It is generally based on the results of life cycle analyses and Environmental Product Declarations (EPDs). The following core aspects have been defined for the assessment of a building's environmental performance (Fig. 4.2, p. 88) [8]:
- environmental impacts
- resource input
- waste categories
- output flows leaving the system

The assessment of the economic performance and social performance of sustainable buildings is to be added by 2012. First drafts of the criteria catalogues are already available. Whereas the main focus of the economic performance is on life cycle costs (construction, opera-

tion and demolition costs) and value preservation, the assessment of social performance considers the following aspects [9]:
- health and comfort
- thermal performance
- humidity
- quality of water for use in buildings
- indoor air quality
- acoustic performance
- visual comfort
- accessibility

International and European system comparison

In recent years numerous studies have been undertaken by certification bodies, research institutes and the building sector with a view to making the contents and results of assessment tools comparable and to enable existing sustainability labels to be used in other countries as well as internationally. For this purpose, multiple assessments of individual build-

ings have been performed using different systems [10]. Worldwide established certification institutions, such as BREEAM, LEED or DGNB, also perform comparisons to improve, further develop and adapt their systems to meet international needs [11]. When developing new, country-specific labels, developers draw on the know-how and experience of available tools. For example CASBEE in Japan and Green Star in Australia have based their systems on LEED and BREEAM respectively. The DGNB certificate also builds upon the know-how of established international systems, however, also incorporates new features into the building's assessment scheme which consider economic, social, technical and process-specific aspects [12].
All studies have clearly shown that building certification requires country-specific assessment systems which are adapted to the local political, social and climatic conditions. However, the studies have also highlighted the need for an interna-

	Methodical basis		Buildings	Building products
Environmental aspects	**ISO 15392** Sustainability in building construction – General principles **ISO/NP TS 12720** Sustainability in building construction – Guidelines for the application of the general principles on sustainability **ISO/TS 21929** Sustainability in building construction – Sustainability indicators – Part 1: Framework for the development of indicators for buildings **ISO/NP 21929-2**		**ISO 21931-1** Sustainability in building construction - Framework for assessment methods for the environmental performance of construction work – Part 1: Buildings	**ISO 21930** Sustainability in building construction – Environmental declaration of building products
Social aspects	Sustainability in building construction – Sustainability indicators – Part 2: Framework for the development of indicators for civil engineering work **ISO/ DTR 21932**			
Economic aspects	Sustainability in building construction – Terminology			

a

Concept Level	Framework Level		Building level	Product level
Environmental performance	**prEN 15643-1** Sustainability assessment of buildings – General framework	**prEN 15643-2** Framework for environmental performance	**prEN 15978** Assessment of environmental performance	**prEN 15804** Environmental product declarations **prEN 15942** Communication format B-B) **CEN/TR 15941** Generic data
Social performance		**prEN 15643-3** Framework for social performance	**WI 015** Assessment of social performance	
Economic performance		**prEN 15643-4** Framework for economic performance	**WI 017** Assessment of economic performance	
Technical performance		Technical characteristics		
Functional performance		Functionality		

b

tional core system, with so-called core indicators, to ensure better comparison of the individual systems and their results. The use of core indicators is already being practised and tested, for example, in the international application of the systems BREEAM (BREEAM International) and DGNB (DGNB International)[13]. The analysis of established systems and the developments in recent years have moreover shown that all methods are subject to substantial shortcomings. Hence, there is a need for further research to add missing content and to define appropriate calculation methods, benchmarks and reference values.

For several years, joint attempts have been made at international and European levels to define these objectives. The aim of umbrella organisations and interest groups, such as iiSBE (International Initiative for a Sustainable Built Environment) or the SB Alliance (see International organisational framework of building certification, p. 27f.), and international standardisation work is a convergence of contents towards uniform core indicators, which consider the environmental, economic and social aspects of sustainability. These efforts are being supported by a variety of research projects.

SBTool (Sustainable Building Tool)
In the context of the introduction and development of the international generic

framework GBTool (now SBTool), the organisation International Initiative for a Sustainable Built Environment (iiSBE) performed comprehensive comparisons of assessment and certification systems at the end of the 1990s [14] (see International Initiative for a Sustainable Built Environment, p. 27f.). The main aim was to develop an assessment tool which could be used in any region and every country, while at the same time allowing comparison of the results [15]. Several nations have used this catalogue of criteria as a basis to develop a country-specific assessment system. Spain, for example, developed the assessment scheme, VERDE; Italy the label, Protocollo Itaca. However, the diversity of national conditions and the various ways of implementing the framework meant that the initial idea of creating international comparability failed during the initial process of adapting and applying the method. Nevertheless, the SBTool still comprises one of the most thorough comparisons of labels throughout the world, and it has provided a comprehensive framework of international core criteria and evaluation rules for the assessment of sustainability in buildings [16].

LEnSE (Label for Environmental, Social and Economic Buildings)
One of the first European research programmes for the sustainability assess-

ment of buildings resulted in the development of the LEnSE methodology (Label for Environmental, Social and Economic Buildings) in 2008 [17] and the practical implementation with case studies on buildings throughout Europe.
Since the approach met little response at a European level, further research projects for the assessment of sustainability in buildings were put out to tender by the European Commission with the aim of developing European core indicators. The main objective of projects, such as OPEN HOUSE [18] and SUPER-BUILDING, which were launched at the beginning of 2010, is to encourage the definition of core indicators and their testing on a range of case study buildings at a European level and to support European standardisation in regard to sustainable building (Fig. 4.3).

SB Alliance (Sustainable Building Alliance)
SB Alliance (Sustainable Building Alliance) [19] is following a similar goal at an international level. Based on already established international assessment methods, the international network of universities, research centres, Green Building Councils and the construction industry are currently developing core indicators and common metrics to assess the sustainability performance of buildings. The definition of core indicators has been undertaken in several predefined steps.

Category	Indicator	Unit
Environmental impact	Global warming potential (GWP)	kg CO_2 eq
	Depletion potential of the stratospheric ozone layer	kg CFC 11 eq
	Acidification potential of land and water sources (AP)	kg SO_2 eq
	Eutrophication potential (EP)	kg PO_4 eq
	Formation potential of tropospheric ozone photochemical oxidants	kg ethene eq
	Abiotic resource depletion potential for elements (ADP_e)	kg Sb eq
	Abiotic resource depletion potential of fossil fuels (including feedstock) (ADP_f)	MJ/kg Sb eq
Resource input	Input of renewable energy resources, primary energy (not including renewable energy resources used as feedstock)	MJ specific heat capacity
	Input of non renewable energy resources, primary energy (not including non renewable energy resources used as feedstock)	MJ specific heat capacity
	Input of secondary material	kg
	Input of renewable secondary fuels	MJ
	Input of non renewable secondary fuels	MJ
	Input of net fresh water	m³
Waste categories	Hazardous waste for final disposal	kg
	Non hazardous waste for final disposal	kg
	Radioactive waste for final disposal	kg
Output flows leaving the system	Components for reuse	kg
	Materials for recycling	kg
	Materials for energy recovery	kg
	Exported energy	MJ

4.2

The first step was to set up a comprehensive catalogue of indicators based on a comparison of already available labels (bottom-up-approach). The following rating systems were compared:
- BREEAM (United Kingdom)
- HQE (France)
- AQUA (Brazil)
- DGNB (Germany)
- Protocollo Itaca (Italy)
- LEnSE (EU research project)
- PromisE (Finland)

An SB Alliance working group sorted the list of indicators according to predefined priorities and selected the first six for the 2009 version (top-down-approach). The next step involved assigning common metrics to assess them (Fig. 4.4). The core indicators are structured according to three main areas [20]:
- Resources depletion: primary energy and water
- Indoor environment quality: thermal comfort and indoor air quality
- Building emissions: greenhouse gas emissions and waste production

The following indicators remain under consideration for the 2009 version:
- Economic performance
- Visual comfort
- Acoustic comfort

The objective now is to add parameters and benchmarks to the defined indicators, predominantly describing the environmental performance of a building. In doing so, all of the building's life cycle phases (design and construction phase, operation and end-of-life phase) are considered. However, since this approach has only been followed through by relatively few rating systems and, at an international level, there is still a lack of assessment and calculation guidelines for criteria such as transportation in the operation phase, several aspects will not be considered in the 2009 version. For this reason, when setting the benchmarks for the individual indicators, information is drawn from a variety of sources:
- Standardised international and European energy assessment processes as well as methods and simulations recognised worldwide today for the life cycle analysis
- Assessment tools already developed and used by established methods, for example material database and Environmental Product Declarations

No.	Categories according to LEnSE	
1	Ecological aspects	Climate change
2		Biodiversity
3		Resource use
4		Environmental and geographical risks
5	Social aspects	Occupant wellbeing
6		Security
7		Social and cultural values
8		Accessibility
9	Economic aspects	Financing and management
10		Whole life value
11		Option appraisal
12		Externalities

4.3

SB Alliance indicators	Unit
Greenhouse gas emissions	kg CO_2 equivalent
Energy	primary energy (kWh)
Water	m^3
Waste	four types: • hazardous goods (t) • harmless materials (t) • inert waste (t) • nuclear waste (t)
Thermal comfort	% of a period during which the room temperature rises above predetermined values (e.g. 2 % of the period above 26 °C)
Indoor air quality	CO_2 in ppm formaldehyde in µg/m^3

4.4

System	Institution	Website
BREEAM	BRE (Building Research Establishment)	www.bre.co.uk
LEED	USGBC (U.S. Green Building Council)	www.usgbc.org
LEED Canada	CaGBC (Canada Green Building Council)	www.cagbc.org
DGNB	DGNB (Deutsche Gesellschaft für Nachhaltiges Bauen)	www.dgnb.de
Green Star	GBCA (Green Building Council Australia)	www.gbca.org.au
CASBEE	JSBC (Japan Sustainable Building Consortium)	www.ibec.or.jp/CASBEE/english/
HQE	Association HQE	www.assohqe.org
	Association Qualitel	www.qualitel.org
	CSTB Centre Scientifique et Technique du Bâtiment	www.cstb.fr
MINERGIE	Geschäftsstelle MINERGIE	www.minergie.ch

4.5

4.2 Key indicators concerning the environmental performance of buildings according to CEN/TC 350 (as of summer 2010)
4.3 LEnSE criteria catalogue, EU research project
4.4 Rating units of the SB Alliance's criteria catalogue
4.5 International rating systems and the corresponding institutions and websites

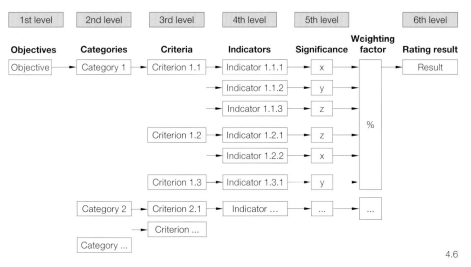

1st level	2nd level	3rd level	4th level	5th level		6th level
Objectives	**Categories**	**Criteria**	**Indicators**	**Significance**	**Weighting factor**	**Rating result**

4.6

Module	Definition/Example
Objectives	Definition: aspired assessment status, which needs to be met Example: maintaining values, protecting the environment
Qualities, categories, aspects	Definition: the sum or topic of criteria, which is used for the assessment Example: environmental quality, functional aspects
Criteria	Definition: features of a building, which are considered in the assessment Example: heating energy consumption, material quantities, operation costs

Indicators	Definition: description of the status quo, definition of the objectives' achievement level
	• Quantitative indicators: through figures and units
	  Example: kWh/m^2a, domestic water consumption m^3/m^2a
	• Qualitative indicators: descriptive
	  Example: maintenance of the construction site's biodiversity

Weighting factor	Definition: significance of the individual categories in relation to each other Example: in %, points, etc.
Significance	Definition: significance of the individual categories and criteria in relation to each other Example: using factors, such as 1, 2, 3
Rating process	Definition: translation of the Information/criteria into one comparable unit Example: grade, number of points

4.7

	LEED	BREEAM	DGNB
1st level: Objectives	national safety objectives	national safety objectives	national safety objectives
2nd level: Qualities, categories, aspects	–	–	6 qualities: • Ecological Quality • Economic Quality • Sociocultural and Functional quality • Technical quality • Process quality • Site quality
	6 categories: • Sustainable Sites • Water Efficiency • Energy & Atmosphere • Materials & Resources • Indoor Environmental Quality • Innovation & Design	10 categories: • Management • Health & Wellbeing • Energy • Transport • Water • Materials • Waste • Land use & Ecology • Pollution • Innovation	11 categories: • Impact on global and local environment • Utilisation of resources and arising waste • Life cycle costs • Value stability • Health, comfort and user satisfaction • Functionality • Quality of the design • Quality of technical configuration • Quality of planning • Quality of construction • Site quality
3rd level: Criteria	43 criteria	76 criteria	49 criteria
4th level: Indicators	qualitative and quantitative	qualitative and quantitative	qualitative and quantitative
5th level: Weightings	with points	in %	with factors of significance and in %
6th level: Result	Certified, Bronze, Silver, Gold, Platinum	Pass, Good, Very Good, Excellent, Outstanding	Bronze, Silver, Gold

4.8

Assessment and certification modules

Tools for the assessment of the environmental, economic and sociocultural performance of buildings are helpful in transforming design objectives into specific quality features. Each assessment process results in the achievement of a particular quality standard and rating level. In essence, the same procedure applies to all systems. However, the routes to get there differ and the assessment is always based on the rating system's own mathematical rules and methodology. The systems also use different terminology, such as categories, points, criteria, sub-criteria, etc. International standards are also not defining a uniform system and currently refer to aspects of the assessment as "indicators". Nevertheless, one can recognise similarities in the structures and related modules (Fig. 4.6–4.8) [21]:

1st level: Objectives

Regional and national safety objectives form the basis and the first level of each assessment method. They are based on social values, political programmes and social trends. Alongside these main protection goals, additional objectives are usually determined for the individual assessment criteria. In so doing, specific design objectives are defined for each criterion, i.e. in each case an individual target is tailored specifically to the characteristics of the criterion.

2nd level: Categories

The safety objectives illustrated on the first level are specified on the second level in the form of assessment categories. The categories rated, often also referred to as qualities or aspects, bring together the individual assessment criteria. Systems and methods that follow a holistic approach (e.g. DGNB Certificate) introduce a further subcategory between this and the next level. Assessment methods, which primarily consider environmental and energy-efficient aspects of a building (e.g. LEED or BREEAM), dispense with an extra subcategory in their structure.

3rd level: Criteria

On the third level, the categories are subdivided into criteria, which describe a specific feature of a building. The criteria catalogues, i.e. the sum of all applied criteria, are the principal constituent of every rating system. The criteria set out which characteristics are important for the assessment and indicate the sustainability level of a building. The contents are dependent on the social, political, climatic and cultural conditions of the rating system.

4th level: Indicators

On the fourth level, the system's assessment and calculation methods are described with the support of indicators. These differ considerably amongst the various methods since they are based on national standards, guidelines and sustainability goals. Indicators either assess buildings in terms of their quality (descriptive) or in terms of quantity (by numbers, units or metered values).

5th level: Weightings

The individual indicators, criteria and categories of established assessment methods are generally subject to different weighting factors. Within the fifth level, these are ranked according to significance, weighted percentages or different point allocations and brought together in the form of a single unit (points, per cent, etc.) which enables comparison.

The determination of weighting and significance factors is dependent on the cultural, economic and environmental conditions of the region. They are generally based on the views of experts, experience and the results of pilot projects.

6th level: Rating

The sixth level leads to the overall result of the assessment and rating process. The determined and weighted partial results established on the fifth level add up to a total sum and the therefore achieved rating. The final value is assigned to a specific rating level and, depending on the system, described as Certified, Silver, Gold or Platinum in the case of LEED, Bronze, Silver or Gold in DGNB's certification system or with school grades such as Pass, Good or Very Good in the case of BREEAM.

Distinctive features

The currently available rating methods differ both in structure and contents (Fig. 4.9, p. 92f.).

Structural differences

The structural arrangement and the assessment processes of the individual

rating methods show resemblance in some aspects, however, the following differences stand out:

Organisational structure
Various establishments are responsible for the introduction and onward development of assessment systems. These function either as not-for-profit organisations or are attached to a government institution (Fig. 4.5, p. 89).
Some organisations carry out the audit of the submitted certification documents themselves, such as BRE for the BREEAM method or DGNB for the DGNB Certificate. Other rating systems, such as LEED or HQE, have a third party perform the audit (Third Party Certification) in order to ensure a transparent assessment process. In this case, the third party institutions responsible are the Green Building Certification Institute (GBCI) for LEED or associations such as Certivéa, Céquami and Cerqual for HQE.

Performance of the assessment process
In the context of certification processes, the sustainability tools are guided by the most recent national construction standards and technologies, and updates for the individual assessment schemes are published regularly. However, the intervals between the updates vary considerably. BREEAM generally updates its versions once a year (e.g. BREEAM Office 2007, BREEAM Office 2008, etc.), LEED every two or three years (e.g. LEED NC Version 2.2, LEED NC Version 3.0) and DGNB according to demand (e.g. DGNB NBV 2008, DGNB NBV 2009).
Every rating system performs the assessment according to different techniques and determines its own specific processes and tools. In the case of BREEAM and DGNB, the assessment can only be carried out by an expert who has taken part in the particular system-specific training at the appropriate certification body (e.g. BREEAM Assessor, DGNB Auditor). In contrast, in the case of LEED, the planning team is entitled to perform the assessment and documentation itself. It is not mandatory to involve a specifically trained LEED Accredited Professional (LEED AP), however, their involvement gains an additional point in the rating.
Following the registration of the respective building at the certification body, the actual certification process is subdivided into two assessment procedures. Under

each of these three rating systems, precertification is not compulsory, but can be undertaken on a voluntary basis (see Certification and life cycle, p. 76f.) [22].
• Pre-certification: determination of design objectives at design stage (not yet mandatory in any of the mentioned systems)
  – BREEAM: Interim BREEAM Certificate
  – LEED: Pre-certification (so far only possible for the variant "LEED Core & Shell")
  – DGNB: Pre-certificate
• Certification: audit of the implemented design objectives on completion of the building
  – BREEAM: Final BREEAM Certificate
  – LEED: LEED Certification
  – DGNB: DGNB Certificate

Rating levels
All certification systems employ different rating levels and awards. The American method LEED, the subsidiary LEED Canada [23] and the DGNB Certificate use Olympic medals such as bronze, silver and gold. LEED has introduced an additional level, the so-called LEED Platinum certificate. Systems, such as BREEAM or the Australian label Green Star, rely on school grades or stars.
In order to determine the overall result, the labels compare the final rating with a degree of fulfilment by stating the result in the form of a percentage or number of points (e.g. BREEAM and DGNB: percentage, LEED: points) (Fig. 4.10, p. 94). The lowest level (LEED "Certified", BREEAM "Pass", Green Star "4 star" or DGNB "Bronze") defines the minimum standard currently applicable (industry standard) for sustainable building.
Due to the different settings of rating levels, it is extremely difficult to compare the results of the assessment methods. If one were only to compare the degree of fulfilment, the rating result of BREEAM Office "Very Good" (above 50 %) in percentage terms would compare roughly with the rating of LEED U.S. "Silver" (above 55 %), LEED Canada "Platinum" (above 52 %) or DGNB "Bronze" (above 50 %) and therefore correspond with German building standards. However, this comparison only

System comparison

	BREEAM	LEED
Assessment method	BRE Environmental Method	Leadership in Energy and Environmental Design
Certification body	BRE	USGBC (United States Green Building Council)
Launch	1990	1998
Internationalisation	BREEAM International BREEAM Europe BREEAM Gulf BREEAM Netherlands BREEAM Spain	LEED Brazil LEED Canada LEED Emirates LEED India LEED Italy LEED Mexico
Updates	according to demand	up until now, according to demand; three-year rhythm is planned
Certification by third party	BRE	GBCI (Green Building Certification Institute)
Auditor	registered and independent BREEAM Assessor training with examination	certification performed by GBCI registered and independent "LEED Accredited Professional" (LEED AP) can support the implementation of the requirements in a project, however, their appointment is not mandatory examination: formal training is not required
Rating process	• design phase: pre-certificate (Interim BREEAM Certificate) • commissioning: certificate (Final BREEAM Certificate) (on completion)	LEED-NC, -CS, -CI: assessment of the relevant criteria after the design phase and the commissioning; certificate on completion; pre-certificate is possible in the case of LEED-CS
Rating levels	Pass (≥ 30 %) Good (≥ 45 %) Very Good (≥ 55 %) Excellent (≥ 70 %) Outstanding (≥ 85 %)	Certified (≥40 points) Silver (≥50 points) Gold (≥60 points) Platinum (≥80 points)
Minimum standards and obligatory criteria	minimum standards, determination acc. to rating levels	predefined minimum criteria (prerequisites) in all categories
Weighting	weighting of the individual categories	no weighting; set number of points for criteria
Assessment categories	• Management • Health & Wellbeing • Energy • Transport • Water • Materials • Waste • Land use & Ecology • Pollution	• Sustainable Sites • Water Efficiency • Energy and Atmosphere • Material and Resources • Indoor Environmental Quality • Innovation & Design – additional points • Regional Credits – additional points
Additional points	innovation points (maximum of 10 points) for predefined criteria selected by the BREEAM Assessor	additional points for the categories "Regional Credits" and "Innovations" (maximum of 6 and 4 points respectively)
Energy	• in UK: Energy Performance Certificate (EPC) based on the European Directive 2002/91/EG (EPBD Energy Performance of Buildings Directive) • outside UK: application of country-specific calculation guidelines, calculation of the Building Energy Performance Index (BEPI), ASHRAE Standard 90.1(2007) or by using provided checklist	US-American standard: ASHRAE Standard 90.1 (2007) – Energy Standard for Buildings Except Low-Rise Residential Buildings

Life cycle analysis (LCA)	dependent on system variant using different approaches:
	e.g. life cycle analysis tool "Green Guide to Specification"
	• based on:
	  DIN EN ISO 14040:2006, DIN EN ISO 14044:2006,
	  DIN ISO EN 21930:2007
	• for the phase: construction
	alternative: national life cycle analysis system based on DIN EN ISO 14040ff.
	• for the phase: construction, operation and recycling
	• calculation of at least three environmental indicators
	• application of the system has to be confirmed by BRE
		up until now only as a pilot credit:
		life cycle analysis of building components and materials during the whole life cycle of the building (Life Cycle of Building Assemblies and Materials)
		• for the phases: construction, transport, upkeep and maintenance, deconstruction and disposal
		• contents:
		  primary energy demand
		  AP – Acidification Potential
		  GWP – Global Warming Potential
		  Human Health Respiratory Effects Potential
		  ODP – Ozone Depletion Potential
		  EP – Eutrophication Potential

Life cycle costs (LCC)	dependent on system variant; for BREEAM Europe, there is an own criterion, which does not define the calculation method • consideration of the construction phase, operation phase, upkeep, maintenance and recycling • LCC calculation based on the design • period: 25 or 30 years, additional 60 years • consideration of at least two of the following building components: structure, envelope, building services, interior fit-out • additional consideration of energy consumption, reduction of upkeep and maintenance work, longer life expectancy of components, reuse of structural building components	Life cycle costs are not considered. The energy costs are merely considered for the operation phase of the building in the context of the mandatory requirement "EA Pre 2 – Minimum Energy Performance" and the criterion "EA Credit 1 – Optimise Energy Performance" by performing comparisons with reference buildings.

DGNB

DGNB Certificate

DGNB (Deutsche Gesellschaft für Nachhaltiges Bauen – German Sustainable Building Council)

2007

Cooperations:
ÖGNI (Austria)
BGBC (Bulgaria)
DGBC (China)
DGNBH (Hungary)
SGNI (Switzerland)
Thailand Council of Sust. Construction (Thailand)

according to demand

DGNB (Deutsche Gesellschaft für Nachhaltiges Bauen – German Sustainable Building Council)

registered and independent DGNB Auditor training and examination

· design phase: pre-certificate
· commissioning: certificate (following completion)

Bronze (≥ 50 %)
Silver (≥ 65 %)
Gold (≥ 80 %)

observance of predefined fulfilment degree in each category dependent on the rating level

weighting of the individual categories, furthermore use of significance factors for criteria

· Ecological quality
· Economic quality
· Sociocultural and functional quality
· Technical quality
· Process quality
· Site quality

–

DIN V 18599 – Energy efficiency of buildings

various life cycle analysis tools based on the national database Ökobau.dat
· life cycle: 50 years
· based on: DIN EN ISO 14040:2006, DIN EN ISO 14044:2006, DIN 18599
· for the phases: construction, upkeep and maintenance, deconstruction and disposal
· contents:
Global Warming Potential (GWP)
Ozone Depletion Potential (ODP)
Photochemical Ozone Creation Potential (POCP)
Acidification Potential (AP)
Eutrophication Potential (EP)
Primary energy demand of non-renewable energies (PE_{ne})
Total primary energy demand and proportion of renewable primary energy (PE_e)

life cycle costs for a period of 50 years based on the present value in €/m² GFA
· selected construction costs:
cost groups 300 and 400 according to DIN 276
· selected operation costs:
cost groups 300 and 400 according to DIN 18960, costs for energy demand according to DIN V 18599, costs for water consumption and waste water according to DGNB criterion 14 "Domestic water"
· life expectancy of structural components acc. to data on www.nachhaltigesbauen.de and the BMVBS's Guideline for Sustainable Building

4.9

illustrates that different levels of building standards apply in the individual countries and that the rating result expressed as a percentage is not applicable for a universal, content-related comparison of systems.

Weightings

Most assessment tools now work with weighted criteria and categories. The weighting factors reflect the importance of the aspects considered and are redefined with every new version of the rating system. The factors invariably differ according to the building type and the timing of the assessment.

The BREEAM method assesses buildings with so-called credits (points) and section weightings expressed as a percentage, which are then multiplied.

Originally LEED based its assessment on a uniform point system. The individual criteria were not weighted according to their importance but were in due proportion [24]. With the introduction of the version LEED 2009 (V3), the former structure was replaced in order to allow a weighted assignment of points [25].

In the case of the DGNB Certificate, the categories are expressed as a percentage (e.g. environmental, economic, sociocultural quality) and the individual criteria are weighted according to significance factors [26].

Minimum requirements and mandatory prerequisites

With the aim of improving the quality of certifications, numerous sustainability labels have developed mandatory minimum standards and compulsory criteria:
· BREEAM: minimum standards [27]
· LEED U.S.: prerequisites [28]
· DGNB: minimum quality performance [29]
· Green Star: conditional requirements [30]

During the course of a certification process, LEED demands so-called prerequisites in all of the five main categories. The fulfilment of a number of criteria is obligatory, in particular with regard to Energy & Atmosphere and Indoor Environmental Quality. Amongst the prerequisites are:
· The involvement of a Commissioning Expert (Cx) (EA Prerequisite 1: Fundamental Commissioning of Building Energy Systems); in detail this means

involving an expert who is responsible for implementing the commissioning of the respective building according to LEED requirements
· The compliance with ASHRAE Standard 90.1 (building energy efficiency – EA Prerequisite 2: Minimum Energy Performance)
· The compliance with ASHRAE Standard 62.1 (requirements concerning the execution of air-handling systems and air distribution – IE Q Prerequisite 1: Minimum Indoor Air Quality Performance) [31]

Under the British method BREEAM, dependent on the achieved rating level, a specified number of points (minimum standard) must be gained in respect of predefined criteria. The lowest rating level "Pass" requires at least one point against each of the following criteria:
· Commissioning (Man 1)
· High frequency lighting (Hea 4)
· Microbial contamination (Hea 12)

In order to meet the requirements for the certificate "Outstanding" (for BREEAM Offices 2008), it is mandatory to fulfil 14 of the 65 criteria. The criterion "Ene 1: Reduction of CO_2 emissions", in particular, demands a minimum result of 14 points [32].

The DGNB Certificate had also originally considered incorporating compulsory criteria. However, this approach was dismissed during the pilot certification phase. Instead, it was agreed to apply minimum standards for each rating level. If a building is awarded a silver certificate, all aspects have to at least receive a bronze rating, in the case of a gold certificate, all aspects have to at least receive a silver rating.

Certification costs

Sustainable building is often associated with a considerable increase in construction costs. However, reference buildings completed in recent years have confirmed that this certainly does not apply to every project. The earlier sustainability aspects are integrated into the design, the lower the additional costs are for the implementation of a sustainable design and certification. The costs for the certifi-

4.9 Comparison of the systems BREEAM, LEED and DGNB

	BREEAM Offices Version 2008	LEED-NC Version 3.0	LEED-NC Canada Version 1.0	Green Star Office Version 3.0	DGNB NBV Version 2009
100%	Outstanding: ≥ 85%				
90%		Platinum: ≥ 80%			Gold: ≥ 80%
80%	Excellent: ≥ 70%			6 Star: ≥ 75%	
70%		Gold: ≥ 60%			Silver: ≥ 65%
60%	Very Good: ≥ 55%			5 Star: ≥ 60%	
50%	Good: ≥ 45%	Silver: ≥ 50%	Platinum: ≥ 52%	4 Star: ≥ 45%	Bronze: ≥ 50%
		Certified: ≥ 40%	Gold: ≥ 39%		
40%	Pass: ≥ 30%		Silver: ≥ 33%		
30%			Certified: ≥ 26%		
20%					

4.10

	BREEAM	LEED	DGNB
Ecological aspects	• energy • water • materials • emission • waste	• energy and atmosphere • efficient use of water • materials and resources	• impact on global and local environment • use of resources and volume of waste
Economic aspects	• management[1]	–	• life cycle costs • value performance
Social aspects	• health and comfort	• comfort and indoor air quality	• health, comfort, occupant satisfaction
	–	–	• functionality
	• additional credits for innovations	• innovations	• quality of design
	–	• regional aspects	–
Other aspects	–	–	• technical quality
	• management	–	• quality of planning • quality of construction • quality of operation
	• land consumption and site ecology • transport	• sustainable site	• site quality

[1] In the case of BREEAM, the life cycle costs are integrated in the category "Management".

a

	BREEAM Offices 2008 (%)	LEED-NC 2009 (%)	DGNB NBV 2008 (%)
1. Ecology	33.6	31.1	16.3
2. Economy	0	0	23.6
3. Social aspects	2.5	4.6	2.5
4. Energy	23.5	32.2	14.4
5. Health and comfort	19.4	16	16.5
6. Functional aspects	0	0	2.5
7. Technical aspects	1.3	0	9.5
8. Design	1.2	6.9	4.2
9. Process/management	18.5	9.2	10.5
10. Site	not considered[1]	not considered[1]	not considered[1]

[1] The site has not been incorporated in the comparison since this is an aspect which is not weighted in the case of DGNB.

b

4.11

cation of a sustainable property, can be broken down into the following parts (see Impact on construction costs, p. 100ff.).
• Registration and certification fees (payable to the certification body)
• Certification costs (payable to the auditor)
• Addtional construction costs (due to sustainable design aspects)

Generally the certification fees are dependent on the size of the building (e.g. €/m²), the type of building (e.g. office, housing, etc.) and the membership of the client in the respective certification system's organisation. The registration and certification fees of the various rating systems differ considerably (Fig. 5.12, p. 104).

Content-related aspects

With regard to their contents, assessment methods can be differentiated according to systems of the first generation and those of the second. Labels described as first generation give priority to the environmental and energy-efficient aspects of buildings (green building approach), such is the case with BREEAM or LEED. These labels do not yet (LEED) or only partially (e.g. the construction phase in the case of BREEAM) consider the life cycle of the building in the certification process. Systems of the second generation, on the other hand, are based on a holistic performance-oriented approach (sustainable building approach). Alongside the environmental and energy-related criteria, these systems also take account of economic, social, technical and process-oriented aspects in the assessment. They furthermore consider the total life cycle of buildings, this means everything from the manufacture of construction materials, through design and construction to the operation and demolition of the building. This approach is still fairly new and is only applied in very few systems, such as the DGNB Certificate.

Comparison of the rating systems LEED, BREEAM and DGNB [33] at indicator level shows that numerous criteria and indicators are already available to assess the sustainability of buildings. Social aspects are included in addition to environmental and economic ones, thus representing the three pillars of sustainability. However, the individual systems differ in the focus and importance of the assessment and in the selection of criteria and

4.10 Rating levels of international systems
4.11 Comparison of BREEAM, LEED and DGNB's rating systems
   a based on the assessment categories
   b based on the rating versions BREEAM Offices 2008, LEED New Construction 2009 and DGNB New builds and administrative buildings V 2009 with main focus items and weighting factors

indicators (Fig. 4.11). The contents featured by BREEAM, LEED and DGNB can be divided into ten main aspects (Fig. 4.12):

- Ecology: environmental load, materials and resources, waste and water
- Economy: life cycle costs, value stability
- Social aspects: safety and security, barrier-free access, regional and cultural criteria
- Energy: CO_2 emissions, renewable energy, energy efficiency, building services, building envelope
- Health and comfort: thermal comfort, indoor air quality, acoustics, lighting, occupants' extent of control
- Functional aspects: site efficiency, suitability for conversion
- Design: architecture, building-related artwork, innovations
- Technical aspects: fire protection, durability, suitability for upkeep, resistance to weather and environmental hazards
- Process/management: design process, construction process, commissioning, operation
- Location: micro location, traffic connection, suitability for cyclists, neighbourhood, situation in regard of planning law, suitability for extensions, site consumption, biodiversity

The comparison of labels highlights the fact that not all assessment methods follow a holistic approach and that buildings are assessed according to different aspects. These depend to a large extent on the respective national, climatic, cultural and political background. This applies to all assessment categories.
Up until now, the DGNB Certificate, an assessment method of the second generation, is the only one to give priority to the following aspects:

- Economy (e.g. SB 17 Value stability)
- Technology (e.g. SB 33 Fire protection, SB 40 Building's suitability for cleaning, upkeep and maintenance, etc.)
- Function (e.g. SB 27 Efficient use of space, SB 28 Suitability for conversions, etc.)

BREEAM and LEED, on the other hand, include criteria which are not part of the assessment for the DGNB Certificate. These criteria principally concern environmental and site-specific aspects:

- Light pollution
- Reuse of the existing structure or preservation of building stock

- Car parking capacity
- Protection of the natural habitat and the biodiversity
- Innovative features

Economic aspects, in contrast, are increasingly taken into account by systems of the first generation. For example, the calculation of life cycle costs (LCC) is not only an aspect considered in the assessment of the DGNB Certificate, but also one considered by BREEAM. However, whereas the LCC calculation is of considerable importance for the German label (SB 16 Building-related life cycle costs), BREEAM applies a slightly simplified method (Man 12: Life cycle costs), which has not yet been incorporated into all of the assessment schemes.
All three certification systems use additional assessment criteria not yet available to the other systems. In the case of BREEAM, these, to a large extent, country-specific criteria, include the demand for water and electricity sub-meters (Wat 2: Water meter, Ene 2: Submetering of substantial energy use), the application of energy-efficient building services, such as cold stores, lifts, elevators, etc. (Ene 7: Cold storage, Ene 8: Lifts, Ene 9: Escalators & travelling walkways) as well as display of local public transport information (Tra 5: Travel plan) (Fig. 2.7, p. 35).
In the case of LEED, these criteria, for example, concern the utilisation of regional construction materials (MR Credit 5: Regional materials), the smoking prohibition in buildings (IEQ Prerequisite 2: Environmental tobacco smoke [ETS] control) and the use of fuel-efficient vehicles (SS Credit 4.3: Alternative transportation, low-emitting and fuel-efficient vehicles) (Fig. 2.22, p. 43).
It is extremely difficult to establish clear parallels between the criteria. Despite all systems applying similar aspects, there are frequently differences in content, indicators and units. One example is the criterion "CO_2 emissions". The DGNB Certificate assesses the greenhouse gas emissions by using criteria in the category "Environmental quality" (SB 1 Global warming potential, SB 10 Proportion of non-renewable primary energy demand and SB 11 Total primary energy demand and proportion of renewable primary energy). In the case of BREEAM, these criteria are incorporated in the categories Energy (Ene 1: Energy efficiency and Ene 5: Low or zero carbon) and Materials

(Mat 1: Materials specification). LEED covers these criteria in the category Energy and Atmosphere (Criteria: EA Pre 2: Minimum energy performance, EA Credit 1: Optimise energy performance and EA Credit 2: On site renewable energy).
Moreover, the CO_2 emissions are determined with different units:

- BREEAM: CO_2 index (Energy Performance Certificate Rating), kg CO_2 equivalent (during a period of 100 years – GWP 100)
- LEED: kbtu/sf/a (kilo British thermal units per square foot per year), savings of annual energy costs in %
- DGNB: $kWh/m^2_{UFA} \cdot a$, kg CO_2 equivalent/$m^2_{UFA}a$

Similar difficulties have been identified in the number and weighting of criteria concerning a particular issue. The aspect "Visual comfort", for example, highlights this disparity. The British method BREEAM applies a weighting factor of 7% to the aspect of "Visual comfort" and uses five separate criteria for its assessment (Hea 1: Daylighting, Hea 2: View out, Hea 3: Glare control, Hea 4: High frequency lighting and Hea 5: Internal and external lighting levels). By way of contrast, the DGNB Certificate assesses this category with 2.5% (a single criterion: SB 22 Visual comfort) and LEED indeed only with 2.3% (two criteria: IEQ Credit 8.1: Daylight and views – Daylight and IEQ Credit 8.2: Daylight and views – Views). This comparison illustrates once more the cultural and climatic differences of the individual labels and highlights the cultural and political significance of the aspects "Daylight" and "Visual comfort" in the UK.
Within the framework of certifications, all assessment methods draw on already established national design tools. The following list describes the most important assessment modules of the individual certification systems (based on the comparison of: BREEAM Offices 2008, LEED New Construction Version 2009 and DGNB Office and Administrative Buildings Version 2008):

- Energy analysis: BREEAM, LEED and DGNB
- Life Cycle Analysis (LCA): BREEAM and DGNB
- Life Cycle Costs (LCC): BREEAM (not yet integrated in all of the occupancy profiles) and DGNB

These modules have, however, not yet been adopted by all labels in a uniform way and are calculated according to different methods [34].

Energy analysis
With regard to the tools to perform an energy analysis of a building, there are fundamental differences between the assessment methods. Without exception, the eco-label systems make use of national tools, standards and legal regulations, which are especially adapted to the climatic, political and cultural requirements of the respective country:
- BREEAM: Energy Performance Certificate (EPC)
- LEED: ASHRAE Standard 90.1 (2007) – Energy Standard for Buildings Except Low-Rise Residential Buildings
- DGNB: DIN V 18599 – Energy efficiency of buildings

What all systems have in common is an energy assessment of the heating, cooling, hot water production, air conditioning and ventilation plant and the lighting of the building. However, the energy demand in these areas is calculated by using different methods, units and climatic data and then the results are assessed according to different computing procedures and benchmarks. With the Energy Performance Certificate (BREEAM) and the DIN V 18599 (DGNB), BREEAM and the DGNB Certificate have both based their energy analysis on the EU Directive 2002/91/EG (EPBD Energy Performance of Buildings Directive), which was passed in 2002. The LEED system, in contrast, is based on the American ASHRAE Standard 90.1, which is specifically adapted to the statutory requirements concerning the energy efficiency of buildings in the USA [35].

Life cycle analysis (LCA)
Up to now, a life cycle analysis (LCA) is only a requirement for the latest BREEAM and DGNB system variants. LEED admittedly makes some provisions for materials, i.e. certain environmental aspects have to be considered within a LEED certification, for example:

4.12 Comparison of the BREEAM, LEED and DGNB assessment methods based on criteria and indicators

- The implementation of low-emitting materials (VOC) (IEQ Credit 4.4: Low-Emitting Materials)
- Reuse of building components and the implementation of recycled materials (MR Credit 3: Materials Reuse and MR Credit 4: Recycled Content)
- The use of regional materials (MR Credit 5: Regional Materials) and renewable resources (MR Credit 6: Rapidly Renewable Materials)
- The use of certified timber products (FSC Timber) (MR Credit 7: Certified Wood)

These requirements, however, refer exclusively to the choice of material and not to the total life cycle of the building. In order to establish the idea of a life cycle approach in the assessment process and to develop a uniform national standard for the life cycle analysis in the context of LEED certifications, the U.S. Green Building Council set up a workgroup in 2004 and started with a pilot credit (test criterion) in 2009. However, a uniform national basis has not yet emerged [36].
The assessment systems currently apply the following tools and databases to perform the life cycle analysis:
- BREEAM: the life cycle analysis tool Green Guide to Specification
- DGNB: life cycle analysis tools, such as GaBi, LEGEP, BAULOOP etc., which are based on the national databases Ökobau.dat and the Guideline for Sustainable Building (Leitfaden Nachhaltiges Bauen) provided by the Federal Ministry for Transport, Building and Urban Development

In BREEAM, the life cycle assessment is dealt with in the category "Material & Resources" (Mat 1: Materials specification and Mat 2: Hard landscaping and boundary protection) and the Internet tool "Green Guide to Specification" [37] is referred to [38]. The results of the life cycle analysis are assessed in 13 criteria (Fig. 4.9, p. 92) according to predetermined component catalogues and environmental databases. Aspects of relevance range from greenhouse gases and eutrophication to acidification. The results are expressed in units such as kg CO_2 equivalent and then transformed into the categories A+, A, B to E for the BREEAM assessment. To date, the life cycle analysis only refers to the construction materials implemented in the respective building. Further life cycle phases,

such as the operation (energy demand and upkeep) or the demolition are not yet considered.
The DGNB Certificate takes account of the life cycle analysis in the category "Ecological quality". The building is assessed over a specified period (e.g. Version 2009 New office and administrative buildings: 50 years) and considers the phases production, operation and demolition (end-of-life). The values required for the life cycle analysis can be determined by using programmes such as GaBi [39] or LEGEP [40]. The results are presented in units per m^2 and year (e.g. CO_2 equivalent/$m^2_{UFA} \cdot$ a). The energy demand for the operation phase of the building is determined according to DIN V 18599; maintenance and upkeep are defined according to the useful life expectancies incorporated in the Guideline of Sustainable Building (Leitfaden Nachhaltiges Bauen) [41] published by the Federal Ministry for Transport, Building and Urban Development (BMVBS).The data for the production and end-of-life phase is based on national figures, derived from BMVBS' database Ökobau.dat [42].

Life cycle costs
Aspects concerning the life cycle costs are currently only incorporated in the assessment process of the DGNB Certificate and the British method BREEAM. Up to now, LEED only considers economic assessment aspects in criteria which have an impact on the energy demand of buildings. For example, the criterion "EA Credit 1 Optimise Energy Performance" evaluates the percentage of annual savings in energy costs in comparison to a reference building (EA Pre 2: Minimum Energy Performance).
In BREEAM, the life cycle costs are calculated by using a simplified method. However, the results are not assessed according to benchmarks. Merely the fact that an LCC calculation is performed is included in the rating (Man 12: Life cycle cost analysis). The life cycle cost calculation has not yet been included in all of the current system variants, for example in BREEAM Offices 2008, BREEAM Industrial 2008, BREEAM Retail 2008 and BREEAM Multi-residential 2008. In the case of all other variants, such as BREEAM Europe 2009, BREEAM provides a uniform calculation method which considers the building's construction, operation and end-of-life phase. This

method examines two periods, the first ranging between 25 and 30 years and then a second period of 60 years.

The life cycle costs have been incorporated in the sustainability assessment of the DGNB Certificate from the very beginning (Category SB 16: Building-related life cycle costs). They are calculated for each system variant individually based on the so-called present value over a predetermined period in Euro/m$^2_{GFA}$ (e.g. New office and administrative building: 50 years). The present value represents the value of assumed future payments discounted back to the present time, allowing for interest and annual price inflation. The assessment is currently based on the costs for construction (selected costs groups of the DIN 271 "Building Costs") and the costs of operation (selected cost groups of the DIN 18960: "User costs of buildings"). The on-going costs incurred for upkeep and maintenance are determined with reference to the following:

- The calculation method incorporated in the DGNB criterion 16 "Building-related costs in the life cycle"
- The BMVBS' Guideline for sustainable building (Leitfaden Nachhaltiges Bauen (life expectancy of materials)
- The energy demand calculated according to DIN V 18599
- The water demand and sewage volume calculated according to criterion 14 "Domestic water consumption and volume of waste water"

The costs for deconstruction and disposal are not yet incorporated in the current version (V 2009).

References:

[1] König, Holger; Kreißig, Johannes; Kohler, Niklaus; Lützkendorf, Thomas: Lebenszyklusanalyse in der Gebäudeplanung. Munich 2009, p.102
[2] ISO TC59/SC17: Sustainability in building construction. http://www.iso.org/iso/iso_technical_committee?commid=322621; CEN/TC 350: Sustainability of Construction Works. http://www.cen.eu/CEN/sectors/technicalcommitteesworkshops/centechnicalcommittees/Pages/default.aspx
[3] Eßig, Natalie: Nachhaltigkeit von Olympischen Bauten. Stuttgart 2010, p. 284
[4] Schmincke, Eva: OPEN HOUSE. Presentation made during "Consense". Stuttgart 2010
[5] ISO 15392: Sustainability in building construction, general principles
[6] see ref. 1, p. 103
[7] ibid.
[8] CEN/ TC 350: prEN 15978, Sustainability of construction works
[9] see ref. 4
[10] Arndt, Jens; Ebert, Thilo: Der Tower 185 – zweimal auf dem Prüfstand. DBZ 03/2010, p. 68–71
[11] Saunders, Tom: A discussion document comparing international environmental assessment methods for buildings. Watford 2008
[12] see ref. 3, p. 230
[13] see ref. 10
[14] Cole, Raymond J.: Building environmental assessment methods. In: Building Research and Information 27/1999, p. 230–246
[15] Cole, Raymond J., Larsson, Nils: Green Building Challenge 2002. http://greenbuilding.ca/down/gbc2005/GBC2k2/GBC2k2_Manual_A4.pdf
[16] Larsson, Nils: An Overview of SBTool 2007. http://www.iisbe.org/down/sbc2008/SBTool/SBTool_notes_Sep07.pdf
[17] http://www.lensebuildings.com
[18] http://www.openhouse-fp7.eu
[19] SB Alliance: Tools& Research. http://www.sballiance.org
[20] Visier, Jean Christophe: Common Metrics for Key Issues. Presentation made during the SBAlliance Annual Conference 2009. http://www.sballiance.biz
[21] Austrian Institute of Ecology : TQ – Total Quality. Vienna 2002.
[22] see ref. 3, p. 270f.
[23] http://www.cagbc.org
[24] U.S. Green Building Council: LEED Reference Guide for Green Building Design and Construction. Washington 2009
[25] Baumann, Oliver: Grün ist nicht gleich Grün. In: Bauphysik, 02/2009, p. 99–105
[26] Eßig, Natalie: Die Bemessung der Nachhaltigkeit. In: db 05/2009, p. 62–65
[27] see ref. 23
[28] BRE GLOBAL: BREEAM Offices 2008 User's Manual. Watford 2008. http://www.breeam.org/filelibrary/BES5055-3_0_BREEAM_Offices1_2008.pdf
[29] German Sustainable Building Council (DGNB): Manual for new office and administrative buildings V 2009. Stuttgart 2009
[30] http://www.gbca.org.au
[31] see ref. 23
[32] see ref. 27
[33] DGNB V 2008 New office and administrative buildings, BREEAM Offices Version 2008 and LEED-NC Version 2009 (all new builds)
[34] see ref. 3, p. 288ff.
[35] see ref. 24
[36] Scheuer, Chris W.; Keoleian, Greg W.: Evaluation of LEED using Life Cycle Assessment Methods. Michigan 2002. http://www.lcacenter.org/library/pdf/LEED-LCA-Wyly.pdf
[37] http://www.bre.co.uk/greenguide/podpage.jsp?id=2126
[38] see ref. 27
[39] http://www.lbp-gabi.de
[40] http://www.legep.de
[41] http://www.bmvbs.de/SharedDocs/DE/Artikel/B/leitfaden-nachhaltiges-bauen.html
[42] http://www.nachhaltigesbauen.de/baustoff-und-gebaeudedaten/oekobaudat.html

		DGNB	BREEAM	LEED
Ecological aspects	Environmental loads/pollution	▪	▪	▪
	Materials/resources	▪	▪	▪
	Waste	▪	▪	▪
	Water	▪	▪	▪
Economic aspects	Life cycle costs	▪	▪	
	Value stability	▪		
Sociocultural aspects	Safety and security	▪	▪	
	Barrier-free accessibility	▪		
	Regional and social aspects			▪
Energy	CO$_2$ emissions	▪	▪	▪
	Energy efficiency	▪	▪	▪
	Renewable energy	▪	▪	▪
	Energy-efficient building envelope	▪	▪	▪
	Building services	▪	▪	▪
	Energy monitoring	▪	▪	▪
	Submetering		▪	
	Electrical building facilities		▪	
Health and comfort	Thermal comfort	▪	▪	▪
	Indoor air quality	▪	▪	▪
	Acoustic comfort	▪	▪	▪
	Visual comfort	▪	▪	▪
	Occupants' extent of control	▪	▪	▪
Functional aspects	Site efficiency	▪		
	Suitability for conversions	▪		
Technical aspects	Fire protection	▪		
	Durability	▪	▪	
	Suitability for upkeep and repair	▪		
	Resistance to weather and environmental impact	▪		
Design/innovation	Architecture	▪		
	Building-related artwork	▪		
	Innovation		▪	▪
Process/management	Design process	▪	▪	
	Construction management	▪	▪	▪
	Commissioning	▪	▪	▪
	Operation		▪	
Site	Micro location	▪	▪	▪
	Traffic connections	▪	▪	▪
	Suitability for cyclists	▪	▪	▪
	Neighbourhood	▪	▪	▪
	Building regulations	▪		
	Suitability for extensions	▪		
	Land consumption	▪	▪	▪
	Protection of nature and landscape		▪	▪
	Biodiversity		▪	

4.12

Economic aspects of building certification

Alongside the ecological and sociocultural dimensions, the economic dimension is one of the three pillars of sustainability. The objective in economic terms is to minimise the costs throughout the whole life cycle at the same time as maximising the income and retaining the desired functionality of the building. The period of observation is not limited to the construction of a property but considers also the costs, risks and income during the operation phase as well as the deconstruction and disposal of the building at the end of its life cycle.

Despite the fact that only a few certification systems, such as the DGNB Certificate, take full account of the economic dimension of sustainability, the positive financial outcome is what the key players in property management actually expect from a green building certificate. At the end of 2009, Roland Berger Strategy Consultants conducted a survey amongst asset managers in Germany, Austria and Switzerland, and two thirds of those questioned regard value retention, or even value increase, of the property followed by a reduction of energy costs and a minimisation of operating costs as the main benefits of creating and using a sustainable property [1] (Fig. 5.1). It is assumed that the consideration of sustainable principles in the execution and management of a building has a positive effect on the property value and that in future sustainability certificates will play increasingly important roles as value drivers [2] (Fig. 5.2 and 5.3).

With the exception of management costs, the extent to which the monetary advantages can be assessed is limited. In particular, the sociocultural objectives are hereby still only attributed minor significance. This is mainly due to the fact that the social dimension of sustainability and the impact it has on the performance are far more difficult to present as economic figures than, for example, the costs for energy. However, this disregard of sociocultural factors, also from an economic viewpoint, is considered to be shortsighted, since these factors, together with those concerning the functional aspects of buildings, have a significant impact on the wellbeing of the occupants. Research in this area has shown that there is an improvement in staff performance, a reduction of health-related absenteeism and therefore an increase in productivity in office buildings with a pleasant, healthy and comfortable work climate [3, 4].

The majority of players involved believe the production costs for sustainable properties to be higher than those of comparable conventional buildings. On the other hand, these people expect the excess costs to be balanced by lower operating costs and raised income during the life cycle of the building [5]. A worldwide survey amongst property investors and tenants performed by the Royal Institution of Chartered Surveyors (RICS) [6] has shown a certain willingness amongst investors and tenants to accept higher costs of between 3 and 8 % for sustainable buildings (Fig. 5.4, p. 100).

This view is supported by the findings of the earlier mentioned survey by Roland Berger Strategy Consultants, in which 70 % of the clients and investors questioned said they would be prepared to pay a premium of on average 8.5 % for a sustainable property [7]. This figure indicates the economic added value market participants expect from a sustainable property.

The question as to whether a sustainable and possibly certified building is financially more viable than a conventional building has to be determined and answered separately for each individual property. If the decision for a certification is to be based on an economic analysis, the additional costs of complying with the certification conditions must first of all be determined. It is then necessary to look at the other side of the equation and assess the additional income or savings deriving from certification as well as the improved suitability for third-party use. Possible external effects, such as the influence on the productivity as well as potential risks in terms of future statutory requirements, should also be brought into consideration (Fig. 5.5, p. 100).

The period used as the basis for the assessment has a significant impact on the economic added value appropriated to sustainable property management. The majority of companies still look at properties in relation to production and not as long-term strategic investments [8]. As a result, priority is given to construction costs despite the fact that, depending on the period under consideration and the building type, these may represent only a fraction of the building's total costs over the complete life cycle. In the case of office buildings, for example, the construction costs are less than 20 % of the whole.

A building certification maps out the pillars of sustainability (economic, ecological and social constituents). The amount of detail and the emphasis given to certain aspects varies according to the structure and sophistication of the selected rating system. Certifications therefore influence the building design and the costs for the construction of the building as well as the costs and income throughout the whole life cycle of a building. Consideration of the life cycle is a particular feature of sustainable building and it is the focus of attention from the very first idea through to the construction and utilisation and finally the deconstruction of the building. The life cycle is continuously reviewed and optimised in terms of sustainability objectives. The overall aim is to mini-mise the life cycle costs during all life phases and to improve the macro-economic success through applying a holistic approach towards perfecting the construction and operation of the building [9].

The international standard ISO 15686-5 [10], which is part of the programme ISO 15686 "Buildings and Constructed Assets, Service Life Planning", provides the basic guidelines for costs and yields during a building's life cycle. The stand-ard differentiates between specific life cycle costs that are exclusively building-related and life cycle costs that are not building-related but linked in broader terms, namely the external costs and financial income (Fig. 5.7, p. 101). The specific, building-related life cycle costs incorporate costs for:
· Construction, including design and consulting
· Operation
· Upkeep, maintenance and repair
· Demolition and disposal at the end of the property's life cycle

In the case of the DGNB Certificate, the assessment of the economic perform-ance is based on a life cycle analysis of specific, building-related life cycle costs [11]. With regard of "other" costs, which are not specifically building-related (non-construction costs), special attention is paid to:
· Land-related expenditure
· Financing charges
· Administration
· Strategic property management

The costs of a property are offset against the income and receipts from third par-ties (rental income) and sales, which tend to be positively influenced by a sus-tainable building certificate.

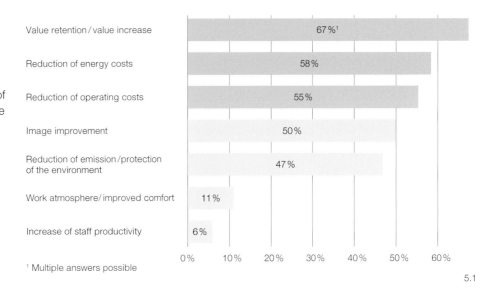

¹ Multiple answers possible

5.1

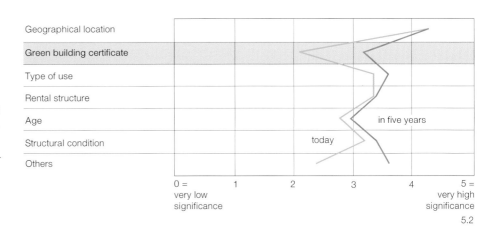

5.2

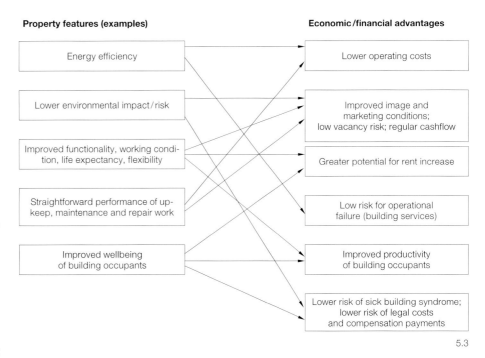

5.3

5.1   Aims of operating a sustainable property (results of a survey performed by Roland Berger Strategy Consultants amongst asset managers in Germany, Austria and Switzerland)
5.2   Current and future drives for the value retention of properties
5.3   Economic advantages of sustainable properties

	Maximum acceptable extra costs		
Country	Tenant/occupant	Investor	Government
All countries	7.2%	6.7%	9.6%
Australia	6%	4%	12%
Canada	8%	5%	14%
Germany	8%	4%	9%
India	7%	6%	5%
Japan	6%	7%	9%
Spain	7%	7%	9%
UAE	7%	6%	10%
USA	6%	6%	12%
UK	6%	6%	12%
China	5%	5%	9%
Brazil	9%	6%	7%
Russia	4%	3%	1%

5.4

Extra effort and expense	Effect
• certification fees • auditor's services • sustainability management • additional certificates and measurements • effort and expense for integrated design approach and design optimisation • systematic commissioning and optimisation of operations • possibly higher construction costs	• lower operating costs • higher rental income • higher resale value • reduced financial charges • longer life expectancy • shorter un-let periods • greater productivity and lower absenteeism • lower risks concerning future regulations in terms of subsequent environmental costs

5.5

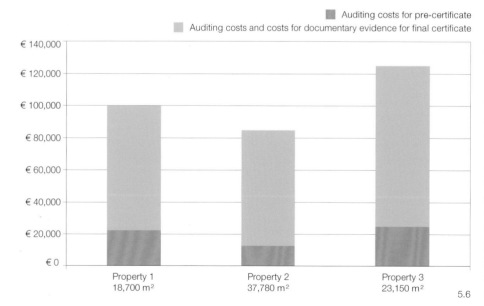

Auditing costs for pre-certificate
Auditing costs and costs for documentary evidence for final certificate

Property 1 18,700 m² — Property 2 37,780 m² — Property 3 23,150 m²

5.6

5.4 Additional price that persons worldwide are willing to pay for a sustainable building (results of a survey performed by the Royal Institution of Chartered Surveyors 2009)
5.5 Comparison of the extra effort and expense for a certification and the effect it has on the building's use
5.6 Costs for the auditor's services and the documentary evidence for a DGNB gold certificate in the case of three office and administrative buildings in Germany. Based on an analysis performed by Fay Projects GmbH, Frankfurt/Main.

DGNB occupancy profile: New office and administration buildings. The costs for the auditor's services include the management of the certification process, the active handling of criteria, the compilation of the project documentation and the submission to the certification body. The costs for the final certificate include the expenses for the performance of: life cycle cost analysis, life cycle analysis, daylight simulation and indoor air measurements.
5.7 Cost structure of a property during its life cycle in accordance with ISO 15686-5

Impact on construction costs

As a rule, certification has an immediate impact on the construction costs of a building. According to DIN 276, the construction costs cover all services and supplies required for the development of the building, including the fit-out consisting of all elements connected to the structure and all technical plant fitted, connected or associated with the building in any other kind of way [12]. In Germany, the costs are structured according to DIN 276. Since all aspects of sustainable building are still generally regarded as a supplementary module, the majority of participants involved automatically associate a certification with additional construction costs.

However, possible added costs are in fact always dependent on the design solution developed specifically for the individual building. The following example illustrates the point: the primary energy demand of a building can either be reduced in a cost-intensive way by using complex technical systems or additional components, such as large areas of photovoltaic cells (PV cells), or by incorporating a well thought out integrated technical concept, which utilises the natural energy sources of the immediate surroundings to provide daylight, passive heating and cooling into the overall building concept. The extent of technical plant can frequently be reduced in comparison to a conventionally designed building leading to a drop in investment costs and the regular costs incurred through operation during the building's utilisation phase. In order to assess the impact of a certification on the construction costs, it is necessary to define a reference value. It should describe the construction costs which would be incurred for such a building without certification. The choice of the reference value has a considerable impact on the proportion of excess or reduced costs which must be included in the budget for a certification. It is furthermore necessary to differentiate between a property market or property sector view and a building-related assessment. In the case of a global consideration, the reference value corresponds to the average construction costs of comparable reference properties in a defined market environment. In contrast, there is the individual, building-related approach. In this case, the reference value refers to the costs of the building to be certified excluding the costs for additional measures required to secure certification. Country-specific building standards can differ considerably. It is therefore difficult to compare the additional construction costs incurred through certification from one country to the next. However, the impact of a certification on the construction costs generally depends on a number of factors:

- Type and scope of the certification system (e.g. LEED, DGNB, BREEAM, EU GreenBuilding)
- Aspired rating level within the selected system (e.g. bronze, silver, gold)
- Individual priorities in the assessment in addition to the minimum requirements or obligatory criteria
- Timing within the project process of integrating sustainable design objectives
- Experience in sustainability management, the quality of the consultants' advice and the dedication of the design team
- General design standard and the client's aspirations

A study performed by the consulting firm, Davis Langdon, has revealed that the costs for a sustainable building are only marginally higher than those for a conventional building. For this purpose, the 2006-conducted survey analysed 221 buildings in the USA. 83 buildings had been completed according to the requirements of LEED; the remaining 138 buildings, offering similar functions and standards, had not been certified according to LEED [13]. Most of the certified buildings involved in the study had been completed with budgets similar to those required by comparable conventional buildings with similar fit-out and equipment.

The earlier the decision for a certification is made within the development process of a property, the greater the possibility is to influence the impact on the investment costs. An integrated planning approach taken at an early stage with a long-term perspective allows for incorporation of sustainability features at much less expense than integrating costly technical supplementary components at a later stage.

Design and consultancy fees
In order to obtain certification, the evidence, calculations and documents must be prepared and compiled in accordance with the documentation requirements of the selected certification system and submitted to the certification body for review. There are considerable differences between the various systems regarding the style and scope of documents. The details concerning these differences are described in "Certification – the systems in detail" (p. 30–75) and in "Design process and documentation requirements" (p. 76–85). In many cases, it is possible to draw on documents which have to be compiled during the course of every project design. The DGNB system, for example, makes use of the legally required document confirming compliance with the German Energy Saving Directive for the assessment of eight criteria. Even so, there is a need for further evidence related specifically to the certification system selected, such as the performance of a life cycle analysis for the DGNB Certificate or, in the case of LEED, a document confirming that the energy efficiency complies with the ASHRAE Standard 90.1 [14].

In terms of a target-oriented approach, it is recommended to involve a sustainability consultant to accompany and support the design and construction process. The consultant gives the client advice regarding the desired rating level, accompanies the project team during the design and construction phase in view of the system's criteria, coordinates the procedure of furnishing proof, compiles the application documents and submits them to the appropriate certification body for the review. Depending on the complexity and the requirements of the selected certification system, the consultant can either be a member of the design team, the client, a sustainability consultant or auditor specifically trained for this purpose. In all of these cases, additional work arises and costs are incurred. The costs are dependent on the selected certification system and project-specific criteria such as type and size of building.

Certification systems do not only rate sustainable buildings, they also provide a sound basis for sustainable building, encourage an integrated planning approach and are effective tools which help define and achieve design objectives. The individual sustainability criteria of the selected system are considered at an early stage and the requirements are determined for the building concerned. The criteria support the decision-making

Whole-life cost (WLC)

1. Non-construction costs

- costs for premises and site preparation
- financing charges
- costs for strategic property management
- utilisation fees
- administrative expenses
- tax
- other costs

2. Income

- income and earnings from sales
- earnings from third parties during operation
- tax on income and earnings
- operating trouble
- other forms of income and earnings

3. Externalities

4. Life cycle cost (LCC)

a) Construction

- design and consultancy fees
- site costs
- construction costs
- costs for fit-out or refurbishment
- tax
- other costs

b) Operation

- rent
- insurance
- costs for external surveillance
- utilities
- tax
- other costs

c) Maintenance

- costs for upkeep and maintenance management
- costs for alterations or renovations during operation
- costs for repair and renewal of smaller components or system parts
- costs for system renewal and exchange of larger components
- costs for cleaning
- costs for upkeep and maintenance of exterior landscape
- costs for redesigning the fit-out
- tax
- other costs

d) End of life

- surveying costs
- costs for demolition and disposal
- costs for the restitution of the original condition
- tax
- other costs

5.7

processes and, at the same time, define the required standards for all participants involved in the design and the construction project.

An integrated design approach is a fundamental requirement to do justice to the complexity of sustainable building and, above all, to identify economic solutions through consideration of various design options in a multidisciplinary work environment. Instead of serial solutions for an individual scheme, the aim of integrated design is to develop a comprehensive, all-embracing concept. This approach requires good coordination between all project participants. Due to measures necessary to encourage the integrated design approach and the need for full and effective communication between team members, this process is more expensive and labour-intensive than a conventional design process with a serial structure. In order to meet the complex requirements of a sustainable building's design, a large number of concepts and variants are drawn up and examined, exceeding the scope of a conventional project's design and construction. This, for example, includes the drawing up of a water supply and waste water concept or the preparation of a comprehensive energy concept. The extra effort and expense has to be rewarded and is therefore regarded as an additional cost item. However, due to the synergies

that can be created through good coordination, the extra effort and expense invested during the design process is frequently compensated for by a positive influence on the construction and operating costs.

The earlier the measures to optimise the building in terms of sustainability are performed and integrated in the design process of a project, the less expensive it is to implement these and maximise the cost-saving potential.

Auditing costs
In the case of DGNB and BREEAM, it is obligatory to include an auditor or assessor in the certification process. LEED does not express this obligation, however, it is recommended to involve an experienced LEED consultant (LEED Accredited Professional) with the appropriate system know-how in the project. The auditor is not only responsible for offering advice and compiling documents, but also for controlling all processes. The services generally include the following tasks:
- Supporting the client in defining the objectives of building features in regard to the aspired rating level
- Evaluating the design and construction solutions
- Instructing the design team and the construction companies in preparing the required documents

- Compiling the project documentation unless this is performed by the design team
- Submitting the documents to the certification body
- Communicating with the certification body
- In the case of BREEAM, confirming that the design approach and intentions concerning the project are actually implemented on site

The fees for the auditor vary according to the selected system, the user profile, the scope of services (active or passive processing of the system's individual criteria), the size of the property, type and number of different building functions, the auditor's experience and the difficulties attributed to the particular design task. The fees are determined individually by the auditor for the specific property. The appointment is usually based on a lump sum agreement. An analysis of auditors' fees for three construction projects completed by the Frankfurt-based Fay Projects GmbH highlights the differences between the projects' auditing fees for the DGNB pre-certificate and the DGNB final certificate. Alongside the auditor's actual services, the auditing costs for the final certificate include the compilation of further documents which are obligatory for the certification of these specific construction projects. The analysed projects are properties in Germany which have either received or are striving for a gold rating (Fig. 5.6, p. 100).

The fees for a BREEAM Assessor for the certification of buildings in the UK vary between approximately £5,000 and £50,000 (€6,000 and €60,000) depending on the scale of the task and project [15].

Costs for sustainability management
Alongside the know-how concerning the application of the selected certification system, a sustainable building concept with a good rating requires multidisciplinary expertise, which must be integrated in the design and construction phase of the building. The expert skills are required during the design and construction stages; especially in the fields of energy and climate design, building services, building physics, building technology and building operation. It is furthermore necessary to properly integrate the certification process into the design and

Type of document	DGNB	BREEAM	LEED
Life cycle analysis acc. to DIN EN ISO 14040 / 14044	■	(■)	
Life cycle cost calculation	■	(■)	
Air quality monitoring for formaldehyde and TVOC acc. to DIN ISO 16000-3, 5 and 6	■		(■)
Determination of airtightness in buildings acc. to DIN EN 13829	(■)	(■)	
Documentation of the applied materials and auxiliary materials	■	■	■
Thermal zone simulation acc. to DIN EN 15251	(■)	(■)	
Calculation of reverberation time DIN 18041	(■)		
Waste management plan during the construction period		(■)	(■)
Building energy simulation acc. to ASHRAE Standard 90.1		(■)	■
Functional quality assurance and systematic commissioning	(■)	(■)	■
Compilation of an erosion and sediment control plan			■

■ obligatory (■) optional

5.8

5.8 Additional documentary evidence needed for DGNB, BREEAM and LEED certifications
5.9 Comparison of certification fees for the system variant "New office and administration buildings" in the case of BREEAM, DGNB and LEED

(US$ 1.3 /€; £0.87 /€; as of March 2010)
5.10 Annual subsequent construction costs in per cent of the construction costs
5.11 Cumulative total costs for various building types during the building's life cycle

construction phase in terms of an appropriate cost, time and quality management plan.

Costs for additional documents, calculations and metering
The documentation requirements of the certification systems determine the various items of documentary evidence, calculations and metering records required. The type of document and the scope depend especially on the selected certification system and the aspired rating. As a rule, the form of the documentation is based on that demanded for conventional design processes in the country of the system's origin. The documents required by DGNB and LEED providing evidence of the energy efficiency are an example for this purpose. The German DGNB system uses the calculation method mandatory in Germany under the Energy Saving Directive as a basis to assess the energy efficiency; LEED bases its calculations on the ASHRAE Standard 90.1, which also serves as evidence to the approving authority for all construction projects in the USA. If LEED is used for construction projects outside the USA, proof according to the ASHRAE Standard 90.1 must be provided in addition. Fig. 5.8 shows an extract from a list of additional documents normally to be provided for building certifications performed in Germany.

Certification fees
The rating systems' agencies charge a fee for the certification. The level and structure of fees differ according to the chosen system (Fig. 5.12, p. 104). They are generally dependent on the selected system variant and usually also the size of the property.
In some cases, such as DGNB and LEED, a reduction is granted if the client or the auditor is a member of the respective agency. The fees cover the time and effort needed to review the submitted documents, the issue of the pre-certificate and final certificate, the onward development of the system and the general overhead expenses of the agency. Fig. 5.9 shows a comparison of fees for three different building sizes for the rating systems DGNB, BREAM and LEED.

Impact on operating costs
In the life cycle of a property, the largest portion of costs is incurred during the operation phase and far exceeds the con-

System	5,000 m² (GFA)		20,000 m² (GFA)		50,000 m² (GFA)	
	Euro	Euro/m²$_{GFA}$	Euro	Euro/m²$_{GFA}$	Euro	Euro/m²$_{GFA}$
BREEAM	2,910	0.58	2,910	0.15	2,910	0.06
DGNB	11,100	2.22	27,600	1.38	34,500	0.69
LEED	3,404	0.68	10,846	0.54	24,000	0.48

a

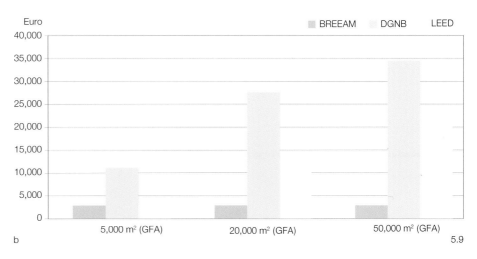

b   5.9

Building type	Annual subsequent construction costs in % of the construction costs	Years
Administration building	8.5%	11–12
Production building	10%	10
Residential building	0.5–2%	20–50
School and kindergarten	31%	3–4
Hospital	26%	4
Indoor swimming pool	21%	4–5
Gymnasium	17%	5–6
Open-air swimming pool	15%	6–7
Transportation facilities	10%	10

5.10

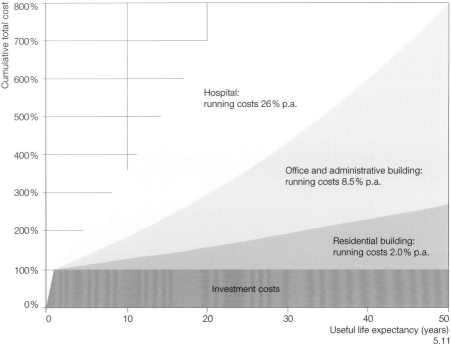

5.11

DGNB fees

Size of property (GFA in m²)	<4,000 m²	4,000–20,000 m²	20,000–80,000 m²	> 80,000 m²
Pre-certificate review: definition of objectives for building features	€4,000	€4,000 + (GFA - 4,000) × €0.35/m²	€9,600 + (GFA - 20,000) × €0.06/m²	€13,000
Certificate review: definition of objectives for building features	€6,000	€6,000 + (GFA - 4,000) × €0.75/m²	€18,000 + (GFA - 20,000) × €0.17/m²	€28,000

Figures without member discount, as of April 2010, system variant: New Office and Administrative Building 2009, pre-certificate is optional

LEED fees

Size of property (GFA in m²)	< 4,650 m²	4,650–46,500 m²	> 46,500 m²
Registration	US$1,200	US$1,200	US$1,200
Pre-certificate (only for LEED-CS) review: definition of objectives for building features	US$4,250	US$4,250	US$4,250
Design submittal review of design-relevant criteria	US$2,250	GFA × US$0.484/m²	US$22,500
Construction submittal review of design-relevant criteria after commissioning	US$750	GFA × US$0.161/m²	US$7,500
Simultaneous review of design and construction-relevant criteria after commissioning	US$2,750	GFA × US$0.592/m²	US$27,500

Figures without member discount, as of April 2010, pre-certificate is optional only for LEED-CS, conversion from imperial to metric units, rounded

BREEAM fees

Size of project (GFA in m²)	all property sizes
Design and procurement review review of design-relevant criteria	£1,500
Post construction review review of construction-relevant criteria	£1,030
Post construction assessment simultaneous review of design and construction-relevant criteria	£1,500

Certification costs for the system variant BREEAM International, as of April 2010

5.12

Cost category	OSCAR 2008 parameters in accordance with rented floor space (Euro/m²a)	DGNB impact on cost category	BREEAM impact on cost category	LEED impact on cost category
Infrastructure service				
Cleaning and upkeep	0.25	▪		
Safety and security	0.31			
Technical service				
Operation	0.29	▪	▪	▪
Maintenance and repair	0.42	▪	▪	
Utilities, local rates and taxes				
Heat	0.46	▪	▪	▪
Electricity	0.33	▪	▪	▪
Water supply and disposal, incl. rainwater	0.12	▪	▪	▪
Waste disposal costs	0.09	▪	▪	▪
Other operating costs				
Property management (staff)	0.25			
Property tax, other charges	0.48			
Insurance	0.14			
Total	**3.14**			
Proportion of operating costs influenced (in relation to OSCAR 2008)		62%	54%	41%

5.13

5.12 BREEAM, DGNB and LEED certification and registration fees for the system variant new office and administration building without member discount (each in their respective currency, as of April 2010)

5.13 Operating costs per m² of rented floor space in an office building according to the OSCAR 2008 survey; furthermore the proportion of operating costs which can be influenced by the different certification systems

struction costs of the building. From Fig. 5.10 (p. 103), it is evident that the accumulated operating costs of an administrative building reach the costs for construction within only eleven to twelve years [16]. The operating costs include all of the expenses associated with the supply of energy and other consumable goods as well as the upkeep and operation of the structure during the building's total life cycle. In Germany, the operating costs are defined either as a sum of costs according to DIN 18960 "User costs of buildings" and the building-independent cost groups accounted for in GEFMA 200 [17] or they are calculated according to DIN 32736 [18] (Fig. 5.11, p. 103).

The high environmental quality of certified buildings, achieved through the generally higher energy efficiency, the use of renewable energy sources and the reduction of water consumption, help to reduce the costs for the utilities (operating supplies). A comprehensive survey of 60 LEED-certified buildings in the USA has, amongst other things, shown that these require approximately 25–30% less energy during their operation phase than comparable conventional buildings [19]. These results are not directly applicable to the German market since standards concerning energy requirements, construction methods and the geographical location have a large impact on the energy costs.

However, it is not only the costs for the utilities that are positively influenced and, depending on the scope of the selected rating system's assessment and the focus of the certification, the expenditure for cleaning, upkeep, operation, maintenance and repair can also be reduced. The intention of an easy to clean and low-maintenance building is not only to reduce the respective costs, but also to ensure the materials have a long lifespan. Fig. 5.13 lists, by way of example, the different categories of operating costs according to GEFMA for an average administration building based on the analysis "OSCAR 2008" for ancillary costs in office buildings. Based on the figures shown, the three systems DGNB, LEED and BREEAM have a significant influence on approximately 40–60% of the operating costs.

Impact on costs at the end of the building's lifespan

The costs for the deconstruction and the disposal of a property at the end of its useful lifespan are currently only considered under certain circumstances, for example in the case of buildings designed and constructed for a short service life or temporary buildings. Due to the, on average, high life expectancy of buildings, most of the building materials and components applied today do not become available as demolition waste and therefore as residual or reusable waste until 50 to 100 years after completion. Today, manufacturers in many sectors of the industry are bound by regulations to observe minimum proportions for reuse and the ability to recover and recycle components and construction materials. According to the EU Directive 2005/64/EG, new motor vehicles, for example, must satisfy a requirement that, based on the weight, at least 85% of a vehicle is reusable and/or recyclable [21]. In the future, a similar regulation could be introduced for properties since approximately 50% [22] of all waste is attributed to the construction industry. The DGNB has drafted some initial requirements in its current certification system regarding a verifiable recycling and waste disposal concept which addresses the subsequent usage of the construction's components. In this regard, the financial responsibilities for the controlled deconstruction and disposal also need to be determined. There is a distinct possibility that it will become necessary to submit a recycling and waste disposal concept as part of the application at the design stage of the building. Easily dismountable, separable and recyclable constructions will in future lead to cost advantages at the end of a building's lifespan.

Impact on income and earnings

The income and earnings are, in a broad sense, also part of the life cycle costs. The income can be separated into regular income, for example rental income in the case of let properties, and irregular income, for example through the sale of a building.

Whereas income is regarded as the receipt of payments, earnings are the result of achievements in terms of business management. The earnings must therefore be balanced with the expenditures; the difference between the two figures is referred to as yield.

A building certificate evidently influences the income and therefore also the earnings since it has a fundamental impact on the characteristics of a building. The question is whether it is the certification itself or the special features of the building achieved through the certification which have this impact on the income and earnings. If it is the certificate itself, the question arises as to how to distinguish between the various certification systems and the corresponding rating levels (e.g. bronze, silver and gold).

Rental income

The findings of surveys, for example those performed in the USA, which record up to 30% higher rents in the case of certified buildings [23], cannot simply be applied to Germany. Due to the relatively low number of certified buildings and the short period since the introduction of the certification system, a general trend towards higher rents in certified buildings has not yet been discerned in Germany. The majority of buildings certified according to current systems are still in their design or construction phase. For this reason, it is difficult to determine the response of the leasing market. Furthermore, it is necessary to exclude all buildings, which have been certified solely at the tenant's request.

In order to provide evidence on their corporate social responsibility (CSR), international-operating companies, in particular, have committed themselves to rent only certified buildings. A higher rent is generally not paid, since other market factors, such as location, quality and number of properties available, have a stronger influence on the price than the certification itself. A rental income, determined by the market, is not applicable to certified buildings occupied by the owner, such as the Federal Environmental Agency in Dessau.

Surveys amongst market participants have confirmed a certain willingness to pay higher rents for sustainable buildings, however, this appears to be slightly theoretical at the moment. Experience over recent months suggests that it is generally only possible to obtain highest rents for certified buildings in prime locations, although this may also be a function of the current financial situation. This therefore does not imply a rent increase due to certification, but the prevention of a rent reduction, as seen for buildings not certified.

However, if only the net rent is considered, i.e. the rent without service charges, it is actually possible to detect an increase. Due to the low service charges, for example for the heating, and a constant level of gross rent, the proportion of net rent rises. The result for let investment properties is therefore a higher return on capital if measures are taken, for example, to improve the energy efficiency in buildings.

Value appreciation
of certified properties
Since green building certificates have a positive influence on the quality of a property and its features are presented in a transparent way, it can be assumed that sustainability labels also have an impact on the value of a property. Research conducted in 2005 led to the conclusion that sustainable features generate additional market value for a property. The difference between this value generated through sustainable features and the value assigned to conventional parts of the building is referred to as "Green Value". According to the RICS, "Green Value is the net additional value obtainable by a green building in the market" [24] (Fig. 5.14).
According to §194 BauGB, the building value is nothing else but the market value. It refers to the price for which a property

should exchange on the date specified in a normal business transaction. A property evaluation is necessary in the case of a sale or forced sale at public auction in order to determine the price of the property. It is furthermore essential as a prerequisite to assessing the value for lending purposes when a mortgage is required. The means to determine the added value of sustainable building features is currently still limited.
Consideration is now being given to application of established valuation methods, such as the hedonic price method, to sustainable building features. However, it is difficult to apply this in practice since there is a lack of reliable statistical information providing evidence as to features which have contributed towards an increase of a certain property's selling price.
When using traditional valuation methods for the assessment of certified commercial properties, the discounted cash flow is a fundamental element. It incorporates quantitative aspects such as the gross annual income, the operating costs, the remaining life expectancy and the risk-adjusted real estate interest rate. However, due to the limited experience in transactions for certified properties, it is currently not possible to establish a relationship between the certification system, the achieved rating and the percent-

age of value increase (such as a Gold LEED certificate increases the building value by 5%).
It goes without saying, that there are also sustainable properties, built according to the sustainability criteria of various rating systems, whose features have not been documented, reviewed and certified. The problem in the case of these buildings is the lack of transparency and documentation, and, although certain features may well be present, the project participants might not yet be aware of them. Nevertheless, these buildings are generally of greater value than conventional properties, despite the absence of a certificate.

Government funding and
tax incentive schemes
In Germany, there are currently no tax concessions or government funds to encourage and facilitate sustainable building or, more specifically, the full range of sustainability. Instead, there are funding schemes to support the implementation of specific technologies and energy-saving measures in general, especially those concerning existing building stock.
These public funding schemes are to a large extent intended for private homes and small and medium-size businesses (SMBs), and their duration is more often than not limited.

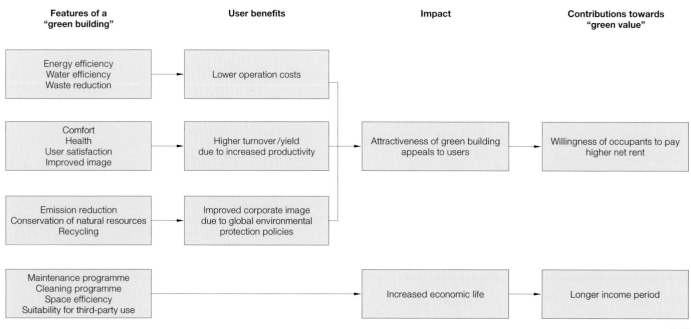

5.14 Impact the features of a (certified) sustainable building have on the property value

In Germany, the groups currently showing the greatest interest in green building certifications are investors and large property companies. Thus, the funding schemes provided for certifications are usually not available for these groups. The following authorities and offices offer financial support:

- BAFA (Federal Office of Economics and Export Control)
- KfW Group (formerly known as: Credit Institute for Improvement)
- Towns, communities and utilities

Non-construction costs

According to ISO 15686-5, the non-construction costs cover, amongst other things, the costs for the land and financing. The impact certifications have on the non-construction costs differs considerably and is dependent on the rating system selected and the actual property.

Land price

At a first glance, certifications have no direct influence on the land price. Other factors, such as the location, far outweigh the impact a certification has on the land price. The owner or project developer will generally not select a certain plot due to an anticipated green building certification. Instead the micro and macro locations with their various factors (e.g. vicinity to amenities, demand for rental space, vicinity to the local transport system, local environment, etc.) are of much greater importance.

Plots with contaminated ground can, in contrast, appreciate in value due to a certification. Since the use and restitution of formerly contaminated ground (land recycling or brownfield redevelopment) is rated positively by the certification systems, these plots have actually become economically attractive for developers. However, the costs for the disposal or decontamination of soil, in the main, exceed the savings achieved through certification. This alone does therefore not lead to an economic advantage.

Financing charges

It goes without saying that the financing charges are influenced by a certified building. Financing charges include the costs for the provision of part of the investment sum by a third party, usually a bank, and are especially important when it comes to the construction of the building. Since most projects, both private and commercial, are hardly ever covered entirely by equity capital, financing charges, which depend on interest rates, loan duration and loan volume, play a major role in the total cost of the project development and construction work.

At the present time, the impact of a green building certification on the financing charges is unpredictable, and there is a lack of representative values based on past experience. Nevertheless, it has been observed that more favourable loan conditions or higher loan sums are sporadically granted for certified properties. As mentioned in "Value appreciation of certified properties" (p. 105f.), there is a direct connection between the value of a sustainable building and the financing charges. A higher real property value (value of the land together with the value of the property thereon) is an important factor of influence in this context, due to the better structural quality deriving from sustainable objectives. A higher market value can also be achieved through sustainable, in this case long-term, rentals or a higher selling price of the property.

In contrast to the market value, these features do not yet influence the fair market value of the property as calculated according to prescribed procedures. Financial institutions, however, have the possibility, on a limited scale, to consider the special features of the sustainable and/or certified property when calculating the loan value, which is the basis for financing the development. Although, the question remains as to which factors cause financial institutions to grant more favourable conditions for a certified property.

In investment property financing, the indirect factors usually have a significant impact on the property valuation and therefore the financing charges. Alongside the already quoted higher net rent and the impact the certification has on the earnings, it is necessary to mention the lower maintenance and upkeep expenses and the longer economic life. The risk of losing rental income is decreased due to the greater attractiveness, the better flexibility and fungibility (suitability for third-party use) of the property. This aspect is, for example, considered in the DGNB Certificate. In the context of the mortgage application, a limited or nonexistent suitability for third-party use is generally regarded as a reason for the credit institution to reject lending.

Alongside these more commercial factors, the quality assurance and documentation of building features achieved through certification play an important role. This tool also helps to reduce the risk and enables the bank granting the loan to either offer more favourable terms and conditions or a higher loan amount.

However, since banks are subject to the control of a supervisory body (in Germany this is the BaFin, Federal Financial Supervisory Authority), they are not necessarily permitted to make a choice on loan terms and conditions. On the contrary, the creditor is then obliged to explain to the supervisory body why they are offering more favourable loan terms and conditions for a certified property. At the end of the day, this is only possible by providing documentation of the respective features which have an immediate impact on the service charges, the expense of upkeep and maintenance or the minimisation of risks, such as energy efficiency or greater flexibility.

Administrative expenses and strategic property management

According to the terms of ISO 15686-5, the administrative expenses include, amongst other things, the costs for commercial facility management. The impact of certification systems on these expenses is identifiable through the systematic and comprehensive building documentation, which differs in scope and depth according to the selected rating system. The provision of systematically structured, up-to-date and above all comprehensive building documents (e.g. maintenance manuals, plans, manuals for occupants and operators, material and product lists) can influence the administrative expenses considerably.

Documents prepared to meet the needs of facility management simplify matters for the administration. These can, for example, include details of the surfaces requiring cleaning with their respective specifications and, in addition, the specific cleaning instructions of the individual surfaces. Comprehensive and up-to-date building documentation can reduce the organisational costs and help to avoid excess costs especially in the case of conversions, alterations and refurbishments.

Furthermore, the strategic property management costs include costs for acquisition, sale and removal (infrastructural building management). A building documentation that is up-to-date and broad in scope is of great value in this context.

Information concerning special building features and qualities, which must normally be ascertained and compiled during the course of a property transaction through a process of due diligence (technical and functional inspection before making an investment), in the ideal case, is already available in adequate form. This documentation will admittedly never be a substitute for an on-site property inspection with assessment of any damage and the state of maintenance work undertaken. However, the documentation does facilitate, for example, research regarding the type of construction materials used and therefore also possible harmful substances, the type of quality-ensuring measures (sound metering, etc.) performed and the scope of structural work executed during the useful life of the building.

The building documentation reduces the buyer's risk since it includes comprehensive information concerning the building's construction and characteristic features that have been reviewed by a third independent body. The fact that positive features are confirmed can lead to a minimised risk surcharge, and a higher selling price may well be achieved as a result. Besides, the costs for the property transaction are reduced since the time and effort required for due diligence is lower.

Externalities

Externalities are expenses that are not immediately related to the costs of the investor or operator of the building. Although they are associated with the property, they are usually beyond the normal limits of an average economic assessment. Examples of externalities are subsequent environmental costs including the removal of a building's environmental load or the impact improved indoor air quality has on salaries and wages, but also the benefits for corporate image and the enhanced market potential. Externalities draw attention to possible cost risks and also highlight potential financial advantages in connection with the property in the near future.

Subsequent environmental costs
Costs are incurred to correct any negative impact a building has on the environment. Today these are to a large extent still borne by the general public. These are damages affecting ground, air, ground and surface water caused by materials used in the building or emissions, such as carbon dioxide, which lead to an accumulation of greenhouse gases in the atmosphere and therefore to an increase of temperature in the air layers near the ground. Most certification systems place great emphasis on the ecological dimension of sustainability, and, in practice, this leads to a considerable reduction in negative effects on the environment with consequent savings in costs for corrective measures. As a result, the risk of costs being levied later for environmental damage are reduced, for example introduction of a special tax or, in the case of carbon dioxide emissions, in the form of emission trading.

Impact of a healthier working environment on the productivity
Good indoor air quality is the basis for a positive and performance-enhancing work environment. A number of factors affect the indoor air quality. In particular, certification systems encourage a healthy work and living environment (e.g. ensuring a good indoor air quality by selecting non-odorous and low pollutant construction materials or improved use of daylight), high user comfort (thermal comfort, visual comfort, acoustic comfort, extent of user control on surroundings) and user convenience (e.g. place to retreat). Studies have shown that absenteeism and the number of sick-days are reduced in sustainable buildings. They furthermore describe the positive influence of a healthy and friendly work environment on long-term productivity [25]. We spend almost 90% of our time in enclosed rooms. The demand for healthy indoor space, together with a comfortable environment, is therefore essential and will continue to gain significance over the next years [26]. The benefits of increased productivity are usually not considered in feasibility or life cycle analyses.
The following "hypothetical" calculation describes the economic effect of a productivity increase of 1.5% brought about by the occupants due to an improvement of the indoor air quality:
A 1.5% increase in productivity corre-

sponds to a daily working time of approximately 7.5 minutes. In terms of a year, this increase of productivity corresponds to an additional working time of approximately 30 hours. At an average wage of € 50 per working hour, the company is able to save € 1,500 per year per employee. Based on an area requirement of 30 m² per employee, this yield in productivity, in terms of square metres, corresponds to an annual saving of € 50/m²a.
This example demonstrates that the impact on the employees' costs can be far in excess of the operation costs of the building.

Conclusion

The economic benefits of a sustainable property in comparison to a conventional building are implicit in the definition of sustainability, which puts economic quality on an equal footing with ecological and social quality. The aim of a life cycle analysis is to determine that the financial advantages (lower costs during the operation phase, higher income and productivity) achieved through sustainable properties exceed the additional costs incurred through their construction. In a study, Flatz [27] determined that operation costs that are 10% lower over a period of 30 years justify a 25% increase in construction costs. However, numerous studies have shown that additional costs need not be incurred when constructing sustainable buildings and that these can actually be completed with a similar cost budget to comparable, conventional buildings if planned intelligently and a holistic integrated planning approach is applied. This highlights the great economic potential of sustainable properties. Current and future property management surveys will have to take on the challenge of quantifying these economic advantages [28]. The necessary transparency and means to compare the characteristic features of sustainable properties are being provided by green building certificates.

Relevance of certificates in the market according to property management experts

Tajo Friedemann

Extreme climate conditions, rising commodity prices, the precarious energy situation, stricter statutory requirements, demographic change, a shift in public awareness and changes in supply and demand will continue to have an increasing impact on the value development, marketability and profitability of properties.
During the course of the last market downturn, the majority of businesses involved in property management grasped the significance of this economic trend. And quite a few market participants have acknowledged the increasing importance of sustainability in everyday business (Fig. 5.15).
Despite this changing awareness, most market players, however, still lack convincing answers or even a clear action plan which they can use effectively in response to this trend. Relatively few market participants have responded to this growing pressure by actually showing a positive interest in the range of products provided by certification systems. Institutional investors, in particular, regard certifications as a suitable first step to adjust early to the changes in supply and demand brought about by the development of sustainable market segments. In the case of new build and refurbishment projects, marketing aspects are generally the main motive. When it comes to existing building stock, value protection and the optimisation of operation costs are also good reasons to systematically record and clearly describe sustainable building qualities in a comprehensive way. The role of certification systems and their application to remain competitive in future markets is subject to much debate. Investors naturally question the time and effort required for the documentation, although it does appear to be justified in the case of large new build or refurbishment projects. The application of complex rating systems, together with the time and expense the assessment of existing building stock involves, are not always worthwhile in comparison to the benefits they actually secure. Especially in association with existing building stock, the relevance of established certification systems in the market is clearly limited.

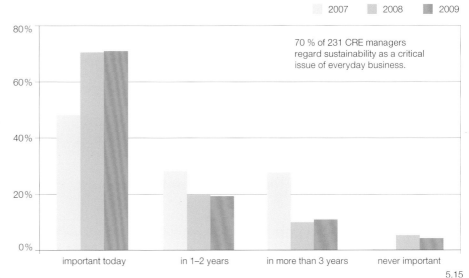

70 % of 231 CRE managers regard sustainability as a critical issue of everyday business.

important today · in 1–2 years · in more than 3 years · never important

2007 · 2008 · 2009

5.15

For a sustainable property, I am willing to pay...

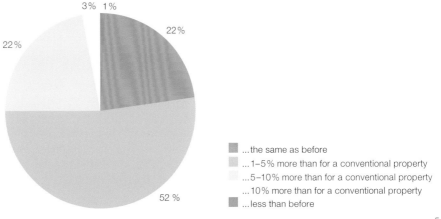

- ...the same as before
- ...1–5% more than for a conventional property
- ...5–10% more than for a conventional property
- ...10% more than for a conventional property
- ...less than before

5.16

Outperformance of certified and non-certified properties[1]

Study performed by	Rent markup	Purchase price markup	
Fuerst, McAllister	11.8%	11.4%	Franz Fuerst, Patrick McAllister: Green Noise or Green Value? Henley Business School, University of Reading, June 2008
Wiley, Benefield, Johnson	18.2–18.8%	$129/sqf	Jonathan A. Wiley, Justin Benefield, Ken Johnson: Green Design and the Market for Commercial Office Space. Journal of Real Estate Finance and Economics, November 2008
Miller, Spivey, Florance	36%	64%	Norm Miller, Jay Spivey, Andrew Florance: Does Green Pay Off? Burnham-Moores Center for Real Estate, University of San Diego, February 2008
Eichholtz, Kok, Quigley	6–9%	16%	Piet Eichholtz, Nils Kok, John M. Quigley: Doing Well by Doing Good? – Green Office Buildings. University of California, Berkeley, April 2008

[1] Economic value increase according to CoStar surveys

5.17

5.15 The increasing importance of sustainability for the property industry (according to the results of a survey performed by Jones Lang LaSalle/CoreNet Global amongst 231 employees responsible for properties in large-scale enterprises, 2009)

5.16 Willingness to pay for sustainable features in properties (according to the results of a survey performed by Jones Lang LaSalle/CoreNet Global, see Fig. 5.15)
5.17 Overview of studies performed to determine the economic performance of green buildings

Tenants have also recognised the importance of certificates, but do not regard these as the only possibility to produce sustainable solutions. When occupying new builds or buildings that have undergone major refurbishments or retrofitting, tenants will start to become accustomed to presentation of a certificate. However, in the course of a rental contract, there is demand for more simple and flexible assessment methods and management structures, which emerge from an effective dialogue between landlord and tenant. According to this, the picture of a certificate's relevance in the market differs considerably between investors and tenants reflecting their specific interests. The following paragraphs examine these differences in more detail.

Investors: Growing market acceptance meets limits in existing building stock
In order to assess the relevance of sustainability certificates in terms of property investment, attention is first of all focused on recent structural and economic shifts in the market. As mentioned before, the attitude amongst investors towards sustainability is generally positive, however, in regard of using certification systems for the assessment of existing building stock, it is slightly more reserved.

Sustainability certificates become established at suitable times
Up until the second half of 2007, the boom on the private equity market contributed towards an extreme rise in prop-

erty prices. Because the rising prices diverged more and more from the corresponding rental income, those who wanted to assert themselves in the market had to purchase more properties. Dwindling yields on single investments could frequently only be balanced by a portfolio of invested assets (in terms of direct or indirect property investments) in order to keep up with the demands of shareholders and creditors. During the course of this development, even lower quality properties and portfolios were purchased.

Since the beginning of the financial crisis, however at the latest since the middle of 2008, a complete reversal has been observed and, as a consequence, property investment has undergone a strategic change of direction. Properties with second-class fit-out, short-term or expiring rental contracts and unfavourable locations are being returned to the market – assuming they were purchased in the first place. Core Assets [29], on the other hand, continue to enjoy great popularity. On the property market, this term refers to investments in properties characterised by stable current returns and long-term value stability. Usually these are properties that are fully let at an average rent, ones that are suitable for third-party use and contemporary buildings. The current returns on this type of investment derive, to a large extent, from the current income of the properties.

The turning point is emphasised by two factors. On the one hand, many compa-

nies were directly affected by the crisis whereby the decline of business was accompanied by a cutback in staffing and a consolidation of sites. The vacation of sites, increase in the number of vacant properties and rent decline have still not come to a standstill. On the other hand, the necessary proportion of external financing for property investments - if at all granted – can only be obtained by providing evidence of long-term securities. Capital-intensive new build projects, refurbishments or structural alterations therefore only materialise if suitable pre-letting agreements, evidence of solvent tenants, a confirmation of the location's quality and first-class structural and technical quality are provided. In future, it will become more difficult and subject to risk surcharges to obtain financing through a bank or borrow liquidity from the capital market.

Hence, the most recent economic and structural changes have contributed towards a revision of investment strategies. These developments have had an effect on the relevance of sustainable properties in the market since investors are hoping for additional security concerning value stability in the investment as well as in the upkeep of buildings by providing verification of sustainable features.

Certified properties -
a separate asset class
Surveys have shown that interest in investment properties with sustainable features has increased during the course of the financial crisis. This is not only because more than half of all institutional investors now recognise sustainable properties as a different class of assets [30], but also because there seems to be greater willingness to liquidate more assets for this kind of investment (Fig. 5.16, p. 109).

A range of studies performed in 2008 gave cause to consider whether sustainability could, other than only for quality assurance purposes, also be used to generate added value. The studies confirm that certified buildings are able to produce higher rental income, have lower vacancy rates and higher returns on sales than could be obtained through conventional reference buildings (Fig. 5.17, p. 109).

Critical voices, amongst others from authors listed in Fig. 5.17 (p. 109), have warned that the results obtained exclusively from transactions in the US Ameri-

Issuer	Fund	Investment strategy
Credit Suisse	CS Real Estate Fund Green Property (closed-end fund)	Upmarket new builds in first-class Swiss business locations (volume: CHF 300 million)
Hesse Newman	Green Building (closed-end fund)	Single asset – Office Building Düsseldorf Airport City (Siemens is the only tenant; purchase price € 36.1 million)
iii Investments	Green Building Fund (closed-end fund)	National or international certified office properties in (West) Europe (volume: € 400 million)
IVG	Premium Green (special open-end fund)	Funds concept for institutional investors, investment in few, certified project developments in German prime locations (volume: € 300 million)
Bank Sarasin	Nachhaltig Immobilien Schweiz (fund from the Sarasin Investment Foundation for institutional investors)	Investment in sustainable new builds, refurbishments of old buildings to fulfil predefined sustainability criteria (volume: CHF 172 million)
Pramerica	TMW Immobilien Weltfonds (open-end fund)	Proportion of certified buildings (at least LEED silver or comparable standard) 50 % up until 2012, 75 % up until 2015; comprehensive data concerning energy/waste/water in the case of 60 % of all assets up until 2012, 85 % up until 2015 (volume: € 840 million)

5.18

can property market cannot simply be inferred to local market conditions. In order to fill this gap, renowned universities and research institutes are trying to compare the structural and operational data of certified properties with those of conventional properties. The intention is to prove that green buildings in Europe are also capable of providing greater added value in the market than conventional properties.

In response to the growing interest of investors in sustainable properties, institutional investors have proceeded in expanding their product range to incorporate alternative types of investment. Consequently, a first generation of "Green Building Funds" is being developed for the German property market with their initiators referring to the stability of sustainable properties (Fig. 5.18).

Some of the products presented here make the presence of a sustainability certificate a condition in the respective investment strategy. The obtainment of documentation in form of a certificate is without doubt advisable in the case of project developments and new builds. Given the continuously decreasing life expectancy of properties, there is the possibility to use a sustainability certificate as a positive factor in resale (investment exit).

However, amongst investors, the generally positive recognition of sustainable features does not automatically correspond to an outright acceptance of certificates. On the one hand, the use of established rating systems to perform inexpensive and time-efficient assessments of building stock is limited and, on the other hand, the contents and methods of the systems do not always satisfy the needs of investors.

Relevance of certification systems is limited for building stock

The success of sustainability certificates is closely linked to project planning and construction. The vast majority of the almost 100 properties in Germany that have obtained either a certificate or pre-certificate have only just been completed or are still under construction. This success highlights that sustainability certificates have gained acceptance as a standard within a very short period for project developments in central locations and primarily for top office properties. The importance of certification systems in these market segments is therefore expected to grow.

On the other hand, if this dynamic development is contrasted with the certification rate for refurbishments, which is below one per cent, the relevance of certifications to the market seems to be clearly limited. For it is precisely the handling of existing building stock which, as the fundamental element of day to day transaction business, is the focus of investors' attention. Certifications for existing building stock will however only gain importance in the market if certificates become significant as an everyday risk and opportunity assessment tool. It remains to be seen if and when certifications might become suitable as an inexpensive, quick and practical method to provide reliable information regarding an existing building's performance. Up until then, with Germany's property market covering 17 million residential and 6 million commercial buildings, the market significance of certifications is hardly worth mentioning. The establishment of uniform standards for the assessment of an existing building's sustainable performance requires a fundamental review and modification of the available rating methods.

In contrast to new builds and refurbishments, a suitable system for existing building stock will not be able to apply the same documentary proof currently demanded if it is to gain relevance in the market. Especially in the case of older buildings, many investors find that the necessary effort to acquire or reacquire documents concerning the property and

the time and effort it entails in terms of staff bears no relation to the expected added value. This is the classic problem following the law of diminishing marginal utility since the marketing advantages and value stability obtained through green building certificates have to be compared with the expenses for due diligence, certification fees, auditors and the possible support received from specialist consultants for simulations and surveys.

Established system variants, such as the British variant "BREEAM In-Use" and the American variant "LEED – Existing Buildings: Operations & Maintenance", pursue a different approach to the assessment of sustainable management but rely on the tenants' pronounced willingness to cooperate. Amongst other things, these variants require evidence concerning tenant fit-out, details on upkeep and maintenance management, disclosure of energy consumption within the rental units and the involvement of the tenant when it comes to optimising property management. Thus the application of these systems gives predominantly tenants themselves or owners occupying their own properties the opportunity to obtain certification. The applicability of the systems by investors is restricted due to the limited access to performance data. Whether the DGNB's variants for the assessment of existing building stock, which are still in development, will offer investors attractive options for a property rating will have to be seen.

The supply of sustainable properties is regarded as...

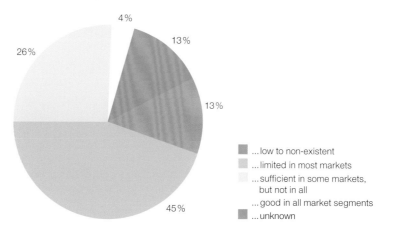

4%
13%
13%
26%
45%

...low to non-existent
...limited in most markets
...sufficient in some markets, but not in all
...good in all market segments
...unknown

5.19

5.18 Green building funds in the German property market
5.19 Opinion regarding the supply of sustainable properties (according to the results of a survey performed by Jones Lang LaSalle/CoreNet Global amongst 231 employees responsible for properties in large-scale enterprises in North and South America, Europe and Asia in 2009)

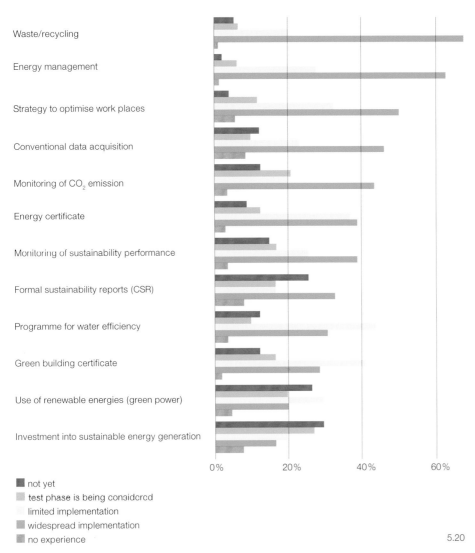

Waste/recycling

Energy management

Strategy to optimise work places

Conventional data acquisition

Monitoring of CO_2 emission

Energy certificate

Monitoring of sustainability performance

Formal sustainability reports (CSR)

Programme for water efficiency

Green building certificate

Use of renewable energies (green power)

Investment into sustainable energy generation

0%   20%   40%   60%

■ not yet
▨ test phase is being considered
□ limited implementation
▨ widespread implementation
■ no experience

5.20

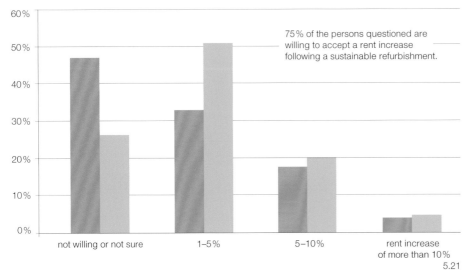

■ 2008   ▨ 2009

60%

50%

40%

30%

20%

10%

0%

not willing or not sure   1–5%   5–10%   rent increase of more than 10%

75% of the persons questioned are willing to accept a rent increase following a sustainable refurbishment.

5.21

5.20 Tenants have proceeded to achieve their self-imposed sustainability objectives by taking the initiative. Measures easily implemented and with short-term saving potential are preferred (result of a survey performed by Jones Lang LaSalle/CoreNet Global amongst 231 employees responsible for properties in large-scale enterprises, 2009).

5.21 Willingness of tenants to accept a rent increase following a sustainable refurbishment

In summary it can be said that structural and economic developments are presumably the cause for a growing acceptance and an incentive for investors to consider sustainable aspects in their investment strategies. Furthermore, a first generation of green property funds highlights increasing interest in sustainable investments. It seems as if green building certificates will become established as a standard for project developments and new builds. At first, however, only in central market segments and top quality product ranges.

Even if surveys point out that investors tend to rely on individual property features when refocussing their business strategies, certification systems offer them only a very sketchy basis for the assessment. This especially applies to existing building stock, which in volume terms dominates everyday property deals. As far as investors are concerned, relevance in the market beyond short-term marketing effects, will only occur if assessment systems can be incorporated as a cost-neutral feature of everyday benefit/risk ratio assessments. Since the rental income is a fundamental factor in these assessments, the way tenants regard the relevance of certificates should also be of crucial importance to investors.

Tenants: Certificates amidst sustainability objectives and rental space management

The economic downturn in the property market has resulted in an increasing number of un-let properties, declining rents and a generally greater risk of rent loss. Those interested in renting property with good financial standing have advanced to a perfect position to negotiate whereby the demand for sustainable site features exceed traditional demands for fit-out and the quality of the location.

Significance of certificates for corporate sustainability objectives

In most cases, the prospective tenants are internationally operating companies whose service providing and administrative divisions are constantly searching for suitable office space in central locations. As part of the development and expansion of corporate sustainability objectives (corporate social responsibility), these groups of tenants are obliged to follow these self-imposed objectives even when making property leasing decisions. Landlords and investors are trying to meet the demand, but are in default due to the considerable effort and expense required to obtain certificates.

And this is exactly the way tenants regard the current supply of sustainable products. The daily experience of broker companies is confirmed in surveys which show that the demand for certified space is outstripping supply (Fig. 5.19, p. 111).

Individual implementation of sustainable measures in rental space management systems

The demand of the above mentioned tenant groups to move into certified sustainable space indicates that tenants too attribute a clear relevance to certificates in the market. However, for the reasons mentioned, certificates can often not be obtained in the time available. Nevertheless, in order to follow the trend of conducting business in a sustainable way, tenants have proceeded to achieve their self-imposed sustainability objectives by taking the initiative and implementing the appropriate measures. This includes developing, and in some cases also implementing, structures to optimise space management. There is a preference for the implementation of simple measures with potential for short-term savings (Fig. 5.20).

The fact that the pressure felt by companies to adopt sustainable objectives far exceeds the scope offered by available systems is also expressed in their willingness to contribute towards the costs of possible optimisation measures. However, looking at the over-supply in the current rental market, it cannot be assumed that this willingness is reflected in the increased readiness of tenants to pay for sustainable features. Provided that the measures designed to offer saving potential actually bring about a reduction in service charges, tenants will show a growing interest in financially shared solutions to the benefits of both landlord and tenant (Fig. 5.21).

A cost-benefit analysis performed for this procedure requires a much higher degree of transparency and cooperation between the contract parties than has been common practice up until now. It is for this purpose that both tenants and landlords are looking for a cooperative approach to incorporate sustainability into the rental management systems. Green rental contracts, memoranda of understanding, the disclosure of consumption

data, coordinated operation and maintenance concepts, guidelines for a sustainable fit-out, green property and facility management solutions and the purchase of renewable energies are examples of the concerted action to increase sustainable potentials.

Especially amongst institutional tenants of commercial properties, there is significant demand for certified rental space. Not least because the presentation of certificates is required in the context of their business reports on sustainable matters. In the case of first occupancy or following major refurbishments, the renewal of building services, the replacement of the facade or other similar capital-intensive measures, potential tenants can now expect a certificate to have been obtained for top quality properties in central locations. In such circumstances, certificates have an immediate impact in the market. In the case of existing building stock, open tenancy agreements or the extension of a rental contract, certificates are not necessarily beneficial since the parties are capable of developing inexpensive, time efficient and flexible solutions adapted to meet the needs of their individual requirements. The relevance of certificates in the market takes a backseat when it comes to individual management solutions.

Conclusion

Investors and tenants have discovered the significance of sustainability certificates to advance their own interests. Consequently, assessment methods have become established as a standard in some market segments. However, the expense and time required as well as the necessity to involve an external consultant (auditor, specialist engineer) are restraining the quick establishment of already marketable certificates in a number of different market segments. In these cases, the parties directly involved have started to develop own solutions. As a result, alternative paths are being taken and new products are being developed limiting the significance of established rating systems to certain market segments. Whether the agencies providing the certificates are able to defend or expand the relevance of their systems in the market is, on the one hand, dependent on their ability to make use of the market players' – primarily investors and tenants - interest to adapt the systems and, on the other hand, on their ability to respond to the changing demand.

References:

[1] Henzelmann, Torsten; Büchele, Ralph; Engel, Michael: Nachhaltigkeit im Immobilienmanagement. Survey by Roland Berger Strategy Consultants. 2010
[2] Lützkendorf, Thomas; Lorenz, David: Nachhaltigkeitsorientierte Investments im Immobilienbereich. Karlsruhe 2005
[3] Miller, Norm: Green Buildings and Productivity. In: Journal of Sustainable Real Estate, 01/2009
[4] Environmental factors affecting office worker performance: A review of evidence. CIBSE Technical Memoranda. London 1999
[5] Drees & Sommer (pub.): Green Building – ein Zukunftsthema der Immobilienbranche, Ergebnisse einer Marktstudie. Stuttgart 2009
[6] Royal Institute of Chartered Engineers (RICS) Economics: Q2 Global Property Sustainability Survey. London 2009
[7] see ref. 1
[8] see ref. 1
[9] Preuß, Norbert; Schöne, Bernhard Lars: Real Estate und Facility-Management. Berlin 2010
[10] ISO 15686-5: Building and construction assets. 2008
[11] König, Holger; Kohler, Niklaus; Kreißig, Johannes, Lützkendorf, Thomas: Lebenszyklusanalyse in der Gebäudeplanung. Munich 2009
[12] DIN 276-1: Building costs, Part 1. 2008
[13] Turner, Cathy; Frankel, Mark: Energy Performance of LEED for New Construction Buildings. Vancouver 2008
[14] ANSI/ASHRAE/IESNA Standard 90.1: Energy Standard for Buildings Except Low-Rise Residential Buildings. 2007
[15] Hornung, Rüdiger: Nachhaltigkeitszertifikate, To BREEAM or not to BREEAM, ist das die Frage? In: Immobilien Zeitung. No. 44, 2009, p. 13
[16] see ref. 9
[17] GEFMA 200: Costs in facility management; cost structure for GEFMA 100. Bonn 2006
[18] DIN 32736: Building management; definitions and scope of services. Berlin 2000
[19] see ref. 13
[20] Jones Lang LaSalle & CREIS (pub.): OSCAR 2009. Office Service Charge Analysis Report. London 2008
[21] EU Directive 2005/64/EG
[22] German Federal Environment Agency: Volume of waste 2008. http://www.umweltbundesamt-daten-zur-umwelt.de/umweltdaten/public/theme.do;jsessionid=0816630066776854A54A5A1A02385285?nodeIdent=2320, as of 28 July 2010
[23] Miller, Norm; Spivey, Jay; Florance, Andy: Does Green Pay Off? San Diego 2007
[24] Royal Institute of Chartered Surveyors: Green Values – Green Buildings, Growing Assets. London 2005
[25] Kats, Greg; Alevantis, Leon; Berman, Adam; Mills, Evan; Perlman, Jeff: The Costs and Financial Benefits of Green Buildings. A report of California's Sustainable Building Task Force USA. 2003; http://www.cap-e.com
[26] Schäfer, Henry: ImmoInvest – Grundlagen nachhaltiger Immobilieninvestments. Stuttgart 2008
[27] Bergius, Susanne: Öko-Bauten bringen mehr Rendite. In: Handelsblatt, 23 Oct. 2006 http://www.handelsblatt.com/finanzen/immobilien/oeko-bauten-bringen-mehr-rendite;1150312
[28] see ref. 26
[29] Core assets: core, value-added and opportunistic strategies define the investment risk classes and the relation between risk and benefit
[30] Survey performed by Union Investment amongst 220 European operating institutional investors (Germany, France, UK), 2010

BREEAM: European Investment Bank, Luxembourg

The new administration building of the European Investment Bank (EIB) in Luxembourg provides space for a staff of 750. From the very start the intention was that the EIB extension building should be a model in ecological terms, while also providing a pleasant working environment for staff and visitors. Using this concept as a basis, the demands in terms of sustainability were comprehensively formulated and assessed in the documentation for the design competition back in 2002. From the ten multi-disciplinary planning teams invited to take part in the competition, the office of Ingenhoven Architects emerged as the winners with their design for a compact and transparent building volume.

In form the building resembles a glass tube that is sliced into the site. The glass roof spans the entire 170-metre-long and 50-metre-wide structure of the building. In combination, the lightweight glass envelope and steel structure provide a maximum amount of daylight and transparency. Inside this envelope the offices are laid out in a meandering pattern and are connected to each other by walkways. This layout creates "V"-shaped atria that face north or south and function as climatic buffers. The north-facing atria, which look towards a wooded valley, are left unheated. In contrast the atria flanking the street in the south are heated and provide public areas free of columns that function as entrances and distributors. Both kinds of atrium, the unheated "winter gardens" in the north as well as the thermally conditioned atria in the south, are naturally ventilated and cooled during the summer months by means of opening elements in the external skin (Figs. 6.1 und 6.4).

6.1

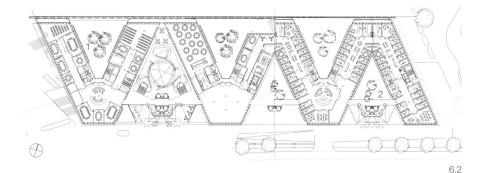

6.2

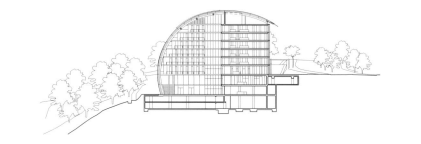

6.3

European Investment Bank (EIB)
Location and completion: Luxembourg 2008
Architect: Ingenhoven Architects, Düsseldorf
Client: European Investment Bank, Luxembourg
Technical building services:
HL-Technik AG, Munich;
IC-Consult, Frankfurt/Main;
pbe-Beljuli, Pulheim; S & E Consult, Luxemburg
Building physics: DS Plan, Stuttgart

Structural design: Werner Sobek Ingenieure, Stuttgart
BREEAM assessor: Faber Maunsell, London
Function: offices, conference areas, restaurant
Number of storeys: ten levels
Gross floor area: 69 996 m²
Certification system: BREEAM
System version: pre-2005 Version of BREEAM Bespoke

A core idea in the concept for this building is the separation of the inner facade that defines and borders space from the actual building envelope, which serves to protect the spaces in the interior from the changing conditions outdoors. Separating the building envelope from the internal spaces creates a buffer zone between the inner facade and the external skin that functions as an additional, insulating climatic layer. The spaces in the interior that border on this zone can thus be naturally ventilated, even in winter, by opening a window onto the atrium. As the internal facades are protected from the effects of the weather it was possible to use wood throughout with all its ecological advantages for the facades and the window frames. For instance the primary energy content or the global warming potential of a timber facade are significantly lower than the corresponding values for a standard aluminium facade. Flexibility, from the construction to the organisational units, is a central characteristic of the design. The spatial structure with its modular floor plans ensures that the building can be easily adapted for different uses. To achieve this end the technical services are placed in easily accessible raised and hollow floors as well as in service shafts. The distribution of the data runs and the connections to them is so flexible that a redesign could be easily carried out with having to reposition them. The floor plan of the building provides junctions between the individual areas which encourage communication and spontaneous interaction between staff members of the different working groups (Figs. 6.2 und 6.3).

Energy and internal climate concept

The outdoor natural energy potential available in the form of daylight, air, wind, water, sun and night-time cooling is consistently integrated and utilised in the overall concept. When the outdoor temperatures are moderate a major part of the usable floor area can be naturally supplied with outside air by opening windows onto the atria, or directly to the outdoors. To cool the halls in summer there are flaps in the facade skin that open or close depending on the internal and external temperatures. A mechanical air supply is provided for internal zones, special areas and for those periods in summer or winter when the outdoor temperatures are extreme. In connection with the internal climate concept this ensures a high level of thermal comfort throughout the year and significantly reduces the amount of energy required to provide fresh air. At the same time the mechanical ventilation system allows highly efficient cold and heat recovery from the exhaust air in winter and summer.

The floor slabs serve as thermal storage mass and are therefore left uncovered for the most part. In summer they are pre-cooled at night by cold external air and thus provide basic conditioning of the building. Pipe coils were laid in the concrete slabs through which water flows at night. The water is directly cooled by cold outdoor air at night, without the use of conventional cooling technology. Peak cooling loads are dealt with by no-drive floor induction units which are integrated in the raised floors so that that they are hidden from view and can be easily accessed in sections for upgrading. They also serve as floor-mounted air outlets as well as static heating elements which are supplied in winter with warm water from a combined heat and power plant via the district heating network.

The technical services, which are housed for the most part in the raised and hollow floors, are laid out in a modular fashion. The work areas receive a basic illumination of 300 lux which combines direct and indirect light, augmented by individual workplace lighting, which the user can switch on if needed. The proportion of artificial light in the basic lighting is reduced evenly by automatic controls so that, in combination with daylight, the required individual lighting level is reached. If there is no-one at the workplace, the artificial light is automatically turned off. The user can individually influence his or her immediate surroundings in terms of the thermal conditions, the lighting level, the position of the protection against sun and glare and, in some areas, also the fresh air supply. The modular layout of the technical systems and the building automation is based on the building axes, in combination with the individual lighting concept this increases flexibility for reconfiguring the workplaces and changing the function of entire areas. In summer heat is drawn from the district heating network across a dessicant cooling system (DEC) to cool the fresh air. This reduces the amount of electrical energy required for conventional cooling. The DEC system is a thermal cooling

process used to condition spaces in which a combination of evaporative cooling and the removal of moisture from the air cools the warm outdoor air directly. When the outdoor temperature is low the technical services rooms, the data processing centre, as well as the conference areas are cooled indirectly through the cooling towers and directly by means of outdoor air; when the outdoor temperature is high by using cooling energy from refrigerating machines (Fig. 6.6, p. 118).

BREEAM certification

During the planning phase the European Investment Bank decided to carry out a sustainability certification of the new building. After examining the various certification systems available at the time such as HQE (Haute Qualité Environnementale, France), LEED (Leadership in Energy and Environmental Design, USA) and BREEAM (Building Research Establishment Environmental Assessment Method, Great Britain) it was decided to use BREEAM. The EIB's new building represents the first use of the BREEAM system on the European continent. The BREEAM certificate of the EIB is

6.4

6.1 European Investment Bank, Aerial view
6.2 Plan of ground floor, Scale 1:1750
    1 Cold atrium
    2 Warm atrium
6.3 Section, Scale 1:1750
6.4 View of facade from inside atrium

Category	Weight-ing	Acronym	Criterion	Maxi-mum score	Building score[1]	Assessment on individual functional levels[2]								
						F1	F2	F3	F4	F5	F6	F7	F8	F9
Manage-ment 15%		Man 1	Commissioning responsibilities	1	1									
		Man 2	Commissioning clauses	1	1									
		Man 3	Seasonal commissioning	1	1									
		Man 4	Guide for building users	1	1									
		Man 5	Construction impact management	6	6									
		Number of credits available per functional area				10	10	10	10	10	10	10	10	10
		Credits achieved per functional area				10	10	10	10	10	10	10	10	10
		Compliance level (score)			100.0%	100%	100%	100%	100%	100%	100%	100%	100%	100%
Health & Well-being 15%		Hea 1	Cooling towers	1	1									
		Hea 2	Drinking hot water – legionellosis	1	1									
		Hea 3	Failsafe humidificiation	1	1									
		Hea 4	Openable windows	1		1	1	1	1	0		1	1	
		Hea 5	Internal air pollution	1	1									
		Hea 6	Ventilation rates	1	1									
		Hea 7	Daylighting	1		0	0	0	0	0		0	0	
		Hea 8	Glare	1			1	1	1					
		Hea 9	High frequency lighting	1		1	1	1	1	1	1	1	1	1
		Hea 10	Electric lighting design	1		1	1	1	1	1	1	1	1	0
		Hea 11	Lighting zones	1		0	1	1	1	1	0	0	1	0
		Hea 12	Lighting control	1					1					
		Hea 13	View out	1			1			1				
		Hea 14	Thermal zoning	1		0	1	1	1	1	1	1	1	1
		Hea 15	Thermal simulation	1	1									
		Hea 16	Internal noise levels	1		1	0	0	0	0	0	0	1	0
		Hea 17	Reverberation times	1						0				
		Number of credits available per functional area				13	15	14	16	15	11	13	13	11
		Credits achieved per functional area				8	11	10	10	9	7	8	10	6
		Compliance level (score)			72.1%	62%	73%	71%	63%	60%	64%	62%	77%	55%
Energy 17%		Ene 1	Sub-metering of major energy uses	1	1									
		Ene 2	Sub-metering of areas	1	1									
		Ene 3	U values	3	3									
		Ene 4	Air permeability	3	2									
		Ene 5	Internal lighting controls	1		1	1	1	1	1	1	1	1	1
		Ene 6	Heating controls	1	1									
		Ene 7	Services control	1	1									
		Ene 8	Internal luminaires	1	1									
		Ene 9	External luminaires	1	1									
		Ene 10	CO_2 emissions of heating system	3	3									
		Ene 11	Heat recovery	1	1									
		Ene 12	Specific fan power	1	1									
		Ene 13	Variable speed drives (ventilators, pumpers)	1	1									
		Ene 14	CHP/Renewable energy feasibility study	1	1									
		Number of credits available per functional area				20	20	20	20	20	20	20	20	20
		Credits achieved per functional area				19	19	19	19	19	19	19	19	19
		Compliance level (score)			95.0%	95%	95%	95%	95%	95%	95%	95%	95%	95%
Transport 8%		Tra 1	Proximity and provision of public transport	5	5									
		Tra 2	Maximum car parking capacity – staff	1	0									
		Tra 3	Maximum car parking capacity – visitors	1	1									
		Tra 4	Cyclist facilities – staff	1	1									
		Tra 5	Travel audit	1	1									
		Tra 6	Staff travel plan	1	1									
		Number of credits available per functional area				10	10	10	10	10	10	10	10	10
		Credits achieved per functional area				9	9	9	9	9	9	9	9	9
		Compliance level (score)			90.0%	90%	90%	90%	90%	90%	90%	90%	90%	90%
Water 5%		Wat 1	Water consumption	3	2									
		Wat 2	Water meter	1	1									
		Wat 3	Mains leak detection	1	0									
		Wat 4	Sanitary supply shut-off	1	0									
		Wat 5	Irrigation systems	1	1									
		Number of credits available per functional area				7	7	7	7	7	7	7	7	7
		Credits achieved per functional area				4	4	4	4	4	4	4	4	4
		Compliance level (score)			57.1%	57%	57%	57%	57%	57%	57%	57%	57%	57%

[1] Score for all functional areas
[2] F1: Foyer with reception, F2: Office, F3: Meeting rooms, F4: Conference area, F5: Library, F6: Archive, F7: Restaurant and cafeteria, F8: Kitchen and serving area, F9: Staff and changing rooms

Category	Weight-ing	Acro-nym	Criterion	Maxi-mum score	Building score[1]	Assessment on individual functional levels[2]								
						F1	F2	F3	F4	F5	F6	F7	F8	F9
		Mat 1	Reuse of structure	1	0									
		Mat 2	Reuse of facades	1	0									
		Mat 3	Use of recycled materials	1	0									
		Mat 4	Embodied impacts of materials	4	0									
		Mat 5	Embodied impacts - external hard surfaces	1	0									
		Mat 6	Floor finishes	2	0									
Materials	10%	Mat 7	Internal walls	1	1									
		Mat 8	Asbestos	1	1									
		Mat 9	Durability	1	1									
		Mat 10	Timber	2	2									
		Mat 11	Storage of recyclable waste	1	1									
		Mat 12	Composting	1								1	1	
			Number of credits available per functional area			16	16	16	16	16	16	17	17	16
			Credits achieved per functional area			6	6	6	6	6	6	7	7	6
			Compliance level (score)		37.8%	38%	38%	38%	38%	38%	38%	41%	41%	38%
		Lue 1	Re-use of land	1	0									
		Lue 2	Use of contaminated land	1	1									
		Lue 3	Use of land of low ecological value	1	0									
		Lue 4	Change in ecological value as a result of development	5	4									
Land use & Ecology	15%	Lue 5	Ecological enhancement advance	1	1									
		Lue 6	Protection of ecological features	1	0									
		Lue 7	Long-term impact on bio-diversity	1	1									
		Lue 8	Topsoil re-use	1	0									
			Number of credits available per functional area			12	12	12	12	12	12	12	12	12
			Credits achieved per functional area			7	7	7	7	7	7	7	7	7
			Compliance level (score)		58.3%	58%	58%	58%	58%	58%	58%	58%	58%	58%
		Pol 1	Refrigerants with zero ODP	1	1									
		Pol 2	Refrigerants with GWP < 5	1	1									
		Pol 3	Refrigerant lead detection	1	1									
		Pol 4	Refrigerant recovery systems	1	1									
		Pol 5	Insulant ODP and GWP	1	0									
		Pol 6	NO_x emissions of heating sources	4	1									
Pollution	15%	Pol 7	Watercourse pollution	1	0									
		Pol 8	Water run-off	1	0									
		Pol 9	Zero emission energy sources	1	0									
		Pol 10	Refrigerant ODP (cold storage equipment)	1									1	
		Pol 11	Refrigerant GWP (cold storage equipment)	1									0	
		Pol 12	Insulant ODP, GWP (cold storage equipment)	1									0	
			Number of credits available per functional area			12	12	12	12	12	12	12	15	12
			Credits achieved per functional area			5	5	5	5	5	5	5	6	5
			Compliance level (score)		41.6%	42%	42%	42%	42%	42%	42%	42%	40%	42%

6.5

based on the pre-2005 version of BREEAM Bespoke. BREEAM Bespoke uses an existing version of the system and adapts it to the specific building and its location in agreement with the Building Research Establishment (BRE). The adaptation of the individual categories is carried out in close collaboration between the BRE, the BREEAM assessor and a local consultant. In this particular case the basis for BREEAM Bespoke was BREEAM Office and Administration Building in the 2004 version. It was applied to the local demands of the location, Luxembourg, and its national standards and was augmented by the use of additional criteria.

The assessment is based on 79 individual criteria which, according to the particular requirement, were applied to the entire building or separately assessed for each functional area. In the latter case the individual assessment was incorporated in the overall assessment by weighting it in proportion to the floor area of the individual functional zones. For the purpose of the assessment the building was divided into the following nine functional areas (Fig. 6.5): foyer with reception area, office, meeting rooms, conference area, library, archive, restaurant and cafeteria, kitchen and food serving areas, as well as staff and changing rooms.

After completion of the design and with the start of construction in 2005 a Design and Procurement Assessment was carried out on the basis of the design stage reached at that time and was submitted to the BRE through the BREEAM assessor. Upon completion of the building this assessment was updated by the BRE at the start of 2009 in the framework of the final examination (Post Construction Review). During the construction phase, the BREEAM assessor regularly examined and documented the implementation of the target values described in the design and procurement assessment on the basis of site visits.

Differences to the design and procurement assessment were found in seven of the 79 criteria. In six of these seven criteria an improvement of the assessment was achieved. This was based essentially

6.5 Detailed certificate result for the EIB according to BREEAM Bespoke

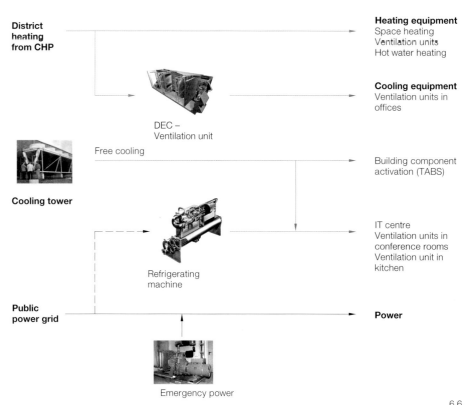

District heating from CHP

Heating equipment
Space heating
Ventilation units
Hot water heating

DEC – Ventilation unit

Free cooling

Cooling equipment
Ventilation units in offices

Cooling tower

Building component activation (TABS)

Refrigerating machine

IT centre
Ventilation units in conference rooms
Ventilation unit in kitchen

Public power grid

Power

Emergency power

6.6

BREEAM Score	Credits Achieved	Credits Available	% of Credits Achieved	Section Weighting	Section Score
Management	10	10	100%	0.15	15%
Health and Wellbeing	6–11[1]	11–16[1]	72.1%	0.15	10.8%
Energy	19	20	95%	0.17	16.2%
Transport	9	10	90%	0.08	7.2%
Water	4	7	57.1%	0.05	2.9%
Materials	6–7[1]	16–17[1]	37.8%	0.1	3.8%
Ecology and Land Use	7	12	58.3%	0.15	8.8%
Pollution	5–6[1]	12–15[1]	41.6%	0.15	6.2%
Final BREEAM Score					**70.8%**
BREEAM Rating					**Excellent**

[1] In assessing these categories the requirements in the individual criteria for some of the nine functional areas of the building differ. Some assessment criteria were not used for all functional areas.

6.7

	25%	40%	55%	70%	100%
Not classified		Passed	Good	Very good	Excellent

European Investment Bank, Luxembourg	Certification result: 70.8% – Excellent

70.8%

6.8

6.6 Energy concept
6.7 Assessment rating according to categories
6.8 Certification and degree of compliance
6.9 Katharinum: perspective from the south, rendering

on a change in the public transport connection and on a new evaluation of the primary energy factor. For example, the assessment of the criterion Ene 10 (CO_2 emissions of the heating system) in the category "Energy" improved from 0 to 3 assessment credits. The reason for this was the re-calculation of the primary energy factor of district heating production by the network operator, which reduced the CO_2 emissions for district heating from 0.1 kg CO_2/kWh to 0.068 kg CO_2/kWh. In addition the EIB had committed itself to carrying out a mobility study and to preparing a mobility plan. The goals were to optimise and reduce private motorised transport to the workplace.

Certification result
The level of the certification is calculated from the degree of compliance achieved in eight individual assessment categories, multiplied by the respective environmental weighting factor. The building achieves the rating "Excellent", which is the highest rating in the version of the system used at the time of the assessment (Fig. 6.8).
The results in the eight main categories and the respective weighting factors are listed in Fig. 6.7. In particular the very good assessments in the categories management, energy, transport as well as health and comfort should be noted, as they reflect the goals that were set by the EIB at the very start.
The overall level of compliance of 95% achieved in the 14 individual criteria of the category "Energy" confirms that, thanks to the architectural design and its energy and climate concept, the new building almost completely meets the high demands made in terms of energy efficiency.
It was only in the criterion Ene 4 ("Airtightness") that just two of three possible credits were achieved. This building improves on the requirements in the English building regulations regarding the air-tightness of the building envelope by 67% but still (just) fails to achieve the target value (75% below the reference air permeability value required by the building regulations). Air-tightness was tested by means of a blower door test in one of the building's wings. This revealed an air volume flow through leaks in the building of 3.3 m^3/h/m^2 of the building envelope at a differential pressure of 50 Pa.

LEED: Katharinum, Leipzig

The Katharinum in the inner city of Leipzig is a mixed use building with retail areas, offices and apartments. It was carried out according to the Dutch building team process. In contrast to the classic approach in which design and construction are separated, in this system the collaboration of all persons involved begins at the start of the design phase, allowing the technical and procedural know-how of those who construct the building to be incorporated in the planning from an early stage.

The individual retail areas on the ground floor and first floor range in size between 90 and 820 m². The offices are distributed throughout the first to the fifth floor; the building is capped off by ten penthouse apartments on the upper levels. In the basement, an underground garage with 43 parking spaces is available for users of the building.

The building footprint utilizes most of the project site and forms the second corner of a block development at the Museum of Fine Arts Leipzig. It is integrated in its inner city setting through its four differently designed facades (Fig. 6.9). The central location means that this building is very well connected to the public transport system, a fact that was positively assessed in the LEED certification.

In opting for certification according to the LEED system, the project developer shows that not only prestige projects such as company headquarters or office high-rises but also conventional construction projects can profit from the certification process that accompanies planning and construction. The Katharinum is the first building in the new German states to be certified according to the system LEED-NC 3.0.

On the site, which comprises 1867 m², there were existing historic cellar walls that had been covered after the war. Before the start of construction, extensive archaeological excavations were carried out on the site in order to secure historic material. Preservation of cultural values is one of the goals of sustainable buildings. Nevertheless, the U.S. Green Building Council (USGBC) did not acknowledge these excavations by awarding one of the innovation credits that are offered by the LEED system.

Contamination from previous uses was one of the major challenges presented by

6.9

this inner city site. Ground samples revealed a high concentration of mercury, making it necessary to remove about 130 tonnes of contaminated soil. On account of the ecological advantages when compared to a greenfield site this decontamination of polluted ground is positively evaluated by LEED.

Extensive planting is envisaged for 60% of the roof area. Planted roofs counteract the heating-up of cities and thus have a positive influence on the assessment of the criteria "Heat Island Effect" and "Protect or Restore Habitat". In addition to the excellent connection to local public transport, which is due to the inner city location, special car parking spaces are designated for carpools and low emission vehicles, and safe areas are provided to park bicycles. In addition there are showers for staff members who, for instance, commute to work by bike.

The LEED requirements regarding water efficiency led to a significant reduction in the drinking water needs for the building. Thanks to water-saving sanitary appliances and fittings, the Katharinum is below the reference value by more than 30% and thus saves approx. 1.37 million litres of drinking water annually.

The requirements in terms of thermal and visual comfort as well as the view out from the work spaces are met in the Katharinum. As the protection of non-smokers plays an important role in LEED, the building has a smokers' area that is ventilated by its own exhaust system. This

made it possible to impose a smoking ban in all other areas, apart from the apartments. LEED allows smoking in residential buildings, if the apartments are sufficiently airtight in relation to each other. The airtightness between apartments is measured by a blower door test. As part of the LEED consulting, stringent demands in terms of indoor air quality in the interior were defined in collaboration with the client, and low-emitting paints and adhesives were used consistently in the fit-out on the basis of the LEED requirements. Air quality measurements before the owner or tenant moves in are used to prove the absence of harmful substances. As an alternative, LEED accepts a flush-out before the building is occupied. In this case, the building is ventilated over a longer period with a defined amount of outside air. However, as air quality measurements are easier to follow and use, the client stipulated that measurements should be used to prove

Katharinum
Location and completion: Leipzig 2010
Architect: Fuchshuber & Partner Architekten, Leipzig
Client: Kondor Wessels Museumsquartier GmbH
Technical building services, building physics, structural design: BAUCONZEPT Planungsgesellschaft mbH, Lichtenstein
LEED AP: Lutz Miersch, Ebert & Baumann Consulting Engineers, Inc., Washington DC, USA
Function: retail, offices, apartments, underground garage
Number of storeys: seven
Gross floor area: approx. 10000 m²
Certification system: LEED
System version: LEED for New Construction and Major Renovations, Version 3.0 (LEED-NC 3.0)

the complete absence or low levels of harmful substances in the Katharinum project from the very start.

Energy and indoor climate concept

The Katharinum is supplied with heat from the city of Leipzig's district heating network. The primary energy factor of district heating (end energy consumed divided by the primary energy used in providing it) is 0.42. Underfloor heating with low supply flow temperatures heats the interior space. A controlled ventilation system with heat recovery minimises the ventilation heating demand of the apartments and in winter offers a high level of hygienic comfort. The residents can, however, still open the windows. The office spaces can be naturally ventilated by operable windows. When the outdoor temperatures in summer are high, the heating load in the office spaces is removed by means of a VRV (variable refrigerant volume) system. In this system a refrigerant, rather than the media water or air, transports the energy out of the space. The windows in the office areas are fitted with electrical contacts which interrupt the cooling system when the windows are opened, avoiding the inefficiency that results from open windows while the air conditioning is running.

The retail areas also have underfloor heating. A ventilation system supplies these areas with fresh air and conditions them by means of a VRV system that is laid out according to the individual spaces and can be operated in both heating and cooling modes.

The energy requirements for the project were calculated during the planning phase according to the German energy saving ordnances EnEV 2007 as well as EnEV 2009. The Katharinum achieves a figure 45% below the legal maximum primary energy requirements as defined in EnEV 2007 and 22% below the maximum figures in EnEV 2009. According to DIN-V 18599, the primary energy demand of the building is approx. 114 kWh/m²a.

In addition to high quality in terms of energy, the client attached particular importance to an energy-efficient operation and carried out the commissioning (enhanced start-up and optimisation of building operation) with own staff. To ensure low energy consumption in the future, the building operator and the facility management team will carry out energy monitoring (measurement and verification). This monitoring is based on a building energy simulation in which the actual and ideal states are compared so as to identify the potential for optimisation and to implement any changes.

The evaluation of the energy efficiency was carried out on the basis of ASHRAE 90.1 -2007, Appendix G. The assessment is based on an hourly year-round simulation of the entire building in which all energy related systems and demands, including office appliances, are taken into account. The ASHRAE Standard assesses the energy efficiency of the building on the basis of energy costs rather than energy demands. This means that the different values of the various kinds of energy are inherently considered. In direct comparison to the minimum requirements of a reference building according to ASHRAE-Standard 90.1-2007, the planned building achieves a saving of 38% in energy costs. In terms of LEED-NC 3.0, this represents 14 out of 19 possible points for the credit "Energy Efficiency". The final energy demand calculated according to ASHRAE-Standard 90.1 is 46% below the figure for the reference building defined in the standard. The fact that the energy savings compared to the baseline defined by EnEV 2007 (45% primary energy saving) and ASHRAE 90.1 2007 (46% final energy saving) are practically the same is coincidental, and cannot be assumed for other projects.

In addition to the characteristics of the building mentioned above, the following aspects are also responsible for the good results in both assessment processes in terms of energy efficiency:

6.10

6.10 Plan of standard floor, Scale 1:1000
6.11 Ring chart showing the achievable certification levels in the planning process
6.12 Radar chart showing the achievable credits per category (result of the LEED assessment in the design phase)
6.13 Assessment result shortly before completion
6.14 Certification result aimed for according to LEED-NC 3.0 (status August 2010)

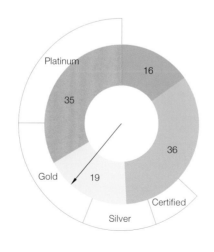

not achievable
possibly achievable
very probably achievable
achievable

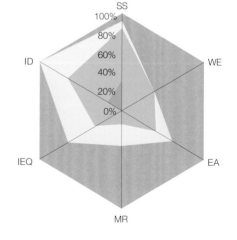

SS   Sustainable Sites
WE   Water Efficiency
EA   Energy and Atmosphere
MR   Materials and Resources
IEQ   Indoor Environmental Quality
ID   Innovations

6.11

6.12

- compact building envelope with good insulation qualities
- external shading devices controlled via a metrological station
- intelligent operation of lighting by means of movement sensors
- controlled ventilation in the living areas
- efficient plant technology
- shutdown of active cooling in office space when the windows are opened

The indoor climate concept applied ensures that the requirements of thermal comfort, as called for in the standard ASHRAE 55 (room temperature, room air speed, radiation asymmetry, vertical temperature asymmetry), are met. The LEED requirements regarding individual control of thermal comfort for at least 50 % of building users are met due to operable windows, as well as thermal control panels in each room.

LEED certification

The client decided upon a LEED certification at the start of the design stage. Specific investments in innovative technology and the resulting focus of the planning on meeting LEED requirements were intended, above all, to reduce operating costs.

The certification of the Katharinum project is based on the version LEED-NC 3.0 for New Construction and Major Renovations. The intention of conducting the assessment in the early design phase, was to define the characteristics of the building to achieve the desired certification level. In the process, the general likelihood of the building to receive certification in the essential criteria (prerequisites) was examined, the possible certification rating was established, along with its potential impact on costs and deadlines, those responsible in the project team were named, and the approach to the certification itself was defined.

The LEED assessment carried out during the planning phase revealed that a silver certification can be achieved without major changes in the design and without additional construction costs. Even a gold certification was seen as possibility. During the planning process, the illustration of the result in the form of a ring diagram showed the certification level that could be achieved (Fig. 6.11). During the planning and construction, the individual criteria of the system were divided into four categories: achievable, very proba-

LEED Category (LEED-NC 3.0)	Maximum credits	Not achievable credits	Achievable credits in the building phase	Credits achieved in the planning phase	Number of credits aimed for [1]	Final compliance level
Sustainable sites	26	3	2	21	23	88.5 %
Water efficiency	10	4	0	6	6	60.0 %
Energy and atmosphere	35	16	5	14	19	54.3 %
Materials and resources	14	10	4	0	4	28.6 %
Indoor environmental quality	15	5	4	6	10	66.7 %
Innovation in design	6	2	3	1	4	66.7 %
Final score	**106**	**40**	**18**	**48**	**66**	**62.3 %**
Certification rating (with the credits achieved in the construction phase)						**Gold**

[1] including credits to be achieved in the construction phase

6.13

6.14

bly achievable, possibly achievable and not achievable. A point or a criterion was assessed as "achievable" if the requirements had already been met and only had to be documented during the implementation. The category "very probably achievable" was chosen where plausible assumptions had to be confirmed by a third person, proofs or calculations were required, or smaller, cost-neutral changes to the design were to be carried out. If moderate, economically viable alterations or a more stringent specification of the qualities were required, the relevant point was categorised as "possibly achievable". The credits that, on account of the circumstances or the design solution, could not be implemented in the Katharinum for a reasonable expenditure were categorised as "not achievable".

In the Katharinum, the compliance levels in the individual categories were depicted in what are known as radar charts, which relate to the assessment points as well as to the compliance level achieved in the respective category (Fig. 6.12).

Upon conclusion of the detail design phase, the documentation of the criteria relevant to the design, known as Design LEED Credits, were submitted to the Green Building Certification Institute (GBCI) to be assessed and checked as part of the design phase submittal. After

the questions from the GBCI in the review had been answered and clarified, the GBCI confirmed all submitted LEED criteria.

To secure the evaluation submitted to the GBCI in the category "Optimise Energy Performance" (credit EA-1), a formal appeals procedure was requested, as the GBCI, even after answers had been given to the questions from the first review, did not award the targeted number of points. The appeal was accepted by the GBCI and the assessment submitted was ultimately confirmed.

Status of certification

Shortly before completion of the building (state August 2010), it can be assumed that the LEED certification rating "Gold" will be achieved. The number of credits and the compliance levels in the individual categories achieved at this stage are shown in Fig. 6.13.

With the 48 credits confirmed by the GBCI in the design phase submittal, the minimum goal, LEED Silver, has already been almost achieved. In the construction phase, a maximum of 18 additional credits is aimed at, so that, with a total of 66 possible credits, a good cushion is provided for achieving the LEED rating "Gold", which is awarded from 60 credits upwards (Fig. 6.14).

LEED: New Headquarters for the Deutsche Börse Group, Eschborn

With a gross floor area of 78000 m² the new headquarters for the Deutsche Börse Group provides work space for a staff of up to 2400. Already in the concept phase the essential demands in terms of ecological, economic and social quality, as well as aesthetics and function, were defined in consultation with the future tenant. Important aims included short routes, low primary energy consumption, surpassing legal standards as well as achieving a bright, light-flooded building (Fig. 6.15). With an investment volume of around 250 million euro, it was clear beyond doubt that, in addition to the ecological and socio-cultural quality of the building, long-term economic efficiency should be made the central focus of all considerations. The sustainability requirements are based on the US certification system LEED (Leadership in Energy and Environmental Design), and were taken into account from the beginning of conceptual design and planning. Integrating this system in the planning process at an early stage had a considerable influence on the solution found.

The cube-like basic form of the building results from two L-shaped volumes, that surround a 21-storey central hall space with a height of about 80 metres (Figs. 6.16 and 6.17). The glass façade and the glass roof of the atrium allow the intensive use of daylight in the atrium and in the adjoining functional areas of the building (Fig. 6.18). At the same time the building has an almost ideal A/V relationship (relationship of the surface area of the thermal building envelope to the heated building volume) of under 0.1.

The atrium is naturally ventilated and cooled in summer by means of opening vents in the facade. Without additional mechanical cooling, the temperature in the area of the entrance hall in summer can be kept around 3-4 Kelvin below the temperature of the outside air. In the ground floor lounge areas during hot summer days an additional underfloor cooling ensures a pleasant microclimate with a felt temperature of 5-6 Kelvin below the outside air temperature. In winter underfloor heating as well as heated façade sections heat the hall to over 17 °C.

The flexible room and circulation concept means that each standard floor can be

6.15

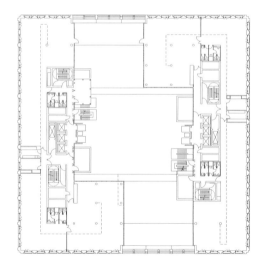

6.16

New headquarters for the Deutsche Börse Group
Location and completion: Eschborn 2010
Architect: KSP Jürgen Engel Architekten, Frankfurt/Main
Project developers: Groß & Partner Grundstücksentwicklungsgesellschaft mbH, Frankfurt/Main; Lang & Cie. Real Estate AG, Frankfurt/Main
Technical building services: Ebert-Ingenieure GmbH & Co. KG, Frankfurt/Main
Building physics: ITA Ingenieurgesellschaft für technische Akustik, Wiesbaden
Structural design: ARGE Lenz Weber Ingenieure,
Frankfurt/Main und Grontmij BGS Ingenieurgesellschaft, Frankfurt/Main
LEED AP: Lutz Miersch, Ebert & Baumann Consulting Engineers Inc., Washington DC
Function: office and administration building, underground garage
Number of storeys: 21 levels of office space, two levels of underground garage with 900 parking spaces
Gross floor area: 78000 m²
Certification system: LEED
System: LEED for New Construction and Major Renovations, Version 2.2 (LEED-NC 2.2)

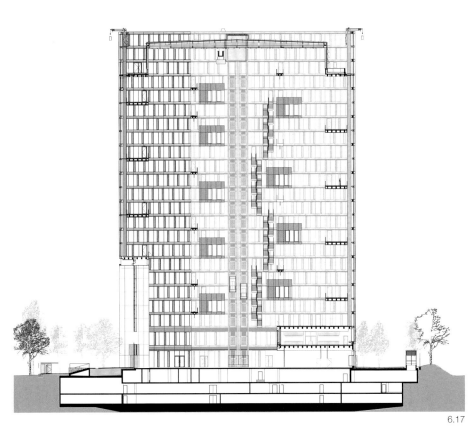

6.17

6.18

separated into eight rental units, each with its own WC core and a connection to the central hall space. Mobile partition wall systems allow the layout of the offices to be easily adapted to suit new requirements.

Bridges and walkways that cross the void are used to implement the philosophy of short routes around the atrium. The effects of both the seasons and the open building structure on the internal climate were evaluated and optimized using CFD (computational fluid dynamics) simulations in various zones.

As desired by the user great emphasis was placed on the use of resource-saving and environmentally sound building materials for both the building shell and the interior fitting-out. This contributes to the overall positive ecological balance and a healthy working environment.

The highly insulated, adaptive building envelope regulates and optimises the energy flows between the outdoors and the inner zones and makes an important contribution to the building's low primary energy demand, which is about 150 kWh/m²a (basis: DIN 18 599). The the facade of the standard floor is constructed as full-height box windows. On the inner face they have triple glazing, on

the outside an additional wind deflector pane protects the adjustable sunshade louver blinds in the façade void from the effects of weather. This window construction minimises heat losses in winter and undesirable heat gains in summer. In the upper area of the sunshade system light-deflecting louvers direct daylight deep into the interior, reducing the need for artificial light.

Staff members can individually and naturally ventilate their own workplace from outside, or through the hall by means of opening vents. The external facade of the atrium consists of a post and beam system with double glazing and external wind-secure metal mesh as sun protection. For the inner façade onto the atrium, single glazing is sufficient.

Energy and internal climate concept

The basic philosophy of the building design combines two aspects: creating the best possible work environment for the staff, and minimising energy consumption. The internal climate concept focuses on thermal comfort in winter and summer, as well as visual, acoustic and hygienic comfort. The work areas are ventilated by a mechanical ventilation system with 4.5 m³/hm² of outside air, and by

means of chilled and heated ceilings. The targeted room temperatures are 22 °C in winter, and a maximum of 26 °C in summer. In winter a heat recovery system uses 80 % of the energy content of the exhaust air to heat the cool outdoor air. In summer the heat recovery system uses the building's exhaust air to pre-cool the warm outdoor air.

Controls based on weather forecasts provide the energy flow required by the building. The high amount of daylight from the light-deflecting elements in the upper area of the sun protection system as well as the daylight provided for the office areas from the hall space helps to reduce the requirement for artificial light. Daylight- and presence-dependent controls of artificial light help to significantly reduce the amount of power consumed. The building is supplied with energy by two gas-fuelled combined heat and power plants on the roof, which provide about 60 % of the power needed, and the

6.15 Street elevation, Rendering
6.16 Plan of standard floor, Scale 1:1000
6.17 Section, Scale 1:1000
6.18 Atrium, Rendering

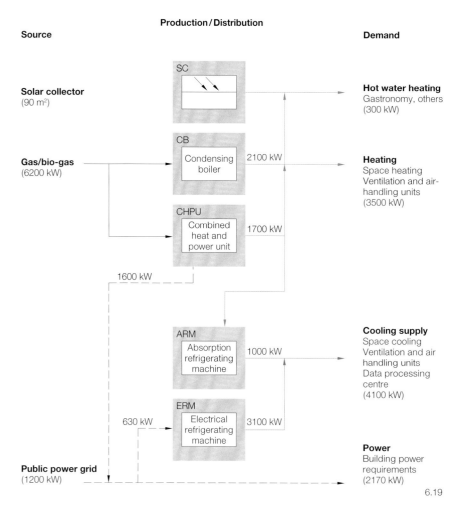

Production / Distribution

Source

SC

Solar collector
(90 m²)

Demand

Hot water heating
Gastronomy, others
(300 kW)

CB
Condensing boiler

2100 kW

Heating
Space heating
Ventilation and air-handling units
(3500 kW)

Gas/bio-gas
(6200 kW)

CHPU
Combined heat and power unit

1700 kW

1600 kW

ARM
Absorption refrigerating machine

1000 kW

Cooling supply
Space cooling
Ventilation and air handling units
Data processing centre
(4100 kW)

ERM
Electrical refrigerating machine

630 kW

3100 kW

Public power grid
(1200 kW)

Power
Building power requirements
(2170 kW)

6.19

base load of the building's heat requirements (Fig. 6.19).

An important goal of the LEED system is to increase the proportion of renewable energies used in supplying energy to buildings. The relevant requirements are more closely defined in the LEED criterion "On-site renewable energy" (EA-2). The higher the percentage of yearly energy costs that can be saved by using locally harvested renewable energies, the higher the rating. The maximum number of points (three) is achieved for energy cost savings of at least 12.5 % (on the basis of an energy calculation according to ASHRAE 90.1). In the new building for the Deutsche Börse Group this is achieved by the use of bio-gas which is obtained from renewable biomass, e.g. straw. Waste heat from combined heat and power units that cannot be used is temporarily stored in a stratified tank, and is fed into the heating system of the building as required. Gas condensing boilers meet peak loads, increase the availability of heat generation, while also offering the advantage that they can be speedily regulated. A solar system covers about 10 %

of the energy required for hot water. Absorption chillers powered by waste heat from the combined heat and power plant provide cooling energy for space and process cooling (e.g. data-processing centre). Electric refrigerating machines cover peak cooling loads, while also guaranteeing the supply for the data-processing centre. When the outdoor air temperature is below 8 °C cooling energy for the computer centre is produced through free recooling from the cooling towers, while chillers are switched off. The primary energy requirement of the building is more than 55 % below the legally permitted maximum in the German energy saving ordnance 2007. To optimise the total energy needs, and to prove energy efficiency according to LEED the building and all energy-relevant systems were depicted in a computer model according to the ASHRAE-Standard 90.1-2004. On this basis the total energy needs including the user-specific energy demand (e.g. for operating office equipment) were evaluated by means of a dynamic year-round whole energy simulation.

LEED certification

The new headquarters of the Deutsche Börse Group is certified according to LEED-NC 2.2 (LEED System for New Construction and Major Renovations, in the version 2.2) by the U.S. Green Building Council. The project developers Groß & Partner and Lang & Cie. wanted to achieve a 'Platinum' rating, which meant that sustainability requirements from six different thematic areas of the LEED certificate system had to be consistently integrated and implemented in the planning and execution of the building. Shortly before the completion of the building an overall compliance level of 84 %, representing 58 of 69 possible credits, had been targeted (Fig. 6.20). The statistics confirm just how ambitious the aims in the area of implemented sustainability quality actually are: only between 5 and 6 % of all LEED certified buildings achieve the rating "Platinum".

Certification results

In the categories "Energy and Atmosphere" as well as "Water Efficiency" the building achieved a compliance level of 100 % and 94 % respectively. By means of the energy year-round simulation according to ASHRAE 90.1, energy cost savings of 43.8 % in comparison to the reference value could be proved and thus the maximum number of credits (10 out of 10) were achieved in criterion EA-1 (Optimized Energy Performance). In both categories in order to achieve a high compliance level it is not just the energy and water concept that are important but also the functional quality assurance implemented in the planning and construction processes. This includes, in particular, systematic commissioning as well as measurement and verification during the first year of operation.

This method is intended to ensure that the energy systems and plants optimised and harmonised with each other during the planning phase are actually operated as planned during operation phase, and thereby achieve the required efficiency. To this end a detailed commissioning plan, which requires input and cooperation from all relevant disciplines, was developed for the energy-relevant systems. It includes extensive test procedures and evaluation methods with which the dynamic operation values could be compared with the ideal values from the planning and, where necessary, corrected. The target values, e.g. to restrict the primary energy requirements to a maximum of 150 kWh/m²a, were translated by means of dynamic whole energy simulations into concrete requirements for the omponents of the overall system (e. g. the efficiency of the refrigeration or the degree of efficiency of motors), and were then incorporated in the specifications. The efficient operation of components is continuously checked by means of monitoring stations and data points, that were integrated in the planning on the basis of the commissioning and operation optimisation strategy.

From the outset the project developers called for building materials that pose no danger to health. Here, the focus was on materials that are in direct contact with the indoor air. The qualities of low-emitting building products are confirmed by the relevant certificates (e.g. Green Label Plus for carpet), or details from the producer (e.g. volatile organic compounds content). This relates to materials such as paints and coatings, floor coverings, composite woods, plant fibre products or adhesives and sealants. The LEED criterion IEQ 4.4 (Low-Emitting Materials, Composite Wood & Agrifiber Products), for example, requires composite wood materials which are used for doors, among other purposes, to be free from added urea-formaldehyde resins. Currently only a few producers in the European market offer such products, which means that procuring them involves more time and additional costs. Nevertheless this requirement was met in the new building for the Deutsche Börse Group. In the meantime the market began to react to the new requirements of the certification systems. Consequently, during the course of the project it was possible to meet the requirements of LEED IEQ 4.3 (Low-Emitting Materials – Flooring Systems). This requires that all the carpet installed in the building must be tested and certified for pollutant emissions according to the standards of the US Carpet and Rug Institute. Whereas at the start of planning in 2008, products with this certificate were not yet available on the German market, the industry has in the meantime responded to the demand, and now offers suitable carpets.

The quality of the building with regard to comfort and internal climate (social dimension of sustainability) is highlighted by its compliance level of over 93% (Fig. 6.21).

LEED Category (LEED-NC 2.2)	Maximum credits	Credits not achievable	Achievable credits in the building phase	Credits achieved in the planning phase	Number of credits aimed for	Final compliance level
Sustainable sites	14	3	1	10	11	78.6%
Water efficiency	5	0	0	5	5	100.0%
Energy and atmosphere	17	1	5	11	16	94.1%
Materials and resources	13	6	7	0	7	53.8%
Indoor environmental quality	15	1	6	8	14	93.3%
Innovation in design	5	0	2	3	5	100.0%
Final score	**69**	**11**	**21**	**37**	**58**	**84.1%**
Certification rating (basis: probable number of credits)						**Platinum**

6.20

0	26	33	39	52	69
Not classified		Certified	Silver	Gold	Platinum

Headquarters of the Deutsche Börse Group, Eschborn 37 credits already awarded (as of August 2010)	Further 21 credits aimed for	Certification goal: Platinum

37   58

6.21

In the category 'Materials and Resources', the new building for the Deutsche Börse Group achieves a compliance level of 54%, which represents 7 out of 13 possible credits. Five of the credits not achieved are related to the re-use of materials and building materials. This relates to recycled building materials (for example used bricks, stone floors etc.), and the re-use of existing building elements such as walls, ceilings, roof or fitting-out elements. In addition, LEED requires that rapidly renewable materials (e.g. straw, cork, bamboo), which can be harvested in a cycle of less than ten years, should make up 2.5% of the total costs of all building materials, which is not realistic in a building of this size. Consequently this point was not pursued further in the project.

The headquarters of the Deutsche Börse Group achieved all four possible innovation credits. These exist to award an additional positive assessment to those buildings where individual criteria are significantly surpassed. In this case the innovation credits were awarded for the following measures and building qualities:

- a potable water consumption figure that is more than 40% below the reference value
- a free and unobstructed view outside from all workplaces
- exceeding the green areas called for in the building regulations by more than 300%
- more than 30% of building materials were regionally produced

6.19 Energy supply concept
6.20 Assessment results according to categories
6.21 Certification result aimed at according to LEED-NC 2.2, status August 2010

DGNB: Zentrum für Umweltbewusstes Bauen (Centre for Environmentally-conscious Building), Kassel

The Zentrum für Umweltbewusstes Bauen (ZUB), which forms part of the University of Kassel, was set up in 1998 as a development association in collaboration with the specialist areas Building Physics (Prof. Gerd Hauser), Experimental Building (Prof. Gernot Minke), and Technical Building Services (Prof. Gerhard Hausladen). The basic idea was to establish a link between applied research, handcraft, industry, architects and engineers, with the aim of fostering environmentally conscious building (Fig. 6.22).

Given the terms of reference of the ZUB, the design of the new building erected in 2001 naturally focused on aspects of ecological building, in particular energy saving and the efficient use of energy. Designed within the framework of the research project "Solar Optimised Building" of the Federal Ministry of Economics and Technology, the intention was, that by taking a holistic approach to the planning, the new building should be a should be a role model, demonstration and research building. The goals, in energy terms, were augmented by guidelines regarding sustainable building, high comfort levels, low energy use, maximum flexibility, as well as low investment and running costs.

The character of the location, a gap on the university site in the inner city, is shaped by late 19th century former industrial buildings. Numerous workshops with students of the University of Kassel led to the development of an elongated building, its footprint measuring 46 × 8 metres, with a single loaded corridor circulation (Figs. 6.23 and 6.24). The building adjoins the neighbouring Kolben-Seeger building to the north, which is under a preservation order, with a light filled atrium space, lit from above and from both narrow end facades (Fig. 6.25). The structure of the new building consists of flat reinforced concrete floor slabs without downstand beams, and circular columns. The triple-glazed south façade has a timber post and beam construction, with exposed wood internally, and aluminium on the external face. The east and west facades are for the most part closed and are made of reinforced concrete, with a red rendered composite thermal insulation system, its colour matching the col-

6.22

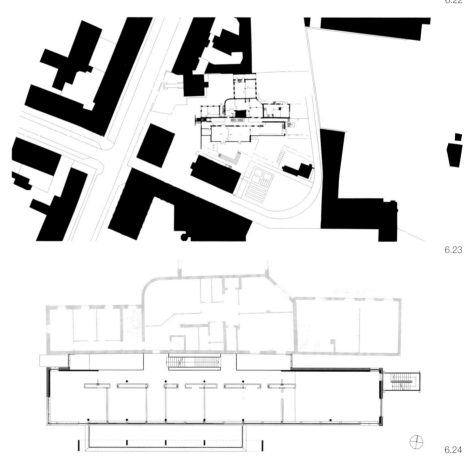

6.23

6.24

Zentrum für Umweltbewusstes Bauen (ZUB)
Location and completion: Kassel 2001
Architect: ARGE ZUB Jourdan & Müller PAS, Frankfurt/Main und Seddig Architekten, Kassel
Client: Zentrum für Umweltbewusstes Bauen e.V., Kassel
Building physics: Ingenieurbüro Hauser GmbH, Kassel
Technical building services: ARGE IB Hausladen GmbH, Heimstetten, and Ingenieurbüro Springl, Ingolstadt

Structural design: Bollinger + Grohmann, Frankfurt/Main
DGNB Auditor: Natalie Eßig, TU Munich, Chair of Building Physics
Function: office, events and laboratory areas
Number of storeys: four levels
Gross floor area: 2293 m²
Certification system: DGNB
System version: New Construction Office and Administration Buildings, V 2008

our of the brickwork of the adjoining buildings. The roof is, in part, a planted roof, on which experiments are carried out on the thermal insulation performance of planted roofs, the other part is a glass roof that lights the atrium below. The presence of the large foyer and lecture hall on the ground floor mean that part of the building projects forward on the south side. Above this projection there is a roof terrace that is partly shaded by a U-shaped reinforced concrete element. The glazed atrium, the central element in the building's circulation, runs the complete length of the building, from the entrance on the west facade to the east facade. To the north it is bordered by a fire wall, to the south by a twin-leaf, non-load bearing wall of unfired clay bricks, which also accommodates service runs. The new building has a foyer and lecture hall on the ground floor which can be combined to form a large hall when necessary, on the upper floors there are offices and experiment rooms, with experiment, storage and service rooms in the basement.

Energy and internal climate concept

The design and use concept for the ZUB building, which began operations in 2001, reflects several criteria of the DGNB certificate. In particular the efficient energy use, the reasonable construction and running costs and the integral planning process had a positive impact on the rating of the ZUB in terms of sustainable building quality. The main thesis of the building physics was first of all to build in a climate-optimised way, then to heat and cool in a way that is suitable for the building. Thus, the energy and climate concept first of all implements passive measures, as far as possible in the location, and only then introduces active measures.

For example, as a passive measure to limit transmission heat losses in winter, particular attention was paid to the installation thermal insulation. This is reflected by the compact enclosing surface area in relationship to the total volume ($A/V = 0.34$ m^{-1}), the low thermal transfer coefficients of the external walls (30 cm insulation, $U = 0.11$ W/m^{2}K), of the roof ($U = 0.16$ W/m^{2}K), of the ground floor slab ($U = 0.26$ W/m^{2}K), and of the triple pane insulated glazing ($U_W = 0.8$ W/m^{2}K) as well as the avoidance of thermal bridges at the joints and connections.

To prevent ventilation heat losses particular emphasis was placed on making the building air-tight. A blower door test resulted in a mean value for the air change rate of $n_{50} = 1{,}0$ h^{-1}, thus confirming that this requirement had been met. The large amount of glazing in the south facade allows solar heat gains from the low winter sun to be exploited in an optimal way. In summer an external sun protection system, part of which is a daylight deflection system, prevents the spaces from overheating. The efficient overall concept of the building is shown in particular in the summer time thermal protection, where thermal insulation, night-time ventilation and the shading of the south facade play leading roles.

The active measures include conventional underfloor heating combined with activated building elements to heat and cool the building. Radiators were fitted only in the sanitary facilities. In each office space there are separate controls for screed and ceiling slab level. To provide greater comfort for the users the room temperature can be individually adjusted by raising or lowering it by 2 degrees Kelvin. Heating is provided by a district heating system, cooling by means of a radiant floor slab cooler. The latter uses the almost constant low temperatures in the area of the ground to condition the building. In much the same way as the activating of the ceiling slabs, pipes were laid in the ground floor slab. The water that flows through them is cooled by the surrounding earth. It then flows into the upper floor slabs and can again take heat from the office spaces.

The flexible ventilation concept combines a number of ventilation strategies. On the one hand all the office spaces can be naturally ventilated by opening the windows, on the other fresh air can be introduced into the office through the ventilation ducts. The stale air moves through flow openings in the door frames with noise and fire baffles into the atrium, where it is centrally exhausted. This air flow could theoretically also move in the reverse direction. In winter, stale air flows across a cross-flow heat exchanger in the basement before leaving the building. In the transitional periods of the year and in summer the heat exchanger can be circumvented by means of a bypass (Fig. 6.26).

The ventilation system with heat recovery is controlled by means of sensors that

6.25

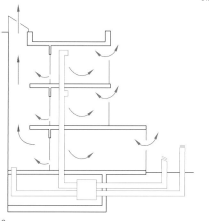

a

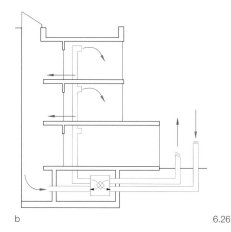

b
6.26

6.22 South elevation
6.23 Site plan, Scale 1:2000
6.24 Plan, Scale 1:500 (existing building in light grey)
6.25 The glazed circulation space is lit from above and takes on the function of an atrium.
6.26 Sections illustrating the ventilation concept, no scale
    a) Fresh air intake through the offices, stale air exhausted through the atrium
    b) Central air supply and exhaust across heat exchangers (winter situation)

127

measure the CO_2 levels in the rooms and in the exhaust air duct, as well as the amount of volatile organic compounds (VOC) in the room air. In addition the night-time ventilation can be used to pre-cool the building in summer.

The almost entirely glazed south facade ensures that the workplaces are provided with an ideal amount of daylight. The daylight factor measured in these spaces is 5 %. The swivelling louvers of the sun protection system allow daylight to be provided without glare. In a number of areas the upper part can also be regulated and directs light deep into the space. The gridded suspended luminaires that combine direct and indirect lighting are also energy optimised. They are dimmed by sensors according to the daylight levels and thus always ensure a nominal illuminance of 500 lux.

DGNB certification and certification result

The Zentrum für Umweltbewusstes Bauen was one of the first 16 projects in Germany to be certified in the pilot phase of the DGNB certificate according to the version "V 2008 New Office and Administrative Buildings". This certification system was developed by the Deutsche Gesellschaft für Nachhaltiges Bauen together with the Federal Ministry for Transport, Building and Urban Develop-

ment (BMVBS). The ZUB, completed in 2001, was selected for the DGNB pilot certification as it still represents an extremely good standard in this building category. In addition a great deal of research was carried out on this building and the results were well documented. This meant that many of the proofs required for certification were already available, for example the documentation of the planning process, thermography records, an air-tightness test and records of the monitoring.

In particular the assessments of the ecological balance (criteria 1 to 5, 10 and 11) and the lifecycle costs (criterion 16) were extremely good. That the ZUB achieved excellent results in 'ecological quality', was due above all to the ambitious energy concept and the building's material efficiency.

The ZUB was planned and built a number of years before the DGNB was developed and consequently there were a number of categories for which no credits could be awarded, as the information required for the assessment was not available at all or only in part. For example, no assessment was possible for 'Internal space hygiene' (criterion 20), as the certificate requires that the air in the rooms must be measured within four weeks of completion at the latest. For reasons of time the alterna-

tive, a report on pollutants listing all the building materials used and with detailed environmental product declarations, was not possible in the framework of the pilot certification. This had a negative impact on the assessment in terms of 'Risks to the local environment' (criterion 6).

The strict standards and the current demands as regards provision of proofs and the tight schedules of the pilot phase of the DGNB certificate, meant that the assessment result for the socio-cultural and functional quality only achieved the rating "satisfactory". However, during the pilot phase it was shown that in particular with regard to the ratings for the socio-cultural and functional quality and the process quality, a number of the DGNB requirements could have been fulfilled without any great additional expenditure if they had already been known during the planning, implementation and commissioning stages of the ZUB. This applies, for example, to the complete documentation of the planning and construction phase that is called for, or, to the holding of an architecture competition (criterion 31), which aims at ensuring a high level of design quality.

Overall the ZUB achieved a compliance level of 67 % and thus obtained the DGNB certificate rating "Silver" (Figs. 6.27 – 6.29).

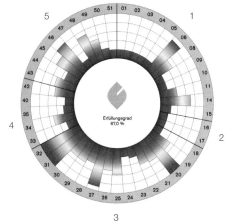

6.27

Main criteria groups	Total weighting	Compliance level	Grade
Ecological quality	22.5 %	67.2 %	1.9
Economic quality	22.5 %	94.0 %	1.0
Socio-cultural and functional quality	22.5 %	43.9 %	3.4
Technical quality	22.5 %	66.6 %	2.0
Quality of the process	10.0 %	59.1 %	2.4
Quality of the location		74.5 %	1.7
Object rating	**100 %**	**67 %**	**1.93**

6.28

6.27 Overview of assessment results
  1 Ecological quality
  2 Economic quality
  3 Socio-cultural and functional quality
  4 Technical quality
  5 Process quality
6.28 Assessment result according to main criteria groups
6.29 Certification result and compliance level
6.30 North elevation
6.31 Plan of 1st floor, Scale 1:1000
6.32 Longitudinal section, Scale 1:1000

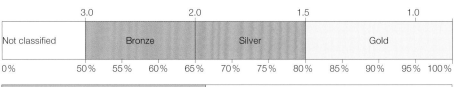

6.29

DGNB/BNB: Federal Ministry of Health, Bonn

In developing its own building projects the Federal Republic of Germany regards sustainable building as a most important theme. With this in mind, the Federal Ministry for Transport, Construction and Urban Development (BMVBS), among others, participated in the development of the Deutsches Gütesiegel Nachhaltiges Bauen (German Seal of Approval for Sustainable Building). The suitability of this system was tested on buildings belonging to the state in two pilot phases. At that time 49 of a total of 63 criteria were 'active', that is, they could be applied to buildings (Fig. 6.34, p.131). Subsequently the newly created assessment method was modified slightly and given the new name 'Bewertungssystem Nachhaltiges Bauen' (Assessment System for Sustainable Building/BNB).

In the second pilot phase the new building for the Federal Ministry of Health in Bonn was certified according to the BNB. This building was completed in 2007, and provides space for 395 staff members. The design by Petzinka Pink Architekten from Düsseldorf had emerged as the winner of a limited entry competition.

The building ensemble consists of a six-storey elongated side wing, a two-storey connecting element containing the main entrance, foyer and library, and a 13-storey high-rise on a square floor plan with offices along the façades and an internal core. The long side wing aligns itself parallel with the surrounding office buildings and subordinate ancillary buildings that are also located on this state-owned site (Figs. 6.30–6.32). The outdoor areas are integrated in the existing park-like complex. Contrary to the requirements of the assessment system, these areas are not barrier-free, but are accessible to the public, which was positively assessed. Credits were also gained by the provision of covered bicycle parking areas. The building itself is a reinforced concrete frame construction, that combines precast and in situ concrete elements. Front-hung, sand-coloured, precast concrete elements with alternating horizontal and vertical butt joints create the facade's characteristic appearance. Alternating opaque and transparent glazing in aluminium frames is fitted between the precast elements. In the case of the roof design (criterion 24, Fig. 6.36) the extensively planted roofs

6.30

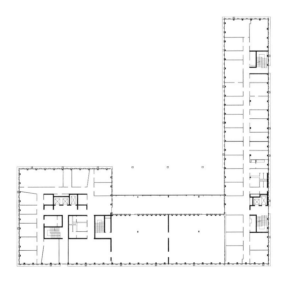

6.31

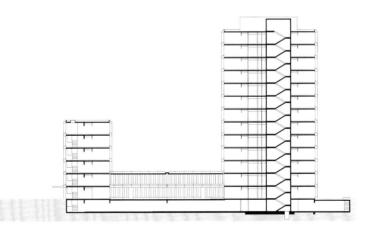

6.32

Federal Ministry of Health
Location and completion: Bonn 2007
Architect: Petzinka Pink Architekten, Düsseldorf
Client: Federal Republic of Germany
Technical building services/Building physics:
DS-Plan, Cologne
Structural design: Weischede, Herrmann und
Partner, Stuttgart

DGNB Auditors: Natalie Eßig, TU Munich;
Thomas Rühle, Integrale Planung GmbH, Munich
Function: office and administration areas, library
Number of storeys: 13 levels
Gross floor area: 17 202 m²
Certification system: DGNB/BNB
System version: New Construction Office and Administration Buildings, V 2008

and the aesthetically designed housing for the services unit on the office tower, ensured that the maximum possible number of credits were achieved. The rainwater from the roofs and the paved outdoor areas seeps away on site, having a positive impact on the water consumption value (criterion 14).

Energy and internal climate concept

A heating supply run from a neighbouring building supplies the ministry building. Radiators in the parapet area below the windows provide heat for the interior spaces. When the outside temperature is particularly low, the ceilings can also be thermally activated. The users can individually adjust the temperatures in their offices. This resulted in the full number of credits in the criterion 'Influence by the user', indicator 'Temperatures during the heating period' (criterion 23) being awarded.

In the area of 'Energetic and moisture-proofing quality of the building envelope' (criterion 35), with average U-values of 1.4 W/m²K for the transparent external building elements and 1.1 W/m²K for the light domes, the building meets the target values for the top assessment rating (1.6 W/m²K and 2.6 W/m²K respectively). In total, however, only a few credits were achieved for this indicator, as the opaque external building elements, which have an average U value of 0.41 W/m²K, only achieved the threshold value for

the lowest assessment rating, which is 0.45 W/m²K. A further indicator in the same criterion, the air-change rate, was given 0 credits, as no measurements were made.

In summer the building is cooled by window ventilation and, in the case of high cooling loads, also by activating building elements. The cooling supply for this system is provided by an evaporation cooling tower with an adiabatic cooling effect. Thermal simulations of the situation in summer were carried out for different facade types. However the facade type developed on the basis of these simulations was ultimately not examined, which meant that in the certification of 'Thermal comfort in summer' (criterion 19) a rating higher than the reference value was not possible.

On the east, south and west facades, passive solar protection is provided by external blinds with aluminium louvers. This protection is automatically activated for each facade and can be individually adapted by the users to suit their needs. The louvers in the upper area also deflect daylight. In addition a curtain fitted in the interior can be individually adjusted to provide protection from glare.

The office spaces are naturally ventilated. To ensure sufficient ventilation without any losses under changing conditions, the performance in summer, in winter, and in windy conditions was examined in commissioned preliminary wind studies. Based

on the results of these studies mechanically operated ventilation windows were fitted from the sixth floor upwards in the high-rise building. In both cases the users can individually regulate the system. The library, conference rooms, toilets and the rooms without windows have additional mechanical ventilation.

The pendant luminaires fitted in the offices combine direct and indirect light radiation (and were therefore positively assessed in the certification). With regard to 'Visual comfort' (criterion 22) credits were also achieved thanks to the individual lighting at the workplace, the proof of glare-free artificial lighting, as well as the high colour rendering indices for the illuminants and the glazing. For other indicators – such as daylight availability for the building as a whole and for the workplaces, or the visual connections to the outdoors – no documentation was available.

DGNB/BNB certification

The building had already been completed and was already in use at the time of the certification. The basis for the rating was provided by extracts from the extensive design documentation, the architects' plans, the general contractor contract, and the digital documentation for cost groups 300 and 400, as well as further reports and data. A calculation according to DIN V 18599 was made retroactively, as this is essential for providing the ecological balance and for calculating life

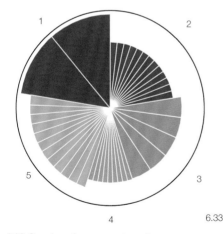

6.33

Main criteria groups	Total weighting	Compliance level	Grade
Ecological quality	22.5%	73%	1.8
Economic quality	22.5%	93%	1.1
Socio-cultural and functional quality	22.5%	46%	3.3
Technical quality	22.5%	58%	2.5
Quality of the process	10.0%	59%	2.4
Quality of the location		78%	1.6
Object rating	**100%**	**66.8%**	**1.94**

6.34

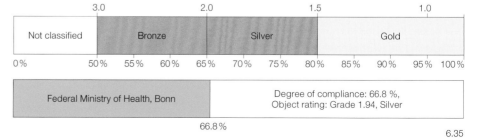

6.35

6.33 Overview of assessment results
(Illustration according to BNB)
   1 Economical quality
   2 Socio-cultural and functional quality
   3 Technical quality
   4 Process quality
   5 Ecological quality
6.34 Assessment results according to main criteria
groups
6.35 Certification result and degree of compliance
6.36 Certification results according to individual
criteria

cycle costs. Other documentation which was unavailable, was not, or could not be produced on account of the regulations in the certification system regarding documentation. This documentation includes, for example, calculations or measurements of the reverberation period in the offices and of the air quality in the interior, thermographic inspections, or a blower door test.

Result of the certification
After the examination of the data by the auditors a number of points were clarified by visiting the building. For a certification that is carried out after completion of the building the 'Silver' rating represents a better than average result. Here particular attention should be drawn to the especially good results in the category 'Economic Quality' with a compliance level of 93 % and a grade of 1.1 (Figs. 6.33–6.35). In the category 'Technical Quality' it was primarily the indicator 'Mean Thermal Transfer Coefficient' in the criterion 'Energetic and moisture-proofing quality of the building envelope' (criterion 35) that prevented the building from achieving a better result. The opaque external building elements only reached the threshold value for the lowest rating (Fig. 6.36). The lack of an air-tightness examination meant that data for the indicator 'Air exchange rate' could not be provided. In this category a total compliance level of 58 % was achieved.

In the category 'Quality of the process' a score of 59 % was achieved. Here, as this category documents the quality of the building process, it was difficult to prove after completion of the building that the targets had been reached. In the category 'Quality of the location' the excellent transport connections, the proximity to facilities and buildings of relevance to the function, as well as media (such as broadband connection) and service supplies (e.g. with district heating) meant that a compliance level of 78 % could be achieved. In contrast the result in the category 'Socio-cultural and functional quality' was comparatively poor with a compliance level of only 46 % and thus the score 3.3. If the 'Bewertungssystem Nachhaltiges Bauen' (BNB) had been known at the time of planning it would certainly have been possible here to devote more attention to the concerns of socio-cultural sustainability and thus to achieve more credits in this category.

		Compliance level	Grade
Ecological quality		**73 %**	
Impact on global and local environment			
1	Global warming potential (GWP)	72 %	
2	Ozone depletion potential (ODP)	100 %	
3	Photochemical ozone creation potential (POCP)	100 %	
4	Acidification potential (AP)	100 %	
5	Eutrophication potential (EP)	100 %	1.8
6	Risks to the regional environment	50 %	
8	Other impacts on the global environment	50 %	
9	Microclimate	100 %	
Utilisation of resources			
10	Non-renewable primary energy demands (PE_{ne})	88 %	
11	Total primary energy demand and proportion of renewable primary energy (PE_e)	61 %	
14	Potable water consumption and sewage generation	93 %	
15	Surface area usage	75 %	
Economic quality		**93 %**	
Life cycle costs			
16	Building-related life cycle costs	89 %	1.1
Value development			
17	Value stability	100 %	
Socio-cultural and functional quality		**46 %**	
Health, comfort and user satisfaction			
18	Thermal comfort in winter	10 %	
19	Thermal comfort in summer	10 %	
20	Indoor hygiene	50 %	
21	Acoustic comfort	0 %	
22	Visual comfort	37 %	
23	Influence by user	63 %	
24	Roof design	100 %	
25	Safety and risks of breakdowns	88 %	3.3
Functionality			
26	Barrier-free accessibility	75 %	
27	Efficient use of area	0 %	
28	Suitability for conversion	64 %	
29	Accessibility	0 %	
30	Bicycle comfort	50 %	
Assuring design quality			
31	Assuring design and urban planning quality in the competition	80 %	
32	Art in architecture	90 %	
Technical quality		**58 %**	
Quality of the technical implementation			
33	Fire protection	83 %	
34	Noise protection	65 %	
35	Energetic and moisture proofing quality of the building envelope	14 %	2.5
40	Ease of cleaning and maintenance	83 %	
42	Ease of deconstruction, recycling and dismantling	46 %	
Quality of the process		**59 %**	
Quality of the planning			
43	Quality of project preparation	70 %	
44	Integrated planning	63 %	
45	Optimisation and complexity of the approach to planning	26 %	
46	Evidence of consideration of sustainability in tender documents and awarding contract	75 %	2.4
47	Establishment of preconditions for optimal use and operation	67 %	
Quality of the construction work			
48	Construction site / construction process	10 %	
49	Quality of the executing companies/prequalification	100 %	
50	Quality assurance of the construction work	50 %	
51	Systematic commissioning	75 %	
Quality of the location		**78 %**	
56	Risks at the micro-location	72 %	
57	Circumstances at the micro-location	53 %	
58	Image and condition of the location and district	75 %	1.6
59	Connection to transport	83 %	
60	Proximity of facilities relevant to building function	88 %	
61	Adjoining media / infrastructure development	94 %	

6.36

DGNB: Office and administration building, Munich (pre-certificate)

In Arnulfpark, a little to the west of Munich's main railway station, a new office and administration building is being erected on the site of a former freight station (Fig. 6.37).

This site had been very detrimentally affected by its previous use. By carrying out a complete decontamination and changing the function of the site to the category 'Building' it was possible to reach the highest compliance level in terms of 'Surface area usage' (criterion 15). In the category 'Quality of the location' the new building achieved a very good result, on account of the good transport access and the numerous facilities and amenities in the nearby surroundings (gastronomy, educational and leisure facilities, local shops).

The building (external dimensions: 82 × 55 m) has six floor levels, above a two storey basement car park, as well as an internal courtyard with auditorium (Figs. 6.38 and 6.39). The roof is a planted roof; the elements housing the technical plant on the roof were reduced to a minimum and they were given a screen. Both these aspects lead to a positive assessment in terms of quality of outdoor space that relates to the building (criterion 24).

The continuous enclosing facade is articulated into two areas. The ground and first floor, accommodating the entrance hall and café, have a flush glass facade. The four upper floors containing the office spaces have full-height fixed-glazing windows alternating with double-glazed openable box-type windows.

The facade onto busy Arnulfstraße exceeds the requirements for airborne sound insulation in the certification system and thus achieves the highest possible number of credits in terms of criterion 34, 'Noise protection'.

Numerous bike parking spaces in front of the building and in the underground garage encourage people to cycle to work. In addition there are changing facilities, showers and drying rooms for the users. Overall this means that the requirements in terms of 'Bicycle comfort' (criterion 30) are met completely.

Energy and internal climate concept

The building draws its heating energy from a connection to the district heating system. The transfer of heating and cooling to the

6.37

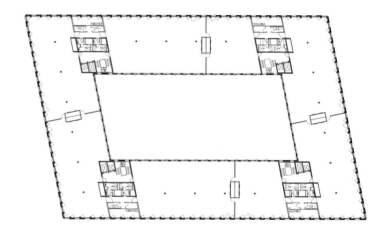

6.38

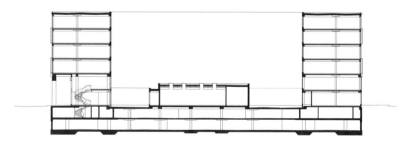

6.39

Office and administration building
Location and completion: Munich 2010
Architect: Ganzer Hajek Unterholzner, Munich, and Thierry Louvieaux, Berlin
Client: ICADE REIM Arnulfstraße MK 9 GmbH, Hamburg
Technical building services: Gruppe Ingenieurbau Technische Gebäudeausrüstung, München; Kuzyl & Sander Ingenieurbüro, Munich; Haustec, Taufkirchen

Building physics: Ingenieure Süd, Munich
Structural design: Seeberger Friedl und Partner, Munich
DGNB-Auditor: Natalie Eßig, TU Munich
Function: offices
Number of storeys: six levels
Gross floor area: 28 487 m²
Certification system: DGNB
System version: New Construction Office and Administration Buildings, V 2008 (Pre-certificate)

offices is by means of heating ceilings, which serve as cooling ceilings in winter, as well as by underfloor convectors in the area of the facade. To achieve the highest number of credits for 'Thermal comfort in winter' (criterion 18) in the indicator 'operative temperature', a thermal simulation was carried out. The data for 'Thermal comfort in summer' (criterion 19) were obtained in the same way. With regard to the other indicators 'Draughts', 'Radiation temperature asymmetry' and 'Floor temperature' as well as 'Air humidity' the project achieves the requisite levels and thus meets all demands as regards thermal comfort. Calculations regarding acoustics and simulations of the lighting conditions at the workplace were carried out at an early design stage, allowing the conclusions drawn to be incorporated in the planning. Thus credits could be collected for 'Acoustical comfort' (criterion 21) and 'Visual comfort' (criterion 22). In the area of acoustics it turned out that the soundproofing in the individual offices is in fact somewhat excessive and that the sound absorption level could be reduced. On the other hand to improve visual comfort a newly developed internal sun and glare screen system was fitted after the examination. Simulations were carried out with the aim of improving energy efficiency. For example in the context of the façade optimisation the use of double and triple glazing was examined. Triple glazing was rejected, as, because of the increased building cooling requirements, it would worsen the overall energy balance. In the

assessment the low energy requirement was proportionally rewarded by a good ecological balance. A further concern of the project developer was that the users should be able to exert a considerable amount of influence over their environment (criterion 23, 'Influence by users'). The users of this building can control light, sun and glare protection as well as the heating and cooling ceilings with a remote control and thus can directly influence their personal comfort. In addition the windows can be opened as and when needed.

An additional mechanical ventilation system is regulated by CO_2 sensors and a new kind of fine dust sensor. A simulation of the ventilation allowed the air outlets to be positioned so that they cause no draughts. To achieve good internal air quality (criterion 20, 'Indoor hygiene'), materials were selected which are, as far as possible, free from pollutants. These include the carpets and adhesives, which were examined by a testing centre for pollutants, emissions and smells. In addition, according the certification guidelines, a measurement of room air should be carried out by, at the latest, four weeks after start up.

To ensure optimal adjustment of the building during the planning phase, a comprehensive measurement and monitoring concept was worked out. For example: in the corner rooms of the uppermost floors that face southwest (the least favourable orientation because they heat up most), the operative temperature in summer was measured and evaluated before the users

moved in, so that, where necessary, subsequent improvements could be made.

DGNB certification and certification result

The building received a DGNB pre-certificate according to the version V 8 2008 'New Construction Office and Administration Buildings', which evaluates the planning status of the project when it is already under construction. In workshops with the client and other members of the project team the aspects of planning already implemented, measurements and simulations were evaluated and, on the other hand, the measures called for by the DGNB criteria that were still to be introduced, were defined in the form of declarations of intent. After commissioning of the building, to obtain the final certification proof must be provided that these have been implemented.

To achieve the DGNB certificate 'Gold' individual aspects of the design were corrected during the execution phase, and new planning targets were determined in collaboration with the auditor. These include, for example, subsequently specified water-saving taps, in order to achieve a better water consumption value for 'Potable water consumption' (criterion 14). Certainly, it is largely thanks to the integral planning of the team and the experience of the project developer, that a score of 1.0 was achieved in the category 'Quality of the process'. Overall the assessments in all categories were 'Good' to 'Very Good' and an overall compliance level of 84.1% was achieved (Figs. 6.40–6.42).

Main criteria groups	Total weighting	Compliance level	Grade
Ecological quality	22.5%	80.0%	1.50
Economic quality	22.5%	88.0%	1.23
Socio-cultural and functional quality	22.5%	85.9%	1.30
Technical quality	22.5%	77.5%	1.58
Quality of the process	10.0%	95.0%	1.00
Quality of the location		85.3%	1.32
Object rating	**100%**	**84.1%**	**1.36**

6.40

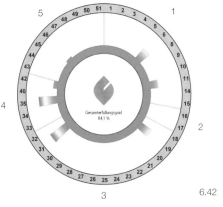

6.42

3.0	2.0	1.5	1.0
Not classified	Bronze	Silver	Gold

0% 50% 55% 60% 65% 70% 75% 80% 85% 90% 95% 100%

Office and administration building, Munich
Degree of compliance: 84.1%, Object rating: Grade 1.36, Gold

84.1%

6.41

6.37 Northwest elevation
6.38 Floor plans of 2nd to 4th floors, Scale 1:1000
6.39 Longitudinal section, Scale 1:1000
6.40 Assessment result
6.41 Certification result and degree of compliance
6.42 Overview of assessment results
  1 Ecological quality
  2 Economic quality
  3 Socio-cultural and functional quality
  4 Technical quality
  5 Quality of the process

Current situation and desired development

Climate change has made many of us rethink our behaviour in terms of sustainability. Ambitious decarbonisation proposals, which describe the transformation of our current economies into "low-carbon economies" as being technically possible and economically worthwhile, are setting the tone in strategic political discussions. Awareness is being raised globally to highlight the importance of sustainable behaviour and its significance is governing our everyday life. In China, for example, inefficient factories are closed regardless of the consequences and the owner's wishes.

Worldwide the building industry leads the field in terms of energy consumption for the air conditioning of interior space as well as the total of mass flow required for the construction and deconstruction of buildings. It follows that the need for change in this sector is especially important. In future, buildings will have to be designed, built, operated and deconstructed in a more sustainable way. As a consequence, throughout the world, there is considerable demand for systems to rate and label the sustainability of buildings and this will continue to grow.

In Germany, the focus of this development was at first on observing a building's performance in terms of energy. And it was in this field that Germany took a leading position. The entry of the American rating system LEED into the German property market coincided with increasing demand for a German system from abroad. As a result, in consultation with the relevant expert groups, a seal of approval to label the sustainability of properties was developed in Germany under serious time pressure between

2007 and the end of 2008. This book contains a detailed description of this system as well as the long-established rating systems, BREEAM and LEED.

The German system, based as far as possible on European standards, has been well received by international expert groups and is on its way to becoming a role model for a European system due to its broad and advanced approach. However, the failure of the Federal Ministry of Transport, Building and Urban Development (BMVBS) and the German Sustainable Building Council (DGNB) to reach an agreement in 2009 led to the introduction of several different German systems all with approval of the BMVBS. This situation could be detrimental to the quality of all systems.

The energy performance certificate (Energieausweis), which was introduced by the federal government as not only a need-based but also a consumption-based energy certificate, is evidence of the effect of these questionable circumstances. The fundamental pillars of a system to label sustainability, i.e. the criteria and all assessment and weighting factors, must be standardised within Germany in order to fulfil the fundamental function of labelling buildings, which is to facilitate the comparison of properties' sustainability.

It would be very unfortunate if the EU member states had to be forced by an EU directive into introducing national systems and, through this, a uniform system in each state. Unfortunately, this wasteful use of resources is foreseeable, as is evident from the development of the energy performance certificate in Germany, which adopted the same course without leading to a positive outcome.

In contrast to this national multi-track approach, an early alignment of all devel-

opments taking place in Europe to rate the sustainability of buildings is desirable. What is more, a harmonised certification system within the European Community would have distinctly better chances confronting international competition.

DGNB Certificate – subject to further research

A system to assess the sustainability of buildings has to be dynamic and, ideally, modular in structure. Due to the permanent increase of knowledge and scientific findings, changing views and social boundary conditions, which are also incorporated in building regulations and recommendations, the criteria describing sustainability must be maintained under constant review.

In the same way as standards, which are subject to constant change, assessment criteria are affected to an even greater extent. This especially applies to the German system, which was developed within a very short period of time and only put into practice recently. The transparency of the German system allows for adjustments and alignments to be made in an exemplary way.

Assessment and weighting factors

The facility to make adjustments is particularly important for the specification of assessment factors (see Certification – the systems in detail, p. 53). The current solution stems from a pragmatic approach needed to establish a German system, but this now requires scientific support and possibly correction. Notably the assessment of the site's quality, as already established in BREEAM and LEED, should be incorporated into the overall rating process. Its separate designation is also due to the time pressure felt during the system's development stages. On the other hand, reasonable arguments were brought forward in favour of a clear and deliberate separation between building and site in order to more clearly define the system's boundaries relevant to the assessment.

The weighting factors, through which consideration is given to the differing importance of individual criteria within a category, must also be based on well-founded scientific evidence. At the same time, as is the case for all assessment factors, different data sets have to be compiled to enable the use of the system in different regions around the globe in a site and society-specific way.

Determination of criteria

The specification of objectives and assessment rules in the individual criteria enables specialists to work in a sequential way which ensures a high degree of effectiveness. This structure, however, requires a great deal of effort and expense to harmonise and align the individual criteria. Maintenance and onward development of the system's criteria requires a clear definition of individual responsibilities reflecting the technical knowledge of those involved. This is the only way to ensure that the latest developments in research, standardisation and legislation are incorporated into the wording of the criteria and their respective assessment rules. Constant reviews and on-going development is essential. From time to time, specific criteria are not applicable to a particular property. In this case, it is not possible to award any points for this aspect and the overall result suffers, despite the criterion being of no significance for the building. This weakness, inherent to all systems, could be resolved if the systems were to allow single project-specific criteria to be excluded from the assessment.

Assessment boundaries extended to incorporate urban districts, estates and towns

For the performance of a property's eco assessment, the evaluation boundary and therefore the observation area of the building itself has been extended to incorporate urban districts, estates, towns and conurbations, since it is difficult to improve the sustainable energy supply of an individual building. This approach was triggered in the 1990s when new housing estates were being developed according to low-energy or passive house requirements and a natural gas connection was sought for these buildings.

Based on the lower specific CO_2 emissions of natural gas, in contrast to heating oil, a new trend developed to move away from oil, which led to a significant increase in the number of natural gas heating systems. However, low levels of gas consumption on estates built according to low-energy or passive house standards, brought into question the blanket supply of natural gas.

Naturally, the same question arises when assessing sustainability. The formulation of assessment boundaries has come to the fore as an important technical issue. Should passive housing estates that are situated on the outskirts of large cities and are therefore the cause for a large amount of private vehicle traffic be favoured, from an ecological viewpoint, over buildings in the town centre, which only meet the legally prescribed minimum requirements regarding energy efficiency but use "walking on foot" as the main means of transportation?

How high is, for example, the value of being able to walk comfortably into the countryside or the town centre? Answers to this question will without fail be very varied, and this highlights the need for research if a way is to be identified which might allow an objective assessment of this criterion within the scope of a certification system.

Government and public buildings

It seems likely that, over the longer term, the differing rating systems at an international level will continue to make it difficult to directly compare certified buildings. Of course the same difficulties apply to national developments. Here experience has shown that certain building categories, despite the same use, are rated with different systems. Government and public buildings must apply the same system as the private sector, otherwise there is no means of comparison.

When performing the certification of a public building's sustainability, it is important to make sure that an impartial and dispassionate attitude is maintained. Using own employees as auditors is therefore regarded as slightly problematic. This does not only apply to government or public buildings, but also to privately financed building schemes, when an employee working for the client or the project developer acts as the auditor.

The role of education in forging a path toward sustainability

Schools as a place of upbringing and education are an ideal place to impart and convey sustainability. At no other time in our lives are we as receptive as we are in our school days. Pupils benefit from the high-quality of room acoustics, noise protection, the provision of daylight and artificial light, good air quality and a high thermal and hygric comfort, due to excellent structural insulation. The eco-

135

logical and economic experience gained encourages them to strive for similar qualities in other locations. The impressions are particularly clear and memorable in the context of refurbishments. In Germany especially, we are encouraged to ensure the best-possible conditions in schools since these are home to our most important, renewable resource – the resource education.

This resource can be used much more effectively in sustainable buildings as is evident from the example describing the dependence of pupil performance on room temperature or room acoustics, in terms of reverberation time [1, 2]. Hence, the meaning and significance of sustainability is conveyed with the greatest possible long-term impact at the same time as achieving the highest possible level of efficiency.

Further education

Sustainable design, building, operation and possibly redevelopment as well as demolition necessitate knowledge of all aspects of sustainable building as described above. It follows that all areas are covered in the assessment of a building's sustainability and there is a requirement for planners and auditors to acquire the appropriate skills. Comprehensive further training programmes are necessary to cover and implement all aspects of sustainable building. No single person will be able to handle all fields in the depth required for the compilation of all individual criteria. However, auditors must be able to apply the criteria and recognise the relationships across the structure.

The appropriate know-how can currently be acquired in training courses specifically designed for auditing. There is furthermore the possibility to take part in advanced training courses to remain up to date. The quality of these training courses and advanced programmes is a vital element affecting the quality of the entire certification system and its acceptance in the market.

In order to meet the challenges of designing a sustainable building, some educational institutions are already offering special courses. Amongst these are, for example, courses at Cornell University and Graz University of Technology or the Summer Academy for Sustainable Building at the ETH in Zurich, Graz University, Delft University of Technology and at the University of Stuttgart. The Technische Universität München is also preparing an interdisciplinary master course for the winter term 2011/2012 called "Energy-efficient and sustainable building".

These educational programmes will support formation of a new professional group, whose main task it will be to consider aspects of sustainability during the course of designing, constructing, operating, possibly also remodelling, and demolishing buildings: the sustainability consultants. The involvement of a sustainability consultant at an early design stage will probably become commonplace in the course of the next few years.

Costs of sustainable building

The increasing demand for detailed and documented design will initially lead to a rise in planning costs. However, once assistance by a sustainability consultant becomes daily routine, it will become evident that the collaboration lends weight to the integrated planning approach, the sustainability aspects will be firmly established as part of the design process and the overall quality of the building will improve. The application of an assess-

ment system may also help in structuring the design phase and accelerate the process. The additional costs incurred for the assessment of sustainability should be outweighed by the cost advantages derived during the building's service life. The total costs of a property, which, to a large extent, are incurred during the building's operation, will decrease.

The very different structures of the established international rating systems, make it difficult to compare the costs associated with their application. The more detailed the assessment is and the more thorough the aspects of sustainability are dealt with by the system, the higher the costs. On the other hand, the optimisation potential is enhanced and benefits ensue during the construction, operation, possibly also the refurbishment and demolition phase.

Outlook on national and international developments

Labelling the sustainability of buildings will become more significant in future as the benefits at the point of sale or when renting gain recognition. The positive image of green labels will also serve to enhance the reputation of the owner of owner-occupied properties.

The consideration of sustainability aspects, in the way that they are defined by currently available rating systems, can be regarded as a classic win-win situation for both the development of a new build as well as the refurbishment of an existing property. Market players will soon come to the same conclusion. We all, the wider community as well as individuals, will benefit from the aspired balance of ecological, economic and social aspects of sustainability. The economic factor, in particular, which is of increasing importance for certification systems, will presumably become the main driver of sustainable building practices.

The pressure put on investors to certify their properties will probably increase worldwide despite different rating systems being used across the regions. Worldwide the most frequently used certification systems are BREEAM and LEED, both of which have been on the market for a relatively long time. They can be applied flexibly in different climate zones and their pragmatic approach makes them easy to integrate into the various design processes encountered worldwide.

The German system, as a system of the second generation, is from a technical viewpoint, regarded as an onward development from existing systems, because it builds on their experience and considers the latest scientific findings. Amongst these are the standardisation activities currently taking place at a European level. Following a very successful start, indeed relaunch, into the field of labelling in Germany in 2007, the initial enthusiasm for the new system has waned somewhat. There is a tendency now either to dispense with a certificate or to have the building assessed according to two systems. The facts and circumstances described in "Current situation and desired development" (p. 134) are the principal reasons for this disappointing trend.

The current situation with rating systems, such as BREEAM, LEED or DGNB, gaining ground is pointing clearly towards internationalisation. Special emphasis is being given to the development and provision of system variants which, due to their structure and the associated assessment scheme, objectives and documentation requirements, are able to cater for the considerable regional differences. With "BREEAM International Bespoke", BRE is already offering a system variant which is capable of assessing and certifying any building worldwide. DGNB and USGBC (LEED) are currently concentrating on the development of corresponding systems whereby LEED is already in use worldwide and (based on American standards) ensures a degree of comparability.

The certification systems are shaped by the building culture customary in the country in which they were originally developed and therefore differ according to the statutory requirements, the design processes and technical particularities. Tried and tested assessment criteria and further developments are being incorporated by other systems so that the current diversity of systems and the sometimes differing areas of focus help to advance and optimise the overall onward development. The trend is for the established systems, each with their individual approach, assessment criteria and objectives, to converge in core areas thereby making it easier to compare results.

After all, the overriding objectives of sustainability are valid throughout the world and the transformation to a sustainable society appears to be globally irreversible.

The application of certification systems and the integration of system-specific sustainability criteria is still, to a large extent, optional and not required by law. However, in the USA, Japan and the UK, documentary proof based on certification systems has been incorporated as a legal requirement, and minimum standards have been established in certain administrative regions or for certain building types. Future developments need to be closely monitored.

The first certification systems were developed through the commitment and dedication of a few individuals whose aim was to encourage and establish sustainable building using a comprehensive approach. Worldwide developments in recent years indicate that these certification systems have already made a significant contribution by triggering a change of awareness amongst property investors. The target values of the individual systems are adjusted regularly by the respective supervisory bodies to improve standards and comply with latest technical developments. The aim is to significantly reduce the impact of negative environmental effects and possibly even achieve net gains in future. USGBC, BRE and DGNB have already set visionary benchmarks for the future versions of their assessment systems (see Certification - the systems in detail, p. 37 and p.47).

It remains to be hoped that national interests will not stand in the way of sustainable building and competition between the certification systems. The primary aim of protecting the environment for future generations must be the driving force of our everyday actions and business activities. If this results in the better planning and development of buildings, this will be to the benefit of not only users and owners, but also the local community and society worldwide.

References:

[1] Danmarks Tekniske Universitet (DTU): Study concerning the impact of room climate on performance. Copenhagen 2006
[2] Klatte, Maria; Hellbrück, Jürgen; Seidel, Jochen; Leistner, Philip: Effects of classroom acoustics on performance and well-being in elementary school children – A field study. Kaiserslautern 2009

Literature (selection)

Principles

Architects' Council of Europe (ACE): Architecture & Quality of Life. Brussels 2009

Architects' Council of Europe (ACE): Architecture and Sustainability. Declaration and Policy of the Architects' Council of Europe. Brussels 2009

Bauer, Michael; Mösle, Peter; Schwarz, Michael: Green Building. Munich 2007

Braune, Anna; Sedlbauer, Klaus; Kittelberger, Siegrun; Kreißig, Johannes: Potenziale des Nachhaltigen Bauens in Deutschland. Leinfelden-Echterdingen 2007

Cole, Raymond J.: Building environmental assessment methods. In: Building Research and Information. Columbia 1999, p. 230–246

Daniels, Klaus; Hammann, Ralph E.: Energy Design for Tomorrow. Stuttgart/London 2009

Eßig, Natalie: Nachhaltigkeit von olympischen Bauten. Stuttgart 2010

EU Commission: Greenbuilding. Improved Energy Efficiency for Non-residential Buildings. Brussels 2010

Federal Government (pub.): Fortschrittsbericht 2008 zur nationalen Nachhaltigkeitsstrategie. Berlin 2008

Federal Office for Building and Regional Planning (BBR) (pub.): Guideline for Sustainable Building. Bonn 2001

Federal Ministry for the Environment, Nature Conservation and Nuclear Safety (BMU) (pub.): EU Strategy for Sustainable Development. Munich 2010

Federal Ministry for the Environment, Nature Conservation and Nuclear Safety (BMU) (pub.): GreenTech made in Germany 2.0 – Umwelttechnologieatlas für Deutschland. Munich 2009

Federal Ministry of Economics and Technology (BMWi) (pub.): Die Entwicklung der Energiemärkte bis zum Jahr 2030 (EWI prognostic study). Berlin 2005

Food and Agriculture Organization of the United Nations (FAO) (pub.): Global Forest Resources Assessment 2005. FAO Forestry Paper 147. Rome 2006

Gauzin-Müller, Dominique: Nachhaltigkeit in Architektur und Städtebau. Basel 2001

German Bundestag (pub.): Final Report of the Enquete Commission. Globalisation of the World Economy – Challenges and Answers. Berlin 1999

German Bundestag, Division of Public Relations (pub.): Konzept Nachhaltigkeit. Fundamente für die Gesellschaft von morgen. Bonn 1997

Gresh, Alain; Radvanyi, Jean; Rekacewicz, Philippe; Samary, Catherine; Vidal, Dominique (pub.): Atlas der Globalisierung. Berlin 2007

Hájek, Petr: Complex Methods for Life Cycle Analysis (LCA) and Life Cycle Cost (LCC) Assessments. Prague 2005

Hauser, Gerd: Mehrwert und Marktchancen von Zertifikaten im Vergleich zu Energieausweisen. Frankfurt 2008

Hausladen, Gerhard; Liedl, Petra; Sager, Christina; de Saldanha, Michael: ClimaDesign. Munich 2005

Hausladen, Gerhard; de Saldanha, Michael; Liedl, Petra: ClimaSkin. Munich 2006

Hegger, Manfred; Fuchs, Matthias; Stark, Thomas; Zeumer, Martin: Energie Atlas. Munich 2007

Huber, Joseph: Nachhaltige Entwicklung. Berlin 1995

Intergovernmental Panel on Climate Change/Fourth Assessment Report (IPCC/AR4) (pub.): Climate Change 2007. Synthesis Report. Geneva 2004

Intergovernmental Panel on Climate Change (IPCC) (pub.): Climate Change and Water. Geneva 2008

König, Holger; Kohler Niklaus; Kreißig, Johannes; Lützkendorf, Thomas: Lebenszyklusanalyse in der Gebäudeplanung. Munich 2009

Lang, Annette: Ist Nachhaltigkeit messbar? Hanover/Stuttgart 2003

Lechner, Robert; Fröhlich, Thomas: Immo-Rate. Leitfaden für das Immobilienrating nachhaltiger Wohnbauten. Melk/Danube 2006

Lewis, Owen J.: A green Vitruvius. Principles and Practice of Sustainable Architectural Design. London 1999

Lützkendorf, Thomas: Nachhaltiges Planen, Bauen und Bewirtschaften von Bauwerken. Karlsruhe 2002

Lützkendorf, Thomas: Umsetzung von Prinzipien einer nachhaltigen Entwicklung im Baubereich. Darmstadt 2003

Meadows, Dennis; Meadows, Donella H.; Zahn, Erich: Die Grenzen des Wachstums. Bericht des Club of Rome zur Lage der Menschheit. Munich 1972

Reed, Richard; Bilos, Anita; Wilkinson, Sara; Schulte, Karl-Werner: International Comparison of Sustainable Rating Tools. San Diego 2009

Stern, Nicholas: Review on the Economics of Climate Change. London 2006

U.S. Energy Information Administration (EIA) (pub.): Annual Energy Outlook 2010. Washington 2010

U.S. Green Building Council (USGBC) (pub.): New Construction & Major Renovation. Version 2.2. Reference Guide. Washington 2006

Union of International Associations (UIA): Declaration of Interdependence for a Sustainable Future. UIA/AIA World Congress of Architects. Chicago 1993

Weizsäcker, Ernst Ulrich von; Lovins, Amory B.; Lovins, Hunter L.: Faktor Vier. Munich 1995

World Commission on Environment and Development (WCED): Our Common Future. New York/Oxford 1987

Certification – the systems in detail

Arndt, Jens; Ebert, Thilo: Der Tower 185, zweimal auf dem Prüfstand. In: DBZ 03/2010, p. 68–71

Baumann, Oliver; Reiser, Claudius; Schäfer, Jochen: Grün ist nicht gleich Grün. Einblicke in das LEED-Zertifizierungssystem. In: Bauphysik 02/2009, p. 99–105

Biernat, Torsten; Schäfer, Jochen: Die wachsende Bandbreite der Gebäudetypen für LEED-Zertifizierungen. In: Bauphysik 03/2010, p. 167–171

BRE Global: BREEAM Europe Commercial 2009 Assessor Manual. Hertfordshire, 2009

Ebert, Thilo; Leipoldt, Dieter: Einflussmöglichkeiten durch Zertifizierung. In: Licht Architektur Technik 03/2009, p. 46–49

Eßig, Natalie: Die Bemessung der Nachhaltigkeit. Das Zertifizierungssystem Deutsches Gütesiegel Nachhaltiges Bauen. In: db Deutsche Bauzeitung 05/2009, p. 62–65

Federal Office for Building and Regional Planning (BBR) (pub.): Guideline for Sustainable Building. Bonn 2001

German Energy Agency (dena): EPBD guideline. Europäische Richtlinie mit verschärften Anforderungen an Gebäude und den Energieausweis. Berlin 2010

German Sustainable Building Council (DGNB): DGNB manual for new builds and administrative buildings. Version 2009. Stuttgart 2009

Gertis, Karl; Hauser, Gerd; Sedlbauer, Klaus; Sobek, Werner: Was bedeutet Platin? Zur Entwicklung von Nachhaltigkeitsbewertungsverfahren. In: Bauphysik 04/2008, p. 244–255

Hegger, Manfred; Fuchs, Matthias; Stark, Thomas; Zeumer, Martin: Energie Atlas. Munich 2007

Hegner, Hans-Dieter: Bewertungssystem als Planungshilfe. In: DBZ 12/2009, p. 46–49

Ingenhoven, Christoph: Der Weg zum BREEAM-Zertifikat. In: Detail Green 01/2009, p. 50–53

Institute for Building Environment and Energy Conservation (IBEC): CASBEE for New Construction. Technical Manual 2008 Edition. Tokyo 2008

König, Holger; Kohler Niklaus; Kreißig, Johannes; Lützkendorf, Thomas: Lebenszyklusanalyse in der Gebäudeplanung. Munich 2009

MINERGIE: 10 Jahre MINERGIE – Die Zukunft des Bauens. Bern 2008

Mösle, Peter; Bauer, Michael; Hoinka, Thomas: Green Building Label. Die wichtigsten Zertifizierungen auf dem Prüfstand. In: Greenbuilding 01–02/2009, p. 50f.

Schweizer Bau Dokumentation: Das Gebäudelabel MINERGIE und MINERGIE-P. Blauen 2006

Swiss Association of Architects and Engineers (SIA): SNARC – Systematik zur Beurteilung der Nachhaltigkeit von Architekturprojekten für den Bereich Umwelt. Zurich 2004

Swiss Federal Office of Energy (SFOE): Assessment system MINERGIE-ECO. Final report. Bern 2008

U.S. Green Building Council (USGBC): LEED Reference Guide for Green Building Design and Construction 2009. Washington 2009

Planning process and documentation requirements

Eßig, Natalie: Nachhaltigkeit von Olympischen Bauten. Stuttgart 2010

Federal Office for Building and Regional Planning (BBR) (pub.): Guideline for Sustainable Building. Bonn 2001

Geissler, Susanne; Bruck, Manfred: Eco-Building. Optimierung von Gebäuden durch Total Quality Assessment (TQ-Bewertung). Vienna 2001

Geissler, Susanne: Gebäudebewertungen mit Nachhaltigkeitsanspruch. Congress Nachhaltig Bauen und Bewerten. Vienna 2009

Geissler, Susanne et al.: Leitfaden zum Umgang mit Energieeffizienz und weiteren Nachhaltigkeitsparametern in der Immobilienwertermittlung. Vienna 2010

Hegger, Manfred; Fuchs, Matthias; Stark, Thomas; Zeumer, Martin: Energie Atlas. Munich 2007
König, Holger; Kohler Niklaus; Kreißig, Johannes; Lützkendorf, Thomas: Lebenszyklusanalyse in der Gebäudeplanung. Munich 2009

System comparison
Baumann, Oliver; Reiser, Claudius; Schäfer, Jochen: Grün ist nicht gleich Grün. In: Bauphysik 02/2009, p. 99–105
BRE Global (pub.): BREEAM Offices 2008 User's Manual. Watford 2008
Bruck, Manfred; Geissler, Susanne; Lechner, Robert: Total Quality Planung und Bewertung (TQ-PB) von Gebäuden. Vienna 2002
Cole, Raymond J.: Building environmental assessment methods. In: Building Research and Information. Vancouver 1999, p. 230–246
Cole, Raymond J.; Larsson, Nils: Green Building Challenge 2002. GBTool User Manual. Vancouver 2002
Eßig, Natalie: Die Bemessung der Nachhaltigkeit. In: db 5/2009, p. 62–65
Eßig, Natalie: Nachhaltigkeit von Olympischen Bauten. Stuttgart 2010
German Sustainable Building Council (DGNB): DGNB manual for new builds and administrative buildings. Stuttgart 2009
König, Holger; Kohler Niklaus; Kreißig, Johannes; Lützkendorf, Thomas: Lebenszyklusanalyse in der Gebäudeplanung. Munich 2009
Larsson, Nils: An Overview of SBTool. Vancouver 2007
Larsson, Nils: Rating Systems and SBTool. The International Initiative for a Sustainable Built Environment. Seoul 2007
Saunders, Tom: A Discussion Document Comparing International Environmental Assessment Methods for Buildings. Watford 2008
Scheuer, Chris W.; Keoleian, Gregory A.: Evaluation of LEED using Life Cycle Assessment Methods. Michigan 2002
U.S.Green Building Council: LEED Reference Guide for Green Building Design and Construction. Washington 2009

Economic aspects and market potentials
Chartered Institution of Building Services Engineers (CISBE): Environmental factors affecting office worker performance. A review of evidence. CIBSE Technical Memoranda TM24. London 1999
Dahlhaus, Ulrich Jürgen; Meisel, Ulli: Nachhaltiges Bauen 2008/2009. Essen 2009
Eichholtz, Piet, Kok Nils, Quigley John M.: Doing Well by Doing Good? Green Office Buildings Working Paper No W08-001. Berkeley, California 2008
German Association for Construction Project Managers (DVP) (pub.): Nutzungskosten als Aufgabe der Projektsteuerung. Berlin 2009
Huff, Thorsten: Fortentwicklung von Bestandsimmobilien. Ein Entscheidungsmodell zur Findung optimaler Lösungen. Berlin 2009
Lützkendorf, Thomas; Lorenz David: Nachhaltigkeitsorientierte Investments im Immobilienbereich. Karlsruhe 2005
Lützkendorf, Thomas; Lorenz, David: Sustainable property investment: valuing sustainable buildings through property performance assessment. In: Building Research & Information 03/2005, p. 212–234
Miller, Norm: Green Buildings and Productivity. In: Journal of Sustainable Real Estate 01/2009
Preuß Norbert; Schöne, Bernhard Lars: Real Estate und Facility Management. Berlin 2010
Waibel, Miriam: Nachhaltigkeitszertifikate bei der Bewertung von Büroimmobilien. Stuttgart 2008

Case studies
Ebert, Thilo: Das natürliche Energiepotenzial von Licht, Luft und Wasser. In: Detail Green 01/2009, p. 48–49
Lang & Groß Management GmbH: Verantwortung Unternehmen. Die Neue Zentrale der Gruppe Deutsche Börse. Eschborn 2010

Links (selection)
Afilog:
    www.afilog.org
American Society of Heating, Refrigerating and Air-Conditioning Engineers (ASHRAE):
    www.ashrae.org
Association pour la Haute Qualité Environnementale (HQE):
    www.assohqe.org
BRE Environmental Assessement Method (BREEAM):
    www.breeam.org
Building Research Establishment (BRE):
    www.bre.co.uk
Canadian Green Building Council:
    www.cagbc.org
Cequami:
    www.cequami.fr
Cerqual:
    www.cerqual.fr
Certivéa:
    www.certivea.fr
Eco-Bau – Nachhaltigkeit im öffentlichen Bau:
    www.eco-bau.ch
European Commission – GreenBuilding Programme:
    www.eu-greenbuilding.org
European Committee for Standardization:
    www.cen.eu
Federal Ministry of Economics and Technology (BMWi) – Energie in Deutschland:
    www.energie-verstehen.de
Federal Ministry of Transport, Building and Urban Development (BMVBS) – Ökobau.dat:
    www.nachhaltigesbauen.de/baustoff-und-gebaeudedaten/oekobaudat.html
German Advisory Council on Global Change (WBGU):
    www.wbgu.de/wbgu_globalerwandel.html
German Energy Agency (dena):
    www.dena.de
German Sustainable Building Council (DGNB):
    www.dgnb.de
Green Building Council Australia:
    www.gbca.org.au
Information portal for sustainable building of the Federal Ministry of Transport, Building and Urban Development (BMVBS):
    www.nachhaltigesbauen.de
Institute for Building Environment and Energy Conservation (IBEC):
    www.ibec.or.jp/CASBEE/english/index.htm
International Initiative for a Sustainable Built Environment (iiSBE) – SB/GB Challenge:
    www.iisbe.org/sb_challenge
International Organization for Standardization:
    www.iso.org
Label for Environmental, Social and Economic Buildings (LEnSE):
    www.lensebuildings.com
MINERGIE:
    www.minergie.ch
Novatlantis – die 2000-Watt Gesellschaft:
    www.novatlantis.ch
OPEN HOUSE:
    www.openhouse-fp7.eu
Qualitel:
    www.qualitel.org
Research for energy-optimised construction:
    www.enob.info
Sustainable Buildings and Climate Initiative – UNEP-SBCI:
    www.unep.org/sbci/index.asp
Sustainable Building Alliance:
    www.sballiance.org
Swiss Federal Office of Energy (SFOE) – EnergieSchweiz: www.bfe.admin.ch
United Nations Population Division:
    www.un.org/popin/data.html
U.S. Green Building Certification Institute (GBCI):
    www.gbci.org
U.S. Green Building Council (USGBC):
    www.usgbc.org
World Green Building Council (WGBC):
    www.worldgbc.org
World Urbanization Prospects – The 2007 Revision Population Database:
    http://esa.un.org/unup

Standards and guidelines
Energy
ANSI/ASHRAE/IESNA Standard 90.1 Energy standard for buildings except low-rise residential buildings. 2007
DIN V 18599 Part 1–10 Energy efficiency of buildings. 2009
EPBD 2002/91/EC European directive on the energy performance of buildings. 2002

Indoor air quality
ANSI/ASHRAE Standard 62.1 Ventilation for acceptable indoor air quality. 2007
ANSI/ASHRAE/IESNA Standard 55 Thermal environmental conditions for human occupancy. 2004
EN ISO 7730 Ergonomics of the thermal environment – Analytical determination and interpretation of thermal comfort using calculation of the PMV and PPD indices and local thermal comfort criteria. 2005

Sustainability
CEN/TC 350 (prEN 15978) Sustainability of construction works – Assessment of environmental performance of buildings – Calculation method. 2010-3
ISO 15392 Sustainability in building construction – General principles. 2008
ISO 21930 Sustainability in building construction – Environmental declaration of building products. 2007
ISO 21931-1 Sustainability in building construction – Framework for methods of assessment of the environmental performance of construction works – Part 1: Buildings. 2010
ISO/DTR 21932 Buildings and constructed assets – Sustainability in Building Construction – Terminology. 2010
ISO/NP 21929-2 Sustainability in building construction – Sustainability indicators – Part 2: Framework for the development of indicators for civil engineering work. 2010
ISO/NP TS 12720 Sustainability in building construction – Guidelines for the application of the general principles on sustainability. 2009
ISO/TC 59/SC 17 Sustainability in building construction. 2002
prEN 15643 Part 1 Sustainability of construction works – Sustainability assessment of buildings – General principles. 2009
prEN 15643 Part 2 Sustainability of construction works – Sustainability assessment of buildings – Framework for the assessment of environmental performance. 2009
prEN 15643 Part 3 Sustainability of construction works – Sustainability assessment of buildings – Framework for the assessment of social performance. 2010
prEN 15643 Part 4 Sustainability of construction works - Sustainability assessment of buildings – Framework for the assessment of economic performance. 2010
prEN 15804 Sustainability of construction works – Environmental product declarations – Product category rules. 2008
prEN 15942 Sustainability of construction works – Environmental product declarations – Communication format – Business to Business. 2009
SIA 112/1 Sustainable building – Building construction (SIA recommendation). 2004

Economy
DIN 276-1 Part 1 Building costs – Building construction. 2006
DIN 18960 User costs of buildings. 2008
DIN 32736 Building Management – Definitions and scope of services. 2000
GEFMA 220-1 Life cycle costing in facility management – Introduction and basic principles. 2006
ISO 18686-5 Buildings and constructed assets – Service life planning – Part 5: Maintenance and life cycle costing. 2008

Picture credits

The authors and the publisher would like to thank everybody who has helped to create this book by providing their pictures, granting permission to reproduce them and supplying information. All diagrams in this book were specifically developed for this purpose. Photographs without credits are taken by architects, are photos of projects or are from DETAIL's archives. Despite intense efforts, it was not possible to identify the copyright owners of some of the photographs, their copyright, however, is not affected. In this case, please contact us.
The numbers refer to the figures in the text.

Principles
1.1 Hegger, Manfred et al.: Energie Atlas. Munich 2007, p. 49
1.4 United Nations Population Division, cf. http://www.un.org/popin/data.html
1.5 Venjakob, Johannes; Hanke, Thomas: Neue Phase im Wettstreit zwischen Energieeffizienz und Wohnraumbedarf. In E & M, 15 May 2006
1.6, 1.8 Colin, Armand: Atlas der Globalisierung. Berlin 2007, p. 41
1.7 see 1.6, p. 38
1.11 see 1.6, p. 39
1.12 EUMETSAT: Climate Monitoring – Meeting the Challenge. Darmstadt 2008, p. 2
1.13 Federal Statistical Office: Zunahme der Siedlungs- und Verkehrsfläche. Press release No. 492 of 23 Nov. 2006, cf. http://www.destatis.de/jetspeed/portal/cms/Sites/destatis/Internet/DE/Presse/pm/2006/11PD06__492__85,templateId=renderPrint.psml
1.14 Federal Environment Agency (UBA): Zunahme der Siedlungs- und Verkehrsfläche in Deutschland vom Jahr 1993 bis zum Jahr 2008. Dessau 2009, p. 9
1.15 German Energy Agency (dena): Thema Energie. Berlin, cf. http://www.thema-energie.de/typo3temp/pics/7c2f97c03a.jpg
1.16 Federal Ministry for the Environment, Nature Conservation and Nuclear Safety (BMU): Erneuerbare Energien 2008 in Deutschland – Aktueller Sachstand 2009. Berlin 2009, cf. http://www.bmu.de/files/pdfs/allgemein/application/pdf/ee_sachstand.pdf, S. 7
1.17 International Energy Agency (IEA): Key World Energy Statistics. Paris 2009, cf. http://www.iea.org/textbase/nppdf/free/2009/key_stats_2009.pdf, S. 6
1.18 Butler, Rhett A.: http://www.mongabay.com. San Francisco
1.19 see 1.6, p. 19
1.21 own illustration acc. to: see 1.1, p. 184
1.22, 1.23 Federal Ministry for the Environment, Nature Conservation and Nuclear Safety (BMU): GreenTech made in Germany 2.0. Umwelttechnologieatlas für Deutschland. Munich 2009
1.24, 1.25 Ernst & Young Real Estate GmbH: Green Building – Ist Zertifizierung für Sie ein Thema? vgl. http://www.competencesite.de
1.26 Fuerst, Franz; McAllister, Patrick: Die nächste Generation. In: Raum & Mehr 01/2009
1.27 see 1.22
1.33 International Initiative for a Sustainable Built Environment (iiSBE), http://www.iisbe.org

Certification – the systems in detail
BREEAM
2.1 Building Reserach Establishment (BRE), Hertfordshire
2.4 Building Reserach Establishment (BRE): BREEAM Europe Commercial 2009 Assessor Manual. Hertfordshire 2009, p. 38
2.8 see 2.4, p. 102
2.10 David Brandt, Dresden; Multi Development Germany GmbH, Duisburg

LEED
2.11, 2.12 U.S. Green Building Council (USBGC), Washington
2.13 own illustration acc. to USGBC
2.14 Green Building Certification Institute (GBCI), Washington
2.16 see 2.11
2.17 see 2.13
2.18 see 2.11
2.21 see 2.13
2.28 see 2.11
2.29 Tishman Speyer, Frankfurt am Main

DGNB
2.30, 2.31 German Sustainable Building Council (DGNB), Stuttgart
2.33 own illustration acc. to: see 2.30
2.35 Federal Ministry of Transport, Building and Urban Development (BMVBS): 12th committee meeting: Round Table on Sustainable Building. Berlin 2009
2.36–2.38 see 2.30
2.39 DGNB: Das Deutsche Gütesiegel Nachhaltiges Bauen. Stuttgart 2009, p. 11
2.40 Eßig, Natalie: Die Bemessung der Nachhaltigkeit. In: db Deutsche Bauzeitung, 05/2009, p. 62–65
2.41 GAP Architekten Generalplaner, Berlin

CASBEE
2.42 Institute for Building Environment and Energy Conservation (IBEC), Tokyo
2.44, 2.45, 2.47, 2.48 own illustration acc. to IBEC
2.50, 2.52 see 2.42
2.55 ingenhoven architects, Düsseldorf

MINERGIE
2.56 MINERGIE, Bern
2.58 see 2.56, cf. http://www.minergie.ch/tl_files/download/Anforderungen_ME.pdf, p. 1; http://www.minergie.ch/tl_files/download/Anforderungen_ME_P.pdf, S. 1
2.59 see 2.56, cf. http://www.minergie.ch/minergie-eco.html
2.60 see 2.56, cf. http://www.minergie.ch/tl_files/images/unterschied.jpg
2.61, 2.62 see 2.59
2.63 Federal Office of Energy (BFE): Systemnachweis MINERGIE-ECO. Final report. Bern 2008, p. 17
2.64 Christine Blaser, Bern

HQE
2.65 Actualités, actus et news en environnement et développement durable, vgl. http://www.actualites-news-environnement.com
2.68 Certivéa, cf. http://www.certivea.com/uk/index.html
2.69 DTZ Research, cf. http://www.paris-region.com/adminsite/objetspartages/liste_fichiergw.jsp?OBJET=DOCUMENT&CODE=42994995&LANGUE=0&RH=PUBLICATIONS, p. 21
2.75 Cerqual, cf. http://www.cerqual.fr/cerqual/nf/prix-des-presentations
2.76 Jacques Le Goff, Paris; Brenac & Gonzales, Paris; ICADE Direction de l'International, Paris

EU GreenBuilding
2.77 German Energy Agency (dena), Berlin
2.78 European Commission, Directorate General GFS Institute for Environment and Sustainability, Department Renewable Energies, Brussels
2.79 German Energy Agency (dena): GreenBuilding[plus] – Leveraging the GreenBuilding Programme to promote energy efficiency and renewables in non-domestic buildings, p. 68; see http://www.eu-greenbuilding.org/fileadmin/Greenbuilding/gb_redaktion/downloads/PublishableReport_GreenBuildingPlus.pdf
2.81 Architekturbüro Franz Bauer, Ingolstadt

Design process and documentation requirements
3.1 Federal Office for Building and Regional Planning (BBR) (pub.): Guideline for sustainable building. Bonn 2001, p. 6.11
3.2 Kleiber, Wolfgang et al.: Verkehrswertermittlung von Grundstücken. Cologne 2002, p. 1511
3.3, 3.4 own illustration acc. to Voss, Karsten et al.: Bürogebäude mit Zukunft. Konzepte, Analysen, Erfahrungen. Berlin 2006
3.6 own illustration acc. to: see 3.1, enclosure 7
3.9 Geissler, Susanne: Gebäudebewertungen mit Nachhaltigkeitsanspruch. Kongress Nachhaltig Bauen und Bewerten. Vienna 2009

System comparison
4.1 own illustration acc. to ISO 15392: Sustainability in building construction – General principles. 2008
4.3 own illustration acc. to Label for Environmental, Social and Economic Buildings (LEnSE), cf. http://www.lensebuildings.com
4.4 Visier, Jean Christophe: Common Metrics for Key Issues, cf. http://www.sballiance.biz

Economic aspects and market potentials
5.1, 5.2 Henzelmann, Torsten et al.: Nachhaltigkeit im Immobilienmanagement. Study by Roland Berger Strategy Consultants. 2010
5.3 Lützkendorf, Thomas; Lorenz, David: Nachhaltigkeitsorientierte Investments im Immobilienbereich. Karlsruhe 2005, p. 12
5.4 RICS Economics: Q2 Global Property Sustainability Survey. New York 2009
5.6 Rapp, Clemens/Fay Projects GmbH, Frankfurt am Main
5.7 own illustration acc. to ISO 15686-5:2008(E) Buildings and constructed assets – Service life planning – Part 5: Life-cycle costing
5.10 Preuß, Norbert; Schöne, Lars Bernhard: Real Estate und Facility Management. Berlin 2010, p. 464
5.11 Makon GmbH & Co. KG, Nuremberg
5.13 Jones Lang LaSalle: OSCAR 2008. Büronebenkostenanalyse. Düsseldorf/Hamburg 2008
5.14 Waibel, Miriam: Nachhaltigkeitszertifikate bei der Bewertung von Büroimmobilien. Stuttgart 2008, p. 68
5.15, 5.16, 5.19 Jones Lang LaSalle, Frankfurt am Main, and CoreNet Global, Frankfurt am Main/Atlanta 2009

Case studies
6.1 Matthias Reithmeyer, Augsburg
6.2, 6.3 ingenhoven architects, Düsseldorf
6.4 Hans Georg Esch, Hennef
6.5 own illustration acc. to Post Construction Review Report by Faber Maunsell, London
6.9 Kondor Wessels, Berlin
6.10 Fuchshuber & Partner Architekten, Leipzig
6.15 Groß & Partner, Frankfurt am Main
6.16, 6.17 KSP Jürgen Engel Architekten, Frankfurt am Main
6.18 see 6.15
6.22, 6.25 Constantin Meyer, Cologne
6.23, 6.24, 6.26 ARGE ZUB Jourdan & Müller PAS, Frankfurt am Main und Seddig Architekten, Kassel
6.27–6.29, 6.40–6.42 German Sustainable Building Council (DGNB), Stuttgart
6.30 Tomas Riehle/arturimages, Cologne; Thomas Pink, Petzinka Pink Architekten, Düsseldorf
6.31, 6.32 Petzinka Pink Architekten, Düsseldorf
6.33–6.36 Federal Ministry of Transport, Building and Urban Development (BMVBS), Berlin
6.37 Visualisation: Kamil Niewelt, Estenfeld; Architects: Ganzer Hajek Unterholzer, Munich, and Thierry Louvieaux, Berlin
6.38, 6.39 Ganzer Hajek Unterholzer, Munich, and Thierry Louvieaux, Berlin

Authors

Thilo Ebert

1967	Born in Schweinfurt
1988–1992	Studied building services engineering at Munich University of Applied Sciences, degree awarded in 1993
1993	Award and prize from the Society for the Promotion of New Technologies for the thesis titled „Development and programming of a heating optimiser"
1993–1998	Project management in the field of technical building equipment, energy and climate design, amongst others in the engineers' practise Prof. Hausladen GmbH, Kirchheim near Munich
1999–2000	International Career Exchange Training at WSP Flack+Kurz Inc., San Francisco, USA
2000–2004	Project management of international construction projects in the field of technical building equipment and future building design at HL Technik AG, Munich
2004–2005	Associate, Advanced Technology Group at WSP Flack+Kurz Inc., San Francisco, USA
since 2006	Managing director and co-partner of Ebert-Consulting Group GmbH & Co. KG; vice president of Ebert & Baumann Consulting Engineers Inc., Washington D.C., USA; accreditation to LEED Accredited Professional of the USGBC
2007	with Ebert-Consulting Group, founding member of the German Sustainable Building Council (Deutsche Gesellschaft für Nachhaltiges Bauen e.V.)
2008	Lecturer at the Technische Universität München in the Master Course of Climate Design and Architecture, DGNB Auditor

Member of the Association of German Engineers (VDI) expert committee for ventilation and air-conditioning
Author of numerous publications in the field of sustainable building, energy and climate design
Management of research projects concerning energy-optimised building
Management of national and international construction projects in the field of sustainable building and technical building equipment using a holistic design approach
Further fields of research: optimisation of design processes in the field of technical building equipment

Natalie Eßig

1977	Born in Fürth
1996–2003	Studied architecture at the Technische Universität Darmstadt
2000–2001	Studied architecture at the Politecnico di Torino
2003–2004	Free-lance work as an architect in the field of energy-efficient and sustainable building
2005–2007	PhD bursary from the German Federal Trust for Environment (DBU) and lecturer at TU Darmstadt, faculty of architecture, in design and energy-efficient building
2006	Research stay at the University of Technology, Sydney, Australia
since 2008	Academic councillor at the faculty for building physics at TU Munich and research assistant at the Fraunhofer-Institute for Building Physics (IBP) in Holzkirchen responsible for the field of sustainable building
2010	Postdoctoral at the faculty of architecture of TU Darmstadt in "Sustainability of Olympic Buildings"

Member of the Bavarian Chamber of Architects and the German Sustainable Building Council (DGNB)
Author of various publications
Selected fields of research: sustainability assessment and certification of buildings (national and international), sustainable sports facilities construction, sustainable concepts and consulting
Support in developing teaching concepts in the field of sustainable design
Further fields of work: support in developing the German green label, chairperson of the Student Network for Sustainable Urban Development (NSE), DGNB Auditor

Gerd Hauser

1948	Born in Bad Kissingen
1967–1972	Studied mechanical engineering at the Technische Universität München
1972–1977	Research assistant at the Fraunhofer-Institute for Building Physics (IBP) in Holzkirchen, theoretical department
1977	Postdoctoral at Stuttgart University in the field of building construction
1977–1983	Senior engineer at Essen University in building physics and civil engineering
1983–2004	Professor for building physics in the faculty of architecture, urban design and landscape design at Kassel University
since 1984	Owner of an engineers' practice for building physics
1990	Chair offered by the Swiss Federal Institute of Technoloy Zurich (ETH), declined
since 2004	Professor for building physics at the TU München in the faculty of civil engineering and surveying and managing director of the Fraunhofer-Institute for Building Physics (IBP) in Holzkirchen

Full professor at TU München
Managing director of the Fraunhofer-Institute for Building Physics (IBP) in Holzkirchen and Kassel
Chairperson of the Society for Rational Energy Use (GRE)
Board member of the Center for Environmentally Conscious Building (ZUB) and the German Sustainable Building Council (DGNB)
Member of the Steering Committee E2B, High-Level-Group, European Construction Technology Platform (ECTP)
Further fields of work: in professional organisations and national and international standardisation committees, such as Renewable Energy Research Association (FVEE), Conseil International du Bâtiment (CIB)

Index

(R)
Life cycle approach to
buildings : principles,
calculations, design tools.

Edition **DETAIL** Green Books

A life cycle approach to buildings

Principles
Calculations
Design tools

Holger König
Niklaus Kohler
Johannes Kreißig
Thomas Lützkendorf

Project management:
Steffi Lenzen, Dipl-Ing. Architect

Editorial work:
Jakob Schoof, Dipl.-Ing.

Editorial assistants:
Sandra Leitte, Dipl.-Ing.;
Kimo Ahmed; Carola Jacob-Ritz; Oliver Oelkers, Dipl.-
Designer; Jana Rackwitz, Dipl.-Ing.; Eva Schönbrunner,
Dipl.-Ing.; Aristotelis Shomper

Translation:
Raymond Peat

English copyediting and proofreading:
Neil D'Souza; Richard Lorch; Roderick O'Donovan

Drawings:
Rana Aminian; Ralph Donhauser, Dipl.-Ing.; Cedric Ehlers;
Evelina Vatzeva

Cover design:
Cornelia Hellstern, Dipl.-Ing.

DTP & layout:
Roswitha Siegler, Simone Soesters

Reproduction:
Martin Härtl OHG, Munich

Printing and binding:
Aumüller Druck, Regensburg
1st Edition 2010

Institut für internationale
Architektur-Dokumentation GmbH & Co. KG
Hackerbrücke 6, D-80335 Munich
Tel.: +49/89/38 16 20-0
Fax: +49/89/39 86 70
www.detail.de

© 2010 Institut für internationale
Architektur-Dokumentation GmbH & Co. KG, Munich
A specialist book from Redaktion DETAIL

ISBN: 978-3-920034-45-4

This book is also available in a German language edition
(ISBN: 978-3-920034-30-0)

Contents

Buildings are long-lived products that in normal circumstances would have life expectancies many times greater than those of their constructors and users. The demand on resources, the resulting effects on the environment and the costs that buildings cause over the course of their service lives exceed those arising during their production and erection. This applies in particular to the energy expended and the CO_2 emitted.

As a consequence of their production, use and management, today's buildings and associated infrastructure cause approximately 30% of the energy and material flows and effects on the environment. Therefore in implementing the principles of sustainable development great significance must be attached to construction in matters of resource conservation and environmental impact. Although significant progress has been made in the field of the energy requirement of new buildings, the main problem lies in the upgrading of the long-lived existing building stock. Control and influence over the life cycle of buildings are therefore key concerns in the sustainable design of the built environment. This presents specific tasks during the design, evaluation and decision-making for buildings and infrastructure, especially those with long service lives and many stakeholders with very different interests involved in their development, design, use and management. Their successful completion requires suitable methods, tools and data, the development, provision and use of which for a long time has failed to keep pace with the level of requirements arising from these tasks.

In the age of the skilled craftsman, buildings were traditionally designed, constructed and maintained on the assumption that their service lives could be extended practically without limit by suitable maintenance measures. However, if a building had to be taken down, then its components and materials were reused. During the building boom between 1955 and 1975, new construction materials and techniques were introduced with very little knowledge of their long-term behaviour. The energy crisis from 1973 onwards initiated a rethink, an increased awareness of the environment and a change of direction towards sustainable development, even in the construction industry, and brought forward the need to consider buildings from the point of view of their life cycles. International standardisation, certification schemes and a more intense perception of our responsibility for the environment and to society have further reinforced this trend.

From the point of view of the stakeholders participating today in the production, use, renovation and management of buildings, the debate about life cycles links seamlessly with efforts to extend and steer the normal construction industry cost-based form of competition, with its one-sided over-emphasis of initial investment costs, towards competition founded on quality and competence through the consideration of life cycle costs. The continuously rising costs for the use of buildings have started an additional process of rethinking. Public authorities and companies in the construction and real estate sectors have begun to show keen interest in follow-on costs and therefore in the use phase of buildings. New approaches have included PPP (public private partnership) and the BOT (build operate and transfer) operator model. This new awareness of the costs, not only in the context of public procurement of buildings but also arising from new cooperative, contract and financial models in the building and real estate industries, has ensured the increasing further development, systematization and application of use costing and life cycle costing. The process has yet to be concluded.

A consideration of the financial flows in the life cycle of buildings is not enough. Payments in and out, value stability and value development are also involved in determining whether and to what extent a building can fulfil today's use requirements and those of the future. Investors and designers, as well as the construction material and construction industries, have to be more committed to their responsibilities to society and for the environment. Society expects information from them about the effects of the construction and use of a building on the user, the neighbourhood, the community and society as well as on the local and the global environment and about how these effects can be intentionally influenced. This type of information about buildings is an additional part of sustainability reporting and companies that fail to pay due attention to these matters place their reputations at risk.

The method of life cycle assessment has long been available as a means of compiling and evaluating energy and material flows and the effects on the environment. Its further development and in particular the availability of the necessary data are now leading to the introduction of life cycle assessment into real design, construction and management processes.

The systems for certifying the sustainability of buildings – in Germany for example the Sustainable Building certification scheme developed jointly by the German Federal Ministry of Transport, Building and Urban Development (BMVBS) and the German Sustainable Building Council (DGNB) – are based among other things on life cycle assessment and life cycle costing and relate this information in a complete evaluation of an individual building's contribution to sustainable development. Architects, engineers, consultants and other stakeholders in the construction, housing, real estate and finance industries are confronted in many different ways with the problem of the collection and interpretation of life cycle costs and life cycle assessment information. For example, this type of information must be taken into account in design decisions, reports to the client and certification applications. Only the simultaneous and interdependent consideration of economic and ecological contexts leads to solutions that can make a contribution to sustainable development. The sustainable development of existing building stock is moving into the centre, time horizons are extending and the interfaces with nature are becoming the new system limits.

A suitable tool is now available which takes the form of integrated life cycle analysis and is introduced in this book. The main emphasis is placed on the presentation and explanation of the methodological principles of life cycle assessment and life cycle costing. The reader gains an overview of the required principles and available tools and applicable knowledge extended by indications of orders of magnitude for assessing apparent validity based on example applications.

The consideration of the life cycle perspective – whether that is in new building design, use, renovation or deconstruction – requires stakeholders to cooperate in new ways. The method of integrated design, which among other things is also founded on life cycle analysis, allows a holistic approach and the continuous consideration of a large number of aspects. However, it needs a new way of describing buildings that must be accessible and suitable for the many stakeholders who enter the life cycle and have very different interests. Only in this way will it be possible to manage the huge quantities of information and fully exploit all the potential for optimisation. The interoperability of design tools, and in particular of the building information model, is therefore a key factor.

In the future the use of the methods introduced in this book will become a permanent constituent part of the design and management of every building and will be oriented towards the entire life cycle of a building – from cradle to grave, from new building through maintenance to dismantling and recycling and reuse.

Sustainability as an objective and general framework

The concept of sustainability goes back to European forestry management in the 17th century. Early pioneers in this field were Jean Baptiste Colbert, who as a minister for Ludwig XIV. published the "Code forestier", and the mining administrator of Electoral Saxony Carl von Carlowitz, who wrote "Sylvicultura oeconomica, oder haußwirthliche Nachricht und Naturmäßige Anweisung zur wilden Baum-Zucht". The sustainable exploitation of resources, in this case forests, has the aim of ensuring the perpetual use of timber, to as consistently high levels in terms of volume and quality as possible [1]. It is made up of four components:
· Long-term view: continuous production of the effect
· Social responsibility: restriction of the usage rights of owners in the general interest
· Economy: resource usage based on the economic principle
· Responsibility: the resource manager's obligation to the future and provision for it.

The definition coined by the Brundtland Commission in 1987 describes development as "sustainable" if it "meets the needs of the present without compromising the ability of future generations to meet their own needs" [2]. The term sustainability therefore describes not merely a quantitative development oriented towards growth but rather more of a qualitative step forward. Sustainable development always encompasses several dimensions.

The dimensions of sustainability

The ecological dimension of sustainability concerns the preservation of our basis for life and means limiting the strain on our resources to an ecologically acceptable level. This level is fixed by the long-term preservation of the stock of natural resources.

The economic dimension, in particular the idea of sustainable development, was defined in "Blueprint for a Green Economy" by three main criteria [3]:
· Consideration of the value of the environment
· Extension of the time horizon
· Equity between people and generations

In this sense ecology can also mean long-term economics. The adaptation of the production and consumption processes to meet ecological requirements therefore works as a long-term cost-avoidance strategy. This must be in complete harmony with the financial objective of efficiency e. g. by internalising external costs and by strategies of long-term use. Resources should be shared fairly between the "rich north" and the "poor south" and between today's generation and future generations. Future generations should have at least the same capital stock available to them as we have ourselves today. This capital stock comprises not only natural resources, but also the possibilities for production, that is to say technologies, knowledge, political institutions and non-material goods.

Social sustainability for its part also contains a number of dimensions. The maintenance of human health and general well-being depends directly on sustainable ecological and economic development. The burden of disease as determined by the World Health Organisation (WHO) includes infectious diseases, epidemics, accidents and hunger [4]. Environmental factors account for about one quarter of the current global burden.

When addressing the built environment, a further important dimension is added to the normal three dimensions mentioned above; the conservation of non-material, cultural values for future generations. Cultural diversity is as essential for the identity of societies as biodiversity is for nature. It is not just a matter of listed monuments and ensembles, but rather the built environment as the product of human history. As architectural heritage, it represents a non-renewable resource.

Sustainable development

Sustainable development can be completely defined by the four dimensions of sustainability: ecological, economic, social and cultural (Fig. 1.1). Using this interpretation, the terms resources or capital, diversity and sustainability appear in various forms. Common to all dimensions is the conservation of capital – natural or manmade, economic or social –, ecological, social or cultural diversity as a long-term guarantee of survival and sustainability (also robustness and resilience) of social and natural systems.

Sustainable development can be carried out at various different levels. General concepts such as sustainable economics or intergenerational equity are defined using analytical methods, which include life cycle analysis.

8

Policy instruments such as labelling or certification schemes allow the objectives of sustainability to be implemented in society. The indispensable foundation is data and information on social metabolism, i. e. the interactions between society and nature, the resources situation etc. (Fig. 1.2)

Sustainability and construction
Construction creates the material basis for life, living space and working environments. Construction is currently responsible for the largest of all man-made material flows. It is a major factor in the sealing of the soil surface, while operating buildings causes very high environmental burdens through the continuing consumption of energy and the building stock represents the largest financial, physical and cultural capital of the industrialised societies [5]. The question of sustainable development therefore acquires special importance for the field of construction.

Certifying the sustainability of buildings
Certifying whether a product or process (behaviour) is sustainable depends on the characteristics of the product or process, on the intentions of the parties involved and on the applied conditions. There is therefore no generally

applicable form of certification. In addition, there are various other dimensions to take into account, which is barely achievable in one step by using a special method. Two types of process that can also be used in combination have emerged in recent years:
- Rating, in which the requirements are given in the form of a checklist and the assessor decides whether each requirement has been fulfilled or not. The result consists of the sum of the weighted or unweighted scores.
- Accounting procedures and methods of estimating effects, which allow various types of resource demands, environmental influences, economic consequences and social and cultural outcomes to be determined.

The accounting processes cover energy, material and financial flows and direct effects on human health (e. g. by a simulation of indoor air quality), on the local ecosystem (by a material flow analysis) or on the social and cultural system (by an impact analysis etc.) (Fig. 1.3, p. 10). Addressing sustainability leads to an expansion of the spatial and temporal system boundaries. While earlier in the field of construction only the direct

capital investment and energy consumption costs were considered for the buildings, the new system boundaries are now the interfaces with nature (extraction of raw materials, recirculation of emissions) and the life cycle (from cradle to grave).

The idea of the life cycle of buildings
Structures, buildings and infrastructure have the longest lives of all man-made products. They have characterised human society since the move from nomadic to permanent settlements. The development of human culture is reflected in its buildings: The still surviving buildings of earlier epochs represent an archive of physical, economic and cultural capital. Durability is a constituent feature of every building. Practically all theories about buildings concern themselves with this aspect. Vitruvius identified three important characteristics of buildings in the first century BC: "venustas" (beauty), "utilitas" (utility) and "firmitas" (firmness) [6]. The creation of buildings, above all prestigious buildings, often spans several generations. Buildings were continuously being maintained and altered, and when new buildings were constructed, the scarce materials from old buildings were reused and recycled. Thus there was no consciousness in this

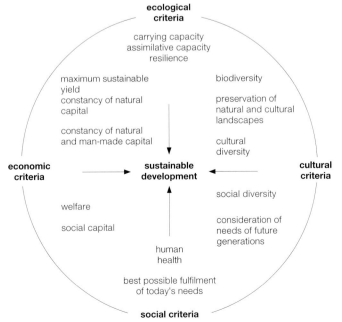

1.1 Various dimensions of sustainable development (after Bächtold)
1.2 Concepts, methods, instruments and data of sustainable development

1.1

Concepts:
- sustainable management
- system ecology
- life cycle perspective
- total cost of ownership
- total quality management
- intergenerational equity

Analytical methods:
- environmental assessment
- urban ecology assessment
- material flow analysis
- risk analysis
- life cycle assessment
- life cycle analysis
- product line analysis
- cost-benefit analysis

Policy instruments:
- sustainability indicators
- environmental accounting
- technology assessments
- strategic environmental assessment
- certification
- labelling

Data

1.2

context of the life of a building in the sense of an end to the life cycle (e. g. as with a living being). As buildings were solidly constructed and the scope of technical systems was very limited and such systems were themselves inherently long-lived, repair and renovation took place continuously and there was no need to carry out periodic renewal in the manner we are familiar with in regard to today's buildings. This form of development changed only at the beginning of the 20th century.

Life cycle phases of buildings
Buildings have a very long life, are subject to constant change (use, renovation, conversion) and a multitude of people are involved in their design, construction and use. Therefore the life cycle of a building does not correspond with that of other objects such as tools, consumer goods etc.
There are in principle four life cycle phases:
• New building: begins with the intention of the client and ends with the commissioning and handover of the building.
• Usage: includes use, operation and maintenance, begins with the commissioning and acceptance of the building and ends with the intention to carry out (periodic) renewal
• Renewal: includes partial or full renewal, conversion. There could be several renewal and usage phases.
• Demolition and disposal: begins with the intention to stop using the building and to demolish it and ends with the complete transfer of

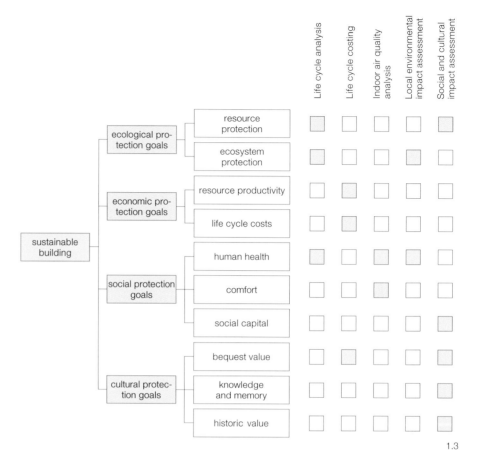

1.3

1.3 Protection goals and certification procedures for sustainable building
1.4 Temporary roof, amphitheatre, Nîmes, 1988
 Structures can last a thousand years and be continuously changed to suit current requirements.
1.5 London Bridge, 1209–1831
 Bridges, which are perceived as eternal and unchanging, are able offer a rich and varied image over centuries and in a post-industrial (car-free) future could again find other uses.
1.6 Swiss Pavilion, Expo 2000, Hanover, Peter Zumthor
 Structures can also be designed to have very short lives. The Swiss Pavilion was made of wooden boards stacked one upon the other, which were reused without waste in other buildings after the exhibition.

1.4

all building materials for subsequent uses (reuse, recycling, power generation, landfill etc.).

Each life cycle phase consists of a number of different process stages:
- Strategy: determination of the objectives, boundary conditions, methods, criteria
- Project management planning: formalising the requirements for the completed building, execution phase planning, cost, programming and quality control
- Implementation: sequence of construction or usage processes

Each phase gives rise to material and energy flows resulting out of the extraction of resources from the environment, energy generation and supply, transport, assembly on site, disposal and use. In parallel to these flows of energy and material, there are also information and financial flows. Life cycle-oriented planning is based on knowledge of the mutual dependencies of flows (Figs. 1.8 and 1.9, p. 12).

New spatial system boundaries: metabolism of the human living space

All life cycle perspectives relate to expanded temporal and spatial system boundaries. The question of system boundaries comes from system ecology and the system theory derived from it. Systems are generally defined by establishing their boundaries with respect to the environment.

Definition of (eco-)systems
The US-American ecologist Eugene Odum suggests a method of modelling ecosystems in which the environment is composed of different elements: microorganisms, soils, forests, lakes, rivers, oceans, living beings (including humans), machines and cities, which are linked to one another by flows of energy, materials and information. Odum has also developed a language of energy in which all the processes within the environment are accompanied by energy conversion. The directed flow of energy from the sun as the only external energy

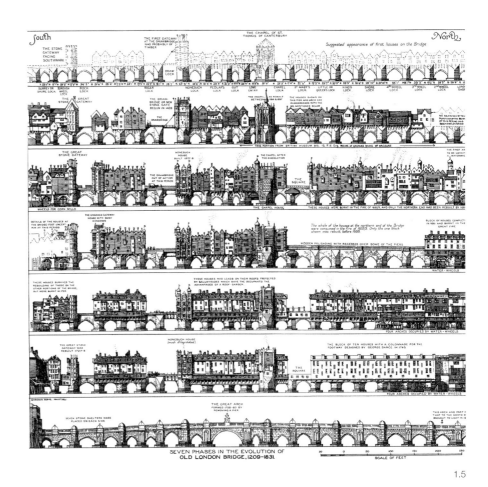

SEVEN PHASES IN THE EVOLUTION OF OLD LONDON BRIDGE, 1209–1831.

1.5

1.6

11

source permeates the environment and gives off heat. At the end of every process there is a reduction in heat energy and an increase in entropy (see Design in the life cycle of buildings p. 30). Within the system, the various flows are either changed by resistances or stored by capacitors (Fig. 1.7) [7].

The system analysis can be applied to various processes, including the functioning of complete cities or regions. Cities change soils, raw materials, energy and water into the built environment, creating wastes, emissions and (waste) heat. The urban metabolism can also be defined as the totality of the technical and socioeconomic processes taking place in the cities. The result is growth of the material stock, energy conversion and emissions.

The need to integrate settlements into the natural cycle had already been advocated in Germany before the First World War by landscape architect Leberecht Migge (Fig. 1.10) [8].

The various material cycles (water, oxygen, carbon, mineral and metallic construction materials, sulphur, cadmium etc.) of the cities are investigated using material flow analysis. This is a form of materials accounting. Odum highlighted the parallel and transitional relationships between flows of material, information and money.

One of the combined techniques was created by the Belgian chemist and biologist Paul Duvigneaud for modelling the Brussels ecosystem

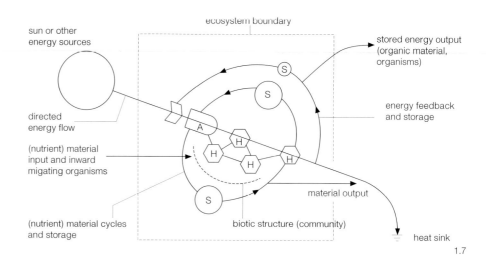

1.7

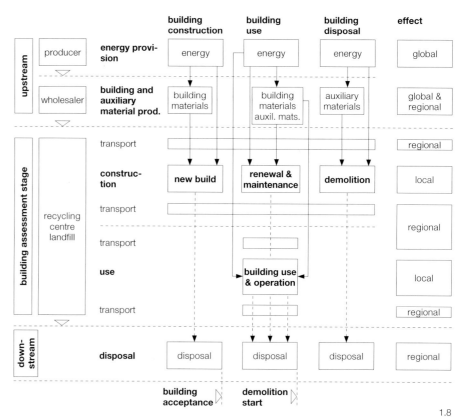

1.8

1.7 Function diagram of an ecosystem (after Odum)
Energy flows, material cycles, storage and nutrient networks play a role along with various organisms in the dynamic of the system.
S storage
A autotroph organisms
H heterotroph organisms
1.8 Split into time-related life cycle phases with several cycles for the usage phase (use, maintenance, renewal, possible conversion) and into process sequences for each phase (from upstream to downstream stages)
1.9 Material and energy flows during the life cycle of a building
1.10 Settlement material cycle by Leberecht Migge
1.11 Ecosystem model of Brussels by Paul Duvigneaud

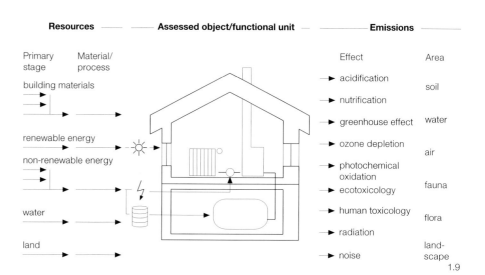

1.9

(Fig. 1.11) [9]. A model representing the material, energy and money flows of a hypothetical small town in central Switzerland was drawn up by environmental chemist Peter Baccini and other scientists [10].

The advantage of modelling is that all the flows in the entire system have to be assigned to a function and therefore nothing can be "forgotten".

New temporal system boundaries: from cradle to grave

The interest in the life cycle of products, in particular of buildings and long-lived industrial products, has developed in parallel in different fields over recent decades and has led to various different methodological approaches. In all cases, new time frames have taken the place of the previously accepted temporal system boundaries, which were of limited applicability to the planning and realisation of new buildings. The idea of the life cycle emerged in different areas at very different points in time. Today the differences between the various methods are rapidly disappearing and the approaches merging. There are five main approaches, each of which are described below.

Life cycle analysis in the sense of Life cycle assessment

Life Cycle Assessment (LCA) – describes a systematic analysis of the resources drawn from nature and the environmental effects of a product over its entire life cycle (from cradle to grave). Today, life cycle assessment

has been widely standardised in international standards such as ISO 14040 "Environmental management – Life cycle assessment" [11]. The idea of a comprehensive assessment of products and processes emerged in the 19th century in the context of the development of thermodynamics, the description of ecosystems and in the field of process engineering, which had its roots in chemical engineering. The methods used in life cycle assessments today can be traced back to ecological accounting [12] and industrial energy analyses [13].

Industrial ecology as the theory of production processes

The theory of industrial ecology was developed within the framework of ecological modernisation. This is an analytical and strategic approach to environmental matters dating from the 1980s and has been adopted by government, commerce and society [14]. The aim of ecological modernisation is the continuous, sustainable co-evolution of man and nature. One of its central ideas is the more productive use of resources and ecological sinks, i.e. using raw materials, energy carriers and environmental media (soil, water, air) in the most efficient and environmentally compatible manner possible. The approach is based on the environmental-economic insight that ecology and economics do not have to conflict. From this are derived manufacturing strategies for an "industrial ecosystem", in which the use of energy and raw materials is optimised, waste and emissions are minimised and natural cycles closed. The

waste from a process becomes the raw material for a subsequent process in the sense of cascade utilisation [15].

Product life cycle in business economics

The product life cycle is a concept of business economics and describes the processes between market introduction or the manufacture of a marketable good and its disappearance from the market. The US-American economist Raymond Vernon divides the life of a product on the market into four phases: the development and introduction phase is followed by growth then maturity and the final phase of saturation, contraction and decline [16]. The product life cycle describes how new products come on to the market (product innovation), how products already on the market are adjusted to match the continuously changing market conditions (product variation), how an existing product line is extended by a further variant (product differentiation), how new product lines are expanded in relation to the existing lines (product diversification) and products which are no longer economically viable are taken off the market (product elimination).

Life cycle costing

Life cycle costs, or whole life costs or total cost of ownership, are considered to include all relevant costs linked with the acquisition or ownership of a good and are systematically recorded in the cost calculation. The definition implicitly covers the complete life cycle of the good. This idea is also not a new

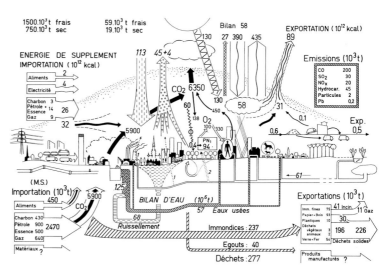

1.10

1.11

one. The pioneering thinkers were the French physiocrats Anne Robert-Jacques Turgot and François Quesnay, who coined the terms "investment capital" and "diminishing returns" at the end of the 18th century, which were then further developed by Adam Smith. The idea was taken up again in the 20th century, for example in a "Manual of the American Railway Engineering Association" dated 1929. The process of life cycle costing was further extended by the US army and other governmental agencies, which used the technique from the middle of the 1960s for public procurement taking into account life cycle costs. The methods have not yet been fully harmonised with one another on the national and international levels. This approach presents only initial recommendations and general principles but permits plenty of scope for interpretation.

The life cycle as a social process

The idea of a social cycle makes use of analogies in nature, in particular with respect to succession models (e.g. the sequence of rapid phases of growth and long phases of saturation). The analysis of complex systems has, in recent years, led to a conceptual linking of natural and social systems [17]. The interrelationship between the physical state and the social conditions within existing buildings can also be understood as succession models (Fig. 1.13).

Stakeholders and points of view

Approaches to describing and modelling buildings and their life cycles are strongly influenced by the particular viewpoint and the way in which the question is framed. First of all a building can be interpreted in the physical

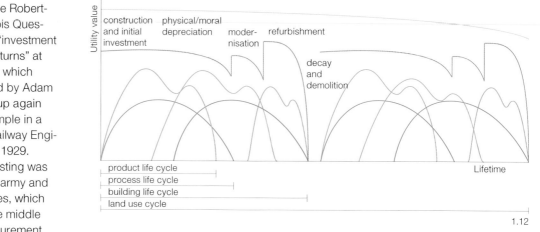

1.12

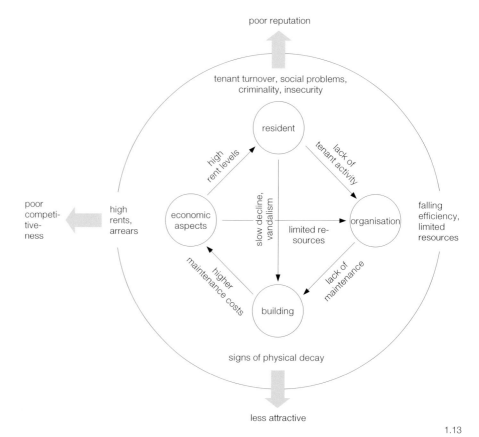

1.13

1.12 Relationship between product, process, building and land use cycles
1.13 The life cycle as a social process
1.14 The time expectations of various stakeholders
1.15 Short, medium and long-term management cycles

Stakeholder	Time expectation
Tenant, residential	5–30 years
Tenant, non-residential	1–20 years
Real estate agent	1–2 years
Building contractor	1–5 years (warranty)
Facility manager	1–5 years (contract period)
Building designers, architects, consulting engineers	1–25 years (1st major repair work)
PPP participants	10–50 years (contract period)
Building owner, general	25–50 years (generation)
Building stock owner (infrastructure, public)	50–100 years
Building stock owner (building, speculative)	1–10 years
Long-term-oriented owner (public, collective, non-profit)	50–100 years
Society (district, city)	considerably more than 100 years
Service life (ISO)	50 years
Planning approval (LCA)	80–100 years

1.14

sense as a product or object, the life cycle as a process and the utility value of the building as a service. On the other hand, a service may be provided without a building (e. g. a virtual library on the Internet).

Buildings as living space and working environments

To their users (occupants, visitors, employees) a building appears as part of the built environment that serves as living space or a working environment. The users are interested in optimum fulfilment of their requirements (from functional quality to comfort) and the avoidance of detrimental health effects or risks.

Buildings as products/end products

A building can be understood as a product consisting of building components and can be described in terms of these. As the objective of a life cycle assessment is to describe, calculate and evaluate the energy and material flows and environmental effects, it is essential to first obtain a description of the physical composition of the building. Information relevant to the environment and health about the components, construction products and processes is at the same time a source of information for assessing effects on and risks to the health of the user, resident and local environment.

Buildings as systems

Buildings can be described using system theory with reference to their input and output flows (energy, material, money flows etc.). In overall terms, the building as a system fulfils functional requirements and therefore has a ben-

efit or utility value, also in the sense of a service. This point of view allows both buildings and measures not involving construction to be considered as solutions. Naturally in this case, the functional equivalents (reference values) and the system boundaries need to be specified in detail. For example, an additional office workplace can either be created by erecting a new building or the employees could work alternately in an open-plan office, on the train, at a customer's premises or from home. As a result the expenditure for the erection of a new building is no longer necessary, though there will be additional expenditure on transport and communication, and on working facilities in the home.

Buildings as cultural capital

The existing building stock represents the largest physical, economic and cultural capital of European societies and includes in particular buildings, which, because of their age, historic or social significance, their craftsmanship or aesthetic qualities, acquire a special value. The total value of a building is established with reference to the sustainable management of existing building stock and its conversion and demolition.

Buildings as initiators of costs and costing units

The erection, use and where necessary removal of buildings gives rise to costs. They are recorded as construction costs, operating costs and costs at the end of the life cycle (end of life). Calculating and assessing them is the subject of life cycle costing.

Buildings as property and investments

As a rule there is a commercial interest in the erection and management of buildings, which influences the judgement made of the income and profit flows, value stability and growth.

The time frames of the stakeholders

Different stakeholders have different perception horizons, which are described as time expectations. They impose time-related requirements on a building, even though in most cases they may not explicitly express these (Fig. 1.14).

Life cycle analyses of packaging, consumer goods or even private cars, can be readily verified if the life expectation is only months or a few years and reliable data are available on survival probabilities (half-lives). The process leads to clear conclusions that are simple to act upon. In the case of buildings, which may have lives of several hundred years, considerations of life cycles may take on a hypothetical character. They are always only very simplified models of the future that represent possible scenarios of long-term developments. The estimate of the technical life of a component or building assesses how long it can be used under normal operating conditions. It says nothing about the actual life. Even under heavy use, a marble floor can last for more than 100 years, provided it is well constructed and maintained. A fitted carpet subjected to light use may last hardly more than 20 years and under normal use, only 10. How long a specific marble floor or fitted carpet will actually be used remains unknown. In principle, the time constants of a

	Interest of user	Interest of designer and contractor	Interest of building owner	Interest of building stock owner	Interest of society
short-term: **5 years**	costs (rent)	design services construction quality (warranty)	usage costs building performance (warranty)	usage costs building performance	Compliance with standards, legal aspects
medium-term: **25 years**	condition (appearance)	design horizon durability	maintenance strategy	options portfolio financial provision	Regulatory objectives (legal, standards, tax legislation)
long-term: **50 years**		design horizon reverse engineering	options	social capital	material resource preservation
Life cycle: **> 100 years**				cultural capital	cultural and material resource preservation

1.15

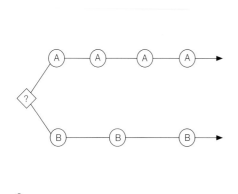

a

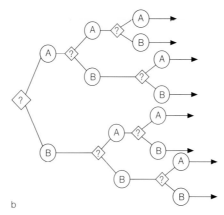

b

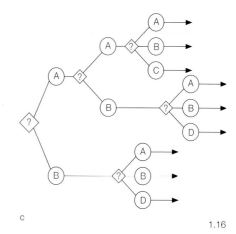

c

1.16

building can be combined with the stakeholders' perception time-frames (Fig. 1.15, p. 15).

Uncertainty about the course of the life cycle

Life cycle scenarios have to be used because it is impossible to predict the life cycle of a building in detail. Two methods can be used for this: trend projection and scenarios with options.

Trend projection

Trend projection assumes that there is a regular sequence of phases. How long the phases last and which changes are associated with them must be explicitly stated. The simplest case consists of projecting forward the currently known life cycle, i.e. the use remains unchanged and the elements are replaced by identical ones at the end of their planned lives. The life of the elements is taken from available empirical values based on experience. The scenario represents the best foreseeable case, i.e. a floor covering of marble has a life of at least 50 years under normal use, while a medium-quality fitted carpet has a maximum life of 10 years under normal use. The elements are replaced in this scenario after 50 and 10 years respectively. This reflects their maximum potential. When they will be actually replaced is not known. Of course an alternative scenario can be evaluated with considerably less durable and consequently cheaper elements in order to compare annual throughputs (cost of provision divided by number of years of life). If a building that was planned

to have a long life is taken down after a shorter period, the remaining life of the building is lost. This case however, must be considered as unplanned and the loss of the remaining life is to a certain extent the penalty for taking the short-term view. If this case were to become the norm for the existing building stock, then it would lead to an unfavourable loss of resources to society and increased environmental effects.

It is also possible to simulate alternative technology scenarios based on reference variants. These can include, for example, the assumption of new technologies such as insulation with very low thermal conductivity. Here the elements may be replaced by non-identical ones at the end of a scheduled renewal cycle. For example the development of insulating glazing units has been considerable years and promises still further improvements in the foreseeable future. Glazing units can be replaced relatively simply in practical terms and without causing damage.

To what extent it is worthwhile analysing such scenarios in individual cases for longer periods of time is open to question. Forecasting technological development is a priori no more accurate than forecasting building life and renewal cycles. It is certainly right to model such scenarios in the context of predictions of estimates of the technical improvement of the existing building stock. The future material properties and their probable future life cycle inventory may be derived from the development of a trend over past years (Fig. 1.18).

A variant of this approach consists of

"backcasting" energy savings or the reduction of environmental effects to determine the time in the future when a specific goal will be attained. This allows assumptions to be made e.g. by 2030 half of all buildings will meet the Passivhaus standard. For this to be so, from now on all new buildings would have to be designed to this standard and the scheduled periodic renewal of older buildings would be carried out to achieve the Passivhaus standard. On-going scenarios would also have to take into account new technologies like the new level of efficiency of energy conversion or improvements in manufacturing processes (Fig. 1.17).

Options

The distinction must always be made between choosing between alternatives today and the temporal shifting of a decision, which is described as an option. A very promising approach to adopt with uncertainties in a building's life cycle is to consider alternative scenarios with options (Fig. 1.16) [18]. In the context of finance, an option may refer to a derived financial transaction or a forward deal. The holder of an option has the right to buy or sell a product at a later time for a previously agreed price. The product does not have to be actually bought or sold; the option may also be allowed to lapse. This traditional form of forward dealing can also be applied in a wider sense in other fields. The term real option describes a method of assessing the advantages of an investment. The method uses various forms of discounted cash flow and risk management.

The distinction is drawn between financial options and real options, i.e. the opportunity but not the obligation to make a decision (e.g. to invest). Unlike financial options, real options cannot be traded. An example of a real option is buying a plot of land of sufficient size and designing a modular factory to allow the factory building to be extended quickly and easily in the future. A special type of option is the quasi-option value. They are defined as the value of the future information made available through the preservation of a resource. In relation to buildings, this means that every generation must be prepared to invest in the preservation of the diversity of the options, the possibility of choice in the further use, conversion, repair and function of a building [19].

References:

[1] Bächtold, Hans-Georg: Nachhaltigkeit. Herkunft und Definition eines komplexen Begriffs. In: SI+A 13/1998, pp. 4–7
[2] World Commission on Environment and Development: Our Common Future. Oxford 1987
[3] Pearce, David W.; Markandya, Anil; Barbier, Edward B.: Blueprint for a Green Economy. London 1989
[4] World Health Organisation: Global Burden of Disease. www.who.int/topics/global_burden_of_disease/en/
[5] Kohler, Niklaus; Hassler, Uta; Paschen, Herbert (ed.): Stoffströme und Kosten im Bereich Bauen und Wohnen. Berlin 1999
[6] Vitruvius Pollio, Marcus: The Ten Books on Architecture. Courier Dover Publications, 1960
[7] Odum, Eugene P.: Fundamentals of Ecology, Brooks Cole Pub Co, 2004 (first edition 1953)
[8] Haney, David H.: Leberecht Migge and the modern garden in Germany. University of Pennsylvania, 2005
[9] Duvigneaud, Paul; Denaeyer-De Smet, Simone: L'ecosystème urbain bruxellois. In: Duvigneaud, Paul; Kestemont, Patrick (ed.): Productivité biologique en Belgique. Paris 1977, pp. 608–613
[10] Baccini, Peter, Brunner, Paul H.: Metabolism of the Anthroposphere. Berlin 1991
[11] DIN EN ISO 14040: Environmental management – Life cycle assessment – Principles and framework.
[12] Müller-Wenk, Ruedi: Die ökologische Buchhaltung. Rüschlikon 1974
[13] Boustead, Ian; Hancock, Gerald Francis: Handbook of industrial energy analysis. Chichester 1979
[14] Fischer-Kowalski, Marina and Weisz, Helga: Society as hybrid between material and symbolic realms: towards a theoretical framework of society–nature interaction, in: Advances inHuman Ecology, 8, pp. 215–251, 1999
[15] Ayres, Robert U.; Simonis, Udo E.: Industrial Metabolism. Restructuring for Sustainable Development. Tokyo 1994
[16] Vernon, Raymond: International Investment and International Trade in the Product Cycle. In: Quarterly Journal of Economics 05/1966, pp. 191–207
[17] Moffat, Sebastian; Kohler, Niklaus: Conceptualizing the built environment as a social-ecological system. In: Building Research & Information 03/2008, pp. 248–268
[18] Ellingham, Ian; Fawcett, William: Options based evaluation of facade refurbishment alternatives. www.bath.ac.uk/cwct/cladding_org/wlp2001/paper5.pdf
[19] Ellingham, Ian; Fawcett, William: New generation whole-life costing. Property and construction decision-making under uncertainty. London 2006

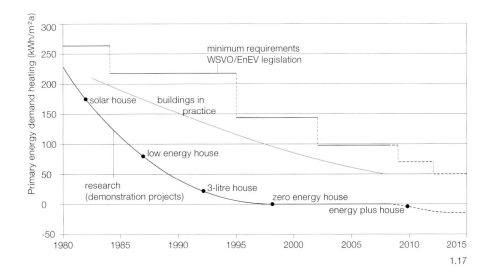

1.16 Consideration of additional variants (options) in detailed scenarios
  a Simple life cycle analysis decision model
  b Model in which the same decision situation between options reoccurs several times. This allows new decisions between two options to be made in the future.
  c A more realistic model in which decisions between different options can be made in the future. Here new options (C, D) emerge in the life cycle of the building and old options disappear.
1.17 Change in heating energy demand since 1980
  The reduction of energy consumption by a factor of 10 in the interest of sustainability has been achieved in full for new buildings. However, the energetic upgrading of the existing building stock will take between 30 and 50 years.
1.18 Example of the technology development for the 2000 watt society. Living according to this energy policy model, the average daily use of energy by each person would be 2000 watts.

The iterative nature of design

Although the built environment is of great significance in supporting society's activities, the holistic process of shaping the environment by planning and design occurs slowly over a long time scale in contrast to sectoral, technical processes such as manufacture and assembly. For a long time, building design was based on the long-established, traditional cooperative working relationship between designers and craftsmen. The function and form of buildings altered only slowly, building technology remained largely untouched by change over generations. The rules of architecture, building legislation, standards, technical regulations and forms of communication were continuously adapted in line with these changes.

In contrast, the post-second world war construction boom from the 1950s to the mid-1970s rapidly led to new methods of design, manufacture and assembly, to new materials and building forms. Compared with the great steps forward made in project management (functional performance specifications, project planning, continuous cost monitoring etc.) and in manufacturing (rationalisation, prefabrication, composite materials etc.), new theories and methods largely failed to materialise in the planning and design of buildings. Traditional industrial optimisation processes are usable only to a limited extent in construction, as they operate with a small number of variables, mostly related to cost-benefit functions.

In modern approaches to planning and design, a multidimensional solution space containing all the solutions that meet the specified target values or limits takes the place of a single, optimised solution. In the case of life cycle considerations, it is a multidimensional solution corridor. The final choice of possible solutions in the solution space depends on social, formal or other criteria considered and adapted on a case by case basis. New design tools integrate this view by establishing life cycle-oriented solution spaces in the briefing/programming phase. Integrated programs employ information about usable floor areas, degree of automation of the building management systems, energy demand target values, new build proportion of the entire project, transport implications and infrastructure equipment to calculate the costs, energy demand and environmental effects for different variants over the whole life cycle.

As the complete information about a building only emerges in the course of the design, the project can undergo continuous refinement through successive iterations. In addition, the various stakeholders need to use a multitude of design tools and assessment processes, some of which have not gained widespread acceptance in practice and are poorly matched with one another. This gives rise to one-off solutions in which every stakeholder remodels the planned project. This repeatedly gives rise to inconsistencies and multilateral dependencies of, for example, environmental burdens and costs, durability and flexibility etc. that until now could not be measured. Significant potential synergies are therefore lost.

Life cycle-oriented design

Current design processes are still oriented towards new buildings. Professional responsibility ends, according to the perception horizons of both the designer and the contractor, when the building is accepted by the client and passes into his ownership on completion. The remaining warranty period can be externalised by taking out insurance. The purpose of the building is narrowly defined at the start of the design process; but paradoxically the service provided starts at the time of handover to the client.

Of course, the actual life of a building, which may last for several hundred years, cannot be easily predicted. To address this concern, one can use scenario planning as a tool. With the help of scenarios, the tasks to be performed on the building throughout its life cycle, such as planned maintenance, refurbishment and change of use can be anticipated and modelled. By doing so, this can eliminate or alleviate possible future problems from the beginning, for example, by avoiding unnecessary air-conditioning systems and troublesome materials.

Buildings can continuously lose part of their overall value through physical aging and the advance of obsolescence. This process can be delayed but not prevented. Nevertheless, buildings vary greatly in the degree of future-proofing they offer, for example, through the number of options they hold for the future.

The life cycle of a building can be represented along two axes (Fig. 2.1):
· Structuring of the building in accordance with the four life cycle phases

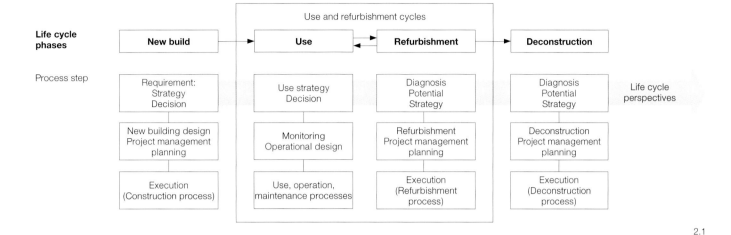

Life cycle phases	New build	Use and refurbishment cycles		Deconstruction	
		Use	Refurbishment		
Process step	Requirement: Strategy Decision	Use strategy Decision	Diagnosis Potential Strategy	Diagnosis Potential Strategy	Life cycle perspectives
	New building design Project management planning	Monitoring Operational design	Refurbishment Project management planning	Deconstruction Project management planning	
	Execution (Construction process)	Use, operation, maintenance processes	Execution (Refurbishment process)	Execution (Deconstruction process)	

2.1

(new build, use, refurbishment and deconstruction), with there being several cycles of change of use
• Structuring of every life cycle phase in terms of process stages (strategy, project management planning, execution)
Strategic decisions made at the beginning of all design processes (typically, when little information is available) always have a great influence on initial performance and on long-term consequences. This is particularly noticeable in the design of new buildings, where the degree of design freedom is very great. In the subsequent life cycle phases (e.g. in a refurbishment) design also assumes a long term impact; it must ensure or recreate the adaptability of the building to meet future needs. The process stages are different in every phase but basically they correspond to the normal service phases in the HOAI (German official scale of fees for services by architects and engineers) or the RIBA Plan of Work in the UK with a strong emphasis on the strategic aspects in the first design stage (Fig. 2.2). To address the concerns about the utility of a building over its whole life cycle, new methods can be used:
• Life cycle-oriented building description (element classification, building product model; see p. 23)
• Scenario techniques (life cycle simulation; see p. 16)
• Option theory (real options, virtual options; see p. 16)
• Value analysis (obsolescence; see p. 30)
• Scalable models (missing data models, product models; see p. 21)
• Reverse engineering (deconstructability; see p. 25, 28)

• Risk analysis (safety, reliability, availability)

Life cycle design entails using scenarios to determine and quantify the development of the requirements, the aging process and the loss of value over the life of the building. Later, these relationships are depicted and the implications made clear for the service life and detailed design. The effects in the form of damage and all types of loss of value are estimated and possible mitigating measures compared and implemented.

Life cycle-oriented building description

The typical building description consists of drawings (floor plans, sections, elevations, 3D models), calculations (cost calculations, energy calculations etc.) and schedules (e.g. specifications and bills of quantities). The various pieces of information are certainly linked at the beginning of this process

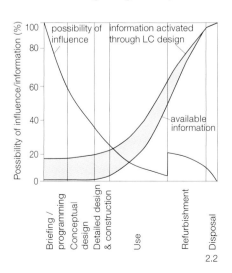

2.2

and some of these links form part of the design team's dialogue. However, there are no mechanisms to consider the effects of a design strategy or operational tactics during the life of a building on the entirety of a building, on how its components impact on the whole building, on its various specific conditions of usage and local context, on its stakeholders or on the various life cycle stages. Linkages like these are essential at the design stage when considering the life cycle of a building. However, they are not implemented because of the enormous complexity of the original data collection, updating and documentation. The only currently available basis for creating and updating energy and material assessments is element-oriented cost planning and the underlying specifications and bills of quantities. They provide enough detailed construction information and schedules of materials to be able to create a link with the inventory of building materials and processes. The data from previously analysed buildings can yield statistical characteristic values,

2.1 Life cycle phases and process steps
2.2 Development of the available information; the information activated by the life cycle design and possible opportunities to exert influence in the various phases of the life cycle. Life cycle design brings a crucial information gain in early project phases when there is less information available and the possibility of exerting influence is high.

19

2.3

which in the form of missing data can allow initial estimates of resource consumption, environmental impacts and overall costs to be made, even in the early design phases. Missing data are assumed values that provide temporary placeholders until the actual values become available. By using an element classification as the superordinate system, the differences in the descriptions of the buildings in the various life cycle phases, although still large, can be overcome (Figs. 2.4 and 2.5).

A life cycle-oriented description of buildings has to fulfil different requirements:

The simultaneous inclusion of energy, material and financial flows with automatic updating of changes

The structure of cost planning uses the bill of quantities as the lowest level of detail. This contains information on layer thickness or volume, material type, cutting and installation wastes, building processes (machine hours, labour hours, tools) as well as details of how to connect layers or parts. Extracts are created from this data, classified according to material or building processes and then linked by inventories with the upstream production stages. This step is very complex and time consuming because there are currently 30 000 items arranged in various catalogues according to the work type or trade.

The next higher level is the fine or process specification elements. They are composed of construction activities but are not classified in accordance with a functional element logic. They act as the link between the works-oriented execution and the function-oriented design. Fine elements can contain a wealth of additional information relating to aspects such as building physics, health, construction sequence and material disposal. They are listed in hierarchic order summarised into (coarse) elements (in accordance with DIN 276 "Costs of buildings") and building macro-elements [1]. The composition of each element depends on the life cycle phase and therefore every element exists in several forms:

• New build element: can also be a recycled or reused component, one-off

• Cleaning element: according to cleaning frequency and depth, continuous

• Maintenance element: according to availability/reliability requirements, or manufacturer's information, periodic

• Refurbishment element: dependent on condition, according to diagnosis, periodic

• Deconstruction element: according to disassembly level and depth, one-off

• Disposal element: according to disposal path, one-off

Integration of life cycle phases into the design

All the cycles of the individual elements come together to form a scenario specific to the project or building. The associated processes for all these elements are initiated every year. Standard scenarios contain average or normative assumptions for the cycles. Each new build element is automatically accompanied by its consequential elements, i.e. effects caused by its presence in the current and later phases. Of course the scenarios are able to be adjusted to create any possible combination of new build, maintenance, refurbishment, transformation and deconstruction. Full and equal consideration of time-dependent processes and alternatives (options) asks a great deal of planning and design tools.

Building projects in the future will consist increasingly of combinations of new build, refurbishment, transformation and deconstruction with the building continuing to be used. This means that these tools must be able consistently to model this diversity. However, there are currently very few truly integrated tools available for performing life cycle analyses.

Scalability

The building description must be scalable, i.e. the information must be structured in such a way that it can cover all life cycle phases and provide for increasing levels of refinement. Missing data must be available for use in the absence of explicit design information. The adoption of the strict hierarchical structure of DIN 276 and 277 makes it possible to define clear interfaces and use a modular process. This allows direct transfer into the Industry Foundation Classes (IFC) building model (see Tools for integrated design, pp. 90f.). The interfaces with the upstream data (energy generation, transport processes etc.) and the downstream stages (ISO/DIN 14050 Environmental management - Vocabulary) can also be clearly defined (Fig. 2.6, p. 22).

Scalable processes
Processes that can be used continuously throughout the various levels of detail are not widespread in building design, in contrast, for example, to the design of ships. Hence in most cases a simplified method is chosen for an early design stage – often only a rule of thumb. This can be replaced several times in later stages by more detailed procedures. Usually, there is not a seamless transition between stages as

the building data has to be compiled again for each procedure.
In contrast, some scalable processes have a high level of detail from the beginning. However, the information available at that time is incomplete, so missing values are replaced by average values, otherwise known as default values or missing data. In each design stage the average values can be replaced by the actual design values (Fig. 2.9, p. 23). This has two advantages: the designer is always working with complete, if not definitive information, and it is possible to consider the whole life cycle from the beginning. Morphological studies of existing building stock show that the formal diversity of buildings is much less than generally assumed. The material diversity (the composition of the buildings), which is crucial for determining the course of

the life cycle, can be foreseen with sufficient accuracy within a relatively limited solution space. This means that uncertainties in the description of buildings in early design stages are about the same size as the average deviation of the characteristics of a large number of buildings. The conclusion from this is that the design process represents a combination of required, planned, derived, simulated, assumed, already known, real and virtual circumstances. The increasing shift of construction activities from new build to existing buildings creates a need for a more accurate conceptual definition of the various activities. The key term in DIN 31051 "Fundamentals of maintenance" [2] is maintenance, which equates to the key term in the corresponding Swiss standard SIA 469 "Conservation of buildings" [3], conser-

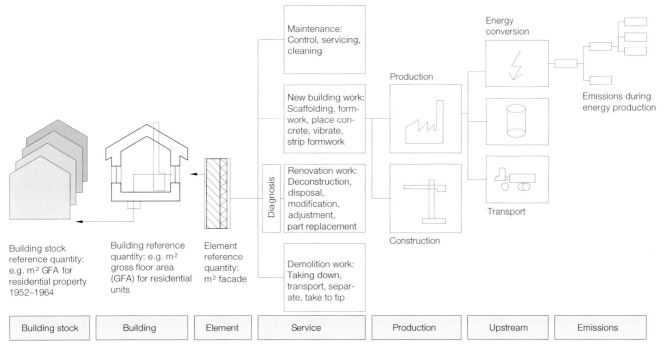

Maintenance: Control, servicing, cleaning

New building work: Scaffolding, formwork, place concrete, vibrate, strip formwork

Renovation work: Deconstruction, disposal, modification, adjustment, part replacement

Demolition work: Taking down, transport, separate, take to tip

Diagnosis

Production

Construction

Energy conversion

Emissions during energy production

Transport

Building stock reference quantity: e.g. m² GFA for residential property 1952–1964

Building reference quantity: e.g. m² gross floor area (GFA) for residential units

Element reference quantity: m² facade

| Building stock | Building | Element | Service | Production | Upstream | Emissions |

2.4

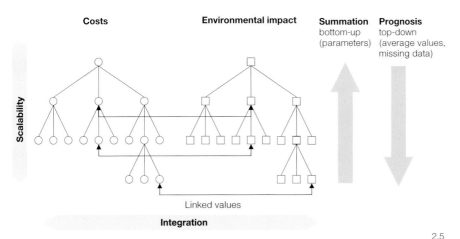

Costs   Environmental impact   Summation bottom-up (parameters)   Prognosis top-down (average values, missing data)

Scalability

Linked values

Integration

2.5

2.3 Life cycle phases of a building
a Construction
b Use
c Refurbishment/renovation
d Disposal
2.4 Linking of element classification, building works services, energy and material flow accounting.
2.5 Element classification
Scalability and integration (and in future Building Information Modelling, BIM) ensure a clear, hierarchical description of the building across all life cycle phases. The scalability ensures consistency and completeness between the design levels and the integration ensures consistency between the characteristics. A modification of the classification triggers an automatic adjustment of its characteristics.

Level	Number	Element type (attribute)	Reference unit	Application
Whole building	1	Ordinary building features (function, dimensions, age etc.)	Gross floor area (and derived areas like usable floor area, circulation areas etc.) in acc. with use (DIN 277)	Construction decisions (stage 1), Management of large building stock
Macro elements	5–7	Loadbearing structure, basement, stairwells, facades, internal walls, stairs, surfaces, building services	Macro-element areas (DIN 276)	Operation and management of building stock based on a diagnosis
(Coarse) elements	25–35	Cost elements, composed of building works for new buildings, cleaning, maintenance, refurbishment, deconstruction, disposal	Element quantities (DIN 276), cycles (cleaning, maintenance, refurbishment), condition (diagnosis codes)	Preliminary design, design (stage 2), operation (facility management), energy analyses, risk assessment
Fine elements	150–250	Cost elements on the basis of layers with loss data, connection type etc.	(Fine) element quantities	Specification, bill of quantities, tender award, construction planning risk identification
Works items		Works-orientated construction process description	Classified in accordance with standard schedule of works	Invitation to tender, construction sequence
Floor plan & materials catalogue		Room neighbourhood, linking of elements, dimensions, fitting out, usage features	Room (or part of a room)	In all life cycle phases

2.6

Conservation (SIA 496):
All the activities and measures for ensuring the continued existence and the material and cultural value of a building

Monitoring	Determination and evaluation of the condition with recommendations for further action	**Conservation**	Preservation or restoration of a building without significant alterations of the requirements	**Alteration**	Intervention in the building for the purpose of adjustment to meet new requirements
Observation	Verification of serviceability by simple and regular checks (usually visual)	**Maintenance**	Preservation of serviceability through simple and regular measures	**Adjustment**	Adjustment of a building to meet new requirements without significant intervention in the building
Inspection	Determination of the condition through systematic investigations, and assessments and indications of consequences	**Renovation**	Renewal of the safety and serviceability for a specified period	**Transformation**	Adjustment of a building to meet new requirements with significant intervention in the building
Inspection measurement	Monitoring by measurement of selected parameters	**Refurbishment**	Renewal of a whole building or component to a condition comparable with the original when new	**Extension**	Adjustment to meet new requirements through adding new components
Function inspection	Systematic check of the functions of systems and of other parts of a building				
Special terms:		**Restoration**	Renovation of a building of special cultural value while preserving the existing building fabric	**Reconstruction**	Reproduction of an earlier building that no longer exists

2.7

Maintenance (DIN 31051):
The combination of all technical and administrative measures and measures during the life cycle of a subject to maintain or return it to a functionally viable state in order that it can fulfil the required function

Maintenance	Inspection	Repair	Improvement
Measures to delay the reduction of the wear margin	Measures to determine and assess the current condition of a subject, including the determination of the reasons for wear, and the derivation of the consequences for a future use	Measures for returning a subject to a functionally viable state but not including improvement.	The combination of all technical, administrative and management measures for increasing operational reliability of a subject but without altering its required function

2.8

vation. The classification system adopted in SIA 469 (Fig. 2.7) is somewhat more detailed and generally more strongly building oriented than that in DIN 31051 (Fig. 2.8).

Life cycle phase 1: New build

In the typical design approach, oriented towards new build, the objective is to create a new individual building, a product, involving the use of resources and the acceptance of by-products and wastes.

Buildings as products or services

For a resource-conscious design, oriented towards the life cycle, the service that the client or user requires is considered from the beginning. Requirements describe first and foremost a service that can then be realised in various ways: through a new building, through the change of use of an existing building, through a non-building solution etc. In a typical design, creating the (new) building is the objective. In a service-oriented design on the other hand, the objective is the optimum satisfaction of the requirements of the client. The whole of the present building stock is therefore regarded as an available resource, the optimisation is measured by the efficiency of the expenditure of the resources to achieve the service. By-products can therefore be minimised or even better considered as available inputs and new resources (Fig. 2.10). From this perspective every design process has three stages in each of which there are clear questions to be addressed (Fig. 2.11, p. 24). At the end of each stage, the client receives a service (e. g. a report, project, building) and can then decide whether he wishes to continue straight away, secure an option or possibly drop the project completely. The traditional HOAI phases are again found throughout the whole process. It is crucial to use scalability reference quantities and characteristic values from a database. The hierarchical information structure can create characteristic impact values by condensing a great deal of different data as well as synthetic target values in the form of average values for buildings and macroelements. Every project

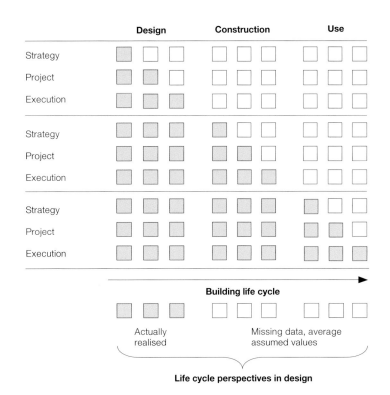

Life cycle perspectives in design   2.9

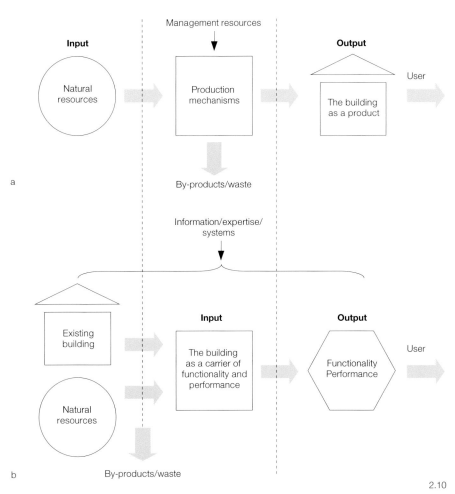

2.10

2.6 Detail levels of the building description according to life cycle phases
2.7 Definition of terms for activities in the building life cycle according to SIA 469
2.8 Definition of terms according to DIN 31051
2.9 Life cycle phases and progression of design. The assumed values are continuously replaced by actual values in every phase over whole life cycle. The design equates to reality at the end of the life cycle.
2.10 The building as a
     a Product
     b Service

produces additional characteristic values that can be reused and combined.

Process step 1:
Strategy, construction decision
In this phase there is a large degree of freedom of decision and it must be made clear which financial, energy and ecological effects the following variants entail:

- New build: creates a long-term demand on resources and has environmental impacts.
- No-build: many forms are possible, for example visualising a building service such as a library made available on an Internet server. Virtual buildings are also conceivable, in which the building metaphor is used as a search system. No-build solutions are always materialised to some extent, the environmental impacts occur in various other places, for example through the operation of a computer centre. If a new building is not necessary, the environmental effects of not building must be compared with those of a new building.
- Continued use of an existing building (with or without renovation)
- Transformation and/or extension of an existing building

The load factor of buildings is becoming an important parameter in the life cycle. Studies of large companies show that the total load factor of office buildings can vary greatly, depending on the employees (Fig. 2.12). If a company introduces widespread hot-desking for example, then in theory one workplace could be shared by 2.23 employees. Starting from the floor space requirements for cellular offices, by changing to an open plan arrangement and systematic hot-desking a saving of 62 % can be achieved. Of course, a more accurate consideration would have to take into account more than just absence times. As work could be performed at several locations – for example at the customers' premises, on the train, at home – these teleworking posts possibly cause a greater energy demand for transport and IT use and are responsible for increased loading of public spaces such as railway stations and homes.

Process step 2:
Design and project management planning
In addition to the ordinary functional, formal and structural requirements, it is essential to investigate the effects of the new system limits. In addition to the efficiency of use of space and occupancy, the costs of transport and infrastructure use assumes considerable importance. The reduction of energy demand and expenditure on energy provision, as well as raising energy efficiency are important to the use phase. Fig. 2.13 shows the relationships between the various influence factors and their indicators and their influence on the life cycle of a building. An accurate determination of the system limits is required to completely fulfil the objectives of sustainability using life cycle analysis (balance procedure). This has to consider the parameters building, context and operation. In order to make comparisons possible, the building is described in terms of functional equivalents (FE), e. g. m^2 gross floor area (GFA) of nursery. The building's performance is determined using performance

Service phase HOAI	Stages RIBA	Step	Aim & content	Questions	Reference unit	Tools	Reference value
1 Establish basic requirements	A & B Appraisal and briefing	1	Fundamental decision over strategy	New build? Change use? No build?	m^2 gross floor area, building units, use units: per person/ student place/ bed etc..	Characteristic values for LC costs, energy demand, environmental impact	
2 Preliminary design 3 Final design 4 Approval design	C, D & E Design	2	Project management planning/ design	Where? What? How much?	m^2 element units	Characteristic values for LC costs, energy requirements, environmental impact	Database with scalable reference values
5 Execution design 6 Tender preparation, invitation and award	F, G & H Preconstruction	3	Execution, commissioning	How? How much?	Construction and use process units	Measured values	

2.11

Employee type	Present at workplace
Consultant	20 %
Sales	47 %
Office-based	67 %
Average occupancy rate	45 %

Occupancy	No. of hours/year
Production	3500–4400
Schools	1200–2400
Higher education	4400
Offices	2200–3200
Hospitals	8760

Use	Average ratio of usable floor area to gross floor area (GFA)	Deviation from average (%)
Offices	0.50	18
Primary school	0.59	15
Nursery	0.55	15
Sportshall	0.65	14
Apartment block	0.53	23
Detached house	052	25
Carehome	0.49	18
Museum	0.59	19
Average	**0.55**	**18**

2.11 Three-step procedure in the design process
2.12 Use efficiency of different spaces
The potentials can be combined and result in considerable lower and upper maximum deviations. Some of them at least have specific environmental effects and resource use demand implications.
2.13 Parameters, indicators and influences on building services (after Bogenstätter and authors)

2.12

indicators. There are also parameters such as space efficiency, use efficiency. The various parameters are in turn defined and evaluated by means of indicators.

Process step 3: Execution
Effects on the local area or at specific points are the focus during the execution phase. Which technologies and auxiliary materials can be used to achieve the objective of this phase must be made clear. The reference units for this are the building works. At this stage the requirements must be set out in a sustainable procurement policy for components , services and operating equipment. Various evaluation methods can be used.
The design of the construction process must be in harmony with the long-term, holistic requirements already defined for the building. Reverse engineering can be applied here to check automatically whether each construction solution can be efficiently and sustainably built, maintained, repaired, inspected, deconstructed and replaced (Fig. 2.14, p. 26). The technique examines in

particular whether these measures and checks can be undertaken safely in an occupied building and without disruption to the users. To ensure that buildings and components can be used sustainably, it is necessary to redefine certain design rules. Reverse engineering is one of the ways in which this can be accomplished.
The safety of the construction workers and building users is considered as a social aspect of sustainability. It mainly concerns pollution and risks for:
• Workers on the construction site
• Future users of the interior of the building
• The immediate surroundings (ecosystem and microclimate)

In contrast to new building projects, refurbishments are often performed on buildings that are in continuous occupation or operation. The occupants are exposed to effects which may be hazardous to health. In some cases, this is for longer than the site workers and yet the occupants do not receive comparable protection. Designers and contractors must take note of the indications

given in the manufacturers' environmental product declarations (EPD) to avoid these dangers.

Life cycle phase 2: Use

Activities during the use phase are defined in a normative way as building management tasks according to the classification in DIN 32736 "Building management" (Fig. 2.15, p. 26) [4].

Life cycle phase 1: Use strategy
As well as achieving high economic returns and resource efficiency, one objective of the concept is to ensure the highest possible load factor for the available floor area. The operating concept establishes the objectives for comfort and the aims for the quality and availability of other services (IT, transport systems etc.). Furthermore it establishes the safety and availability requirements that the building equipment must achieve, defines the target values for the consumption of energy and other media (drinking water, waste water etc.) and the cleaning requirements.

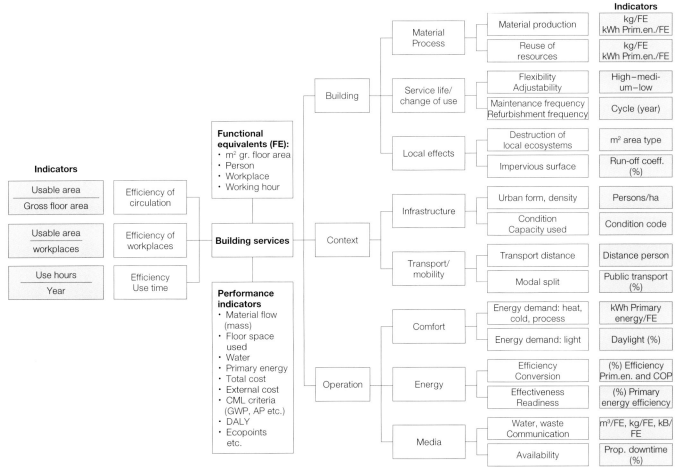

2.13

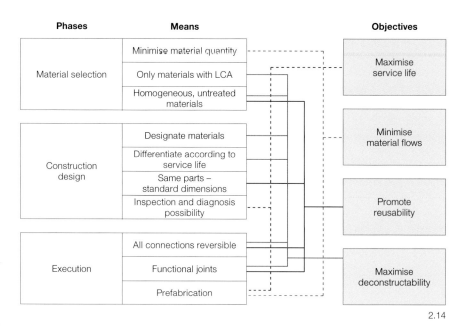

2.14

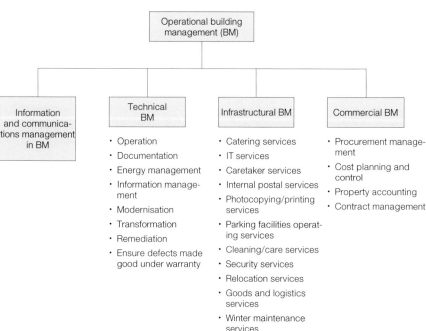

2.15

Process phase 2: Use design
Use design divides the operational building management system (BMS) into technical, infrastructural and commercial activities (Fig. 2.15).

Optimised operation
The development of the quality concept in environmental management indicates extensive integration with the many objectives of sustainable building. The client or his representative must therefore ensure that the selected designer and contractor have established their own quality assurance procedures in order to demonstrate the comprehensive long-term quality of the building, particularly its performance over time and fitness. In particular, this applies to demonstrating and fine-tuning the actual performance of the building's environmental management system(s). While the ordinary contractual criteria (completion to programme and within budget) when the building is handed over can be audited, it is not possible to verify the predicted complex dynamic parameters of building performance at that time. Therefore optimisation of the building's operation during the first year is vitally important for actually achieving the target values, the fine-tuning, and the continuous checking and optimisation of the systems and the building (as well as for understanding how the users and facility managers actually use the building and resolving problems that they may identify). The basic requirement structure of the life cycle analysis can be updated and adjusted according to the requirements of the subsequent life cycle phase and building management (Fig. 2.16). Among the various ways of dealing with these problems, the "Soft Landings" [5] process is interesting because it increases designer and constructor involvement before and after handover, and directs the "supply side" to greater involvement with users and a careful assessment of building performance in use. As the originators of this new form of professionalism state: "The objective is more certainty in delivering buildings that achieve a close match between the expectations of clients and users and the predictions of the design team. A Soft Landings team (designer and builder) is resident on site during the move-in period in order to deal with

2.14 Principles of design for durability and reverse engineering
2.15 Components of building management in accordance with DIN 32736
2.16 Process flow in building operations optimisation (BO)

emerging issues more effectively. It then monitors building use and energy performance for the first three years of occupation, identifying opportunities both for fine-tuning the building and for future projects. This process also creates a coordinated route to post-occupancy evaluation" [6].

Maintenance design
Various maintenance strategies are available, depending on the objectives. As far as components are concerned the strategies may be based on failure, prevention or inspection. The first strategy is the most favourable in the short term but harbours a high risk of consequential damage. A preventative strategy could result in overinvestment. An inspection strategy is generally considered ideal for buildings (Fig. 2.17, p. 28).

Process phase 3: Use
The main issues during the use phase of a building are the adherence to the maintenance cycles, achieving the optimum operation, continuous monitoring and benchmarking against the target values of the building. The safety and availability of the systems must be guaranteed and detrimental consequences avoided as far as can be foreseen.

Maintenance cycles
Maintenance cycles are important above all for components that have to be maintained for reasons of safety, due to expensive replacement costs or where high quality maintenance contributes greatly to saving costs or where its omission would have expensive consequences.

Avoidance of consequential damage
The renovation of a building element that is only slightly damaged may be more urgent than one that is severely damaged or has already failed. The urgency of a maintenance task therefore depends on the consequences of omitting to perform the renovation and the costs of these consequences (Fig. 2.18, p. 28).

Life cycle phase 3: Refurbishment/renovation

There are several basic strategies available for the maintenance of buildings. They may be focused on the whole building or its components.

Process phase 1: Conservation strategy
In general terms there are four main conservation strategies for buildings:

Value conservation strategy (reference strategy)
The main goal of the value conservation strategy is to preserve the serviceability at the original level of comfort and maintain the original use. The utility value of a building can fall if its standard is not improved or the changing comfort requirements of the tenants are not taken into account.

Value increase strategy (also referred to as refurbishment strategy or transformation strategy)
A value increase strategy entails widespread interventions to adapt the usability to match increasing demands. Forecast future developments are anticipated in planned redesign and improvement measures.

Low-level maintenance strategy
This strategy is chosen when the funds for a reference strategy are not available or if there is uncertainty over the further development of the general location at the time. A low-level strategy cannot be followed in the long term.

Decay strategy (dereliction strategy)
Allowing a building to degrade is usually done with the objective of achieving an increase in the value of the site with a suitable new building. However the price of the land does not always rise and reductions in values can occur in neglected areas. This can lead to urban decay and general loss of value.

Process phase 2: Planning the project management of a refurbishment
In a refurbishment project, the creative input of the designer is a combination of diagnosis and estimation of the long-term potential of a building The sequence of steps in the design process is therefore changed. With new build there is a smooth transition from the preparation for construction phase into the construction phase itself in order to be able to start building as soon as possible after obtaining the building permit. The documents required for the construction to progress (drawings, tenders etc.) are usually prepared successively in parallel with the works. With a refurbishment project, typically the building continues to operate, so usually time pressure during the design phase is reduced. However, an operating building offers few opportunities for sudden departures from the agreed plan (even for good reasons) and planning the

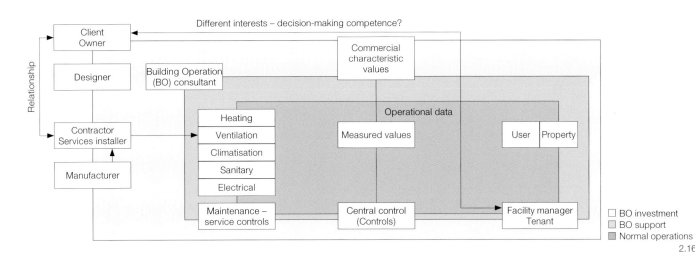

2.16

sequence of the works becomes critical for the success of the project.
A building condition diagnosis consists of dividing the building into elements, ascertaining the state of aging of each element in accordance with predefined degradation scales, estimating any consequential damage and establishing the limitations imposed by the building and its surroundings (e. g. access possibilities, building occupancy rates etc.) Furthermore the urgency of immediate interventions in the interest of safety or avoiding consequential damage must be defined. The next stage is to plan the refurbishment measures, task by task. The various tasks can then be bundled together into packages of measures. The criteria for forming these packages could include, for example:
- Functional dependencies, e. g. a refurbishment of the exterior render also makes repainting necessary
- Logical interrelationships, e. g. optimum use of scaffolding
- Reduction of detrimental effects on utility, e. g. by dirt, noise

In forming these packages of measures, it is important to consider residual life, present value, renovation costs and common cost components. There is always a question about how much residual value is discarded when an element is prematurely renovated.
A use diagnosis is carried out in parallel with the building condition diagnosis. On the basis of these diagnoses, an assessment is made of whether the building has serious functional (e. g. rooms too small) or formal deficiencies or, on the other hand, whether it has options such as offering opportunities for a further, ongoing use, perhaps with additional storeys, a more flexible circulation system, or has a facade with a high design or historic value etc. A number of variants with different cost-benefit ratios and abilities to meet future needs arise from a consideration of the building condition diagnosis, the package of reinstatement measures, use diagnosis, usability defects and possible options for measures. (Fig. 2.19).

Process phase 3: Undertaking the refurbishment (building in use)
In view of the large number of refurbishment tasks arising directly from a composition of the building, it is normally not possible to clear the building before refurbishment. Refurbishment during occupancy is the normal situation. The project management planning and preparation time exceeds the actual construction time of a structural refurbishment by a factor of about four. The preparation time is made up of the time required for drawing up the documents by the architect, periods of notice required by tenancy agreements, time taken by the client to make decisions, time to process official applications, time to find suitable contractors and the time required to manufacture prefabricated components (Fig. 2.20).

Life cycle phase 4: Deconstruction

The preparation of a deconstruction project (planning for selective dismantling or "construction in reverse")

Strategy	Measures
Damage-dependent firefighting or failure strategy	Renovation as a reaction to failure or acute damage
Objective-dependent interval strategy	Determination of the intervals for regular maintenance and renovation
Condition-dependent inspection strategy	Determination of conditions likely to initiate intervention; regular inspection with maintenance as the reaction
Service-life-oriented replacement strategy or preventative strategy	Classification of components according to their average service life; preventive replacement
Safety-oriented technical strategy	Classification of components according to safety aspects; hazard-based strategy
Return-oriented economic efficiency strategy	Classification of buildings; strategy selection according to anticipated return on investment (ROI) and quality standard
Standard-oriented sustainability strategy	Classification of buildings and components according to importance and quality standards; always using the inspection strategy

2.17

	Window	Plaster	Floor covering	Heating plant
Maintenance intensity	Regular repainting	Occasional repainting	Frequent cleaning (floor cleaning)	Legally stipulated servicing
Influence of component location	Important (weathering)	Important (weathering)	Important	Unimportant
Influence of use	Neutral	Unimportant (little difference)	Important	Neutral
Influence of non-material aging	Low	Low	Medium (fashion obsolescence)	High (technical obsolescence)
Consequential damage	Very high	Very high	High	Low (if building well insulated)
Average service life	20 to over 100 years	20–60 years	Depending on floor covering type between 10 to over 100 years	Heat generation 15 years, heat distribution 40–80 years
Important reasons for refurbishment	Component condition	Component condition Package of measures	Component condition Change of use	Technical obsolescence

2.18

requires careful planning, which is achieved by cooperation between the client, designer, specialist demolition contractors and any parties interested in the subsequent use of building components or materials.

Process phase 1: Deconstruction strategy

The strategic objective of every deconstruction is to ensure the highest possible level of subsequent reuse for all components, the minimisation of losses during deconstruction, transport and reinstallation and to control the risks of the whole demolition process by the exercise of design, technical and organisational measures [7]. This is best accomplished by a detailed analysis of the structure. The hierarchy of objectives for this is:

- Subsequent use at the element level (e. g. windows)
- Subsequent use at the component level (e. g. bricks, parquet)
- Material recycling at the highest possible level, minimisation of downcycling
- Thermal recycling
- Landfill

Process phase 2: Project management planning for deconstruction

Compared with conventional building demolition, deconstruction covers a complex spectrum of activities. The method of implementation of strategic design objectives (including fundamental deconstruction strategies or cost-optimised levels of disassembly) must often be devised within a short time frame of just a few days or hours. The results of the above series of steps yield framework data that are important for the rapidly devised operational design, as they circumscribe the range of available alternatives. The specification of the levels of disassembly is particularly important in this context. In addition to economic efficiency, the final disassembly plan takes particular account of technical and environmental aspects. This brings the operational questions increasingly into focus. In particular, the sequence of works on site, their estimated duration, the type, quantities and timing of the resources (personnel and equipment) to be made available on site for deconstruction work and the associated costs of

deconstruction and disposal (Fig. 2.21, p. 30).

At the time of demolition planning, the available information about the materials present within the building is usually inadequate. An important starting point for a systematic dismantling of a building is therefore an investigation of the materials it contains as part of a building diagnosis, in the course of which the materials in the building are identified, measured and evaluated. Problematical areas such as contaminated parts of a building components or components that are difficult to disassemble can be identified and their effects limited.

Process phase 3: Disposal and recycling processes

A design incorporating an integrated disassembly and recycling plan can result in higher quality secondary building materials. The plan should seek to ensure coordination between disassembly and material processing. A key factor is the coupling of the outward transfer of foreign materials and pollutants with the downstream building ma-

2.19

2.20

2.17 Maintenance strategies related to objectives
2.18 Maintenance of different building elements
2.19 Combination of technical and use diagnoses
The process does not usually run straight though from beginning to end. There are optimisation loops.
2.20 Process steps in the design and construction of a refurbishment project

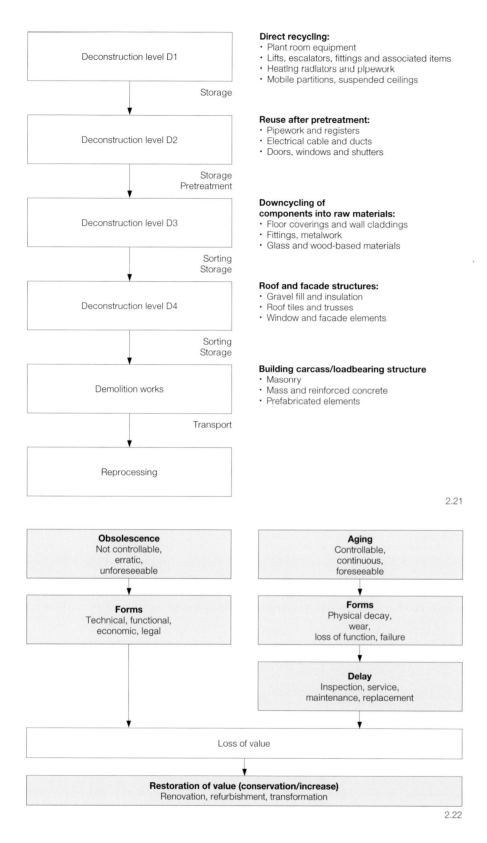

Deconstruction level D1

Storage

Deconstruction level D2

Storage
Pretreatment

Deconstruction level D3

Sorting
Storage

Deconstruction level D4

Sorting
Storage

Demolition works

Transport

Reprocessing

Direct recycling:
· Plant room equipment
· Lifts, escalators, fittings and associated items
· Heating radiators and pipework
· Mobile partitions, suspended ceilings

Reuse after pretreatment:
· Pipework and registers
· Electrical cable and ducts
· Doors, windows and shutters

**Downcycling of
components into raw materials:**
· Floor coverings and wall claddings
· Fittings, metalwork
· Glass and wood-based materials

Roof and facade structures:
· Gravel fill and insulation
· Roof tiles and trusses
· Window and facade elements

Building carcass/loadbearing structure
· Masonry
· Mass and reinforced concrete
· Prefabricated elements

2.21

Obsolescence Not controllable, erratic, unforeseeable	**Aging** Controllable, continuous, foreseeable

Forms Technical, functional, economic, legal	**Forms** Physical decay, wear, loss of function, failure

	Delay Inspection, service, maintenance, replacement

Loss of value

Restoration of value (conservation/increase) Renovation, refurbishment, transformation

2.22

2.21 Deconstruction levels
2.22 Types and successive stages of
    obsolescence and aging
2.23 Survival curves for
    a Windows
    b Heating systems

terial processing as part of the building disassembly plan. A central part of the plan would be that soot-contaminated components (e. g. chimneys) and materials containing gypsum are extracted and recycled separately from the remainder of the materials during the disassembly of the building.
In the medium term, the objective should be to develop regional recycling chains that are linked to the deconstruction activities on site. The chains combine the determination of the quantities of elements and building materials with the opportunities for reuse and subsequent use in the region. These recycling centres would have appropriate equipment for assisting with deconstruction and reuse of components.

Aging and loss of value

The term 'aging' embraces a large number of phenomena that can lead to loss of value over the life of a building.

Aging and obsolescence as causes of loss of value

The triggers for loss of value and obsolescence may be very diverse: physical aging of the building material, aging through use, environmental influences or inappropriate maintenance (Fig. 2.22). Losses, but also gains of value arise from commercial valuation: when this is negative it can be accompanied by increasing shabbiness and aging (obsolescence), when positive the building instead develops a patina. In the case of listed buildings, the age and appearance of property have an eminently positive significance. Obsolescence (Latin obsolescere: loss, dilapidation, decline of appearance and value) expresses the two roots of the word: value and appearance.
The physical basis of the phenomenon of aging is described in the second principle of thermodynamics by the terms energy and entropy.
The process of aging is founded in the inevitable increase in entropy. Entropy can be thought of as a measure of "order" or "disorder".

Reference aging and risk
The reference condition is a state of physical aging that has been delayed

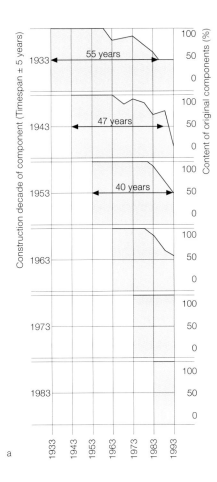

by normal planned maintenance and repair. Additional loss of value can arise through:

- Overuse (compared with the planned level of use)
- Inadequate maintenance (compared with the best possible maintenance)
- Premature replacement (natural catastrophe, planned demolition etc.)
- Consequences of delayed replacement

Triggers may be direct influences (e.g. earthquakes) or indirect influences from other processes (e.g. the owner's decay or dereliction strategy, lack of competence of the tradesmen involved). The result in both cases is a physical loss of fabric of a building with possible associated economic, cultural and information losses.

The risk is defined as the product of the probability of occurrence and the extent of destruction or damage. From the point of view of risk however, the only losses that are considered are either determined by external (natural) events or losses due to outdated use, management, design or construction of the building. The loss of value that arises through aging and changes in requirements is not seen as risk but rather as a normal occurrence. Although losses resulting from natural causes cannot in principle be avoided, the magnitude of the losses can be mitigated in certain circumstances, for example by increasing the earthquake resistance of the building. Consequential effects can likewise be limited. Knowledge and information are required in both cases. All losses of value are taken into account in the case of indirect influences through societal processes, as far as they are known and can be anticipated.

There are of course contradictions: the replacement of perfectly functional windows by much more energy-efficient windows represents, on the one hand, a loss of physical and economic capital. On the other hand, it is a gain in natural capital through the reduction of environmentally harmful emissions. Likewise carefully renovating homes may certainly lead to loss of perfectly functional componentsbut allows the homes to be better suited to changes in living preferences.

Survival functions

The aging process can be described as a survival function within the context of a survival analysis. The survival function can always be used where there is 'mortality', (i.e. successive withdrawal of measured objects from the statistical database). This can occur through the failure of mechanical systems, disuse or destruction. The key issue is the survival or survivor function. This describes the probability of survival at least as far as a particular point in time. For technical systems, this can also be described as the reliability function. The survival function is usually assumed to approach zero as age increases. However, a number of studies on building component service life arrive at very widely different conclusions. A comparative study into the survival of identical components of various ages shows a relatively clear result [8]. The half-life of a component (i.e. the number of years until 50% of the initial life will have passed) reduces dramatically with each new construction decade.

The survival curves for different components plotted according to their year of manufacture show that the survival probability of the components in the last 50 years has decreased continuously. Windows installed in 1933 had a half-life of 55 years, while windows installed in 1953 only had a half-life of 40 years (Fig. 2.23) [8]. What can be seen is that robust statements about service lives cannot be made without having specific information about the year of manufacture, construction, exposure, and the quality of installation and maintenance.

Loss of value through obsolescence

What decides whether buildings survive or which buildings survive? Obviously their physical durability plays only a subordinate role. The statement: "Buildings are not demolished because they are in a poor condition, buildings are in a poor condition so that they can be demolished" sums up this finding, as there are other 'drivers' that influence obsolescence.

Why components are prematurely replaced and buildings demolished can be explained to some extent through differentiation of the term obsolescence. Certain products lose their economic value over the long term,

2.23

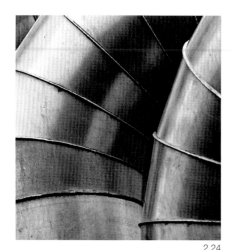

2.24

Aging of a material, for example zinc

Layer thickness: 20 µm = 0.02 mm

Mass loss (ML)
Unprotected exposure: $4ML = 14.5 + 0.043 \times TOW \times [SO_2] \times [O_3] + 80 \times Rain \times [H+]$
Protected situation: $4ML = 5.5 + 0.013 \, TOW \, [SO_2] \times [O_3]$

Influence factors:

$4ML$ = Mass loss after 4 years' exposure in µg/m^2
TOW = Period of humidity (RH > 80 %, T > 0 °C) as fraction of a year
$[SO_2]$ = Concentration in µg/m^3
$[O_3]$ = Concentration in µg/m^3
Rain = Rainfall in m/year
$[H+]$ = Concentration in g/l

Example of use:
$ML = 14.5 + 0.043 \times 0.377 \times 10 \times 55 + 80 \times 0.7 \times 0.4 \times 4 \times 102 = 25.7$ µg/m^2

Thickness of zinc: 7.2×106 g/m^3
Thickness loss per year = $25.7/(4.7 \times 7.2 \times 106) = 0.89$ µm/year
The service life equals $20/0.89 = 22$ years.

2.25

they become obsolete and therefore are thrown away or destroyed. In order to judge the chances of survival of a building it is necessary to estimate the risk of its obsolescence.

This can be done statistically by very complex analyses of demolitions (i. e. the end of life a vast range of different buildings). More accurate estimates can be made if the half-life time is known. This half-life method does not differentiate between the reasons for the loss of value and the underlying reasons for its end of life. It is important to understand whether the loss of value takes place due to aging or obsolescence. Obsolescence can take place for several reasons:

Functional obsolescence
Some buildings cannot fulfil new functions (e. g. residential buildings from the 1950s with very small apartments, office buildings with deep plans or low ceiling heights etc.). This obsolescence threatens considerable numbers of post-war residential and office buildings.

Physical obsolescence
Poor maintenance causes the state of a building to deteriorate to such an extent that its repair is no longer worthwhile. Of course, poorly constructed buildings are also under great threat but these faults can be usually be rectified.

Technical obsolescence
Technical obsolescence occurs when buildings cease to comply with current technical standards. This is an unavoidable consequence of technical development. The unavailability

of replacement parts is one of the reasons why repairs and maintenance can become difficult. This can also happen if the technical systems are intimately linked with the building and cannot be repaired or easily replaced.

Legal obsolescence
In many cases buildings can no longer be economically upgraded to meet new regulations. More stringent requirements for thermal and sound insulation figure highly in cases of legal obsolescence. Other examples include buildings contaminated with asbestos or new requirements for disabled access.

Economic obsolescence
Economic obsolescence means that, for example, the income from a building has failed to keep up with the return that could be made from developing the plot. This is the most common reason for demolition. This form of obsolescence affects an increasing number of buildings.

Style obsolescence
Buildings often find themselves no longer in accord with the "taste" of an epoch. Particularly affected are fashionable buildings, which have to live with the discrepancy that what is trendy and modern today is outmoded tomorrow. The problem is primarily one of the building's external appearance. What becomes apparent is that, for example, the facades from Germany's "Gründerzeit" (the period of economic growth in the mid to late 19th century), which were once considered overelaborate, are now seen as less obsolete than the "timeless" white boxes of the Modern Movement.

The aging of building materials
The aging of building materials is described as the loss or reduction of physical properties (loadbearing capacity, air- and watertightness, transparence, elasticity etc.) through the actions of physical, chemical and biological influences such as water and other liquids, water vapour (damp), heat and cold, salts in solution, vibra-

Component quality	A	Quality of the component	Manufacturing method, storage, transport conditions, materials, protective coatings
	B	Quality of the construction	Joints, protective construction details
	C	Execution quality	
Environment	D	Indoor influences	Indoor air conditions
	E	Outdoor air influences	Weather, vibration, outdoor air quality
Conditions of use	F	Intensity of use	Mechanical effects, type of use, wear
	G	Maintenance quality	Type and frequency of maintenance, accessibility,

From the above:
$ESLC = RSLC \times A \times B \times C \times D \times E \times F \times G$

$ESLC$ = Estimated service life of a component
$RSLC$ = Reference service life of a component

2.26

tion, light, microbiological pro esses, natural or man-made catastrophes or accidents. The extent of the influence is a function of the following factors:
• Cycle: the number of occurrences, frequency, amplitude
• Dose: flow, deposition, concentration, exposure time
• Occurrence: probability of occurrence

Aging can generally be expressed as a dose function (Fig. 2.25). This involves the measurement of material loss while recording the various influences such as moisture and pollutants over the period of measurement at locations of different exposure. In this way, the loss of coating thickness and therefore the life of the coating can be determined, for example.
This process is important for infrastructure buildings and is suitable for all kinds of surface coatings in which the building material and the component are for all practical purposes identical. There are a whole range of studies being carried out on this topic as part of European Union and international research projects [9].

The aging of building components
The information available about the service life of all sorts of building components is extensive, diverse and very inconsistent. The most important methods of collecting it are described below:

Factor method in accordance with ISO 15 686
In order allow a larger number of factors to be taken into account, the International Organisation for Standardisation (ISO) devised the factor method in accordance with ISO 15 686 "Buildings and constructed assets – Service-life planning – Part 8: Reference service life". The service life of any product can be estimated using seven factors which cover the aspects of building component quality, environment and utility (Fig. 2.26).
The key questions are what to assume as the reference service life and where to obtain the values for the factors. When applied to industrially manufactured goods with assessable service lives based on empirical data (e.g. computers, washing machines), the

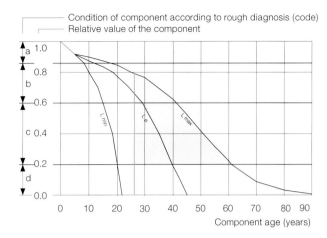

Age known:
The accepted age of the component under consideration is 26 years.
It can only be said that it will probably lose its ability to function in the next 35 years if it is not already in this condition

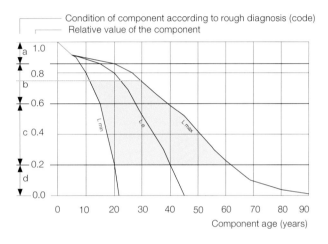

Condition known:
The accepted condition factor of the component under consideration is 0.75 (condition code b).
From the aging curve, it can be said that the component has still another 8–30 years until it loses its ability to function.

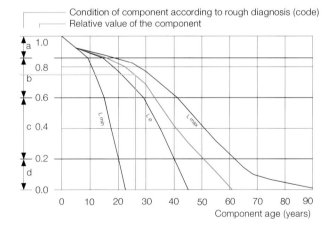

Age and condition known:
If age and condition are known, it can be seen from the curves that the aging of component will follow the green curve. According to the green curve the component has a residual service life of about 34 years.

2.27

2.24 Galvanised ventilation ducts
2.25 Calculation of the aging of a material, here a zinc coating, using a dose function
2.26 Estimation of the component service life using the factor method in accordance with ISO 15 686
2.27 Interpretation of aging curves

method leads to plausible results and is suitable for comparing variants or estimating consequential costs. However, the method can also provide meaningful results for laminated components. A large number of sources are available, in particular the publicly accessible BMVBS database [10]. It is difficult to obtain clear results for complex components that have to comply with many different criteria.

Loss of value

Another method uses data on element type and service life to create specific aging curves. By linking the loss of value to the service life, each component can be assigned its own aging curve.

It has been shown that methods based on aging curves (depreciation curves) lead to better results. Different aging curves for a large number of residential buildings are analysed in relation to the effects of the environment and standards of construction and maintenance. The initial data are obtained from diagnoses of components in relation to deterioration state, quality and age [11]. Various aging curves relating to type, exposure, and the quality of installation and maintenance can be derived from the results (Fig. 2.28). These curves allow the residual service life of components to be calculated. Comparison with information about service life in the literature (Fig. 2.27, p. 33) shows that the combination of a larger number of values from the literature certainly forms the same aging spectrum (maximum, minimum and mean values) but cannot explain the reasons for the resulting deviations (e. g. in the case of the installation quality).

The aging of buildings

The aging function a building cannot be described independently of the interventions made during its life. "Pure" aging without any maintenance would lead relatively rapidly to a combined loss of value through consequential effects and failure to meet the threshold values of utility (usability, safety, hygiene etc.). Regular maintenance makes it possible to slow this process. In theory one could imagine that a building would last practically for ever if it were given continuous maintenance and its parts continuously renewed. This applies for example to major structures or items of infrastructure such as the Arena in Nîmes, which has been in use for 2000 years. The need for periodic maintenance is usually determined by the limited service life of technical systems and surfaces. A distinction is drawn between partial refurbishment (after 20–30 years) and complete refurbishment (after 40–60 years). Renovation positively impacts on the restoration of value of the original.

The tasks of maintenance, partial refurbishment and complete refurbishment can often be combined into similar packages of measures that lead to cyclic refurbishment (Fig. 2.29, 2.30 and 2.33, p. 37).

In many cases however, the standards acceptable to society change over time. Instead of a pure renovation by replacement using identical components, an improvement as compared to the original standards of the building (e. g. new kitchen units, rewiring etc.) or an upgrade to meet new regulatory standards (energy consumption, environmental pollution) will occur.

The aging of building stock

Studies of the long-term development of mixed building stock show a paradoxical trend of reduction of the average service life within each age class. The newer the building, the shorter its half-life time. Residential buildings have a much higher service life than non-residential buildings. Industrial buildings, on the other hand, have even shorter half-lives (Fig. 2.32, p. 37).

The tasks of maintenance, partial refurbishment and complete refurbishment can often be combined into similar package of measures that lead to cyclic refurbishment (Fig. 2.31, p. 36).

Estimated service life of buildings

In order to estimate the probable service life of buildings, it is necessary to differentiate between:
· Prognosis
  How long will a building last? This is difficult to answer because it depends on many factors that are not predictable.
· Potential
  How long can a building continue to exist based on its constructional characteristics?
· Hypothesis
  What assumptions should be made in life cycle costing for its service life?

In making a prognosis, a number of characteristics have been identified which have led to existing buildings surviving, being durable, simple to maintain and adaptable to several cycles of change. Adaptability is determined by morphological characteristics

Construction of loss of value curves with reference to parameters

In general form:

$$W = 1 - t^a$$

W = Relative value of the component
t = Relative age of the component
a = Exponent in the depreciation formula

Division into two phases gives:

$$W = \begin{cases} 1 - t_{\ddot{u}} \times (t/t_a)^{a1} & \text{for } t < t_{\ddot{u}} \\ W_{\ddot{u}} - W_{\ddot{u}} \times [(t - t_{\ddot{u}})/W_{\ddot{u}}]^{a2} & \text{for } t > t_{\ddot{u}} \end{cases}$$

Paul Meyer-Meierling quotes the following parameters (see adjacent table):

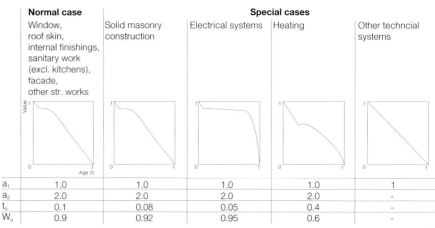

	Normal case	Special cases		
	Window, roof skin, internal finishings, sanitary work (excl. kitchens), facade, other str. works	Solid masonry construction	Electrical systems	Heating	Other techncial systems
a_1	1.0	1.0	1.0	1.0	1
a_2	2.0	2.0	2.0	2.0	-
$t_{\ddot{u}}$	0.1	0.08	0.05	0.4	-
$W_{\ddot{u}}$	0.9	0.92	0.95	0.6	-

2.28

(building depth < 12 m; storey height > 3.5 m), a circulation system that allows the building to be divided in many ways into directly accessible sections, and a clear system of load distribution within the main loadbearing structure and structural components.

In terms of potential, it can be said that buildings can last in theory for hundreds of years, provided they are well maintained and regularly repaired. The durability of the loadbearing structure is hardly reduced, except perhaps in the case of some lighter wooden or steel structures. Most important for the building envelope and fit-out systems are good design, installation and maintenance, protection against harmful external influences and overuse, material selection (tile roofs, mineral render, floor coverings of stone, ceramic tiles or solid parquet, hardwood windows etc.). Other systems, such as technical plant (e. g. burners, boilers etc.), have only a short service life due to continuous technical development. Here it is particularly important to ensure that these systems can be inspected, maintained and replaced easily.

A hypothesis of the building service life in life cycle costing requires accounting processes to be based on cyclic replacement models and the service life of the loadbearing structure to be the same as that of the building. The frequency of partial refurbishment (20–30 years) and complete refurbishment (40–60 years) results in the long term, (at the latest in 60 years though probably after 50 years), in a practically continuous cycle of replacement. If the building is demolished shortly before this point in time and the total cost divided by 50, the resulting figure is an average annual expenditure over the service life (e. g. expenditure of primary energy or mass per year). If the building is demolished shortly after the complete refurbishment, for example in year 52, then the expenditure is much greater but the divisor not much changed. The result in this case is above all dependent on the assumptions made in the calculations. In principle this "depreciation" for the long-term durable components, such as the loadbearing structure is lower the longer the building remains in use, and after 100 years it is negligible. Then there is only the regular maintenance expenditure

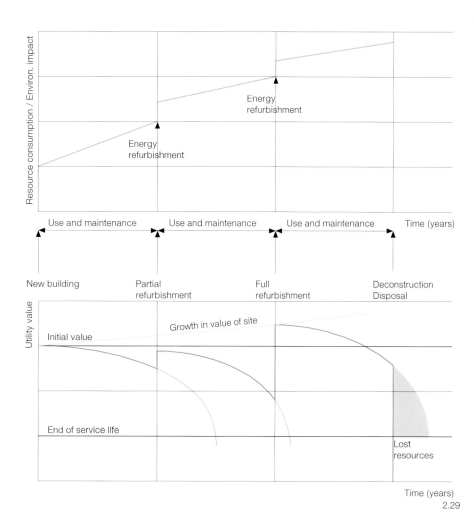

2.29

Type of use/ problem	General strategy	Reaction of the building/ building measures	Reaction of the user/use measures	Additional measures
Lack of use	Abandon	Demolish	Abandon use, move out	Recycling and reuse of elements and building materials, Replace existing
Non-conforming use	Modify	Extend, transform: refurbishment and raise standard	Adjust use, Modify programme	Use changes in surroundings
Indeterminate use	Adjust	Increase flexibility, Exploit multipurpose potential	Wait, improvise risk	Influence surroundings
Uncertain use	Improvise	Minimum maintenance, wait	Reinterpret, neutralise, increase flexibility	Observe surroundings and react to them

2.30

2.28 Construction of loss of value curves with reference to parameters
2.29 Aging of buildings and influence of age on the maintenance, renovation and value-increasing measures
The slowing down of pure aging and the maintenance of functionality requires continuous resource expenditure (money, building materials, energy etc.).
2.30 Measures to maintain equilibrium between use and building

on the non-structural components. This means that the annual average expenditure falls continuously until the first complete refurbishment takes place. Even with the often-assumed service life of 80 or 100 years, the figures for annual expenditure are similar.

If the aim is to achieve a lower long-term consumption of resources, it is therefore better to observe certain simple rules and to plan for a number of real options. The first important criterion in decision making is whether a building is a temporary structure, which will stand for less than 50 years and can be disassembled according to plan, or a long-term structure, intended to last for over 100 years.

In the first case (temporary building) the following requirements are recommended:

- Basement of not more than one storey or no basement
- Pad foundations that can be easily removed
- A loadbearing structure that can be completely dismantled and consists of at least 80 % reusable components
- Internal fitting-out with high flexibility. It is assumed that no complete refurbishment will be necessary and, if applicable, no partial refurbishment either, and that the building will be continuously adapted to changing needs.
- Building technical services equipment should as far as possible be separate and independent of the loadbearing structure and finishes.

In the second case (long-term building) the following requirements are recommended:

- Loadbearing structures with a technical service life of more than 100 years
- Building envelope and internal walls with a service life of more than 40 years to provide a substantially longer partial refurbishment interval
- No use of fit-out components with a service life of less than 30 years
- Easy inspection of all fit-out components. Replacement and restoration designed to be anticipated and accomplished without disruption
- Simple replacement for all energy system components (glazing, window frames, shading, thermal insulation, controls, energy converters) without special site equipment (as part of ordinary maintenance)
- External surfaces and roofs designed to achieve a run-off coefficient of < 10 % (option for decentralised, autonomous water management of the site)
- Reserved surfaces (roof, facades, external surfaces) as an option for the installation of future solar energy
- Very low energy demand, achievement of the Passivhaus standard as an option for a future refurbishment
- Creation of a detailed life cycle management plan for 50 years and a comprehensive building maintenance manual that must form part of the supplied building and remain accessible and readable for over 50 years.

Normative terms of service life

The following terms and definitions are based on those listed in International Standard ISO 15686 and are applied

here in the context of the service life of a building, depending on the approach and objective.

Technical service life of a building
This is primarily used for engineering structures and describes the technical (design code) service life of the principal components or the period until they fail to satisfy the design code requirements. In buildings the components of the loadbearing/primary structure are principal components.

Economic service life of a building
The economic service life is defined as the period during which it is economically worthwhile to use the building. This period is determined by the commercial considerations of the client or investors as well as the question of how long a demand for this building will continue at its location (utility value).

Design life
The planned (residual) design life is explicitly or implicitly defined by the client and forms the basis of the requirements for the design brief. It is also used in defining the functional equivalent. Provided technical aspects predominate, it can also be interpreted as the anticipated service life.

Residual service life
This covers the period from the point in time under consideration up to the end of the building's use (i. e. remaining service life). The residual service life can be determined from technical or economic considerations.

Differentiated terms are used for the service lives of buildings.

Element	Type	Package of measures
External plaster	Mineral External Thermal Insulation Composite System (ETICS)	Complete refurbishment Partial refurbishment
Roof covering	Tile, window	Complete refurbishment
Basement	Screed	Complete refurbishment
Sanitary systems	Down pipes; distribution systems (sanitary, heating)	Complete refurbishment
Floor coverings	Stone, ceramic tile, solid parquet	Complete refurbishment
Carpet	Synthetic	Partial refurbishment
Wall, ceiling covering	Plaster, gypsum plaster, wood; stair wells (residential buildings)	Partial refurbishment
Kitchen fittings	Furniture, appliances	Partial refurbishment
Bathroom/WC		Partial refurbishment
Heating, ventilation	Heat generation, central plant	Partial refurbishment
Electrical installations		Partial refurbishment
Wall coverings	Wallpaper	Maintenance

2.31 Frequency of replacement of elements according to partial and complete refurbishment
2.32 Survival probabilities of German building stock
2.33 Distribution of maintenance, partial and complete refurbishment in building stock

2.31

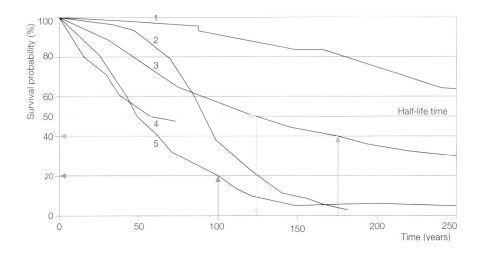

1 Residential
2 Water infrastructure
3 Non-residential
4 Industrial buildings
5 Industrial plants

—— Survival probability
after 100 years: 20%

—— Half-life time:
120 years

—— 40% of existing buildings
still surviving after
175 years

2.32

Reference service life (RSL)
The average technical service life of components assuming standard conditions of use and loadings. This value is used in life cycle analysis as the starting point for calculating the estimated service life.

Estimated service life (ESL)
Unlike the average technical service life, the estimated or assumed technical service life takes into account the actual context of use and load. The approach is based on the factor method in accordance with ISO 15686-8 (see p. 33). The factors take into account the quality of the product (inherent performance level), the quality of the design (design level), the quality of the manufacture and installation (work execution level), the loads from the indoor environment and outdoor environments, the usage conditions and the scope and quality of the maintenance (maintenance level).

Economic service life of components
The end of service life may be precipi-

tated by economic considerations. The economic service life covers the period during which it is economically worthwhile to use the component (e. g. a heating system). As a rule the economic service life is shorter than the technical service life and may be linked to financial planning in relation to investment or market demands.
Further reasons for replacing a component before the end of its technical service life include functional, formal, cultural and regulatory obsolescence.

Calculated service life of components
The service lives of components must be calculated following the principles of VDI 2067 to allow a life cycle costing to take place.

Reference study period
A reference study period for the life cycle analysis must be stipulated by or agreed with the client. For certain cases the reference study period is set out by convention (e. g. certification system).

References:

[1] DIN 276 Building Costs. 2006
DIN 277 Areas and volumes of buildings. 2005
[2] DIN 31051 Fundamentals of maintenance. 2003
[3] SIA 469 Conservation of buildings. 1997
[4] DIN 32736 Building management – Definitions and scope of services. 2000
[5] UBT and BSRIA: the "Soft Landings" Framework . BSRIA BG 4/2009 http://www.soft-landings.org.uk
[6] Way, M. and Bordass, B. Making feedback and post-occupancy evaluation routine 2: Soft Landings - involving design and building teams in improving performance. Building Research & Information (2005) 33(4), pp. 353–360
[7] Schultmann, Frank, Rentz, Otto. Environment-oriented project scheduling for the dismantling of buildings. OR Spektrum (2001) 23: 51–78
[8] Meyer-Meierling, Paul; Christen, Kurt: Optimierung von Instandsetzungszyklen und deren Finanzierung bei Wohnbauten. Zurich 1999
[9] Project Cluster LIFETIME: Lifetime Engineering of Buildings and Civil Infrastructures. European guide for life time design and management of civil infrastructures and buildings. Espoo 2005. lifetime.vtt.fi/delivrables_of_project_cluster/european_guide.pdf
[10] www.nachhaltigesbauen.de
[11] Bundesamt für Konjunkturfragen: Alterungsverhalten von Bauteilen und Unterhaltskosten. Grundlagendaten für den Unterhalt und die Erneuerung von Wohnbauten. Bern 1994.

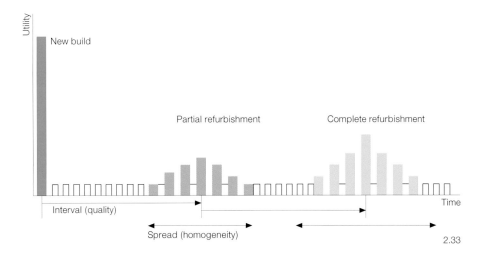

2.33

Method of life cycle assessment

The intellectual principles behind life cycle assessment (LCA) represent a paradigm shift in the consideration of products and services. In the past only the direct effects of manufacturing at a location or use were considered and then minimised as much as possible. Today the assessment adopts a holistic approach that is intended to take into account and reduce the shifting of problems to other places or into other environmental media (Fig. 3.1). This approach includes the whole life cycle, i. e. besides the manufacturing, it also covers the use and disposal of the product – from cradle to grave. This way of viewing the life cycle is known as life cycle thinking.

In economic terms this approach corresponds to life cycle costing (LCC); see Assessment of the economic advantages, pp. 59f.).

The concept of life cycle assessment is based on the following fundamental ideas:

- The whole life cycle comprising raw material extraction and processing, manufacturing and use, right up to recycling and disposal is considered. This requires the development of scenarios for the future phases in the life cycle.
- All the environmental effects connected to the life cycle, such as emissions into the air, water and soil, resource consumption, as well as land use impact, are determined and aggregated.
- The environmental impacts are classified according to their potential effects and listed in a comprehensible manner for evaluation.

ISO 14 040 "Environmental management – Life cycle assessment" defines the term life cycle assessment as follows: "Life cycle assessment is the compilation and evaluation of the inputs, outputs and the potential environmental impacts of a product system throughout its life cycle." [1]

Life cycle assessments make it possible to explicitly include environmental aspects in decisions that have to consider a wide range of diverse influencing factors. However, life cycle assessment is unsuitable for the assessment of the risks for and effects on the user and the environment at a specific location. There are other tools available for this task, including the environmental impact study and risk assessment. Therefore life cycle assessment cannot adequately evaluate e. g. the risks of using nuclear energy nor the toxic effect on building occupiers of a particular emission into the indoor environment.

The scientific principles of life cycle assessment

System analysis, a practical method of system theory, is the scientific basis of life cycle analysis. System theory is an interdisciplinary cognitive model in which the system can be made to describe and explain many different, complex phenomena [2].

The theory of systems (or general system theory) was developed by the biologist Ludwig von Bertalanffy in the 1920s. His system concept describes a number of elements and their relationships. Bertalanffy describes the organised complexity of systems as the interaction of individual phenomena that are linked together in a non-linear manner. In addition to the system concept, the basic building blocks of system theory also include cybernetics (which focuses on the regulation and control of systems) and information theory (the statistical collection and communication of information).

In system analysis a model of a system is designed first as a black box and then refined as far as is necessary to achieve the desired quality of result. The model is composed of elements and relationships. It can be expressed graphically as a flow diagram of processes connected by relationships (flows). The process describes the quantity that e. g. must be made available by the flow in the preceding process.

A model is always an abstract, reduced image of reality but it allows for a mathematical description to be made and therefore the use of computerised techniques for processing the model. A modular approach that permits the use of predefined modules or sub-modules is recommended in order better to handle the large amount and diverse scope of information.

Life cycle assessment in construction
The use of life cycle assessment in the building sector generally goes hand in hand with efforts to develop suitable methodologies. However, almost all this has been happening exclusively in the academic field. The following aspects have hindered the wider acceptance of life cycle assessments in the building sector:

- The unavailability of adequate data for a complete description of buildings.
- The lack of consistency in the basic

data led to large uncertainties in the analysis of the results. Differences encountered when comparing buildings or scenarios could be merely due to inconsistent basic data.

· In the past, the dominance of the use phase naturally drew focus on the energy consumption of the operating building.
· The effort involved in providing a complete description of the building was much too great to convince the market of the advantages of life cycle assessment.

The recent discussions about climate change have escalated the importance of life cycle assessments. The relationship between the basis for life, welfare and long-term thinking is seen in much clearer terms today. It forms the basis for the discussion of more complex relationships.
Until now consideration of building life cycles has not been a feature of the market, but the climate is set for it to become one in the future. The discussion of sustainability contributes to this, as does the increasing interest shown in the German Sustainable Building Council (DGNB) and its building certification scheme, the first in the world to completely integrate life cycle assessment and costing.

International standards

Life cycle assessment is covered by the 14000 series of environmental management standards published by the ISO (International Organization for Standardization). The overarching standard, ISO 14040 "Environmental management – Life cycle assessment – Principles and framework", was published as early as 1997. The standards 14041–14043 dealing with inventory analysis, environmental impacts and interpretation of the results of life cycle analyses were published up to the year 2000 and after that, revisions were republished in consolidated form in 2006 as ISO 14044 "Environmental management – Life cycle assessment – Requirements and guidelines".
The basic structure of a life cycle assessment in accordance with ISO 14040 can be seen in Fig. 3.3 (p. 40). This diagram clearly shows that the parts of the life cycle assessment; inventory, classification and interpretation assessment, interact with one another and that life cycle assessment must be treated as an iterative process.
The application of the results of life cycle assessment is not within the scope of life cycle assessments according to ISO 14040. It, however, recognises the point that life cycle assessments can be used in many different ways and the applications should not be limited to a few examples mentioned in a standard. The authors of the standard also wished to avoid creating the impression that the results of a life cycle assessment can be processed in an automatic manner, without specific consideration of the particular circumstances.

3.2

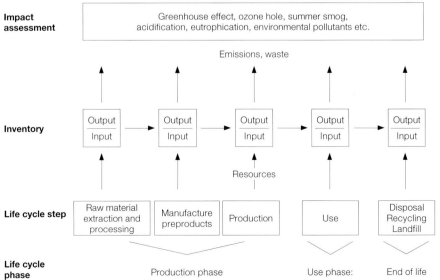

| Impact assessment | Greenhouse effect, ozone hole, summer smog, acidification, eutrophication, environmental pollutants etc. | | | | |

Emissions, waste

| Inventory | Output / Input | Output / Input | Output / Input | Output / Input | Output / Input |

Resources

| Life cycle step | Raw material extraction and processing | Manufacture preproducts | Production | Use | Disposal Recycling Landfill |

| Life cycle phase | | Production phase | | Use phase: | End of life |

3.1

3.1 Modular structure of life cycle assessment with the creation of inventories and determination of environmental effects
3.2 Solving problems not shifting them – get the whole picture with life cycle assessment.

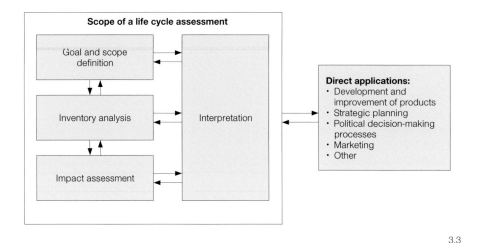

Scope of a life cycle assessment

Goal and scope definition

Inventory analysis

Impact assessment

Interpretation

Direct applications:
· Development and improvement of products
· Strategic planning
· Political decision-making processes
· Marketing
· Other

3.3

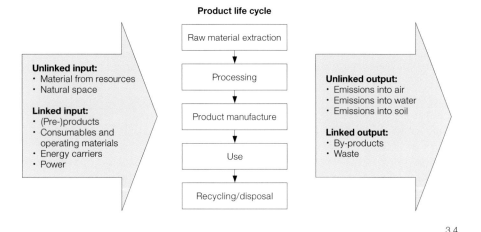

Product life cycle

Raw material extraction

Processing

Product manufacture

Use

Recycling/disposal

Unlinked input:
· Material from resources
· Natural space

Linked input:
· (Pre-)products
· Consumables and operating materials
· Energy carriers
· Power

Unlinked output:
· Emissions into air
· Emissions into water
· Emissions into soil

Linked output:
· By-products
· Waste

3.4

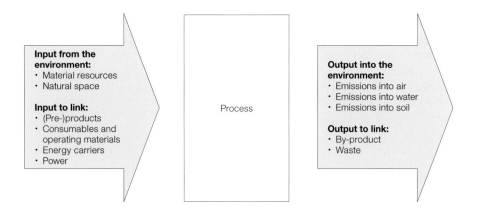

Process

Input from the environment:
· Material resources
· Natural space

Input to link:
· (Pre-)products
· Consumables and operating materials
· Energy carriers
· Power

Output into the environment:
· Emissions into air
· Emissions into water
· Emissions into soil

Output to link:
· By-product
· Waste

3.5

Description and boundaries of the life cycle

In system analysis, all material and energy flows arising from the system components throughout the whole life cycle are quantified and aggregated. The calculation takes direct account of the extraction of materials and energy out of the environment and emissions into the environment. The products and energy used from other processes are linked to the corresponding manufacturing process for each product. Wastes are taken to the appropriate waste treatment facility (Fig. 3.4). The reference value for the calculation is the utility of the system, i.e. all the partial systems are scaled up to the quantity that is required to provide a utility unit. In the consideration of the whole life cycle, this utility is called a "functional unit". The term utility is used here to describe a service e.g. a product. In this way it is possible to compare different products that provide the same utility. A good illustration is the classic example of the utility "hand drying": The utility can be provided by disposable paper towels, reusable cotton towels or a hand dryer.

System boundaries

Many different materials are normally required to manufacture a product. These materials could be resources, pre-products, consumables and operating materials, energy carriers etc. Most of these constituents must be prepared and manufactured in upstream stages, which in turn results in the use of more materials and energy. The chain of upstream stages can be long and varied. They can be broken down into processes, which also have effects on the environment, and all these effects must be taken into account. The inputs and outputs of a process are called flows (Fig. 3.5).

Taken to the limit, it would be possible to connect almost all processes together in one vast worldwide network. However, in order to arrive at a conclusion and "not have to assess the whole world", the assessment is limited to those parts of the system with effects that are significant and relevant to the subject of interest. Specific truncation criteria are defined to achieve this. The distinction is drawn between linked input and output flows within the tech-

3.3 Phases of a life cycle assessment
3.4 Input and output flows along a life cycle analysis
3.5 Input and output flows of a process

nosphere on the one hand, and flows out of the environment (resources) and into the environment (emissions) on the other. The transition between the technosphere and the environment forms the system limits at which the individual flows of the inventory are aggregated (black frame in Fig. 3.6 (p. 42). This happens without consideration of the time and place, i.e. a cumulative result cannot be "resolved" to relate to the actual effect at a particular place. The impact analysis therefore deals with potential effects on the environment (e.g. the potential greenhouse effect), as the information relating to time and place is displayed with unified models.

Truncation criteria
It is obvious that some input flows have no significant influence on the result of the life cycle assessment. Truncation criteria are drawn up in order to avoid overburdening the assessment with irrelevant data and to reduce the amount of calculation required. Establishing these criteria involves identifying which material and energy flows have to be taken into account in the assessment. At the same time it is important to check which upstream stages belong to the flows and the extent to which they need to be taken into account.

Tracing of all the upstream stages of a product is often possible only with some difficulty, as they are not in the immediate sphere of influence of the direct manufacturer (e.g. the factory) The more distant the upstream stage in the assessment is from the process actually being considered and the smaller its contribution (by proportion), the smaller in general is its influence on the assessment result.

The truncation criteria are defined for building materials at the process level in the rules for environmental product declarations (EPD) published by the German construction product manufacturers' certification body, the Institute Construction and Environment e.V (IBU) as follows [3]:

- All input flows of the product system that are greater than 1 % of the total mass of the input flows or contribute more than 1 % to the primary energy consumption are taken into account. Estimates are permitted but they must be justified.

- All material flows that leave the system (emissions) and whose environmental effects are greater than 1 % of the total effects of an effect category considered in the assessment are to be taken into account.
- The sum of the masses of the disregarded material flows must not exceed 5 % of the product under consideration. Departures from this rule must be substantiated.

Allocation
Allocation divides processes with more than one utility, making them suitable for use in systems that only require part of the "basket" of utilities. The purpose of allocation is to distribute the inputs and outputs of a process to the products in order to be able to quantify the pollution burdens and resource consumption for each single product. The general principle is that allocations should reflect the process intention. A number of examples of allocation are given below:

- A process has several products as its output (multi-output process) and production cannot take place in separate steps (e.g. sawmill, refinery, many chemical processes).
- A process has several products as input (multi-input process) and these products can only be assessed together (e.g. domestic refuse incineration plant).
- At the end of the life cycle, the material is recycled in a subsequent life cycle (open loop and closed loop recycling, e.g. as happens with many metals).

Recycling potential
If the allocation crosses life cycle boundaries then the production and the recycling components must be considered separately. The modelling of the production is based on the situation today with respect to the ratio of primary material to used recycled material. As the recycled material enters the system without creating ecological burdens, a recycling potential reflecting the ecological value of the product must be shown in parallel. This represents the future avoidable primary production. The recycled material already required for today's secondary production is subtracted beforehand to limit the assessment and avoid double counting.

Production and recycling potential together describe the life cycle and therefore they form the basis for an assessment.

Products that consist entirely of secondary materials (e.g. reinforcement steel) have no subsequent recycling potential. Their advantage is already reflected in the lower cost of today's production.

Scenarios
For long-lived products, the description of a complete life cycle normally requires the formation of scenarios for the sections of the life cycle still to take place. Mostly, this relates to the use and subsequent use phases. Scenarios are used to compare the effects of different options. They describe the assumptions that have been made for a particular consideration. They should be as scientifically based as possible, but that cannot always be guaranteed. Scenarios usually involve servicing and maintenance, the service life of components, the elimination of future transport, recycling and reuse paths.

While prognoses extrapolate future developments from past events, scenarios can also point to future breaks in trends. One such break in trend could, for example, be triggered by the installation of a new replacement heating system after 20 years or even the introduction of a waste gas reduction system.

Establishing a balance
A balance is normally performed in several stages:
- Establishing a process balance (gate to gate)
- Establishing an inventory balance, e.g. for a manufacturing product (cradle to gate) An example of this can be found in Fig. 3.6 (p. 42). It illustrates the modular make up of an inventory balance using the fictional example of the simplified production of stone in a quarry.
- Establishing the inventory balance for the life cycle. This consists of the production and scenarios for use, recycling or disposal (cradle to grave).

The life cycle consists of the production of the individual products, the con-

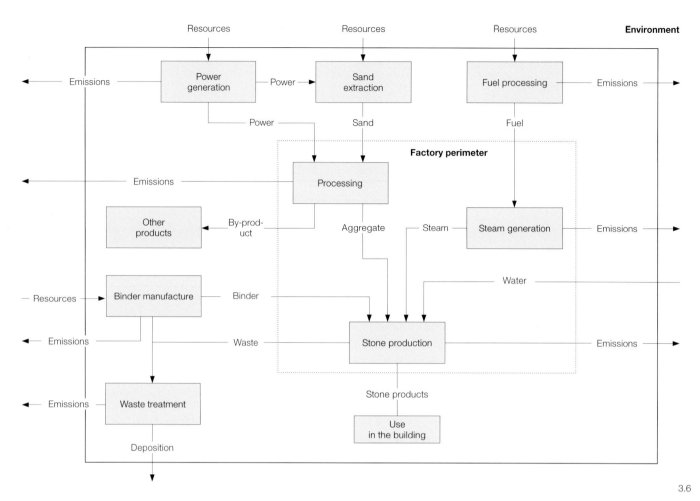

Resources   Resources   Resources   **Environment**

3.6

struction process, use phase and recycling/disposal.

It is important that the actual uses are considered in the use phase, otherwise comparisons can often include variants with different performance characteristics. Construction products do not usually have a use phase that is independent of the building. Normally they develop their characteristics in conjunction with the building and its location.

Recycling and disposal, on the other hand, can be described as a first approximation based on the component materials. This permits a modular approach to be adopted as with production. The products from recycling generally flow back into the construction sector. Occasionally therefore, the term "cradle to cradle" can be applied to the system, which makes refers to the avoidance of a "grave" for the recycled material.

Establishing the inventory
According to ISO 14040, the assessment uses information from the inventory as well as the results of the impact

analysis. Indices are calculated in order to be able to interpret the results of the inventory sensibly. They address areas of the inventory that have no direct effect on the environment (e. g. primary energy consumption).

Resources
"In essence, sustainable development is a process of change in which the exploitation of resources, the direction of investments, the orientation of technological development, and institutional change are in harmony and enhance both current and future potential to meet human needs and aspirations." [4] This definition from the United Nations' Brundtland Commission makes it clear that the use of resources is not viewed as fundamentally evil. However, this use of resources must be targeted.
Resource consumption in itself has no ecological effect. If sufficient resources are available then in that case only the energy consumption required to extract the resources and their effects on the environment need to be taken into consideration. On the other hand if

resources are scarce (no longer available, cannot be found or inaccessible), then the consumption of the resources must also be included in the calculation. The cost of exploiting resources increases as their availability reduces. Furthermore, the development opportunities open to future generations are severely restricted by dwindling resources.
Resources in this sense include the following categories:
· Finite abiotic resources, such as ores, minerals or fossil-based energy carriers
· Finite biotic resources, such as wood from primary forests or threatened species
· Renewable abiotic resources, such as fresh water
· Renewable biotic resources, such as wild plants and animals
· Natural space and its associated usable areas

The degree of scarcity determines whether the consumption of a particular resource is included in the assessment. Scarcity is described as a situation in the economy in which the supply can no longer satisfy the demand. Scarcity is generally accompanied by a rise in prices.

Higher prices make additional investment in exploration for and extraction of the raw material more attractive, which leads to an increase in the supply and to a return to lower prices. If consumption of the resource increases more than the development of new deposits, then long-term plans should allow for greater price rises, if the demands cannot be satisfied in other ways.

The question then is: Which resources are now subject to scarcity and where are the problems of resource consumption?

The value of material resources is mainly determined by their concentration or purity and the accessibility of the deposits. Dissipation of a material after use leads to a reduction of the future availability of that resource. Viewed from the point of view of chemistry, the individual elements are just as present as before, however they are present in other concentrations and often in different chemical compounds. The same applies to energy: it is not "consumed", since the quantity of energy remains constant, according to the first law of thermodynamics. Energy consumption in this context is commonly understood as a devaluing of energy, i. e. the reduction of its capacity to perform work. This process converts energy, which is chemically bound in energy carriers (e. g. oil, gas, coal or biomass), into heat by combustion. This finally becomes environmental heat, in which state it loses its capacity to perform work and can no longer be used.

Non-renewable primary energy consumption is defined as the total heating value (using the lower heating value, LHV) of the energetic resources (oil, natural gas, coal, lignite and uranium) used or devalued. The primary energy consumption of fossil energy carriers is equal to the product of their heating value (LHV) and mass.

Renewable energy can be used, to a certain extent, without resulting in a scarcity of the resource. Renewable energy includes direct forms (solar, geothermal and tide) and indirect forms of solar energy, such as wind, water and biomass. With renewable forms of energy, the limiting factor is not the scarcity of the resource but the shortage of economically usable locations or the competition for their use. Areas of the earth's surface or natural space that can form the basis for the use of renewable resources are themselves of limited availability. Natural space fulfils a host of functions, which depend on the type of surface use. Nature (soil, flora and fauna) regulates the replenishment of ground water deposits, soil erosion, biotic production and local climate, and acts as a buffer for numerous environmental influences [5]. It is clear from this that competition for the use of nature comes into focus in many respects. An area of land covered with solar cells is no longer available for cultivation with crops to provide food or biomass energy. Likewise the spread of urban development diminishes the stock of land that could support agriculture or forestry.

Aggregated indicators from the inventory

Indices can be created from the inventory of resources as part of the life cycle assessment and are discussed below.

Non-renewable primary energy consumption

The aggregate value "non-renewable primary energy consumption" (expressed in MJ) characterises the use of finite abiotic energy resources natural gas, oil, lignite, coal and uranium (Fig. 3.7). As well as being energy carriers, natural gas and oil are used as materials in their own right as ingredients of e. g. plastics. Coal is mainly used for energy creation. Uranium is used exclusively for generating electricity in nuclear power stations.

In arriving at the total, the energy contents/heating values of energy carriers are added. In this way some interchangeability of the energy carriers can be assumed. This corresponds to an exergetic evaluation of chemically bound energy.

Characterisation of the other finite abiotic resources (ores and minerals) can be based on their estimated scarcity/abundance. A suitable method is described in the section about classification (see p. 45).

a

b

c

3.7

3.6 Flow chart of production at a quarry from cradle to gate
3.7 Non-renewable primary energy from fossil energy carriers
    a Brown coal
    b Natural gas
    c Mineral oil

43

a

b

c

3.8

Renewable primary energy consumption

The aggregate value "renewable primary energy consumption" (expressed in MJ) is established independently of the non-renewable primary energy consumption and includes predominantly energy from wind and water, geothermal, solar and biomass energy (Fig. 3.8,). If renewable primary energy is to be used to a greater extent, then the capacity of the sustainable supply should be verified.

It is important to note that the end energy used (such as electricity or space heating) and primary energy are not confused, since the end or consumed energy does not include the impact of its production or provision. For example, in Germany the creation of 1 kWh of electricity requires the use of over 3 kWh of primary energy.

Water use

Water usage is usually expressed as the aggregate value of ground and surface water in kg. Apart from some chemical processes, the use of water is not irreversible. Water is often only evaporated or bound up in the environment as water of crystallisation or in biomass.

A brief examination of the earth's available water shows that most of it is present in the oceans, as deep ground water and polar ice (Fig. 3.9). With water there is always the question of availability.

In evaluating water use it is important to know whether the use in a region exceeds the rate of replenishment. Only if this is true does water become a scarce resource. In Germany this aspect is only seldom investigated in practice and it is ignored in the calculations of an aggregate value.

Use of natural space

Work is continuing on establishing a consistent method of characterising the use of natural space. It demonstrates that surface transformation in addition to surface allocation (in this case, land use) must be taken into account for illustrating use competition (measured in m² per year). Surface transformation can model a range of effects, such as the potential influence of ecological quality (landscape qual-

ity) as well as pollution or use flows This method is well known from environmental impact studies. However, it is a matter of debate whether or not the surface transformation could be described in terms of the changes in biodiversity (species diversity, genetic diversity and ecosystem diversity).

Waste

In addition to considering resources, the inventory can also establish some waste quantities. Waste can be classified according to its qualities. In accordance with the German Waste Management Act section 1 clause 1 p. 1, waste is defined as "mobile matter that the owner wishes to dispose of" or "the proper disposal of which is advisable to safeguard the well-being of the general public, in particular the protection of the environment".

The treatment of waste must be integrated into the system boundaries, so that the aggregate values for the quantities of waste that remain after waste treatment (refuse incineration, regulated landfill) can be described. All effects arising from waste treatment, i. e. the resulting emissions into the air, water and soil, are therefore included in the inventory. Subdividing waste into categories is beneficial, since the scarcity of landfill capacity varies according to type.

• Excavated and stockpiled material: This category comprises the overburden of soils excavated to extract the raw material and the ash and other materials arising from its exploitation. There are also the residues from ore processing, such as gangue, slag, red mud from the Bayer process, etc. The availability of areas for the landfill ing of the excavated and stockpiled materials is generally adequate.

• Domestic refuse and similar commercial waste: This index includes the quantities of waste deposited in domestic waste tips.

• Special waste: This category contains aggregate values of materials that are taken to special waste tips for disposal, such as filter dusts or other (mainly solid) special waste, radioactive waste from operating nuclear power plants, including material arising from fuel rod manufacture and preparation.

3.8 Renewable primary energy from the use of regenerative energies
  a Water power
  b Wind power
  c Biomass
3.9 Distribution of the earth's natural water resources
3.10 Principle of estimating effect through classification of the inventory value

Impact assessment

In an attempt to make the information in the inventory more accessible for evaluation and interpretation, the various flows were summarised according to their effects. However, the structure of the results of the inventory, in which the different flows are added together irrespective of time and place, means that the impact assessment cannot create a direct cause and effect relationship. The inventory yields no conclusions about e. g. the concentrations of a pollutant at a specific location.

Therefore the various different potential environmental effects should, in future, be included in the impact assessment with their mechanisms of action modelled using scientific methods.

An approach has been established in life cycle assessment that calculates the potential environmental effect of each inventory item and makes these available for further calculations. In this approach, the emissions are characterised based on the environmental media that they enter: soil, water and air. To do this the flows are assigned characterisation factors that relate the effectiveness of the emissions in causing potential environmental damage in comparison with or relative to a reference substance. The potential effect of an emission is then obtained by multiplying its quantity by the corresponding characterisation factor. The potential effects of all emissions are then aggregated and the result is used as an effect indicator (Fig. 3.10).

This concept of inventory flow characterisation has been applied in the standards in the life cycle assessment standard ISO 14040/44 and the draft European standard for construction product environmental declarations (prEN 15804

"Sustainability of construction works – Environmental product declarations") [6]. A summary of the method with references to the most important background data was published in 1992 by CML (Centrum voor Milieukunde) in Leiden [7] and revised in 2002 [8]. Today the following five environmental problem areas are evaluated in life cycle assessments in Germany:
· Global warming potential (GWP)
· Ozone depletion potential (ODP)
· Acidification potential (AP)
· Eutrofication potential (EP)
· Photochemical ozone creation potential (POCP)

To these can be added, to some extent, the abiotic depletion of resources (ADP) and the potential for human and ecological toxicity. The models used for studying the above problem areas are a subject of some controversy in discussions and have not achieved international consensus.

Global warming potential

The mechanism of action of the global warming effect can be observed at a smaller scale in cars, living rooms or greenhouses. The incident short-wave solar radiation penetrates the glazing almost unimpeded. When it strikes the enclosing non-transparent surfaces or objects in the room, the radiation is converted into long-wave infrared radiation. The resulting infrared radiation cannot leave the room unimpeded. The energy from solar radiation entering the room is greater than the energy leaving it. The room temperature rises as a result.

This effect can also be observed on a global scale. Short-wave solar radiation strikes the earth's surface. Here part of the radiation is absorbed, which

warms the surface directly, and part is reflected as infrared radiation. The reflected proportion is absorbed by the so-called greenhouse or climate gases in the troposphere (the lower part of the atmosphere that extends up to an altitude of approximate 10 km). From there it is radiated again, this time in a diffuse form, and some of that diffuse radiation returns to the earth. This leads to further warming. Without this natural greenhouse effect, the average temperature at the surface of the earth would be approximately -18 °C instead of today's +15 °C. Life, as we know it, would not be possible on the earth in these circumstances.

In addition to the natural greenhouse effect, there are signs that human activities are responsible for causing an anthropogenic greenhouse effect (Fig. 3.11, p. 46). Greenhouse gases released by Man include, for example, carbon dioxide (CO_2), methane (CH_4) and chlorofluorocarbons (CFC). The estimated contributions of climate gases to the greenhouse effect can be seen in Fig. 3.13 (p. 46).

The global warming potential (GWP) of these gases is given in terms of their carbon dioxide equivalent, which allows the potential greenhouse effect of any emission to be related to that of CO_2. As the length of time that the gases will persist in the atmosphere (the lifetime) is relevant for the calculations, it must always be quoted with the time horizon chosen for the assessment. An integration period of 100 years is commonly used (GWP 100).

Ozone depletion potential (ODP)
in the stratosphere

Ozone is created at high altitudes in the atmosphere by the irradiation of

Resource	Proportion
Open water, oceans, seas, lakes	83.51 %
Inaccessible ground water (too deep)	15.45 %
Polar ice	1.007 %
Rivers	0.015 %
Accessible ground water	0.015 %
Atmosphere	0.0008 %

3.9

Inventory value	×	GWP factor	=	Potential effect

| 25 kg CO_2 2 kg CH_4 ... | × × × | 1 21[1] ... | = = = | 25 (kg CO_2 equivalent) 42 (kg CO_2 equivalent) ... |

[1] 1 kg CH_4 has the same effect as 21 kg CO_2

Total: | 67 (kg CO_2 equivalent) |

3.10

3.11

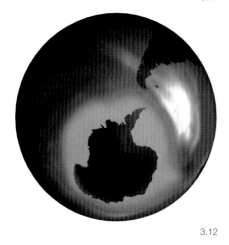

3.12

oxygen molecules with short-wave UV light. This leads to the formation of the ozone layer in the stratosphere (15–50 km above the earth). About 10% of the ozone enters the troposphere though various mixing processes. In spite of its low concentration, the effect of the ozone is important for life on earth. Ozone absorbs short-wave UV radiation and releases its energy again in the form of diffuse longer wavelength radiation. Only part of the UV radiation reaches the earth. Anthropogenic emissions result in the depletion of the ozone layer (Fig. 3.12). Two groups of compounds, chlorofluorocarbons(CFC) and nitrogen oxides (NO_x), are particularly responsible for ozone depletion.

One effect of ozone depletion is the warming of the earth's surface. Another factor to take into account is the sensitivity of humans, animals and plants to UV-B and UV-A radiation. Possible outcomes are e.g. plant growth changes or reductions in harvest yields (interference in the process of photosynthesis), increases in cases of cancer (skin or eye cancers) and the reduction in sea plankton numbers, which could have considerable knock-on effects on the food chain.

A calculation of the ozone depletion potential also requires knowledge of the emissions of anthropogenic halocarbons, which can act as catalysts in the destruction of a large number of ozone molecules. Model analyses for the various substances that interact with ozone have produced characterisation factors for ozone depletion potential. As a result, it is possible to express the ozone depletion potential of various substances in terms of their R11 equivalents (a specific chlorofluorocarbon called trichlorofluoromethane, freon-11 or CFC-11).

Acidification potential (AP)
The acidification of soil and water arises mainly from the transformation of atmospheric pollutants into acids. The result is a reduction of the pH value of rain water and fog from 5.6 to 4 and below. The acids formed by sulphur dioxide and nitrogen oxides (sulphuric and nitric acids respectively) make a significant contribution to acidification. The most noticeable direct damage to ecosystems is forest death or tree dieback (Fig. 3.14). Damage may be direct or indirect. Examples include nutrients being washed out of the soils and increased solubility of metals in the ground. However, buildings and construction materials are showing signs of increasing damage. For example, metals and natural stone corrode or decompose at greater rates.

The acidification potential of a substance is expressed in terms of its sulphur dioxide equivalent (SO_2 eq.). When assessing acidification, it is important to realise that this is a global problem, the local effects of which may vary from place to place due to the local buffering capacity of the soil.

Eutrophication potential
Eutrophication or nutrient input is the enrichment of nutrients at a particular location. Atmospheric pollutants, waste water and the use of agricultural fertilisers contribute to eutrophication.
The consequences for bodies of water include increased algae growth (algal bloom) (Fig. 3.15). As a result, less sunlight reaches the deeper layers of water, and photosynthesis and oxygen production decrease. This can lead to fish death and anaerobic decomposition (without oxygen). Areas of water where this has occurred are known as dead zones.

3.11 Melting of polar ice-caps
   a North polar sea in summer 1979
   a North polar sea in summer 2003
3.12 Ozone hole (computer graphic from satellite data collected on 24 September 2006)
3.13 Contributions of climate gases to the anthropogenic greenhouse effect
3.14 Forest dieback due to acid rain and soil acidification
3.15 Algal bloom caused by eutrophication
3.16 Summer smog due to photochemical ozone creation

	Proportion of anthropogenic global warming effect	Increase in concentration per year	Most significant anthropogenic sources
Carbon dioxide (CO_2)	50%	0.5%; trend unchanging	Burning fossil fuels, deforestation
Methane (CH_4)	20%	0.5%; trend falling	Rice cultivation, livestock, refuse tips, extraction of fossil fuels
Chlorofluorocarbons (CFC)	17%	< 0; trend falling	Propellant gases, refrigerants, flameproofing, foams
Nitrous oxide (N_2O)	6%	0.3%; trend unchanging	Over-fertilisation, deforestation, biomass burning

3.13

Plants growing in eutrophic soils are observed to be more susceptible to pests and diseases, and to have weaker support tissues. In addition, a higher nutrient input can occur as a result of the leaching process, which produces increased nitrate levels in ground water and therefore also in drinking water. Nitrates in small amounts cause no harmful toxicological effects themselves, however their reaction products, nitrites, are toxic to humans.

The eutrophication potential is taken into account in the assessment as phosphate equivalent (PO_4 eq.) values. As with acidification potential, it should be realised that the effects of eutrophication vary greatly from region to region.

Photochemical ozone creation potential (POCP)

In contrast to the protective function of ozone (O_3) in the stratosphere, ozone at or near ground level is a damaging trace gas. Photochemical ozone formation in the troposphere, also known as summer smog, stands accused of causing damage to vegetation and materials (Fig. 3.16). Ozone in higher concentrations is toxic to humans. Ozone and other corrosive reaction products arise from the effect of solar radiation on nitrogen oxides and hydrocarbon emissions. The latter arise from incomplete combustion and leakages of gasoline (storage, handling, refuelling etc.) or solvents. As the presence of carbon monoxide (CO), which is produced mainly by traffic, reduces ozone (O_3) to carbon dioxide (CO_2) and oxygen (O_2), the highest concentrations of ozone are not often found in close proximity to the sources of CO emissions. Higher ozone concentrations are found in areas of clean air (e.g. forests), where there is hardly any CO present. The summer smog or photochemical ozone creation potential (POCP) of a substance is expressed in terms of its ethylene equivalent (C_2H_4 eq.). In an assessment it must be realised that the actual ozone concentrations depend on the weather and vary from place to place.

Abiotic resource consumption

This impact category can be used to indicate the scarcity of the basis for life for future generations. It concentrates on the dissipative use of resources. The quantities of resources consumed, i.e. no longer available in the technosphere, are entered into the inventory. Abiotic resource consumption characterises the resources according to their scarcity. The rarer the resource, the higher is its weighting in a normalised assessment. The reference value is the antimony equivalent (Sb eq.).

This impact category is heavily dominated by fossil energy carriers and therefore double-counting with primary energy consumption occurs. Discussions about omitting fossil energy carriers from the abiotic resource consumption impact category and adopting iron equivalent (Fe eq.) as the reference value are ongoing. No consensus on this has yet been reached among environmental professionals.

Human and ecotoxicity potentials

The early aim in calculating human and ecotoxicity potentials was to describe in the life cycle assessment the potential of a substance to damage humanity and the environment. However, because the inventory lacks the ability to resolve the information down to time and place, it is necessary to develop models to describe the movements of pollutants between the compartments (air, water, different soils) and their propagation. No models have so far been developed that can be applied uniformly to all classes of substances. This continues to be the subject of controversy in discussions between environmental professionals. For metals in particular, the models yield results that cannot be verified.

In the case of buildings, the toxicity of the indoor air is far more relevant to human toxicity than the upstream chains. Ecotoxicity for aquatic and terrestrial ecosystems is an important impact category in every case and should be accommodated in the assessment.

Optional components of the impact assessment

After calculation of the individual impact categories, ISO 14044 can be used for further optional steps to put the results together before the assessment. These mainly concern norming and ranking or weighting of the results.

3.14

3.15

3.16

Norming
Norming seeks to determine how the contribution in an impact category relates to the total result for the impact category within a specific reference area. In this way, e. g. the global warming and acidification potentials of a building can be compared with the total global warming potential or acidification potential in Germany. It reveals which indicators make the greatest contribution to the relevant overall problem field.

Weighting
The question of how the various indicators should be weighted with respect to one another has not yet been answered. This weighting cannot be determined using scientific methods as it involves making subjective judgements. Therefore weighting or prioritising is neither "wrong" nor "right". It should, however, be acceptable to society, as otherwise the results of a weighting may not be recognised.
A weighting usually produces a numerical end result that is calculated from a large number of weighted or weighted and normed indicators. Whatever system is used, the weighting key must be made clear.
ISO 14044 does not allow weighting in comparative studies; the discussions must centre on the individual results.

Interpretation
In the interpretation of a life cycle assessment, ISO 14040 requires the results of the inventory and the impact assessment to be evaluated with the aim of deriving conclusions and providing recommendations. The interpretation is divided into three phases:
- Identification of the critical parameters from the inventory and impact assessment
- Assessment of completeness and data quality
- Formulation of conclusions. The conclusions and recommendations should also contain a clear indication of the limits of applicability of the recommendations.

The best way of recognising the critical parameters of a life cycle assessment is by performing a dominance analysis. This shows which life cycle sections and which processes within them make the largest contributions with regard to

an indicator. It is then possible to concentrate on the critical influences. Normally however, the description of the life cycle, in addition to considering production from a retrospective point of view, also examines scenarios for use and subsequent use. In all cases, the parameters assumed for the scenarios must be subject to critical analysis, as they often have a determinant influence on the results.
The calculation should be checked for completeness in a further step, in order to ensure that all the relevant contributions have been taken into account. As estimated values (conservative at best) are always inserted where information is missing, scenario analyses should demonstrate the influence of these estimates.
The second part of this "quality assurance" stage entails assessing the consistency of the assumptions and base data. The parameter sets in the scenarios must be compatible with one another and the methodology specified for the study has been applied consistently. This is particularly important for the base data, as data in databases are often collected from diverse sources, vary in quality and are used by everyone with access to the database. Examples of databases that have been developed along consistently methodical lines include the European Commission's ILCD database [9] or the internationally accessed GaBi database [10]. Conclusions and recommendations primarily relate directly to the investigated product system. Transferability to other systems (e. g. other buildings) must be verified by proof of compatibility of the buildings and parameters upon which the scenarios are based.

Limits of life cycle assessment
The applicability of life cycle assessment comes up against limits if, in addition to ecological questions, it is expected to handle technical, societal or economic matters. The decisions associated with non-ecological questions are outside the scope of investigation of a life cycle assessment.
A further restriction applies when relating life cycle assessment to the product life cycle. For ecological matters (e. g. the environmental assessment of production facilities or companies) that diverge from the ideal, it is necessary

to check on a case by case basis whether there are better, more authoritative instruments available. Examples include e. g. environmental indices, environmental impact assessments (EIA), eco-audits and regional balances.

Life cycle assessments of buildings

The following sections explore the special aspects of life cycle assessments of buildings. As life cycle assessments also form the basis for certification under the DGNB Sustainable Building certification scheme, the documentation requirements for achieving certification are also considered here.

Principles
In life cycle assessments of buildings particular attention must generally be paid to the exact definition and documentation of the functional unit, as results are often highly dependent on the selected scenarios. For example, the assumed service life has considerable influence of the overall result.
Also of relevance is the design or life cycle phase of the building at the time of consideration. At the early planning stage, when the available information about the building is relatively sparse, it is still possible to make fundamental design changes, i. e. there is a large conceptual scope of action. In the detailed design stage, and even more so during construction, the designer's room for manoeuvre in relation to the building as a whole is severely restricted.
In the determination of the functional unit, the function and form of construction of the building must be described. This is essential to achieve an adequate use scenario and only in this way are future comparisons to other buildings possible. The important parameters for this include:
- Location and integration into the environment
- Building type
- Volumes and areas (gross enclosed volume, number of storeys, gross floor area, net usable floor area, technical services floor area)
- Type of construction
- Type and intensity of use
- Assumed service life

The level of detail of the study of a life cycle phase depends very much on the when and why it was done. As the design advances, so does the amount of available information, which becomes increasingly accurate and capable of allowing authoritative opinions to be drawn from it. However, at certain points in time during life cycle assessments it is typical to be faced with various levels of detail and a wide range of different issues.

Concept/preliminary planning
The objective of this type of assessment may be the comparison of different solutions from a life cycle point of view, i. e. the creation of scenarios relating to energy supply concepts, the building volume or energy performance requirements.
A dominance analysis allows the identification of crucial contributions in the life cycle and provides starting points for potential optimisation. At the same time, results in the preliminary design phase are still linked with relatively high levels of uncertainty, as many decisions about design, construction and materials have yet to be made.
It is best to enter mean data for materials, material groups or forms of construction into estimates of life cycle analyses at this stage. They are most likely to correctly represent the decisions that are to be made in the future. If DGNB certification is an aim, then life cycle assessment is beneficial in this phase to bring the building into line for a precertificate application.

Detailed design
All the variants have to be evaluated during the detailed design to further improve the building. Although a

change of the overall concept is usually no longer possible in this phase, components can still be modified, which can have a large influence on the use phase. Variants may relate to different forms of construction that provide the same utility or to the use of products from different manufacturers. The life cycle assessment makes clear the consequences of decisions. Economic and ecological considerations run parallel to one another.

After completion
The verification of ecological performance after the building is complete provides the documentation and the starting point for monitoring.
The verification is necessary for the building certification. It confirms the successful implementation of the design. It is now possible to consider the production of the building specifically in terms of the products involved. A prerequisite for a product-specific assessment is the appropriate base data in the form of environmental product declarations (EPD) for all the products. The actual use of the named products has to be confirmed though, and this can be substantiated with invoices or audits. The tender documentation alone is not adequate proof. The building itself is described by the elements that form its geometry. For the production of the building the classification in DIN 272 is definitive; for the use phase, DIN 18960
For the DGNB Sustainable Building certification scheme (2009 version), it is sufficient to consider construction works (cost group 300 in accordance with DIN 276) and structures – services (cost group 400). During the use phase, the focus lies on the building

services (cost group 310 in accordance with DIN 18960) and structural repair (cost group 410) as well as the repair of building services (cost group 420) (Fig. 3.17).

Validation, reliability and sensitivity of the methods
Proof of fulfilment of sustainability objectives can be demonstrated using a number of different methods, some of which use the same base data and are linked to some extent (Fig. 3.18 p. 50). A number of the requirements can be validated empirically using balance procedures (costs, energy consumption) or directly measured (indoor climate, noise). Other requirements are calculated with the help of base data, hypothesis and assumptions in addition to specific algorithms. These results cannot be directly validated; only their apparent validity can be checked. One way of doing this is by cross comparison: The quantities of building materials in the elements can be found (and validated) in the cost accounting records and therefore reference can be made to them in the life cycle assessment. Many energy consumption figures can be obtained from available databases containing assessments of large numbers of reference objects. These figures can be adopted as standard values or as comparative values for use in validations.
Another method is comparison with the results of national economic figures (top-down analyses). Thus relatively detailed energy consumption figures for various building types per m² and year are available and have been validated by total energy consumption figures. This means that large errors would immediately stand out by comparison.

Reliability of life cycle assessment results
The question of reliability can be viewed in two lights:
• Do the results appear valid when viewed on the large scale, i. e. are the results of the calculation of the total national building stock (based on individual typical buildings) of the

Production	Use	Reuse
• Cost group 300 (construction works) • Cost group 400 (services) in accordance with DIN 276	• Cost group 310 (building services) • Cost group 410 (structural repair) in accordance with DIN 18960	• Metal recycling • Wood and plastic incineration • Mineral recycling • Landfill residual waste

3.17

3.17 Framework for the life cycle assessment for the DGNB Sustainable Building certification scheme

same order of magnitude as the annual building material production or energy consumption figures?
- Are the results of the calculation for two building variants significant, i. e. does a difference in the overall balance of 5 % of the global warming potential really mean that one variant is better than the other, or does the reason for the difference lie in the inaccuracies of the base data, hypotheses or simplifications of the calculations?

The first question can only be answered by comparison with the national building material flow balance (building production figures, total measured or derived values for emissions). A feasibility study on calculating national building material flows in Switzerland is available [11]. The circumstances in Germany are probably similar. Therefore the overall values can be taken – when adjusted for the higher population – to be 10.6 times the Swiss values (Fig. 3.19 and 3.20).

Sensitivity of the method
Various errors can occur during the creation of a combined life cycle assessment and life cycle costing (Fig. 3.21 p. 52). They have very different degrees of effect in the construction and use phases. In the construction phase, the deviations have relatively little effect in terms of costs or the environment. However, in the use phase the differences in costs and energy consumption are high. This means that errors in the assumptions and calculations of energy requirements and operating costs in the assessment can lead to large deviations. As these values can be compared with measured values as early as after one year of use, the discrepan-

Dimension	Indicator	Method	Directly validated?	Apparent validity
Ecological	Resource consumption (mass)	Life cycle assessment Material flow analysis Total energy use	Possible	Comparison with top-down and material flow analyses (MFA) Comparison with quantities from building cost data
	Resource consumption (energy)	(End) energy consumption	Yes	Comparison with indices
	Environmental effects global	Inventory and impact balance	No	Comparison with top-down results (regional, national emissions data)
	Environmental effects local	Environmental impact assessment (EIA)	Some aspects (e. g. noise)	Comparison with indices from environmental impact assessment (EIA)

3.18

cies are only problematic in the short term and can be corrected quite quickly.
The uncertainty arises principally not from the base data or the life cycle assessment of the construction process but rather from the assumptions about the (future) operating processes. Relatively small standard deviations of ± 8 % arise during the construction processes. Even combining errors in further simulations only produces standard deviations of well under ± 20 %.

Requirements for the calculation of the life cycle assessment for the DGNB Sustainable Building certification scheme
The German Sustainable Building Council (DGNB) requires the life cycle assessment for the building to follow the principles of ISO 14040 and 14044. The standards allow the use of a simplified or a full calculation method for the building production phase.
In the simplified calculation, the construction process, the building technical services (including the generation of heat) and the connections between the components are integrated into the calculation by applying an additional 10 % to the cost of production.

Using the full method, the building technical services and the connections between the components must be fully balanced and recorded in the calculation. This can only be done at a relatively stage for building technical services in particular, as this is when many of the necessary details are established.

Use
The use of the building is examined using scenarios in which energy requirements and renovation play a significant role. The final energy requirement from the calculations for the demonstration of compliance with the German energy saving regulations (EnEV) is multiplied by the specified period of observation and linked with the corresponding usage datasets for power and heat in the Ökobau.dat database.
The renovation measures are integrated into the balance, using defined service lives to calculate the renewal rates. The disposal of the items renewed during the use phase must also be included in this calculation. The term items covers surfaces as well as removable components. The loadbearing structure of a

3.18 Methods of demonstrating fulfilment of sustainability objectives
3.19 Estimate quantities of materials in the existing built environment in Switzerland, by type (in million t)
3.20 Average quantities of materials in various building types in Switzerland, (in kg per m² gross floor area)

	Material total	Gravel, sand	Asphalt	Concrete	Masonry	Wood	Metals
Materials in buildings	1460	260	20	730	380	30	27
Materials in civil engineering	840	500	120	170	20	5	15
Other infrastructure	160	Unknown	Unknown	160	Unknown	Unknown	5
Total:	2460	760	140	1060	400	35	46

3.19

building has generally been designed for the assumed service life and is not renewed. The same applies to inaccessible components, such as building envelope insulation. Suitable values for service lives can be taken from the sustainable building guide "Leitfaden Nachhaltiges Bauen" (average values) [12] and guideline VDI 2067 "Economic efficiency of building installations" [13] for building technical services. Any departures must be separately documented and substantiated. This allows constructional measures that result in increased durability to be taken into account.

Deconstruction, recycling and disposal
Deconstruction, recycling and disposal of the building are examined according to material groups in scenarios. All the materials making up the building taken separately for recycling, thermal recycling or landfill.
A subsequent use or recycling potential is determined for the subsequent use phase based on present technology. This potential represents the remaining "ecological value" in each material or component.
In the first stage of the calculation, the building is divided according to material groups or products. In the second stage, specific account is taken of composite combinations of more than one material. If combinations of materials cannot be separated, then they may have to follow a different recycling or disposal path, which generally reduces the efficiency of the process. The datasets for recycling potential are based on typical collection rates that assume that large, valuable components are almost completely recycled and small or worthless components are recycled or reused to a lesser extent. So for example, large format aluminium

facade parts have an assumed recycling rate of over 99 %, but the rate is considerably lower for aluminium corner profiles embedded in plaster.

Validity and auditing of a life cycle assessment for the DGNB Sustainable Building certification scheme
For quality assurance purposes, the results of the calculations produced by the auditors are submitted to an accredited auditing body. There conformity testing is performed on the results, which also increases their credibility. This testing checks in particular the following aspects, which are decisive in the assessment of quality:
• Completeness of the collected data at the building level
• Correctness in the performance of the calculation with respect to the linking of the life cycle assessment background data with the building data
• Use of life cycle assessment background data with higher quality and representivity
The conformity testing can be divided in line with the life cycle phases.

Production phase
The building must be completely described for the calculation. Any judgement of the completeness of the production phase depends primarily on whether the building is to be assessed using the full or simplified method. In the simplified method, the masses of the components of following elements are determined:
• Foundations
• External walls and basement walls including coatings
• Windows and technical facades
• Roof
• Floors/ceilings including floor construction, coverings and coatings

• Ground floors including floor construction and coverings, and floors/ceilings over open space
• Internal walls including coatings and columns
• Doors
• Heat supply systems

The layers of the components must be specified and recorded in a component catalogue along with the necessary conversion factors, such as bulk density or quantity required per m^2. Assignment of the correct dataset is of primary importance. The assignments must be documented. If there is no suitable dataset available, then a conservative estimate must be made and the details recorded. In performing the assignment, it is always advantageous to use software in which the assignment has been set up by experts. Summaries related to the various surface areas must be used to verify that the building has been fully described. The building envelope areas calculated for the EnEV compliance analysis and the areas mentioned in DIN 277 can be compared with the areas used for the life cycle assessment. The areas of the internal walls must be checked for validity against the figures derived from the storey heights and linear metre lengths of internal wall on each floor.

Use phase:
For the use phase, the life cycle assessment must consider renovation as well as energy consumption. Cleaning, inspection and maintenance on the other hand play a subordinate role. The calculation of operating costs does not require a separate check of the EnEV calculation, although it is important to ensure that the data are in accordance with the current approved version of the EnEV performance certi-

Building type	Material total	Gravel, sand	Asphalt	Concrete	Masonry	Wood	Metal (Fe, Al, Cu)	Gypsum, glass, ceramics	Mixed materials
Detached house	2253	333	10	846	708	54	21	148	133
Apartment	1687	151	10	728	509	31	19	135	103
Office	1836	184	20	977	310	27	47	128	143
Retail	1896	190	21	1009	321	28	48	132	147
Hotel	1969	198	22	1047	333	29	50	137	153
Industrial/ warehouse	1604	305	29	871	179	22	57	76	65
Agricultural	1350	371	19	477	304	63	23	67	26
Infrastructure	2994	844	106	1361	369	24	38	122	131

3.20

fication document. In addition, the selected datasets for power and heat have to be shown to correspond with the actual situation. The regenerative proportion of district heating must be documented with a certificate from the supplier. The adjustment of the dataset for district heating to the supplier's local situation is described on p. 54. Renovation must cover all components with service life (according to "Leitfaden Nachhaltiges Bauen" and VDI 2067) that is shorter than the defined period of observation. To simplify matters in the use scenarios, it is assumed that products are renovated by replacement with the same products. This should always be based on the individual replacement intervals. Moreover the disposal of the replaced components should be handled correctly in the determination of the end of life process. All components renewed during the renovation measures must be taken for recycling or disposal and this should be reflected in the assignments of the datasets used.

End of life

For the end of life (EOL) calculation, the individual materials of the components are assigned to the appropriate material-specific scenarios.

Most recycling of metals take place without altering their fundamental material properties. As the recycling potential of a product depends on the proportion of scrap used in its production, it is important to ensure that the dataset used is appropriate for the production process. The amount of scrap already used in production is subtracted in the calculation of the recycling potential before granting the credit.

The disposal in landfill of untreated waste that does not meet the landfill acceptance criteria has been prohibited by law in Germany since 1 June 2005. The indicator for landfill disposal is the total organic carbon (TOC) of the waste, which must be less than 1 % by weight for landfill class 1 and less than 3 % by weight for landfill class 2. Therefore all combustible materials such as plastic, wood or other renewable raw materials are taken for thermal recycling. If a suitable dataset is available in the Ökobau.dat, it can be used. If not, the combustion can be estimated on the basis of general domestic waste.

Mineral waste is taken to a centre for processing building rubble and subsequently reused. The smallest proportion possible is taken to landfill. All non-assignable waste must be sent to landfill and taken into account with the relevant dataset.

A full mass balance showing which recycling scenario applies to which fraction must be undertaken for the end of life. A balance of the masses with production must also be performed.

Construction materials and processes

As well as all the materials used in the construction of a building, the life cycle assessment must also cover all the relevant processes of energy provision (e. g. for heating, air-conditioning and ventilation).

Construction materials

Almost every conceivable material can be found somewhere in a building. The

data pool has therefore also to be suitably comprehensive to allow the building to be fully described. However, it is necessary to design the data structure so that the user can quickly find the correct datasets. The dynamic database Ökobau.dat provides a good example. Its structure was developed in conjunction with various trade associations from the construction materials industry. More details of the concept for the database, how it is maintained and its links with environmental product declarations can be found on p. 57 and p. 86. Ökobau.dat is divided as follows:

1. Mineral construction materials
2. Insulation
3. Wood products
4. Metals
5. Coatings
6. Plastics
7. Window, door and curtain wall components
8. Domestic and sanitary services
9. Site processes, transport, energy carriers and waste treatment

In many cases classification based on function may be both appropriate and worthwhile. The problem often is that a material is used in many different areas and this causes the data structure to become bloated. An appropriately assigned, function-based relationship system (e. g. floor coverings, facade panels or waste water pipes) should therefore be included in the application software.

In order to be able to compare constructional solutions, it is very necessary to think in terms of functional equivalents, i. e. the focus must remain on use. For example, "1 m² of floor covering" imparts no comparable use

3.21 Effects of errors in life cycle assessments and life cycle costings
3.22 Fuel mix in Germany: Gross electricity generated by various energy carriers in 2008
3.23 Projected development of electricity generation from regenerative energy in Germany up to 2030
3.24 Scenario for composition of fuel mix in Germany up to 2030

Category		Error	Effect on overall life cycle	Effect on construction phase
Building description	Element quantities	Deviation of element quantities	Low	High
	Element type	Replaced with nearby element	Low	High
Use	Energy requirement	Deviation of calculated quantities	High	Low
	User behaviour	Deviation in electricity use	High	Low
Life cycle	Element life cycle	Wrong replacement interval	Medium	Low
	Building life cycle	Wrong service life	Medium	Low
Base data	Construction materials balance	Deviation of inventory	Low	Medium
	Energy carrier inventory	Different fuel mix	High	Low

3.21

information. The use situation (loading, desired level of comfort), period of observation and the level of cleaning to be achieved must be integrated into the functional equivalent. The functional equivalent would then be e. g. "floor covering in hotel corridor with high level of comfort, daily cleaning and a period of observation of over 30 years".
Comparisons can now be made using this functional equivalent over the whole life cycle, i. e. the service lives with the required renovation, recycling and reuse or disposal.

Energy provision
As the heating energy demands of buildings fall, power consumption and therefore power generation continue to gain in importance. While power consumption can be influenced by the user through the efficiency of the plant and equipment in the building, the generation of the electricity is in the hands of the grid operator and his generating plant.
The user can choose to be supplied with standard electricity or obtain his power from selected sources. As a rule these additional choices include some form of ecological tariff. Small hydropower plants or wind turbines are the main generators of green electricity. Green electricity can also be obtained from biogas, photovoltaic, solar and geothermal systems.
Most of Germany's mains electricity is generated in large power plants using fossil energy carriers and nuclear energy. A fuel mix disclosure indicates the percentage of each energy carrier used to generate the electricity being sold to the consumer by the provider. In Germany electricity generation mainly relates to fossil energy carriers and nuclear energy (Fig. 3.22).
While the proportion of regenerative energies is certainly increasing, at approximately 15% it is still low. Fig. 3.23 shows the anticipated development of electricity generation from regenerative energy in Germany. The scenario highlights the growth potential of wind energy in particular.
In scenarios for the use phase of buildings, it is important to consider, as well as today's electricity generation, the future changes in the composition of fuel mixes and the effects of these

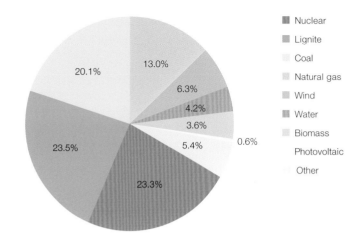

3.22

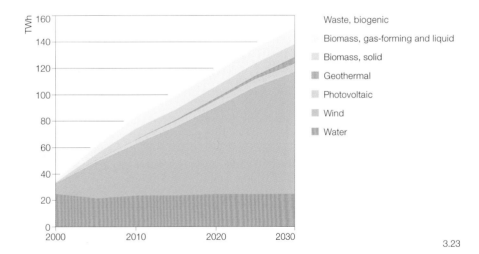

3.23

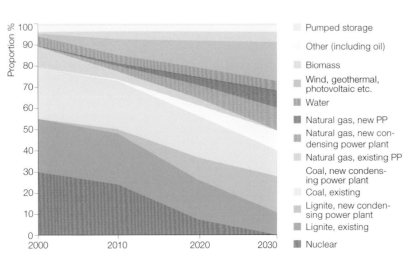

3.24

Heat energy generator		Weight	Primary energy, non-renewable (MJ)	Proportion recycling potential to primary energy, non-renewable	Global warming potential (kg CO_2 eq.)	Proportion recycling potential to global warming potential
Gas condensing boiler < 20 kW (wall-mounted)	Each	43 kg	2304	21 %	157	21 %
Gas low-temperature boiler < 20 kW (floor-standing)	Each	118 kg	3327	16 %	271	12 %
Oil condensing boiler < 20 kW (wall-mounted)	Each	85 kg	4554	21 %	311	21 %
Oil low-temperature boiler < 20 kW (floor-standing)	Each	221 kg	6210	18 %	503	15 %
Pellet boiler < 20 kW	Each	335 kg	9994	33 %	719	33 %
Gas condensing boiler 120–400 kW (floor-standing)	Each	974 kg	42459	27 %	2967	25 %
Gas low-temperature boiler 120–400 kW (floor-standing)	Each	937 kg	23100	19 %	1948	14 %
Woodchip boiler 120–400 kW	Each	3399 kg	70683	43 %	5198	42 %
Oil condensing boiler 120–400 kW (floor-standing)	Each	1504 kg	64588	27 %	4522	26 %
Oil low-temperature boiler 120–400 kW (floor-standing)	Each	992 kg	25168	20 %	2094	16 %
Electric heat pump (brine/water, horizontal ground loop) 10 kW	Each	2259 kg	177636	1 %	5383	3 %
Electric heat pump (brine/water, horizontal ground loop) 70 kW	Each	15745 kg	1260473	0 %	37397	0 %
Electric heat pump (brine/water, vertical ground loop) 70 kW	Each	7713 kg	421464	0 %	20999	0 %
Electric heat pump (water/water) 70 kW	Each	1411 kg	102374	3 %	3440	6 %
District heating transfer station	Per kWh	1 kg	57	26 %	3.9	26 %
Solar panels	Per m²	18.2 kg	1416	46 %	110	51 %

3.25

changes on emissions. Lignite and coal will continue to play the dominant role in electricity generation in Germany in the future, too (Fig. 3.24, p. 53). Renewable energy will make up for the planned abandonment of the use of nuclear energy in Germany. The amount of electricity generated from renewable energy is anticipated to rise as a proportion of the total to 27 % by 2030.

Transferring the predicted changes in fuel mix on to the picture for CO_2 emissions would only produce a reduction in CO_2 emissions of about 10 % by 2030 due to the improved efficiency of new power stations.

Building use
In addition to renovation, the life cycle assessment of the building use should take into particular account energy-transforming processes, such as space heating, hot water production, air conditioning and ventilation. In some types of building use, equipment such as lifts, escalators or lighting may be the crucial components.

Air conditioning and ventilation
Electric current is the energy carrier for air conditioning and ventilation as a rule. Consequentially the efficiency of the equipment and electricity generation is of great significance. The need to reduce dependence on electricity and the associated poor efficiency of the production chain has advanced the development of solar cooling in recent years. The combination of solar energy and cooling is attractive for use in buildings, particularly in southern Europe, where the hours of greatest radiation coincide with the highest cooling energy requirement.

Heat production
Hot water is produced either in combination with space heating or by decentralised continuous water heaters or small boilers. No single variant is generally preferred. The choice usually depends on the required quantities and distances between the draw-off points and where the hot water is produced.

Thermal solar systems can make a sig-nificant contribution to hot water production. They pay off from an ecological view in every case, as, apart from the electricity used in their manufacture, they require only a very small amount of electricity for operation. Flat plate or vacuum collectors are used for hot water production. Vacuum collectors have the advantage of better efficiency during periods of low outdoor temperatures in spring or autumn and therefore attain a higher efficiency over the whole year.

The heat energy for the central hot water supply generally comes from heating apparatus with fossil or renewable fuels, heat pumps or district heating. The same sources can also be used for space heating in buildings. They have some fundamental differences and differ also in their ecological performance.

District heating
District heating mainly finds use in large buildings, as long as they are close to a power station and it is worthwhile connecting it to an already exist-

ing infrastructure. District heating is usually connected either to a coal-fired power station or – as is happening increasingly nowadays – to a gas or steam turbine plant. As well as electricity, most refuse incineration plants also produce process steam, which is fed into the district heating network. The waste heat from nuclear power stations is generally not used.

District heat represents a worthwhile complementary activity for the electricity supplier as he can make use of energy of lower exergy (capacity to do work). District heating improves the overall efficiency of power stations but is nowhere near as effective as it is with smaller, local combined heat and power plants. The main reasons are that the distribution losses are too great and that a power station is operated to produce electricity, which means that the use of heat is seen as more of a by-product.

In practice the district heating supplier publishes a primary energy indicator, information about the proportion of renewable energy and the fuel mix of the power plant from where the district heat comes. The use of district heating can be calculated from this information in the following stages:

· Determine the proportion of renewable energy in the district heat fuel mix
· Set the non-renewable proportion of the heat requirement of the building against the dataset "non-renewable district heat" in the database Ökobau.dat. This dataset describes a mix of 35 % coal and 65 % natural gas.
· Set the renewable proportion against renewable district heat. At the moment Ökobau.dat has no suitable dataset available for this. The propor-

tion can instead be approximated using the figures for a woodchip boiler.

Alternatively it could be based on the actual mix of the energy carriers used. This calculation requires information about the energy carriers used, the power-heat ratio and fuel use of each of the plants.

Heat pumps
Geothermal energy is used in many regions of Germany as a conveniently exploited source of heat (Fig. 3.26). There are three types of cost-effective ground heat pumps:
· Heat pumps with downhole heat exchangers and brine/water media
· Heat pumps with ground loops and brine/water media
· Heat pumps with ground water wells and water/water media

Heat pumps consist of pipework (heat exchanger, ground loop or well and feeder pipes), cold carrier circuit, heating circuit, buffer store, expansion tank, housing and controls. The ground loops and downhole heat exchangers are very costly to manufacture. With the current state of technology, it cannot be assumed that the downhole heat exchangers and ground loops can be recycled at the end of their service lives. This is reflected in the low values for the recycling potential of heat pumps (Fig. 3.25).

Heat pumps currently work using the vapour compression principle [14]. In this process a volatile medium warmed by a heat source (soil, ground water) is compressed and transported to condenser where, by removal of the latent heat of liquefaction, it is turned into a

liquid again. Then it is returned to the heat source, where it is rewarmed. The heat of liquefaction is transferred through a heat exchanger to a consumer (e. g. heating circuit). The performance factor is the ratio of the heat output to the electrical energy input. It depends largely on the ratio of the heat source temperature and the inlet temperature of the heating circuit. The general rule is: The higher the temperature of the heat source and the lower the heating circuit inlet temperature, the better is the performance factor of the heat pump.

There are suitable datasets for various heat pump types and temperature levels available in the Ökobau.dat database.

Fig. 3.27, p. 56 shows the end effect of various performance factors. A water-water system with a 35 °C inlet temperature requires only approximately 2 MJ of primary energy per kWh of generated heat (1 kWh = 3.6 MJ), while systems with an inlet temperature of over 50 °C only just recover the primary energy used. Compared to creating the heat directly, even this is better by a factor of 3.

Oil and gas heating
Gas and oil heating systems form the greatest proportion of heating systems in existing building stock. In addition to the different energy carriers, the systems are classified according to low temperature and condensing boilers.

3.25 Life cycle assessment indices for the manufacture of various heat energy generators and their recycling and global warming potential
3.26 Use of various heat sources by heat pump systems

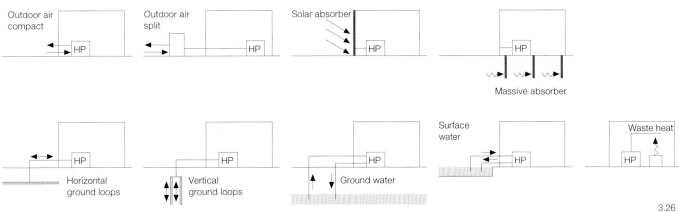

3.26

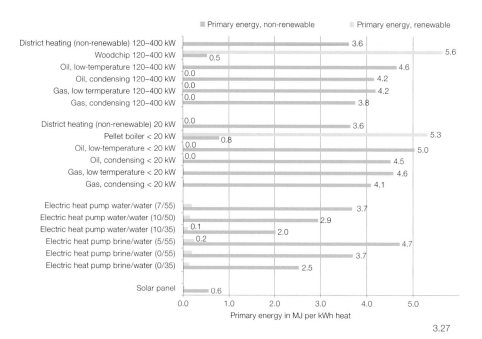

3.27

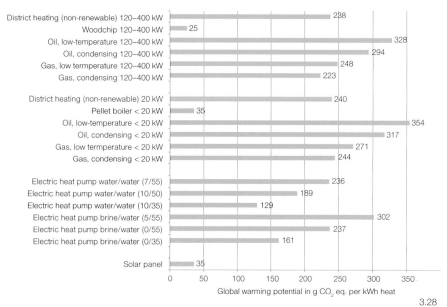

3.28

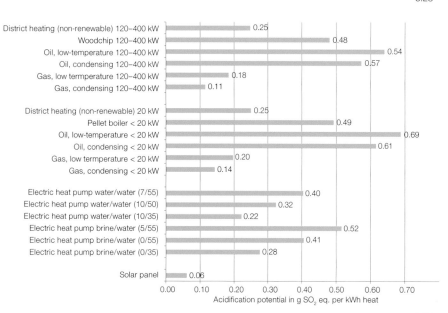

3.29

The manufacture of the systems has much less influence on materials and energy compared with use. They are constructed mainly of metal and can be recycled at the end of their service lives (Fig. 3.25, p. 54). Weight and performance are approximately proportional for heat generators.

For use, the efficiency can be calculated in accordance with DIN 4701-10 "Energy efficiency of heating and ventilation systems in buildings" [15]. The calculation takes into account the auxiliary power used for blowers, pumps and electronics. Extensive measurement records are available for emissions from firing appliances. They are suitable as base data for estimating the direct emissions during the use period. Ökobau.dat contains datasets that summarise the whole process chain (fuel provision and distribution, plant efficiencies, auxiliary energy consumption) per kWh of heat. Fig. 3.27 gives an overview of some important heat generators; Fig. 3.28 shows the global warming potential of different variants. From the point of view of emissions, the higher SO_2 and particulate emissions from oil heating compared with gas heating as a result of the higher sulphur content of oil must be taken into account. This is reflected in a considerably higher acidification potential (Fig. 3.29). The CO_2 emissions are also about 30 % higher compared with gas because of the higher carbon and lower hydrogen proportions in the fuel.

Pellet and woodchip heating
In contrast to gas and oil boilers, the constant starting up and shutting down of the burners in pellet and woodchip heating systems leads to significantly increased efficiency losses and high carbon monoxide emissions. An intermediate storage tank with a capacity appropriate for the rated output of the boiler should therefore always be used in biomass heating systems to ensure they can operate efficiently.

As well as the efficiency of the system, the calculation of the biomass con-

3.27 Primary energy consumption of various heat energy generators
3.28 Global warming potential of various heat energy generators
3.29 Acidification of various heat energy generators

sumption must take into account the heating value of the pellets or wood-chips. The use datasets in the Ökobau.dat database contain information on combustion emissions, biomass provision and auxiliary energy consumption. Non-renewable sources must provide only a small part of the energy. As a consequence, the greenhouse gas emissions are correspondingly low. Pellet and woodchip boilers perform less well than oil and gas boilers when it comes to carbon monoxide and particle emissions.. On the other hand, their advantages lie in significantly lower greenhouse gas emissions, as most of their CO_2 emissions are of biogenic origin and are removed from the atmosphere by the growing trees (Fig. 3.28).

Data in Ökobau.dat

The Ökobau.dat database forms the basis for the calculation of the life cycle assessment for buildings in the context of the DGNB Sustainable Building certification scheme. It was conceived as a dynamic database and is continuously augmented by environmental product declarations (EPD) in accordance with the system devised by the Institute Construction and Environment e.V. (IBU) [16]. The Ökobau.dat database is always kept up to date as the environmental product declarations in the IBU system have to be audited every three years by an independent expert committee.

A starter database was developed for Ökobau.dat in order to allow full descriptions of buildings to be made from the beginning. This starter database contained the existing environmental product declarations, as well as datasets from the GaBi life cycle assessment database [17] and other literature sources.

Ökobau.dat contains datasets provided by several manufacturers as well as company-specific datasets.

Use of datasets in Ökobau.dat

The datasets from Ökobau.dat are always related to a reference unit. This could be 1 kg, 1 m^2 or 1 m^3 of a product or a specific system. In a similar way, the use datasets could relate to 1 kWh of electricity or heat.

Irrespective of the reference unit, the dataset should always be capable of being scaled up linearly to suit the required quantity.

The dataset should be briefly but adequately documented to help ensure the correct dataset is chosen. Without these details it is difficult to ensure the that the selected dataset is representative in terms of location, time and technology.

Data format

As well as the documentation, a fully specified data format is necessary so that the base data is suitable for use with the various tools for building evaluation and therefore by the design team. The data format in Ökobau.dat contains a short assessment of the quality of the dataset as well as a unique identifier (UUID) and the indicators themselves. A dataset contains:

- General information about the product/process (declared unit)
- Assessment of the data quality (representivity and review)
- Indicators (aggregated results of the inventory and impact balances)

The format is XML and can be displayed in a standard browser using a stylesheet. It is compatible with the European Commission's life cycle assessment data format ILCD, which was drawn up in consultation with European manufacturers' associations.

Quality assurance of the data

The quality of the data in the harmonised database must be regularly audited to maintain the credibility of the results of building evaluations over the long term. All data must be collected in accordance with the agreed rules. At the moment Ökobau.dat contains data only part of which has been adequately quality assured through an external review. This mainly applies to datasets based on IBU environmental product declarations.

There are therefore three levels of quality:

- Fully reviewed by an independent third party: IBU environmental product declarations that have been checked by an independent expert committee for correctness, completeness, appropriateness and conformance with standards meet this requirement.

- Internal review: datasets e. g. from the field of the GaBi-4 database that undergo an independent in-house quality check.
- Not reviewed

Datasets not reviewed by an independent third party are in the database with a preapplied "safety surcharge" of 10 % and are adequately documented.

References:

[1] DIN EN ISO 14 040, Environmental management – Life cycle assessment – Principles and framework. 2006
[2] http://de.wikipedia.org/wiki/Systemtheorie
[3] IBU: Allgemeiner Leitfaden zur Erstellung von PCR-Dokumenten.
[4] Hauff, Volker (ed.): Our Common Future. Brundtland Report of the World Commission on Environment and Development. Greven 1987
[5] Baitz, Martin: Die Bedeutung der funktions-basierten Charakterisierung von Flächenin-anspruchnahme in industriellen Prozessketten. Aachen 2002
[6] prEN 15 804 Sustainability of construction works – Environmental product declarations – Product category rules. 2008
[7] Heijungs, Reinout et al.: Environmental life cycle assessment of products. Guide and backgrounds. Leiden 1992
[8] Guinée, Jeroen B. et al.: Handbook on Life Cycle Assessment. Operational Guide to the ISO Standards. Dordrecht 2002
[9] lca.jrc.ec.europa.eu/lcainfohub/index.vm
[10] www.gabi-software.com
[11] Rubli, Stefan; Jungblut, Niels: Materialfluss-rechnung für die Schweiz. Feasibility study Bern 2005
[12] Bundesamt für Bauwesen und Raumordnung (pub.): Leitfaden Nachhaltiges Bauen. Berlin 2001
[13] VDI 2067 Economic efficiency of building installations. Fundamentals and economic calculation 2007
[14] Kunz, Peter et al.: Wärmepumpen. Planung, Optimierung, Betrieb, Wartung. Zurich 2008
[15] DIN 4701-10 Energy efficiency of heating and ventilation systems in buildings – Part 10: Heating, domestic hot water supply, ventilation 2003
[16] www.bau-umwelt.com
[17] www.gabi-software.com

Tasks and objectives as seen by the stakeholders

This chapter provides a conceptual and practical explanation of the processes involving the calculation of life cycle costs in order to understand and compare economic efficiency. In the context of this book, a distinction is made between life cycle analysis (see preceding chapter) and life cycle costing.

Although this chapter is based on the German system of building procurement (in particular that the German system is scaleable from whole buildings to smaller dimensions or components), the ideas and processes can also be applied to other countries.

One of the fundamental tasks of life cycle analysis is to describe and evaluate the economic advantages of investments and different design solutions (particularly in terms of specification). This description and evaluation is assigned to the investment appraisal. The assessment is usually based on the equivalent yield (e. g. the growth in value expressed in monetary terms) and the financial resources expended to attain it. The objective is therefore to achieve an intended yield with the smallest possible expenditure or to achieve the maximum yield for a given expenditure.

The description and assessment of the economic advantages are closely related to the economic dimension of sustainability. In transferring these ideas to the construction industry, it is important to demonstrate the economic profitability of investment in order to obtain the capital. This requires the assessment of the financial risks and

the payment flows (payments in and payments out) over the complete life cycle as well as the analysis of the stability and growth of the economic value. A further objective formulated in this context is the reduction of life cycle costs. Other objectives are set out in the final report "The Concept of Sustainability" published in 1998 by the German Bundestag [1]: the relative reduction in the costs of investment in the transformation and conservation of existing buildings compared with creating new buildings, the optimisation of the expenditure for technical and social infrastructure, and the decrease in state subsidies.

Economic advantage cannot be assessed in isolation from the views, objectives and motives of the various stakeholders. Above all, the approach to the measurement of expenditure and utility (normally the yield) varies considerably according to the position of each stakeholder. Thus for example, in the case of a tenant the basic rent (not including building services costs such as heating and therefore often referred to as the cold rent) is a payment out in the sense of a financial expenditure and for the landlord a payment in (and therefore the prerequisite for the generation of a yield). Life cycle costs are as a rule only analysed in their entirety and incorporated into decision-making by the owner-occupier, while the landlord or tenant only takes into direct account certain parts of life cycle costs (some specific cost types or apportionable and non-apportionable costs). Fig. 4.1 gives some examples of the interests of selected stakeholder groups in the economic assessment of constructional solutions, investments or deci-

sions on the management or development of properties.

The various points of view, interests and motives of the stakeholder groups affect the approach and methodology applied to the economic assessment of real estate. The selected method of evaluating the economic efficiency (see pp. 71f.) should be adjusted to suit the circumstances surrounding the particular aspect or property being examined. Furthermore, the calculation of the money flows (payments in and payments out) forms the basis for the assessment of the economic advantages, although the money flow data are included the decisions of each stakeholder group in different ways and to different extents. Life cycle costing therefore represents an indispensable element in life cycle analysis.

The methods of life cycle costing and the evaluation of economic efficiency form the foundations for investment decisions and for the certification of buildings.

Life cycle costing

The calculation and assessment of costs in the life cycle of a property is a significant task in life cycle analysis. The analysis treats the capital investment as a one-off or initial cost and the operating costs as continuous follow-up costs. Life cycle costing supports the decision-making process in relation to investment as well as management accounting.

The date and scope of the life cycle costing, and the object under consideration must be taken into account. Depending on the task and objective, life cycle costing can be used at various stages in the design (e. g. in the individual HOAI service phases or in the RIBA Plan of Work) and in different phases of the life cycle (e. g. during the use phase in preparation for transformation or modernisation projects). The focus of assessment can be either whole buildings or building components and technical services systems. systems. The period of observation, basis, assumptions and methods of calculation, as well as the type, scope and level of detail of the cost types considered may be different in each case.

The method of life cycle costing can be used for:

- Informing investment decisions by analysing the most advantageous variants of buildings, parts of buildings, building components or technical services systems in terms of cost or economic efficiency
- Understanding the trade-offs [2] between investment and operating costs
- Establishing the principles for the ranking of alternative solutions for buildings, parts of buildings, building components or technical services systems
- Establishing the principles for the creation, checking and evaluation of tenders for PPPs (public private partnership), PFI projects (private finance initiative) or BOT models (build operate transfer)
- Analysis of comparative data for assessment of PPP, PFI or BOT models for a reference project as a standard for comparing the economic efficiency of proposed projects (public sector comparator, PSC)
- Creation, assessment, evaluation and selection of tenders in the EMAT process (economically most advantageous tender)
- Preparation of additional information for building components and technical systems by the product provider
- Establishment of the principles for sustainability certification (e. g. whole life costing is one of the credits considered in the BREEAM schemes

The long service lives of buildings give rise to uncertainties, above all in the calculation of operating costs. It is therefore a matter of debate whether and to what extent the calculated operating costs are suitable for budget planning. If this approach is followed, it is important to indicate in a suitable form the applicable boundary conditions (including the selected maintenance strategy and the service life of the building components assumed in the calculation) and to represent them in a transparent manner.

A similar discussion is taking place on the question of benchmarking. The comparison of solutions with absolute values is made considerably more difficult by uncertainties in the prognoses, the large differences in the principles of the methodologies of and approaches to performing life cycle costing. If this procedure is possible, it is only possible on the basis of uniform principles and conventions such as those currently being developed for sustainability certification, among other things.

If the principles and approaches are known and comparable to one another, then life cycle costs are also suitable for formulating limits and target values. In industry, there are already concepts available for setting out, specifying and determining life cycle cost limits such as "design to life cycle cost" and "life cycle target costing". These concepts can in principle be transferred to the planning and design of buildings and can therefore become part of budget and cost planning in requirements planning. In Germany, this is done in accordance with DIN 18205 "Brief for building design" [3].

Principles

The terms life cycle costing (LCC) and life cycle cost analysis (LCCA) are used to describe a method of systematic calculation and evaluation of costs of real estate over its complete life cycle or a defined period of observation. A distinction is drawn between life cycle costing in the narrower sense, which includes exclusively costs (payments out), and life cycle costing in the wider sense, which, in addition to costs, also takes monetary benefits

4.1 Interests of selected stakeholder groups in the economic assessment of constructional solutions

Interest / Stakeholder	Functional quality	Short-term risks	Long-term risks	Value stability and growth	Rental income	Return on investment	Life cycle cost	Level of rent	Non-apportionable ancillary costs	Apportionable ancillary costs	External costs
Project developer	☐	■				■					
Client / owner of rented property	☐	■	■	■	■	■			☐	■	☐
Client / owner-occupier	■	■	■	■			■				
Occupier with long-term interests		■	■	■		■					
Occupier with short-term interests		■		■		■					
Tenant	■								■		■
Banker / financier	☐	■	■	■	☐						
Fund manager	☐	■	■	■	■	■			☐	☐	☐
Society / public body	■	■	■	☐			■				■

■ Direct interest ☐ Indirect interest

4.1

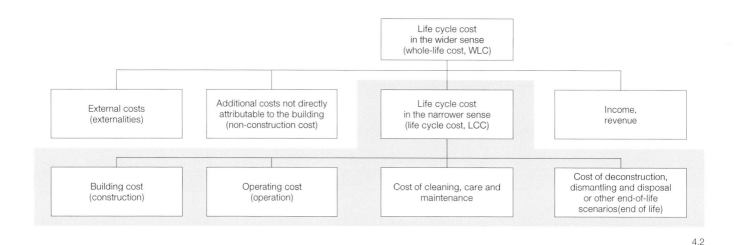

4.2

(payments in) into account. Life cycle costing in the wider sense can be interpreted as a life cycle-oriented calculation of economic efficiency. Its outcome is also described as the life cycle result.

ISO 15686-5 represents an international standard for life cycle costing [4]. It is part of the ISO 15686 series of standards "Buildings and constructed assets – Service life planning" and provides definitions of the terms as well as the principles of the method. By differentiating between "life cycle cost" and "whole life cost", this standard also recognises the difference between the narrower and wider senses of life cycle costing (Fig. 4.2). A detailed classification of life cycle costs with an extensive schedule of the cost types to be taken into account can be seen in Fig. 4.3. As ISO 15686-5 offers considerable scope for interpretation in the selection and consideration of cost types in a life cycle costing, they can be combined in a manner appropriate to the particular application and circumstances.

In Germany, life cycle costing has never been based on a set of harmonised principles. Initial orientation is offered in particular by the current edition of the "Sustainable Building Guide" published by the Federal Ministry of Transport, Building and Urban Development (BMVBS) [5]. Guidance on the application of LCC to construction

projects in the UK is provided by the Office of Government Commerce (OGC) in the "Achieving Excellence Guide 7: Whole-life Costing" (see http://www.ogc.gov.uk/implementing_plans_introduction_life_cycle_costing_.asp) When carrying out an assessment of the economic efficiency of a real estate investment according to this document, the initial investment and subsequent costs of the building (as defined in the guide) may be combined and incorporated as an assessment criterion in the overall assessment. The guide gives advice on the use of the net present value method, on the discount rate and how to calculate selected cost types. It forms the basis for the development of criteria, calculation principles and standards of assessment for the German Sustainable Building Certificate quality mark awarded by the German Sustainable Building Council (DGNB).

The two standards DIN 276 "Building costs – Part 1: Building construction" [6] and DIN 18960 "Running costs of buildings" [7] can be used together to determine life cycle costs – in the narrower sense – of buildings. DIN 276 provides the basis for calculating the design and construction costs at the beginning of the life cycle and – in as far as they are included – the costs of deconstruction and remediation at its end. DIN 276 can also be used to include the costs of a modernisation, extension or a transformation into the life cycle costing calculations (see pp. 64f.). A transformation in the sense of a change of use is frequently already allocated to a subsequent cycle.

The structure and classifications of DIN 18960 are generally compatible with

DIN 276. DIN 18960 provides a basis for calculating running costs (capital, management, operating and repair costs).

It is important to avoid "double-counting" construction costs in the calculation of life cycle costs.

In Germany, the provisions of the Second Computation Ordinance (II. BV) must be taken into account when calculating the economic efficiency of residential buildings [8]. This includes the cost classification and notes on how to calculate the costs of capital, property management, depreciation, administration, maintenance and the allowances to be made for risk of rent loss. The principles and classifications to be used in the calculation of operating costs in rented residential property are set out in the German Utilities and Operating Costs Ordinance (BetrKV) [9].

One useful aid to decision-making and in carrying out cost analyses over all the life cycle phases is the draft edition of GEFMA 220, which addresses life cycle costing in facilities management and is published by the German Facility Management Association (GEFMA) [10]. This guideline contains advice on the definition of terms, examples of applications and model calculations.

A snapshot in summer 2009 showed that considerable efforts had been made in Germany to overcome uncertainties, narrow the scope for interpretation and ensure the directional certainty and comparability of results in life cycle costing. The working groups set up by the BMVBS, DGNB and GEFMA are particularly involved in this and the accompanying intensive exchange of information.

4.2 Difference between life cycle costing in the narrower sense (LCC) and in the wider sense (WLC) according to ISO 15686-5
4.3 Classification of life cycle costs and the cost types to be considered in accordance with ISO 15686-5. Crossing the boxes in the left-most column indicates whether or not the costs are included in the calculation

Life cycle costs in the wider sense (whole-life cost, WLC)

1. Other costs not directly attributable to the building (non-construction costs)

	Examples of cost types
☐ Cost of the land and preparation of the plot	Plot price (construction site and any existing buildings)
☐ Finance costs	Interest or other financing costs and further financial instruments
☐ Costs of strategic property management	Includes internal resources, real estate/property management/general inspections, purchase, sale, moving in and out
☐ Utility charges	General charges, parking fees, charges for communal amenities
☐ Administration costs	E. g. costs of reception, information counter, telephone switchboard, IT, library, catering, vending machines, workplace equipment, furniture, plants (plant care and maintenance), stationery, waste disposal, janitorial and portering services, security, internal alterations to information and communications technology, winter maintenance
☐ Taxes	Taxes for non-building-related costs
☐ Miscellaneous costs	

2. Income and revenue (income)

☐ Income and revenue from sales	Residual value on the sale of portions of the site, construction equipment, surplus materials, including subsidies, grants etc.
☐ Salaries of third parties during operation	Rent and ancillary costs
☐ Taxes to be paid on income and revenue	E. g. on land transactions
☐ Interruptions in operation	Non-availability, loss of income
☐ Other income and revenue	

3. Costs in conjunction with external effects (externalities)

4. Life cycle cost in the narrower sense (life cycle cost, LCC)

a) Building costs (construction)

☐ Costs of design and technical consultancy services	Project design and engineering services, official approvals
☐ Costs of plot	Site clearance
☐ Construction costs	Including infrastructure, fixed installations, internal fit-out, commissioning, asset valuation and handover
☐ Costs of first modification or renovation	Including infrastructure, fixed installations, internal fit-out, commissioning, asset valuation and handover
☐ Taxes	Taxes on construction products and services, (e. g. VAT)
☐ Miscellaneous costs	

b) Operating costs

☐ Rent	
☐ Insurance	For building owner and/or user
☐ Costs of external monitoring	Fire inspections (fire safety and escape routes)
☐ Supply and disposal services	Including fuel for heating, cooling, electricity, lighting, fresh water and waste water charges
☐ Taxes	E. g. land taxes, community charges, environmental charges
☐ Miscellaneous costs	

c) Cost of cleaning, care and maintenance

☐ Costs of care and maintenance management	Regular inspections, planning of the necessary measures, management/award of planned maintenance contracts
☐ Costs of modification or renovation during building operation	Including infrastructure, internal fit-out, commissioning, acceptance and handover
☐ Costs of repair and refurbishment of minor components and parts of systems	Defined by the value, the size of the system parts, contractual conditions
☐ Costs of renewal of systems replacement of major components	Including associated design and project management
☐ Costs of building cleaning	Including routine, regular cleaning and periodic special cleaning measures
☐ Costs of care and maintenance of external facilities	Within the boundaries of the plot
☐ Costs of internal refurbishment, incl. redecoration, refit etc.	Including routine periodic and special internal refurbishment measures
☐ Taxes	Taxes on care and maintenance goods and services
☐ Miscellaneous costs	

d) Costs at the end of the service life (end of life)

☐ Costs of technical reports	End condition reports
☐ Costs of demolition and disposal	Including disposal of materials and site clearance
☐ Costs of reinstatement to the contractually agreed state	Costs of compliance with the contractual conditions applicable at the end of the contract
☐ Taxes	Taxes on goods and services
☐ Miscellaneous costs	

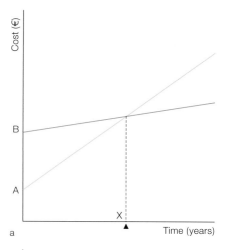

a

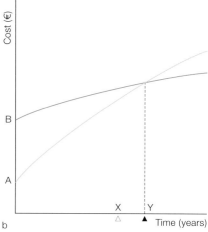

b

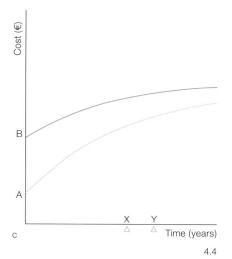

c

4.4

The calculation principles, rules and evaluation standards set out in the current version of the German sustainable building certification scheme (DGNB) for the specific building and types of use in question are mandatory for the certification of an individual building's contribution to sustainable development in the calculation and evaluation of building-related costs in life cycles.

Procedure and input variables

Different procedures can be used in life cycle costing. These procedures often require their own specific input variables.

Procedures

Although stakeholder groups such as tenants and landlords only perceive and take into account certain specific sections of life cycle costs of buildings, they share a general perspective of life cycle costing, namely that of the owner occupier, in the form of the "total cost of ownership". This concept provides the basis for an overall assessment of the economic advantages of a project, but does not expressly replace the stakeholders' own assessments of the investment, its economic efficiency and the attendant risks.

The normal case is life cycle costing in its narrower sense, which covers exclusively costs (payments out). A life cycle costing in the wider sense takes into account payments in (income or revenue) and offers the opportunity to consider the income from feeding solar electricity into the public network as well as rent and other income [11].

A typical approach found in life cycle costing is to consider the time-related value of future payments by discounting them to the analysis date. With life cycle costing in the narrower sense, the capital value is calculated as the cash value of all payments out without taking into account any payments in (see pp. 73f.).

The choice and basis of the rate of

interest or discount rate used in the calculation are particularly important in this process. A discount rate of 0 % corresponds to a static calculation, which can be used to perform sensitivity analyses in exceptional cases for long-term considerations or discussions relating to fairness to subsequent generations.

The choice of discount rate has considerable effects on the present value of a payment. The effect of "discounting" is a relative reduction of the significance and the proportion of operating costs to the life cycle cost. Payments scheduled to be made in the very distant future (e. g. for deconstruction , dismantling or demolition) may, depending on the selected discount rate, be almost insignificant in terms of their net present value.

Information about the ratio of the costs of construction and operation should therefore only be used as the basis for general statements on the significance of operating costs, even if the selected assumptions, boundary conditions, cost types considered and, in individual cases, the discount rate are known. In an example described in GEFMA 220 [12], the proportion of the "initial cost" (investment costs including land costs) to the life cycle cost of a commercial and residential property is calculated for various sets of boundary conditions (Fig. 4.5). The type of calculation (static/dynamic), the assumed rate of inflation and the selected discount rate are varied. The estimated service life is 90 years and is assumed as the period of observation. There is no credit for the possible sale of the land at the end of use.

The selection of the boundary conditions and in particular the discount rate has a great influence on the ratio of initial to follow-up costs. At the same time, the boundary conditions also influence the trade-off between initial and follow-up costs.

Fig. 4.4 compares two variants of a

4.4 Effects of the choice of discount rate on the trade-off between initial and follow-up costs
   a Without discounting
   b Low discount rate
   c High discount rate
4.5 Effects of different discount rates on the ratio of initial and operating costs
4.6 Required input variables for life cycle costing

Calculation type	Inflation	Discount rate	Proportion of initial costs (building costs incl. land) in the life cycle cost	Proportion of follow-up costs (operating costs) in the life cycle cost
Static	0.0 %	0.0 %	36 %	64 %
Dynamic	1.5 %	0.0 %	17 %	83 %
Dynamic	1.5 %	real 3.5 %	60 %	40 %

4.5

possible investment assuming different discount rates. In this comparison, variant A always has lower initial costs and higher follow-up costs (steep curve), while variant B is an investment with higher initial costs and lower follow-up costs (flatter curve). Fig. 4.4 a shows a simplified consideration without discounting and with regular follow-up costs. Until time X the total costs of variant A are lower than those of variant B, at time X they are both the same and from time X variant B offers a greater advantage. And with a low discount rate, Fig. 4.4 b) shows a point in time at which the advantage passes from variant A to variant B (Y). This is later than in Fig. a) as the follow-up costs are discounted. Time X is marked on the horizontal axis for comparison. With a high discount rate (Fig. 4.4 c) variant A remains advantageous due to the heavy discounting of the follow-up costs, the higher initial investment of variant B does not prove worthwhile. The times X (from a) and Y (from b) are shown for comparison purposes.

As the graphs show, the choice of discount rate has an influence, including on directional certainty. Even the ranking of the solutions according to their economic advantage can be influenced by the discount rate.

The effects described here have led to questions about how to treat investments that contribute to energy savings, resource conservation, climate protection or health. These types of projects are generally characterised by high start-up costs and long-term use and are therefore detrimentally affected by a high discount rate. Some appropriate suggestions are put forward introduced and discussed on p. 76.

Another important aspect in life cycle costing is the period of observation. Due to the increasing uncertainty of prognoses and the effects of discounting, the planned design life of buildings is, as a rule, not chosen as the period of observation where the building life is well over 50 years. In the calculation of life cycle cost (for certification in accordance with the German sustainable building certification scheme, DGNB, e.g. the period of observation for office buildings) is set at 50 years. It has frequently been the case in the past that financing costs were not taken into account in life cycle costing.

The assessment of the advantages of a building were not allowed to become entwined with the advantages of the financing. While the sustainability of a building will gain more influence in the future on the conditions for financing and insurance (this is sometimes already the case), taking into account the financing costs and demonstrating the advantages of sustainable building relating to this can still be of interest today. In the section dealing with operating costs, the proportion of finance costs to the operating costs is included in a whole life cost calculation for the owner-occupier (see pp. 68f.).

There are resources and tools available to ease the task of determining and interpreting the life cycle cost (see Resources for integrated design, pp. 80f.).

Input variables
Life cycle costing requires the input variables listed in Fig. 4.6, which must either be selected with care or allow comparison with others. The DGNB evaluation criterion for building-related costs in the life cycle gives guide values, sets out methods of calculation and identifies data sources.
From this information, a list of documents and checks can be developed that detail the important assumptions and principles for life cycle costing necessary to ensure its results can be meaningfully compared with others.
A further prerequisite for the comparability of results and conclusions is the demonstration of the completeness of the description of the building and its life cycle in the level of detail appropriate for the purpose.

Integration into the processes of planning, design and decision-making
Questions of the determination and assessment of life cycle cost as a component of life cycle analysis pervade the whole life cycle of real estate.
Even in the early phases of requirements planning – and here the general principles of DIN 18205 should be followed – when formulating the financial framework, it is important to state the basis of the life cycle cost and in particular the operating costs so that follow-up costs can be properly considered.
Requirements relating to life cycle cost are becoming increasingly common in

Input variables required or to be determined for life cycle costing

Building and use type, functional equivalents, service level

Conditions and peculiarities of the location

Period of observation in years

Information on the type and scope of cost types to be considered
· Building costs
· Operating costs

Determination of the type and treatment with
· Costs of deconstruction and removal
· A residual value (end of period of observation)
· Income and revenue
· Outputs

Stipulation or information on the level of detail of the cost appraisal

Reference values

Discount rate (%)

Price level of construction costs

Price level of operating costs

Information on how VAT is to be handled

Principles and assumptions for determination of
· Building costs
· Energy costs
· Fresh and waster water costs
· Cleaning costs including surfaces
· Operating costs
· Costs of maintenance and inspection
· Renovation costs
· Costs of deconstruction and removal

Sources for the calculated service life of the components, if necessary including increases or reductions

Hourly rates for selected services (e. g. cleaning) (€/h)

Prices or tariffs for
· Energy supply
· Water supply
· Waste water disposal

Annual price increase, if necessary separately for various cost types (%) for
· Heating energy
· Electrical energy
· Water and waste water
· Hourly rates (cleaning)
· Operational management
· Inspection and maintenance work
· Renovation work

4.6

architectural competition documents. In some cases life cycle costs and operating costs are estimated and examined as part of a first selection stage of the competition process. This provides the information on the economic viability of each entry and is taken into account by the competition jury.

The life cycle cost may be specified or calculated in the preliminary design (HOAI service phase 2 / RIBA Work Stage B or C) in order to be able to agree objectives and clarify commercial relationships. In this service phase, the estimation of the construction costs in accordance with DIN 276 is part of the direct performance profile.

In the final design phase (HOAI service phase 3 / RIBA Work Stage D), the calculated life cycle cost plays a role in the working up of the design concept and influences the assessment of its economic efficiency. The calculation of the construction costs in accordance with DIN 276 is part of the direct performance profile in this service phase.

In the execution design (HOAI service phase 5), the life cycle cost can act as an aid to decision-making in the examination of variants and the assessment of economic efficiency This impacts in particular on the economics of the efficient use of energy and the use of

renewable energy. In addition to the life cycle cost of the whole building, this phase may also include the analysis of the life cycle costs of parts of buildings, building components and technical systems [13]. Here it is particularly important to pay attention to the appropriate choice of system limits.

Tenders that contain information on life cycle cost can be checked and evaluated as part of assisting with the award of the contract (HOAI service phase 7 / RIBA Work Stage H). A comparative analysis of tender items, preparation of a final estimate and cost control (comparison with the costs of similar works) are part of the performance profile in this service phase. The design of modernisation, alteration, conversion or extension projects may be approached in a similar way.

Environmental labelling schemes, such as the German DGNB, require the preparation of LCC figures for precertification and certification. This approach may be adopted elsewhere and become more widespread. The determination of the precertification life cycle cost can be assigned to HOAI service phase 4, while the actual certification life cycle cost can become part of service phase 9.

The commonalities and differences

should be observed in a parallel application of life cycle assessment and life cycle costing (Fig. 4.7).

Determination of construction costs

In Germany, DIN 276 "Building costs – Part 1: Building construction" provides a basis for calculating construction costs – the term being used here in the sense of investment costs. DIN 276 not only sets out how to classify costs, it also provides advice on how to integrate cost estimates in the process of planning, design and decision making.

Cost classification in DIN 276

Construction costs of a building can be classified according to building components or work categories. A building component-related classification is based on main parts or elements of the building, such as foundations, external and internal walls etc. (Fig. 4.8). A work category-related classification takes an execution-oriented or trades-oriented approach and is based on the work categories contained in the German library of specification texts for standard construction works (STLB-Bau, which is similar to CI/SfB indexing system) (Fig. 4.9).

A building item-related cost group

Aspect	Life cycle analysis	Life cycle costing
Building description	Standard model based on elements used to describe the building	
Period of observation	Selection of a standard possible and recommended	
Consideration of the design phase	Life cycle phases normally considered without the design phase as the energy and material flows are not taken into account in the design	Life cycle phases considered with design phase as the costs of the design can be taken into account
Consideration of the production phase	Life cycle phases normally considered with energetic and material upstream phases and the production stage for the consideration of the resource use and environmental effects as a consequence of the construction products	Life cycle phases normally considered without the production phase as the material costs are already included in the building price, if necessary the material costs can be shown separately
Consideration of transport	Modelling of the life cycle normally taking into account transport	Modelling of the life cycle without transport, transport costs included in the building prices
Consideration of erection	Modelling of the life cycle normally taking into account the erection phase and the building processes	Building costs include production, supply and erection, if necessary the labour costs can be shown separately
Consideration of use phase	General agreement (cleaning costs are normally always included in the consideration of use costs, whereas cleaning costs are sometimes not included in a life cycle analysis).	
Consideration of deconstruction and disposal	Deconstruction and disposal are normally considered	Deconstruction and disposal are often not taken into account as they are hardly of any consequence in a dynamic observation
Discounting	Not possible	Possible and commonplace
Evaluation according to trades	Sometimes possible, in certain cases	Possible
Evaluation according to elements	Possible	Possible
Checking of results	Not possible, as the results are calculated values	Possible on the basis of submitted invoices

4.7

classification is most suitable for the early stages in the design (preliminary estimate, approximate estimate). Experience shows that the use of elements in accordance with the element method of cost calculation is very compatible with a building item-oriented approach to the planning and design of a building. A trades-oriented cost classification in accordance with the types of work performed is particularly suitable for cost fixing or determining the costs actually incurred, as its structure is a good match for the format of the incoming invoices and final accounts customarily submitted for construction projects. In the ideal case, use can be made of costing tools and indices that provide good support in the early stages of a building item-oriented approach to designing a project and allow a later restructuring into a trades or work performed approach for the later stages. DIN 276 (like other similar standards elsewhere) divides the costs into the following cost groups:

100 Site
200 Clearance and development
300 Structure – construction works
400 Structure – services
500 External works
600 Furnishings and artistic appointments
700 Incidental building costs

The classification level contains at least three levels, which are each identified by three digit numeric codes:
300 Structure – construction works
  310 Building pit
    311 Excavation

The summation of cost groups 300 and 400 gives the cost of the structure. They are frequently used as the basis for comparison of buildings or variants and can also be used as the basis for benchmarking (in the sense of orientation, limiting, average or target values).

Creation, use and interpretation of indices

Creating a cost index involves relating estimated or actual costs to a value of suitable dimensional quantity. Suitable reference values include surface areas, room volumes or usage units (e. g. places in student halls of residence, beds in hospitals or desks in offices). In the creation, use and interpretation of indices for building costs, the following information must be provided or be made clear:

- In the numerator (quantity):
  - Unit of quantity (currency)
  - Price or cost level (quarter and year)
  - Treatment of VAT (including/excluding)

No.	Work category
000	Site installations
001	Scaffolding
002	Earthworks
003	Landscape works
012	Masonry
013	Concrete work
014	Natural stone and cast stone work
016	Carpentry and woodwork
017	Structural steelwork
020	Roofing work
021	Roof waterproofing work
022	Plumbing work
023	Plastering and rendering
024	Floor and wall tiling work
025	Screeding
026	Windows, external doors
027	Joinery
028	Parquet flooring, wood block flooring
031	Metalwork, locksmith's work
032	Glazing
034	Painting and varnishing
036	Laying of floor coverings
037	Application of wallcoverings
039	Dry walling
040	Heating systems / central hot water supply systems
042	Gas and water installations work (pipework and fittings)
050	Lightning protection and earthing systems
051	Construction work for cable systems
053	Low voltage systems
062	Telephone systems
069	Lifts, moving staircases and ramps
070	Building automation
075	Ventilation and air-conditioning systems
080	Roads, paths and squares
905	Thermal insulation composite systems
920	Demolition works
921	Dismantling/removal of building services

4.9

No.	Cost group
100	**Site**
110	Site value
120	Incidental site costs
130	Disencumbrance
200	**Clearance and development**
210	Clearance
220	Public development
230	Private development
240	Compensations
250	Transitional measures
300	**Structure – construction works**
310	Building pit
320	Foundations
330	External walls
340	Internal walls
350	Floors and ceilings
360	Roofs
370	Structural fitments
390	Other construction-related activities
400	**Structure – services**
410	Sewerage, water and gas systems
420	Heat supply systems
430	Air treatment systems
440	Power installations
450	Telecommunications and other communications systems

No.	Cost group
460	Transport systems
470	Function-related equipment and fitments
480	Building automation
490	Other services-related work
500	**External works**
510	Ground surfaces
520	Hard surfaces
530	External construction works
540	External services
550	External fitments
560	Water areas
570	Planted and seeded areas
590	Other external works
600	**Furnishings and artistic appointments**
610	Furnishings
620	Artistic appointments
700	**Incidental building costs**
710	Client's responsibilities
720	Preliminary project planning
730	Services of architects and engineers
740	Assessments and consultations
750	Art
760	Financing
770	General incidental building costs
790	Other incidental building costs
980	Site
990	Incidental building costs

4.8

4.7 Similarities and differences between life cycle analysis and life cycle costing
4.8 Cost groups in DIN 276 for item-related classification
4.9 Example of a work category-related classification in accordance with the Standard Library of Descriptions of Building Works (STLB; selection)

No.	Cost groups on 1st level	Unit[1]	from	€/ unit	to	from	% of 300+400	to
100	Site	m² BGF						
200	Clearance and development	m² BGF	6	20	44	0.7	2.1	4.0
300	Structure – construction works	m² GFA	750	1004	1,380	69.2	77.4	83.0
400	Structure – services	m² GFA	191	316	604	17.0	22.6	30.8
	Structure (300+400)	m² GFA	955	1320	1,915		100.0	
500	External works	m² AUF	49	114	614	2.7	6.3	11.7
600	Furnishings and artistic appointments	m² GFA	21	62	122	1.2	4.6	8.4
700	Incidental building costs	m² GFA	151	206	325	14.1	16.7	19.6

No.	Cost groups on 2nd level	Unit[1]	from	€/ unit	to	from	% of 300	to
310	Building pit	m³ BGI	13	24	49	1.2	2.5	5.1
320	Foundations	m² GRF	183	260	362	6.3	8.9	14.8
330	External walls	m² AWF	333	487	706	26.5	31.8	38.5
340	Internal walls	m² IWF	193	256	374	14.2	19.2	23.4
350	Floors and ceilings	m² DEF	219	294	412	10.9	18.2	22.7
360	Roofs	m² DAF	235	327	519	8.7	12.7	21.5
370	Structural fitments	m² GFA	6	27	78	0.3	2.1	5.8
390	Other construction works	m² GFA	25	49	96	2.4	4.5	7.3

No.	Cost groups on 2nd level	Unit	from	€/ unit	to	from	% of 400	to
410	Waste water, water, gas	m² GFA	30	49	90	9.0	16.2	25.9
420	Heat supply systems	m² GFA	43	65	106	13.2	21.8	34.0
430	Air treatment systems	m² GFA	15	56	151	1.7	10.4	23.2
440	Power installations	m² GFA	68	111	192	25.5	33.0	41.7
450	Telephone systems	m² GFA	11	37	93	2.1	9.0	17.1
460	Transport systems	m² GFA	12	26	46	0.6	4.4	12.0
470	Function-related equipment and fitments	m² GFA	4	20	59	0.2	2.7	10.3
480	Building automation	m² GFA	41	86	212	0.0	2.1	16.9
490	Other technical systems	m² GFA	3	15	55	0.0	0.6	7.2

[1] Key to Units column: BGF plot area, AUF outside surface, BGI building pit volume, GRF foundation area, AWF external wall area, IWF internal wall area, DEF ceiling area, DAF roof area, GFA gross floor area.

4.10

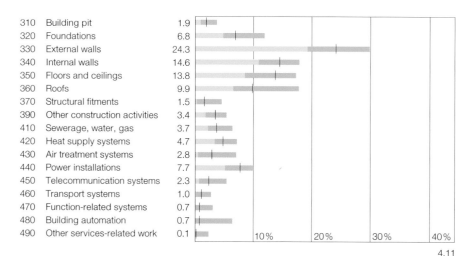

310	Building pit	1.9
320	Foundations	6.8
330	External walls	24.3
340	Internal walls	14.6
350	Floors and ceilings	13.8
360	Roofs	9.9
370	Structural fitments	1.5
390	Other construction activities	3.4
410	Sewerage, water, gas	3.7
420	Heat supply systems	4.7
430	Air treatment systems	2.8
440	Power installations	7.7
450	Telecommunication systems	2.3
460	Transport systems	1.0
470	Function-related systems	0.7
480	Building automation	0.7
490	Other services-related work	0.1

4.11

4.10 Cost indices for office and administration buildings (cost groups on 1st and 2nd levels of DIN 276, incl. VAT; dated: 1st quarter 2009, German average)

4.11 Percentage proportion of cost groups in accordance with DIN 276 of the building costs for office and administration buildings

(including VAT, dated: 1st quarter 2009, German average)

4.12 Integration of cost appraisal into the planning and design process

4.13 Integration of the appraisal of the building and operating costs in the life cycle

- In the denominator (reference value):
  - Unit of quantity (m², m³, number etc.
  - Reference value (gross room volume (BRI), gross floor area (GFA), usable floor area (NF))
  - Rules for calculation (e.g. for living space)

The reference value quoted is much more than a floor area, room volume or number and type of usage units. It represents a comparative value in the sense of a functional unit or a functional equivalent. In particular for interpretation of the cost indices available in the literature, it is important to have at access to least a certain amount of additional information about the building. This would include information in particular on:

- Areas and volumes
- Building use, if relevant details of different types of use
- Intensity of use (hours or days per year)
- Service level
- Any special conditions at the location

Building costs are subject to the influence of many factors, including the following:

- Form and type of building
- Difficulty of setting up site installations
- Topographical peculiarities such as sloping ground
- One-off or serially produced buildings or items
- Regional peculiarities (cost structures, market situation)
- Fluctuations in economic conditions

In as far as the above boundary conditions are known, the values available in the literature can be adjusted to suit the date of observation and the particular characteristics of the actual project. The following may be useful:

- Price indices for updating to the current price level
- Factors for taking into account the economic situation
- Factors for taking into account the peculiarities of the market (e. g. size of the local population)
- Factors for taking into account the peculiarities of the region (e.g. state or region of the country)

Phase	RIBA Work Stage	Stage of cost appraisal	Task	Classification level	Indices used[2]
Requirements planning		Outline budget	Determination of an outline budget or establishing cost guidelines	Overall costs, structure costs separated	€/m² GFA; €/m² NF; €/m³ BRI; €/Usage unit
1 Establish outline requirements	A & B				
2 Preliminary design	C	Cost estimate	Basis for decision on the preliminary design	At least 1st level	€/m² GFA; €/m² NF; €/m³ BRI; €/Usage unit €/Building element (e. g. macro-element)
3 Detailed design	D	Approximate estimate	Basis for decision on the detailed design	At least 2nd level	€/m² GFA; €/m² NF; €/m³ BRI; €/Usage unit €/Building element (e. g. coarse element)
4 Building approval design					
5 Execution design	E & F	Final estimate	Basis for decision on the execution design and preparation of tender documents	At least 3rd level	€/m² GFA; €/m² NF; €/m³ BRI; €/Usage unit €/Building element (e. g. fine element)
6 Preparation of the tender documents	G				
7 Assistance with the tender award	H		Cost control by comparison of final estimate and approximate estimate		
8 Site supervision		Cost fixing	Calculation of the costs actually incurred	At least 3rd level	
9 Site administration and documentation	J & K	Cost evaluation[1]	Creation of cost indices for comparison and record purposes, if relevant also for certification		€/m² GFA; €/m² NF; €/m³ BRI; €/Usage unit
Commissioning[1]	L				
Use and operation[1]	M				

[1] The terms commissioning, use and operation, and cost evaluation are not mentioned in DIN 276. They have been added by the authors.
[2] Key to 'Indices used' column: GFA gross floor area, NF usable floor area, BRI gross building volume.

4.12

Phase	RIBA Work Stage	Stage of the cost appraisal Building costs	Stage of cost appraisal usage costs	Task	Classification level
Requirements planning		Outline budget	Operating cost outline budget	Basis for decisions about requirements planning (DIN 18205) Basis for considerations of economic efficiency Basis for considerations of financing Basis for determination of operating cost guidelines	
1 Establish outline requirements	A & B				
2 Preliminary design	C	Cost estimate	Operating cost preliminary estimate	Basis for decision on the preliminary design Basis for decision on the financing	At least up to 1st level
3 Detailed design	D	Approximate estimate	Operating costs approximate estimate	Basis for decision on the detailed design Basis for decision on the financing (continuous updating until creation of operating costs final estimate as the planning and design progress.	At least up to 2nd level
4 Building approval design					
5 Execution design	E & F	Final estimate			
6 Preparation of the tender	G				
7 Assistance with the tender award	H				
8 Site supervision		Cost fixing			
9 Site administration and documentation	J & K	Cost evaluation[1]	Operating costs final estimate	Setting out all the foreseen costs of building operation	At least up to 3rd level
Commissioning[1]	L				
Use and operation[1]	M		Operating costs fixing Cost control[1]	Setting out all the foreseen costs of building operation For the first time after an accounting period then on a continuous (annual) basis	

[1] The terms commissioning, use and operation, and cost evaluation are not mentioned in DIN 276. They have been added by the authors.

4.13

The literature contains various types of cost indices for a diverse range of buildings and building uses as well as for new build, alteration, conversion and modernisation projects. They can be used for cost calculations and as orientation or comparison values (Fig. 4.10 and 4.11).
The assignment of the stages of the cost calculation to the HOAI service phases is illustrated in Fig. 4.12.

Determination of operating costs

One of the tasks involved in integrated life cycle analysis and the drawing up and evaluation of life cycle costs is the determination of operating costs. In DIN 18960 the term running cost planning includes measures to determine, control and manage operating costs and the comparison of these values.

Cost classification in DIN 18960
There are a number of different ways and principles for classifying the costs arising in the use phase of a building (DIN 18960, GEFMA 200 [14], German Utilities and Operating Costs Ordinance (BetrKV)). One method in

DIN 18960 is particularly suitable for taking into account operating and life cycle costs in the planning and design of buildings. It is close to DIN 276 in terms of content and yet is decisive in its clear reference to building-related running costs.
DIN 18960 (2008) classifies running costs into the following groups (Fig. 4.14):
  100 Cost of capital
  200 Building management costs
  300 Operating costs
  400 Repair costs

The classification level contains at least three levels, which are each identified by three digit numeric codes:
400 Repair costs
  410 Structural repair
    411 Substructure

Creation, use and interpretation of indices
The following information is important for the creation, use and interpretation of indices for operating costs:
• Type of building and use
• Conditions and intensity of use, service level
• Peculiarities of the building use

• Peculiarities of the location
• Date of cost determination, price level
• Period of observation
• Scope of the considered cost groups and types
• Type of summation (static or dynamic observation)
• Method of considering sales tax (with = gross value, without = net value)
• Special conditions of supply or contract with utilities companies

Without knowing the above mentioned information, it is not possible to interpret the data available in the literature. If used carefully they can provide an initial indication of the order of magnitude of the figures and are therefore useful for feasibility assessments.
In the case of ancillary costs, Fig. 4.15 lists and analyses the operating costs that arise for the tenant. A similar treatment of the full costs, Fig. 4.16 shows the situation for the owner occupier. When comparing ancillary and full costs, it is important to take into account the level and share of interest payments, depreciation (allowance for wear and tear) and maintenance (building maintenance) in the variant

No.	Operating cost group
100	**Cost of capital**
110	Cost of loan capital
120	Interest on own funds
130	Depreciation
190	Cost of capital resources, other items
200	**Management costs**
210	Labour costs
220	Non-labour costs
230	Cost of work input by others
290	Management costs, other items
300	**Operating costs**
310	Building services, supply
320	Building services, disposal
330	Cleaning and care of buildings
340	Cleaning and care of external works
350	Operation, inspection and maintenance
360	Monitoring and security
370	Statutory charges and contribution
390	Operating costs, other items
400	**Repair costs**
410	Structural repair
420	Repair of building services
430	Repair of external works
440	Repair of furnishings and equipment
490	Repair costs, other items

4.14

Type of ancillary costs (data in euro/m² net floor area (NGF) month)	Simple	Medium	High
Public charges and fees	0.44	0.48	0.48
Insurance	0.12	0.14	0.15
Servicing	0.31	0.37	0.43
Electricity	0.23	0.29	0.35
Heating	0.42	0.43	0.47
Water, sewage	0.12	0.11	0.12
Cleaning	0.21	0.28	0.25
Security	0.22	0.27	0.33
Administration	0.24	0.25	0.27
Janitor	0.27	0.29	0.30
Other	0.05	0.09	0.09
Total	**2.63**	**3.00**	**3.24**

4.15

Type of full costs (data in euro/m² net floor area (NGF) month)	Simple	Medium	High
Interest	8.69	9.48	12.76
Public charges and fees	0.44	0.49	0.55
Insurance	0.12	0.13	0.15
Servicing, renovation, janitor	0.99	1.15	1.36
Electricity	0.56	0.59	0.64
Heating, cooling	0.46	0.49	0.56
Water, sewage	0.11	0.13	0.14
Cleaning, other	0.74	0.85	0.92
Security	0.36	0.42	0.51
Administration	0.33	0.39	0.44
Sub-total	**12.8**	**14.12**	**16.03**
Wear and tear	2.35	3.22	4.34
Building maintenance	0.31	0.38	0.47
Total	**15.46**	**17.72**	**22.84**

4.16

	< 8 storeys	High-rise building
Public charges and fees		
Insurance		
Servicing		
Electricity		
Heating		
Water, sewage		
Cleaning		
Security		
Administration		
Janitor		
Other		

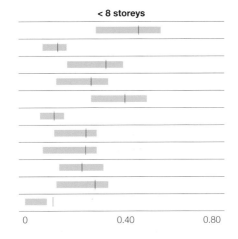
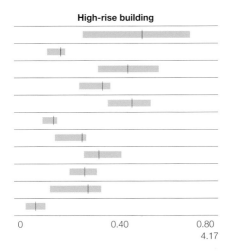

€/m² and month   0   0.40   0.80   0   0.40   0.80
4.17

full costs as well as the slightly different collection of considered cost types (e. g. "Cleaning and other costs" in the full costs). Considerable variations occur in the values of ancillary and full costs overlap (Fig. 4.17). Orders of magnitude for average operating costs of residential properties can be taken from Fig. 4.18.

Integration of cost appraisals in the design, management and decision-making processes
The integration of the appraisal of operating costs in the design, management and decision-making processes can be seen in Fig. 4.13 (p. 67). In the use phase it is recommended for operating cost fixing that the actual consumptions are examined in parallel with the costs for energy and water. Only in this way can it be determined whether the cost deviations result from changes in the consumption data or price changes.

Determination of the costs of supply and disposal
The determination of the costs of energy provision, drinking water requirements and the piping away of waste water, and if appropriate rainwater, is calculated on the basis of local prices and tariffs or the use of preset prices for specific energy carriers and media supply and disposal companies. The preset calculated prices for each medium and service should be used in order to ensure comparability of results for certification. In the cost appraisal, the costs of energy and drinking water requirements and the costs of waste and rain water handling must be taken into account in the appropriate calculations and linked with the prices.

Determination of cleaning costs
Cleaning costs include the costs of maintenance cleaning, glass cleaning, facade cleaning and, where appropriate, the cleaning of technical equipment. The determination of the cleaning costs requires an appropriate calculation of the relevant areas. In glass cleaning it is important to note that the areas of glass to be cleaned (inside and outside faces) usually works out at double the area of the glazed facade surface. The basis for the cost appraisal is the cost of the labour hours involved in cleaning, which in turn is linked to the cleaning cycle and the hourly rate.
The example of cleaning costs clearly illustrates the interplay of different data and information from various sources. The intensity of use for the building as a whole depends on the type of building and its use, and for each area of the building on its individual usage zones. The quality requirement results from the user's wishes expressed in the service level. A required cleaning cycle can be calculated from this quality

Property tax	0.19 €
Water incl. waste water	0.40 €
Heating	0.77 €
Hot water	0.22 €
Lift	0.14 €
Street cleaning	0.05 €
Refuse disposal	0.19 €
Building cleaning	0.15 €
Garden upkeep	0.09 €
Electricity general	0.05 €
Chimney sweeping	0.04 €
Insurance	0.12 €
Janitor	0.20 €
Aerials/cables	0.12 €
Other	0.04 €

4.18

requirement and the intensity of use. Each of the surfaces to be cleaned in turn influences the type and method of cleaning, its position in or on the building determines the accessibility and the associated costs, which may lead to possible supplements for difficulty being applied.

Determination of renovation costs
In general speech there is seldom clarity in the correct use of the terms servicing, maintenance, renovation, modernisation or refurbishment. The use of the terms in the various relevant standards and legislative texts is also not uniform. This leads among other things to problems in determining and setting the boundaries for the costs of renovation. Following the principles of DIN 32736 "Building Management – Definitions and scope of services" [15] and DIN 31051 "Fundamentals of maintenance" [16] is recommended (see Design in the life cycle of buildings, pp. 21f.).
In order to be able to determine renovation costs as a constituent of operat-

4.14 Cost groups for operating costs in accordance with DIN 18960
4.15 Example of ancillary costs related to the quality of fit-out and building (for office buildings, values in euro per m² net floor area (NGF) month, excl. VAT, financial year 2007)
4.16 Example of full costs related to the quality of fit-out and building (for office buildings, values in euro per m² net floor area (NGF) month, excl. VAT, financial year 2007)
4.17 Spread of values of ancillary costs relating to number of storeys (horizontal bars: average 50% quartile; vertical line: average values; values in euro per m² net floor area (NGF) month, excl. VAT, financial year 2007)
4.18 Example of typical values of operating costs of residential buildings in Germany (values in euro/m² net floor area (NGF) month; data from 2007)

ing costs, it is necessary to have established assumptions or stipulations about the period of observation of the life cycle analysis, about the calculated service life of the component (see Tools for integrated design, pp. 84f.), about the possibility of increasing or decreasing the calculated service life and about the required level of detail. Furthermore the replacement investment (deconstruction and disposal, supply and installation) after the expiry of the use or service life of components must be correctly taken into account.

Approximate calculation
Approaches that calculate the costs for renovation on an annual basis as a percentage of the investment cost of each component and technical system are frequently used to arrive at an approximate figure for the renovation costs. As a result of this, components with high investment costs automatically bring with them high maintenance costs. This approach cannot express the advantages of high-quality, more expensive components and systems that entail low renovation costs. Furthermore the percentages should be checked to see whether they exclude (regular) renovation and whether they include the replacement investment at the end of the service life of the component or system.

Detailed calculation
The detailed calculation includes the costs of regular renovation and the costs of replacement investment at the end of the service. This affects all components in cost group 300 in DIN 276 in the form of cost group 410 "Structural repair" in accordance with DIN 18960 and all components in cost group 400 in DIN 276 in the form of cost group 420 "Repair of building services" in accordance with DIN 18960.
For a detailed calculation, it is recommended that the regular renovation costs be expressed in annual terms in the financial plan and the costs of the replacement investment be added to them in the year of replacement. As much use as possible should be made of the manufacturer's information about the level and costs of regular maintenance. Integrating the replacement investment into the year of replacement

allows proper account to be taken of high-quality components and systems with a long service life and benefits budget planning. High-quality maintenance (e. g. ensured through maintenance contacts) can in certain circumstances result in a demonstrable increase in the calculated service life. VDI 2067 guideline "Economic efficiency of building installations" [17] provides a basis for a detailed calculation of renovation costs, in particular domestic, technical and building services. The guideline contains information on the calculated service life in particular and on the calculation of the expenditure on renovation, maintenance and operation of heating systems, air-conditioning plants and drinking water supply systems. Fig. 4.20 shows an example of the principle of building up a detailed calculation. When applying VDI 2067 it should be noted that the guideline interprets renovation as the continuous maintenance of operational availability but considers refurbishment as a replacement investment. The estimation of the expenditure for the (regular) renovation does not include the expenditure for the replacement investment. The latter must therefore be separately calculated.
The use of cost indices relating to new buildings – if necessary including allowances for anticipated price increases – for replacement investments in the use phase is not completely correct. In addition to the supply and installation of components in the context of replacement investment, the expenditure for deinstallation and disposal of the part to be replaced must also be taken into account.
As far as possible, the replacement investment should take into account the cost indices for maintenance and modernisation, which should include the cost of deconstruction and removal of the components and systems to be replaced. This is intended to ensure that renovation elements as well as new build elements are considered when applying complex planning, design and evaluation tools.

Alternative methods
Alternatively the calculation of renovation costs can be taken from the rates for full service contracts (maintenance contracts). They cover the costs of

servicing, repairs (including replacement parts) and consumables. This variant has the advantage of an even cash flow. There is also the possibility of adopting an approach based on calculated costs (e. g. in accordance with the Second Computation Ordinance (II. BV)).

Determination of the costs of operation, inspection, servicing and maintenance
Costs for operation, inspection, servicing and maintenance of technical systems and for inspection, servicing and maintenance of building structures arise throughout the whole life cycle. VDI 2067 provides useful information for domestic, technical and building services systems. It should be noted that the operating costs are given in hours and have to be multiplied by the appropriate hourly rates to arrive at a total cost.
Alternatively the costs can be taken from servicing and maintenance contracts.

Accounting for externalities

The erection, use and disposal of buildings have effects on the environment. The consequences and secondary effects are not always borne by their originators but shift on to third parties or society. They are not reflected in market prices. Therefore they do not feature in investment decisions and hence lead in certain circumstances to distortion in the comparison of variants. Undesirable effects on the environment cause damage which can be either described directly or characterised by the costs of their avoidance, reduction, remediation and insurance. Losses in value may be incurred or expenditure may be necessary to mitigate the undesirable effects in the future. These cases usually result in negative external effects.
At the same time, the need to take action is often underestimated. This is the case with the improvement of the energy performance of buildings or with environmental measures. There are sometimes positive external effects to be seen.
A monetary evaluation of the negative external effects can be made in terms of costs. These costs relate to e.g. pollution, avoidance, evasion or costs to

cover long-term risks. The first question to be addressed is the estimation of the level of external costs that arise for third parties or society. A second step is to discuss whether and how external costs can be taken into account in assessments of economic efficiency [18].

The literature contains numerous approaches, values and orders of magnitude for the estimation of external costs. The great spread of these figures made earlier attempts to integrate them into economic efficiency assessments and the investment decisions based upon them difficult. Examples of implementable methods were developed in Switzerland, where external costs are taken into account in investment decisions in the form of supplements applied to energy prices. Germany is developing studies for similar proposals. (Fig. 4.21 shows the resulting orders of magnitude for Germany and Switzerland.

4.19

Assessment of economic efficiency

The assessment of economic efficiency is part of the process of investment appraisal. The investigation compares the expenditure and yield (utility) to take a view of the advantages of the planned investment. In a narrower sense, the assessment of economic efficiency concentrates on consideration of monetary values. In a wider sense it also investigates the advantages of measures in terms of non-monetary values and mixtures of non-monetary and monetary values. Fig. 4.19 gives an overview of the main ways of comparing expenditure and utility. In assessing economic efficiency the distinction is drawn between static and dynamic processes.

Static processes
Static processes assess the economic efficiency based on a comparison of costs and/or yields of an investment without taking account of the point in time when they arise. Their simplicity

System component	Nominal service life[1]	Renovation cost[2]	Servicing costs[2]	Operating costs[3]
1 Heating				
1.1 Benefit transfer				
1.1.1 Heating surface with accessories (valves, threaded connections, brackets)				
Cast iron radiators	40	1	0	0
Steel radiators	35	1	0	0
Panel radiators, steel	30	1	0	0
Convectors with cladding	30	2	0	0
Radiator paint	10	0	0	0
Ceiling heating with suspended steel pipes and heat conduction plates	20	1.5	0.5	0
Hot water underfloor heating	30	1	0	0

[1] In years
[2] In percentage of investment sum per year and component
[3] In hours per year. Operating cost is always added to the creation cost.

4.20

Mode of supply	Energy price supplement (in cent/kWh)		
	Excluding upstream processes	Including upstream processes	For comparison: Switzerland
Heating oil	2.0	2.7	2.6
Heating gas	1.4	2.0	1.9
Wood burner without particle filter	1.1	1.3	1.0
Wood burner with particle filter	0.0	0.4	
Combined heat and power plant (CHP)	0.0	1.4	
Heat pump	0.0	0.6	
Biogas	1.4	1.4	
Solar thermal	0.0	0.5	

4.21

4.19 Economic efficiency from different viewpoints
4.20 Example of calculation principles for renovation costs in accordance with VDI 2067
4.21 Suggested values for energy price supplement for taking into account external costs

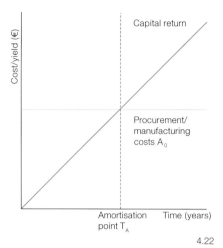

Cost/yield (€)

Capital return

Procurement/
manufacturing
costs A_0

Amortisation   Time (years)
point T_A

4.22

makes them extraordinarily popular in
practice. Static processes are only of
limited use in the field of real estate
because they disregard the exact
point in time when payments in and
out occur. They cannot adequately
address the typical situation of high initial investments at a few specific points
in time, compared with comparatively
small incomes or cost reductions in
many points in time. The use of static
processes alone can easily result in
false assessments. This must always
be borne in mind when evaluating the
results.
Typical processes for static investment
appraisal are:
• Cost comparison
• Profit comparison
• Return on investment
• Amortisation to determine the
  repayment period.

Different opportunities and limits apply
to the use of each of these processes.
Thus a static calculation of the repayment period is in very widespread use
in practice. It can be used to evaluate
individual investments in which a high,
one-off payment out (cost) made in the
beginning is compared with regular
payments in (through higher income or
lower costs) in the future. The repayment period defined as the length of
time before the cost of procurement or
production is exceeded by the income
or savings (capital returns). According
to the decision rule: choose the alternative with the shorter repayment period
(Fig. 4.22).
However, the static amortisation process is problematical in many respects.
Firstly all payments in and out that
occur after the repayment period are

omitted from the calculation. These
ignored payments could be a longer
service life of an alternative or higher
disposal costs. One possibility of incorporating the service life is offered by
the calculation of the amortisation
ratio. This value indicates the number
of times the measure is amortised in
its life or period of use. Secondly the
timing of the payments – as with other
static processes – is not taken into
account.
These two weaknesses mean that a
comparison of several alternatives
based on their static amortisation periods cannot ensure that the variant with
the most overall advantage is selected.
In addition the term suggests that a
specific time has to pass before an
investment pays off. Unfortunately the
index cannot reflect a situation such
as an investment in energy saving
measures in which there are gains
from lower energy costs and therefore
a lower energy price risk as well as
increased comfort. The statement that
a period of 10–15 years must pass
before an investment pays off would
have a deterrent effect on private
clients and landlords.
Overall the use of a static amortisation
period for individual investment
appraisals should be strongly advised
against because of these weaknesses.
The annuity method, which is more
suitable for modelling the actual payment flows, is recommended instead
(see p. 74).
In conclusion, dynamic processes are
preferred to static processes. The work
involved in the calculation, particularly
when using computer-aided methods,
is hardly more than for the equivalent
static process, and therefore the directional certainty of the results is assured.

Dynamic processes
Dynamic processes take into account –
in contrast to static processes – the
exact points in time of payments in and
out in the time line of the investment.
One advantage of the dynamic investment appraisal is its unlimited suitability for undertaking absolute and relative
evaluations of investments. An absolute
evaluation ascertains whether an
investment is worthwhile, whereas a
relative evaluation is used to select the
best of several alternatives. Furthermore all the indicators come to the

same conclusion if applied correctly,
i.e. an investment that is shown to pay
off by the net present value method
also generates a positive equivalent
annuity. This also ensures the directional certainty of the results.
The basis for the dynamic processes is
simple and compound interest. In contrast to static processes, with dynamic
processes it is possible to select a suitable discount rate. In the simplest case
this rate applies to the investment and
to the credit payments and remains
the same for the time line of the investment. However, it is possible to take
variable discount rates into account.
The basis for the selection of a discount rate could be:
• The discount rate of a 10-year
  government bond
• An average hypothetical discount
  rate for investments in real estate
  predominantly made by third parties
• The relevant return on property
• A discount rate appropriate to the
  particular risk (the higher the risk,
  the higher the discount rate)
• A discount rate based on a company's own defined or desired return
  on capital

With standard methods of calculation,
the discount rate is stipulated.
The basis of the evaluation of an investment using a dynamic process is the
cash flows of the various alternatives.
This is expressed in tabular form showing all the different points in time of the
costs and revenues arising. Values
used purely within the calculation that
do not require payments, such as
write-downs, are not considered.
With a dynamic investment appraisal,
a distinction can be drawn between
the indices explained in more detail
in the following section and between
appraisal methods. As a rule, any
index can calculated with any of the
appraisal methods. Appraisal methods
can be calculated:
• On the basis of individual values
• Using standard calculated factors
• Using complete financial plans

The complexity of the situation governs
the choice of method. If it is matter of
a series of payments on a tenancy
agreement or a similar case of equal
payments at regular intervals (such as
a rent or interest and repayment of a

loan) at a constant interest rate, then the calculation can be performed using standard calculated factors. These factors can be obtained from tables or calculated using formulae in spreadsheets. Calculation on the basis of individual values is suitable only for simple series of payments with varying payments, different intervals between payments or with interest rates that change over time. However, if an appraisal of an investment with a combination of different types of serial payments is required, (e.g. a sporadic series of payments for modernisation and a regular rental income, or taxation needs to be taken into account, or the investment involves a number of different sources of finance such as loans, owned capital or subsidies), then a complete financial plan is the recommended method. Spreadsheet programs are a very convenient way of performing this type of appraisal. The above methods can be used to calculate a wide variety of specific dynamic indices. In particular:

- Net present value
- Equivalent annuity
- Internal rate of return

Further, more specific indices can be calculated to include parameters such as end value. The following sections give a brief explanation of the net present value and annuity methods.

Net present value method
With the net present value method, all payments in and out are related to their cash or present value at the time of the original investment. The net present value is the basis of various tools used in the real estate sector, among other things for assessing an investment using the capitalisation valuation method. It is also often used as the basis for appraising the life cycle cost of a building. The associated decision rule is: select only investments with positive net present values or select the alternative with the higher net present value. The net present value can also be interpreted as the capital growth or loss at the time of investment.
In the calculation of the net present value, all payments that occur at a later date are not entered as their nominal amount but as the sum which would

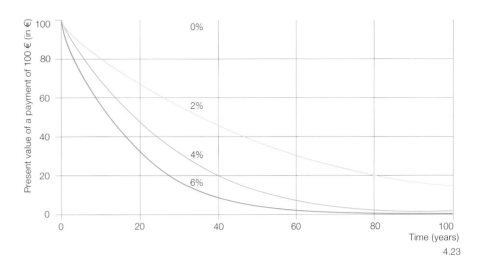

4.23

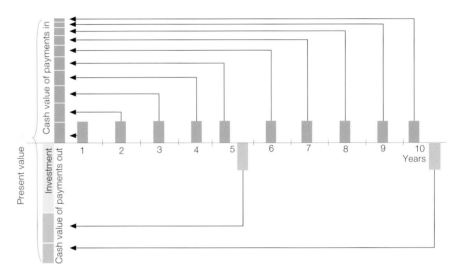

4.24

Time	Discount factors (present value of annuity factor) for an interest rate of								
(years)	2.0%	3.0%	4.0%	5.0%	6.0%	7.0%	8.0%	9.0%	10.0%
1	0.98	0.97	0.96	0.95	0.94	0.93	0.93	0.92	0.91
5	4.71	4.58	4.45	4.33	4.21	4.10	3.99	3.89	3.79
10	8.98	8.53	8.11	7.72	7.36	7.02	6.71	6.42	6.14
15	12.85	11.94	11.12	10.38	9.71	9.11	8.56	8.06	7.61
20	16.35	14.88	13.59	12.46	11.47	10.59	9.82	9.13	8.51
25	19.52	17.41	15.62	14.09	12.78	11.65	10.67	9.82	9.08
30	22.40	19.60	17.29	15.37	13.76	12.41	11.26	10.27	9.43
35	25.00	21.49	18.66	16.37	14.50	12.95	11.65	10.57	9.64
40	27.36	23.11	19.79	17.16	15.05	13.33	11.92	10.76	9.78
45	29.49	24.52	20.72	17.77	15.46	13.61	12.11	10.88	9.86
50	31.42	25.73	21.48	18.26	15.76	13.80	12.23	10.96	9.91
60	34.76	27.68	22.62	18.93	16.16	14.04	12.38	11.05	9.97
70	37.50	29.12	23.39	19.34	16.38	14.16	12.44	11.08	9.99
80	39.74	30.20	23.92	19.60	16.51	14.22	12.47	11.10	10.00
90	41.59	31.00	24.27	19.75	16.58	14.25	12.49	11.11	10.00
100	43.10	31.60	24.50	19.85	16.62	14.27	12.49	11.11	10.00

4.25

4.22 Principle of a static amortisation period
4.23 Effects of the level of the discount rate on the present value of a payment
4.24 Principle of the net present value method
4.25 Discount factors (present value of annuity factor)

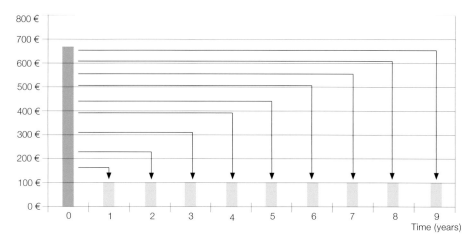

4.26

Time	Annuity factors for an interest rate of								
(years)	2.0%	3.0%	4.0%	5.0%	6.0%	7.0%	8.0%	9.0%	10.0%
1	1.020	1.030	1.040	1.050	1.060	1.070	1.080	1.090	1.100
5	0.212	0.218	0.225	0.231	0.237	0.244	0.250	0.257	0.264
10	0.111	0.117	0.123	0.130	0.136	0.142	0.149	0.156	0.163
15	0.078	0.084	0.090	0.096	0.103	0.110	0.117	0.124	0.131
20	0.061	0.067	0.074	0.080	0.087	0.094	0.102	0.110	0.117
25	0.051	0.057	0.064	0.071	0.078	0.086	0.094	0.102	0.110
30	0.045	0.051	0.058	0.065	0.073	0.081	0.089	0.097	0.106
40	0.037	0.043	0.051	0.058	0.066	0.075	0.084	0.093	0.102
50	0.032	0.039	0.047	0.055	0.063	0.072	0.082	0.091	0.101
60	0.029	0.036	0.044	0.053	0.062	0.071	0.081	0.091	0.100
70	0.027	0.034	0.043	0.052	0.061	0.071	0.080	0.090	0.100
80	0.025	0.033	0.042	0.051	0.061	0.070	0.080	0.090	0.100
90	0.024	0.032	0.041	0.051	0.060	0.070	0.080	0.090	0.100
100	0.023	0.032	0.041	0.050	0.060	0.070	0.080	0.090	0.100

4.27

4.26 Principle of the annuity method
4.27 Annuity factors
4.28 Example calculation for the determination of
     an equivalent energy price
4.29 Example of an equivalent energy price with
     an increase of energy efficiency in buildings

Equivalent energy price for a measure to provide thermal insulation (example)

Boundary conditions	Period of observation: 25 years Discount rate (%) 4% Annuity factor for 25 years and 4%: 0.064 Measure: 12 cm ext. thermal insulation composite on uninsulated brick wall Energy saving: 110 kWh/m² external wall Full costs of the measure: 100 €/m² external wall Costs of renovation (plaster refurbishment): 60 €/m² external wall Additional cost of the energetic improvement[1]: 40 €/m² external wall
Full cost approach	100 €/m² × 0.064 1/a : 110 kWh/m²a = 0.06 €/m² [2]
Additional cost approach	40 €/m² × 0.064 1/a : 110 kWh/m²a = 0.02 €/m²

[1] With the renovation costs deducted as already incurred costs
[2] Values rounded

4.28

have to be set aside at the present time in order to yield the actual later amount through the application of a preset interest rate (Fig. 4.24).
In this way e. g. a sum of 1000 € received today, by the application of an interest rate of 4%, grows to an amount of 1040 € in one year and to 1081.60 € in two years. In reverse it means that payments of 1040 € and 1081.60 € expected to be received in one and two years' time respectively will each have a present value of 1000 €.

All payments are discounted to the time of the start of the investment and are thus assessed in the appraisal calculation as their cash or present values. The further off in the future a payment is made and the higher the interest rate, then the lower its present cash value is (Fig. 4.23, p. 73).
It is easy to see that payments scheduled to be made more than 50 years in the future have hardly any effect on the net present value. Herein lies the difficulty of using this method to assess very long-term investments, such as those normally found in real estate.
The net present value is the sum of the cash values of all the payments. The cash value of a constant series of payments (e. g. from rental income) can be calculated very simply using a discount factor (present value of annuity factor). The factors can be taken from a suitable set of tables, provided the interest rate and period are known (Fig. 4.25, p. 73). In order to calculate the net present value, all that needs to be done is to multiply the regular payment by the appropriate discount factor (present value of annuity factor).
As the net present value is determined by addition, even a complex series of payments can be split into regular and irregular payments, then their present values can be calculated separately and finally added together. This is particularly useful when creating complete financial plans, which take into account all the relevant effects such as subsidies, taxes, rental income, operating costs etc. This is achieved by modelling them as separate series of payments in a table, then calculating the present value of each part and adding them to form the whole net present value of the project.

Annuity method

The annuity method focuses on determining the level of regular income to be obtained from the investment. The method is particularly suitable for the assessment of investments in which an initial payment at the start of a project is compared with later regular income or savings. This is the case with the improvement of the energy performance of buildings or with environmental measures, where a one-off expense is balanced by a regular yield – in this case in the form of energy cost savings. This approach can be used in particular for the owner-occupier. For the landlord the yield is in the higher rent that can then be commanded. According to the decision rule: select only products with a positive annuity or those alternatives with the highest annuity. To calculate the annuity, the one-off payment at the start is converted into a regularly recurring payment over the period (Fig. 4.26).

This is done by multiplying the one-off payment by the annuity factor, the reciprocal of the discount factor (the present value of annuity factor). If the discount rate and the period are known the annuity factor can be taken from a set of suitable tables (Fig. 4.27).

As can be readily appreciated, the calculated result equates to the interest on and capital repayment of a loan equal to the initial cost of the investment that would fully repay the loan within the period of observation, assuming the interest rate remained unchanged. This can be added to the other continuously occurring costs such as servicing and the regular income from sources like rent or energy savings over the period. If additional irregular payments in or out occur at later points in time, for example due to the need to replace short-lived parts, then the cash value of these payments must first be calculated and then distributed to all the points in time with the help of the annuity factor in order to calculate the annuity.

In principle the annuity is equivalent to the net present value. Each calculated net present value can be converted immediately into the equivalent annuity by multiplying it by the appropriate annuity factor. In this respect the results are directly comparable. A project shown to be economically viable by the

net present value method will also be economically viable by the annuity method, and the same applies to a series of alternatives. From the psychological point of view, it is interesting to examine their use. Private clients in particular do not normally have an established point of reference when considering large sums of money, such as those commonly needed for the construction or refurbishment of a house, and hence cannot make "rational" decisions. When choosing between alternatives, the annuity method can be used to convert the various sums, for example for the additional installation of a solar water heating system, into a monthly credit or debit, which can be compared with the income. Furthermore a positive equivalent annuity makes it clear, for example with an energetic refurbishment, that the investment is linked to direct advantages, something which cannot be done with a static amortisation period. Therefore the annuity method is attractive in these circumstances, even if it is in principle the equivalent of net present value and is sometimes more complex to calculate.

Special forms of advantage analysis

In addition to the traditional methods for assessing the advantages of proposed projects, a number of special forms of analysis to assess the advantages of energy-saving and emission-reduction measures. This includes individual measures on components and systems, as well as packages of measures in new build and modernisation projects. These special forms are discussed in the following section of this chapter.

Costs of the saved kWh energy (equivalent energy price)

The equivalent energy price (cents per saved kWh) can be calculated on the basis of the useful energy (for heating requirements) or the final energy (energy requirement or demand on end energy carriers) taking into account the conversion chain. As the energy savings is expressed in kWh/year, the measure-related costs must be distributed over the service life or use period and given in euros, dollars or pounds per year. The costs of the measures can be incorporated as full costs or – when linked with renovation works which may well be successful in their own right – as additional costs, rather than just defect rectification costs. Using the annuity factor, the expenditure – with the costs of servicing and maintenance added where applicable – can be converted into the annual charge for full financing of the measures. The period of observation here is normally chosen to be the same as the service life of the component or the system. This annual charge is compared with the annual reduction of the annual useful or end energy demand in energy units (i.e. savings as kWh/year) resulting from the measures. In the analysis of packages of measures, the measure that takes place first in the analysis has an advantage, as its savings potential is available for longer. The calculated equivalent energy price is completely independent of the energy carrier, energy tariff and efficiency of energy conversion. Only the actual investment costs and interest terms encountered in practice go into the calculation. The results show the cost of realising the meas-

Measure	Energy saving (kWh/m²a)	Investment (euro/m²)	Equivalent energy price (euro/kWh)
Insulation (roof, basement ceiling, external wall)	50–150	50–250	0.02–0.20
Window	20–50	30–150	0.06–0.30
Boiler replacement	20–120	20–80	0.02–0.20
Comfort ventilation	10–30 (max.)	20–70	0.08–0.25
Solar drinking water heating	5–20 (max.)	35–50	0.10–0.30
Solar drinking water heating and background space heating	10–25 (max.)	50–80	0.10–0.40
Hydraulic balancing and heating optimisation by building modernisation	10–20	1–6	0.02–0.04

4.29

ures in terms of each kWh of energy saved.

The equivalent energy price can then be compared with average or specific costs of provision of useful or end energy incorporating the actual energy carrier and conversion information and, if relevant, supplements to take into account any external costs. The measure is financially advantageous if the expenditure to achieve a saving of a unit of energy is smaller than its cost of creation or provision. Examples of the orders of magnitude are given in Figs. 4.28 (p. 74) and 4.29 (p. 75). The values in Fig. 4.28 relate to the component surface area, the values in Fig. 4.29 relate to the area of heated living space.

However, the equivalent energy price is not suitable for selecting one measure from several mutually exclusive alternatives. In this case the net present value method should be used. In future, measures could and should be evaluated not only in accordance with the equivalent energy price. In this approach the savings potential of the measures compared with the initial situation should be given in absolute or relative quantities.

Using estimated values, it is possible to establish the average energy price over the service life of a variant which indicates the variant becoming economically viable.

Energy/ecology amortisation period
A calculation of the energy (ecological) amortisation period starts with the thought that the expenditure for a measure consists not only of the investment costs but also the resources (energy) to be deployed and/or the environmental impacts caused (emission of pollutants/depletion of raw materials). First the energy (as a rule measured in terms of primary energy) or the environmental impact (as a rule measured in terms of CO_2 emissions) invested or caused in the manufacture, realisation, commissioning and, if relevant, maintenance of the improvement measures is determined. Then the payback period, after which the energy savings or general relieving of the pollution load on the environment resulting from the measures will have covered the investment, is calculated. This method is suitable for performing a relative comparison of different variants.

In a similar fashion to the cost-oriented amortisation index, it is possible to calculate an energy or ecological amortisation index often referred to as the harvest factor. In average conditions in Germany, the energetic amortisation period for insulation is of the order of weeks or months, for solar water heating system it is about two years and for solar electricity generation (PV) systems anything up to four years. Assuming PV systems have a service life of 20 years, this represents a harvest factor of 5.

CO_2 avoidance costs
A number of different ways exist to calculate and interpret CO_2 avoidance costs. One of these, the net avoidance cost approach, is introduced here (Fig. 4.30).

As a rule, CO_2 avoidance costs are based on the net costs of emissions reduction. There may be positive (additional costs) and negative (reduced costs) values. Negative net costs or reduced costs for emission reductions always arise if the additional costs for a measure are less than the cost reductions resulting from this measure with other, similarly considered costs of the same system. This gives rise to an additional utility.

In general with this approach to calculating the specific net avoidance costs, the quotient is composed of the difference of emissions and a cost difference linked with the measure.

In conjunction with the determination and interpretation however, there are a series of preconditions to create, questions to clarify and assumptions to describe. Therefore, for example, it must be stated whether the cost model follows a social or economic approach. An initial situation (reference case or system) must first be defined in order to be able to calculate the differences. This process is also described as a system comparison through difference analysis with a reference system.

Influences on boundary conditions
The results of dynamic economic efficiency assessments are strongly influenced by the chosen assumptions and applied boundary conditions. Processes have been developed, in particular in connection with measures to save energy, reduce emissions and environmental impacts, which seek to compensate for the disadvantages of dynamic methods in their consideration of long-term effects. They include in particular:

- Analytical methods to achieve a reduction of investment costs for measures to save energy and reduce emissions
- Consideration of external costs (price supplements for energy)
- Selection and use of modified discount rates

The choice of the discount rate has a decisive influence on the result of a dynamic economic efficiency assessment. A decision must be made as to whether market interest rates are to be used, whether an overall economic approach should be adopted or whether the discount rate should reflect the risks involved. This decision depends on the circumstances of the project, the field of application and the period of observation.
For an assessment of economic efficiency, the discount rate used for low-risk situations should be the capital market interest rates, which are usually lower than the average market rates. This approach is appropriate for short- to medium-term assessments with a period of observation of up to 20 years and leads to discount rates of 3 to 4 %. The method convention published by the German Federal Environment Agency (UBA) suggests that a discount rate of only 1.5 % is used for observation periods of over 20 years and a discount rate of 0 % is used for sensitivity analyses of schemes with observation periods that span generations [19]. By adopting this rate the expenditure and utility for today's and future generations are given equal weight for ethical reasons. The discount rates are used for the whole of the period of observation.

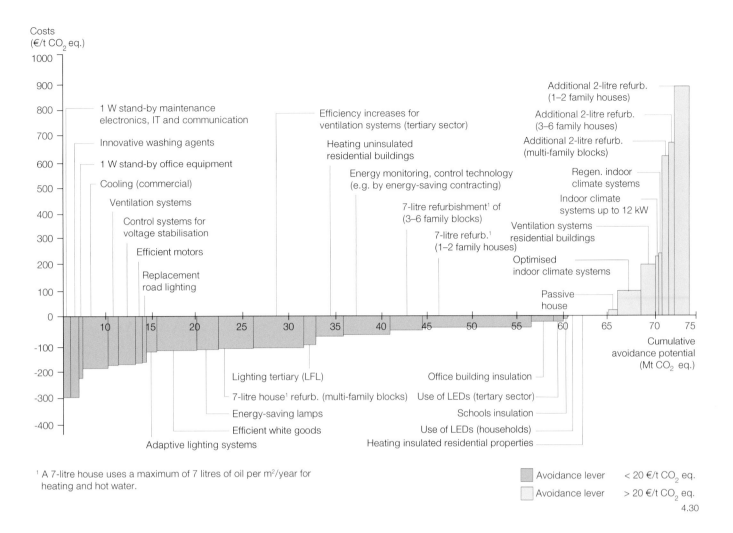

Costs
(€/t CO$_2$ eq.)

1 W stand-by maintenance electronics, IT and communication

Innovative washing agents

1 W stand-by office equipment

Cooling (commercial)

Ventilation systems

Control systems for voltage stabilisation

Efficient motors

Replacement road lighting

Efficiency increases for ventilation systems (tertiary sector)

Heating uninsulated residential buildings

Energy monitoring, control technology (e.g. by energy-saving contracting)

7-litre refurbishment[1] of (3–6 family blocks)

7-litre refurb.[1] (1–2 family houses)

Additional 2-litre refurb. (1–2 family houses)

Additional 2-litre refurb. (3–6 family houses)

Additional 2-litre refurb. (multi-family blocks)

Regen. indoor climate systems

Indoor climate systems up to 12 kW

Ventilation systems residential buildings

Optimised indoor climate systems

Passive house

Cumulative avoidance potential (Mt CO$_2$ eq.)

Lighting tertiary (LFL)

7-litre house[1] refurb. (multi-family blocks)

Energy-saving lamps

Efficient white goods

Adaptive lighting systems

Office building insulation

Use of LEDs (tertary sector)

Schools insulation

Use of LEDs (households)

Heating insulated residential properties

[1] A 7-litre house uses a maximum of 7 litres of oil per m^2/year for heating and hot water.

Avoidance lever   < 20 €/t CO$_2$ eq.

Avoidance lever   > 20 €/t CO$_2$ eq.

4.30

References:

[1] Enquete Commission "Schutz des Menschen und der Umwelt" of the 13th German Bundestag: Konzept Nachhaltigkeit – vom Leitbild zur Umsetzung. Final Report 1998

[2] Trade-off in the sense of an investigation into whether higher investment costs lead to lower operating costs.

[3] DIN 18205 Brief for building design. 1996

[4] ISO 15686-5:2008 (E): Building and constructed assets – Service life planning – Part 5: Life cycle costing. Berlin 2008

[5] German Federal Ministry of Transport, Building and Urban Development (BM-VBS): Sustainable Building Guide. Berlin 2001 (under revision, access to current version i. a. at www.nachhaltigesbauen.de)

[6] DIN 276-1 Building costs – Part 1: Building construction. 2006

[7] DIN 18960 User costs of buildings. 2008

[8] Verordnung über wohnungswirtschaftliche Berechnungen nach dem Zweiten Wohnungsbaugesetz (Zweite Berechnungsverordnung/II. BV)

[9] Verordnung über die Aufstellung von Betriebskosten (Betriebskostenverordnung, BetrKV). 2003

[10] GEFMA e. V. German Facility Management Association: GEFMA 220 Life cycle costing in FM. Introduction and fundamentals. Draft 2006 (in German)

[11] Life cycle costing does not take into consideration other costs and risks to others resulting from externalities (such as environmental costs), carbon trading, water framework, waste regulations, etc.

[12] as ref. 10

[13] The possibilities offered by having a scaleable technique that can be used at different levels (systemic, strategic and detail level) means that optimisation can be assessed at different times and at different scales, as well as comparing different strategies. It does raise questions about integrating the parts into the whole. It also means that different actors (clients, designers, contractors, subcontractors) will be able to analyse their role and their value added more closely.

[14] GEFMA e. V. German Facility Management Association: GEFMA 200. Costs in facility management. Cost classification structure Draft 2004 (in German)

[15] DIN 32736 Property management. Definitions and scope of services. 2000

[16] DIN 31051 Fundamentals of maintenance. Berlin 2003

[17] VDI Guideline 2067, Part 1 Economic efficiency of building installations – Fundamentals and economic calculation. 2000

[18] Maibach, Markus, et al.: Praktische Anwendung der Methodenkonvention. Möglichkeiten der Berücksichtigung externer Umweltkosten bei Wirtschaftlichkeitsrechnungen von öffentlichen Investitionen. Zurich/Cologne 2007.
www.umweltdaten.de/publikationen/fpdf-l/3194.pdf
Umweltbundesamt (pub.): Ökonomische Bewertung von Umweltschäden. Methodenkonvention zur Schätzung externer Umweltkosten. Dessau 2007.
www.umweltdaten.de/publikationen/fpdf-l/3193.pdf

[19] Umweltbundesamt (pub.): as ref. 16

4.30 Avoidance costs for greenhouse gases emissions in the German building sector (after McKinsey)
The technical report "Kosten und Potenziale der Vermeidung von Treibhausgasemissionen in Deutschland" evaluates a total of 300 technical avoidance levers, of which 32 are in the building sector. The graph gives the forecast for the year 2020. The potential for avoidance of greenhouse gases and the foresee net addition or reduction in costs compared with the reference technology in current use.

Life cycle analysis taking life cycle assessment and life cycle costing into account presents the designer with a complex task. It requires the combination of various methodological principles and procedures, which are described in this chapter. Life cycle analysis is suitable as a tool for integrated design, which adopts a holistic approach that can cope with the complexity of the task.

Integrated design

In particular since the 1973 energy crisis, the requirements applied to buildings have become continuously more stringent while the buildings themselves have become increasingly complex. This increase in complexity can no longer be effectively managed by the conventional sequential method of design, in which the design team divides up the work and only becomes fully formed at the end of the design process after the responsibility has been continuously shunted from one project stakeholder to another. The concept of integrated design was developed to overcome this problem and is finding increasing acceptance.
Integrated design has come to mean a procedure in which the design team is assembled at the beginning of the design, the client's representatives are involved and in certain circumstances even the main contractor can be brought in at an early stage in the design [1]. This provides the foundations for integration along interdisciplinary lines (horizontally) and throughout all life cycle phases (vertically). The responsibility for the design decisions is assumed by the design team, which

generally requires specific forms of contract (e. g. lead or project consultant). The cooperative working of the team is based firstly on an extensive, explicit alignment of their aims with the requirements of the project and secondly on a common image of the planned building [2].
Integrated design is a process in which the acquisition of knowledge and its optimisation take place in alternate steps. This requires that all the participants in the design exchange information honestly and impartially. The solution process demands coordination without prejudice or favour towards one discipline or another, so that quality, continuity and a design complying with the objectives are guaranteed.
The design process inevitably raises conflicts of objectives. "They arise from the divergent perspectives and areas of competence of the participating parties – but also through their different objectives. Quantitative objectives – for example remaining within budget – can be defined in unambiguous terms and incorporated relatively easily into the design process. [...] Additional difficulties find their grounds in the inherent conflicts of objectives in the tension between ecology and economy that accompany and combine with the conflicts of interests of the participants in the design and construction," as it says in the book "Bürogebäude mit Zukunft" [3]. Completely new methods and tools are necessary to overcome these difficulties. This need stems from the following requirements and aspects:
- The requirement-oriented approach is based on the formulation, auditing and agreement of systems of objectives [4].

- The horizontal (disciplinary) integration needs special tools that link several specialist areas (e. g. energy requirement and costs).
- The planned building must be described in scalable form capable of being used by all the design participants (e. g. element cost classification).
- The exchange and synchronisation of the data must be carried out as a continuous process. This can only be fully achieved by adopting a common building information model (BIM). The use of central project servers and web-based project rooms allows a high standard of design consistency to be maintained.

Integrated design methods have not yet gained complete acceptance because the necessary working environments (project rooms), building product models (building information models), integrated project planning programs and comprehensive databases have not been universally available.
The traditional approach to project design, even on major projects involving several different architects, designers and engineers, is for each of these agents to work using their own preferred software. This way of working is characterised by high costs of data collection and entry combined with inevitable data inconsistencies (Fig. 5.1). This realisation has prompted several research projects from which a working approach with the following objectives has been developed:
- The integration of quantitative design approaches (manufacturing and use costs, energy requirement and costs, environmental impact) into one software solution

- The consideration of the building's over all life cycle phases (construction, use, disposal)
- The use of a modular element construction to ensure data consistency and allow work to progress smoothly and without interruption throughout the project

A decisive step forward was made with the agreement of a means of dividing the tasks between the CAD dimensional information (with the graphical information) and the building cost information (with the database for the building description); the solution being a shared interface, the building information model, (BIM). The design team now has a digital tool available that links the design process with cost information. The modular structure of the data model allows the information to be updated to the current state of the building design at appropriate aggregation stages. Databases with modular structures have also been developed in parallel with the programs and interfaces (Fig. 5.2).

The principles and stages of the design must be documented to allow third parties to understand and interpret the project. Therefore all aspects of the databases, standards, legislative and technical guidelines used must be automatically recorded and carried forward. An example of a complete listing is shown in Fig. 5.3. Listing all the necessary constructions and technical services systems in the form of a digital chain is a worthwhile and not too laborious way of easing the task of summarising all the project information.

Scalability and accuracy in the design process

The main task of the architect is the development or one or more ideas with an abundance of possible variants to create a solution to a declared project objective. The necessary high flexibility maintained in the preliminary design phases means that many questions of detail addressed in these early stages have to take into account a great deal of uncertainly and lack of definition. The

Building data	Design team member	Tools used	Documents created
Areas and masses Elements Building technical services by area	Architect	CAD Construction costs Building catalogue	Construction costs in acc. with DIN 276 (cost estimates, Cost supplement)
Masses for elements Items Building technical services selection	Architect	Tender and accounting program	Construction costs by trades (cost calculation, Cost fixing)
Envelope modelling Assignment Area calculation Building technical services selection	Engineer	Energy program	Energy requirement certificate
Area calculation Building technical services Furnishing Open areas	Facility manager	FM program	Follow-on costs Maintenance Cleaning Renovation
Building elements LCA modules	LCA specialist	Life cycle analysis	Inventory balance Impact balance

5.1

Building data	Design team member	Tools used	Documents created
CAD model with IFC export	Architect	Consistent element-based scalable data model	Working drawings Tender
	Quantity surveyor		Building costs in acc. with DIN 276 and by trades
	Building services engineer	Integral software or complex interface for all applications software	Energy performance certificate in acc. with Energy Performance of Buildings Directive (EPBD)/heat load calculation in. acc. with EN 832
	LCC planner		Use costs in acc. with DIN 18960
	LCA planner		Inventory and impact balance in acc. with ISO 14040 and ISO 14044

5.2

Construction costs	Construction price database Cost classification in accordance with DIN 276
Energy requirement	Calculation rules in accordance with EnEV or DIN V18599 Energy costs in accordance with market prices Construction materials database in accordance with DIN 4108
Life cycle costs, use costs	Construction price database Cleaning cycles Maintenance cycles Building component renovation cycles (BMVBS) guidelines Renovation of building installations (VDI 2067) Deconstruction in accordance with the selection variants Disposal in accordance with waste recycling legislation Thermal or material recycling Cost classification in accordance with DIN 18960
Life cycle assessment	Data collection in acc. with ISO 14040 and ISO 14044 Inventory and impact assessment database (Ecoinvent 2.0, Ökobau.dat, GaBi) Environmental product declaration (EPD)

5.3

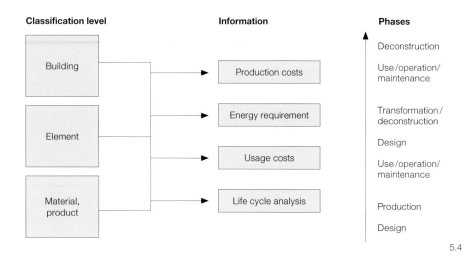

Classification level — Information — Phases

Classification level	Information	Phases
Building	Production costs	Deconstruction
		Use/operation/maintenance
Element	Energy requirement	Transformation/deconstruction
		Design
	Usage costs	Use/operation/maintenance
Material, product	Life cycle analysis	Production
		Design

5.4

		Application in the life cycle phase		
		Production	Use	Disposal
Building physics	Coefficient of thermal conductivity		■	
	Water vapour diffusion resistance		■	
	Specific heat capacity		■	
	Bulk density	■		
	Material class		■	
	Sound absorption		■	
	Total solar energy transmittance		■	
	Light transmittance		■	
	Solar absorption		■	
LCA data	Inventory	■	■	■
	Impact balance	■	■	■
	European waste catalogue (EWC)			■

5.5

Levels	Stakeholders	Activities
Environmental product declaration (EPD) programme	List maintenance: mainly by industrial associations or societies	Organisation of PCR development Invitation of experts and interested groups Registration of PCR and EPD Organising the checking of PCR and EPD
Declaration requirements for product groups (Product Category Rules, PCR)	Industry experts: industry, LCA experts	Determining the PCR: Scope and objective of the life cycle assessment e. g. allocation, truncation or calculation rules Data quality for specific data and background data
	Interested groups: authorities, NGOs, scientists, users	Commenting on the PCR: Evaluation from the point of view of environmental politics and science
	Checkers: LCA and industry experts	Checking the PCR for conformity with the programme, appropriateness and completeness
Environmental product declaration (EPD)	Manufacturer of the declared product in conjunction with LCA experts	Drawing up/publication of the EPD Data procurement Calculating the life cycle assessment indicators Representation of the additional information
	Reviewers: LCA and industry experts	Checking the EPD for conformity with the PCR, apparent validity and completeness

5.6

5.4 Classification levels, information areas and phases in the life cycle of the building
5.5 Data for construction material data and their relevance in different life cycle phases

5.6 Stakeholders and activities involved in creating the EPD
LCA = Life Cycle Assessment;
PCR = Product Category Rules;
EPD = Environmental Product Declarations

wide choice of variants and the imprecise nature of much of the information about the project also create great difficulties in the use of conventional computer programs for drawing or calculating, as they require exact, unambiguous information. The demands of the client for relatively precise information at an early stage in the design, e. g. about areas, volumes, room schedules, functional sequences, costs, development opportunities, programme dates or the likely results of precertification, add to the difficulties of this working approach. The contradiction between diversity of variants and indistinctness on the one hand and the exact information and accurate cost estimates on the other has considerably sharpened over recent years. The client finds a need for more and more information with the increasing complexity of decision making, particularly in the field of property investment. With this need for information goes a sharp increase in the time spent on its preparation by designers and project developers.

The consequences are considerably increased costs in data collection and processing for all participants in the planning, design and construction of a building and an increase in errors through the use of inconsistent data. This leads to a rise in demand for computerised tools and analysis programs to help with the iterative design process and substantiate the design results with relevant information and reports.

Principles and tools

The design team and the client have access to a number of principles and tools that can provide support in integrated design and, in particular, life cycle analysis. The following principles and tools lie within the scope of this book:
• Data, base data and databases
• Information systems
• Element catalogues
• Computer programs
• Tools (in the sense of planning, design and evaluation software)

They are further discussed in the sections below. Other recommended tools, not considered in detail in this book, but nevertheless equally useful include labelling schemes (e. g. for hazard, quality, environmental labels), positive and negative lists, criteria for recommendation or banning, model tender documents, energy performance certificates and building passports. The website www.ecobau.ch gives a good overview of the design tools available in Switzerland.

National and international standards are another good basis for ensuring the methods used are consistent and compatible with others. Life cycle analysis results also find use in certification schemes. The state of standardisation and the DGNB Sustainable Building certification scheme are therefore considered separately at the end of the chapter.

Data

"No data, no business" – this slogan from an EU declaration on the new European chemical regulation REACh sums up the future situation facing everyone with a role in the construction industry. Data are the starting point for every analysis or evaluation process. This data must describe, as accurately as possible, the subject of the design, its functions and all the construction products it contains.

The extension of the period of observation from the production of the building to include the complete life of real estate and the shifting of the focus of observation from manufacturing costs to life cycle costs and life cycle assessment require the preparation of additional data.

The following section shows an example of a data structure that is oriented towards the bottom-up approach.
· Construction materials
· Items of work
· Building elements

The following information must be made available to be able to consider different aspects in the life cycle design of real estate.
· Information giving a detailed description of a building, covering the construction materials, building products and elements, right up to the complete building
· Information to be able to calculate the costs of production and use, the energy requirement and the life cycle assessment of the building

· Information about the various phases that may occur during the period of observation of the building (Fig.5.4).

Construction materials data
The basis for every built object is the construction material or the building product. The building in the sense of an end product is made up of building products. For construction material information to be capable of being used for aspects of a life cycle assessment, at least the following information must be available (Fig. 5.5).
· Building physics properties such as bulk density, thermal conductivity, water vapour diffusion resistance, specific heat capacity, building material class, sound absorption
· Additionally for translucent construction materials: total solar energy transmittance, light transmission, solar absorption
· Life cycle assessment data (inventory and impact balances)
· Data describing recycling and disposal, such as the European waste catalogue (EWC) code, differentiated according to the various deconstruction and disposal variants

Life cycle assessment data are one form of building product information urgently needed for life cycle analysis. The following section introduces unevaluated product information, for example environmental product declarations. They summarise the environmental and health-related information on a uniform basis.

Example: Environmental product declarations
Environmental product declarations (EPD) provide the base data for the ecological assessment of a building. This is currently the subject of the European standardisation project "Sustainability of construction works" (CEN TC 350). EPDs are based on ISO standards and therefore are in accordance with international practices (see p. 95).
The objective of an EPD is to provide credible and comparable data on the environmental and health-related properties of products. The simplification of the procedures has been intended to make it easier for smaller companies to declare in a systematic manner the environmental and health-related informa-

tion about their products. The use of this data in building assessment, product development and environmental communication improves the environmental quality of the assessed building and individual products. Furthermore EPDs also allow purchasers and users to make informed comparisons between products when considering product applications. An EPD does not contain any comparative statements. The whole system of environmental declarations is based on three steps. First the requirements of the declaration of a product group (the Product Category Rules (PCR)) are developed. The PCR are then reviewed by an independent expert and made available for comment to a group of interested parties. The individual EPDs are created based on the PCR and examined again for their completeness and apparent validity by an independent expert. Fig. 5.6 gives an overview of each stakeholder's duties.

Most building products are used with other building products in a system, namely the building. Building product EPDs that also contain life cycle assessment data are therefore a prerequisite for the life cycle assessment of buildings. Life cycle assessments provide a systematic and standardised source of base data with which to create an ecological assessment of a building by means of a modular approach using the declarations for the individual building products (Fig. 5.7, p. 82).

The declaration contains statements about the use of energy and resources and the extent to which a product contributes to the greenhouse effect, acidification, eutrophication, depletion of the ozone layer and summer smog formation. Information about technical properties is also given. This is necessary to evaluate the performance of the building product in the building and includes information such as service life, thermal and sound insulation properties or the influence on indoor air quality. An abridged version contains an overview of the content of the declaration and lists some important parameters.

The wider public is not generally aware of environmental product declarations. Professionals, such as environmental protection officers, purchasers and product developers, make use of them

5.7

Item	1012005228	**Short description**	HLz 12-0.9; 0.24 W, AW, d = 36.5 cm, basement		
Short description GAEB 2000	Vertically perforated brick HLz 12-0.9; 0.24 W/mK, external wall, d = 36.5 cm, basement				
Cost group	331	Loadbearing external wall			
Unit of quantity	m²				
Construction prices	65.1 €	**Average**	74.4 €	**to**	82.2 €
Long description	Vertically perforated brick masonry in external wall, with blocks				
	Masonry unit type		HLZ 12-0.9		
	Perforation type		...		
	Masonry unit format		...		
	Thermal conductivity		0.24 W/mK (acc. to certification)		
	Mortar group		NM II a (DIN V 18580)		
	Mortar class		M 5 (EN 998-2)		
	Basic permissible compressive stress		1.6 MN/m²		
	Wall thickness		At least 36.5 cm		
	Proposed manufacturer		...		

5.8

		Application in the life cycle phase		
		Production	Use	Disposal
Construction costs	Labour time	■		
	Machine time	■		
	Material quantities and waste	■		
	Price	■		
	Separability		■	■
Building physics	R_T value		■	
	Equivalent air layer thickness		■	
	Heat storage capacity		■	
Life cycle assessment	Inventory	■	■	■
	Impact balance	■	■	■
	Water hazard class (WHC)	■		■

5.9

Building component	Building costs		Life cycle analysis	
	Main works (€/m²)	Ancil. works (€/m²)	Main works (%)	Ancil. works (%)
ETICS	60	40	75	25
External plaster	24	12	85	15
Lead sheeting	101	48	70	30

5.10.

5.7 Example of an environmental product declaration (EPD; abridged version)
5.8 Contents of a bill of quantities item
5.9 Data from bill of quantities and its use in different life cycle phases

5.10 Typical figures for main and ancillary works
5.11 Principal sequences of LCA modelling based on the example of an external wall

to ensure their supply chains are more ecologically compatible. EPDs represent a solid base for manufacturers of building products to comply with the information requirements of their users. They are used to consider environmental aspects during product development, as product-related and energy management resources as well as providing basic information about future requirements from climate protection agreements.

Institut Bauen und Umwelt e.V. (IBU) organises the environmental declaration system in Germany. IBU is a producer's organisation open to all interested construction material manufacturers. The IBU's declaration system allows EPDs to be created for all building products. If no basic requirement document (PCR) is available, a group of industry experts is convened to produce one.

Environmental declarations at IBU are valid for three years, after which time they must be reviewed and updated if necessary. All valid EPDs and the associated PCRs are published on the IBU website (www.bau-umwelt.de).

Items of work data
The key element of the building description in the UK, Germany, Austria and Switzerland is the bill of quantities. With public construction projects, all construction works to be carried out on a building must be fully and exhaustively described in a tender document and issued to contractors for pricing by open tender. In earlier times, the information was compiled in various volumes of loose-leaf sheets. Today tender documents are mainly distributed in digital format. Modern comprehensive databases containing over 30000 text modules for bill of quantities items can describe virtually all the activities usually encountered in the building industry (Fig. 5.8). The catalogue contains calculated construction costs or market-related prices. It can be used with the aggregated quantities of the works to produce an estimate of the expected spread of tender bids. Cost calculations in a bill of quantities takes into account the following:

· The labour hours expended at the relevant hourly rate
· Machine hours for plant and equipment used

• Construction material quantities and prices including wastage

This compilation of information can be use to create further linkages. If the construction material information is taken from a suitable construction material database and linked to the thickness declared in the bill of quantities, then the heat transmission coefficient R_T can be calculated at any time in the future. If the construction materials used are recorded with details of their weights, and the associated machinery, waste and transport are taken into account, then the inventory and impact balance data can be calculated. Through this linking of information, a bill of quantities can provide precise base information for calculating:
• Prices
• Building physics parameters
• Life cycle assessment parameters (Fig. 5.9).

Building component data
The cost calculation during the tender process leaves no room for later large-scale corrections, as all the significant details of the building have already been fixed. However, in the earlier design phases, the designer needs information about the more complex building components to allow him to develop time-saving variants and to obtain pre-

cise results. These results should relate to the building component, but still allow calculations to be made for a fully described building.

1. Data for the production phase
A change of data structure is necessary in order to obtain information relating to aggregated building components from the information in the tender document. The classification is no longer based on trades; it must now relate to building components. The classification structure can be taken from DIN 276 (see Assessment of the economic advantages, pp. 64f.). The required works must be prepared from the tender documents at the item of work level (Fig. 5.8). This precisely describes the completion of e.g. the internal plastering according to material type, quantity and machine use. The functional unit in the case of building components is usually 1 m² of area. Exceptions include e.g. balustrades or hand rails, which may also be described by the linear metre. For technical services, the functional units are the cost per m² and per item. Crucial for the quality of the building component information is the inclusion of the ancillary work and materials also required for each building component. These additional works influence costs greatly and can amount to 40–50% of the main works (Fig. 5.10).

The same applies to the influence of ancillary construction materials on the life cycle assessment. Research by Daniel Kellenberger and Hans-Jörg Althaus shows that additional construction materials (ancillary materials, adhesive, fastenings) can contribute 15–30% of a building component's environmental impact [5].
These findings are of fundamental importance to the question of completeness of the building component information. If all the additional materials required for the completion of the items of work are not accurately recorded, then the life cycle assessment may considerably distorted.
Only the component classification used in DIN 276 can localise the components in the building. This provides further opportunities for linking information. For example, the U-value of the component or the Glaser diagram for moisture analysis in the building can be calculated from the heat transmission coefficient R_T.
Individual building component layers can be fitted together by further aggregation to the second classification level in DIN 276. A life cycle assessment (LCA) for an external wall is carried out e.g. in the following stages (Fig. 5.11):
Building level (top level)
• Break down the component into its separate layers

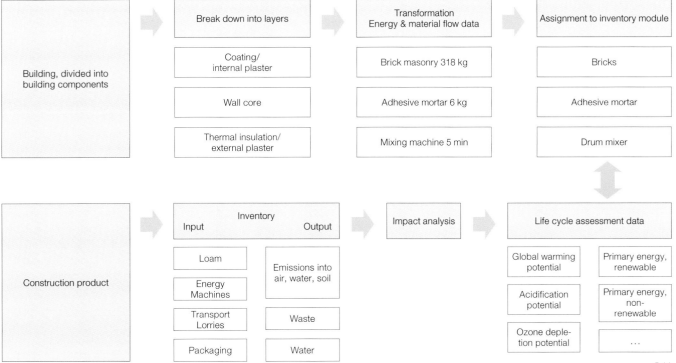

5.11

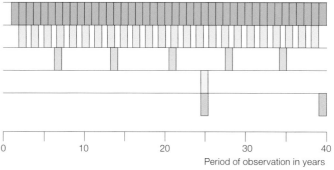

Service	Relative frequency
Window cleaning annually	
Maintenance every 2 years	
Repainting every 7 years	
Renovation glazing	
Deconstruction and disposal	

Period of observation in years

5.12

		Application in the life cycle phase		
		Production	**Use**	**Disposal**
Construction costs	Price/costs	■		
Use costs	Cleaning costs		■	
	Maintenance costs		■	
	Renovation costs		■	
Deconstruction	Separability			■
	Deconstruction costs			■
	Landfill costs			■
Building physics	U-value		■	
	Phasenverschiebung		■	
	Fire protection class		■	
	Sound insulation class		■	
Life cycle assessment	Inventory	■	■	■
	Impact balance	■	■	■

5.13

Non-loadbearing construction, internal

Building component/component layer	Expected life from–to (years)	Average expected life (years)
21. Dividing walls		
Clinker, brick, lime-silica, lightweight concrete, aerated concrete with plaster	80–150	100
Plasterboard on subconstruction: Light metal, wood	35–60	50
22. Internal screeds		
Lime wash	10–20	15
Loam and synthetic dispersion paints	10–25	15
Mineral paints	15–25	20
Oil-based paints and varnishes, latex	20–25	18
Glazes, stains	10–15	12
23. Internal doors		
Steel, softwood, fire protection class T 30, T 90	60–80	70
Plate glass	55–65	60
Plywood, light metal	40–60	55
Simple hardware	55–70	60
Panic locks, door closers, sliding and folding door hardware	30–40	35
24. Handrails, grills, ladders, grids, internal		
Steel, aluminium	60–90	70
Wood, wood-based materials	50–80	60
25. Window sill, internal		
Natural stone, ceramic, hardwood	80–150	100
Softwood, aluminium, steel, plastic	30–60	50
26. Floor constructions		
Floor and subfloors (Bonded screed and screed on separating layer)	60-100	80
Screed as finished floor wear surface: (cement, hard aggregate and mastic asphalt screeds)	40–60	50
Floating screed	25–50	30
Sprung floor, wood	40–50	45
27. Floor coverings		
Natural stone, hard	80–150	100
Natural stone, soft, cast stone, artificial stone	60–100	70
Hardwood, ceramic	50–70	60

5.14

- Calculating the material quantities and the machine times
- Assignment of the materials and machines to a suitable life cycle assessment dataset

Life cycle assessment level (bottom level)
- Creating the inventory balance
- Calculating the impact balance
- Creating a full life cycle assessment dataset

2. Data for the use phase
The distinction must be drawn between component-related works and services and building-related services for the supply and/or disposal of energy and water. The costs for the use phase are classified in DIN 18960 (see Assessment of the economic advantages, p. 68).

3. Component-related services
During the period of use of a building an abundance of building component-related construction works and services are undertaken, all of which have further environmental impacts. These works and services include:
- Cleaning
- Maintenance and inspection
- Repairs
- Renovation, associated with:
- Deconstruction and disposal
- Transformation
- Refurbishment
- Demolition and disposal

Fig. 5.12 shows an example of the different frequency of services during the life cycle assessment and the possible results:
- Cleaning (daily to annually)
- Maintenance (monthly to biennially)
- Renovation, dependent on the service life of the building element (every 5–50 years)
- Deconstruction as part of renovation or removal of the building
- Accidental damage such as fire, flood, improper use (no time frame).

Cleaning, maintenance, renovation and deconstruction work are all foreseeable and calculable. The critical influence on the level of expenditure over the period of use is the cycle in which these operations take place. This information is currently not standardised. By linking the information, a building component can supply precise figures for

- Construction prices/costs
- Use costs
- Building physics parameters
- Life cycle parameters for production, use and disposal (Fig. 5.13)

Databases can be of help in providing of this data.

Databases

Important data for a life cycle analysis may be available to the user from publicly accessible databases The following section identifies some of the databases that can be used to provide data for calculated service lives and the life cycle assessment of building products.

Databases for the service lives of building components

The calculated service lives are used to create scenarios for the renovation of buildings over the period of observation. The databases perform an important function in life cycle assessment and life cycle costing, in particular of buildings with long service lives. Service lives are of great interest in this context.

Base data can be obtained from numerous publications in a wide range of fields. However, they all have the disadvantage that they are not based on a common methodology and the values in their tables are often only compositions of existing data from various sources. Even most of the new tables are based on relatively old data. This creates problems because some building methods and materials have changed greatly over the last 20 years. With most of the assessments of products and materials so far completed, it must be taken into account that in practice a great many components never achieve their technically possible service life (based on their durability). This happens because they either no longer fit in with changed aesthetic tastes or they have had to be removed with an-

5.12 Services over the life cycle of a window component (service life 40 years)
5.13 Data for construction components and their relevance in different life cycle phases
5.14 Examples of service lives of building components (after Appendix 6 of "Leitfaden Nachhaltiges Bauen")
5.15 Dataset from Ökobau.dat database

Dataset: 1.3.11 Concrete roof tiles – Eternit; 2100 kg/m³ (de)

Content: Dataset information – Modelling and validation – Environmental indicators

Dataset information

Dataset core information

Geographical representivity	DE
Reference year	2006
Name	Base name: 1.3.11 Concrete roof tiles – Eternit; 2100 kg/m³
Technical field of use	Concrete roof tiles; approx. 4.5 kg/item; 40–50 kg/m²
Reference flow (flow dataset)	Concrete roof tile
Quantity	1 kg (mass)
Advice on application of dataset	This environmental profile contains the applications for the life cycle stages "cradle to gate". It is based on the directly submitted data from Eternit AG.
Classification product group	1 Mineral construction materials / 1.3 Masonry and building elements / 1.3.11 Roof tiles
	Copyright? Yes	Dataset owner (contact dataset) Eternit

Quantitative reference

Reference flow (name and unit)	Concrete roof tile (usable good) – (usable material) – (mineral material) – kg (mass)

Representivity (with respect to time)

Dataset valid until	2011
Further details on representativeness (w.r.t. time)	Annual average

Technical representivity

Technical representivity including background system	The life cycle analysis of 1 kg roof tiles covers the life cycle section "cradle to gate", i.e. the production of raw and auxiliary materials are taken into account, such as roof tile production including factory operation. The main raw materials are quartz, flyash and Portland cement. The system boundary is the ready to ship product at the factory gate. Transport to the site is not taken into account and must be added to the consideration of the system.

Modelling and validation

Dataset type	EPD

Data sources and representivity

Data sources (sources)	IBU declaration Eternit AG: Concrete roof tiles (IBU-ETE-2008211-D), 2008 GaBi4 software and database

Validation

Review type	Independent third-party review
Reviewer (name and institution) (contact dataset)	IBU

Administrative Information

Data input

Data input date & time	2009-08-06 12:19:33 +01:00
Data input by (contact dataset)	PE INTERNATIONAL

ID

Dataset UUID	6add6215-39c8-4992-92f9-4e17dac04080
Dataset owner (contact dataset)	Eternit

Environmental indicators

Inventory indicators

	Direction	Value	Unit	Proportion
Inputs				
Primary energy, non-renewable	Input	2.35	MJ	
- Lignite				7%
- Coal				16%
- Natural gas				29%
- Oil				32%
- Uranium				16%
Primary energy, renewable	Input	0.0295	MJ	
- Water				45%
- Wind				49%
- Solar (solar energy)				6%
- Solar (biomass)				0%
Secondary fuels	Input	0	MJ	
Water use	Input	0.801	kg	
Outputs				
Excavation and ore preprocessing residues	Output	0.457	kg	
Domestic and commercial waste	Output	0.0084	kg	
Special waste	Output	0.00128	kg	

Impact indicators

Indicator		Value	Unit
Abiotic resource consumption (ADP)	Input	0.00095	kg Sb eq.
Eutrophication potential (EP)	Output	6.22E-5	kg PO$_4$ eq.
Ozone depletion potential (GWP 100)	Output	9.95E-9	kg R11 eq.
Global warming potential (GWP)	Output	0.255	kg CO$_2$ eq.
Acidification potential (AP)	Output	0.000567	kg SO$_2$ eq.
Photochem. ozone creation potential (POCP)	Output	5.67E-5	kg C$_2$H$_4$ eq.

5.15

other component, e. g. they cannot be mechanically separated from it or they are part of the same product or building system.

Published tables must have a compatible classification system, otherwise the service life data in them cannot be used for life cycle assessments and life cycle costings. DIN 276 provides a suitable basic structure. However to be able to properly represent calculated service lives it requires enhancement, for example with function and material levels.

Example: The service life table in "Leitfaden Nachhaltiges Bauen"
In Germany most people working in the field of sustainable construction use the table "Lebensdauer Bauteile und Bauteilschichten" from Appendix 6 of "Leitfaden Nachhaltiges Bauen" [6]. This has the advantage of not having been drawn up by any one special interest group. (Fig. 5.14 p. 84) shows an extract from the guideline covering the field of non-loadbearing constructions for use inside the building.

The service lives are given in the database as figures based on past experience. The spread of values takes into account different designs of compo-

nents, installation sites and loadings by including a minimum, maximum and average service life. Furthermore, the values for every building component layer or component part are given in the case of multilayer or assembled building components, whose individual components could have different expected service lives.

The service life database is designed to be an open system so that values may be added or expanded, for example to reflect new knowledge. The database can be found at www.nachhaltiges-bauen.de.

Databases for life cycle assessment data
Databases for life cycle assessment data contain the results of an environmental impact balance for building products. Some of this information is extended with information from selected results from the inventory. Recognised databases include Envest2 (UK), Athena Ecocalculator for Assemblies (Canada), GaBi, probas, Ökobau. dat (Germany) and ecoinvent (Switzerland) (Fig. 5.16). ecoinvent and GaBi are used internationally in numerous life cycle assessment programmes for modelling building products (e. g. SimaPro, Umberto).

Attempts to move forward with the foundations for life cycle assessments using EPDs and setting up similar databases are ongoing in many countries, including France, United Kingdom, Norway and Finland. It is a very dynamic process, which will continue after the publication of this book. An overview of relevant databases can be found on the web pages of the EU's Joint Research Centre [7]. The website has a search form, which can be used to find the required databases. The user can enter e. g. the country and the sector "Construction" to obtain information about relevant databases.

Example:
Database Ökobau.dat
Life cycle assessment data about building products are an essential starting point for the life cycle assessment of buildings. Therefore the German Federal Ministry of Transport, Building and Urban Development (BMVBS) has initiated a database with the necessary indicators. The database is being continuously extended. Industry makes available life cycle assessment data in the database in the form of environmental product declarations (EPD) (see p. 81). These documents can relate to average or typical products as well as to manufacturer-specific or regional products (Fig. 5.15, p. 85). The data in Ökobau. dat are suitable for analyses carried out in early design or planning stages and for carrying out life cycle assessments of completed buildings, such as is necessary as part of the DGNB Sustainable Building certification scheme.
The database Ökobau.dat is accessible at the German Sustainable Building Council (www.dgnb.de) and from the BMVBS' sustainable building information portal (www.nachhaltigesbauen.de) (for content classification see Life cycle assessment, p. 52).

Information systems and element catalogues
Information systems provide information (e. g. about hazardous substances and construction materials) and can normally be viewed by the public. Linking makes

Country	Database	Link
Canada	Athena Ecocalculator for Assemblies	www.athenasmi.org/about/
Germany	Ökobau.dat	www.nachhaltigesbauen.de/baustoff-und-gebaeudedaten/oekobaudat.html
Germany	probas	www.probas.umweltbundesamt.de/php/index.php
Germany	GaBi	www.pe-international.com/deutsch/gabi
Switzerland	ecoinvent	www.ecoinvent.org
Switzerland	KOB-Ökobilanzdaten	www.bbl.admin.ch/kbob/00493/00495/index.html?lang=de
UK	Envest2	http://envestv2.bre.co.uk/
USA/Canada	Companion LCI Database	www.athenasmi.org/tools/impactEstimator/companionLCI DatabaseReports.html

5.16

Country	Building material information system	Link
Germany	WECOBIS	www.wecobis.de
Switzerland	SIA Deklarationsraster	www.sia.ch/d/praxis/bauprodukte/index.cfm
Austria	baubook	www.baubook.at

5.17

Country	Element catalogue	Link
Germany	Element catalogue	www.legep.de/index.php?AktivId=1069
Austria	Catalogue for Passivhaus elements	www.baubook.info/phbtk
Austria	baubook calculator for elements	www.baubook.at/BTR/?SW=5
Switzerland	Element catalogue	www.bauteilkatalog.ch/11.asp
UK	Green Guide for Specification	www.thegreenguide.org.uk

5.18

5.16 Databases containing life cycle assessment data (overview)
5.17 Construction material information systems (selection)
5.18 Element catalogues for the ecological assessment of high-rise buildings (selection)

addition information available. Additional indirect electronic processing of the information is however not usually required.

Hazardous substances information system
Information about hazardous substances is processed and made available in hazardous substances information systems. In some systems the structure of the information allows the information to be filtered so that the results match the needs of particular target groups (e. g. site managers, occupational health practitioners). Hazardous substances information systems can be used for hazard assessment during the planning, design, tendering and supervision on site of a project.

Example: Hazardous substances information system WINGIS
WINGIS is a freely available Internet-based hazardous substance information system (www.wingis-online.de). It was developed and is operated by construction industry occupational health insurance bodies. It makes available information about the environmental and health compatibility of substances and products and can be used to assess the hazards in connection with their direct use. The information focuses on the preparation and use phase of the substance or product (Fig. 5.15, p. 85).

Construction material information systems
Construction material information systems generally provide information that relates to building product groups and are neutral with respect to both product and manufacturer. They follow the style of the well-established building product declaration matrix. Internationally there are various systems that contain building product information and support ecologically based choice (Fig. 5.17).

Example: Construction material information system WECOBIS
WECOBIS is a web-based information system that in particular provides ecologically oriented information about construction materials. It is directly linked to the hazardous substances information database WINGIS and is accessible from www.nachhaltigesbauen.de. There the user can access environmental- and

health-related information that is neutral with respect to both product and manufacturer.
The environmental- and health-related information provided by WECOBIS covers the whole life cycle of product groups. The advice on the risks to the environment and health from the production, application, use and disposal of product groups is a worthwhile addition to the life cycle assessment data. Information from WECOBIS can therefore be applied in this way to assess the risks to the health of construction workers, building users and the local environment around the site.

Element catalogues
Element catalogues contain descriptions with the complete layer construction of functional units and functional equivalents (e. g. external walls). The information mainly relates to technical features and properties, e. g. in the form of building physics parameters. This allows comparisons to be made between variants within a building component group. The element catalogues published to date have generally concentrated on providing information of help in the ecological assessment of high-rise buildings. The SIA document D 0123 "Hochbaukonstruktionen nach ökologischen Gesichtspunkten" provides an early example of the structure and possible applications of an element catalogue [8].
Typical information – always related to an element unit (e. g. 1 m^2) – contained in an element catalogue includes:
• Primary energy requirement, non-renewable
• Primary energy requirement, renewable
• Global warming potential
• Acidification potential

The information relates to production and renovation within a specific period of observation. The information is transferred from the life cycle assessment and augmented with qualitative information on the processing, use and disposal phases.
The Austrian Institut für Baubiologie und Bauökologie is one body that has published an element catalogue with a comparable data system [9]. In the UK, the Construction Emissions Community of Practice (CECoP; www.cecopnetwork.

org.uk has conducted research on whole-life carbon footprinting in buildings and on embodied energy in building materials. There are also some other examples available on the Internet (Fig. 5.18).
The information from element catalogues can be combined in an ideal way with data on construction costs that are compiled according to the element method and are made available. They create the basis for element catalogues in electronic form and can be further processed in complex design and evaluation tools (Fig. 5.19, p. 88).

Design tools and computer programs
Design tools play a primary role in the planning and design process. Computer Aided Design (CAD) programs are used in the design and realisation of a building. Designers rely on them when producing outline concepts, building designs, construction solutions and drawings. In addition to graphical output, drawing tools give information about volumes, areas and, to a limited extent, component mass. Until now they have not allowed the calculation of, for example, the cost or energy requirements, and therefore the quantitative comparison of variants. Further specific software is generally required to obtain this type of information.
With these programs the design team can calculate:
• Energy requirements
• Construction costs
• Use costs
• Life cycle assessment

These programs assist the designer in the calculation of quantitative data. Most design offices use programs for the calculation of energy requirements and for the processes involved in the tendering, tender award and billing of construction contracts.
Programs to calculate energy requirements are based on the relevant standards covering the energy use of buildings and demonstrate compliance with nationally applicable limits. Tendering and billing software (for which the term "AVA" is becoming increasingly accepted in German-speaking countries and beyond) is used for producing preliminary cost estimates for projects, for comparing variants and choosing the optimum solution. They can also access

Floor slab construction reinforced concrete (RC) C 20/25 (B 25), d = 20 cm, thermal insulation to unheated rooms, polystyrene 120 mm, floating cement screed, linoleum covering

Costs

Long description	Unit	UP (€)	Factor	TP (€)
Floor slab, linoleum covering natural materials 4 mm, skirting spruce, varnished 20/80 mm	m²	38.67	0.800	30.94
Floating screed on floor as cement screed CT 20-S 50, polystyrene 22/20 and polystyrene 100, construction depth 170 mm	m²	28.2	0.800	22.56
Floor slab C 20/25 (B 25), fair-faced formwork, d = 20 cm	m²	94.81	1.000	94.81
Total for 1 m² RC floor slab, thermal insulation, linoleum covering				148.31

a

Ecology
Period of observation 80 years

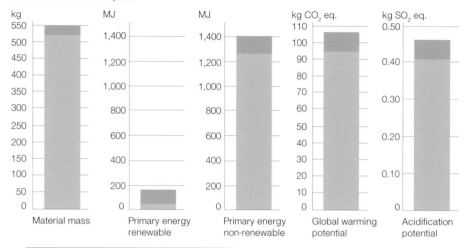

Material mass
527.38 kg

Material mass
542.90 kg over 80 years

Primary energy, renewable:
1.75 MJ/year

Primary energy, non-renewable:
17.29 MJ/year

Global warming potential:
1.30 kg CO₂ eq./year

Acidification potential:
0.01 kg SO₂ eq./year

b

5.19

Country	Design tool	Link
France	Equer	www.cenerg.ensmp.fr/english/index.html
Netherlands	ECOQUANTUM (IVAM)	http://ecoquantum.com.au/
Switzerland	OGIP	www.the-software.de/ogip/einfuehrung.html
UK	Envest (BRE)	http://envestv2.bre.co.uk/
USA and Canada	ATHENA impact estimator	www.athenasmi.org/about/lcaModel.html

5.20

5.19 Datasets from an element catalogue
(example: LEGEP)
a Construction costs
b Ecological impact balance
The white bars represent the bandwidth of
all products within the same cost group,
the green dot the value for the actual
product being considered.

5.20 Integrated design tools (selection)
5.21 Data interchange for an integrated
design tool (example: LEGEP)
5.22 Results of an international questionnaire
(% agreement) among construction
professionals about the current and future
significance of various models of IT tools

external databases that are updated annually to provide users with costing information from the latest tender documents.

Results in the areas of production costs, use costs and energy requirement can be checked empirically (by measuring them). In order to assess the whole of the figures, the design team can provide decision-makers with target and limiting values for the comparison of alternative solutions, e. g. cost parameters and energy indices. These requirements place clearly defined limits on the design and allow clients to check that the limits are being observed, including during the design process, and compare them with existing buildings (benchmarking).
This approach cannot be applied for the time being to life cycle assessment, as the necessary system for the base data has yet to be established.

Design and assessment tools
Unlike the programs described above, design and assessment tools allow the user to create information actively, then manipulate, link and evaluate it. These tools vary greatly in their complexity. Some of them can work in one dimension, concentrating on a single aspect of sustainability, while others are multidimensional and can address all aspects. They may work using different methods and be capable of linking to databases and information sources to varying extents. Furthermore, not all tools are able to create the correct forms of data and documents to fulfil all the information needs, e. g. of certification bodies.

Tools for integrated design
Which design aids and tools are the most appropriate will depend on the project stakeholders, the sorts of issues to be faced and anticipated flow and sequence of the design processes. The recommended approach to the division of the planning and design work is one which makes the most of the possible uses and advantages of the available design aids and tools. Complex tools can be used in this way throughout the whole of the building design.
The use of integrated design and analysis tools that can handle costs and energy requirements as well as the life cycle assessment of a building ease

the task of bringing the quality of the empirically based sectors (costs and energy requirement) into the formal design system and allows the ecological assessment results to be checked for the completeness of the building description. This approach avoids the weaknesses of separate monofunctional programs for cost estimating, energy requirement analysis and life cycle assessment, whose results can only be checked with difficulty for validity.

Examples of tools
A series of different tools have already been developed for integrated design and sustainability assessment that have been capable of being used for the life cycle assessment of buildings, life cycle cost determination or a combination of the two. Some examples are listed in Fig. 5.20.

Complex tools with linked analysis programs and databases
Tools that are linked to analysis programs and databases and at least partially to information systems can be described as complex design and assessment aids. The support of these digital tools throughout the design process eases the task of life cycle assessment

Example: Design and analysis tool LEGEP
LEGEP is a tool for integrated life cycle analysis and provides support to the design team in the conceptual design, technical design and evaluation of any built object. The program and its connected databases can be used to prepare the following calculations and demonstrations of compliance:
• Building description (building component catalogue) and the calculation of quantities
• Cost calculation (construction costs in accordance with DIN 276)
• Life cycle costing (production and use costs in accordance with DIN 276, DIN 18960) classified according to cost type (cleaning, maintenance, renovation)
• Direct energy requirement (heating, hot water, electricity)
• Operating costs
• Compilation of the energy requirement certificate (EnEV 2007 and DIN 18599 for non-residential buildings)
• Life cycle assessment

The recorded project data can be compared with the reference data from other projects, comprehensive analyses and evaluations produced and graphics created. The documents cover the construction process and the future use phase of the building (Fig. 5.21).

Data models, data interchange and data maintenance

The vision of the digital information chain has long remained an unfulfilled promise. In contrast to other industries, (e. g. mechanical engineering), the necessary data interchange between programs and databases has only been accomplished to a moderate extent, even after 20 years of development work. This has led to a considerable increase in the costs of data collection in all design and construction processes, and a rise in the number of errors due to inconsistent data. Different approaches and regulations on national and intentional levels influence data interchange between different programs and databases in the construction industry.

Information models (BIM) for the building life cycle
The demands on buildings and there-

fore on the design, construction and operating processes have massively increased over the last ten years, among other reasons through the expansion of the spatial and temporal system limits. The transition from a construction (description)-oriented to a requirement-oriented methodology leads to changes, above all in information technology (IT) tools. With regard to the increased consideration of the building life cycle phases, there is also a general shift towards more complexity. Fig. 5.22 shows the results of an international survey of IT specialists working in the construction sector. The percentages indicate the importance that these specialists attach to a number of different information models, today and in the future.
And in the medium term, the traditional methods of reducing complexity, i. e. subdividing problems into smaller parcels (design packages), eliminating the long-term dynamic (separation of new build and life cycle) and allowing design teams to organise and allocate the work between themselves (integrated design and network-based design) are not longer capable, when used on their own, of fulfilling society's new requirements. The digitalisation of design processes has brought about consider-

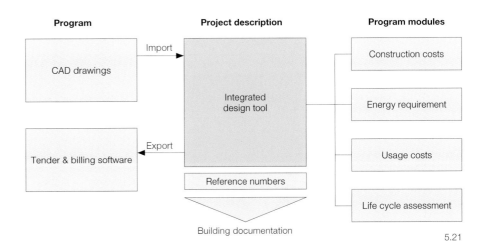

5.21

Function	Information flow	Requirement model	Design model	Construction model	Delivery model	Operating model
Client requirements today	Construction-oriented		10 %	75 %	10 %	5 %
Client requirements future	Requirement-oriented	20 %	5 %	5 %	10 %	60 %
IT tools today	Construction-oriented		50 %	30 %	5 %	15 %
IT tools future	Requirement-oriented	30 %	5 %	5 %	10 %	50 %

5.22

able increases in productivity in some areas (CAD, cost and project programming, communications), but has not always led to a higher quality of design and even less frequently to a better quality of construction. The faster the march of digitalisation, the higher the demands on communications. At the moment this results in further problems, with interaction between project stakeholders being cumbersome and prone to error.

Interfaces
An initial answer to these problems was the attempt to create interfaces between data processing applications. Substantial progress has been made in the field of communication with Internet protocols and browser interfaces. In other areas, such as building technical services, several new standards have been introduced and this has prevented the conclusion of these developments. Data interchange formats for geometric and graphical information (e. g. drawing interchange format, dxf) are not comprehensive or reliable enough, which has always limited their use in the design process. There has been a need for universal interfaces for 20 years, which was reasonably well satisfied with introduction of STEP (Standard Exchange Procedures). In contrast to industrial products, which consist of a number of relatively independent individual components, buildings are more complex, as they have to satisfy many, often conflicting, requirements, have a long service life and a large number of stakeholders are involved in the planning and design process. The complexity of this process is made even more so by many feedback loops and incomplete or imprecise information.

As geometric aspects dominate in the building industry, it has so far not been possible to develop a general drawing-oriented data structure (Fig. 5.23). Researchers have certainly continued to develop proposals for this, such as transferring the ideas of product modelling into the building industry, but their implementation in practice and the development of suitable software have not been successful. In principle there are several possibilities for solving the problem of inadequate interoperability of the tools, including:
• The loose coupling of a number of interfaces
• A universal interface that links all programs with one another
• A central interface in the form of an abstract model to which all applications can refer and through which they can communicate with one another

One such central interface is the building information model (BIM), which is also called the building product model. This model consists of a semantic computer-readable description of a building.
A building is divided into objects that are assigned attributes (properties) and relationships with other objects. All such objects, which are designated as classes, form the Industry Foundation Classes (IFC) and are the current international standard of the large CAD software publishers who are members of the International Alliance for Interoperability (IAI). [10]
In this product model an entity "window" (IfcWindow) contains all the information about a window necessary to describe it, in theory over the complete life cycle. The attributes of the entity

"window" (type, dimensions, components, U-value, cost etc.) are unambiguously described in a formal manner and are used for interchanging information between different applications (Fig. 5.24).
For each phase (e. g. preliminary design) and specialist discipline (e. g. architect) there is a separate view on the object window. An application program for calculating the heat requirement of a building obtains the initial values for its calculation through the central document management system (DMS) from the building information model and exports the results again through the DMS to a graphical interface, which displays the performance of the building at a specific point in time. All the important properties of a building are stored in the building's document management system (DMS) and can be archived or displayed in any number of ways. The central file storage facility always displays the latest version. Earlier versions are also stored there (Fig. 5.25).
The important advantages and possibilities are:
• Complete separation of content and form of information
• Contradiction-free, complete, up-to-date, continuously secure data
• Ability to check the consistency of the project using the model (e. g. check of standards)
• Ability to query the model
• Immediate determination of the effects of a change in one element/ property on other elements/properties
• Ability to display the same basic data in any number of different ways (whatever the type and form of the information, such as e. g. in a hand-drawn sketch)

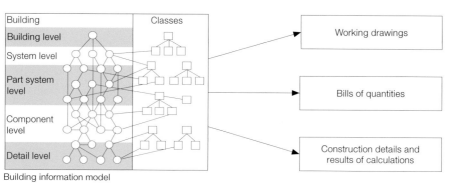

Conventional, drawing-oriented data structure
All information is available in original document form.

Product model-oriented data structure
All information is contained explicitly in semantic form in the product model.
Documents are available as freely selectable extracts from the product model in original document form.

5.23

- Ability to develop a number of fairly sophisticated tools in a very short time and make them available to a large circle of users. The tools only have to be compatible with a comprehensive interface (IFC) and are no longer dependent on having particular versions of particular programs.

Extension of the building information model to the life cycle phases
A first extension is the integration of life cycle analysis and life cycle costing programs into the existing data model. The integration of cost planning and other applications, such as energy requirement, into the model prove problematical. There are already suitable applications in Australia (LCA-Design, www.construction-innovation.info). Work on linking life cycle analysis, life cycle costing and CAD software over the IFC interface is already under way. It must be appreciated that the calculation of the service life of the structure is limited to the state of the description of the building at the design stage. If the various life cycle phases are really to be considered within the building model, then there must be a particular description for each phase (e. g. "building as designed" or "building as built"). This would also mean that the building as a whole "ages" to a certain extent. Furthermore such a model must also take into account the material flows, in particular the upstream and downstream steps Fig. 5.26).

Long-term archiving
Digital archiving has advantages, but it also carries hidden risks. Life cycle-oriented design and management tools, like those now possible with the availability of high-performance computers, make it possible to expand the temporal and spatial system limits and consider all the various life cycle phases in a consistent and comprehensive

5.23 Difference between the traditional, drawing-oriented data structure and the product model approach
5.24 Requirements of the architectural model for windows in the design phase (according to the Industry Foundation Classes, IFC)
5.25 IFC data transfer for the various design processes, stakeholders and their specific IT tools
5.26 The "Building as built" state in the centre of this representation. Each state causes upstream flows (resource extraction) and downstream flows (environmental impacts).

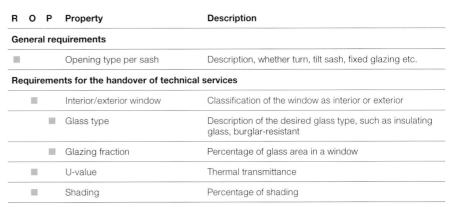

R	O	P	Property	Description
General requirements				
■			Opening type per sash	Description, whether turn, tilt sash, fixed glazing etc.
Requirements for the handover of technical services				
	■		Interior/exterior window	Classification of the window as interior or exterior
		■	Glass type	Description of the desired glass type, such as insulating glass, burglar-resistant
		■	Glazing fraction	Percentage of glass area in a window
	■		U-value	Thermal transmittance
	■		Shading	Percentage of shading

R = requiredt   O = optional   P = possible (by special agreement in the project)

5.24

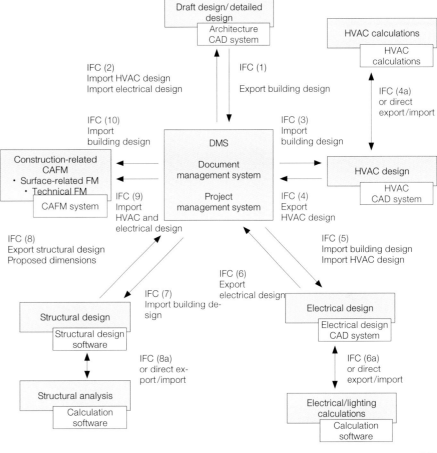

5.25

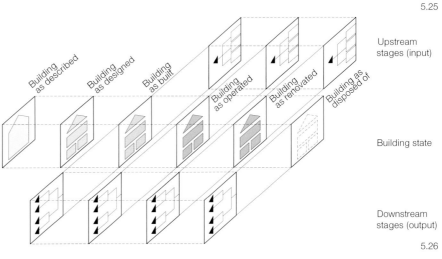

5.26

manner. On the other hand, data can become lost when using computer-based tools, along with the user's information and knowledge. Information may become lost for a number of different reasons:

- Loss due to limited service life of the data carrier (e. g. CD): information disappears
- Loss due to obsolescence of the data carrier, device or operating system: information no longer readable
- Loss due to obsolescence and the disappearance of the application software: information no longer readable
- Loss due to lack of knowledge of the system user, which is the equivalent of loss of craftsmanship skills: information becomes unintelligible

Loss of data can also occur through:

- Incomplete building documentation (unfortunately very frequently the case)
- Loss of building documentation by the building owner
- Missing documentation for the use and renovation phases (due to lack of knowledge of the building owner or there being no requirement)
- Loss of building documentation as a result of frequent change of ownership

The cost to individuals and society of current and future losses are considerable. As with the building industry, there is currently no simple solution to the problem of loss of information in other fields (product liability, product documentation). Steps that can be taken to counter the risk of information loss include:

- Use of a few standard formats (IFC, pdf etc.)
- Print out important documents on a long-lived, durable data carrier (paper, printing ink)
- Ensure redundancy of documentation (by distribution to several stakeholders) to allow the documentation to be reconstituted at least partially in the event of loss
- Distribute the documentation on different data carriers and in different locations, e. g. central server at a service provider, complete documents with several stakeholders (client, architect, building owner/

manager, building administration), on the Internet
- Product liability for owners, clear guidelines for real estate business and PPP projects to ensure the retention of building documentation etc.

Contribution of standardisation

The description and assessment of the contribution of buildings to sustainable development is the subject of international (ISO), European (CEN) and national (DIN) standards. On the international and especially on the European level, the principles, terms and boundary conditions for an assessment of the sustainability of a building are regulated in the relevant standards. The same applies to the description and communication of building product information relating to environment and health. Many people are working on this in Germany.

Standards are particularly important for the content and objectives of a building life cycle analysis. The standards should cover the following aspects:

- The description and modelling of the life cycle of buildings
- The principles of predicting the service life of building components
- The development and use of criteria and indicators for describing, evaluating and assessing the contribution of specific structures to sustainable development
- The contribution of life cycle assessment to the evaluation of ecological quality (environmental performance)
- The contribution of life cycle costing to the evaluation of ecological quality (environmental performance)
- The fundamental importance of collection, processing and making available of product information to life cycle assessment and the estimation of other effects on the environment and health

A short selection of relevant standardisation projects and results follows:

Principles of life cycle analysis

The ISO 15 686 "Buildings and constructed assets – Service life planning" series of standards provides an important foundation for life cycle analysis (Fig. 5.27 and 5.28). The series was

developed and agreed as part of the work of the international standards committee ISO TC 59 "Building construction"/SC 14 "Design life" and consists of:

- ISO 15 686-1: General principles
- ISO 15 686-2: Service life prediction procedures
- ISO 15 686-3: Performance audits and reviews
- ISO 15 686-5: Life cycle costing
- ISO 15 686-6: Procedures for considering environmental impacts
- ISO 15 686-7: Performance evaluation for feedback of service life data from practice
- ISO 15 686-8: Reference service life and service life estimation
- ISO 15 686-9: Guidance on the provision of reference service life data (in preparation)
- ISO 15 686-10: Assessing functionality and serviceability (in preparation)

The ISO 15 686 series sets out principles relating to the following points:

- Description of the life cycle
- Prediction of life and service life
- Determination of life cycle costs in the narrow and wider senses
- Consideration of the formulation of user requirements and the description of their degree of fulfilment

Principles of the sustainability assessment of buildings

The principles for the assessment of the sustainability of buildings are currently under examination in international (ISO) and European (CEN) standardisation projects.

State of international standardisation (ISO TC 59/SC 17)

The scope of the standardisation committee ISO TC 59 "Building construction"/SC 17 "Sustainability in building construction" includes the establishment of principles for the evaluation and assessment of the contribution of individual buildings to sustainable development.

Along with the provision of principles and the definition of terminology for the assessment of sustainability of build-

5.27 Overview of a life cycle analysis, extract from ISO 15 686-5 (2008), p. VII
5.28 Structure of a life cycle analysis, extract from ISO 15 686-3 (2002)

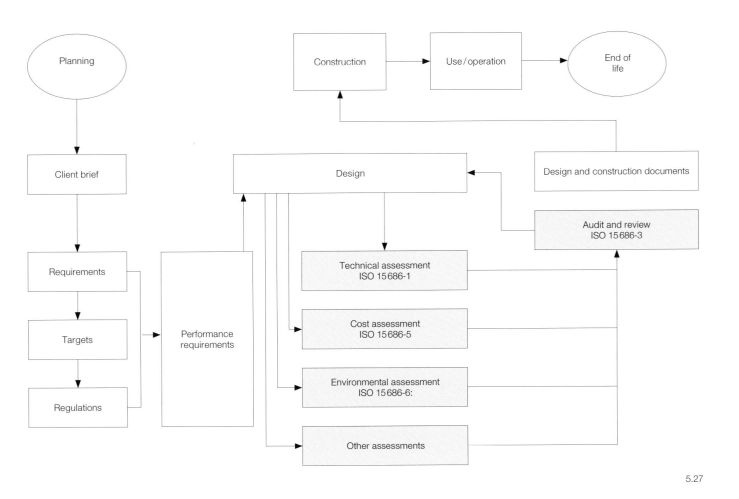

5.27

Life cycle phase	Type of check/audit	Priority	Task and objective of the audit
Project initiation	Pre-commission audit	Key task	Check and ensure that the use phase has been adequately considered in the decision to build and in the selection of the location
Project definition	Commission audit	Key task	Check and ensure that there is adequate basis for a life cycle-oriented design in the preliminary design and the detailed design documentation
Preliminary design	Preliminary design audit	Secondary task	Analysis of the influences and consequences arising from the preliminary design for the rest of the life cycle
Design	Design audit	Key task	Check and ensure that the design accords with the life cycle-related use requirements of the project brief and that adequate information about the construction and commissioning is available to the other participants in the project
Construction	Construction audit	Secondary task	Check and ensure that the intended and correct construction materials and components have been used and whether the installation instructions have been fully observed
Acceptance and handover	Acceptance and handover audit	Secondary task	Check and ensure that the acceptance inspection instructions have been fully observed and that adequate information is available for the operation and maintenance of the building
Use	Use and maintenance audit	Secondary task	Check and ensure that maintenance instructions have been properly carried out and check whether the maintenance measures are adequate
Renovation, adjustment, transformation, change of use	Audit of the renovation, adjustment, transformation, change of use	Secondary task	Check and ensure that proposals/instructions for renovation/adjustments/transformations/changes of use accord with the life cycle-related requirements of the project brief Check and ensure that suitable instructions have been issued for the carrying out of the work Check and ensure that the instructions have been fully observed
Disposal, decommissioning, deconstruction, recycling and reinstatement of the site	Audit of the disposal, decommissioning, deconstruction, recycling and reinstatement of the site	Secondary task	Check and ensure that proposals for the disposal, decommissioning, deconstruction, recycling of materials and reinstatement of the site etc. accords with the requirements of the disposal contract and/or the original project contract and the detailed design Check and ensure that the disposal works carried out comply with the relevant instructions

5.28

ings, advice is being created for the development and use of indicators. The work is based on the three column model of sustainability. The important features and characteristics of the building and its impacts are assigned to the economic, ecological and social dimensions of sustainability. The distinction is drawn between indicators that relate to the location, the site and the building itself.

The information about the assessment of sustainability of the building and the building systems themselves currently concentrates on the description and the assessment of the environmental quality. Principles are identified and advice is available for performing a more precise assessment, but there are no defined benchmarks.

Furthermore, the principles and procedures for the formulation and content of declarations that are used to describe a building's environment- or health-related features and characteristics are set out. The building products themselves are not the actually assessed objects. Instead, in most cases, the environmental product declarations (EPD) represent an important source of information for life cycle assessment and the description and assessment of the building's environmental quality that stem from it. Fig. 5.29 shows the structure of ISO TC 59/SC 17.

Work has begun on the development of principles and procedures for the assessment of sustainability of engineering structures (infrastructure and other constructed assets).

Information on the current state of standardisation can be found at www.iso.org.

State of international standardisation (CEN TC 350)

The state of development of European standards can be obtained from the relevant project reports from the working group CEN TC 350 "Sustainability of construction works". In the context of sustainability of buildings and the determination and provision of building product information relevant to the environment and health, CEN TC 350 represents one of the principles and prerequisites for the description and assessment of the environmental performance of buildings.

The work of CEN TC 350 starts with the user's specified requirements of the building or the requirements arising from legislation and standards. These requirements include:
- Technical performance
- Functional performance
- Environmental performance
- Economic performance
- Social performance

On a conceptual level, the overall performance can be disaggregated into five separate aspects of performance. The series of standards that are scheduled to arise from CEN TC 350 directly concern the development of the principles for the assessment of sustainability of buildings. This assessment covers the determination, provision and interpretation of information that is assigned to the three dimensions of sustainabil-

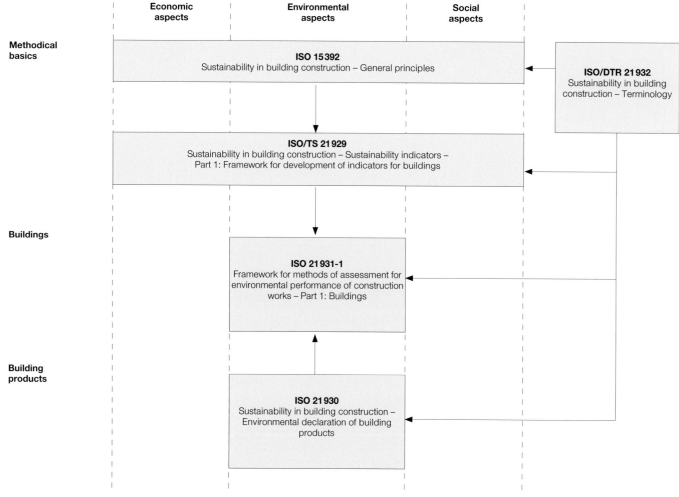

5.29

ity. The assessment does not involve ranking or sequencing, nor a comparison of limiting, reference or target values (benchmarks). This is left to national standards. Three parts of standards describe and identify the appropriate criteria for the description and assessment of the ecological, economic and social performances of buildings as well as the general procedures and principles.

Advice concerning actual principles and sequences of calculation are currently being developed for the description and assessment of the ecological performance. One of the aspects being discussed is the selection and determination of impact categories of the life cycle assessment.

One part covers the use of environmental product declarations as sources of information for the life cycle assessment of buildings.

A separate part of the series of standards deals with the principles for the determination, preparation and representation of the environment- and health-relevant features and characteristics of building products and the basic data used for this. This part is of particular interest to building product manufacturers. Some of its more important content has already been discussed in a separate section of this chapter (see pp. 81 f.).

Fig. 5.30 shows the structure and overall concept of CEN TC 350. The current state of the work on standards at CEN is available at www.cen.eu/cenorm.

Conclusions from the state of standardisation

The state of development in international and European standardisation within the remits of ISO TC 59/SC 17 and CEN TC 350 in summer 2009 can be summarised as follows:

Standardisation is oriented towards the consideration of ecological, economic and social dimensions on the three column model. This takes into account and assesses, while attaching equal importance to all three aspects, the environmental, economic and societal aspects of the design, construction and operation of buildings. Technical requirements and functional requirements / functionality are taken into account in the scope of the formulation of the use requirements and included in the description of the functional equivalents. The subject to be considered and assessed is the building including the site, derived from the sphere of responsibility and competence of the investors or owners. The building and its complete life cycle consisting of the design, manufacture, construction, use, management and end of life can be defined as follows:

- A trigger for a demand on resources and impacts on the global and local environment, as well as on flora and fauna due to the flows of energy and materials, and further effects arising from the presence of building (e.g. shadow, wind suction, heat island)
- An initiator of financial flows (payments in and out) and other impacts on business and the national economy

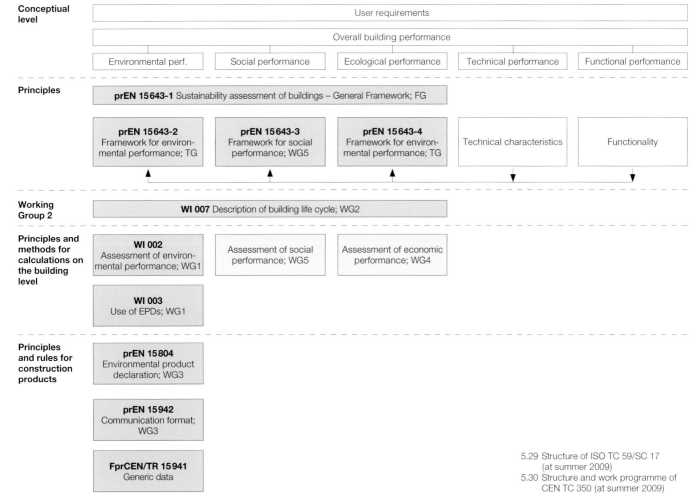

5.30

5.29 Structure of ISO TC 59/SC 17 (at summer 2009)
5.30 Structure and work programme of CEN TC 350 (at summer 2009)

• An initiator of impacts on the health, comfort and satisfaction of the user, occupants, visitors and residents

Also important to some extent are the impacts and interrelationships with the neighbourhood, the settlement or township and society as a whole.

The assessment of the environmental performance of a building should and will in the future be aided by the results of the complete life cycle assessment of the building. Environmental product declarations (EPD), which are drawn up for products, product groups and processes according to the product category rules (PCR), are an important basis and source of information for building-related life cycle assessments. The assessment of the economic performance of a building should and will in the future be aided by the results of the complete life cycle costing of the building. Whether income, value stability, growth or financial risk should also be taken into account is not stipulated.

The assessment of social performance should concentrate on aspects such as indoor air quality, comfort, barrier-freedom, accessibility and safety. To what extent the cultural value and urban planning qualities of the building design should be taken into account is also the subject of debate.

The systematics of the assessment of sustainability and the description of the life cycle of buildings is also determined, including aspects such as calculation methods and basic data. Also covered are the principles and requirements (transparency, verifiability and traceability, forms of representation and reporting requirements). On the other hand, there is no guidance on assessment standards or benchmarks These should be defined in national standards or remain to be judged by assessment systems not regulated by public bodies. In this respect – as it is with life cycle assessment – the determination and assessment of energy and material flows are covered by the standards, but not included in the assessment in the narrower sense.

The description and assessment of the technical and functional performances/serviceability are outside the scope of ISO TC 49/SC 17 and CEN TC 350. European standardisation, however,

allows their description through a representation of the overall result. An aim of international and European standardisation is the provision of principles and main procedures for the description, evaluation and assessment of the contribution of buildings and constructed assets to sustainable development. They ensure the transparency and comparability of the results of different design and assessment tools. It is important that new or further developed tools for the description, evaluation, assessment and representation of the contribution to the sustainability of buildings are in line with the state of standardisation.

Sustainability certification of buildings

There are several reasons for the growing demand for instruments and forms of description, representation and communication of the design and process performance for buildings in combination with themes of sustainability. Designers and construction companies are showing an increasing interest in the development of an alternative to competition based on cost and therefore redressing the unbalanced concentration on the level of design and construction costs in investment decisions. The ideal instruments would be those suitable for the transition to competition based on quality and expertise. In these circumstances labels and certification schemes become indicators of quality.

There is also an interest among the general public in the implementation of the principles of sustainable development through sustainable production and consumption patterns. These approaches are based on the ideas of increasing efficiency. Labels and certification schemes are used here as information instruments.

At the same time, project developers, investors and other stakeholders in the construction, housebuilding and real estate industries would like to integrate the perception of responsibility for the environment and society, i.e. corporate social responsibility, more fully into building and decision-making processes. Should a building not be sustainable or its sustainability not be verifiable, then this would result

in financial risks or possible loss of reputation. It is therefore in the interest of the stakeholders to publicise their commitment to sustainability by e.g. the global reporting initiative, sustainability reporting.

Public authorities and the state would like to set a good example and are looking for their own ways of expressing their particular commitment. In these circumstances, investment in buildings becomes a part of green public procurement.

The principles and objectives of certification are discussed below along with the state of international development. The distinction must be drawn between today's widely distributed first-generation certification methods and the second-generation certification methods that are already mainly based on life cycle analysis. The DGNB Sustainable Building certification scheme is introduced below as an example of a comprehensive second-generation assessment and certification system, along with a view of the possibilities for future development.

Principles

Certification can be described as a process to ensure that the compliance with standards of products and services and their associated production processes can be verified and documented. Certification generally consists of a check on conformity and the issuing of a certificate. This certifies a positive outcome to a compliance audit performed by an independent, accredited examining body.

The certification of buildings combines several procedures and methods of describing and evaluating different features and qualities in a transparent process with the aim of providing the designers, investors, owners or users of buildings with an assessment of the contribution of their buildings to sustainable development. The findings are summarised in an assessment report, usually in the form of a statement of the degree of fulfilment or a points score, which enables a ranking or a specific level of award (e.g. gold label) to be made. It seeks to demonstrate above all, whether, where and how the certified building distinguishes itself from the average or reference buildings. The result has been the development of a process that allows comparisons and classifications to be made (distance to target, benchmarks).

State of international development

The first certification process for green buildings, BREEAM, (BRE Environmental Assessment Method) was introduced in the United Kingdom by the BRE (Building Research Establishment) in 1990 [11]. A first attempt to develop a comprehensive method of assessment was the "Green Building Challenge 98" [12], which gave rise to the GB-Tool developed by iiSBE (International Initiative for a Sustainable Built Environment) [13], [14]. Following on from this, evaluation methods have developed from just having a generally environmentally related orientation ("green") into comprehensive objectives that take into account all aspects of sustainability.

The most well-known of these systems are (Fig. 5.31):
- BREEAM, the BRE Environmental Assessment Method owned and operated in the UK by BRE Global.
- CASBEE, the Comprehensive Assessment System for Building Environmental Efficiency owned and operated in Japan by the Japan Sustainable Building Consortium.
- GREEN STAR, owned and operated in Australia by the Australian Green Building Council.
- HQE, Haute Qualité Environnmentale (High Environmental Quality). The method is owned by the Association HQE. Certification bodies are empowered by AFNOR.
- LEED, Leadership in Energy and Environmental Design owned and operated in the USA by the US Green Building Council.
- Protocollo ITACA, owned and operated in Italy by ITACA the Federal Association of the Italian Regions.
- DGNB, the German Sustainable Building certification scheme, run by the German Gesellschaft für Nachhaltiges Bauen e.V. and the German Ministry of Transport, Building and Urban Development.

A publication by UNEP-FI and SBCI [15] gives a good overview of the current systems.

Certification systems are based on a number of hierarchically structured ob-

jectives, criteria and assessment standards that cover the different aspects of sustainability. Generally these objectives and assessment standards are defined in terms of limiting and target values (benchmarks). The auditing and verification is performed in many cases using existing standards and rules (Fig.5.32).

Fig. 5.32 shows that the examined certification processes are highly dependent on national legislation, national certification processes and the average conventional building performance

(reference building process). Therefore comparison of the results is possible only with difficulty.

All the certification processes employ a system of weighting of the requirements in order to be able to arrive at a simply communicable, comprehensive assessment result. In turn this leads to large differences between processes.

Fig. 5.33, (p. 97) shows for example that with BREEAM and LEED, the environmental aspects are weighted highly (58.5 and 64.9 %), while the weighting system used by the DGNB assumes

Selected assessment and certification systems

BREEAM	United Kingdom	www.breeam.org
LEED	USA	www.usgbc.org
LEED Canada	Canada	www.cagbc.org/leed/what/index.php
GREEN STAR	Australia	www.gbca.org.au/green-star/
CASBEE	Japan	www.ibec.or.jp/CASBEE/english/
HQE	France	www.assohqe.org
DGNB	Germany	www.dgnb.de www.nachhaltigesbauen.de
Protocollo ITACA	Italy	www.itaca.org

5.31

Benchmarks	Definition	%
Against national regulation	Performance measured as an improvement over national building regulations	11.8
Against national codes/standards	Performance measured against national codes as BS, ANSI, NF etc.	4.7
Against national best practice	Performance measured against national industry best practice such as CISBE, ASHRAE etc.	34.2
Against international codes/ standards	Performance measured against international codes such as CEN,ISO etc.	2.9
Against international best practice	Performance measured against industry best practice from another country	2.9
Bespoke rating system	Performance measured against a benchmark unique to assessment system (or a combination of the above benchmarks)	43.5

5.32

Certification system	1st generation		2nd generation
Criteria	BREEAM	LEED	DGNB
Ecological	58.5 %	64.9 %	22.5 %
Economic	0.0 %	0.0%	22.5 %
Social	14.0 %	14.5 %	14.0 %
Functional	5.0 %	0.5 %	6.5 %
Technical	5.0 %		22.5 %
Planning process	1.0 %	2.0 %	5.0 %
Construction process	7.0 %	8.0 %	5.0 %
Operational process	4.0 %	1.5 %	0.0%
Location	5.5 %	9.5 %	Separate evaluation

5.33

5.31 Assessment and certification systems for buildings (selection)
5.32 Type of benchmarks and their proportionate role in existing certification processes. The

percentages are average values from the comparison of many certification processes.
5.33 Weighting for different certification systems for new office buildings

equal weighting of economic, ecological, social and functional aspects (they are brought together in the system into one criteria group). As can be seen, the differences are fundamental.

Based on the comprehensive lists of criteria of the EU research body LEnSE [16], Fig. 5.34 compares the most common processes.

Sustainability certification: top-down or bottom-up approach?

Two basic forms of process can be discerned among the certification systems with respect to methodology, the type and scope of the criteria considered and with regard to life cycle analysis.

Bottom-up process

Building on the numerous predecessors developed particularly in universities and research institutions, the first generation of evaluation and certification systems found successful commercial use in the real estate industry in the early 1990s. The objective was to provide "green buildings" with a unique selling proposition by displaying their ecological performance and through this contribute to their competitiveness and popularity. The criteria and assessment standards were developed to concentrate primarily on environment- and health-related aspects. At the same time, it was attempted to compensate for or augment the missing or inadequate normative or legal requirements with these criteria and assessment standards. The criteria lists were assembled using a "bottom-up" process. Many were developed and completed step by step through adjustment and supplementation. They were frequently focused on the characterisation of technical features and properties, the availability of selected components and systems or the evaluation of selected design and management processes. Weighting systems were mostly based on the findings of surveys of experts. The long-term behaviour was hardly ever considered, while, as a rule, life cycle analysis was not used at all. The relationship between the assessment result and energy requirement or energy consumption of the building is not clear. The result concentrates mainly on the state achieved at the completion of construction and start of use.

More recent developments have led to solutions that deal with the assessment of the ecological advantages of modernisation and transformation measures or concentrate on the description and evaluation of parameters from the use phase (e.g. energy consumption, water consumption, waste generation, and user satisfaction, if relevant).

Top-down process

Second-generation assessment and certification systems such as the DGNB Sustainable Building certification scheme are being introduced. These systems are based on the concept of sustainable building. Since they consider ecological, economic and socio-cultural aspects of all dimensions of sustainability, these systems cover and supplement these dimensions through the assessment of the technical, functional and, where relevant, design performance. In this respect, the approaches and concepts of sustainable building and performance-based building have been amalgamated. The determination and structuring of the criteria take place in a top-down process and are derived from predefined protected assets and objectives. The weighting factors of the main criteria groups representing the dimensions of sustainability are determined on the basis of a convention of equivalence of the economic, ecological and socio-cultural dimensions. There is a clear separation of the building performance (as the actually assessed object) and the performance of the design, construction and management processes that contribute to the building's production, maintenance and improvement. In Germany, process performance is therefore only included in the system as a supplementary item, to make a component available to motivate the stakeholders, in addition to the aspect of the description and assessment of the building performance. According to the current state of the debate in international and European standardisation, the full life cycle is considered in assessment and certification systems and in the evaluation of new building works, and a life cycle assessment and a life cycle costing are carried out within the scope of a life cycle analysis. In this respect the second-generation systems comply with standards.

Third-generation processes

A possible third generation could still fill the gaps in the areas of the assessment of risks to the environment, health and value stability, if applicable take more account of the mutual dependencies between the criteria and overcome the perceived contradiction between double counting and multiple impacts in the adjustment of weighting factors. Furthermore it is important to be able to make adjustments for local, cultural and climatic conditions within an integrated framework consistently, while ensuring the essential comparability and interpretability of the results.

Differences between the building certification processes

The various assessment and certification processes for buildings differ in detail in the following respects:

Scope of consideration

Ecological and social objectives and criteria are generally always taken into account in all processes, while only a few processes consider economic objectives and criteria. Until now cultural aspects, as part of the social dimension of sustainability, have only rarely been taken into account, despite their importance in the context of the existing building stock. The issues of technical, process and location performance are either not consistently considered or not considered at all.

Number of criteria

The LEnSE project [16] produced a long list of 120 criteria, which was then reduced to about 50. Most processes have around this number of criteria. The criteria are usually placed into fewer than 10 groups for weighting. The number of criteria is not always easy to determine. Sometimes the criteria are subdivided into partial or secondary criteria.

Type of weighting, handing of minimum and secondary requirements

The weighting procedures differ as does the division in categories. The possibility of compensating points in one group with points in another has been criticised in many ways.

Consideration of the life cycle of the building

Most processes consider the aspect of service life implicitly or by means of a single criteria (e. g. durability). Only the second-generation processes that are based on life cycle simulations consider the building life cycle.

Type of building

The longest established methods such as BREEAM and LEED have also developed the largest number of specific variants for different building types. The assessment of existing buildings (renovation) forms part of only a few processes. Some processes (LEED, BREEAM, HQE) have also begun to propose system variants for communal housing developments [17].

Time (scope) of certification

In most cases, certification covers new build at the time of its completion. They are extensively based on data from the design and calculated values. Some processes call for an additional or stand-alone assessment to be carried out during the use phase based on measured data.

There are also attempts to consider the criteria in advance – by means of

precertification – during the early design phases. This type of certification in the design or use phase is performed by designers as a special service. To what extent it could be treated as part of design, project management or controlling is yet to be decided.

In principle however, the existing methods are oriented towards the description, assessment and representation of the state of the building in relation to aspects related to sustainability in connection with new buildings or real estate marketing.

As the available assessment processes are voluntary in nature and are based on design documentation, the significance of their validation and most importantly of their warranty liabilities is not great. If however, as with second-generation methods, binding statements are made about aspects of the life cycle (environment, costs, risks), then the responsibility for the performance of these services and the achievement of the specified characteristics must be defined.

Consideration of life cycle analysis, life cycle assessment, life cycle costing

Only the second-generation processes consider these aspects from the begin-

ning. The agreement of the results of a life cycle analysis and the assessments of first-generation certification processes cannot be automatically assumed. The extension to life cycle analysis continues to be the centre of debate [18].

However, life cycle analysis requires considerably more detailed information about the building than the first-generation certification methods, making this extension no simple task.

Agreement with stand-alone assessments, e. g. energy performance certificates

It is possible for the actually measured energy consumption or the information on an energy performance certificate and the results of an assessment certification to differ. The body responsible for the "Energy Star" system points out, for example:

"None of the major green certification programs currently require buildings to meet a set of core green requirements

5.34 Basic features, mode of implementation and issues covered by different certification schemes. The indications about the number of certified buildings can change considerably depending on the source and year.

Name	BREEAM	CASBEE	GREEN STAR	HQE	LEED	ITACA	DGNB
Year launched	1990	2003	2003	2005	1998	1996	2009
Country	UK	Japan	Australia	France	USA	Italy	Germany
Information gathering	Design/management team or assessor	Design/management team or accredited professionals	Design team	Design team	Design/management team or accredited professionals	Design/management team or assessor	Design/management team or assessor
Assessment	Licensed assessor	Accredited professional	Accredited professional	Approved professional	USGBC	Licensed assessor	Licensed assessor
Third party verification	BRE Global	JSBC and similar	GBCA	Assessor in situ	N/A	N/A	N/A
In situ	N/A	N/A	N/A				
Certifying body	BRE Global	JSBC	GBCA	CERTIVEA QUALITEL	USGBC	ITC-CNR	DGNB BMVBS
Mode of implemenation	Voluntary	Voluntary	Voluntary	Voluntary	Voluntary	Voluntary	Voluntary Compulsory for federal buildings
Self-assessment possible	no	yes	no	no	no	yes	no
Rating scale	Pass, Good, Very Good, Excellent, Outstanding	C, B-, B+, A, S	One to six stars	Profile with 14 criteria	Certified, Silver, Gold, Platinum	-1, 0, +1, +2, +3, +4, +5	Gold, Silver, Bronze
Number of units certified (up to 2009)	> 100 000	Approx. 2000	> 50	> 1000	> 20 000	> 20	> 80
LCA compulsory							Yes
LCC compulsory							Yes
Risk assessment							Partial (EPD)

5.34

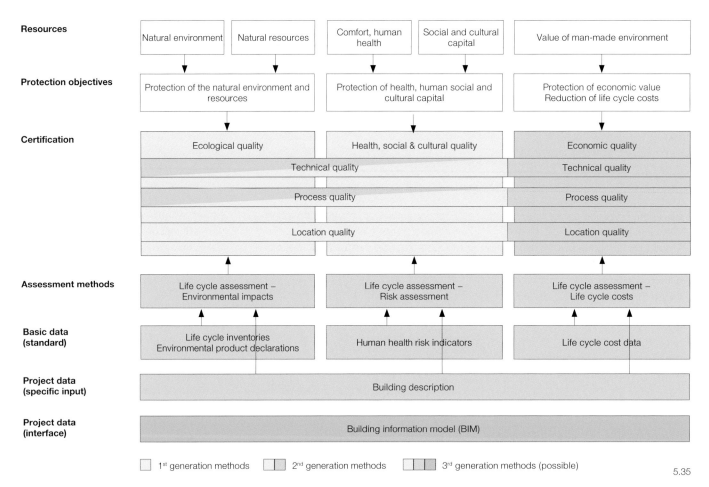

Resources	Natural environment	Natural resources	Comfort, human health	Social and cultural capital	Value of man-made environment
Protection objectives	Protection of the natural environment and resources		Protection of health, human social and cultural capital		Protection of economic value Reduction of life cycle costs
Certification	Ecological quality		Health, social & cultural quality		Economic quality
	Technical quality				Technical quality
	Process quality				Process quality
	Location quality				Location quality
Assessment methods	Life cycle assessment – Environmental impacts		Life cycle assessment – Risk assessment		Life cycle assessment – Life cycle costs
Basic data (standard)	Life cycle inventories Environmental product declarations		Human health risk indicators		Life cycle cost data
Project data (specific input)	Building description				
Project data (interface)	Building information model (BIM)				

☐ 1st generation methods   ☐☐ 2nd generation methods   ☐☐☐ 3rd generation methods (possible)

5.35

beyond code, instead, they allow builders flexibility to meet the green threshold by accumulating a minimum number of points from any of the various categories. ... Consequently, one of the strongest selling points for green construction is reduced operating costs from increased energy efficiency. In fact, much of the 'business case' for green buildings is founded on the assumption that a certified green building will be more energy efficient than a conventional building. ... Unfortunately, it is possible under some rating systems to achieve a green rating without actually achieving meaningful energy efficiencies. As a result, some property owners are now finding that their green buildings are actually less energy efficient than many conventional buildings." [19]

The various processes in future will have to correspond with one another to the extent that there must be reasonable agreement between the energy requirement and the CO_2 footprint values in the use phase, which are presented in the energy performance certificate, and the information and assessments from the certification process.

Comparability of the results
The continuously increasing number of systems and variants make achieving comparability of results ever more difficult. In the field of real estate there is a pressing interest in bringing the approaches together and uniting them. It remains to be seen whether these processes can be successfully fashioned through the competition of existing systems, the international and European standardisation projects, organisations such as World Green Building Council (WGBC) [20] and International Initiative for a Sustainable Built Environment (iiSBE) [21] or initiatives such as Sustainable Building Alliance (SB Alliance) [22]. It is, however, scarcely possible to design the first and second generation processes to be compatible, They are based too rigidly on national standards and verification systems (e. g. ASHRAE, DIN etc.) and have very different scopes and weightings.

Second-generation certification methods
Second-generation certification methods, for example the DGNB Sustainable Building certification scheme, are notable for the integration of additional crite-

ria and for the methods of integrated life cycle analysis upon which they are based. The health risks of construction materials and the aspect of aging of building components can be incorporated by linking with publicly accessible databases (e. g. WECOBIS [23]). The scope of the data required for certification is therefore very much greater than for first-generation methods. The collection of this data involves a great deal of time and expense, except when it has already been created as part of the design process and hence can be made available more quickly and at less cost. If an integrated life cycle analysis is incorporated into the design process then this reduces the additional costs.

Strict element classification and the consequent scalable process create the opportunity of including the requirements of the certification process in the very early design stages, of continuously checking conformity with the objectives and of transferring the method at the end of the design into the facility management process. The life cycle of the building then becomes an integral part of the processes at the levels of objective fulfilment, design and management.

DGNB Sustainable Building certification scheme

The DGNB Sustainable Building certification scheme was jointly developed by the German Federal Ministry of Transport, Building and Urban Development (BMVBS) and the German Sustainable Building Council (DGNB). The system was introduced first of all for application to new buildings in 2009. Development for use on existing building stock and further building types and uses is ongoing. The current state of these developments can be seen at www.dgnb.de. The available resources and tools can be found at www.nachhaltigesbauen.de. This Internet site offers life cycle assessment data for construction products, information on estimated service lives of building components and systems, as well as tools for presenting ecological information about products (WECOBIS database).

Principles and objectives of the quality label

The starting point for certification under the DGNB Sustainable Building scheme is the protected assets and objectives (Fig. 5.35) that were formulated for the three dimensions of sustainability. Proper treatment of the theme of sustainability in all its complexity can be ensured by considering and observing the following points.
- Ecological, economic and socio-cultural aspects
- Technical, functional, formal and urban planning performance
- Design, construction and management performance
- Assessment of the site features

The salient feature of the DGNB Sustainable Building certification scheme is the equality of treatment of the ecological, economic, social, functional and technical aspects, which is expressed in the weighting factors (Fig. 5.36). The process performance is included as 10% of the total evaluation. The site performance is evaluated separately but is not included in the overall evaluation. The subject being evaluated and assessed is the building including the site. This is considered as the trigger for energy and material flows, environmental impacts and financial flows. The complete life cycle is included, both in the physical sense (production,

construction, use and management, end of life) and from the point of view of project management.
The following points describe the essential form of a relationship between the life cycle analysis and the content of an assessment of the sustainability of real estate based on the criteria of the DGNB Sustainable Building certification scheme.

Life cycle assessment
The description and evaluation of the impacts on the global environment and the resource demand for non-renewable energy carriers based on the results of a complete life cycle assessment for the real estate. The following parameters are calculated in the 2009 version:
- Global warming potential
- Ozone depletion potential
- Acidification potential
- Eutrophication potential
- Primary energy requirement, non-renewable
- Primary energy requirement, and the contained proportion of renewable energy

The important principles for life cycle assessment within the scope of certification are:
- The phase model to describe the life cycle (see Design in the life cycle of buildings, pp. 19f.)
- Assumptions for the estimated service life of building components and building technical systems (see pp. 85f.)
- Calculated values for life cycle assessment data (see pp. 86f.)
- Suitable design aids and tools (see pp. 88f.)

Life cycle costing
The 2009 version describes and evaluates selected costs in the life cycle with a direct relationship to the building based on the life cycle costing. According to DIN 276 (2006) this includes the following construction costs:
- Cost group 300 Structure – construction works
- Cost group 400 Structure – services

According to the principles of DIN 18960 (2008) the use costs are listed in the following use cost groups:
- 310 Building services, supply
- 320 Building services, disposal
- 330 Cleaning and care

- 350 Inspection and maintenance
- 410 Structural repair
- 420 Repair of building services

The investment costs for the replacement of those parts of the construction works and the building services systems with service lives less than the period of observation are also calculated. The basis for the evaluation is the cash value of the use costs over the selected period of observation using stipulated assumptions and boundary conditions, which is calculated and included with the sum of the construction costs (cost groups 300 and 400 in accordance with DIN 276). The result is evaluated by comparison with limiting, reference and target values.

Assessment of design quality
The type and scope of the comparison of variants is included in the description and evaluation of the design quality as a component of process quality. The complexity of the approach to the design is audited and evaluated by its inclusion in the life cycle analysis and by an analysis of the comparison of variants as part of building and building component optimisation. This demonstrates that the variants have been investigated and evaluated with respect to their economic and ecological advantages.
The life cycle assessment and life cycle costing are performed using the most suitable complex tools for the comparison of variants. The combined life cycle assessment and life cycle costing allows the apparent validity and completeness of the data to be verified. If the construction and use costs lie within

Ecological quality	22.5%
Economic quality	22.5%
Social and functional quality	22.5%
Technical quality	22.5%
Process quality	10%
Overall performance (building and processes)	100%

5.36

5.35 Scope of the first-, second- and possible third-generation methods. The distinctions between the methods are schematic. Certain extensions (e.g. risk issues) are not yet fully implemented. The consideration of cultural and social aspects is still in evolution.
5.36 Weighting factors for the main criteria in the DGNB Sustainable Building certification scheme

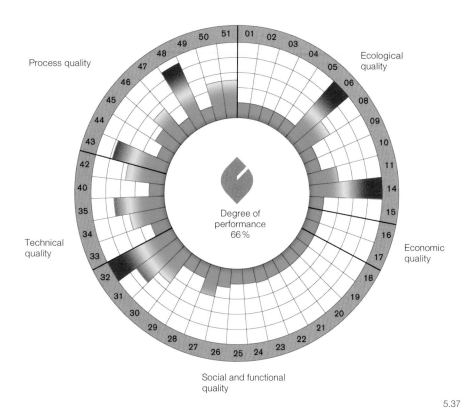

Process quality

Ecological
quality

Technical
quality

Degree of
performance
66 %

Economic
quality

Social and functional
quality

5.37

5.37 Representation of the overall result in the
DGNB Sustainable Building certification
scheme

an anticipated order of magnitude then
it can be assumed that the building
has been completely described. This
conclusion can be applied to the result
of the life cycle assessment.

Added value of the system
The DGNB Sustainable Building certification scheme has long since been
more than a system for the description,
evaluation, certification and presentation of the contribution of a building to
sustainable development. It can also
be used as a:
• Common basis for understanding
the project objective with the client
• Check list for the design
• Tool for comparing variants
• Information source for rating buildings, calculating value and real estate
analysis

The scope of the sustainability assessment performed as part of a certification process should also include the
preparation, evaluation and making
available for use by third parties of
findings of the life cycle analysis. It is
recommended that, in addition to the
evaluation points, the direct results of
the life cycle analysis are recorded in
the documentation.

Outlook
While the first- and second-generation
certification methods continue to be
used in practice, development of the
tools of the future is taking place in research and methodology development
centres. The main areas of development are seen as:

*Development of the energy requirement
level of buildings*
As discussed in previous chapters the
end and primary energy requirement of
buildings is moving increasingly in the
direction of the Passivhaus standard,
net-zero-energy and net-zero-emission
buildings. The consequences are not
only new technologies and building
processes, but also new, life cycle-oriented, integrated design methods. The
massive reduction of the primary energy requirement of buildings in the use
phase, the assurance of user comfort
in winter and summer through passive
measures and the simplification of the
building technical systems are only
possible by the adoption of integrated
design processes that incorporate production. It is expected that energy labels such as Passivhaus [24] or Minergie-P [25] will not be awarded only for
services in the building use phase. On

the other hand, there are processes
that have lost their credibility because
their use is restricted to the fulfilment of
a single set of requirements at the end
of the design process. Life cycle analyses of Passivhaus standard buildings
and the energy upgrading of buildings
to meet that standard [26] show that
environmental impacts during the use
phase reduce compared with the impacts during the construction phase.
This also raises the need for some
adjustment in the field of building
certification.

New buildings or existing stock
From the point of view of sustainability,
the existing building stock is of much
greater significance than new buildings. The management of building
stock and the planning of refurbishment
or transformation works needs special
tools for assessing the state of a building and estimating its long-term potential. This brings to light an increasing
number of constructional, social, cultural and design issues [27]. Building
researchers and heritage conservation
bodies have developed procedures
and methods for the careful exercise of
their responsibilities for existing building stock. Similarly there are a number
of diagnosis instruments that are used
today in the design and management of
buildings. As these methods demand
considerable specialist knowledge and
are very difficult to separate from design services, it remains to be seen to
what extent adjustments can be made
to certification methods that rely heavily
on standards for new construction. At
the same time, more design aids are
needed to support decisions between
renovation, transformation and replacement investments in new buildings.

*Integration of design, construction
and management through building
information models:*
The emerging new communications
and integration levels created by the
building information model (BIM) and
the associated IFC interfaces allow the
multiple use of building-specific information (element formulation, dimensions, room schedules etc.). Life cycle
analyses (life cycle assessments, life
cycle costings, risk assessments) can
be carried out practically on a continuous basis and adjusted for compliance

with other requirements of the certification systems (see pp. 89 ff., Information models for the building life cycle). The breaks between the life cycle phases (new building, operation, renovation, disposal) can be avoided and it is possible to prepare the information in the same sequence as the phases and in a format to suit the user. Continuously updated information and a wide choice of additional information (e.g. about allergies) can be obtained by linking with databases over the Internet. The first prototypes for such systems are already in operation, e.g. LCADesign [28].

Instead of a multitude of certification systems, labels and databases, new performance-oriented methods of design and building management that are based on common agreed standards and are suitable for all buildings and life cycle phases are being developed. They can use detailed benchmark-oriented assessments and comprehensive parameters that can be aggregated to suit the intended purpose. The sustainability certification can be transferred into the "normal" design and management process – there are no longer any "non-sustainable" buildings.

Scalability of the process
LEED, BREEAM and HQE [29] processes are currently used for the certification of sustainable housing projects. These methods have no clear system limits and do not refer to a life cycle analysis of the buildings and infrastructure or to the energy and materials flows, the urban metabolism of a city. If the perception horizon is extended from individual to groups of buildings, then the infrastructure systems, the mobility and lifestyle of the residents, the social aspects (social capital), the city's ecosystem and the cultural aspects must be taken into account. This poses a number of problems with respect to system limits, administrative and political responsibilities, involvement of the local residents in decision making etc. On the level of larger residential developments, communities and cities, there are already processes available to assess energy use and degree of sustainability [30, 31, 32]. However, these processes are clearly moving in the direction of political and social self-organisation and not the certification

of buildings. Certification is as a rule only relevant in the case of new housing projects (e.g. sustainable residential districts) where they are planned and marketed.

This illustrates that the sustainable development of a community, city or region is only realisable through the cooperation of many stakeholders and on different levels. Objectives and stakeholders are different on each level; the problems in many cases run continuously from bottom to top. For this reason, a balance (urban metabolism) needs to be created, which should be as comprehensive and consistent as possible and incorporate the energy, material, financial and information flows. Biodiversity must also be brought into the scope of urban ecosystems. The next step is the investigation of local microclimates and the interaction of buildings, their use, open spaces and climate. In this context the certification of buildings, groups of buildings and infrastructure will require a new approach. Only if pertinent information on material and energy flows is available across all scales of development can objectives and strategies for individual and groups of buildings be coordinated. In this respect, the mainly qualitative methods presented here for the certification of larger urban developments are not capable of being integrated. Second-generation certification methods could in the future be incorporated into a larger system because of their quantitative life cycle base. In this event, the linking of building product models (BIM) with geographic information system (GIS) information would allow full and consistent data integration and spatial-temporal modelling.

References

[1] Wiegand, Jürgen: Handbuch Planungserfolg. Methoden, Zusammenarbeit und Management als integraler Prozess. Zurich 2004
[2] Performance Based Building Thematic Network (PeBBu), www.pebbu.nl
[3] Voss, Karsten et al.: Bürogebäude mit Zukunft. Cologne 2005, p. 154
[4] von Both, Petra: Ein systemisches Projektmodell für eine kooperative Planung komplexer Unikate. Karlsruhe 2006
[5] Kellenberger, Daniel; Althaus, Hans-Jörg: Relevance of simplifications in LCA of building components. In: Building & Environment 4/2009, pp. 818-825
[6] Bundesamt für Bauwesen und Raumordnung (pub.): Leitfaden Nachhaltiges Bauen, Appendix 6: Bewertung der Nachhaltigkeit von Gebäuden und Liegenschaften, pp. 6.11–6.18, Bonn/Berlin 2001
[7] ec.europa.eu/dgs/jrc/index.cfm
[8] SIA Document D 0123: Hochbaukonstruktionen nach ökologischen Gesichtspunkten. Zurich 1995
[9] Waltjen, Tobias et al.: Ökologischer Bauteilkatalog. Vienna/New York 1999
Waltjen, Tobias et al.: Passivhaus-Bauteilkatalog. Ökologisch bewertete Konstruktionen. Vienna 2008
[10] IAI (International Alliance for Interoperability), www.buildingsmart.de
[11] www.breeam.org
[12] http://greenbuilding.ca/gbc98cnf/
[13] www.iisbe.org
[14] Cole, R.J. and Larssen, N.K. (2000) GBC '98 and GB Tool, background.Building Research & Information 27(4-5), pp 221-229.
[15] Lowe, Clare; Ponce, Alfonso: UNEP-FI / SBCI'S Financial & Sustainability Metrics Report. An international review of sustainable building performance indicators & benchmarks. BRE/CSTB, 2008
[16] LEnSE Methodology Development towards a Label for Environmental, Social and Economic Buildings (2008). An EU Project inside the 6th Framework Program. www.lensebuildings.com
[17] BREEAM Communities: www.breeam.org/communities
LEED for neighbourhoods: www.usgbc.org
HQE2R for neighbourhood: hqe2r.cstb.fr
[18] Scheuer, Chris W.; Keoleian, G.A.: Evaluation of LEED Using Life Cycle Assessment Methods. Center for Sustainable Systems, University of Michigan 2002. www.bfrl.nist.gov/oae/publications/gcrs/02836.pdf
[19] Energy Star Newsletter Summer 2006, p. 7
[20] www.worldgbc.org
[21] www.iisbe.org
[22] www.sballiance.org
[23] www.wecobis.de; www.wingis.de
[24] www.passivhaus.org.uk
[25] www.minergie.ch/home_en.html
[26] Kohler, Niklaus; Wagner, Andreas; Lützkendorf, Thomas ; König, Holger: Life Cycle Assessment of Passive Buildings with Legep, an LCA tool from Germany. Tokyo 2005.
[27] Hassler, Uta: Long-term building stock survival and intergenerational management: the role of institutional regimes. Building Research and Information.Vol. 37, No. 5-6, 2009, pp. 552-558; download at www.rbri.co.uk
[28] www.ecquate.com
[29] as [16]
[30] Agenda 21 Web Site of the United Nations Division for Sustainable Development; www.un.org/esa/dsd/agenda21
[31] Association of European Local Authorities promoting local sustainable energy policies; www.Energie-Cites.eu
[32] Kohler, Niklaus: Life cycle analysis of buildings, groups of buildings and urban fragments, in: M. Deakin, G. Mitchell, P. Nijkamp and R. Vrekeer (eds): Sustainable Urban Development: The Environmental Assessment Methods, pp. 348–372. London 2006

Working methodology

The application of life cycle analysis to actual design issues on real projects is a task that demands an expansion of the perception horizons of all participants. Which methods, tools and data are used depends on the sort of questions posed by the design. If e. g. during the establishment of the details of the brief with the client, the question is one of whether the project should be built at all, or whether an existing building could be put to new use, then metadata on the building level should be collected and compared. On the other hand, if an on-going design needs to be optimised, then there is highly refined information already available from which precise data can be prepared and compared.

Top-down versus bottom-up

Conventional working methodologies have given rise to two approaches with which the designer can match the extent and complexity of the necessary research, information and analysis to the issue being addressed.
- Top-down
- Bottom-up

Top-down approach
The top-down approach (Fig. 6.1) makes it possible, on the basis of highly aggregated indices, to generate guidance values for an actual project. The results can provide the foundation for investment decisions. Depending on the composition and content of the information source used (tables, databases), the data can be adjusted to varying extents to provide the necessary answers. While smaller architec-

tural practices make use of generally accessible publications, larger companies maintain their own databases with values compiled from experience. A housing association with a large building stock, for example, plans to build some new housing blocks. The association's internal database contains the following data:
- Construction costs per m² gross floor area (GFA) for 80-unit blocks
- Data age: 3-25 years
- Energy standard of the building: WSVO 82–EnEV 2003

The calculated building cost and its operating cost are required for an observation period of 15 years.
In order to be able to provide correct information, the construction costs are projected to present day levels. The German federal statistics office (Statistisches Bundesamt) publishes flat-rate net asset value indices for this purpose [1]. Three additional costs for increased thermal insulation in accordance with EnEV 2009 or for more efficient building technical services systems can only be estimated.

The top-down approach does not allow the assessment of innovations, as there is no information about them in the data pool, nor is it suitable for evaluating variants at the level of detailed changes, as the aggregated parameters only permit decisions of principle. The data pool is subject to aging, which means that the data upon which a decision is made may have changed considerably over as little as three to five years as a result of the high speed of innovation in the industry. The German Energy Conservation Regulations (EnEV), for exam-

ple, are currently being upgraded every three years, which has reduced the permissible energy requirement for new buildings by 20–30 % on each occasion. Therefore after about five years, new buildings can no longer be used to provide base data for considerations of building type, building technology, construction cost or services media supply and disposal costs.

Bottom-up approach
The bottom-up approach (Fig. 6.2) is used, in addition to deciding between different building variants, for considering certain limited issues, e. g. for selecting between different constructional solutions. Calculating the construction costs and energy requirement for a completed building certificate using separate computer programs is usually too time consuming and uneconomic. In the example of the residential block mentioned above, the new building was first drawn up as a feasible variant (compliant with the currently applicable EnEV) and assessed.
For other variants, the energy requirement is then reassessed and the additional costs estimated, e. g.:
- Variant with 20 % lower energy requirement
- Variant with additional use of a pellet-fired combined heat and power plant

Both approaches, top-down and bottom up, have been in use for decades. However, they have changed considerably with the development of high-capacity computers and the available databases. The limit to the amount of data that could be managed economically has been removed for the top-down approach. This means the current parameters for completely described buildings can be generated at very little cost. In addition, the building can be modified to satisfy any specific requirement by the replacement of or addition of building components.

The prerequisite for this in every case is the complete description of the building using the bottom-up method and the continuing availability of these data (Fig. 6.3). In order to be able to ensure the completeness of the building description, every level of the description must take into account the modular construction of the building, its components, layers and materials. The structure of the description must, on the one hand, permit anything from highly aggregated elements up to complete building components, and, on the other hand, the dismantling of these elements into their smallest constituent parts, e. g. all the materials used, to be able to trace the interactions and the reasons for them. Scalability of the data is essential for this (see Design in the life cycle of buildings, p. 21). The completely modular descriptions of buildings are stored in databases.

Ensuring comparability

In order to be able to compare buildings with respect to their performance data by means of indices, then the buildings must be classified according to use type.

In Germany the classification system used by the German federal statistics office (Statistisches Bundesamt) divides construction works into two groups; structures and civil engineering works [2]. Structures are further subdivided into buildings and other structures; buildings are in turn divided into the two subgroups; residential buildings and non-residential buildings. The classification system used by the building and construction authorities of the German federal states is explained in the building classification catalogue (Bauwerkszuordnungskatalog (BWZK)). This catalogue is published by the building committee of a working group of German states (LAG) under the supervision of the building ministers' conference, a consortium of ministers and senators responsible for urban planning, construction and housing in Germany's 16 states, known as the ARGE-BAU. 6.4, p. 106) [3]. This catalogue

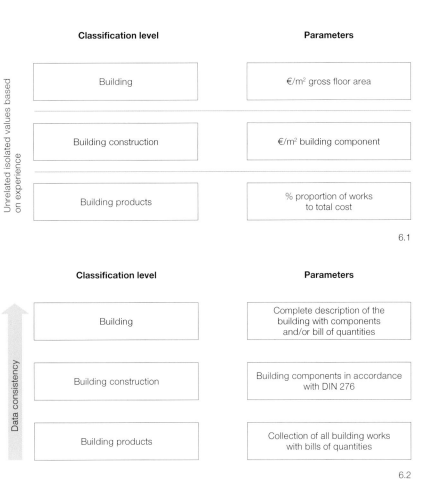

6.1

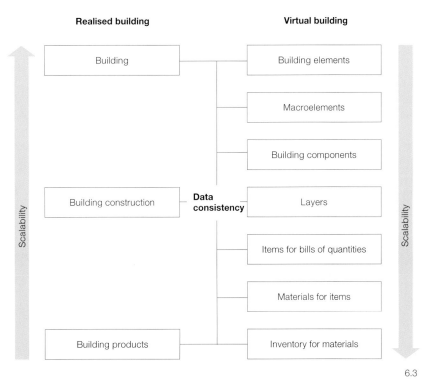

6.2

6.3

Procedures for life cycle design
6.1   Top-down approach
6.2   Bottom-up approach
6.3   Complete scalability of all data in
         every phase of work

No.	Building types
10000	Parliament, justice and administration buildings
20000	Scientific teaching and research buildings
30000	Health service buildings
40000	Schools
50000	Sports buildings
60000	Housing/communal buildings
70000	Production, distribution, maintenance and storage buildings
80000	Technical buildings
90000	Other types of buildings

6.4

6.4 Classification of the ARGEBAU building classification catalogue
6.5 Heinrich Böll Siedlung, Berlin: Plan 1st/2nd floors and ground floor, scale 1:400
6.6 General view
6.7 Street view

considers mainly public authority property. It differentiates only to a limited extent between commercial structures and residential buildings. Furthermore the catalogue is not used in the same way in all the federal states.

The building classification catalogue is very important as its classification is referred to in documentation, standards and rules, e. g. in the calculation of the standard construction costs for a property valuation procedure. The standard construction cost catalogue published by the German Federal Ministry of Transport, Building and Urban Development (BMVBS) provides its users with data for valuing buildings in Germany [4].

Additionally, the uses are listed according to building groups, and area- and requirement-related indices provided for electricity requirement etc. in the supplement to DIN 18599 "Energy efficiency of buildings". The assignment of the building to a specific use group also allocates various parameters that are of crucial importance in the subsequent calculation of limiting values of the reference building.

Important international building certification systems, such as LEED, BREEAM or the DGNB Sustainable Building certification scheme (see Tools for integrated design, pp. 96f.) are developed in a similar way specifically for particular buildings and use types, and assign the building being assessed to a building class.

Boundary conditions of the assessments

As explained in the previous chapters, different scenarios, databases and reference values for parameters may be selected and used for the calculation of life cycle costs and life cycle assessments. A precise description of the input variables and boundary conditions of the assessment is therefore of critical importance for the evaluation of the values by third parties.

The following boundary conditions were applied for the assessments of the buildings discussed in this chapter:
- The system limit is the building and its components:
  – Cost groups 300 and 400 in accordance with DIN 276 (see Assessment of the economic advantages, pp. 64f.).
- Period of observation:
  – For residential buildings, 80 years
  – For office buildings, 50 years
  – For industrial buildings, 15 years
- Information about cycles:
  – Cleaning cycles in accordance with life cycle costs in the DGNB Sustainable Building certification scheme (DGNB)
  – Renovation cycles for building elements in the sustainable building guide "Leitfaden Nachhaltiges Bauen" published by the German Federal Ministry of Transport, Building and Urban Development (BMVBS)
  – Renovation cycles for technical systems in accordance with VDI 2067
- Additional assumptions for the life cycle costing (LCC):
  – Cost groups included: production, services media supply and disposal, cleaning, maintenance, renovation
  – Prices for media: in accordance with BMVBS tables
  – Energy price increase: 4 % per year
  – Construction cost increase: 2 % per year
  – Discount rate 5.5 % (nominal) or 3.5 % (real)
  – Present value over all life cycle phases
- Additional assumptions for the life cycle assessment (LCA):
  – Phases included: upstream steps, production of the building, renovation, disposal, media supply and disposal

  – Not taken into consideration: transport, waste, cleaning process, supply and disposal with water
  – Fuel mix: Germany
  – Ecology database: GaBi (project NiroSan Production Hall, Schmiedefeld) or ecoinvent 2.0 (all other projects)
- Assumed disposal scenarios for the deconstruction and disposal phases (end of life, (EOL)):
  – Mineral construction materials: material recycling
  – Metal/glass: material recycling
  – Synthetic construction materials: material recycling, incineration
  – Plant-based construction materials: material recycling
  – Paper, cardboard: thermal recycling, incineration
  – Paints: residues taken to landfill
  – No credit for recycling potential, balancing at lowest energy point of recycling. Another scenario was used in the example of the NiroSan Production Hall (see p. 120). The metal recycling potential for this project was included in the assessment.

Project comparison

The buildings discussed on the following pages are intended to illustrate the use of life cycle design in various design situations:
- Heinrich Böll Siedlung, Berlin: New housing – development of construction alternatives
- Normand Barracks, Speyer: Existing housing – decision to demolish or convert, energy standards
- Lebenshilfe, Lindenberg im Allgäu: New commercial building and offices – decision between a standard building design and solar building project
- NiroSan Production Hall, Schmiedefeld: New industrial building – development of energy variants
- Barnim Administration Centre, Eberswalde: New office building – energy-optimised construction (EnOB) project, integrated design, certification.

All projects have been reassessed using the above-described 2009 boundary conditions. The prices used for the calculation of the production costs, energy process and follow-on costs are based on the current values.

Example 1: Life cycle cost-oriented variant comparison – Heinrich Böll Siedlung, Berlin

In 1992, the Gemeinnützige Siedlungs- und Wohnungsbaugesellschaft (GSW), a communal housing association in Berlin, decided to build an ecologically oriented residential development with around 650 housing units on a large plot in Berlin-Pankow (Figs. 6.5–6.7). The new buildings were to be built as part of the programme to satisfy the city's social housing need. At the same time, the project also sought to undertake a critical examination of the conventional approach to the design and construction of housing. Architects Architektengemeinschaft Brenne-Eble (Berlin) were awarded the commission and instructed to carry out a preliminary study. The study was to examine the potential for the ecological measures that could be implemented within the economic constraints of the social housing programme in Berlin.

Design concept

The ordinary standard construction (variant 1) in sand-lime brick masonry units with an external thermal insulation composite system (ETICS) for the external walls, concrete ceiling slabs and timber truss gable roof with mineral fibre insulation – complying with the insulation standards of the time – was to be compared with two further variants. The concept for variant 2 was to have the objective of achieving an improved standard of thermal insulation for the external walls and other areas of the building envelope. In particular, the simplified, single-skin construction of the external walls and the roof was to be augmented with additional thickness of insulation. This variant was to improve on the thermal insulation ordinance (WSVO) by 20 %.

Variant 3 would ascertain the extent to which it would be possible, within the constraints of the social housing budget, to take additional measures to improve the life cycle assessment of the buildings. The construction for this variant would also comprise a single-skin masonry unit wall, but in this case incorporating a mineral aggregate with the very low coefficient of thermal conductivity of 0.13 W/mK. The separating ceilings were designed as a stacked

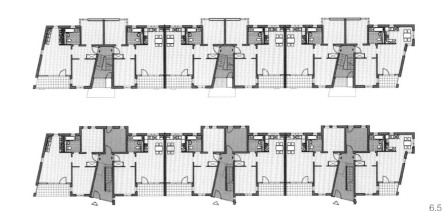

6.5

6.6

6.7

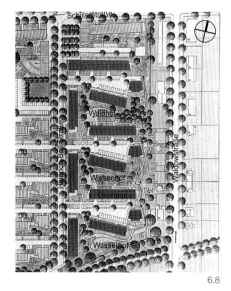

6.8

plank and concrete top slab construction, while the external and internal walls in the top storey were also designed as stacked planks. The internal walls on all storeys were given a internal coating of loam plaster, which was finished with a paint based on renewable raw materials. The technical fitting-out included water-saving wall heating systems.

As part of the scope of the initial feasibility study, the construction costs, life cycle costs, energy requirement and life cycle assessment were calculated for all three options. The investigations and calculations prove that the higher investment for the additional measures are amortised over a long period according to the life cycle phases of the building.

As a result of these findings and based on the building designs and calculations, twelve blocks were completed in a second phase, among which one (a north-south block with 24 apartments, of which 19 were three-bedroomed, 3 two-bedroomed and 2 single-bedroomed units) was of the variant 3 design (Fig. 6.8). The photovoltaic system installed on the roofs of the development was Berlin's largest at the time. 6.6, p. 107).

Documentation

In view of the new building materials and techniques, the construction phase was documented, with special attention being paid to cost trends and any problems encountered in the course of construction. A support and measurement phase was instigated after the first occupancy period in 1999 in selected apartments in variants 1 and 3. This involved the determination of the energy consumption and the heating and ventilation conditions in the differently constructed buildings.

The concept phase in 1995, with its considerable expenditure on calculations and simulations, showed that buildings could only be analysed in future at a reasonable cost using integrated software for cost determination, life cycle costing, calculation of energy requirement and life cycle assessment. The foundations for such software were laid down with extended databases during the research project looking into life cycle design for buildings from an ecological point of view or "Lebenszyklusplanung für Gebäude unter ökologischen Gesichtspunkten (LEGOE)" undertaken by the German federal foundation for the environment, the Deutsche Bundesstiftung Umwelt (DBU). The Heinrich Böll Siedlung development was assessed in 2002 and the three variants compared. By that time actual figures for the first year of use were available for the analysis

(construction and energy costs), which allowed an initial credibility check to be carried out on the results of the calculations. The results of the database-based cost calculations were identical with the billed construction costs.

In the comparison of the life cycle costs for the three variants, the advantage of the improved building envelope showed itself in the clearly lower operating costs. The long-term economic viability of variant 3 was also apparent from the almost 25% better net present value compared to variant 1 (Figs. 6.9 and 6.10). If today's energy and construction prices are used as the basis for the assessment of all three variants, then the static amortisation period for variant 3 is less than ten years (Fig. 6.11). The client had selected this static method of calculation for the assessment even though this approach does not take into account the economic effect of late-onset material flows (see Assessment of the economic advantages, pp. 71f.). Variant 3 exhibits three clear advantages in the life cycle assessment over a use period of 80 years. The assessment takes into account all expenditure for use, deconstruction and disposal (Fig. 6.12).

Variant 3 performs the best with all indicators. The difference is between 10–15%. To bring out this information clearly, with identical volumes and areas and similar specified performance figures reflecting the narrow economic room for manoeuvre, the building description and evaluation must be undertaken carefully and precisely.

Summary

The high quality residential development Heinrich Böll Siedlung sets an impressive

Values in €	Variant 1 (standard)	Variant 2 (improved thermal insulation)	Variant 3 (improved life cycle assessment)
Gross floor area (GFA) in m²	2897	2897	2897
New building costs (CG 3 and 4) incl. other costs	1803117	1959348	2135999
per m² GFA	622.41	676.34	737.31
Cleaning costs/year	29558	33302	30392
per m² GFA	10.20	11.50	10.49
Operating costs/year	46190	38345	26200
per m² GFA	15.94	13.24	9.04
Renovation costs/year	30165	32167	29624
per m² GFA	10.41	11.10	10.23
Maintenance costs/year	3241	3401	3501
per m² GFA	1.12	1.17	1.21
Net present value	7821148	7361134	6226829
per m² GFA	2699.74	2540.95	2149.41

6.9

standard. The selection of materials and construction makes a considerable contribution to reducing CO_2 emissions. The ten-year-old building accords with today's policy requirements and current legislative limits.

The expectations of all the project participants about the reduction of time spent on the life cycle design were fulfilled through the use of suitable software. The digital modelling of the three variants required the following:

- Capturing the dimensions of the surface of all building components: 3 man-days
- Assignment to the element catalogue: 1 man-day
- Creation of special construction elements for the different residential unit types with construction materials,

specification and bill of quantities information and layer elements: 5 man-days
- Evaluation of the results: 2 man-days
- Summarise and report: 3 man-days

Project data for Heinrich Böll Siedlung
- Building: Heinrich Böll Siedlung
- Location: Berlin-Pankow
- Client: Gemeinnützige Siedlungs- und Wohnungsbaugesellschaft (GSW), Berlin
- Architect: Architektengemeinschaft Brenne-Eble, Berlin
- In collaboration with: Franz Jaschke
- Construction: 1999
- Use: multistorey housing
- No. of floors: 4

Volumes and areas (1 block):
- Enclosed volume: 8608 m³
- Thermally conditioned volume: 6687 m³
- Gross floor area (GFA): 2896 m²
- Area occupied by construction elements e. g. walls etc.: 579 m²
- Net floor area: 2317 m²
- Circulation area: 150 m²
- Technical systems area: 60 m²
- Usable area (UA): 2108 m²
- Ancillary use area: 0 m²
- Residential area: 1661 m²
- Efficiency: UA/GFA = 0.73
- Heat transfer envelope area: 2970 m²
- A/V ratio: 0.44

- Analysis software: LEGEP

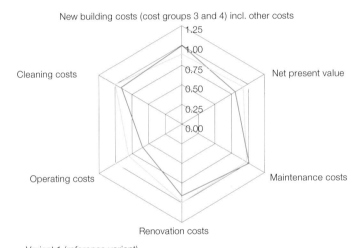

Variant 1 (reference variant)
Variant 2 (improved thermal insulation)
Variant 3 (improved life cycle assessment)

6.10

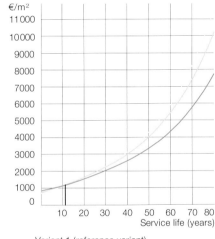

Variant 1 (reference variant)
Variant 2 (improved thermal insulation)
Variant 3 (improved life cycle assessment)

6.11

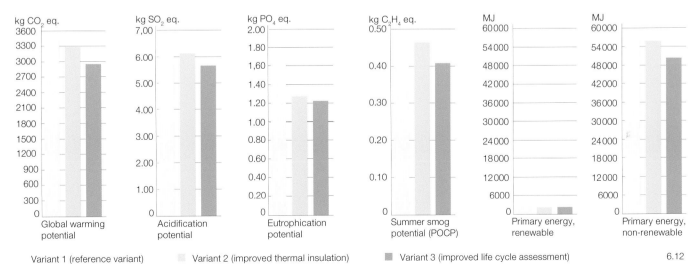

Variant 1 (reference variant)　　Variant 2 (improved thermal insulation)　　Variant 3 (improved life cycle assessment)

6.12

6.8　Heinrich Böll Siedlung, Berlin: layout plan
6.9　Life cycle costs for the three variants. Colour-shaded cells indicate the most favourable variant.

6.10　Relative comparison of life cycle costs
6.11　Comparison of life cycle costs (static amortisation period) of the three variants

6.12　Results of the life cycle assessment over a period 80 years (per m² GFA)

109

6.13

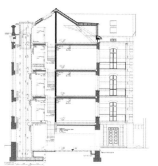

6.13 Normand Barracks, Speyer:
 Layout plan (situation after alterations)
 scale 1:600
6.14 Section (situation after alterations)
 scale 1:600
6.15 Facade elevation
6.16 General view after alterations
6.17 Strategic options and basis for decisions for
 existing properties
6.18 Requirements of EnEV 2009 for the
 thermal insulation of the building envelope

6.14

Example 2:
Renovation strategies –
Normand Barracks, Speyer

Following the withdrawal of the French military forces, the majority of the buildings of the old barracks dating back to the 19th century in Speyer were taken down. The soldiers' quarters, which was built in 1888, had been retained and was a listed building. The difficulty facing the investor was how to develop a marketable residential property with the very few interventions in the building fabric tolerated by the conservation authorities (Figs. 6.13–6.16).

The retention of the external facing brick facade presented a particular challenge. The listed building would not have to meet the requirements of the German Energy Conservation Regulations (EnEV), but would still have to comply with the even more stringent energy standards of the government-owned KfW development bank and the associated CO_2 emission reduction requirements in order to receive favourable grants. Since the external facade could not be altered, the design team had to develop complex building physics solutions and monitor the site work to ensure their correct implementation.

Strategic design

The strategic design was to include consideration of the following scenarios that correspond with the conventional options applicable for existing buildings (Fig. 6.17):
• Sale
• Deconstruction
• Renovation
• Modernisation

Each aspect contains further, more detailed options:
• Deconstruction: not replaced, or replaced by new buildings
• Renovation: remediation of the security defects or full resolution of the whole renovation backlog
• Modernisation: energy modernisation or extension by structural modernisation

Sale

The possible sale price of a property (current market or marketable value) is determined by a valuation. This may be ascertained using comparison, depre-

6.15

6.16

Strategies	Variants	Basis for decisions (supported by software and database)			
		Billing / manual	Building data	Building documentation	Additional evaluation
Sale	Sale	Estimated price			
Deconstruction	Deconstruction, demolition without replacement		Deconstruction costs	Deconstruction B of Q Landfill quantities	
	Deconstruction and new build	Construction costs / m³	Demolition and new build costs	Deconstruction B of Q Landfill quantities	
Renovation (Basis: technical diagnosis)	Safety defects only	Safety-relevant elements	Renovation costs	Plan of works	Rent risk
	Extensive renovation		Renovation costs	Plan of works	Reference solution
Modernisation / use options	Energy modernisation	Rent apportionment	Construction costs	Plan of works	Cost-utility analysis
	Structural modernisation	Rent increase	Construction costs	Plan of works	Cost-utility analysis

6.17

ciated replacement cost or investment capitalisation valuation methods. The depreciated replacement cost is used for parcels of land with buildings that provide rental or lease income (e.g. multiple dwelling units). The valuations are based on the German Federal Ministry of Transport, Building and Urban Development (BMVBS) guidelines [5]. In the case of the Speyer residential development, this option was not followed through because of the serious value reduction factors represented by the poor state of the buildings and the conditions imposed by the conservation legislation.

Deconstruction (demolition without replacement)
This option was not taken further because of the listed building requirement to retain the building.

Deconstruction with replacement with new building
This variant was evaluated for comparative purposes. The demolition cost for the whole volume and disposal costs for the residual construction materials were calculated based on local conditions. To this was added the cost of a new building based on a multiple dwelling unit with the same gross floor area. This cost was checked for apparent validity against a cost calculated on the basis of conventional construction estimation rates. In order to be able to carry out a life cycle cost comparison, the use phase costs of the new building over the period of observation – 80 years for residential buildings – have to be included in the calculations.
In addition to the costs, the environmental impact of these measures must be

determined over the same period (Figs. 6.22 and 6.23, p. 112).

Renovation of the existing building
Extensive renovation of the existing building is required for this variant. This variant is no longer permissible today, as the revised German Energy Conservation Regulations (EnEV) 2009 require energy improvement measures to be incorporated in projects involving comprehensive modernisation of roofs and facades. The building component requirements of EnEV (Fig. 6.18) apply if at least 20% of a building component is changed. This means that all the windows on a building must be replaced if more than 10 m² out of a total of 50 m² of window area are replaced. If the roof is recovered than the whole area must be insulated.
A calculation of the heat requirement should make it clear to the building occupant that the high energy costs reduce the value of the property and in the long term will make it unrentable.

Modernisation in accordance with EnEV
Modernisation in accordance with EnEV is the most frequently performed measure in existing buildings. The limiting value for the building envelope must be observed and the heating requirement of a comparable new building must not be exceeded by more than 40%. Modernisation in accordance with EnEV reduces the heating costs for the user and therefore favourably curtails the amortisation period of the investment, which is very important, in particular to the owner-occupier. As these measures also improve thermal comfort in the dwellings, the landlord gains from the

better and more rapid rentability and higher rental income.

Structural modernisation
The internal plan layouts of the building are completely redesigned and the technical services systems, including the distribution networks, are renewed. The building envelope surfaces are brought up at least to the U-value standard of a new building. This is intended to achieve a building performance that satisfies future requirements over a time frame of 50 years.

Comparison of variants
The description of the components and technical systems of existing buildings starts from a different point compared with new buildings. While the construction and commissioning of a new building provides a succession of information, there is frequently no relevant information about existing buildings. Building records get lost or simply do not comply with modern description standards. The survey of existing buildings is augmented through building catalogues with records of historic building construction. These catalogues contain the

Component	Max. permissible U-value (W/m²K)
External walls	0.24
External windows, window doors	1.3
Roof windows	1.4
Glass roofs	2.0
Ceilings, roofs and pitched roofs	0.24
Ceilings and walls against unheated rooms or earth	0.3
Floor components	0.5
Ceilings with outside air below	0.24

6.18

111

Values in €	Variant 1 (Structural modernisation)	Variant 2 (Deconstruction and new build)	Variant 3 (Modernisation in accordance with EnEV 2007)	Variant 4 (Renovation of existing building)
New building costs (cost groups 3 and 4) incl. other costs	2 530 026	3 678 096	1 604 811	1 196 198
Operating costs/year	31 497	36 714	40 288	75 296
Renovation costs/year	50 599	69 912	37 284	41 360
Maintenance costs/ year	14 452	10 658	2 678	3 251
Deconstruction costs	1 585 201	2 121 987	1 266 068	1 389 537
Net present value	7 934 690	9 926 088	6 148 035	10 202 957

6.19

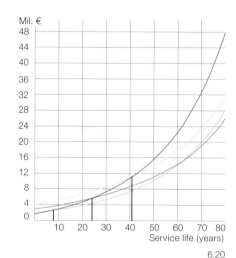

6.20

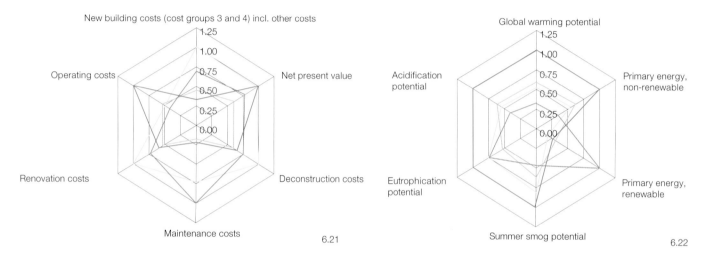

6.21

6.22

—— Variant 1 (structural modernisation)   —— Variant 3 (modernisation to EnEV 2007)
—— Variant 2 (deconstruction and new building)   —— Variant 4 (renovation)

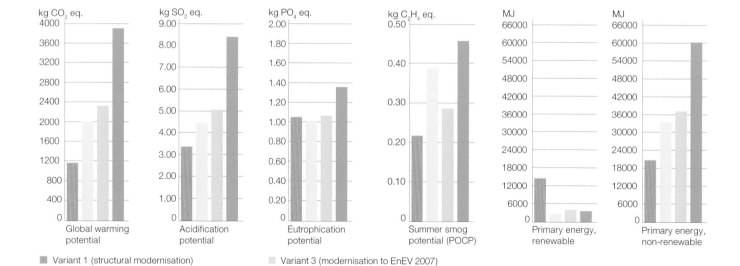

■ Variant 1 (structural modernisation)   ■ Variant 3 (modernisation to EnEV 2007)
■ Variant 2 (deconstruction and new building)   ■ Variant 4 (renovation)

6.23

6.19 Life cycle costs of the four variants over a period of 80 years
6.20 Comparison of life cycle costs (static amortisation period) of the four variants

6.21 Relative comparison of life cycle costs
6.22 Relative comparison of life cycle assessments
6.23 Results of the life cycle assessment over a period of 80 years (per m² GFA)

construction details normally encountered in residential property in Germany and covers all generations of buildings from 1890 to 1990 [5].

Building components and technical systems of new buildings are generally described as being in ideal condition. On the other hand, components in existing buildings have been subject to aging processes. Their characteristics could have significantly changed since the time of their installation, with the result that they may no longer or only partially fulfil technical or building physics standards. An external risk occurs if the component has safety defects, e. g. a stair rail no longer prevents a fall.

If a building with all its elements is described completely and a building component diagnosis and market analysis performed, then this allows different variants for the preservation or improvement of the existing building to be evaluated. The necessary measures are then determined and brought together to form an overall concept.

Integrated software was used to develop the following variants for the housing development in Speyer and then to compare their economic and ecological aspects.

- Variant 1: Energy modernisation (primary heating energy requirement 30 kWh/m²a) and a complete redesign of the layout of the dwelling units
- Variant 2: Demolition followed by erection of a new building with the same volume (energy rating 20 % less than EnEV)
- Variant 3: Modernisation to the standard of EnEV 2007 (energy requirement = 140 % of a new building complying with EnEV; renovation measures)
- Variant 4: Leave the existing building unmodified but complete the outstanding backlog of renovation measures built up over past years.

A comparison of variants was carried out to allow conclusions to be drawn about life cycle costs, taking account of all expenditure over a use period of 80 years (Fig. 6.19–6.23). A life cycle assessment over the same time period was performed for each variant. The assessment consisted of the following steps:

- Description of the building and its variants and their components
- Determination of the costs of the construction measures
- Calculation of all services media requirements for the use phase of the building (energy for heating and hot water, electrical power, water)
- Cost calculation for the building management in the use phase with information about operation, cleaning, maintenance, renovation and deconstruction
- Determination of the impacts on the environment caused by construction, use and removal

The following indicators were taken into account for the balance of life cycle costs:

- Construction costs in accordance with cost groups 3 and 4
- Operating costs for services media supply and disposal
- Maintenance costs
- Renovation costs
- Deconstruction costs
- Net present value

The variant comparison shows the complexity of the investigation in that no variant scores positively with all indicators (Fig. 6.21):

For construction costs, the investment cost for the renovation of the existing building (variant 4) and the simple energy modernisation (variant 3) is the lowest. The most expensive would be the variant involving demolition and new build (variant 2).

The costs for supply and disposal of services media are the highest for the existing building variant (variant 4). The variant based on modernisation with layout changes (variant 1) achieves the lowest value.

Maintenance costs are high for the new build variant (variant 2), as solar shading has to be installed in front of all windows. The same applies to the plan layout modernisation (variant 1), which requires two lifts to be installed.

The renovation costs for these two variants are similarly higher than for the renovated existing building (variant 4) and the simple modernisation variant (variant 3), as the robust construction of the existing building is relatively inexpensive to renovate.

In the net present value calculation, the simple modernisation (variant 3) and the high quality modernisation (variant 1) are the most favourable solutions.

The static amortisation of the investment costs shows the advantages of the only energy modernisation variant (variant 3, Fig. 6.20). Note that in this assessment of life cycle costs only the payments out have been considered. Possible rental or sales income is not taken into account in this comparison. These aspects must be included in a risk assessment of the investment in the evaluation.

The following indicators are taken into account in the life cycle assessment:

- Primary energy, non-renewable in MJ
- Greenhouse gases as kg CO_2 equivalent
- Acidification as kg SO_2 equivalent
- Europhication potential as kg PO_4 equivalent
- Photochemical ozone creation potential (POCP) in kg C_2H_2 equivalent

The comparison relates to 1 m² gross floor area and a use phase of 80 years. The layout redesign modernisation (variant 1) performs best with all indicators except renewable primary energy (Fig. 6.22 and 6.23). The differences between all the variants are clear in most cases and the ranking of the variants is generally the same for all indicators.

With the renewable primary energy indicator, the very large deviation of the layout redesign modernisation (variant 1) can be attributed to the installation of a woodchip heating plant. The three other variants use a fossil fuel, natural gas. This example clearly underlines that life cycle assessments can provide accurate evaluations but also points out the need for detailed knowledge in order to interpret the results.

Building realisation

On the basis of the concept comparison and taking into account the market potential, the investor decided in favour of a transformation concept that combined a completely new plan layout with a future-oriented very low energy rating. The heat requirement and energy costs were calculated using the procedure for residential buildings in accordance with EnEV 2007. The extensive construction works involved in the modernisation measures, which affected the whole of the building envelope, and the innovative technical systems (e. g. woodchip heating, building ventilation with heat recovery) result in very low end energy (27.08 kWh/m²a) and non-

renewable primary energy requirements (11.66 kWh/m²a).
This was achieved with the following measures:

- Reduction of the building's heat losses:
  - Internal insulation to the external walls
  - Ceiling insulation to ground floor slab
  - Roof insulation
  - Window replacement
- Regenerative/recuperative building technical services components:
  - Controlled ventilation with 80% heat recovery
  - Heating boiler with regenerative fuels (woodchip)

The woodchip-fuelled heating system reduces the requirement for non-renewable primary energy to a minimum.
The graphical representation of the primary energy requirement (Fig. 6.24) shows the heat gain from the ventilation heat recovery system (dotted line column on the input side).
The comparison of the energy requirement (end energy) for heating, hot water and electrical power of the two variants with plan layout modernisations (variant 1) and the existing building without energy modernisation (variant 4) shows the possibilities for savings (Fig. 6.25).
This reveals an important phenomenon: the heat energy requirement can be very substantially reduced by a wide range of measures. Hot water and electricity requirements, on the other hand, remain the same or even rise as a result of some user comfort measures in the refurbishment.

In view of the high cost of the plan layout modernisation, it would seem reasonable to know about the ecological amortisation. A separate calculation over the life cycle must be performed for each variant and life cycle indicator. For the global warming potential indicator, the comparison calculation for variants 1 and 4 showed that the initially higher energy consumption for the plan layout modernisation (variant 1) is amortised in only three operating years. The reason for this is the very low annual energy requirement of this variant.

Summary

The barracks conversion in Speyer clearly demonstrated that even the transformation of a 120-year-old listed building into a high quality residential property is possible. Low energy-loss construction measures were able to be incorporated, even while respecting the old building fabric.
Whether an investment is economically advantageous depends on regional real estate market conditions, i.e. the selling price that can be obtained. The continuing viability of the building for the future is ensured by the building's technical services concept with its very low end energy requirement and the resulting low energy costs.
The ecological amortisation shows the future-proof character of the design of the overall concept. Prerequisite for a positive project result is the intensive co-operation between the concept and detailed design architects, the cost planners and energy consultants. In addition when considering proposals for listed buildings, the conservation authorities must make concessions within reasonable limits and e.g. permit roof storey extensions. In the case discussed here, this allowed the successful revitalisation of the building.
Through the low energy requirement and the use of regenerative energy sources, a considerably lower environmental impact is achieved over the observed period of building operation compared to conventional residential buildings.

Project data for Normand Barracks
- Building: Normand Barracks former troop accommodation
- Location: Speyer
- Client: Osika GmbH, Mannheim
- Architect: AAg Loebner Schaefer Weber, Heidelberg
- Construction: 2007/08
- Use: Multiple dwelling unit building
- No. of floors: 5

Volume and area:
- Enclosed volume: 17087 m³
- Thermally conditioned volume: 12438 m³
- Gross floor area (GFA): 4601 m²
- Area occupied by construction elements e.g. walls etc.: 779 m²
- Net floor area: 3822 m²
- Circulation area: 650 m²
- Technical systems area: 100 m²
- Usable area (UA): 3072 m²
- Ancillary use area: 0 m²
- Residential area: 3004 m²
- Efficiency: UA/GFA = 0.67
- Heat transfer envelope area: 4700 m²
- A/V ratio: 0.38

Analysis software: LEGEP

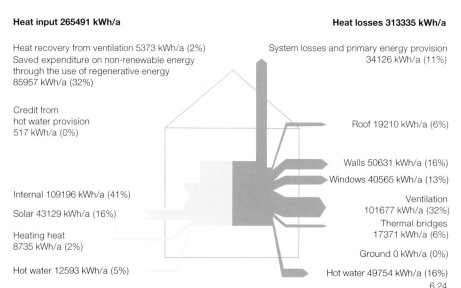

Heat input 265491 kWh/a

Heat recovery from ventilation 5373 kWh/a (2%)
Saved expenditure on non-renewable energy through the use of regenerative energy 85957 kWh/a (32%)

Credit from hot water provision 517 kWh/a (0%)

Internal 109196 kWh/a (41%)

Solar 43129 kWh/a (16%)

Heating heat 8735 kWh/a (2%)

Hot water 12593 kWh/a (5%)

Heat losses 313335 kWh/a

System losses and primary energy provision 34126 kWh/a (11%)

Roof 19210 kWh/a (6%)

Walls 50631 kWh/a (16%)
Windows 40565 kWh/a (13%)
Ventilation 101677 kWh/a (32%)
Thermal bridges 17371 kWh/a (6%)

Ground 0 kWh/a (0%)

Hot water 49754 kWh/a (16%)

6.24

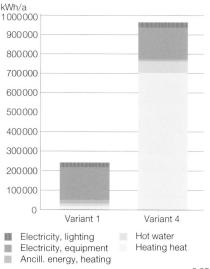

kWh/a

Variant 1   Variant 4

- Electricity, lighting
- Electricity, equipment
- Ancill. energy, heating
- Hot water
- Heating heat

6.25

Example 3: Evaluation of the economic efficiency of building standards – Lebenshilfe, Lindenberg im Allgäu

In 2002 Lebenshilfe für Behinderte e.V., a German organisation providing support to people with disabilities in Lindenberg, Allgäu, held an architectural competition for a workshop building, which was won by Munich architects Lichtblau. The concept convinced the competition jury through its integration of manufacturing process flows into a solar-assisted energy concept. The new workshops for people with disabilities are located on the eastern edge of Lindenberg. The spatial programme includes craft and assembly workshops, support and training areas, office and administration units, a dining hall, catering kitchen and janitor's residence. Two elongated blocks in the south (single storey) and north (two-storey, with an office floor over the workshops) are complemented to the east by a two-storey communal building with an integrated janitor's residence (Fig. 6.26–6.28).

Design concept
Two variants were developed in the preliminary design phase in order to justify the initial additional investment for an energy-efficient new build to the funding institutions and the client:

Variant 1 (standard variant, eligible for grant funding)
This building would employ a selection of commonly used materials and construction methods, e.g. reinforced concrete frame with a solid masonry skin. The energy requirement is roughly in line with the limiting values in the then applicable EnEV, but would not improve on them.
The following concept was selected:
- Reinforced concrete (RC) frame with RC floor slabs and roof
- External and internal walls of masonry units
- Facade with polystyrene external thermal composite insulation system (ETICS)
- Plastic window with thermal glazing
- Central heating and hot water provision from natural gas

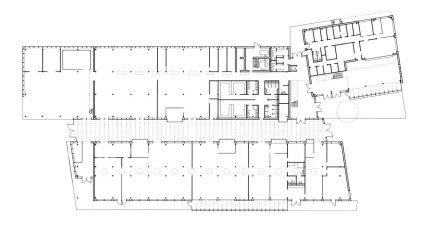

6.26

6.24 Normand Barracks, Speyer: Heat flow diagram (primary energy) of the built variant 1
6.25 Primary energy requirement (no substituted energy), comparison of variants 1 and 4
6.26 Workshop building, Lebenshilfe Lindenberg: layout plan ground floor, scale 1:1000
6.27 General view
6.28 Internal view of main circulation corridor on ground floor

6.27

6.28

115

Variant 2 (SolarBau, solar-optimised building programme)
This alternative would comply with the grant eligibility rules for SolarBau projects stipulated by the German Federal Ministry of Economy and Technology (BMWi) [6]. In detail the rules require:
- Primary energy requirement for heating, ventilation, air-conditioning and lighting below 100 kWh/m²a
- End energy requirement for heating, ventilation, air-conditioning and lighting below 70 kWh/m²a
- Heating energy requirement below 40 kWh/m²a
- No thermally activated building component cooling
- Enhanced use of natural light
- Integration of renewable energy sources into the building services media supply systems

The architects selected the following concept:
- Use of electrical geothermal heat pumps, with a wood pellet boiler to cover peak loads
- Reduction of the electricity require-

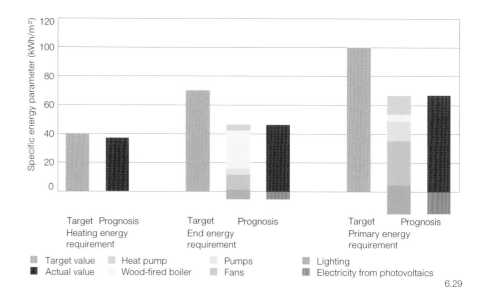

Target Prognosis
Heating energy
requirement

Target Prognosis
End energy
requirement

Target Prognosis
Primary energy
requirement

| ▦ Target value | ▦ Heat pump | ▦ Pumps | ▦ Lighting |
| ■ Actual value | ▦ Wood-fired boiler | ▦ Fans | ▦ Electricity from photovoltaics |

6.29

ment through good daylight provision, e. g. by means of skylights and light redirection through reflective light tubes (Fig. 6.30)
- Photovoltaic systems

As each building had to contain the highest possible proportion of regenerative raw materials, the architects opted for the following forms of construction:
- Timber frame system: floors and roof in stacked plank construction, facade as timber frames with cellulose insulation
- Wooden windows with triple glazing, window spandrels and doors insulated with vacuum insulation panels

Both variants were fully modelled. Energy simulations were carried out and reports submitted on life cycle costs (LCC) and life cycle assessments (LCA). The results provided further evidence in support of the submissions to authorities and banks concerning the continuing viability of the project in the future. The computer-aided preview of the building performance over the life cycle convinced all the project stakeholders, and the forward-looking SolarBau variant was approved for construction. The project was developed as an example of the use of integrated design with the help of funding from the German Federal Ministry of Economy and Technology (BMWi) (SolarBau design 05/2002–01/2005). A monitoring programme was in force up to 2007 (SolarBau monitoring 10/2003–01/2007), to check that the calculated requirements agreed with the actual consumption figures.

The architects Florian + Wendelin Lichtblau describe the building ensemble in the following way: "Consisting almost entirely of wood and glass, the building stands on a piled foundation and was CO_2-neutral in its production. High quality insulation and seals alongside intensive use of passive solar energy minimise the heating requirement. Ground water heat pumps and a wood-fired boiler provide the residual heat by means of heated screeds, through which cold ground water flows in summer. Controlled ventilation with heat recovery, overall daylight autonomy and minimum, solar-provided electricity requirement complete the energy and ecological balance."

Results of the life cycle analysis
Integrated software was used to keep the design phase costs as low as possible. The software allowed an analysis of the integrated life cycle performance of the buildings to be carried out based on the element method. After the input of the project and its elements, information about the production and use costs, energy requirement, the anticipated operating costs and environmental impact was then available for both building variants. The required assessments and decisions were made on the basis of these results.

Construction costs
The total construction costs in cost groups 1–7 were 8 882 000 € gross for variant 1 and 9 433 000 € for variant 2. The additional costs for variant 2 were approximately 550 000 € or 6.2 %. They

6.30

had to be financed by the client with loans. To secure the loans it was necessary, among other things, to demonstrate the low annual costs of energy provision, which, with the continuing rise of energy costs, would ensure the financial viability of the overall concept.

Heat and energy
The energy requirement was calculated using a simulation program. After input into the element program, the data was available for the determination of the operating costs, amortisation and environmental impact. The operating costs were calculated on the basis of the cost values for wood pellets, electricity and water in the client's contract with the services media suppliers. An important design objective was to comply with the SolarBau limiting values. This meant:
• Heating requirement below 40 kWh/m²a
• End energy requirement below 70 kWh/m²a, including electricity for lighting
• Primary energy requirement below 100 kWh/m²a, including electricity for lighting

Fig. 6.29 illustrates the results of the computer analysis of the energy requirement for all three load cases. The left column (Target) in each case shows the specified limiting value, the right (Prognosis) shows the predicted energy requirement, subdivided according to the various consumers. Due to conversion losses, the primary energy requirements of the electrical consumers are three times their end energy requirements. The generation of electricity from photovoltaic systems reduces the electricity requirement. The negative parts of the columns represent end and primary energy generation.
The primary energy requirement of the heating heat created from wood pellets is only around a fifth of its end energy requirement. The reason for this is the primary energy factor of 0.23 for renewable raw material-based fuels specified in EnEV.
The limiting values of the SolarBau programme are not exceeded by any of the indicators of the considered variants.
The comparison of the life cycle costs clearly shows the lower annual building

operation costs for variant 2 (Fig. 6.33). These savings allow the higher production costs to be amortised (Fig. 6.32). As the heating energyheat requirement of the building is already very low, the principal effect of the SolarBau strategy is a reduction of the electricity used for lighting. The limiting value of 100 kWh/m²a cannot be achieved without a substantial reduction in this area. For this reason illuminance simulations were carried out in the design phase. In order to allow daylight to enter the rooms despite their great depth, skylights were fitted in the single storey buildings. Wood and reflective foil light deflection tubes were installed to pass through the first floor from the rooflight into the hall area on the ground floor (Fig. 6.30)
To improve confidence that the final cost would agree with the design estimate, the operating costs were calculated in accordance with DIN 18960 over a period of observation of 50 years, as well as under the standard operating cost heading items. Fig. 6.37 shows the production costs at the base of the graph and the cumulative annual

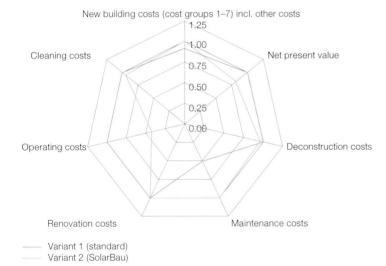

Variant 1 (standard)
Variant 2 (SolarBau)
6.31

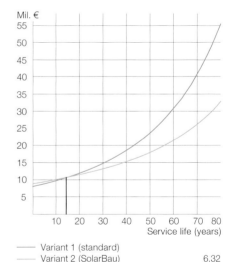

Variant 1 (standard)
Variant 2 (SolarBau)
6.32

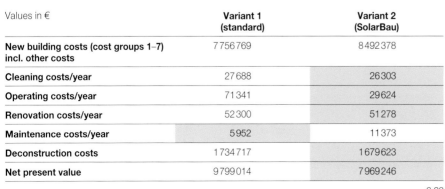

Values in €	Variant 1 (standard)	Variant 2 (SolarBau)
New building costs (cost groups 1–7) incl. other costs	7 756 769	8 492 378
Cleaning costs/year	27 688	26 303
Operating costs/year	71 341	29 624
Renovation costs/year	52 300	51 278
Maintenance costs/year	5 952	11 373
Deconstruction costs	1 734 717	1 679 623
Net present value	9 799 014	7 969 246

6.33

6.29 Comparison of energy requirements: variant 2 (SolarBau) and limiting values of the SolarBau programme
6.30 Administration room on upper floor with "light chimney"
6.31 Relative comparison of individual cost types
6.32 Comparison of life cycle costs (static amortisation period) of the two variants
6.33 Life cycle costs for variants 1 and 2. Green-shaded cells indicate the most favourable variant.

expenditure on operation, cleaning, maintenance, renovation and deconstruction plotted above them. Fig. 6.31 (p. 117) explains the relative differences between the individual cost types. Based on operating costs, variant 2 is clearly less expensive, but it has maintenance costs twice those of variant 1. This is related to the considerably more extensive technical systems and controls.

Life cycle assessment
As the two assessed variants have totally different material concepts, it is revealing to assess only the production phases of both buildings as a first stage (Fig. 6.34). The values relate to 1 m^2 GFA. The mass of material used in variant 2 is almost one third less than variant 1, which is largely due to the use of wood for the primary structural elements. Likewise the lower CO_2 value of variant 2, which is only one quarter of the value for variant 1, can be explained by the credits from the use of wood.

These credits are lost upon deconstruction and final thermal recycling. If the wood is reused as a material, then some of the CO_2 credits can be retained. The two variants hardly differ at all in their indicators for acidification and eutrophication potential. On the other hand, the renewable primary energy indicator for variant 2 drops noticeably due to the structural concept being based on renewable raw materials. Overall it can be seen that the life cycle assessment indicators for the different construction material concepts do not relate to one another in a linear manner, i. e. a reduction or increase does not affect all indicators to the same degree. The most striking congruence between the non-renewable primary energy input indicator and the global warming potential impact indicator does not occur with a completely different construction material concept. The difference between the variants is even more apparent in the life cycle assessment of the building over a 50-year

period of observation. Here, variant 2 does distinctly better in all the indicators. The reasons are the lower energy requirements and the use of regenerative energy sources to cover them (Fig. 6.35).

Comparison of construction material use
Calculating the amount of construction materials used, measured by weight (in t or kg), is helpful in checking the apparent validity of the building input data. The classification of the construction materials takes into account firstly the structural carcass of the building and its principal materials:
• Mineral
• Plant-based
• Metal
• Plastic

Secondly by describing the fitting-out components according to their function:
• Sealants
• Floors
• Insulation

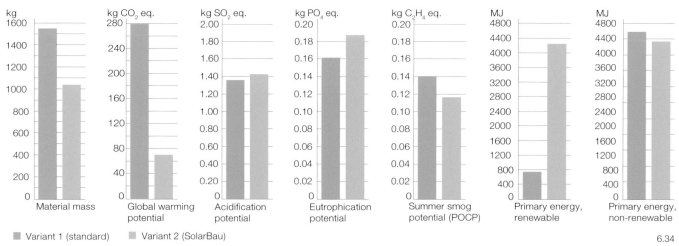

6.34

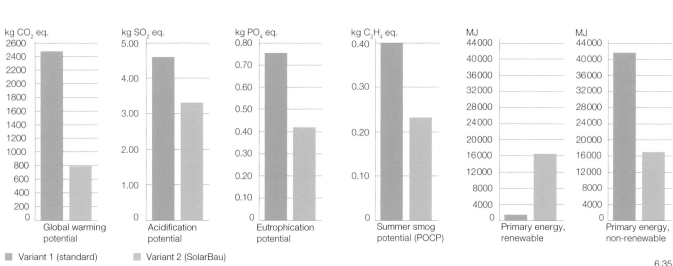

6.35

- Coatings
- Technical systems

Fig. 6.36 shows all the materials in the building weighted according to their proportion by mass. The higher proportion of renewable raw materials in the structural carcass of variant 2 can be clearly seen. Similarly clear is the higher proportion of insulation. This material mix produces a building with a substantially lower overall weight. The standard variant achieves a medium value at 1.550 t/m²GFA. While, at 1.060 t/m²GFA ,variant 2 undercuts this value by 30%.

Summary

For a relatively small additional financial expenditure of approximately 6%, a building has been created in Lindenberg that the architects describe as "fit for the future". It sets itself apart by:
- Very low energy requirements
- Coverage of the residual heat requirement from regenerative sources

(wood pellets, photovoltaics)
- Material concept based on renewable raw materials

The results impress through their low energy costs and environmental impacts. Through the low energy requirements and the use of regenerative energy sources, a considerably lower environmental impact is achieved, even over a short period of building operation, compared to conventional administrative and commercial buildings.

Project data for Lebenshilfe Lindenberg
- Building: New workshops for people with disabilities
- Location: Lindenberg im Allgäu
- Client: Lebenshilfe für Behinderte e.V., Kreisvereinigung Lindau
- Architect: Lichtblau Architekten BDA, Munich, Florian + Wendelin Lichtblau
- In collaboration with: A. Reichmann, C. Rein
- Construction: 2005
- Use: Workshops for people with disa-

bilities with production, offices, communal areas (kitchen with dining hall)
- No. of floors: Production 1, storage/administration 2

Volume and area:
- Enclosed volume: 25 160 m³
- Thermally conditioned gross volume: 21 503 m³
- Gross floor area (GFA): 5247 m²
- Area occupied by construction elements e.g. walls etc.: 624 m²
- Net floor area: 4623 m²
- Circulation area: 545 m²
- Technical systems area: 541 m²
- Usable area (UA): 3537 m²
- Ancillary use area: 340 m²
- Efficiency: UA/GFA = 0.67

Analysis software: LEGEP

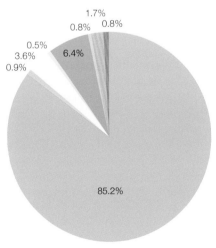

Variant 1 (standard)

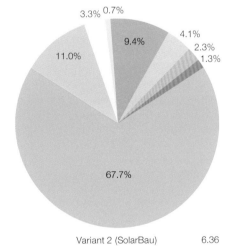

Variant 2 (SolarBau)　　6.36

Plant-based construction material, renewable
Metals
Sealants, adhesives, roof coverings
Floor coverings, screeds
Insulation materials (sound/heat/cold)
Plaster, external panels, facade cladding
Translucent building components
Mineral construction materials
(excluding glass and metal)

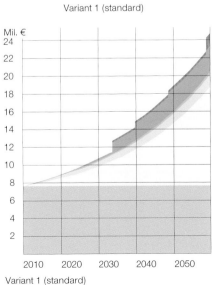

Variant 1 (standard)

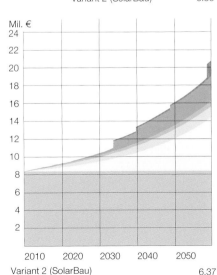

Variant 2 (SolarBau)　　6.37

Deconstruction
Renovation
Maintenance
Cleaning
Operation
New building

6.34 Life cycle assessments of both variants during the production phase (per m² GFA)
6.35 Life cycle assessments of both variants over the life cycle (per m² GFA)
6.36 Summary of the construction materials used, weighted according to proportion by mass
6.37 Comparison of cumulative life cycle costs, classified by cost types

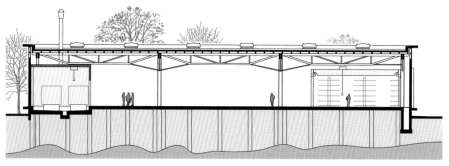

6.38

6.38 NiroSan Production Hall, Schmiedefeld:
   section
6.39 General view
6.40 Internal view
6.41 Results of the life cycle analysis and reduction potential for variant 1
6.42 Non-renewable primary energy requirements
   for variants 1 and 2
6.43 Mass balance and environmental effects of
   production, classified by component group

6.39

6.40

Example 4:
Energy concepts in industrial buildings – NiroSan Production Hall, Schmiedefeld

Increasing importance is being attached to sustainable construction in the field of industrial buildings as well. One example is the company NiroSan Multifit, who had a new production facility for the manufacture of high quality stainless steel parts for the assembly industry erected in Schmiedefeld near Dresden (Fig. 6.38–6.40).

The production hall stands alongside a stream on a site that had been used for industrial purposes for more than 100 years. As the European Union had only recently declared the area a site of community importance (SCI), it was necessary for the design of the production hall to radiate its closeness to nature. Furthermore the production processes and the operation of the building had to demonstrate a high level of energy efficiency.

Design concept
Wuppertal architects Juhr Architektur-büro für Industriebau- und Gesamtplanung designed a transparent production hall with a post and beam construction made from untreated wood sourced from the region. The exposed media pipes and ducts on the roof are concealed from the viewer on the ground by a continuous raised frame. The top chord of the structure supporting the roof is glued laminated timber; the bottom chord is steel. The superstructure is supported internally and externally by reinforced concrete columns.

Large glazed areas in the timber facade were composed of double glazed solar protection glass and allow a high degree of daylight usage. 6.40). The large number of transparent skylights with light deflection lamellae admit light from above. The energy requirement for artificial lighting was substantially reduced by daylight sensing controls. The building is thermally conditioned by hot water underfloor heating. The machinery for stainless steel production is cooled with river water. In winter the river water is warmed by the waste heat and fed through the underfloor heating system. In summer the cold from the river water is used directly for the underfloor cooling system. The innovative building technical services systems greatly reduces the energy requirement of the building and the associated operating costs.

The ground floor production hall contains the production lines, a portal crane for handling goods, a pickling tank for surface treatment and a tool-making shop. On the upper storey, which is accessed by an internal staircase, are offices and sanitary facilities.

Defining the system for the life cycle analysis
Life cycle analysis was used with the aim of comparing and contrasting the two alternative variants in terms of their energy provision. In addition to the variant based on the exploitation of waste heat (variant 1), a scenario using gas-fired overhead radiant tube heaters (variant 2) was considered. The primary energy intensity and the environmental impacts of both variants were com-

pared. This was intended to determine the potential for the reuse of energy from the production processes. Furthermore the ecological effect of timber construction is analysed and the results used to indicate how the environmental impact of the production phase could be reduced.

System limits
The construction costs for the industrial building were calculated using the building components in cost groups 300 and 400 in DIN 276. Unlike in the case of office buildings, the use phase of industrial buildings can vary immensely. While production halls for the automobile industry may be used for only 5–10 years, depending on the model and company, logistics facilities can look forward to up to 40 years of use. A use phase of 15 years was assumed for this production hall and adopted as the basis for the life cycle

phases (production of the building, its operation including maintenance, renovation and disposal).
The assessment of the production of the building considers the upstream stages of the production of the individual building components, from the extraction of the resources to the finished product (cradle to gate), and the transport to the site. The use phase contains the requirement for energy carriers such as electricity and natural gas for the operation of the building. These values were able to be taken from the building's energy requirement certificate. To forecast the renovation measures, the renovation cycles were analysed and compared with the values in the "Leitfaden Nachhaltiges Bauen" published by the German Federal Ministry of Transport, Building and Urban Development (BMVBS). Due to the short period of observation, only one repainting of the building was

	Variant 1 (Waste heat recovery)				Variant 2 (Gas-fired overhead radiant tube heaters)	Saving (relative)
	Production	Use	End of life	Total	Total	
Primary energy requirement, non-renewable (MJ)	12 183 113	1 168 128	- 7 344 830	6 006 411	25 106 423	76 %
Primary energy requirement, renewable (MJ)	5 316 623	58 753	- 463 134	4 912 241	4 921 450	0 %
Primary energy requirement, total (MJ)	17 499 736	1 226 881	- 7 807 964	10 918 652	30 027 873	64 %
Global warming potential (kg CO$_2$ eq.)	826 535	75 562	86 815	988 913	2 127 368	54 %
Ozone depletion potential (kg R11 eq.)	0.052	0.012	- 0.071	- 0.007	- 0.0058	28 %
Acidification potential (kg SO$_2$ eq.)	2982	131	- 500	2612	3580	27 %
Eutrophication potential (kg PO$_4$ eq.)	397	11	6	413	545	24 %
Ozone creation potential (kg C$_2$H$_4$ eq.)	340	9	- 43	306	424	28 %

6.41

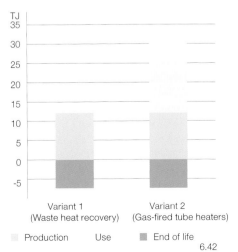

Production   Use   End of life
6.42

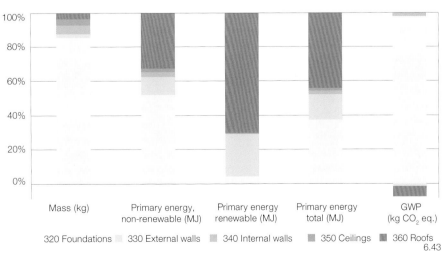

320 Foundations   330 External walls   340 Internal walls   350 Ceilings   360 Roofs
6.43

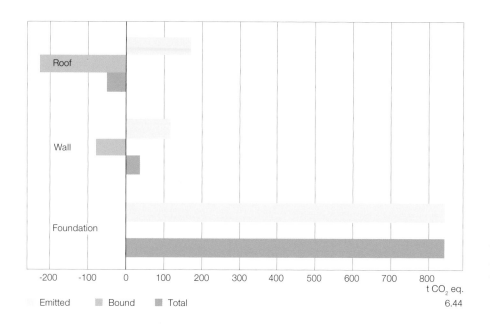

Emitted	Bound	Total

6.44

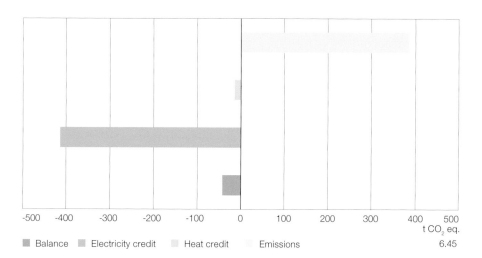

Balance	Electricity credit	Heat credit	Emissions

6.45

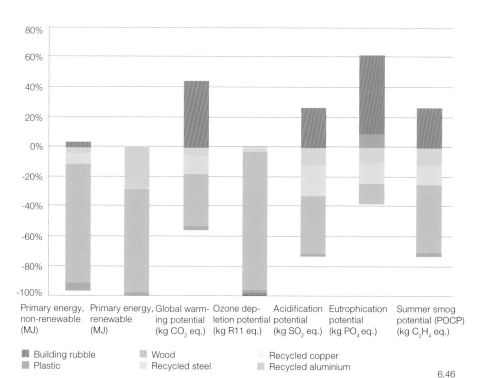

Primary energy, non-renewable (MJ) / Primary energy, renewable (MJ) / Global warming potential (kg CO₂ eq.) / Ozone depletion potential (kg R11 eq.) / Acidification potential (kg SO₂ eq.) / Eutrophication potential (kg PO₄ eq.) / Summer smog potential (POCP) (kg C₂H₄ eq.)

Building rubble	Wood	Recycled copper
Plastic	Recycled steel	Recycled aluminium

6.46

assumed in the renovation scenario. The concept of balance credits was used for the end of life phase (EOL) in the life cycle assessment. The construction materials in the balance may attract credits if the industry can prove that the materials will be recycled. In this way, e. g. a rate of recycling of 55 to 95 % is achieved for metals, depending on type. This concept is currently in use in the German life cycle assessment database maintained by the BMVBS. It allows the credits set out in Fig. 6.41 (p. 121) for end of life. The degree of prefabrication of the prefabricated building parts is very high. Therefore material waste is not taken into account. The process of stainless steel component production including process engineering was not part of this assessment as a universally applicable comparison for the industry is not possible due to the different levels of resources (water, energy etc.). The cleaning of the hall was not included in the analysis, as was also the case with the construction site operation, dismantling and reinstatement, as well as the materials in the external works.

Functional unit

The functional unit for this analysis is the production building (gross floor area 3007 m², gross enclosed volume 23 801 m³) related to the period of observation of 15 years. The primary energy requirement and the environmental impacts of the production of the building, its use and disposal are considered cumulatively and related to the functional unit.

Results and interpretation of the life cycle analysis

As the energy requirement for the production of the process engineering equipment is of marginal significance, it can be considered as making no difference to the environmental impacts of either variant during the production phase. On the other hand, the differences are clear in the consideration of the use phase. Fig. 6.42 (p. 121) shows the non-renewable primary energy requirements of both variants related to the whole life cycle.

Variant 2 requires much more primary energy for the use phase than it does for the production of the building. In the completed variant 1, the waste heat from the existing production equipment is used for the thermal conditioning of the new building. The required primary energy is assigned to the production process. Thus the exploited heat is entered without penalty into the balance of the use phase of the building. The fossil primary energy consumption is reduced in comparison with variant 2 by 19.1 TJ or 76%. In relation to the other environmental impact categories, the scenario involving the exploitation of waste heat gives rise to an enormous reduction, which, followed by the global warming potential at 54%, is the greatest. Over the period of observation of 15 years it would save 1.1 t CO_2 equivalent for the entire building. The analysis of variant 1 reveals that the production phase uses 91% of the non-renewable primary energy requirement (Fig. 6.42, p. 121). This illustrates the great importance of the choice of construction material for the life cycle assessment.

Production
A total of 5185 t of construction materials were used in the erection of the production hall. The greater part of this, 85%, was allocated to cost group 320 in DIN 276, in which e. g. the ground slab and the foundations are summarised. External walls (cost group 330) contribute 2%, internal walls (340) 5% and floors and ceilings (350) with roof elements (360) 4% to the result (Fig. 6.43, p. 121).
This distribution of mass is typical for industrial buildings. Analyses of logistics, warehousing and production halls reveal that the proportion of cost group 320 is normally about three-quarters of the total cost. In the consideration of the environmental impacts the ratio is completely different.
Although the roof construction in Schmiedefeld is only a small proportion of the total mass of the building, it is responsible for 33% of the embodied fossil-fuel primary energy requirement. The external walls as well contribute more to the energy requirement than they do to the mass of the building. One of the reasons for this is that the materials used; mineral wool, polyethylene film and PVC roof waterproofing membrane, have considerably higher energy intensities than the concrete placed in the foundations. The other environmental categories considered show a similar

relative distribution of the building component groups as the non-renewable primary energy requirement.
The global warming potential (Fig. 6.44) is largely determined by the materials in the foundations, which emitted a total of 805 t CO_2 equivalent (CO_2 eq.) during their production. The construction materials in the external and internal walls are responsible for 35 t CO_2 eq. The roof components have a negative global warming potential of -50 t CO_2 eq. in the summation, which arises from the binding up of CO_2 during the growth of the wood. The credit of a total of 215 t CO_2 eq. represents the emissions that would have been arisen if the materials had been produced from fossil resources.

End of life
The high primary energy credit at the end of the service life (end of life (EOL)) stands out in the more precise consideration of variant 1. It results from the wooden materials used. During the growth phase the wood takes up and binds solar energy. At EOL the wood is taken to a waste incineration plant and thermally recycled, releasing the stored energy, which is used in the form of electricity and district heat. It substitutes for the fossil resources that would otherwise have been necessary for electricity and heat generation. The approximately 5 TJ of regenerative primary energy in the production contribute a considerable part of the EOL credit in the non-renewable primary energy requirement (Fig. 6.46).
In the impact categories of the life cycle assessment as well, the use of wood is responsible for most of the credit at EOL. The metal and plastic used also attract credits, because a proportion of them can be recycled (Fig. 6.46).
Fig. 6.45 shows an example of how the released emissions and the credits relate to one another at the end of the service life. In the thermal use of wood in the waste incinerator, the carbon bound up in the wood during the growth phase is emitted mainly in the form of CO_2 back into the atmosphere. At the same time the resulting production of electricity and district heat from the wood also substitutes for the fossil fuels otherwise used. Thus the credits further increase in significance and the final negative grand total is 425 t CO_2 eq.

Summary
Through the realisation of this innovative energy concept, which makes use of the waste heat from the manufacturing processes on the production floor, it has proved possible to build a environmentally compatible production hall. In the use phase the completed building, as compared with the variant with gas-fired overhead radiant tube heaters, achieves a very large reduction in the fossil-based primary energy requirement and in the global warming potential. This shows where the potential lies in the use of production process energy. The multiple use of the material wood has a positive influence on the environmental impacts as renewable primary energy has been "built in" and substitutes for the use of fossil resources when the wood is thermally recycled at the end of the building's service life.

Project data for NiroSan Production Hall
- Building: Production hall of solid timber construction
- Location Schmiedefeld near Dresden
- Client: NiroSan Multifit GmbH & Co. KG, Schmiedefeld
- Architect: Juhr Architekturbüro für Industriebau- und Gesamtplanung, Wuppertal
- Construction: 2004
- Use: Stainless steel production
- No. of floors: 1–2

Volume and area:
- Gross floor area (GFA): 3007 m²
- Net floor area: 2900 m²
- Area occupied by construction elements e. g. walls etc.: 107 m²
- Primary use area: 2900 m²
- Thermally conditioned net plan area: 2800 m²
- Heat transfer envelope area: 7456 m²
- External building volume: 23801 m³
- A/V ratio: 0.31

Analysis software: GaBi

6.44 Global warming potential of building component groups over a period of 15 years
6.45 Calculation of the greenhouse gas emissions from the wood in the structure at end of life
6.46 End of life assessment of the materials used

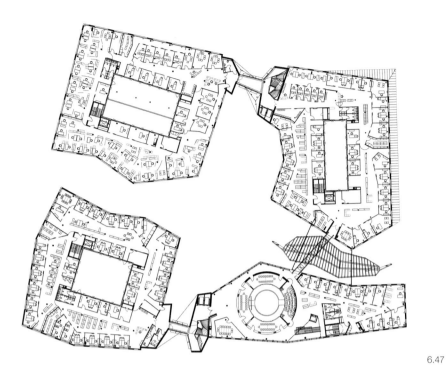

6.47

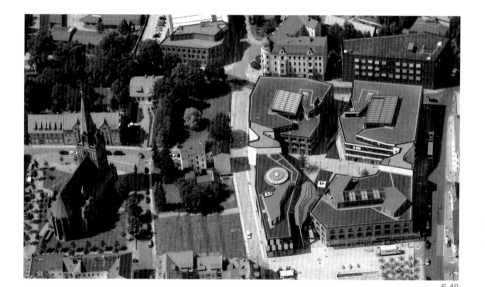

6.48

6.49

Example 5: Integrated design as the basis for certification – Barnim Administration Centre, Eberswalde

In 2001 the local council, Landkreis Barnim, decided to build a services and administration centre in Eberswalde to the north-east of Berlin. The heart of the town had been badly damaged in the last days of the second world war. During the time of the German Democratic Republic (GDR), the town centre had been redeveloped only on a piecemeal basis, with the result that many areas of land were left derelict up to the end of the millennium. The new services and administration centre for the Barnim district would fill a vacant plot of over 1 ha in the middle of the historic old town (Figs. 6.47–6.49).

Design concept

Berlin architects sol·id·ar planungswerkstatt were responsible for the project from determining the contents of the initial brief, through the design and construction right up to and including the monitoring of the first use phase. From the very beginning with the European-wide invitation to participate in the design competition, the requirement had always been for an energy efficient and sustainable building. The winner of the competition was another firm of Berlin architects, GAP Gesellschaft für Architektur & Projektmanagement mbH. From an early stage, efforts were made to assemble a broad-based design team under the management of the architects, who adopted the role of lead consultant. In January 2004 the council resolved to build the competition-winning design and decided on a new name for the building: Paul Wunderlich House. Works of the artist would be on permanent exhibition in the rooms of the new building. The project was accepted by the German Federal Ministry of Economy and Technology (BMWi) into its "Energy-optimised building" (EnOB) programme and would have to satisfy additional requirements relating to economy, ecology and comfort. The EnOB programme is a reinterpretation of the earlier SolarBau programme (see p. 115). Its requirements are generally equivalent to those of its predecessor.

• Primary energy requirement for heat-

ing, ventilation, air-conditioning and lighting below 100 kWh/m²a
- End energy requirement for heating, ventilation, air-conditioning and lighting below 70 kWh/m²a
- Heating energy requirement below 40 kWh/m²a
- No thermally activated building component cooling
- Enhanced use of natural light
- Integration of renewable energy sources into the building services media supply systems

Important urban design objectives included the completion of the block structure, re-emphasis of the existing building lines as well as the linking of open spaces and the recreation of the historic street structure. Four three- to four-storey individual buildings were constructed on Pavillonplatz (council, building and departmental blocks I, II and III, Figs. 6.47 and 6.48). In addition to the district administration offices, official headquarters with a council chamber and space for retail and commercial premises, there is also a small museum. As the building could not incorporate an underground car park, a neighbouring plot was used for a multistorey 290-space car park with an end block for further office space.

Energy efficiency and user comfort
Paul Wunderlich House is forward-looking; not only because of its energy efficient building technical services concept and its transparent spatial structure, but also because of the successful symbiosis of administration, services and exhibitions of art. It is remarkable for its characteristic minimal primary energy requirement and enhanced level of user comfort. The early involvement of the specialist design engineers and the use of thermal and lighting modelling drove up design costs. The development of the building climate concept was handled jointly by the architect and specialist design engineers, who worked together in an interdisciplinary manner using integrated design and design optimisation techniques to achieve the best solution.

The following constructional measures were implemented:
- Reinforced concrete frame with a low proportion of reinforcing steel

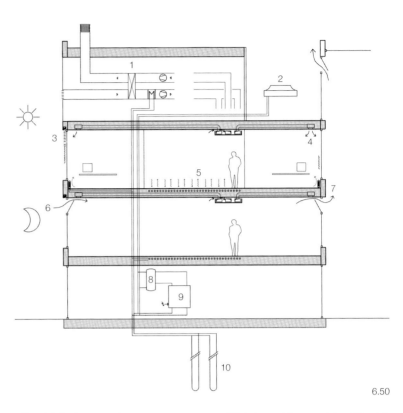

6.50

- Facades with a high degree of prefabrication involving timber frames with cellulose insulation, fibre-cement boards and rendered facade panels
- Wooden windows
- Flat roof of reinforced concrete with cork insulation (cut-to-falls slabs with expanded polystyrene (EPS))
- Internal walls: glass wall in parts with sliding glass doors to reduce corridor lighting (Fig. 6.49)
- Ceilings with activated concrete cores, left unplastered and without suspended ceilings
- Building technical services routes in the corridors are clad with wood-wool lightweight building boards to reduce noise

In addition, as part of the research project, the following innovative construction products were used:
- Vacuum insulation panels on the underside of the upper storey cantilevers
- Storage panels with latent heat storage based on paraffins (phase change materials, PCM)
- Floor lamps in the offices with indirect and controlled direct working light

Paul Wunderlich House has a particularly favourable ratio of external surface area to volume. The daylight entering the building is optimised by the ab-

sence of lintels and favourable ratios of storey height to room depth.
The building technical services concept avoids the use of air conditioning over large areas. The concrete ceiling slabs are fitted with ventilation ducts to allow concrete core activation. The bored piles in the foundations are designed as energy piles, which supply heat or cold to temper the building. The basic load for space heating is covered by the ventilation system. When heat is required it blows in supply air at a temperature of 10 K above the ambient into the rooms (heating load approx. 10 to 15 W/m²). Radiators cover the peak loads and regulate the room tempera-

6.47 Barnim District Services and Administration Centre: Plan 1ˢᵗ floor, scale 1:750
6.48 Aerial photograph of the whole site (photomontage). The car park building with end block is on the top edge of the image above the green space.
6.49 Part of the daylighting concept: office floor with glass dividing walls
6.50 Section with energy and ventilation concept
   1 Ventilation system with 80% heat recovery
   2 Recooling plant
   3 Light deflecting blinds
   4 Ceiling thermal storage mass cooling through inlet air hypocausts
   5 Underfloor heating/cooling
   6 Night ventilation
   7 Exhaust air through atrium
   8 Buffer storage
   9 Reversible heat pump (heating and cooling)
  10 Energy piles

125

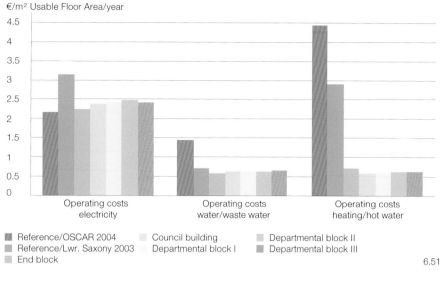

€/m² Usable Floor Area/year

■ Reference/OSCAR 2004   ■ Council building   ■ Departmental block II
■ Reference/Lwr. Saxony 2003   ■ Departmental block I   ■ Departmental block III
■ End block

6.51

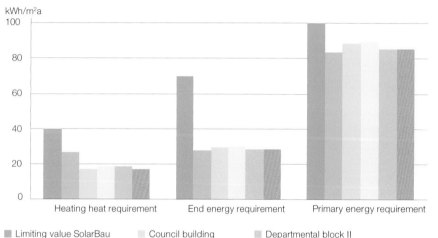

kWh/m²a

■ Limiting value SolarBau   ■ Council building   ■ Departmental block II
■ End block   ■ Departmental block I   ■ Departmental block III

6.52

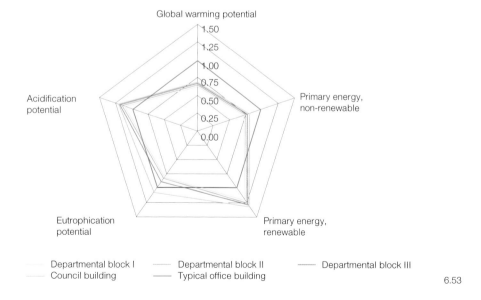

—— Departmental block I   —— Departmental block II   —— Departmental block III
—— Council building   —— Typical office building

6.53

6.51 Comparison of operating costs of the four building parts and values for standard office buildings (in accordance with OSCAR and Lower Saxony reference values)

6.52 Comparison of the energy consumption of the four building parts and limiting values of the "Energy-optimised building" programme (EnOB)

6.53 Relative comparison of environmental effects

tures. Underfloor heating or cooling can be switched on when necessary in the corridors and multi-use areas (Fig. 6.50, p. 125).

The building achieves levels 75 % below the limiting values in EnEV at the time of calculation in 2005. As the EnEV calculation would not be able to take adequate account of the special design options, the energy flows were also modelled. This was able to prove that even the very low limiting values required to qualify for grants under the EnOB/SolarBau programme were very easily met (Figs. 6.52 and 6.53).

Results of the life cycle costing and life cycle assessment

The budgeted construction costs for the building were only slightly exceeded in spite of intervening changes in the boundary conditions. The specified objectives of the competition were originally 1350 €/m² of usable floor area for the building's construction and technical system. Four years later the building was calculated at 1400 €/m² of usable floor area. When the aspects of the general rise in construction costs and the achieved building quality are considered, it is a very good result. For comparison: according the German building cost indices (BKI), construction costs for high-standard office buildings in 2007 were between 1480 and 2430 €/m² GFA.

The predicted costs from the estimating software for services media supply and disposal with electricity, water and gas were substantially lower than the parameters for comparable office buildings (Fig. 6.51). For a first comparison a value was taken from the literature (see Assessment of the economic advantages, p. 68), and for a second comparison a reference value for an administration building belonging to the state of Lower Saxony.

The life cycle assessment of the four main buildings in the ensemble showed a considerably lower value than that of a comparable standard office building over the 50 year period of observation. The representative building type "Bürogebäude" (Office building), which was developed on behalf of the German Federal Ministry of Transport, Building and Urban Development (BMBVS) for determining life cycle assessment indices for the DGNB Sustainable Building certification scheme was used as a benchmark for this comparison.

The values for the indicators for global warming, photochemical ozone creation and eutrophication potentials are 25–50 % lower. As expected because of the use of renewable raw materials for heating, the acidification and renewable primary energy indicators are higher.

Certification in accordance with the DGNB Sustainable Building certification scheme

Paul Wunderlich House was certified by the LKL audit team (Günter Löhnert, Holger König and Thomas Lützkendorf) in accordance with DGNB Sustainable Building certification scheme. The building certification is the last link in the information chain.

The DGNB certification scheme was developed jointly by the BMVBS and the German Sustainable Building Council (DGNB). The key objectives of certification cover six aspects:
- Ecological performance
- Economic performance
- Social and functional performance
- Technical performance
- Process performance
- Site performance and location

These sub-aspects are weighted differently within the overall system (see Tools for integrated design, p. 101). The overall quantitative character of the evaluation criteria in the DGNB system moves the direct assessment of individual components and systems (e. g. rain water use, green roofs) and construction products (e. g. use of recycled construction materials) into the background. Instead these can and must bring in their advantages in the context of a quantitative evaluation (e. g. by means of life cycle assessment and life cycle costing) or indirectly by the effect on comfort and user satisfaction. In this respect there is a need for suitable information and evaluation or calculation rules relating to this. Building products themselves are therefore not the subjects of direct assessment, but rather a source of information that is evaluated in terms of its effect on the building and its life cycle. The desired "sustainable" influence of design and investment decisions assumes, among other things, that the significant features and characteristics of buildings can be described, evaluated and, if necessary, communicated to

third parties. This includes the demands on resources, impacts on the environment, life cycle costs, influence on value stability and development, the performance of the functional solution, influence on user satisfaction and selected technical characteristics.

The assessment of sustainability is not reduced to the recommendation or exclusion of construction products. It is rather the case that all products must demonstrate, through the provision of suitable information, that they contribute – verified in terms of quantity – to the advantages (e. g. to ecological and economic advantages) of buildings. This also applies to products, and in particular to construction products, made from renewable raw materials that up to now were frequently seen in a positive light and perceived as contributing to sustainable development. Since the introduction of the DGNB certification scheme, this must also be substantiated, quantified and demonstrated. This must include all life cycle phases of a building:
- The production and erection of the building including all energy and material resources
- The maintenance over a 50-year period of observation including energy and material upstream stages, production, on-site processes, deconstruction and disposal processes
- The costs of heating, hot water provision, cooling, air conditioning, lighting including primary and auxiliary energy over a 50-year period of observation
- Deconstruction and disposal

16 office buildings were erected in a first pilot phase of the DGNB certification scheme. Six of these buildings qualified for the gold award of the DGNB certification scheme with a minimum fulfilment rating of 80 % of the weighted individual aspects. To receive the silver award the building must fulfil 65–80 %, and for the bronze 50–64 %. In the pilot phase, Paul Wunderlich House achieved a fulfilment rating of 92 %, which corresponds to a score of 1.18 – the best assessment of all 16 office buildings.

Summary

The Barnim District Services and Administration Centre was handed over to the client on 1 July 2007. The modern building complex sets new standards

in many respects and gives the Eberswalde town centre a completely new character.

The architect, Thomas Winkelbauer, describes the final design as follows: "Paul Wunderlich House sweeps away current thinking about administration buildings. Instead of long, dark corridors devoid of people, our design presents a transparent, forward-looking administration centre at the heart of the community. The basis for this success was the emphasis on sustainability and economic and social compatibility. Thermally effective storage masses, a compact building geometry and the use of natural resources for heating, cooling and ventilation mean Paul Wunderlich House consumes 70 % less energy than comparable buildings. Glass provides transparency and natural light. References to the historic urban planning context ensures integration into the old town district.

Project data Barnim Administration Centre
- Building: Barnim District Services and Administration Centre
- Location: Eberswalde near Berlin
- Client: Landkreis Barnim
- Architects: Gesellschaft für Architektur & Projektmanagement mbH (GAP), Berlin (Thomas Winkelbauer, Wolfgang von Herder)
- In collaboration with: Reinhard Groscurth, Michael Abramjuk
- Construction: 2007
- Use: Administration centre, commercial
- No. of floors: 4

Volumes and areas (ensemble, five buildings):
- Enclosed volume: 90 300 m³
- Thermally conditioned enclosed space: 75 000 m³
- Gross floor area (GFA): 22 000 m²

Volume and area of the assessed building components (Departmental building III):
- Enclosed volume: 23 383 m³
- Thermally conditioned volume: 20 549 m³
- Gross floor area (GFA): 5445 m²
- Area occupied by construction elements e. g. walls etc.: 566 m²
- Net floor area: 4879 m²
- Circulation area: 815 m²
- Technical systems area: 354 m²

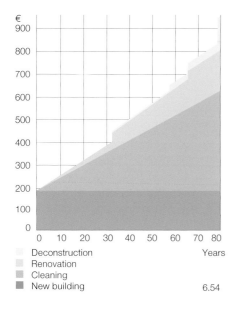

Deconstruction
Renovation
Cleaning
New building   6.54

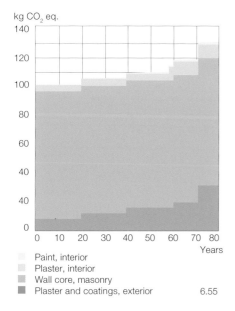

Paint, interior
Plaster, interior
Wall core, masonry
Plaster and coatings, exterior   6.55

6.54 Life cycle costs of a building component
     (upper storey ceiling) over a period of 80
     years
6.55 Environmental effect, indicator global warm-
     ing potential (kg CO_2 eq.) of an external wall
     over a period of 80 years (per m²)
6.56 Environmental effect of four external thermal
     insulation composite systems (ETICS) in the
     production phase
6.57 Environmental effect of four external thermal
     insulation composite systems (ETICS) in the
     production and renovation phases over a pe-
     riod 80 years (per m²)

- Thermally conditioned net plan area:
  4874 m²
- Usable area (UA): 3710 m²
- Ancillary use area: 210 m²
- Efficiency: UA/GFA = 0.67
- Heat transfer envelope area:
  5500 m²
- A/V ratio: 0.27

Analysis software: LEGEP

Extended consideration of buildings

In addition to the examples discussed earlier in this chapter, design teams are frequently faced with further recurring issues in which life cycle analysis can make a significant contribution to decision making. Five such cases are explored in the following sections.

Case a: Life cycle analysis of building components

The building is analysed on the basis of its components and the services it provides. The building components can also be investigated for the purpose of comparison independently of the installation situation. However, it must be pointed out that although a standard situation may be assumed, it could be changed in the building. In this way e. g. the installed situation for a window could lead to it being subjected to more or less weathering.

Life cycle analysis works with the information about the life cycle provided by the building components. This information must include cycle times, which determine the frequency of an event over a defined period of time. Fig. 6.54 shows the annual costs arising from a building component (in this case: an intermediate storey ceiling slab) plotted cumulatively over an 80-year period of observation.

A similar graph can also be selected for the environmental balance of a building component (in this case: an external wall) (Fig. 6.55). The graph can always be used only for one indicator (in this case: global warming potential).

Component comparison

Only with the definition of a functional unit and an unambiguous service spectrum can comparable analyses of life cycle costs and life cycle assessments be worthwhile. So that sense can be

made of the results produced by third parties, it is essential that the boundary conditions and the situation under which the investigations were carried out are fully defined. Figs. 6.56 and 6.57 show a comparison of the environmental impacts of four external thermal insulation composite systems (ETICS). The following assumptions have been made:

- Functional unit: 1 m², applied over the full area on any substrate
- Construction materials: adhesive, insulation, dowels, mesh, base plaster, finishing plaster, paint
- U-value: approx. 0.33 W/m²K
- Period of observation: 80 years
- Base data database: ecoinvent
- Phases: production to renovation (no end of life)
- Indicators:
  – Material mass (check on apparent validity)
- Input indicators:
  – Primary energy, non-renewable (MJ)
  – Primary energy, renewable (MJ)
- Output indicators:
  – CO_2 (kg) (with credits for renewable raw materials)
  – SO_2 (kg)

The system used consists of:
- Polystyrene 25 kg/m³, 100 mm, mineral plaster, epoxy resin dispersion paint
- Mineral fibres 150 kg/m, 120 mm, mineral plaster, silicate paint
- Softwood fibres 130 kg/m³, 120 mm, mineral plaster, silicate paint
- Mineral foam 115 kg/m³, 120 mm, mineral fine plaster, silicate paint

System comparison in the production phase

If the production phase alone is considered, then a different environmental impact can be determined for each type of construction which may also be different for every indicator for any particular product (Fig. 6.56). The polystyrene system is the lightest form of construction, while the mineral wool system, due to the heavy facade insulation boards and the two-layer plaster system, is the heaviest. The renewable primary energy is the highest with the wood fibre insulation boards as they are made of renewable raw material, while the non-renewable primary energy of the mineral foam boards made of aerated concrete is the lowest. The wood fibre insulation boards attract a credit in the greenhouse gas indicator.

System comparison in the production and renovation phase
Using a period of observation of 80 years without considering deconstruction and disposal evens out some of the differences. In the case of the mineral board system only the plaster and paint are renewed, the insulation boards are not replaced. Therefore the material mass is only slightly higher. With the wood fibre system the CO_2 credit is reduced by the plaster and paint reno-

vation. The ETICS with mineral boards clearly shows the influence of the renovation cycles as this system has much longer renewal intervals than the others (Fig. 5.57).

Case b: Life cycle analysis of Passivhaus-standard buildings
Passive houses (Passivhaus-standard buildings) are buildings "for which thermal comfort (ISO 7730) can be achieved solely by post-heating or post-cooling of the fresh air mass that is required to fulfil sufficient indoor air quality conditions (DIN 1946) – without a need for recirculated air" [7]. The Passivhaus standard stipulates an annual heating heat requirement of

≤ 15 kWh/m^{2}a and a primary energy requirement of ≤ 120 kWh/m^{2}a (including all electrical consumers). These values are achieved through a combination of measures that seek to reduce demand (thermal insulation, window performance and airtightness of the outer skin) and through efficient waste air heat recovery and hot water production. In principle passive houses are able to function without additional static heating.
The environmental impacts of passive houses in the operating phase are small in every case. Differences arise mainly through the type of electricity used. The question inevitably arises as to whether the additional construction work involved in passive houses causes higher

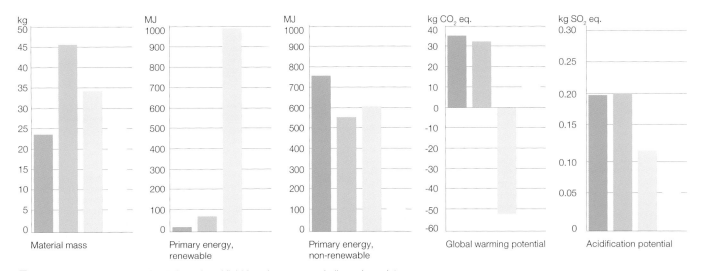

ETICS, 100 mm polystyrene insulation, mineral finishing plaster scraped, dispersion paint
ETICS, 120 mm mineral wool insulation, mineral finishing plaster rubbed, silicate paint
ETICS, 120 mm wood fibre board, mineral finishing plaster rubbed, silicate paint
ETICS, 120 mm mineral board, fine finishing plaster, silicate paint

6.56

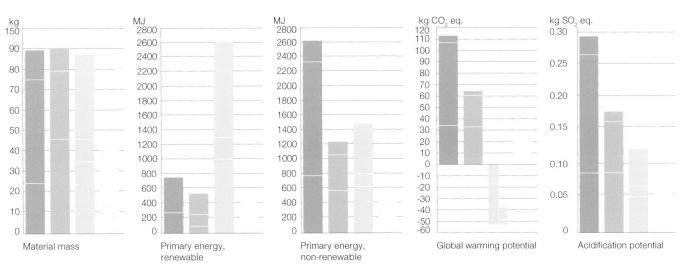

ETICS, 100 mm polystyrene insulation, mineral finishing plaster scraped, dispersion paint
ETICS, 120 mm mineral wool insulation, mineral finishing plaster rubbed, silicate paint
ETICS, 120 mm wood fibre board, mineral finishing plaster rubbed, silicate paint
ETICS, 120 mm mineral board, fine finishing plaster, silicate paint

6.57

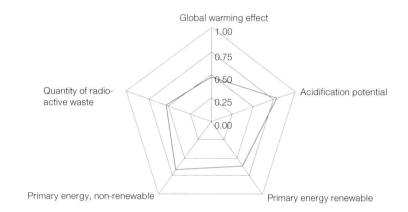

— Construction of a Passivhaus office building   ⋯ Construction of a conventional building

6.58

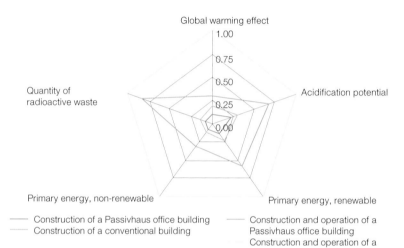

— Construction of a Passivhaus office building
⋯ Construction of a conventional building

— Construction and operation of a
Passivhaus office building
⋯ Construction and operation of a
conventional building

6.59

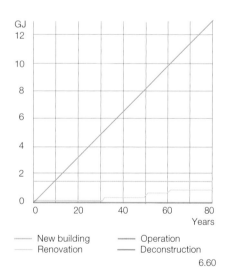

— New building   — Operation
— Renovation   — Deconstruction

6.60

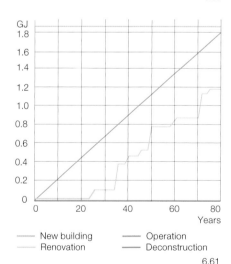

— New building   — Operation
— Renovation   — Deconstruction

6.61

6.58 Environmental effects of the construction
of a conventional office building and a
Passivhaus-standard office building
6.59 Environmental effects of the construction and
operation during the service life of a conventional office building and a Passivhaus-standard office building

6.60 Primary energy expenditure
(Basis: European average fuel mix UPCTE)
for a conventional office building over a
period of 80 years
6.61 Primary energy expenditure, non-renewable
(Basis: use of PV electricity) for a
Passivhaus-standard office building

environmental impacts through its production, maintenance and renovation.
A detailed investigation shows that the
environmental impacts arising from the
construction of a comparable conventional building are clearly higher [8].
The widespread belief that, because
of their necessarily higher insulation
standard, passive houses require more
primary energy and impact more on the
environment than conventional buildings was not confirmed. In the passive
house studied here, certain components were superfluous (heating system), other components were very
carefully designed and the various materials were used in the optimum manner to exploit their properties (wooden
walls, roof, concrete floors etc.). The
conventional house is oversized in
many of its details and contains numerous redundant components. This increases the on-going energy requirement and the amount of energy required for construction and maintenance of the building fabric. Moreover,
the complexity of the building technical
services systems lays them open to
serious risks regarding availability,
aging and obsolescence.
Environmental impact is therefore not
a question of energy standards or material selection, but much more about
optimum construction and design (Fig.
6.58). If the environmental impacts of
these two buildings are considered
assuming a service life of 80 years,
then the impacts of the passive house
can be expected to be significantly
less than those of the conventional
building (Fig. 6.59).
The type of electricity generation has a
great influence on the possible environmental impacts caused by operating
the building. If the European fuel mix
(UPCTE) is used, then the environmental impacts of the passive house are
about one third those of the conventional building. If the French fuel mix,
which has a greater proportion of nuclear power, is used, then the result is
a lowering of the greenhouse effect but
an increase in the quantity of radioactive waste (Fig. 6.59). The advantages
of photovoltaic electricity are apparent
particularly in the primary energy consumption and radioactive waste categories, where up to 90% of the environmental impacts are avoided.
A comparison of the development of

the primary energy requirement for the construction and the operation of both buildings over 80 years shows that, with conventional buildings, the operational energy exceeds the energy expended in constructing the new building in just 14 years. For a passive house with photovoltaic electricity, the cost of operation is still less than the cost of production, even after 80 years (Figs. 6.60 and 6.61).

Life cycle analysis shows that priorities will shift between production and operation in the coming years. Only by extending design to include life cycle analysis will the industry be in a position under the changed conditions outlined above to minimise the total impacts caused by production, renovation and disposal.

Case c: Management of existing building stock
The development of housing construction always reflects the prevailing wider situation in society. So it was with the rebuilding in the post-war period, the expansion of the building stock in the following 30 years up to today's era of consolidation and renovation, which is the current subject of observation here. The latter period is characterised by a rising number of smaller households, which has led to a shift in demand in housing construction. At the same time, there is a general need for renovation across the whole range of older building stock.

The short-term need for renovation of residential properties in Germany was estimated to be 20 billion € in 2000 [9]. From a longer-term view, the potential is much higher still. The main focus for construction in the future will therefore be on the conception and implementation of combined new building, transformation and renovation strategies.

In these conditions two most likely main tasks are emerging for design engineers, architects and the construction industry for the next decades. On the one hand there is an extensive challenge ahead in building maintenance and therefore in renovation and modernisation. On the other hand the analysis of the existing building stock will provide important aids to decision-making in the fields of deconstruction or demolition. A high level of specialist knowledge and experience is required for everyone involved with design and construction in existing buildings. Dealing with different forms of construction and in some cases construction materials that are no longer in common use requires care and expertise. The reasons for damage or defects in buildings and the sources of possible pollution must always be analysed on a case by case basis. Frequently old buildings are inappropriately refurbished or prematurely replaced simply through lack of thought or the necessary knowledge, which results in the irreversible loss of resources.

Different starting points for life cycle analysis
The starting point for describing existing buildings, their components and technical systems differs from that of new buildings. While with new buildings information is collected and compiled successively from the design phase through construction and operation, the relevant data and information for describing an existing building is often unavailable. Building documentation sometimes gets lost, is not kept up to date or no longer represents the current situation, which sets the design team a problem, even before deciding on how the building should be improved. It is understandably not worthwhile bringing a building up to modern standards in every respect if the client has decided in favour of demolition on the basis of its valuation. In these circumstances the design team has to approach the task with particular economy.

With existing buildings the collection of information has to take place incrementally, in stages. These stages must be tailored to ensure that the results lead to clear decisions by the client and provide the starting point for further work. The element and building catalogues are the essential basis for increasing the depth of knowledge about a building step by step. They allow the description of a building to start with general, rather vague data that can be made more precise in subsequent steps. The collector and complier of this information needs software that allows, at the element as well as the building level, the complete building to be described in all its practical reality in order to make this very complex task somewhat easier.

Building components and technical systems in new buildings generally fulfil constructional, building physics or technical requirements, i.e. they describe an ideal situation. On the other hand, components in existing buildings have been subject to aging processes. Their characteristics have significantly changed since the time of their installation, with the result that they no longer or only partially fulfil technical or building physics standards. However, a crucial fact to be noted in the creation of an element catalogue for an existing building is that the construction methods used for residential property have undergone considerable change as a result of historical and technological developments.

Tools for designing works in existing buildings
As well as the building catalogues of the various German states [11], there are also reference works on the analysis of existing construction [10] available to help the designer in his task. However they are mainly focused on heating technology aspects and relevant above all to energy consultants. On the other hand, collections of data are available that are intended to support architects in determining the costs of construction works in existing buildings [12]. The variety of forms of construction in existing buildings and the range of possible renovation measures make it possible to compile work item catalogues with cost information for only the most important areas of work. On the other hand, electronic work item catalogues can offer work items for all areas of work with an appropriate width of variations [13]. Yet here there is still a lack of support in relation to assignment to building age classes.

A good introduction to cost appraisal can be found in an appendix on cost elements by Rolf Neddermann [14]. The appendix can be applied very well to cost estimating and calculation by elements but does not deal with the assignment to building age classes. Historic building catalogues can be of help in estimating the costs of building works [15]. These documents contain published information about the evaluated buildings and their costs. The data are specific to each particular building and are not made more generally applicable.

On the other hand the previously mentioned building catalogues of the various German states and the papers published by the Institut Wohnen und Umwelt (IWU) [16] attempt to make their data on the measures to improve the heating performance of buildings more generally applicable. The typology upon which they are based allows the connection to be made between building age class and element constructions. Suggestions for improving design and construction techniques are developed for these examples. Cost information about the measures and their financial efficiency, on the other hand, is not available.

Existing buildings
A building age catalogue was developed as part of the study "Material flows and costs in the areas of building and housing" for the Enquete Commission "Protection of man and the environment" of the German Bundestag [17]. This building age catalogue was developed with the aim of establishing a classification system that would be capable of the detailed consideration of the boundary conditions relating to

historical developments in construction methods and standards, society and culture. Different sources have been consulted for classifying buildings into age classes [18] and augmented by some thoughts of the author (Fig. 6.62). A number of existing building elements for the cost groups in DIN 276 are required for the building age classes:
320 Foundations
330 External walls
340 Internal walls
350 Floors and ceilings
360 Roofs
400 Structure – services

The existing building elements must be adequately differentiated to allow information to be entered later about individual building component layers. Using the building elements available in the reference works, which can likewise be assigned to particular building age classes, existing buildings can be sufficiently accurately described without the need for more detailed investigation. The assignment of the building elements is performed by comparing the drawings and the building description with the catalogue and the collection of suitable elements.

Construction materials with health risks (materials, items, elements)
Building products that contain pollutants are a particular problem in existing

buildings. They have to be identified and removed before the building can be put to further use. An investigation strategy intended to provide project stakeholders with practical guidance on construction in existing buildings was developed in the research report "Investigation strategy and scope for demolition works/materials auditing of environmentally relevant construction materials" [19]. The results of the research project were taken up by ministries in Baden-Württemberg and Bavaria and distributed in their ministerial information systems [20]. The Bavarian Environmental Agency (LfU) makes the information available to the public on the Internet. This risk information was linked with the hazardous material.

Existing building elements with hazardous materials
If these hazardous materials are linked with existing building elements in a database, then they can supply the appropriate information for every existing building, e. g. facade cladding with asbestos cement boards or wood parquet flooring with a tar-containing adhesive. This creates an information chain that extends from the external wall element through the facade cladding up to the asbestos cement material and the information stored with it about hazardous materials.

6.62 Classification of buildings into ten building age classes
6.63 Modernised housing in Karlsruhe, 2006
6.64 Project stakeholders and process flow for the modernisation of buildings in use

Building age class	Period	Special constructional, social, political and economic characteristics
AK-1	Before 1835	Pre-industrial construction involving manual building methods and little use of energy-intensive materials
AK-2	1835-1870	Establishment of industrialised building elements made from iron and steel
AK-3	1871-1918	Industry, in particular the iron and steel industry, took over the leading role in the German economy; Steel became the predominant material for long-span construction; start of reinforced concrete construction from 1900; National standards introduced; rapid urban concentration and urbanisation (modern German state born)
AK-4	1919-1933	War and post-war years use of substitute materials; "Roaring twenties" with high growth rates, investment and foreign debt; 1929–1932: World economic crisis with falling production and high unemployment
AK-5	1934-1949	Economy of scarcity with use of substitute materials of previous pre- and post-war years, rise of nationalism, growth of war industries: road building, chemical industry, vehicle building and armaments with employment creation policy; 1945–1949: Era of need and uncertainty; occupying powers issued 1948 Housing Order No. 8 for rectification of housing shortage
AK-6	1950-1964	1950-1956: Post-war years with material shortages. construction and building methods similar to inter-war period; change in design approach due to reinforced concrete slabs; 1951: DIN 18011 "Space requirements for furniture, cooking and heating appliances in social housing"; 1957: DIN 4108 "Thermal insulation and energy economy in buildings" came into effect
AK-7	1965-1976	Reconstruction with Germany's "economic miracle" and full employment; German Democratic Republic (GDR) concrete panel construction method (from 1965); precast construction, new materials from the chemical industry, more engineering and transportation infrastructure; from 1971 increasing building conversions
AK-8	1977-1994	1973: first oil crisis; 1st + 2nd thermal insulation ordnance (WSchVO) made effective ; 1989: Reunification of German Federal Republic (GFR) and GDR
AK-9	1995–2001	3rd WSchVO made effective (WSchVO 95)
AK-10	2002–to date	01.01.2002: EnEV came into effect; EnEV 2007 and 2009

6.62

Modernisation example

Finished to a very basic, simple standard with inexpensive rents, five nine-storey individual blocks of multiple dwelling units stand in a Karlsruhe district. They are typical examples of 1970s architecture. The reinforced concrete structure was faced with calcium silicate masonry and incorporated 2 cm of mineral fibre insulation. A curtain wall facade of asbestos cement boards forms the weather protection layer.

High energy costs and the prospect of balcony and facade refurbishments led to the drawing up of a comprehensive modernisation plan. Following extensive scenario analyses, the housing company decided on the following variants:

- Demolition of two of the blocks
- Structural modernisation and refurbishment of the remaining three buildings (Fig. 6.63).
- High CO_2 savings through low energy requirement and the use of a combined heat and power plant

A design office worked up three modernisation concepts (Mini/Plus/Maxi) and produced a cost estimate, energy requirement calculation and financial concept. The objective was to attract funding from the government-backed KfW development bank on the strength of the CO_2 emissions savings. As part of the research project, a building was entered into an integrated analysis program with links to a building element

database. The modernisation costs, energy savings and environmental impacts were calculated for all three concepts. The construction variant was a mixture of all three concepts.

In addition the design team was notified of the hazardous materials with the relevant building elements. The information concerned the following construction materials:

- Asbestos cement boards
- Mineral fibre insulation
- Tar-containing adhesives
- Cushion vinyl floor coverings

The asbestos cement facade presented a serious problem for this refurbishment of an operating building. Appropriate additional precautions (dust binding etc.) had to be taken so that it could be removed.

The modelling of a renovation scenario variant was particularly useful for the calculation of the apportionable modernisation costs. This cost appraisal related to the renovation costs e. g. painting the windows, renewal of the balcony waterproofing membrane or refurbishment of the roof water inlets. The works carried out included complete window replacement, demolition and replacement of the balconies. The apportionable modernisation costs were able to be calculated precisely and verified in accordance with the "construction costs less renovation costs" method.

6.63

Stakeholders in the modernisation

One of the factors that should never be underestimated when carrying out refurbishment and modernisation of existing buildings is the building user. The significant difference between new build and renovation lies not in the construction materials or the processes (concrete is still concrete) but rather in a different approach to planning and coordination of the measures to be undertaken and in the active involvement of clients and users.

The scope for improvisation in a building in use is limited and the financial

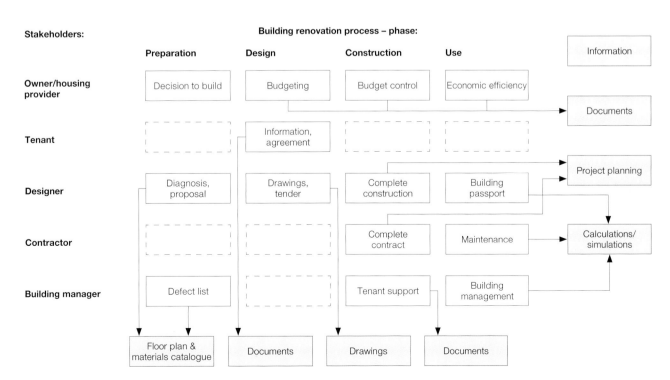

6.64

6.65

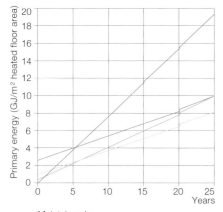

—— Maintain only
—— Replace with new to Minergie standard
—— Refurbish to Minergie standard
—— Refurbish to Minergie new building standard

6.66

consequences of detrimentally affecting the operation of the building can be many times the construction costs. The anticipated sequence of work on site assumes great significance at a relatively early stage in the design. A new category of design tool is required to evaluate whether a project is realisable, i.e, technically feasible and compatible with the operation of the building. This tool must provide continuous support to the design and construction processes from the beginning and integrate into the long-term management strategy of the existing building.

Fig. 6.64, p. 133, shows the complex organisation of the construction process for the modernisation of a building in use. Communication between all stakeholders during the various stage is a necessary prerequisite for the successful completion of the project. The content of the documents (green boxes) required for the information exchange should be structured so as to be mutually consistent.

This was done in an exemplary manner for the building in Karlsruhe. The project was completed in a very short construction period of only eight months.

Case d: Demolition or conservation of value?

The decision whether and under what circumstances it is worthwhile demolishing the building is complex and raises questions about the reasons, the stakeholders, the boundary conditions and generally about the possibility of a complete valuation of a building.

The demolition question arises in very different ways and occurs at the level of individual buildings and existing building stock as well as at a regional and national level (Fig. 6.65). It is very difficult to draw any generally applicable conclusions.

Demolition rates in Europe are on average very low and demolition continues to be a rare occurrence (Fig. 6.67). There are of course regional exceptions. The intention to demolish has usually to do with the building standing empty or having too low a rate of return in relation to the market value of the site. With decisions to renovate, as soon as the cost of the renovation of a building becomes significantly more than one third of the cost of a new building, then a demolition or a complete transformation, which in some cases is almost the equivalent of a demolition, is considered. Functional or technical obsolescence is often given as the reason for demolition (e.g. rooms too small, very poor sound insulation). Architectural form is also an often-quoted reason, after buildings have been judged as being old-fashioned or ugly. In these cases it becomes difficult to achieve a satisfactory rent. A last ground may be legal obsolescence. Here a structure is no longer capable of complying with the currently applicable requirements (energy consumption, environmental impact etc.).

As a rule, lower rents result from a building being seen as obsolete and having real defects. On the other hand this actually helps lower income groups find somewhere to live, albeit for the short or medium term. In almost every case, demolition of housing therefore translates into cheaper accommodation disappearing and being replaced by more expensive. Replacing obsolete buildings by inexpensive new ones at low rents can only be accomplished with subsidies or by adopting collective ownership models.

Boundary conditions also have a great influence on demolition rates. Empty

6.65 A failed policy of subsidised demolition has placed heritage buildings from the late 1800s under threat while renovated panel system housing estates remain empty in east German cities.

6.66 Development of primary energy expenditure for different variants of refurbishment and replacement new buildings

6.67 Demolition and new building rates for housing construction in various European countries

Country	New building rate (%)	Demolition rate (%)
Belgium	No information	0.075
France	1.1	0.07
Germany	0.6	0.14
Netherlands	0.6	0.225
Sweden	0.5	0.05
Switzerland	1.0	0.03
United Kingdom	0.75	0.075
Austria	1.4	No information
Finland	1.0	No information
Europe overall	**1.1**	**0.095**

6.67

buildings in the former German Democratic Republic (GDR) combined with demographic decline and migration within Germany will lead to an increase in the already high numbers of unoccupied buildings over the coming decades.

In principle the new build rate in Europe is about 1 % of the existing building stock, while the demolition rate is below 0.1 %. In some countries for various reasons the rates are above average – e. g. in the Netherlands, because of the poor quality of the social housing put up after the second world war or in France, where buildings have been taken down in an attempt to deal with social problems in large housing estates. In parts of the former GDR where the proportion of empty properties may amount to 20 % over the long term, the demolition rate can be assumed to be 1 % (Fig. 6.67) [21].

In the interests of saving energy and protecting the climate, it has already been proposed to demolish significant parts of the existing building stock and replace them with buildings offering better energy performance. However, studies at the level of individual buildings show that from an energy use point of view, demolition and replacement is only a worthwhile option in the long term and with certain prerequisites (very low energy requirement, as much recycling of all construction materials as possible etc.) (Fig. 6.66). With existing buildings, a systematic demolition strategy first of all produces a clear increase in total energy consumption. A model study, in which the primary energy requirement during production and operation of housing properties were measured, shows that the substitution of an existing building by a replacement new building causes a massive increase in consumption in the first few decades and only pays off from an energy use point of view over a very long period (> 30 years). In the same time frame, systematic renovation strategies achieve a greater reduction of environmental impacts, as they also cause considerably smaller material flows [22].

Conservation value of buildings
The question of demolition is not easy to answer for individual buildings nor for larger property portfolios. Demolition

decisions are still made on a case by case basis in many areas. Economic and demographic contraction can lead to widespread demolition. A differentiated process involving a comprehensive definition and determination of the conservation value of individual buildings should be adopted in every case. SIA Document 2017 "Conservation value of buildings" proposes one such process, which differentiates between tangible and intangible values (Fig. 6.69) [23].

Tangible values include primarily the value of the location of the building, based on the possibilities for use of the site. The utility value arises from a combination of fitness for purpose and adaptability or developability (future potential). The value of the building fabric depends on the type and condition of the building and its infrastructure, structural stability and durability, and its need of renovation or rehabilitation. The building owner should also consider social and economic aspects, which are influenced by society and the environment (e. g. the effects of the closure of a factory on a community). The economic value of a building is composed of the market value and the income, utility, taxable or insurance value. Buildings are becoming increasingly important to the environment as well. Relevant aspects here include the environmental impacts due to production and use of the building, durability, disposal, and the ability to recycle the building and its constituent materials.

Intangible values are more difficult to quantify. They encompass the situation value, which arises from the effect of the building on its surroundings, the historic-cultural value of a building as representative of a specific cultural epoch and lastly its architectural value. Furthermore, the craftsmanship or engineering technology value invested in the original fabric of a building, its socio-cultural value, which arises from its suitability for use by specific occupational, societal, age or ethnicity groups, should also be taken into account. Finally the emotional value also takes on a certain significance.

The process put forward in SIA 2017 can be used to provide support to decision groups during decision-finding and represents an interesting expansion of the usual short-term and profit-

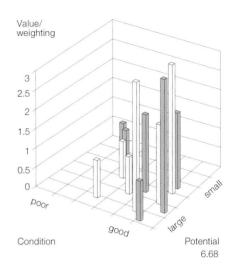

Condition   Potential
6.68

Tangible values:

Location (site)
Use
Building fabric
Society
Economic efficiency
Environment

Intangible values:

Situation value
Historic-cultural value
Architectural value
Craftsmanship-technical value
Socio-cultural value
Emotional value   6.69

Development potential	Condition	
	Poor	**Good**
Large	Some conservation value, high potential	Upward trend in conservation value
Medium	Situation too unclear for a decision	
Small	Downward trend in conservation value	Some conservation value, low potential

6.70

6.68 Example of the determination of the conservation value of a building (after SIA 2017). In this case the evaluation shows a limited conservation value (good condition, but low potential).
6.69 Tangible (green) and intangible values (yellow) in the assessment of existing buildings (after SIA 2017)
6.70 Conservation decision based on condition and development potential (after SIA 2017)

oriented methods commonly found in practice.

The current value (poor to good) and the potential (small to large) are determined for every value category and positioned in the matrix (Fig. 6.68, p. 135). The subjective or location-specific weighting of the values is expressed in the height of each column. The evaluation can also be performed by several stakeholders working independently of one another. The evaluation can be shown visually or in tabular form. There are five possible cases, depending on which quadrant of the matrix has most of the evaluation columns (Fig. 6.70, p. 135).

Case e: Industrial buildings
About a half of the estimated costs of all construction activities in Germany are expended in the construction of new buildings and in works within existing buildings in the non-housing sector. When it is considered that factories and workshops together with retail and warehousing space make up more than 40% of new non-housing building activity, then it becomes clear how important sustainable industrial buildings are in the achievement of sustainability targets in the construction and real estate sectors. [24]
The design and construction of industrial buildings are founded on different premises to other building types. As could be seen in the example of the production hall at Schmiedefeld (see

pp. 120f.), the period of observation of 15–25 years is short in comparison with that of other building use categories. Frequent and fundamental changes of use as well as the difference in the normal service life of building components, production systems and product generations lead to a complex web of interrelationships in the sphere of industrial building.

In addition for example logistics buildings have a very low energy requirement during the use phase. From the point of view of life cycle assessment, the production and disposal of the buildings therefore play a much greater role than in e.g. housing. As a result it is worthwhile optimising the design and examine variants for constructional elements. For the reasons outlined above, the focus is increasingly moving towards ensuring recycling-compatible deconstruction and reusable materials in industrial buildings. From an economic point of view it maximises the potential for use by third parties. Building for a multiplicity of diverse uses is immensely important here, in order to avoid ecologically and economically senseless demolition following a change of use.

Research project "Life cycle engineering in industrial buildings"
On the other hand, the high degree of standardisation in industrial building concepts and the resulting very short design times open a window of oppor-

tunity to develop alternative concepts. In the course of the research project "Life cycle engineering (LCE) in industrial buildings" an attempt was therefore made to develop a design tool that would produce results, from relatively little input and a few subject-specific information sheets, that would allow the designer to compare different project variants in the early stages of planning and design on the basis of the following aspects [25]:
• Production costs
• Use costs
• Energy requirement
• Environmental impact
• Comfort
In many cases when planning new investment projects, it is noticeable with the current situation that a synchronous, interdisciplinary agreement between factory designers, industrial building designers and town planners under the umbrella of an overall consideration of economic, ecological, social and technical requirements does not take place or only takes place to some extent. This method of working frequently leads to uneconomic building configurations and system concepts. Even in the early planning phases, the analysis tool developed as part of the research project provides information as a result of a systematic combination of production and building design with an urban planning dimension.
Designers normally adopt a requirement-oriented, top-down approach in

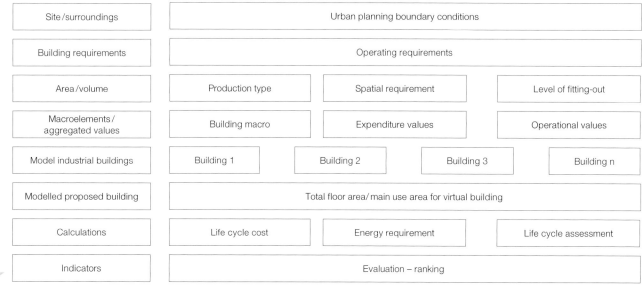

Process level	Process step/results		
Site/surroundings	Urban planning boundary conditions		
Building requirements	Operating requirements		
Area/volume	Production type	Spatial requirement	Level of fitting-out
Macroelements/ aggregated values	Building macro	Expenditure values	Operational values
Model industrial buildings	Building 1 / Building 2	Building 3	Building n
Modelled proposed building	Total floor area/main use area for virtual building		
Calculations	Life cycle cost	Energy requirement	Life cycle assessment
Indicators	Evaluation – ranking		

6.71

which an ever more precise image of the completed building emerges from the progressive refining of details based on initially fuzzy, ill-defined information. On the one hand, this process permits a large number of variants and differences. On the other, the information at the beginning of the process is vague and insubstantial.

Improvement of the top-down approach can only be achieved if the initial data at the beginning of the project has already been analysed and evaluated using a bottom-up approach (see p. 104). Highly aggregated indices or software-generated macrodata from over 60 industrial buildings that have been recorded completely in all their detail are available for the analysis of variants. In addition, info-boxes open to provide specific expert knowledge as an aid to decision-making (Fig. 6.71).

The urban planning boundary conditions of a commercially zoned area or parcel of land normally allow the design team to create a requirement-oriented building model.

The LCA tool is already capable of examining the following aspects for the development of variants at the establishment of the project brief stage:

- The suitability and feasibility of different plots for development
- Maximum extendibility
- Tailoring the site
- Possible development concepts
- Parking provision
- Connection to transport infrastructure

The LCE tool also allows the design team to examine different building variants (e.g. roof truss spans, columns, spacings and system heights of the buildings). At the design stage, the tool allows in-depth investigations to determine the preferred variant, which can then taken forward for the detailed design.

- Loadbearing structure (spans, column grids, structural material)
- Materials for the roof and external walls
- Specification of the heating, ventilation and cooling system, and air conditioning
- Regenerative energy use

The analysis and evaluation of project data describes the whole life cycle of the building and is oriented towards the three themes of sustainability:

- Economy (production costs, use costs, operating costs)
- Ecology (environmental impact production, operating expenditure, environmental impact operation, environmental impact production and operation per year)
- Social aspects

This information forms the basis for an evaluation of the absolute value expressed per unit of volume or area and allows the comparison with orientation, limiting or target values.

Summary

The practical examples presented in this chapter clearly show that life cycle analysis provides a means of extending the whole spectrum of the design process. Buildings, not only new buildings and those falling into the use category "office real estate", can be developed and evaluated from the point of view of their life cycles. Moreover, life cycle analysis provides valuable advice to stakeholders involved in the renovation of existing buildings and in new industrial buildings.

The economic and ecological advantages of individual design decisions cannot be described nor evaluated without the use of life cycle analysis. The applied examples in this chapter show that the knowledge and technical prerequisites are available to make life cycle analysis a part of everyday design office practice.

References:

[1] Statistisches Bundesamt Deutschland (pub.): Preisindizes für die Bauwirtschaft. Fachserie 17. Wiesbaden 2007
[2] Statistisches Bundesamt (pub.): Systematik der Bauwerke, Signierschlüssel für Gebäude. Issue 1978
[3] ARGEBAU-Hochbauausschuss, Fachkommission Baukostenplanung und Baukostenkontrolle
[4] Bundesministerium für Verkehr, Bau und Stadtentwicklung (pub.): Normalherstellungskosten 2000. Berlin 2000. www.bmvbs.de/Anlage/original_965507/Anlage-7-NHK-2000.pdf
[5] IWU Institut Wohnen und Umwelt: Die Heizenergie-Einsparmöglichkeiten durch Verbesserung des Wärmeschutzes typischer hessischer Wohngebäude. Darmstadt 1997 König, Holger: Altbausanierung leicht gemacht. Kissing 2008
[6] www.solarbau.de
[7] Passivhausinstitut Darmstadt, www.passivhaus.de
[8] Moosmann, Cornelia et al.: Lebenszyklusanalyse von Passivhäusern. Frankfurt/Main 2005
[9] Oswald, Rainer et al: Systematische Instandsetzung und Modernisierung im Wohnungsbestand. Final report. Stuttgart 2003
[10] Böhmer, Heike: k-Werte alter Bauteile. Eschborn 1999
[11] Gertec GmbH, UTEC GmbH: Gebäudetypologie Schleswig-Holstein. Wärmetechnische Gebäudesanierung in Schleswig-Holstein. Kiel 1999
[12] Schmitz, Heinz et al.: Baukosten 2004, Instandsetzung, Sanierung, Modernisierung/Umnutzung. Essen 2004
[13] sirAdos: "Altbau-Elemente" im sirAdos-Wohnungsbau. Kissing 2008
[14] Neddermann, Rolf: Kostenermittlung im Altbau. Munich 2005
[15] BKI Baukosteninformationsdienst (pub.): BKI Objektdaten Altbau. Stuttgart 2001
[16] Eike-Henning, Werner; Siepe, Benedikt: Die Heizenergie-Einsparmöglichkeiten durch Verbesserung des Wärmeschutzes typischer hessischer Wohngebäude. Darmstadt 1997
[17] Kohler, Niklaus; Hassler, Uta; Paschen, Herbert (pub.): Stoffströme und Kosten in den Bereichen Bauen und Wohnen. Enquete Commission "Schutz des Menschen und der Umwelt" 13th German Bundestag. Berlin/Heidelberg/New York 1999
[18] Gertec GmbH, UTEC GmbH: as Ref. 17 IWU Institut Wohnen und Umwelt: as Ref. 11
[19] Weber Ingenieure GmbH: Untersuchungsstrategie und -umfang bei Rückbaumaßnahmen. Stoffkatalog umweltrelevanter Baustoffe. Pforzheim 2001
[20] Landesamt für Umweltschutz (pub.): Arbeitshilfe kontrollierter Rückbau. Munich 2003
[21] Gruhler, Karin et al.: Sanierung und Umbau versus Neubau? IÖR Texte 155. Dresden 2008
[22] Behnisch, Martin; Aksözen, Mehmet: Die kulturellen und sozialen Werte von Gebäuden mitberücksichtigen. In: Thema Umwelt 01/2008.
[23] Schweizer Ingenieur- und Architektenverein (pub.): SIA Merkblatt 2017: Erhaltungswert von Bauwerken. Zurich 2000
[24] Statistisches Bundesamt: Bautätigkeit, Fachserie 5, Reihe 1. Wiesbaden 2007
[25] www.win-lce.de

6.71 Improved top-down approach through use of macroelements

The requirements of the description and assessment of buildings have risen enormously. Increasingly themes such as climate change and conservation of resources, demographic change, globalisation, value stability and development are having to be considered in the early stages of design. Awarding authorities, clients, owners and users of buildings expect robust statements, not only about the quality and performance of buildings, but also about their behaviour during the life cycle, about their effects on the environment and human health as well as their economic advantages.

The traditional problems will continue to play a role in design, e. g. in urban planning, architectural, functional and technical matters, as well as in the design and control of the manufacturing, construction and management processes. In addition there are more requests for information about energy consumption, environmental impact, the users' health and comfort as well as the long-term behaviour of building components. These new requirements and their mutual interactions have to be documented and the quantitative and qualitative terms of reference made verifiable. This development has yet to reach its conclusion.

For some years now research on the economic, energy and environmental assessment processes has turned its attention towards the life cycle of buildings and has generally been described as life cycle analysis. This preliminary work was intended to further develop the methods of life cycle analysis and their practical applica-

tion. However, the integration of this process into the design, construction and use phases of a building has proved difficult. The calculations to do this require a wealth of information about buildings that often is not available or has to be newly defined for each aspect and then collected. A breakthrough in this area can only be achieved by a universally applicable, multipurpose, scalable description of the building. It builds on the results of research on building information modelling.

Higher requirements of design
For some years the requirements of buildings have been increasingly influenced by assessments of their sustainability. The associated long-term perspective was already contained in life cycle analysis and allowed its seamless integration with sustainability certification. Both combine to form, together with the building information model, the boundary conditions for a new, integrated design methodology. This by no means applies only to the design of new buildings: life cycle analysis is also a valuable tool for design and construction in existing building stock.

Everyone participating in the design must meet certain prerequisites in order to be able to use life cycle analysis in the design process: they need to be able think in terms of models and scenarios to describe the life cycle of buildings and be prepared to expand the earlier spectrum of problem definition, methods and the information to be processed. Life cycle analysis has extended the spatial and temporal system limits of all design and management processes. These new limits are the basis for long-term scenario planning. With this comes the need to consider the aging process and in particular the risks of obsolescence.

The circle of stakeholders, those who design and manage real estate, has also become larger. The various points of view and interests must be analysed and set in relation to the applicable system limits, and the consideration and decision horizons. Arising from this are numerous consequences for the description and modelling of buildings and the interpretation of results of the life cycle analysis. These aspects have been demonstrated and discussed in earlier chapters.

This book has not been able to cover all possible themes and discuss all of the questions to the fullest extent. In addition to the content introduced here, the authors recommend addressing the influence of design decisions on the health, comfort and satisfaction of building users. The actual status of the identification, assessment and control of risks in the life cycle of real estate (e. g. the risks to safety, availability, loss in rental income) from the point of view of the affected stakeholders have still to be reviewed.

Life cycle analysis is gaining acceptance
The question to be addressed now is whether life cycle analysis in its current form and under the present boundary conditions has achieved a definitive form and will become an

accepted method, which of course would be very desirable. It can be assumed from this that in future two further developments will run in parallel. Firstly in the design and management processes recourse will increasingly made to the methods and tools already available. Secondly research and development processes will deliver new knowledge and tools that at present are yet to be identified. To keep pace with these developments, it is necessary to keep abreast of the latest knowledge and extend it in a systematic manner.

What follows is a considered prediction of the expected developments: Estimates of the damage to ecosystems and human health as well as comprehensive predictions of the expenditure of resources will increasingly emerge to take the place of the effect-oriented indicators used today, such as e. g. global warming potential. This forms an inclusive bridge between life cycle analysis and risk assessment. In the general field of sustainability, new methods of control and evaluation of the complex long-term conservation of value are being developed. They are indispensable in defining and evaluating the strategies of sustainable management of buildings and infrastructures, housing developments and cities. It is assumed that these evaluation methods will be built upon a comprehensive life cycle analysis.
If product modelling becomes further accepted in design and management processes, in the future – among other things to improve confidence in the

estimated costs of projects – then automated checks are possible, for example the automatic check for conformance with standards based on an IFC model. These processes are currently being evaluated.

From this overall picture it can be assumed that the consideration of life cycles of buildings will become accepted in the future. It is perhaps not obvious at the moment how it could be possible with so little information, such limited options for evaluation, the short-term design and management horizons and so little understanding of the complicated interactions to design such complex and long-lived products as buildings.

The authors are convinced even today that an intensive discussion of the subject of sustainability and life cycle analysis can deliver a significant contribution to a expansion of the services provided by design consultants, an improvement of long-term building performance and comprehensive conservation of resources through long-term building management. These objectives can however only be achieved by means of massively improved cooperation between the participants and through the optimum use of new design methods and information technologies. The authors hope to have made a contribution to these objectives with this book.

Literature (selection)

Principles
Baccini, Peter; Brunner, Paul: Metabolism of the Anthroposphere. Berlin 1991
Enquete Commission of the German Parliament on the Protection of Humanity and the Environment (ed.): Konzept Nachhaltigkeit. Fundamente für die Gesellschaft von morgen. Bonn 1997
Grunwald, Armin; Kopfmüller, Jürgen: Nachhaltigkeit. Frankfurt/New York 2006
Kohler, Niklaus et al.: Stoffströme und Kosten im Bereich Bauen und Wohnen. Berlin 1999
Nentwig, Wolfgang et al.: Ökologie. Heidelberg 2009

Design in the life cycle of buildings
Halter, Martin: Bauerneuerung. Projektieren mit Methode. SIA Document D 0163. Zurich 2000
Hassler, Uta; Kohler, Niklaus; Wang, Wilfried (eds.): Umbau. Über die Zukunft des Gebäudebestandes. Tübingen 1999
Meyer-Meierling, Paul: Gesamtleitung von Bauten. Ein Lehrbuch der Projektsteuerung. Zurich 2002
Ronner, Heinz et al.: Vom Zahn der Zeit. Basel 2008

Life cycle assessment
Meadows, Dennis et al.: The limits of growth; a report for the Club of Rome's project on the predicament of mankind. New York 1972
Volker Hauff (ed.): Our Common Future. Report of the World Commission on Environment and Development. Greven 1987
Eyerer, Peter; Reinhardt, Hans-Wolf (eds.): Ökologische Bilanzierung von Baustoffen und Gebäuden. Wege zu einer ganzheitlichen Bilanzierung. Basel 2000
Fullana, Pere et al.: Communication of Life Cycle Information in the Building and Energy Sectors. United Nations Environment Programme. 2007
Kotaji, Shpresa et al.: Life-cycle Assessment in Building and Construction. A State-of-the-Art Report of SETAC Europe. Brussels 2003
Klöpffer, Walter; Grahl, Birgit: Ökobilanz (LCA). Ein Leitfaden für Ausbildung und Beruf. Weinheim 2009
Guinée, Jeroen B. (ed.): Handbook on Life Cycle Assessment. Operational Guide to the ISO Standards. Berlin 2002
Remmen, Arne et al.: Life Cycle Management. A Business Guide to Sustainability. Nairobi 2007

Assessment of economic advantage
Principles of real estate management
Bogenstätter, Ulrich: Property Management und Facility Management. Munich 2008
Maier, Kurt: Risikomanagement im Immobilien- und Finanzwesen. Frankfurt/Main 2007
Möller, Dietrich-Alexander: Planungs- und Bauökonomie. Munich 2007

Assessment of economic efficiency
Kruschwitz, Lutz: Investitionsrechnung. Munich 2000
Möller, Dietrich-Alexander: Planungs- und Bauökonomie. Volume 1: Grundlagen der wirtschaftlichen Bauplanung. Munich 2007

Determination of construction costs
BKI Baukosteninformationszentrum (pub.): Kostenplanung im Hochbau. Stuttgart 2008
BKI Baukosteninformationszentrum (pub.): Bildkommentar DIN 276/DIN 277. Stuttgart 2009
BKI Baukosteninformationszentrum (pub.): BKI Baukosten 2009 – Part 1: Statistische Kostenkennwerte für Gebäude; Part 2: Statistische Kostenkennwerte für Bauelemente. Stuttgart 2009
Dahlhaus, Ulrich Jürgen; Meisel, Ulli: Nachhaltiges Bauen 2008/2009. Bauelemente, Kostenkennwerte, ökologische Bewertung, Ausführungshinweise. Essen 2009
König, Holger; Mandl, Wolfgang: Baukosten-Atlas 2008. Bauen im Bestand Wohnungsbau. Kissing 2007
Mandl, Wolfgang; König, Holger: Baukosten-Atlas 2008. Neubau Wohnungsbau. Kissing 2007
Schmitz, Heinz et al.: Baukosten 2008. Preiswerter Neubau von Ein- und Zweifamilienhäusern. Essen 2008
Schmitz, Heinz et al.: Baukosten 2008. Instandsetzung, Sanierung, Modernisierung, Umnutzung. Essen 2008

Determination of use and life cycle costs – principles and parameters
Institut für Bauforschung e.V. (pub.): Baunutzungskosten-Kennwerte für Wohngebäude. Stuttgart 2006
Herzog, Kati: Lebenszykluskosten von Baukonstruktionen. Technische Universität Darmstadt – Institut für Massivbau, vol.10. Darmstadt 2005
Pelzeter, Andrea: Lebenszykluskosten von Immobilien, Schriften zur Immobilienökonomie, Volume 36. Cologne 2006
Riegel, Gert: Ein softwaregestütztes Berechnungsverfahren zur Prognose und Beurteilung der Nutzungskosten von Bürogebäuden. Technische Universität Darmstadt – Institut für Massivbau, vol. 8. Darmstadt 2004
Zehbold, Cornelia: Lebenszykluskostenrechnung. Wiesbaden 1996

Tools for integrated design
Integrated design
Löhnert, Günter: Auf dem Weg zur Integralen Planung. In: Deutsches Architektenblatt 01/2002
Schweizer Ingenieur- und Architektenverein (pub.): TOP – Team orientiertes Planen. www.energie.ch/bfk/ravel/305D.pdf

Voss, Karsten et al.: Bürogebäude mit Zukunft, Cologne 2005
Wiegand, Jürgen: Handbuch Planungserfolg: Methoden, Zusammenarbeit und Management als integraler Prozess. Zurich 2004

Design tools
Koordinationskonferenz der Bau- und Liegenschaftsorgane des Bundes (KBOB): Umweltmanagementsystem von Hochbauprojekten. Bern 2000

Certification systems
Frensch, Stefanie: Green Building. Ist Zertifizierung für Sie ein Thema? Stuttgart 2008
Mösle, Peter et al.: Green Building Label. Die wichtigsten Zertifizierungen auf dem Prüfstand. In: greenbuilding 01–02/2009, pp. 50ff.

Building information models
Eastman, Chuck et al. (ed.): A Guide to Building Information Modeling for Owners, Managers, Designers, Engineers, and Contractors/BIM Handbook. New Jersey 2008
Krygiel, Eddy; Nies, Brad: Green BIM: Successful Sustainable Design with Building Information Modeling. New Jersey 2008

Life cycle analysis in practice: Examples and areas of application
Passivhaus and refurbishment
Schulze Darup, Burkhard: Energetische Gebäudesanierung mit Faktor 10. Osnabrück 2003. www.dbu.de/phpTemplates/publikationen/pdf/151208015825dea0.pdf

Demolition and conservation of value
Hassler, Uta; Kohler, Niklaus; Wang, Wilfried (ed.): Umbau. Über die Zukunft des Gebäudebestandes. Tübingen 1999
Brand, Steward: How buildings learn. What happens after they're built. New York 1995

Links (selection)

Construction data for cost planning and tendering:
www.sirados.de
Centre for construction cost information of the
German Chamber of Architects (BKI):
www.baukosten.de
BRE Environmental Assessment Method
(BREEAM):
www.breeam.org
Deutsche Gesellschaft für Nachhaltiges Bauen e.V.
(DGNB):
www.dgnb.de
Research for energy-optimised construction:
www.enob.info
Hazardous substances information system of the
German construction industry employer's liability
insurance association:
www.wingis-online.de
German Facility Management Association –
Deutscher Verband für Facility Management e.V.
(GEFMA):
www.gefma.de
International Alliance for Interoperability (IAI):
www.buildingsmart.de
International Initiative for Sustainable Built Environment (iiSBE):
www.iisbe.org
Informationsportal Nachhaltiges Bauen of the
German Federal Ministry of Transport, Building
and Urban Development (BMVBS):
www.nachhaltigesbauen.de
Institut Bauen und Umwelt e.V.(IBU):
www.bau-umwelt.com
Integrated life cycle analysis:
www.legep.de
Web-based ecological building material
information system (Wecobis):
www.wecobis.de
Performance Based Building Thematic Network:
www.pebbu.nl
Process-oriented basic data for eco-management
instruments (ProBas):
www.probas.umweltbundesamt.de
SB Alliance:
www.sballiance.org
Software and databases for sustainability analysis:
www.gabi-software.com
Software for energy and material flow analysis of
buildings:
www.the-software.de/ogip/einfuehrung.html
Swiss Center for Life Cycle Inventories:
www.ecoinvent.ch
U.S. Green Building Council:
www.usgbc.org
Wolfsburger Industriebau Netzwerk für LifeCycle
Engineering:
www.win-lce.de
World Green Building Council (WGBC):
www.worldgbc.org

Standards and guidance documents (selection)

The EU has issued directives for a number of
products with the aim of ensuring the safety and
health of users. These directives have to be implemented in the EU member states as compulsory
legislation and regulations. The directives themselves do not contain any technical details, but
instead only lay down the underlying mandatory
requirements.
The corresponding technical values are set out in
associated technical rules and in harmonised
European standards (EN standards).
In general, the technical rules are not legally binding provisions but are aids to decision-making.
Only when they are included in national law, regulations or statutory instruments are their requirements legally binding (e. g. in the construction regulations). Specific standards may be made legally
binding in contracts between project partners. The
latest version of a standard, which is intended to
represent the latest state of the art, always applies.
The origin and sphere of influence of a standard is
apparent from its reference number. In Germany,
a document referred to as DIN plus a number
(e. g. DIN 4108) is primarily of national significance. DIN EN plus a number (e. g. DIN EN 335)
is a German edition of a European standard that
has been adopted unamended by the European
Committee for Standardization (CEN). A reference
beginning DIN EN ISO (e. g. DIN EN ISO 13786)
reflects the national, European and worldwide
sphere of influence of the standard. A European
standard can also be created based on a standard published by the International Organization
and adopted as a DIN national standard. DIN ISO
plus a number (e. g. DIN ISO 2424) refers to an
ISO standard adopted unamended as a national
standard.

Determination of costs, construction and life cycle costs
ISO 15686-5 Buildings and constructed assets –
Service life planning – Part 5: Life cycle costing.
2008
DIN 276-1 Building costs – Part 1: Building con-
struction. 2006
DIN 277 Areas and volumes of buildings – Part 1:
Terminology, bases of calculation 2005
DIN 18960 User costs of buildings. 2008

Investment and economic analysis
VDI 6025 Economy calculation systems for capital
goods and plants. 1996
VDI 2067, Part 1 Economic efficiency of building
installations – Fundamentals and economic calculation. 2000
SIA 480 Wirtschaftlichkeitsrechnung für Investitionen im Hochbau. 2004

Maintenance and operation
DIN 32541 Management of machines and similar
technical equipment – Terminology associated
with activities. 1977
DIN 32736 Building Management – Definitions
and scope of services. 2000
DIN 31051 Physical assets maintenance – Defini-
tions and actions. 1985
DIN 40041 Dependability – concepts. 1990
VDI 3801 Operation of air-conditioning systems.
1982
VDI 3810 Operation of heating systems. 1997
GEFMA 108 Betrieb – Instandhaltung – Unterhalt
von Gebäuden und gebäudetechnischen
Anlagen – Begriffserläuterungen. 2001
GEFMA 122 Betriebsführung von Gebäuden,
gebäudetechnischen Anlagen und Außenan-
lagen. 2001

SIA 269 Grundlagen der Erhaltung von Trag-
werken. 2007

Energy parameters
VDI 3807, Part 1 Characteristic value of energy
and water consumption in buildings – Fundamentals. 2007
VDI 3807, Part 2 Characteristic values of energy
consumption in buildings – Heating and electricity 1998
VDI 3807, Part 3 Characteristic values of water
consumption inside buildings and on adjacent
ground. 2007
VDI 3807, Part 4 Characteristic values of energy
and water consumption of buildings – Characteristic values for electrical energy. 2008

Life cycle design and sustainable construction
ISO 15686-1 Buildings and constructed assets –
Service life planning – Part 1: General principles
2000
ISO 15686-2 Buildings and constructed assets –
Service life planning – Part 2: Service life predic-
tion procedures 2001
ISO 15686-8 Buildings and constructed assets –
Service life planning – Part 8: Reference service
life and service life estimation. 2008
ISO 15686-10 Buildings and constructed assets –
Service life planning – Part 10: Assessing func-
tionality and serviceability (in preparation)
ISO 15392 Sustainability in building construction
– General principles. 2008
ISO TS 21929-1 Sustainability in building
construction – Sustainability indicators – Part 1:
Framework for development of indicators for
buildings. 2006
DIN 18205 Brief for building design. 1996
SIA 469 Erhaltung von Bauwerken. 1997
SIA 112/1 Nachhaltiges Bauen – Hochbau (SIA
recommendation). 2004
SIA 493 Deklaration ökologischer Merkmale von
Bauprodukten. 1997
SIA-Merkblatt 2017 Erhaltungswert von Bau-
werken. 2000

Life cycle assessment and environmental information
ISO 15686-6 Buildings and constructed assets –
Service life planning – Part 6: Procedures for
considering environmental impacts. 2004
ISO 21930 Sustainability in building construction
– Environmental declaration of building products.
2007
BS EN 15804 Sustainability of construction works
– Environmental product declarations – Product
category rules (in preparation)
EN TR 15941 Sustainability of construction works
– Environmental product declarations – Method-
ology and data for generic data (in preparation)
DIN EN ISO 14040 Environmental management –
Life cycle assessment – Principles and frame-
work. 2006
DIN EN ISO 14044 Environmental management –
Life cycle assessment – Requirements and
guidelines. 2006
DIN EN ISO 14020 Environmental labels and dec-
larations – General principles. 2002
DIN EN ISO 14021 Environmental labels and dec-
larations – Self-declared environmental claims
(Type II environmental labelling). 2001
DIN EN ISO 14024 Environmental labels and dec-
larations – (Type I environmental labelling) –Prin-
ciples and procedures. 2001
DIN EN ISO 14025 Environmental labels and dec-
larations – (Type III environmental declarations)
– Principles and procedures. 2007
E DIN EN ISO 14050 Environmental management
– Vocabulary. 2009
DIN EN ISO 14001 Environmental management
systems – Requirements with guidance for use.
2009
DIN EN ISO 14015 Environmental management –
Environmental assessment of sites and organiza-
tions (EASO). 2009

Picture credits

Photographs without credits are from the authors or architects or from the archives of "DETAIL, Review of Architecture". Despite intense efforts, it was not possible to identify the copyright owners of some of the photographs. Their rights, however, remain unaffected and we request them to contact us. The numbers refer to the figures in the text.

Principles
1.3   ifib, University of Karlsruhe
1.4   Patrice Blot, photo-aerienne-france.fr
1.5   deutsche bauzeitung, Vol. 103/1969, No. 1, p. 14
1.6   Frank Kaltenbach, Munich
1.7   Odum, Eugene P.: Prinzipien der Ökologie. Lebensräume, Stoffkreisläufe, Wachstumsgrenzen. Heidelberg 1991, p. 52
1.10 Migge, Leberecht: Der soziale Garten. Das grüne Manifest. Berlin 1926 (1999)
1.11 Duvigneaud, Paul; Denaeyer-De Smet, Simone: L'ecosystème urbain bruxellois. In: Duvigneaud, Paul; Kestemont, Patrick (ed.): Productivité biologique en Belgique. Paris 1977, p. 589
1.12 Wirth, Stefan; Hildebrand, Torsten: Die Fabrik der Zukunft. In: IndustrieBAU 04/2001, p. 56
1.13 after Skifter Andersen, Hans: Self-perpetuating processes of deprivation and decay in 500 Danish social housing estates. Copenhagen 1999
1.16 Ellingham, Ian; Fawcett, William: Options based evaluation of facade refurbishment alternatives. Cambridge, p. 42
1.17 Fraunhofer Institute for Building Physics, Holzkirchen
1.18 Spreng, Daniel; Jochem, Eberhard: Research & Development Needs of Tomorrow as a Contribution to a 2000 Watt Per Capita Society. Zurich 2003

Design in the life cycle
2.3a bilderbox/fotolia
2.3b Ingo Wiederoder/fotolia
2.3c mj-foto/fotolia
2.3d Jakob Schoof, Munich
2.11 Bogenstätter, Ulrich: Propertymanagement und Facilitymanagement. Munich 2008, p. 142
2.16 Bundesamt für Energie: Grundlagen für die Betriebsoptimierung von komplexen Anlagen (BOk). Bern 2002, p. 5
2.17 Engelbach, Wolf: Instandhaltung als Strategie des bestandsorientierten Stoffstrommanagements. In: Die Wohnungswirtschaft 09/2000, pp. 79–82
2.19, 2.20 author's diagrams after Bundesamt für Konjunkturfragen: Projektierungshilfen. Von der Grobdiagnose zum Vorprojekt. Bern 1995
2.21 Landesanstalt für Umweltschutz Baden-Württemberg (ed.): Abbruch von Wohn- und Verwaltungsgebäuden. Handlungshilfe. Karlsruhe 2001
2.23 Bundesamt für Konjunkturfragen: Alterungsverhalten von Bauteilen und Unterhaltskosten. Grundlagendaten für den Unterhalt und die Erneuerung von Wohnbauten. Bern 1994, pp. 49, 55
2.24 Pixler/fotolia
2.27, 2.28 Meyer-Meierling, Paul; Christen, Kurt: Optimierung von Instandsetzungszyklen und deren Finanzierung bei Wohnbauten. Zurich 1999
2.29 after Ronner, Heinz et al.: Zahn der Zeit. Baukonstruktion im Kontext des architektonischen Entwerfens. Basel 1994

Life cycle assessment
3.1   PE International, Leinfelden-Echterdingen
3.2   Jan-Paul Lindner, Leinfelden-Echterdingen
3.7a mompl/pixelio
3.7b apfelweile/fotolia
3.7c Natalia Bratslavsky/fotolia
3.8a Lianem/fotolia
3.8b Otmar Smit/fotolia
3.8c Sergej Toporkov/fotolia
3.11a, b NASA Goddard Space Flight Center, Greenbelt/Maryland (USA)
3.12 Greg Shirah, GSFC Scientific Visualization Studio/NASA Goddard Space Flight Center, Greenbelt/Maryland (USA)
3.13 Umweltbundesamt (pub.): Daten zur Umwelt, Charakteristika und Emissionen der Treibhausgase.
3.14 Werner David/fotolia
3.15 F. Lamiot/wikimedia.org
3.16 Eric Isselée/fotolia
3.19 Rubli, Stefan; Jungbluth, Niels: Materialflussrechnung für die Schweiz. Machbarkeitsstudie. Neuchâtel 2005
3.20 author's calculations after: as 3.19
3.22 de.wikipedia.org/w/index.php?title=Datei:Strommix-D-2008.png&file timestamp=20090315182703
3.23, 3.24 Markewitz, Peter; Matthes, Felix Ch.: Politikszenarien IV: Szenarien bis 2030 für den Projektionsbericht 2007. Jülich 2008

Assessment of the economic advantages
4.2, 4.3 author's tables after ISO 15686-5:2008(E) Buildings and constructed assets – Service life planning – Part 5: Life cycle costing
4.4   Ellingham, Ian; Fawcett, William: New generation whole-life costing. Property and construction decision-making under uncertainty. London 2006, p. 19
4.8   DIN 276-1:2006-11 Building costs – Part 1: Building construction
4.9   DIN.bauportal GmbH (ed.): STLB-Bau – Dynamische BauDaten. Berlin 2009
4.10, 4.11 BKI Baukosteninformationszentrum (ed.): Baukosten 2009 – Part 1: Statistische Kostenwerte für Gebäude. Stuttgart 2009, p. 55
4.12 author's table based on DIN 276-1 Building costs – Part 1: Building construction
4.13 author's table based on DIN 18960 User costs of buildings
4.14 DIN 18960 User costs of buildings
4.15 Jones Lang LaSalle: OSCAR 2008. Büronebenkostenanalyse. 2008, p. 10
4.16 as 4.14, p. 17
4.17 as 4.14, p. 12
4.18 Deutscher Mieterbund e.V. in cooperation with mindUp GmbH
4.19 Möller, Dietrich-Alexander: Planungs- und Bauökonomie. Volume 1: Grundlagen der wirtschaftlichen Bauplanung. Munich 2007, p. 5
4.20 VDI 2067 Economic efficiency of building installations, p. 20
4.21 Maibach, Markus et al.: Praktische Anwendung der Methodenkonvention: Möglichkeiten der Berücksichtigung externer Umweltkosten bei Wirtschaftlichkeitsrechnungen von öffentlichen Investitionen. Zurich/Cologne 2007, p. 63
4.29 Dieter Wolff: Optimierung von Heizanlagen. OPTIMUS-Studie 2006. Cologne 2006, p. 7
4.30 McKinsey & Company (ed.): Kosten und Potenziale der Vermeidung von Treibhausgasemissionen in Deutschland. Sektorperspektive Gebäude. 2007, p. 49

Tools for integrated design
5.7   Institut Bauen und Umwelt e.V., Königswinter
5.8   author's table after sirAdos-Baudaten 2009. Kissing 2009
5.14 Bundesamt für Bauwesen und Raumordnung (ed.): Leitfaden Nachhaltiges Bauen. Bonn/Berlin 2001, Appendix 6
5.15 author's table after Ökobau.dat
5.19a, b author's diagrams after Bauelementekatalog LEGEP Software GmbH, Karlsfeld
5.22 Huovila, Pekka; Porkka, Janne: Decision Support Toolkit (DST). A step towards an Integrated Platform for Performance Based Building. 2005, p. 28.
5.23 author's diagram after Björk, Bo-Christer: The RATAS project – developing an infrastructure for computer integrated construction. p. 6
5.25 Thomas Liebich/IAI Industrieallianz für Interoperabilität
5.27 after ISO 15686-5:2008, p. VII
5.28 after ISO 15686-3:2002, p. 4
5.29 author's diagram after ISO TC 59/SC 17
5.32 Lowe, Clare; Ponce, Alfonso: UNEP-FI / SBCI'S Financial & Sustainability Metrics Report. An international review of sustainable building performance indicators & benchmarks. BRE/CSTB, 2008
5.33 Graubner, Carl Alexander; Schneider, Carmen; Schulte, Carsten; Mielecke, Torsten: Umwelt- und Nachhaltigkeitszertifizierungssysteme für Gebäude im Vergleich. »Bauingenieur« vol. 84, issue 7/8. Düsseldorf 2009.
5.34 author's table after 5.32 and www.breeam.org
5.36 Deutsche Gesellschaft für Nachhaltiges Bauen e.V., Stuttgart
5.37 Deutsche Gesellschaft für Nachhaltiges Bauen e.V.: Das Deutsche Gütesiegel Nachhaltiges Bauen. Stuttgart 2009, p. 10

Life cycle analysis in practice: Examples and areas of application
6.4   own table after Bogenstätter, Ulrich: Bauwerkszuordnungskatalog. Synopse. Nürtingen 2007. p. 2
6.5, 6.8 Architektengemeinschaft Brenne-Eble, Berlin
6.6, 6.7 Winfried Brenne Architekten, Berlin
6.13–6.16 Osika GmbH, Speyer
6.18 Bundesministerium für Verkehr, Bau und Stadtentwicklung: Energieeinsparverordnung (EnEV) 2009, Berlin 2009
6.26, 6.27 Lichtblau Architekten, Munich
6.28, 6.30 Frank Kaltenbach, Munich
6.38 Juhr Architekturbüro für Industriebau und Gesamtplanung, Wuppertal
6.39, 6.40 Jörg Lange, Wuppertal
6.47, 6.48 GAP Architekten und Generalplaner, Berlin
6.49 Marco Maria Dresen, Berlin
6.50 teamgmi, Vienna/Vaduz
6.62 own table after Kohler, Niklaus et al. (eds.): Stoffströme und Kosten in den Bereichen Bauen und Wohnen. Berlin/Heidelberg/New York 1999
6.65 www.stadtforum-leipzig.de
6.66 econcept AG/FHBB (ed.): Neubauen statt Sanieren? Schlussbericht. Zurich 2002, p. 5
6.67 OTB Research Institute for Housing, Urban and Mobility (ed.): ERABUILD. Building Renovation and Modernisation in Europe: State of the art review. Delft 2008, p. 33
6.68–6.70 author's diagram and table after SIA-Merkblatt 2017 Erhaltungswert von Bauwerken. Zurich 2000

Authors

Holger König
1951 Born in Munich
1971–1977 Studied architecture at TU Munich, graduated 1977
1977 Founded an urban and regional planning consultancy in Munich
1984 Founded Holz-König GmbH, Freising (1994 transferred management of the company)
1986 Founded an architectural practice, Gröbenzell near Munich
1986 Founded Ascona GbR Gesellschaft für ökologische Projekte
1995 Founded ÖkoPlus AG, Fachhandelsverband für Ökologie und Bautechnik
1996 Chairman of the supervisory board, ÖkoPlus AG
1998–2001 Executive board member, ÖkoPlus AG
2002 Founded LEGOE Software GmbH, executive board; published LEGOE software and database – integrated economic and ecological software for construction
2004 LEGOE renamed as LEGEP Software GmbH (life cycle & building design)
2005 Accreditation for ECOS (European Citizen Organisation for Standardization) in European Committee for Standardization CEN TC 350 "Life cycle design of buildings"
2008 Member of the German Federal Ministry of Transport, Building and Urban Development (BMVBS) task force participating in diverse workshops in the preparation of the DGNB's Sustainable Building certification scheme (DGNB)

Leader of numerous research projects in the field of life cycle design and environmental parameters for building design. Author of many specialist publications, guest lectures at universities in Karlsruhe, Paris and Naples, and at the European Business School.

Niklaus Kohler
1941 Born in Zurich
Studied architecture in the USA and Switzerland; graduated 1969 at ETH Lausanne
1970–1978 Research assistant at ETH Lausanne, then F&E manager in facade industry and system building
1978 – Visiting lecturer at ETH Lausanne and visiting professor at Ecole Spéciale d'Architecture, Paris
1978–1982 Senior research assistant at the faculty of material science at ETH Lausanne
1985 Doctorate on the overall energy use of buildings during their service lives
1982–1992 Researcher and visiting lecturer at the faculty of physics, solar energy laboratory, ETH Lausanne
1978–1992 Member of the project management teams for several technology transfer programmes (impulse programme)
1993–2007 Professor at the University of Karlsruhe (TH), manager of the Institute for Industrial Building Production
2005 Schelling Medal for Architectural Theory

Member of scientific advisory committees in Germany, United Kingdom, France and Switzerland. Selected fields of research: Life cycle analysis of buildings and building stock, product modelling and shared, cooperative design.

Johannes Kreißig
1967 Born in Ulm
1987–1993 Studied mechanical engineering at the Universities of Stuttgart and Arizona in Tucson, USA
1994 Research assistant at the Institute for Plastic Testing and Science of the University of Stuttgart
1998 Department head of Holistic Life Cycle Assessment at the Institute for Plastic Testing and Science of the University of Stuttgart
2001 Joined consultants PE INTERNATIONAL GmbH, Director of Sustainable Construction
2004 Elected to the LCA Steering Committee of SETAC (Society of Environmental Toxicology and Chemistry)
2005 Member of DIN NABau NA 005-01-31 AA working committee on sustainable construction
2006 German delegate at CEN TC 350 "Sustainability of construction works", Leader of the subgroup "Generic data"
2007 with PE INTERNATIONAL initiator and founder member of Deutsche Gesellschaft für Nachhaltiges Bauen e. V. (DGNB), member of executive committee; 2007–2009 deputy chairman (honorary)
2008 Auditor, trainer and compliance auditor with the DGNB

Thomas Lützkendorf
1957 Born in Merseburg
1977–1981 Studied civil and structural engineering at what is now Bauhaus-Universität Weimar, graduated 1981
1981–1988 Research assistant to the chair of business economics in construction, Bauhaus-Universität Weimar, Faculty of Construction Engineering.
1985 Doctorate in the field of energy-optimised buildings
1988–1990 Employed in the field of site management/site supervision
1990 Working and studying at ETH Lausanne
1990–1992 Research assistant to the chair of construction economics and management, Bauhaus-Universität Weimar, Faculty of Construction Engineering
1992-2000 Research assistant to the chair of building climate and ecology, Bauhaus-Universität Weimar, Faculty of Architecture; creation of building-ecological profiles.
2000 Habilitation on the implementation of the principles of sustainable development in the construction field
2000 – Appointed to the chair of economics and ecology of housing of the scientific faculty of the University of Karlsruhe (TH)/KIT, simultaneous membership of the Faculty of Architecture

Member of the Deutschen Gesellschaft für Nachhaltiges Bauen (DGNB), research advisor to the round table for sustainable construction at the BMVBS, chairman at Deutsches Institut für Normung e. V. (DIN)
Selected fields of research: Development and testing of design and assessment aids, and systems for assessment and certification

Subject index

Appendix